DATE DUE

NO 27 99			

DEMCO 38-296

California Soul

California Soul

Music of African Americans in the West

EDITED BY

Jacqueline Cogdell DjeDje
and
Eddie S. Meadows

UNIVERSITY OF CALIFORNIA PRESS

Berkeley   Los Angeles   London

University of California Press
Berkeley and Los Angeles, California

University of California Press, Ltd.
London, England

© 1998 by
The Regents of the University of California

Library of Congress Cataloging-in-Publication Data

California Soul: music of African Americans in the west / edited by Jacqueline Cogdell DjeDje and
Eddie S. Meadows.
        p.   cm. — (Music of the African diaspora ; 1)
    Includes bibliographic references and index.
    Contents: Music in an urban environment — Music and the media — The musician as
    innovator — Source materials.
    ISBN 0–520–20627–4 (alk. paper). — ISBN 0–520–20628–2 (pbk.: alk. paper)
    1. Afro-Americans—California—Music—History and criticism.   2. Popular music—
    California—History and criticism.   I. DjeDje, Jacqueline Cogdell.   II. Meadows, Eddie S.
    III. Series.
  ML3479.C37   1998
780'.89'960730794—DC21   96–49288
                                                                             CIP
                                                                             MN

Printed in the United States of America
9 8 7 6 5 4 3 2 1

CONTENTS

ILLUSTRATIONS, CHARTS, AND TABLES

FIGURES

vii

ACKNOWLEDGMENTS

We are indebted to many people and organizations that assisted us in the long and arduous process of completing this project.

To the Society for Ethnomusicology (SEM), we are grateful for the opportunity to organize and co-chair the 1990 SEM Pre-Conference Symposium ("The Challenge of Change: Approaches to the Study of African-American Music"). Because this collection of essays is the outgrowth of the symposium, we want to thank the many people and organizations that made contributions to the pre-conference. These include the Cultural Arts Division of the City of Oakland, the California Council for the Humanities, SOLAR Records, the BEEM Foundation, Capitol Records, the UCLA Department of Ethnomusicology, the San Diego State University School of Music and Dance, the UCLA Center for African-American Studies, the SEM Pre-Conference Symposium Planning Committee, and the SEM Local Arrangements Committee.

To our editors Doris Kretschmer and Rachel Berchten, who both encouraged and supported us, we are especially grateful. From the beginning Doris saw the significance of this book to the study of American culture. We commend her for supporting a book on a topic that has received little scholarly attention.

To the anonymous referees who critically assessed early drafts of the manuscript, we offer thanks for helpful insights and comments.

To the numerous musicians who provided penetrating insights and information about themselves, their music, and the context in which they performed, we are eternally indebted. We thank them for graciously allowing us to use their photographs and memorabilia without renumeration.

To the many research assistants, students, staff, and colleagues who helped us to prepare this volume for publication, we give our thanks. Without their assistance and support, it would have been difficult to bring this project to closure.

To the contributors to this volume, we are especially grateful. Without their encouragement, patience, and prompt response to our numerous inquiries, it would have been difficult to publish a volume of such complexity and magnitude. We appreciate their willingness to be part of this work and beg their indulgence should there be errors, while accepting full responsibility commensurate with our roles and functions as editors.

To our families, especially Dominique and Eddie Jr.: thank you for your unwavering support.

Introduction

Jacqueline Cogdell DjeDje and Eddie S. Meadows

This book represents an introduction to the musical creativity and experience of African Americans[1] in California. It demonstrates not only that California blacks have a rich and complex musical heritage that has stirred the hearts and souls of many but also that much diversity exists in this music. On the one hand, California blacks have maintained and built on musical styles and concepts from different parts of the United States (for example, the highly rhythmic, African-based, down-home melodic sounds identified primarily with the South, as well as the European-based art music traditions found throughout the country). Also, African Americans in California have created a performance style that can be described as smooth, mellow, laid-back, with less emphasis on rhythm. In addition, black California musicians have not been afraid to experiment, a feature that is in sync with one of the underlying characteristics of African-American culture.

Tolerance of diverse musical traditions is not unusual in urban environments, which is the context in which most African Americans in California have lived. In large, dense, and heterogeneous settings,[2] adaptation to changing circumstances is a necessity. Descriptions of Los Angeles can be applied to cities in the rest of state. Anthropologist Jacques Maquet says Los Angeles is "fluid and ever-changing: constantly there are new musics, new ideas, new trends."[3] Los Angeles city planner Con Howe comments: "We certainly have a more diverse population than most cities. And we have kind of a willingness to take on new ideas and the best ideas from different cultures."[4] Each city in California has its own history and personality, of course, so there are variations in the degree to which these characteristics apply.

Unlike urban areas in the Northeast and Midwest as well as rural and urban settings in the South, which have historically had segregated African-American communities, California featured ethnically diverse communities during its early history. Independent African-American communities in California did not evolve until much later, in the twentieth century. Whether this unique historical foundation gave rise to expressive forms that differ from those created by blacks in other areas of the country is difficult to ascertain. The findings from studies in this book are mixed, underscoring the complexity of the African-American musical experience in California.

Many works that focus on music of the city discuss urbanization in terms of dichotomies: folk/modern, rural/urban, or country/city.[5] This approach sometimes implies that urbanization is evolutionary, linear, and unidirectional, which is not always the case. Also, few studies take into consideration the fact that urbanization is continuous and may occur in stages. The manner in which city life affects musicians and their music, as well as how the musicians and their music affect the city, needs to be examined. Thus, urban music and culture must be discussed from several viewpoints simultaneously.

Because the migration patterns of California African-American musicians were sometimes circuitous, this book broadens our understanding of urbanization as it relates to music. Though many California performers were born in the rural South, a large number lived in southern, midwestern, or northeastern cities before finally settling on the West Coast. Thus, their sensibility and self-image were different from those of people who simply moved from a rural to an urban environment. In addition, the music and culture some musicians brought to California were distinct from traditions associated with their birthplace. More important, because of the constant influx of visitors and the distant travels of Californians, California musicians frequently interacted with individuals outside the state. Also, performers within the state often intermingled with each other. California is one of the few states in the United States with substantial black populations in several cities, and each city has a thriving music culture. Finally, the opportunity for black Californians to control and participate in media institutions (radio, record, and television industries) normally dominated by mainstream society made California an attractive place to live, and these media had a significant impact on music developed in the state.

California serves as an excellent context in which to examine not only the multiplicity of musical traditions but also the sociocultural differentiations and tendencies within black culture. For too long, the different cultural expressions emanating from the experiences of African Americans in the United States have been discussed as a monolithic entity. The chapters in this volume demonstrate that the situation is quite complex, particularly when regional variations are taken into consideration. Before we examine how the social dynamics and different layerings of black culture in California relate to music making, however, a historical overview of African-American presence in the state is in order.

A SOCIAL HISTORY OF AFRICAN AMERICANS IN CALIFORNIA

Although black presence in California dates to the sixteenth century,[6] African-American communities did not become established there until the mid-nineteenth century. Large-scale African-American migration from the South and Southwest into California began later than that to the North because of the state's geographical distance from nineteenth-century population centers. The first U.S. Census for California, conducted in 1850, lists the black population as 962. Whereas about twelve blacks lived in Los Angeles,[7] approximately 464 San Francisco residents were African American. These numbers demonstrate a trend that continued until the late 1800s—that is, the number of blacks living in San Francisco was much larger than the number residing in Los Angeles, Oakland, or San Diego.

The discovery of gold in 1848 was one of the primary reasons both blacks and whites were attracted to Northern California. By 1870, San Francisco was the ninth-largest U.S. city, with a strong manufacturing industry and a port that rivaled those of New York, Boston, and New Orleans. Also, in the 1890s, black service workers of the Spanish-American War, as well as black sailors, boat workers, and railroad men, saw San Francisco as an excellent place to advance. Many found employment as laborers in households, hotels, and restaurants. Because of their numbers, black San Franciscans exercised considerable influence in African-American affairs on the West Coast in the nineteenth century. The establishment of black institutions in California cities and towns often depended on leading San Franciscans, who were frequently invited to cultural events to deliver speeches or to promote interest in various projects.[8]

Yet San Francisco was a paradox. In spite of the influence of African Americans, the number of blacks in San Francisco was small in comparison to that of whites. According to historian Douglas Henry Daniels:

> A number of factors kept the Black population small in the nineteenth and early twentieth centuries. The Blacks' lack of power and influence in [white communities in] San Francisco and the distance from the south accounted for the size of the population before 1880. After 1880, powerful white labor unions prevented Negroes from winning jobs, while white immigrants took many of their traditional service positions. Industrialists and financiers rarely lent aid to the Black community and did not promote its growth through migration schemes. They only used Blacks occasionally as strikebreakers, the last kind of situation to lead to permanent residency or power. Finally, by 1900 Oakland grew and attracted Blacks, including San Franciscans, but then other new Pacific coast cities offered more opportunities to Afro-Americans and other migrants.[9]

Moreover, local officials made little effort to encourage migration of blacks because California already had an abundant supply of unskilled Chinese, Japanese, and Mexican laborers.[10]

By 1900, Los Angeles had surpassed San Francisco as the most populous African-American community in the state. Whereas San Francisco's black community decreased in size between 1890 and 1910, in Los Angeles the population grew from 102 in 1880 to 7,990 in 1910. By the early twentieth century, black political and socioeconomic advocacy organizations in the state found their power based in Southern California. The Afro-American Congress met in Pasadena in 1906, signalling that the noise and numbers of recent arrivals finally overshadowed the history and achievements of the pioneer era.[11] The phenomenal rise in the black population in Los Angeles resulted from the Great Migration that earlier had occurred in cities in the Northeast and Midwest. Most California blacks were recruited as agricultural workers. However, they tended to cluster in large urban areas and sought employment in service jobs, particularly domestic work and transportation, not in agriculture.[12] Comparing Northern and Southern California, Daniels states, "This mass movement of Blacks to urban areas around World War I formed a picture of Black urban America that is usually accepted as standard. But it did not affect San Francisco, Oakland, Berkeley, or Richmond to any considerable degree until the 1940s."[13] Several factors encouraged blacks to move to Los Angeles: the possibility of employment in the interurban railway that was being built in Los Angeles County; the destruction of the cotton economy by the boll weevil in south central states such as Texas; and heightened racial tensions in the South that had become intolerable. Thus, the rate of increase of the black population in Los Angeles during the early 1900s was higher than that of whites.[14]

In addition to the intolerable conditions in the South, there are other reasons blacks chose Los Angeles over other cities on the West Coast. Daniels states, "Compared to the eastern and newer far western cities, San Francisco extended very limited economic opportunities to Blacks after the spectacular boom days of the mid-nineteenth century. The sparse Afro-San Franciscan population, numbering approximately 1,600 until World War I, suggests the stiff economic competition they then endured."[15]

As Los Angeles's African-American population increased, so, too, did racial restrictions and discrimination. In 1918 white hostility resulted in the confinement of African Americans to specific residential areas, and by 1930 close to 70 percent were concentrated in one assembly district around the main Central Avenue business area, with a majority of the remainder percent residing in adjacent neighborhoods. Overcrowding and a decrease in the overall standard of living contributed to the process of ghettoization that continued through subsequent decades. Aside from the residential restrictions, the expression of anti-black sentiment took many otherforms. There was growing receptivity for the Ku Klux Klan, with its "message of hate and anger in new and longtime white residents of the city."[16] African Americans were denied access to many restaurants, hotels, theaters, and public areas, including certain beaches and bathhouses. In response to the city's growing racism, organizations such as the NAACP (National Association for the Advancement of Colored People) and Marcus Garvey's UNIA (Universal Negro Improvement Association) became increasingly active. The Los Angeles chapter of the NAACP was founded in 1913, the UNIA chapter in 1921.

By comparison with black communities in San Francisco and Los Angeles, those of San Francisco's East Bay[17] were very small during the late nineteenth century. Not until the early 1900s did the East Bay's African-American population surpass San Francisco's. Much of the growth in Oakland and surrounding areas can be attributed to 1) the earthquake and fire that destroyed San Francisco in 1906, sending thousands of refugees to the East Bay, and 2) the development of Oakland's shipbuilding and railroad industries. Black-owned businesses benefited from the general prosperity of the East Bay, which caused Oakland and other areas to become more attractive to Northern California black residents.[18]

When California entered the union in 1850, only eight blacks in a total population of 798 resided in San Diego County. In 1870 the county still had only seventeen African-American denizens, but by 1880 the number had risen to fifty-five.[19] Thus, the growth of the black community in San Diego between 1860 and the 1880s differed from that of other cities in California. Not only was the number of blacks in the southernmost part of the state extremely small in comparison to the total population, but most blacks settled in rural areas, where they worked as farmers. About 0.2 percent of the total population of San Diego was black, whereas African Americans in the rest of the state constituted just under 1 percent of the population: "Of the fifteen blacks listed in the 1870 census for San Diego County, only one lived in the city; of the fifty-five listed in 1880, only three lived in the city."[20] Also, many of the blacks who settled in San Diego (and Southern California in general) were born in slave states. In Northern California, "especially San Francisco, the proportion of blacks born in slave states was much lower."[21]

Several factors help to explain the growth pattern of the black population in San Diego. With mountains and desert to the east, the city was poorly situated for the building of a railroad, leaving it a port without a hinterland. Also, it was not until 1869 that an important gold strike (started by Fred Coleman, a black) was made in San Diego County, and this caused only a minor boom. While San Diego's black population increased between 1885 and 1900, it remained less than 1 percent of the total, rising to 289 in 1890.[22] However, it is noteworthy that the majority of blacks in San Diego County during the late nineteenth century lived in or near downtown San Diego, where they rented, lived with their employers, or lived on their employers' property.[23] Most were cooks, laborers, servants, housekeepers, or women of the evening, though a few were involved in business.[24] After the 1890s the economic status of blacks improved, and blacks fanned out in all directions and settled in the more expensive urban neighborhoods, such as Logan Heights.

During the early twentieth century, there was little variation in life for blacks who lived on the West Coast; it was the same in Seattle, Portland, San Francisco, Los Angeles, and San Diego. Most lived in neighborhoods that were ethnically mixed with Asians, Mexicans, and various European groups; because "blacks migrated as individuals and over a long period of time, they scattered over a wide area."[25] Compared to their counterparts in the South, Californian blacks enjoyed considerable freedom on public transportation and in public. By the mid-1920s, black wage scales across occupations in California were among the highest in the nation,[26] making the state an attractive destination for African Americans. In Los

Angeles, the period from 1900–1929 is referred to as the "Golden Era" because African Americans enjoyed a higher standard of living there than was possible in the states of their birth. While some maintained businesses, most worked in service trades, as domestics, or as unskilled laborers. Many were able to purchase their own homes.[27] It was not until the stock market crash of 1929 that blacks were subjected to the policies and obstacles (such as restrictive residential covenants) that forced them into segregated communities.

The process of ghettoization that developed in eastern and midwestern cities between 1916 and 1920 began to accelerate in Los Angeles and San Diego in the late 1920s. In San Francisco and other western cities, this trend was delayed between twenty-five and thirty years.[28] Yet in spite of the diversity of these communities, most whites, particularly those in San Francisco, perceived blacks as inferior and restricted their progress socially, politically, and economically.[29] Recounting life in the twenties and thirties, one black San Diegan states, "Many restaurants downtown had signs up saying that they refused to serve blacks. Hotels didn't have signs up, but they wouldn't serve Negroes either."[30] In spite of racism and hardships, large numbers of blacks migrated to the West Coast in the thirties. Those who migrated to California tended to come from Louisiana, Oklahoma, and Texas, whereas those from Mississippi and Alabama more commonly moved north to Chicago or Detroit.[31] African Americans entering California during this time tended to concentrate in the Los Angeles area,[32] making the city and its environs the logical destination of most subsequent black migrations.

Between 1942 and 1945, "340,000 Blacks settled in California, two hundred thousand of whom migrated to Los Angeles."[33] The first large influx of black workers came in the spring of 1942, when the Southern Pacific Railroad Company began to import railway workers. The migration reached its peak in June 1943, when between 10,000 and 12,000 African Americans entered Los Angeles in a single month. As in earlier years, the main source of these and other migrants was mostly the south central states and Mississippi, with the greatest number coming from Texas.[34] In his study of Watts, California, Keith Collins conducted interviews with 275 men and women who migrated to Los Angeles during the war. One hundred seventy-one came from the same states as most of the musicians who entertained them: Louisiana, Oklahoma, and Texas.[35]

Blacks who migrated sought a different way of life and a better future, for many believed that obtaining a job in the wartime industry would lead to better socioeconomic conditions.[36] Also, the West Coast seemed free of the poverty and tenements of New York or Chicago. Though they did not leave discrimination or segregation behind them, Southerners felt they would be able to escape Jim Crow laws and humiliation.[37] Although the move to California was beneficial for southern migrants, the influx had a negative impact on the established communities of blacks[38] because few accommodations were made for the new migrants. As the black population grew in Los Angeles, it remained confined by prewar boundaries, and restrictive housing covenants were more tightly enforced. Betty Reid

Soskin, a Berkeley record-store owner who moved to the Bay Area from Louisiana in 1925, recalls, "There were so many blacks suddenly settling in the area and people were coming in by the trainloads that they were building housing, emergency housing, like crazy. The area was suddenly becoming a black metropolis."[39] It is also noteworthy that by 1940, the black population in Oakland (8,462) was nearly twice the size of that in San Francisco (4,846). According to Lawrence Crouchett, "Oakland's black population grew from 8,462 in 1940 to 37,327 in 1945 and 47,562 in 1950; Berkeley's from 3,395 in 1940 to 13,289 in 1950; and Richmond's from a mere 270 in 1940 to 14,000 in 1950."[40]

The 1950s and 1960s can be regarded as a period of change within the social history of blacks in California. By the fifties, migration into the Los Angeles area had increased substantially, making it a major metropolitan center for black America. Servicemen who were discharged from the military during the forties and fifties decided to stay in San Diego and other cities on the West Coast rather than return to their hometowns.[41] Like blacks who settled in Los Angeles during the early twentieth century, the new migrants felt the West Coast offered greater opportunities for social mobility than the South did. Many believed that unlike blacks of the South, "the people of color in Los Angeles were guaranteed some basic liberties, such as the right of suffrage, the right to seek legal recourse, and freedom from the worst effects of residential segregation."[42]

The period from the fifties and sixties was also important because it was this time that African Americans actively protested against discrimination and inequities. Although the civil rights movement helped to change the laws, blacks continued to suffer many injustices. For example, even though restrictive covenants were outlawed in 1948, blacks in Los Angeles still did not live in "integrated" communities during the fifties. Yet when African-American settlement patterns changed, black customers who had had no alternative choices prior to integration began to patronize businesses that had previously been restricted to whites.[43]

Between 1960 and 1970, California's black population increased from 900,000 to 1,400,000.[44] However, by the mid-sixties, the popular image of California as a "wonderful land of easy wealth, good health, pleasant living, and unlimited opportunities"[45] for blacks no longer existed. For blacks who migrated to the state in the forties and earlier, life had changed between the end of World War II and the beginning of the 1960s. Also, recent migrants (those who arrived in the sixties) quickly discovered their road to success to be more difficult than they had anticipated. As Lapp explains: "Frustration and bitterness were becoming obvious to many. In California, the problems of decent housing, jobs (especially for youth), and police brutality were chronic. The continued migration of blacks to California increased the population density of already crowded black ghettos. Young blacks grew up separated from the larger white world, and their own world became one of de facto segregation with declining educational advantages."[46] Though dreams may have come true for some African Americans in California, many became disillusioned, ultimately causing their aspirations to burst into flames in the Watts (Los Angeles) and Logan Heights (San Diego) rebellions of 1965.[47] In other areas of the state, grassroots organizations such as the Black Panthers (established in Oakland in 1966) came into existence to deal with problems.[48]

Dramatic changes occurred in the demographics in California during the seventies and eighties. Because of the large influx of Asians and Latinos, the percentage distribution of blacks in the state fell. The situation in Los Angeles exemplifies what occurred in other urban areas in California. Eugene J. Grigsby explains:

> By 1970 . . . the Los Angeles area began to experience a totally different set of immigration patterns. Chicanos and Latinos comprised 14 percent of the region's population in 1970. By 1980, their numbers had increased to 24 percent, and today they constitute 28 percent of the population. Forecasts for the year 2010 indicate that the Chicano and Latino population is expected to reach 40 percent of the area's residents.
>
> The size of the Asian and "other" population—Japanese, Chinese, Koreans, Vietnamese, Filipinos, Iranians, Russian Jews, Armenians—doubled between 1970 and 1980 and is projected to grow at a slow but steady rate over the next 10 to 15 years.
>
> The Black population, on the other hand, reached a plateau during this same time period. In 1970, Blacks represented 17.3 percent of the city's population and dropped to 12.6 percent in 1980. Today, Blacks comprise approximately 10 percent of the city's population and are not expected to exceed this number in the foreseeable future.[49]

California cities in the 1990s have maintained their diversity and many of the characteristics that have historically been associated with them. An article that appeared in the January 26, 1995, issue of the *Los Angeles Times* provides an interesting description of urban areas in the state. Though San Francisco and San Diego have their differences, the article states, similarities exist; they are thought to be civic jewels in the Golden State's crown, port cities of great beauty and great promise, cities that have remained livable while much of urban America appears in rapid decline. Both are mission cities with military and maritime traditions. Interestingly, San Francisco, with a population of 723,959, has also retained its aura as a sophisticated city with a European aristocratic tradition. By contrast, San Diego, a newcomer to the ranks of big-citydom (population 1,110,549), is more middle American, with a lifestyle revolving around hearth and home. Residents of San Diego and San Francisco criticize Los Angeles, the largest city in the state (population, 3,485,398), because of its sprawl, unchecked growth, rush, and turmoil.[50] Though Los Angeles may draw the ire of many, few cities have such range of choices in cultural traditions. Also, because of its proximity to Hollywood, it is the entertainment capital of the world, giving the city enormous social, political, and cultural influence. In the words of Mike Davis, "this essentially deracinated city has become the world capital of an immense culture industry, which since the 1920s has imported myriads of the most talented writers, filmmakers, artists and visionaries."[51] In addition, Los Angeles continues to be the hub of California's black community, with the state's largest population of African Americans, although Oakland has the largest percentage distribution of blacks (see Table I.1 for statistics on population in California). The chapters in this volume show that the distribution and diversity of California's population has had a considerable impact on the music of African Americans in the state.

STRUCTURE AND SCOPE

The contributors have used a variety of approaches in the presentation of their material. Most focus on a specific genre (blues, jazz, gospel, rhythm and blues, or soul) as the basis for the discussion of a historical period, issue, or individual. Others use interviews to examine important institutions, such as the music industry and radio. Because limited scholarly material exists on the music and social context of African Americans in California (see source materials in Appendix compiled by David Martinelli), all authors have had to rely on oral history, in addition to archival sources, for their research. This is not unusual for music investigations concerning people of color, women, urbanism, and regional musicians who have not received much documentation. Although the authors have identified several layers of musical styles and tendencies associated with California blacks, the interplay of these tendencies among various performers within different contexts is interesting. For example, some California musicians are noted for their down-home performance style, whereas others perform music that can be regarded as "laid-back," mellow, and smooth, and still others play music in the European art music tradition. Experimentation and openness to new ideas are also important features of African-American music in California.

When a work covers such a diversity of topics and issues, it can be organized in a number of ways: geographically, historically, or according to genre. We have decided to use several themes—"Music in an Urban Environment," "Music and the Media," and "The Musician as Innovator"—as the basis for organizing the book. Though these themes are the primary focus of some papers, issues concerning urbanism, media, innovation, and multiculturalism are intrinsic to the California region,[52] so they are discussed to some extent in each of the articles. For example, Meadows and Browne provide contextual information about San Diego and Los Angeles, respectively, before their discussions of the media and the musician. Similarly, the chapters by Bakan, Browne, DjeDje, Hildebrand/Moore, and Kidula address the impact of the media on trends, as well as personalities involved in the record industry and black radio.

As indicated above, the majority of African Americans in California historically have lived in urban environments; therefore, it is apropos to have a section entitled "Music in an Urban Environment." Cities give rise to a certain type of dynamic that can have a dramatic effect on culture and music making.[53] Chapters by Bakan, DjeDje, Eastman, and Hildebrand/Moore show how migration trends,

TABLE I.1   1990 Population and Percentage Distribution
of Ethnic Groups in Four Cities in California

	Los Angeles	Oakland	San Diego	San Francisco
Total population	3,485,398	372,242	1,110,549	723,959
Number of blacks	487,674	163,335	104,261	79,039
Percentage distribution of blacks	14.0	43.9	9.4	10.9
Number of American Indians, Eskimos, or Aleuts	16,379	2,371	6,800	3,456
Percentage distribution of American Indians, Eskimos, or Aleuts	.5	.6	.6	.5
Number of Asians or Pacific Islanders	341,807	54,931	130,945	210,876
Percentage distribution of Asians or Pacific Islanders	9.8	14.8	11.8	29.1
Number of Hispanics (of any race)	788,704	29,725	121,159	41,345
Percentage distribution of Hispanics (of any race)	22.6	8.0	10.9	5.7
Number of whites	1,841,182	120,849	745,406	387,783
Percentage distribution of whites	52.8	32.5	67.1	53.6

United States Department of Commerce, *1990 Census of Population. General Population Characteristics, California, Section 1 of 3* (Washington, DC: Bureau of the Census, 1990).

settlement patterns, and support institutions affected musical activity. Also, the networking of individuals and organizations and the spatial arrangement of buildings (homes, businesses, churches, entertainment venues) make the music in one community differ from that in another.

Together, the chapters by Bakan and Eastman chronicle the activities of several jazz musicians who were active in Los Angeles from the mid-teens to the end of World War II. The authors refute the sobriquet that musicians go to Los Angeles to die. In the article, "Way Out West on Central: Jazz in the African-American Community of Los Angeles before 1930," Michael B. Bakan explains that much activity in the early development of jazz took place in Los Angeles. He shows that noted New Orleans musicians who migrated to the West Coast during the early twentieth century became leaders in the Los Angeles jazz scene, making historic recordings and performing at a variety of social events, thus providing a unifying force for the community during a period of considerable political instability and change. Although jazz musicians who migrated to California continued to perform down-home music, it is also noteworthy that migrant musicians had to adapt to the conservative aesthetic sensibilities of Los Angeles's black establishment. Early jazz musicians in Los Angeles who were "well schooled" (trained in European art music) tended to enjoy greater success than musicians who only performed "hot" jazz styles from the South and Midwest.

In "'Pitchin' up a Boogie': African-American Musicians, Nightlife and Music Venues in Los Angeles, 1930–1945," Ralph Eastman discusses the development of jazz and black popular music in the city during a period when Central Avenue had become a jewel of success for musicians and entrepreneurs. The details he provides about the spatial arrangement of clubs, demographics, and political environment in Los Angeles help to explain how a separate community emerged and became one of the most famous settings for the exchange of musical ideas and establishment of new trends. In addition, he suggests reasons for the decline in the popularity of music venues and musicians who performed on Central Avenue.

The chapter on "Oakland Blues" gives two perspectives on the development of the tradition: one from Bob Geddins, an insider who was a producer and composer of the art form, and another from Lee Hildebrand, a journalist who, through artistic criticism, helped to promote the music. The first part of the chapter, by Hildebrand, includes a historical overview of the Oakland blues tradition from the forties to the nineties, focusing on the contributions of several noted figures, including Geddins, Lowell Fulson, and Jimmy McCracklin. Hildebrand explains that Oakland has a southern musical character and personality, which makes the city's blues tradition different from that associated with San Francisco and other urban areas in the state. Part two of this chapter is a conversation between James C. Moore and Bob Geddins. Geddins explains why and how blues evolved as it did in Oakland. His discussion of the aesthetics of blues and the techniques he used in recording sessions to create a particular quality of sound are issues rarely discussed by scholars. The interview is now of particular value because it documents Geddins's last public appearance before his death in early 1991.

California residents were slow in their acceptance of gospel, a type of music whose beginnings date to the early twentieth century. The manner in which the form was promoted and disseminated in the state is documented in "The California Black Gospel Music Tradition: A Confluence of Musical Styles and Cultures" by Jacqueline Cogdell DjeDje. She not only discusses context and the social factors that caused the adoption of the art form to differ in various areas of the state but also shows how the connections between Chicago and the various urban areas in California made the gospel music tradition on the West Coast distinct from that of other areas in the United States. As a result, it was not long before Los Angeles became as important a center for gospel music as cities in the Midwest and East. DjeDje also demonstrates that the fusion of a down-home performance style with the European art music tendencies of some California gospel musicians helped make the state's gospel music a model that was imitated by others throughout the country. Subsequently, California gospel musicians became known as major innovators.

The media (the record industry and radio, in particular) have given the music of California a distinctive ambience. Moreover, they are partly responsible for the new ideas and trends that have been incorporated into various musical forms (e.g., gospel, rhythm and blues, and jazz). Therefore, the section entitled "Music and the Media" as it relates to the African-American experience in California is particularly important.

"Insider Perspectives on the American Afrikan Popular Music Industry and Black Radio" provides interviews with Al Bell and Pam Robinson, individuals who are involved in the business aspects of the music industry. Kwaku Person-Lynn's interview with Bell, a Los Angeles music executive who has been an important innovator within the popular music industry since the 1950s, not only includes information about Bell's life and contributions but also touches on the role and importance of Los Angeles to the record business. In addition to recounting the history of Stax Records, Bell elaborates on trends in the popular music industry, future directions of black music, black radio, creativity, black music marketing, and differences between Stax and Motown (a Los Angeles–based record company from the 1970s to the 1990s). Of particular note are Bell's comments on the challenges facing a black male executive in a multibillion dollar industry dominated by white males. Though Bell feels it is important to maintain an Afrocentric approach to music making, he also believes it is critical that black musicians continue to be innovators rather than allow themselves to become imitators. Robinson, one of the few female program directors in Los Angeles radio during the 1980s, discusses the complexities of running a radio station in a changing market, as well as the role and influence of radio in the black community and in the promotion of new artists. Like Bell, Robinson comments on the challenges that black women executives face in the music industry as well as the need to experiment with new ideas to be successful within the music business.

In "California Rhythm and Blues Recordings, 1942–1972: A Diversity of Styles," Willie R. Collins uses a sample of fifty-one recordings to discuss the stylistic trends and song texts of rhythm and blues. Collins argues that California rhythm and blues is a confluence of several genres. Whereas some Californians embraced music forms from the South and Midwest (e.g., rhythm and blues based on Kansas City jazz, boogie woogie, and gospel), other artists created a laid-back, smooth, ballad style generally associated with California. The differentiation in styles within the state exists because musicians have been conditioned by local phenomena. Thus, music aesthetics is directly related to context.

In "African Americans and 'Lites Out Jazz' in San Diego: Marketing, Impact and Criticism," Eddie S. Meadows examines the impact of KIFM radio on jazz preferences in San Diego. Meadows states that shrewd marketing, along with live community presentations, caused "lites out jazz" to become one of the most popular radio program formats in San Diego from 1986 to 1990; the radio station received high ratings among both African Americans and whites. The author suggests that a corollary relationship exists between the education and income levels of African Americans and their ability to participate in "lites out jazz" activities. "Lites out jazz" reflects the smooth, laid-back musical tendencies within California—what Carl Evans, a "lites out jazz" performer from San Diego, refers to as "vanilla" music. By exploring new directions, the performers developed a performance style that met the musical tastes of the African-American middle class.

The section entitled "The Musician as Innovator" examines the lives of three Los Angeles musicians who have been pioneers and trailblazers in their fields. As individuals, they fought against the odds and were not interested in maintaining the status quo. Their desire to be different, experiment, and introduce new ideas eventually led to notoriety that they would have not achieved if they had followed tradition. Danica L. Stein discusses the life and experiences of Clora Bryant, one of the few females who, in spite of the odds, decided to become a professional jazz musician. Bryant, as a jazz trumpet player, experienced numerous obstacles within her career because of the marginalization of women as well as the negative attitudes and perceptions that exist among male musicians and society at large.

In "The Gospel of Andraé Crouch: A Black Angeleno," Jean Kidula discusses what she believes are the characteristics of Los Angeles. According to Kidula, not only does Crouch symbolize the multicultural and multiracial environment of Los Angeles, his music involves integration and synthesis as well as collaboration and compromise. In demonstrating Crouch's uniqueness in the field of gospel music, Kidula describes Crouch's upbringing in the Church of God in Christ, his exposure to secular music, his role in the development of contemporary gospel, and his involvement in the white Christian community, which helped to bridge the gap between white and black gospel. Crouch was not afraid to challenge the status quo or explore new directions, which is one of the reasons that he became one of the primary architects of contemporary gospel in the seventies and eighties.

In "Brenda Holloway: Los Angeles's Contribution to Motown," Kimasi L. Browne discusses the circumstances and issues that made Brenda Holloway, a Motown recording artist of the 1960s, special and different. As an innovator, Holloway was one of the first performers in California to separate from the Motown family. Her career at Motown is noteworthy because the context in which she grew up was so different from that of other Motown artists. Also, her early training in European art music greatly influenced her performance style, which indirectly affected other Motown artists because Holloway was used as a model. The chapter touches on history of the Motown label, Holloway's early life and musical training, her role as a fashion innovator, and her contributions to the Motown sound.

The Appendix, prepared by David Martinelli, is a comprehensive compilation of source materials on African-American music, musicians, and culture in California. As we have indicated, the amount of *scholarly* literature on the music of African Americans in California is minimal when compared to the documentation that exists on the musical activity of blacks in the South, East Coast, or Midwest. Though *The Negro Trail Blazers of California*[54] by journalist Delilah Beasley provides useful social, cultural, and musical information about the art music community during the early twentieth century, most general works and histories that concern black music in the United States—e.g., *Music and Some Highly Musical People*, by James M. Trotter; *Negro Musicians and Their Music*, by Maude Cuny-Hare; the second and third editions of *The Music of Black Americans: A History*, by Eileen Southern; or *Black American Music: Past and Present*, by Hildred Roach—contain little discussion of California.[55] Except for two publications by the Center for Black Music Research *(Black Music Research Bulletin* and *Black Music Research Journal)*,[56] few scholarly journals or anthologies contain extensive discussion of black music activity in California. Tom Reed's *The Black Music History of Los Angeles—Its Roots: A Classical Pictorial History of Black Music in Los Angeles from the 1920s–1970* is one of the first attempts to examine in a comprehensive manner the musical forms created and performed by African Americans in Los Angeles. Unfortunately, aside from his brief comments on the numerous photographs included in the book, there is little discussion of the music or musicians.[57] Two books by Bette Yarbrough Cox provide an excellent overview of musical activity in Los Angeles during the early part of the twentieth century. Cox's introduction in *Central Avenue—Its Rise and Fall (1880–c.1955)* focuses on the development of the African-American music in the city, and the second part contains valuable oral history accounts from music educators, art music, jazz, and religious musicians. Her edited work, *Music in the Central Avenue Community 1890–c. 1955*, contains essays on jazz, gospel, church music, art music, and the black musicians' union in Los Angeles.[58]

Although noted performers who were born in California have been the focus of monograph-length studies,[59] only a handful of biographies about California performers are included in the *Biographical Dictionary of Afro-American and African Musicians, The New Grove Dictionary of Music and Musicians, The New Grove Dictionary of American Music, The New Grove Dictionary of Jazz*, and *Jazz Research and Performance Materials: A Select Annotated Bibliography.*[60] The University of California, Los Angeles (UCLA) Oral History Program has begun to compile oral histories from Los Angeles African-American musicians (see Martinelli's source materials), filling many of the gaps that have heretofore existed. So far UCLA's oral history project has been devoted primarily to musicians in the jazz world.[61]

A similar lack of documentation exists with regard to specific music idioms. Except for publications by Hansonia L. Caldwell, Bette Y. Cox, William Duncan Allen, Marion D. Schrock, and Jacqueline Cogdell DjeDje,[62] only brief references have been made to the development of art music and various religious genres in California. Though much has appeared in music trade journals about blues, jazz, and popular music—e.g., *Down Beat, Billboard, Variety, Record Changer, Coda, Metronome, Melody Maker, Cadence, Village Voice, Option*—scholarly discussion of these forms has been scanty. Lee Hildebrand, Arnold Shaw, Portia Maultsby, and Ralph Eastman are among those who have produced works concerned with rhythm and blues.[63] The few books that have appeared on jazz (e.g., works by William Claxton, Tom Stoddard, Robert Gordon, Burt Wilson, and Ted Gioia) have dealt with developments in Los Angeles, San Francisco, and Sacramento during the 1950s and later.[64] Also, other than Stanley Dance's[65] brief discussion of jazz in San Diego, no scholarly sources are available on the southernmost city within the state. Therefore, the situation Floyd and Reisser found during the 1980s has not changed: "Aside from what has appeared in biographies and a few reference books . . . , not much has been written about the black-music activity that took place in California in the late nineteenth and early twentieth centuries, and not many research tools and materials exist for those wishing to research the black-music history of the state."[66]

This volume helps to fill the void that now exists with regard to scholarly materials on African-American music in California. We believe it is appalling that so little has been done when one considers that California is one of the most important regions in the United States for black social and political activity. Also, it is ironic that although Los Angeles and its surrounding communities can be regarded as the mass media capital of the world because of the region's involvement in the creation and promotion of popular culture, little attention has been given to the city's African-American culture, the foundation for most musical creativity in world culture.

This collection in no way attempts to be complete in its coverage of the music of African Americans in California. Although black Californians have a long history of involvement in art music, spirituals, rap, and other performance idioms, including film, television, and theater,[67] the chapters in this volume are limited to a discussion of blues, gospel, jazz, rhythm and blues, and soul. The contributors show that African-American musicians in California use down-home, laidback stylistic tendencies in many genres. Whether these phenomena can be defined as a California aesthetic, or the expression of a particular identity, is debatable. Until more research is done on music in the region (which we hope this book will inspire), we can only suggest that such a definition might be applicable. African-American musical preferences are conditioned by local cultural phenomena as well as national concepts. Instead of focusing on the well-known, established musicians and geographical areas, scholars of African-American music need to investigate regions of the United States where little research has been done so we may have a more holistic view and better understanding of the creativity and performance practices of *all* African-American musicians.

NOTES

1. Throughout this volume, the terms African American, Afro-American, black, and black American are used interchangeably.

2. This definition for urban is based on a discussion in Edwin Eames and Judith Granich Goode, *Anthropology of the City: An Introduction to Urban Anthropology* (Englewood Cliffs, NJ: Prentice-Hall, 1977), 38–41.

3. Jacques Maquet, "L.A.: One Society, One Culture, Many Options," in *Selected Reports in Ethnomusicology, Volume 10: Musical Aesthetics and Multiculturalism in Los Angeles,* ed. Steven Loza (Los Angeles: Department of Ethnomusicology and Systematic Musicology, UCLA, 1994), 15.

4. Con Howe and Aaron Curtis, "Chat Room: Future Is in the Neighborhood," *Los Angeles Times* (19 September 1995): B2.

5. See Bruno Nettl, "Preliminary Remarks on Urban Folk Music in Detroit," *Western Folklore* 16 (1957): 37–42, and "Aspects of Folk Music in North American Cities," in *Music in the Americas*, ed. George List and Juan Orrego-Salas (Bloomington: Indiana University Research Center in Anthropology, Folklore, and Linguistics, 1967), 139–146; Charles Keil, *Urban Blues* (Chicago: University of Chicago Press, 1966); and James T. Koetting, "The Effects of Urbanization: The Music of the Kasena People of Ghana," *The World of Music* 17, no. 4 (1975): 23–31.

6. The history of African Americans in San Diego County dates to 1519. "During the Spanish and Mexican periods blacks, who accompanied Cortéz in 1519 and had been slaves until 1829, as well as mixed-blood Caliornios, were found at all levels of society" (Robert Fikes Jr., Gail Madyun, and Larry Malone, "Black Pioneers in San Diego: 1880–1920," *Journal of San Diego History* 27, no. 2 [Spring 1981]: 91–92). The founding of the city of Los Angeles in 1781 is surrounded by controversy because, of the forty-four *pobladores*, or settlers from Mexico, "twenty-six were either Black or of mixed racial ancestry." See further discussion in Lonnie Bunch III, *Black Angelenos: The Afro-American in Los Angeles, 1850–1950* (Los Angeles: California Afro-American Museum Foundation, 1988), 10.

7. Bunch, *Black Angelenos*, 11; William Mason and James Anderson, "The Los Angeles Black Community, 1781–1940," in *America's Black Heritage*, ed. Russell E. Belous. (Los Angeles: Los Angeles County Museum of Natural History, History Division, Bulletin No. 5, 1969), 42–64.

8. Douglas Henry Daniels, *Pioneer Urbanites: A Social and Cultural History of Black San Francisco* (Philadelphia: Temple University Press, 1980), 13–14.

9. Ibid., 17.

10. Keith E. Collins, *Black Los Angeles: The Maturing of the Ghetto 1940–50* (Saratoga, CA: Los Angeles Century 21 Publishing, 1980), 5–8.

11. Daniels, *Pioneer Urbanites*, 120–121.

12. Collins, *Black Los Angeles*, 8.

13. Daniels, *Pioneer Urbanites*, 13.

14. Jacqueline Cogdell DjeDje, "Gospel Music in the Los Angeles Black Community: A Historical Overview," *Black Music Research Journal* 9, no. 1 (Spring 1989): 36.

15. Daniels, *Pioneer Urbanites*, 31.

16. Bunch, *Black Angelenos*, 29.

17. In this chapter, "San Francisco Bay Area" and "Bay Area" are used interchangeably and include the cities of San Francisco, Oakland, Berkeley, Richmond, and surrounding communities. However, the phrase "East Bay" refers only to Oakland, Berkeley, and Richmond.

18. Lawrence P. Crouchett, Lonnie G. Bunch III, and Martha K. Winnacker, *Visions Toward Tomorrow: The History of the East Bay Afro-American Community 1852–1977* (Oakland: The Northern California Center for Afro-American History and Life, 1989), 17.

19. Fikes, et al., "Black Pioneers in San Diego," 91–92.

20. Robert L. Carlton, "Blacks in San Diego County: A Social Profile, 1850–1880," *Journal of San Diego History* 21, no. 4 (Fall 1975): 8.

21. Ibid.

22. Fikes, et al., "Black Pioneers in San Diego," 92.

23. Robert Fikes, "Black Pioneers of San Diego, 1850–1900: Out of Sight, Out of Mind," *San Diego Voice News & Viewpoint* (5 July 1978): A6; Fikes, et al., "Black Pioneers in San Diego," 102.

24. Robert Fikes, "Black Pioneers of San Diego, 1850–1900: An Introduction," *San Diego Voice News & Viewpoint* (15 February 1978): 8.

25. Daniels, *Pioneer Urbanites*, 99.

26. Collins, *Black Los Angeles*, 8.

27. Bunch, *Black Angelenos*, 21–22, 29–34; Patricia Carr Bowie, "The Cultural History of Los Angeles: From Rural Backwash to World Center" (Ph.D. diss., University of Southern California, 1980), 367.

28. Albert S. Broussard, *Black San Francisco: The Struggle for Racial Equality in the West, 1900–1954* (Lawrence, KS: University Press of Kansas, 1993), 5; Bunch, *Black Angelenos*, 21; Fikes, "Black Pioneers: Out of Sight," A16.

29. Broussard, *Black San Francisco*, 6.

30. Nolan Davis, "From Wilderness to Mansions: Southeast San Diego History Key to Area's Problems Now," *San Diego Evening Tribune* (3 April 1965).

31. Collins, *Black Los Angeles*, 44.

32. Ibid., 6.

33. Bunch, *Black Angelenos*, 38.

34. Lawrence B. DeGraff, "Negro Migration to Los Angeles, 1930–1950," (Ph.D. diss., University of California, Los Angeles, 1962), 257.

35. Collins, *Black Los Angeles*, 44.

36. DjeDje, "Gospel Music in the Los Angeles Black Community," 46.

37. Daniels, *Pioneer Urbanites*, 163.

38. Bunch, *Black Angelenos*, 39.

39. Betty Reid Soskin, personal interview with Jacqueline Cogdell DjeDje, 21 June 1989.

40. Crouchett, et al., *Visions Toward Tomorrow*, 45.

41. Julie Cheshire, "The World According to Art," *San Diego Downtown Newsweekly* (28 May 1984): 1; and V. M. McPherson, personal interview with Jacqueline Cogdell DjeDje, 17 February 1992.

42. Bunch, *Black Angelenos*, 21.

43. Bowie, "Cultural History," 368–372.

44. Rudolph M. Lapp, *Afro-Americans in California*, 2nd ed. (San Francisco: Boyd & Fraser Publishing Company, 1987), 84.

45. Norris Hundley Jr. and John A. Schutz, "Editors' Introduction," in Rudolph M. Lapp, *Afro-Americans in California*, 2nd ed. (San Francisco: Boyd & Fraser Publishing Co., 1987), iii.

46. Lapp, *Afro-Americans*, 77–78.

47. John Hope Franklin and Alfred A. Moss Jr., *From Slavery to Freedom: A History of African Americans*, 7th ed. (New York: McGraw-Hill, 1994), 514; and Jean E. Hoffman and Sydney D. Hammond, "A Documentary Study of the 'Logan Heights Riot' of August 1965" (A Research Project Report, San Diego State College, 1966).

48. Lapp, *Afro-Americans*, 75; Crouchett, et al. *Visions Toward Tomorrow*, 59.

49. Eugene J. Grigsby, "The Rise and Decline of Black Neighborhoods in Los Angeles," *UCLA Center for Afro-American Studies Report* 12, nos. 1 & 2 (Spring/Fall 1989): 16–17.

50. Tony Perry and Richard C. Paddock, "Super Bowl Hype Reflects a Tale of Two Different Cities," *Los Angeles Times* (26 January 1995): A1, A18–A19.

51. Mike Davis, *City of Quartz: Excavating the Future in Los Angeles* (New York: Vintage Books, 1990), 17; also see Cowe and Curtis, "Chat Room," B2.

52. Steven Loza, "Musical Aesthetics and Multiculturalism in Los Angeles: An Introduction," in *Selected Reports in Ethnomusicology, Volume 10: Musical Aesthetics and Multiculturalism in Los Angeles*, ed. Steven Loza (Los Angeles: Department of Ethnomusicology and Systematic Musicology, UCLA, 1994), 1–13.

53. For some of the works concerned with the city, music, and culture, see Koetting, "The Effects of Urbanization; Steven Loza, ed., *Selected Reports in Ethnomusicology, Volume 10: Musical Aesthetics and Multiculturalism in Los Angeles* (Los Angeles: Department of Ethnomusicology and Systematic Musicology, UCLA, 1994); Bruno Nettl, ed., *Eight Urban Musical Cultures: Tradition and Change* (Urbana: University of Illinois Press, 1978); Burton Peretti, *The Creation of Jazz: Music, Race, and Culture in Urban America* (Urbana: University of Illinois Press, 1992); Adelaida Reyes Schramm, "Ethnic Music, the Urban Area, and Ethnomusicology," *Sociologus* 29, no. 2 (1979): 1–21, and "Explorations in Urban Ethnomusicology: Hard Lessons from the Spectacularly Ordinary," *Yearbook for Traditional Music* 14 (1982): 1–14; Thomas Turino, "The Music of Andean Migrants in Lima, Peru: Demographics, Social Power, and Style," *Latin American Music Review* 9, no. 2 (1988):127–150, and *Moving Away from Silence: Music of the Peruvian Altiplano and the Experiment of Urban Migration* (Chicago: University of Chicago Press, 1993). For a few of the works related to the city as a context for research, see Eames and Goode, *Anthropology of the City*, 38–40; Richard G. Fox, "Rationale and Romance in Urban Anthropology," *Urban Anthropology* 1, no. 2 (1972): 205–233; John Gulick, "The City as Microcosm of Society," *Urban Anthropology* 4, no. 1(1975): 5–15; Kenneth Moore, "The City as Context: Context as Process," *Urban Anthropology* 4, no. 1 (1975): 17–25; and Robert Redfield and Milton Singer, "The Cultural Role of Cities," *Economic Development and Cultural Change* 3, no. 1 (1954): 53–73.

54. Delilah Beasley, *The Negro Trail Blazers of California* (Los Angeles: Times Mirror Printing and Binding, 1919).

55. James M. Trotter, *Music and Some Highly Musical People*, reprint ed. (New York: Johnson Reprint Corp., 1968 [1881]); Maude Cuny-Hare, *Negro Musicians and Their Music* (New York: Da Capo Press, 1974 [1936]); Eileen Southern, *The Music of Black Americans: A History*, 2nd ed. (New York: W.W. Norton, Inc., 1983; 3rd ed., 1997); Hildred Roach, *Black American Music: Past and Present* (New York: Crescendo Publishing Co., 1973), and *Black American Music: Past and Present, Volume II: Pan-African Composers Thenceforth and Now* (Malabar, FL: Robert E. Krieger Publishing Co., 1985).

56. Samuel A. Floyd Jr., ed., *Black Music Research Bulletin* 10, no. 1 (Spring 1988), and *Black Music Research Journal* 9, no. 1 (Spring 1989).

57. Tom Reed, *The Black Music History of Los Angeles-Its Roots: A Classical Pictorial History of Black Music in Los Angeles from the 1920s–1970* (Los Angeles: Black Accent Press, 1992).

58. Bette Yarbrough Cox, *Central Avenue—Its Rise and Fall (1890–c.1955), Including the Musical Renaissance of Black Los Angeles* (Los Angeles: BEEM Publications, 1996); and Bette Cox, ed., *Music in the Central Avenue Community 1890–c. 1955* (Los Angeles: BEEM Foundation, 1996).

59. See names of some of these musicians in Samuel A. Floyd Jr. and Marsha J. Reisser, "On Researching Black Music in California: A Preliminary Report about Sources and Resources," *Black Music Research Journal* 9, no. 1 (Spring 1989): 112.

60. Eileen Southern, *Biographical Dictionary of Afro-American and African Musicians* (Westport, CT: Greenwood Press, 1982); Stanley Sadie, ed., *The New Grove Dictionary of Music and Musicians* (London: Macmillan Publishers, Ltd., 1980); H. Wiley Hitchcock and Stanley Sadie, eds. *The New Grove Dictionary of American Music* (London: Macmillan Publishers, Ltd.,

1986); Barry Kernfeld, ed., *The New Grove Dictionary of Jazz* (London: Macmillan Publishers, Ltd., 1988); Eddie S. Meadows, *Jazz Research and Performance Materials: A Select Annotated Bibliography*, 2nd ed. (New York and London: Garland Publishing, Inc., 1995).

61. Jazz historian Steve Isoardi has conducted the majority of the interviews for the UCLA Oral History Program.

62. Hansonia L. Caldwell, "Music in the Lives of Blacks in California: The Beginnings," *Black Music Research Bulletin* 10, no. 1 (Spring 1988): 5–7; Bette Y. Cox, "A Selective Survey of Black Musicians in Los Angeles," *Black Music Research Bulletin* 10, no. 1 (Spring 1988): 7–10; William Duncan Allen, "An Overview of Black Concert Music and Musicians in Northern California from the 1940s to the 1980s," *Black Music Research Journal* 9, no. 1 (Spring 1989): 81–92; and Marion D. Schrock, "Aspects of Compositional Style in Four Works by Olly Wilson," *Black Music Research Journal* 9, no. 1 (Spring 1989): 93–108. See also Jacqueline Cogdell DjeDje, "An Expression of Black Identity: The Use of Gospel Music in a Los Angeles Catholic Church," *The Western Journal of Black Studies* 7, no. 3 (1983): 148–160; "Change and Differentiation: The Adoption of Black American Gospel Music in the Catholic Church," *Ethnomusicology* 30, no. 2 (Spring–Summer 1986): 223–252; "A Historical Overview of Black Gospel Music in Los Angeles," *Black Music Research Bulletin* 10, no. 1 (Spring 1988): 1–5; "Gospel Music in the Los Angeles Black Community: A Historical Overview," *Black Music Research Journal* 9, no. 1 (Spring 1989): 35–79; "The Beginnings of Gospel Music in the Bay Area," in *African-American Traditional Arts and Folklife in Oakland and the East Bay: A Collection of Essays*, ed. Willie R. Collins (Oakland: Cultural Arts Division, City of Oakland, 1992), 1–3; and "Los Angeles Composers of African American Gospel Music: The First Generations," *American Music* 11, no. 4 (Winter 1993): 412–457.

63. Since the 1970s, Lee Hildebrand has documented music making in the Bay Area; he has written numerous articles for local newspapers, liner notes for recordings, and reviews of recordings, films, and concerts. Also, he has coauthored and written books on two noted popular musicians from the Bay Area: M. C. Hammer and Johnny Otis. Martinelli's compilation of source materials includes a wealth of material published by Hildebrand. Also see Arnold Shaw, *Honkers and Shouters: The Golden Years of Rhythm and Blues* (New York: Collier Books, 1978), and "Researching Rhythm and Blues," *Black Music Research Journal* (1980): 71–79; Portia K. Maultsby, *Black American Popular Music: Rhythm and Blues, 1945–1955* (Washington, DC: Smithsonian Institution, 1986); and Ralph Eastman, "Central Avenue Blues: The Making of Los Angeles Rhythm and Blues, 1942–1947," *Black Music Research Journal* 9, no. 1 (Spring 1989): 19–33.

64. William Claxton, ed., *Jazz West Coast: A Portfolio of Photographs* (Hollywood: Linera Productions, 1955); Tom Stoddard, *Jazz on the Barbary Coast* (Chigwell, Essex: Storyville Publications, 1982); Robert Gordon, *Jazz West Coast* (New York: Quartet Books, 1986); Burt Wilson, *A History of Sacramento Jazz, 1948–1966: A Personal Memoir* (Canoga Park, CA: Burt Wilson, 1986); and Ted Gioia, *West Coast Jazz* (New York: Oxford University Press, 1992).

65. Stanley Dance, "Jazz Musicians in San Diego," *Black Music Research Bulletin* 10, no. 1 (Spring 1988): 10–11.

66. Floyd and Reisser, "On Researching Black Music," 110–111.

67. In the absence of chapters on these subjects in this volume, we refer the reader to source materials in the Appendix.

PART ONE

Music in an Urban Environment

Way out West on Central

Jazz in the African-American Community
of Los Angeles before 1930

Michael B. Bakan

In *West Coast Jazz*, Ted Gioia writes: "Conventional jazz history tells how jazz first traveled from New Orleans by riverboat up to Chicago. Yet just as early, jazz came by railroad from the Crescent City to California."[1] Jazz—understood in this article to be urban, brass-band inspired, blues-centered, ragtime-derived, improvisation-oriented, syncopated dance band music created by African-American musicians prior to 1930; music that began crystallizing into a distinct genre in New Orleans and other cities around the turn of the century, spreading throughout the United States over the next couple of decades and becoming most conspicuously developed during the 1920s in Chicago, Kansas City, and New York—did indeed travel west from New Orleans to California as early as it traveled north to Chicago and other major midwestern and northeastern cities. That music—"Louisiana-style or ragtime or jazz or whatever you want to call it," as it has been described by one of the most prominent California jazz musicians of the early days, Benjamin M. "Reb" Spikes[2]—was already alive and thriving on the West Coast by the second decade of this century.

Yet the story of jazz, as it has been told from so many perspectives in thousands of books, essays, and articles, has scarcely touched upon the rich history of the music's early development in California. Perhaps the most conspicuous area of neglect within this largely ignored area has been the African-American jazz scene that flourished in the Central Avenue district of Los Angeles during the 1920s and the years immediately preceding. Jazz historians, with few exceptions, have treated the early Los Angeles jazz scene as little more than a footnote to the New Orleans–Chicago–New York mainstream of early jazz development. It merits mention only as a place where certain prominent musicians spent some time before, after, or in between more historically significant phases of their careers in major jazz centers.

Thus, in reading the literature, one might discover in passing that the Creole

Band (a.k.a. the Original Creole Band), which played a major role in disseminating New Orleans–style jazz throughout the nation during the World War I era, was actually formed in Los Angeles; that both Ferdinand "Jelly Roll" Morton and Edward "Kid" Ory resided in Los Angeles for extended periods of time after leaving New Orleans and before moving on to Chicago (and that both ultimately died in California); that the first recordings ever made by an African-American jazz band, featuring a group led by Ory, were recorded in Los Angeles; that the first published compositions of Jelly Roll Morton were published in Los Angeles; that trombonists Britt Woodman and Lawrence Brown established themselves professionally in Los Angeles before moving east and achieving fame as members of Duke Ellington's orchestra; or that the great jazz vibraphone pioneer and bandleader Lionel Hampton spent most of the early part of his musical career playing drums in Los Angeles dance bands of the 1920s.

Beyond such cursory references, there is little to be found about the Los Angeles activities of these musicians, whose best-documented career accomplishments occurred in other parts of the country rather than in Southern California. As for those musicians who came from or migrated to Los Angeles and chose to stay there rather than move on to Chicago or New York, most have been all but forgotten, their musical careers documented in a handful of scattered writings by jazz historians; a small number of rare and obscure recordings; notices in African-American newspapers of the day, especially *The California Eagle* (a.k.a. the *Eagle*), and other archive-preserved documents; and the autobiographical recollections of a few musicians whose careers date back to the early days of Los Angeles jazz.

Drawing together these varied sources, this chapter presents a sociomusicological history of jazz in Los Angeles's African-American community before 1930, with particular focus on the years 1917–1929. This was a complex and fascinating period of transition and ambiguity during which jazz musicians and the music they performed helped to define the collective identity and social life of black Los Angeles, as well as the dynamics of that community's interaction with the city's dominant white population. In placing the musicians and their music within their sociocultural context, I hope not only to provide a much-needed account of a largely ignored chapter in the history of American jazz but also to make a contribution to the study of African-American cultural history in Los Angeles.

PRE-1930 JAZZ IN LOS ANGELES: A REVIEW OF THE LITERATURE

Jazz historians have devoted a good deal of attention to the study of "West Coast jazz," but this term, despite the broad and diverse frame of reference it implies, has come to be associated almost exclusively with one small slice of a very large pie: the "cool jazz" phenomenon of the 1950s, spearheaded by Miles Davis with the release of his album *Birth of the Cool* and developed mainly by California-based white artists such as Chet Baker, Dave Brubeck, and Shelly Manne. Even during this period, when Los Angeles achieved at least brief recognition as a major center of jazz innovation, the city's African-American jazz musicians received little notice beyond the local level. Ted Gioia's *West Coast Jazz* and Robert L. Gordon's *Jazz West Coast*[3] have particularly filled the void by providing balanced and complete accounts of modern (i.e., post–World War II) jazz in Los Angeles. Among the autobiographies and oral histories that provide important information about African-American culture and the Central Avenue jazz scene of the forties and fifties are Red Callender's *Unfinished Dream*[4] and Roy Porter's *There and Back*.[5] Though both Gioia and Gordon delve into the pre–World War II era of African-American jazz in Los Angeles in order to establish a historical context for their discussions of later developments, only Gioia goes as far back as the 1920s and preceding years, and his coverage of this early period, though informative, is minimal.[6]

Tom Reed's *The Black Music History of Los Angeles—Its Roots*[7] makes a concerted effort to explore the emergence and early history of African-American jazz and the Central Avenue–based cultural scene in which it flourished. This book is a veritable treasure-trove of rare photographs and other archival documents (newspaper and magazine notices, advertisements, promotional flyers, record jackets and labels, etc.) covering a period of fifty years, from 1920 to 1970. This impressive, attractive volume is a wonderful tribute to Central Avenue and to the musical and cultural history of Los Angeles's African-American community. Through its assemblage of photographs and other documentary materials, it paints an evocative portrait of that community's musical legacy. However, as a scholarly resource, it has severe limitations. The organization of materials is somewhat haphazard, and the text, mainly limited to captions and short introductory and transitional essay passages, provides valuable chunks of information but leaves a great deal unaccounted for, jumping about without much regard for chronological coherence. Bette Yarbrough Cox's *Central Avenue—Its Rise and Fall*,[8] despite its somewhat anecdotal presentation, is one of the few works that provides a more extensive discussion of jazz in Los Angeles prior to 1930. Cox includes excellent photographs of jazz musicians and venues as well as oral histories of Los Angeles musicians who personally experienced the Central Avenue jazz scene during the early 1900s.

Albert McCarthy's *Big Band Jazz*[9] is the only comprehensive jazz history text that provides reasonable documentation of Los Angeles's 1920s jazz scene, devoting a full seven pages to discussion of the careers, bands, and music of four performers who dominated that scene: Reb Spikes (as well as his brother and business partner John Spikes), Sonny Clay, Paul Howard, and Curtis Mosby.[10] Noteworthy here are McCarthy's assessments of recordings by these artists.[11]

Articles by jazz historians Floyd Levin and Lawrence Gushee represent some of the most important contributions to the literature on early jazz in Los Angeles. Levin has written about both "local" musicians of the period, such as Reb Spikes and Andrew Blakeney, and expatriate New Orleans jazz masters who resided in the city during the 1920s, particularly Kid Ory and Jelly Roll Morton.[12] Gushee's important research on the New Orleans–Los Angeles jazz connection includes an annotated list of New Orleans musicians who worked in California for extended periods between 1908 and 1925;[13] a fascinating study of the legendary Creole Band;[14] and a report on the early career of Jelly Roll Morton which chronicles Morton's activities in Los Angeles between 1917 and 1922 and suggests Jelly Roll may have spent time in the city as early as 1911.[15] Morton's Los Angeles years— along with those of Ory and cornetist Mutt Carey, another transplanted New Orleans jazz master—are also documented in Martin Williams's *Jazz Masters of New Orleans*.[16] Morton's own account of his tenure in Los Angeles prior to and during the early 1920s appears in a chapter entitled "I Took California" from the book *Mister Jelly Roll*,[17] a condensed and edited version of the jazz master's autobiographical oral history, transcribed by Alan Lomax from a lengthy series of recordings for the Library of Congress. *Mister Jelly Roll* represents Lomax's reduction of Morton's voluminous personal history into a concise, informative, and highly entertaining book.

Mister Jelly Roll and other autobiographies and oral histories of jazz musicians who resided in Los Angeles prior to 1930 inform a profound understanding of the period and its music. The autobiography of Pops Foster,[18] a bassist who began his career in New Orleans and is most remembered for his work with Louis Armstrong, contains valuable information on the author's experiences in Los Angeles during two periods when he was based there, the first in 1922–23 and the second around 1927–28. His colorful remembrances vividly recapture the lifestyle and musical activities of the period, especially with reference to expatriate New Orleans musicians such as Kid Ory, Ed "Montudie" Garland,[19] and Papa Mutt Carey. Lionel Hampton's autobiography, *Hamp*,[20] is both evocative and provocative. The third chapter, "Hollywood."[21] traces the development of the vibraphonist's career from the time of his arrival in Los Angeles from Chicago as an ambitious teenage drummer around 1923 or 1924 to his membership in Les Hite's Los Angeles–based big band beginning around 1930. Tom Stoddard's *Jazz on the Barbary Coast*,[22] the only book devoted exclusively to a study of early jazz history in California, delves even further into Los Angeles's musical past by including a autobiographical sketch of Reb Spikes. Spikes settled in the city in 1919, which, according to Stoddard, was right about the time when "the West Coast jazz scene shifted [from San Francisco] to Los Angeles."[23]

In addition to the sources already discussed, there are a few others worthy of mention. Bette Cox's "A Selective Survey of Black Musicians in Los Angeles, 1890–ca. 1945," William Claxton's photographic essay on West Coast jazz, a brief survey of early West Coast jazz by Leonard Kunstadt, and William Kenney's *Chicago Jazz: A Cultural History, 1904–1930* all contain references to pre-1930 African-American jazz musicians with Los Angeles ties.[24] Works by Lonnie Bunch[25] and Lawrence B. DeGraaf[26] explore the economic, political, and cultural conditions surrounding the musical life of the era.

The principal primary source for research in this area is *The California Eagle*, the African-American community's main newspaper during the period under investigation. Notices and advertisements published in the *Eagle* between 1917 and 1929 announcing performances by area jazz bands, as well as occasional reviews and articles, provided the blueprint of early Los Angeles jazz history from which this study was built. Personal interviews that I conducted in 1988 with two jazz musicians whose careers began in 1920s Los Angeles, trumpeter Teddy Buckner and saxophonist/clarinetist Jack McVea,[27] were also of fundamental importance.

What follows is a historical study of a jazz lifeworld. It features a few famous musicians who are remembered mainly for what they did before they moved to Los Angeles or after they left, a host of others who are barely remembered at all, and a city that has hardly been recognized as having had a jazz scene at all, let alone one worthy of serious interest, prior to 1930. Regardless of their overall impact on the historical development of jazz, however, the musicians and bands of Los Angeles in the early days of jazz were a major force in the life of the city's African-American community, and the stories of their musical lives add new depth and perspective to our understanding of the United States's musical and cultural legacy. Furthermore, on the basis of the few recordings that still survive, it is evident that the leading 1920s Los Angeles bands were highly accomplished musical outfits—with some fine "hot" soloists and talented composers and arrangers among their ranks—who lent considerable verve and style to the instrumental blues, rags, stomps, novelty numbers, and popular songs that constituted the jazz repertoire of the day.

JAZZ BEGINNINGS IN CALIFORNIA

In the early years of this century, San Francisco was the main center for "hot" music on the West Coast. Most African-American musical activity was centered in a district known as the Barbary Coast, the city's answer to New Orleans's Storyville district. An abundance of nightclubs, brothels, and other spots that featured music in a variety of contexts provided ample work opportunities for local players and drew African-American musicians and other entertainers from throughout the country.

A touring band of New Orleans musicians led by bassist Bill Johnson first brought the new jazz style of New Orleans to the Barbary Coast in 1908, and their impact on more conventional dance music styles of locally based bands such as Sid LeProtti's So Different Orchestra (see Figure 1.1) was soon felt.[28] The "ragged," syncopated, driving four-beat rhythmic style of the New Orleans jazz musicians transformed the more squared-off, heavy two-beat feel of local rhythm sections. Quasi-polyphonic, improvised embellishments of the main melody by a "front line" of cornet, clarinet, and trombone gained currency. Instrumental blues, rags, and stomps were added to the usual repertoire of quadrilles, waltzes, polkas, and popular songs, stimulating the development of new dance styles. By the outbreak of World War I, San Francisco had already given birth to several jazz dances that became popular nationwide, including the Texas Tommy, Turkey

Figure 1.1. Original So Different Band. Left to right: Pete ?, drums; Adam Mitchell (also known as "Slocum"), clarinet; Reb Spikes, saxophone; Sid LeProtti, piano; Gerald Wells, flute; and Clarence Williams, bass. From Floyd Levin's Jazz Archives. Used by permission.

Trot, Grizzly Bear, and Bunny Hug.[29] Even the word "jazz" came to have an important connection with San Francisco, that being the city where, in 1913, the term first appeared in print with reference to music.[30] Jazz music and jazz bands became increasingly important parts of the very active Barbary Coast entertainment scene up until the government closed the district down in 1921 as part of a Prohibition-era effort to curtail vice.

Even before the closing of the Barbary Coast, the pendulum of jazz activity on the West Coast had begun to swing southward to Los Angeles. Though jazz took longer to germinate in the conservative African-American community of Los Angeles than it had in San Francisco, the community experienced rapid growth and change, and the Central Avenue district of the city was "a musical hotbed by the start of the 'Jazz Age' in the 1920s."[31] The closing of the Barbary Coast was the decisive event that established Los Angeles as the premiere center for jazz on the West Coast. As Stoddard explains, "The Barbary Coast had closed and the centre of Bay Area jazz disappeared. . . . It was far easier to make it in Los Angeles and many musicians went south, some staying for the rest of their lives."[32]

With the largest and fastest-growing African-American urban community in the West, as well as the growing Hollywood movie industry and an emerging recording industry, Los Angeles also became a magnet for jazz musicians from other parts of the country, especially New Orleans, where jazz players suffered a devastating blow with the closing of Storyville in 1917. Without question, Chicago and then New York served as the main new centers for the growth and development of jazz in the 1920s and years immediately preceding, with Kansas City, St. Louis, and Memphis also figuring prominently in the music's ascent. But jazz also thrived in Los Angeles, where an interesting mix of local players, New Orleans expatriates, and itinerant and resident musicians from all over the country contributed to an active and exciting musical culture. Jazz became a major component of the social life of Los Angeles's African-American community; it played an important role in that community's efforts to establish a sense of identity during a rather turbulent historical period marked by growth, pride, and prosperity, on the one hand, and by external pressures and internal strife and confusion, on the other.

Black Los Angeles, 1915–1930: An Era of Growth, Change, and Paradox

It was in 1988 that I first became aware of the early history of African-American jazz in Los Angeles. I was reading a catalog for an exhibit at the California Afro-American Museum in Los Angeles: *Black Angelenos: The Afro-American in Los Angeles, 1850–1950.*[33] The catalog was written by the then curator of the museum, historian Lonnie Bunch. It was the following passage about jazz on Central Avenue during the final years of what Bunch defined as the "Golden Era of Black Angelenos," an era spanning the three decades from 1900–1929, that piqued my curiosity:

> For many Black Angelenos, the plethora of musical establishments, jazz dens and nightclubs located in this area made Central Avenue the entertainment center of the city. . . . It was the jazz clubs that brought the evening crowds to Central Avenue, where new migrants[,] established residents and "White Nordics" rubbed elbows on the dance floor. Nightclubs such as the Kentucky Club at 25th Street and Central with its Kentucky racing decor, the Club Alabam, the Savoy at 55th Street and Central . . . , the Apex Night Club at 4015 Central Avenue, . . . and many other establishments, all provided opportunity for Black musicians to develop a following, and a chance for the patrons to have "cool, clean, scads of fun."[34]

Bunch's discussion of this evidently active and exciting jazz scene did not extend beyond this one paragraph, and it ultimately proved to be a bit misleading: my subsequent research would reveal that the specific clubs mentioned opened no earlier than 1928, just a year before the end of the so-called Golden Era. But even given the sparseness of Bunch's account and the questionable accuracy of his chronology of the development of Central Avenue's jazz venues, the subject matter was fascinating.

My interest was strengthened all the more by Bunch's discussion of the complex social, cultural, and political environment of Los Angeles's African-American community in the 1920s. "Central Avenue was in its heyday as the center of both the Black business and residential communities"[35] and also host to a flourishing musical and literary movement similar to the Harlem Renaissance but smaller in scale.[36] Black businesses, doctors' and dentists' offices, beautiful homes, publications (including *The California Eagle*), nightclubs, theaters, and hotels were sources of pride and symbols of prosperity and opportunity.[37] The pinnacle of entrepreneurial accomplishment was the opening of the glamorous, black-owned Hotel Somerville in 1928, "the Jewel of Central Avenue," renamed the Hotel Dunbar in 1929 when economic hardships brought on by the Depression forced its owner, Dr. John Somerville, to sell the establishment. In the political arena, the election of African American Frederick Madison Roberts to the office of state assemblyman in 1919, an office he held until 1934, represented "the crowning achievement of the Golden Era of Black Los Angeles."[38]

Though Los Angeles had historically been one of the best American cities for black residents in terms of freedoms, opportunities, and standards of living, conditions decisively worsened during the twenties. Lionel Hampton, the most celebrated musician to emerge from the 1920s Los Angeles jazz scene, moved west from Chicago as a teenager around 1924. His arrival in California rudely awakened him to the ugliness of racism:

> Hollywood was a pretty town, but I didn't think much of the attitude toward blacks there. It was my first real experience with discrimination. Back in Chicago, the black population was so big that you could live and go to school and work and never even have to talk to a white person. And even if you went downtown, you didn't have to sit in the back of the bus or anything. But out in Hollywood, it was like the South in some ways. You had to sit in the back of the bus, go into the white nightclub by the back door. Taxis wouldn't stop for you. Also, black musicians didn't get paid as much as white musicians—in fact, blacks got about 20 percent of what whites made.[39]

The 1920s and the years immediately preceding them, constituted a dynamic and turbulent period in the history of black Los Angeles. The internal pride, achievement, and determination of the African-American community were challenged by escalating racism, oppressive political conditions, overwhelming population growth, and socioeconomic diversification. The establishment of distinctly African-American cultural icons became important in the promotion of some sense of cultural identity and integrity for the community. Jazz helped to facilitate social integration, and jazz musicians became symbols of the energy, spirit, pride, and struggle of a new kind of African-American culture. There was a sense of liberation and fresh vitality in the new sound of jazz, valued qualities for a community trying to move forward at the same time that it was being forced to close in upon itself.

The Pre-1930 African-American Jazz Scene in Los Angeles: A History

The year 1917 stands as an important landmark in U.S. history and in the history of jazz. The United States entered World War I; the first jazz recording was made—"Livery Stable Blues," by the Original Dixieland Jazz Band (a white group); and Storyville, the famed red-light district of New Orleans, where the pioneers of jazz had honed their craft and earned their livelihood, was closed down.

With the closing of Storyville, many of New Orleans's musicians found it necessary to go elsewhere to make a living. Following the general migrational trends of African Americans of the period, most headed north to major urban industrial centers, especially Chicago and New York. Chicago became the new center of "hot" jazz music, with musicians including Joe "King" Oliver arriving in 1918 and Louis Armstrong joining him there a few years later. Some of the musicians, however, went west, and their principal destination was usually Los Angeles, the fastest-growing African-American community in that part of the country.

Even before 1917, New Orleans jazz musicians began migrating to Los Angeles on a temporary or permanent basis. A group of New Orleans jazzers led by bassist Bill Johnson, who would later become the leader of the Creole Band, reportedly played a one-month engagement at the Red Feather Tavern in Los Angeles in 1908, after which time they returned to New Orleans. The band's cornet player, Ernest Coycault, stayed in Los Angeles for good,[40] becoming a leading figure in the city's jazz scene from the outset.

By 1912, Bill Johnson had returned to Los Angeles and set up residence there. Joining forces with several other New Orleans expatriates who had moved to California either independently or at his invitation, he formed the Creole Band in 1914. Along with Johnson on bass, the band featured the legendary cornetist Freddie Keppard, clarinetist George Baquet, violinist James Palao, trombonist Edward Vincent, and drummer Ollie "Dink" Johnson. Performances by the band, billed alternately as the Creole Orchestra, the Imperial Band of New Orleans, and Johnson's Imperial Band of Los Angeles and New Orleans, are documented by announcements in *The California Eagle* between April and July 1914 for events such as a truck drivers' outing, an Emancipation Day carnival, and a Fourth of July all-night ball at the Dreamland Hall.[41]

The Creole Band got its big break at a heavyweight prize fight between Leach Cross and Joe Rivers in Los Angeles on August 11, 1914. In attendance was Carl Walker, manager of the Pantages theatrical company. He was so taken by the group's performance between the undercard and the main event that he arranged for an audition with his boss, Alec Pantages, the famous theatrical impresario. Clarinetist George Baquet recalled the incident years later in a 1965 address to the New Orleans Jazz Club: "[W]hen we played the then popular 'Mandalay,' Freddie Keppard, our cornetist, stood up with his egg mute and an old Derby Hat on the bell of the instrument. The crowd stood up as one man and shouted for us to get up into the ring, and screamed and screamed. When we got down, Mr. Carl Walker, Mr. Alec Pantages' manager, stepped up asking for our card."[42]

The audition for Pantages was an unqualified success, resulting in an offer to perform on the Pantages vaudeville tour circuit. Baquet remembers that at the audition Pantages was so impressed that "he jumped up on the stage and asked us to form an act, he did not care what, so long as he had that music. So, going into a huddle we formed a plantation act with a comedian, the character of Old Man Mose."[43]

Over the next four years, the Creole Band was a fixture on the American vaudeville circuit, introducing the sounds of New Orleans jazz to many parts of the nation even before the advent of jazz recordings or the diaspora of New Orleans jazz musicians to Chicago and elsewhere in the wake of Storyville's demise. According to Eileen Southern, "It was this band, the Original Creole Band, that carried the jazz of New Orleans to the rest of the nation."[44]

It was around the time of the Creole Band's 1914 performance at the Cross-Rivers boxing match that New Orleans–style jazz began to make inroads into the small and conservative African-American music scene of Los Angeles. Up to that time, Los Angeles had remained a rather sleepy town in terms of nightlife and music making. Pioneer Los Angeles musician Reb Spikes reported to Stoddard that "Los Angeles had mostly just piano players in the early days before 1913. I know when I used to go to dances here they just had a piano player. He had all the dance jobs and his name was Sam McVea. He finally got up to three pieces: piano, mandolin, and drums. That's the only Negro I remember around here, and you couldn't have a dance unless you had McVea. We didn't have any dance halls in Los Angeles so there weren't any places for musicians to play. San Francisco had the dance halls for the bands."[45]

The Sam McVea referred to by Spikes was likely related to (or perhaps was himself) the father of Jack McVea. Jack got his start as a musician playing banjo for his father's group, McVea's Howdy Band, in the 1920s, joining the band when he was only eleven years old. According to Jack, the Howdy Band always played from written arrangements in a straight style "without ragging." Most of Los Angeles's black dance-band musicians were formally trained in European art music, to a greater degree than their counterparts elsewhere in the country,[46] and music-reading ability was a prerequisite for professional success on the society dance-band scene. Black Angelenos were, on the whole, more affluent and more formally educated during the first part of the century than any comparable African-American community in the country, and this was reflected in musical training and tastes.[47]

Prior to a large-scale expansion of railroad service to California around 1915, only the wealthiest of southern blacks could get to the West Coast. Los Angeles remained a rather exclusive enclave for African Americans of high economic and social standing, with an inordinately low percentage of unskilled urban workers, farmers, and others representing lower economic brackets.[48] Such a community had no desire to be identified with a larger "black American culture" and especially abhorred the notion of association with poor blacks of the rural South. The valued symbols and cultural practices of black Los Angeles reflected the community's adaptations of white middle-class culture. Measures of sophistication and prestige were largely held in common by both groups. In terms of musical taste,

European art music and popular mainstream dance music—played by musicians who "were expected to read music and to play the music as written" with "very little improvisation or embellishing of melodies"[49]—were seen as far more appropriate to the values and aspirations of the established community than were musical forms coming out of the South, such as blues and jazz. Paul Howard, who moved to Los Angeles from Ohio in 1910 when he was about fifteen years old and became one of the city's major musicians and bandleaders in the 1920s, recalled in an interview with Berta Wood that before 1915 the main entertainment in the city's clubs involved German beer garden music, which, along with church music, the symphony, and an occasional brass band, "was all the music there was in those days."[50] Before and during the 1920s, musicians such as John Gray and William T. Wilkins ran music schools that provided conservatory-type musical training for young African-American musicians. Art music recitals by local musicians and internationally renowned black concert artists, including Roland Hayes and Florence Cole-Talbert, were presented quite regularly.[51]

Against the background of this conservative musical environment, it is perhaps no coincidence that the particular New Orleans jazz musicians who enjoyed the greatest success in Los Angeles in the early days of the city's jazz scene—for example, Jelly Roll Morton, Kid Ory, William Johnson, and Ernest Coycault—were light-skinned Creoles with excellent formal musical training. The specific significance of such formal skills within the context of the particular demands of the city's jazz scene will be explored later in this chapter.

As southern blacks began migrating to Los Angeles in ever-increasing numbers in the middle part of the 1910s, the Los Angeles African-American community not only grew dramatically, it also changed dramatically, and the musical climate of the time followed suit. Reb Spikes states that in 1913, "The only Negro-owned place [for music] in Los Angeles was the Dreamland at Fourth and Standard [but] durin' the war, from 1914 on, there was four or five Negro-owned places."[52] Spikes mentions the Cadillac Cafe and Murray's Cafe (at 56th on Central) as two such places, both of which were owned by "a Negro fella named Murray."[53] The Dreamland Hall at Eighth and Spring Street, first of the black-owned Los Angeles dance clubs, was, incidentally, the venue for one of the Creole Band's early Los Angeles performances prior to the group's discovery by Pantages.[54]

As the community grew on and around Central Avenue and the demand for music for social occasions grew in response, bands began to form. They were made up of local musicians, New Orleans musicians, and players from other parts of the country, especially Texas and, somewhat later, Chicago. By February 1916, Central Avenue was host to a number of black-owned businesses: two hotels, a dry goods store, the Angelus motion picture theater (advertised in the March 10, 1916, *California Eagle* as the "Only Show House Owned by Colored Men in the Entire West"),[55] the Booker T. Washington Building, a drugstore, and numerous smaller businesses. Central Avenue was growing quickly, and, as Gioia points out, "From the first, black music was part of this economic expansion."[56]

The demand for jazz and "syncopated music" grew as a result of both the influx of African Americans from Louisiana and other parts of the South and the excitement felt by more adventurous Angelenos who had been intoxicated by the hot sounds of the Creole Band and touring groups who came through town. Even local bands that had not traditionally played in a true jazz style got in on the jazz vogue. The Wood Wilson Band, for example, which was already active as a local dance band by 1913 (at which time Reb Spikes played with the group),[57] did not include any bona fide jazz players; yet by 1916, when a young Paul Howard joined the group, doubling on saxophone and clarinet, bandleader Wilson had renamed the group Wood Wilson's Syncopators, and the band was being billed as a "Famous Jass Band" at such events as Los Angeles's first-ever automobile show, which took place at the Watts Country Club.[58]

It was about a year prior to his joining Wilson's band (his first music job) that Howard first caught the jazz bug, hearing the Creole Band for the first time at the Pantages Theater in Los Angeles. Howard recalls, "I had never heard anything like it in my life. I was working at Bullock's department store and going to school and I cut both of them to hear the band. During their two-week engagement I didn't miss a performance."[59] After a brief stint with Wilson's Syncopators, Howard moved on to McVea's Howdy Band at the Dreamland Hall and in 1918 joined the Black and Tan Jazz Orchestra. The Black and Tan was originally from Texas, a ten-piece "cake-walking ragtime brass band that came to Los Angeles with a carnival"[60] in 1916 or earlier. A notice in the January 8, 1916, edition of *The California Eagle* announces a dance at 19th and Central featuring the Black and Tan Orchestra.[61]

In 1918 local trombonist Harry Southard, who had been active in Los Angeles dance bands since at least 1913, when he and Reb Spikes were both members of the Wood Wilson Band,[62] took over leadership of the Black and Tan. As Howard puts it, Southard "reshuffled" the group into a jazz band,[63] changing its name from the Black and Tan Orchestra (or Band) to the Black and Tan *Jazz* Orchestra (the billing used in the *Eagle* for an October 12, 1919, appearance at the Dreamland Cafe).[64] Unlike Wilson's band, the Black and Tan did have at least one "genuine" jazz musician, Ernest Coycault, the cornet and trumpet player who had come to Los Angeles in 1908 with Bill Johnson's first New Orleans touring band and stayed.[65] In addition to Coycault, Southard hired Howard to play clarinet and tenor saxophone. The Black and Tan became one of the busiest groups in Los Angeles through the first half of the twenties, posing the most serious competition to bands led by newly arriving New Orleans musicians, especially those of Jelly Roll Morton and Kid Ory.

Jelly Roll Morton and Kid Ory: Resident New Orleans Jazz Masters

Jelly Roll Morton, the highly influential pianist, composer, bandleader, and self-proclaimed "inventor of jazz," was the first of these two jazz luminaries to move

west. Though he had been to California as early as 1912 and possibly even earlier,[66] it was not until 1917[67] that Morton actually stationed himself in the state.
Based primarily in Los Angeles, he also performed in San Diego and San Francisco touring as far south as Tampico, Mexico, and as far north as Vancouver,
Canada, over the course of the next five years. Often his touring activities centered around cabaret and dance-hall performances of his vaudeville show, which
featured the famous entertainer Bert Williams.[68]

Beginning in 1917, Morton worked the cabarets along Central Avenue, such as
the Cadillac Cafe (553 Central—see Figure 1.2), the Newport Bar, and the Penny
Dance Hall (Ninth Street at Central). Reed notes performances by Jelly Roll at
George Brown's Little Harlem and Baron Long's (both in Watts), at the U.S. Grand
Hotel, and at the Jump Steady Club, where he appeared with the great blues
singer Jimmy Rushing. Reed also notes Morton's employment as pianist for a
house of prostitution in an area of downtown Los Angeles called "Nigger Alley."[69]

Of these establishments, the only one that advertised in the *Eagle* was the Cadillac Cafe, which beginning in November 1917 promoted itself in newspaper ads as
having "The Highest Class Entertainers, Music and Service."[70] Though Morton's
name does not appear in the ads, his autobiography[71] indicates that the Cadillac was
his first main gig after he arrived in Los Angeles in 1917 and that the band he played
with there initially was composed of local (at least, non–New Orleans) players:

> The Cadillac was again in bloom. Of course, the musicians couldn't play the tunes
> we could in New Orleans; they didn't have the ability. So we had to play what we
> could—*The Russian Rag, Black and White, Maple Leaf Rag, Liza Jane* (a little comedy
> song, the whole Coast went for that), *Daddy Dear, I'm Crying For You, Melancholy Baby*—
> these were quite prominent in 1917, if I don't get the years mixed up. Then I wrote a
> tune and called it *Cadillac Rag* that we used to do with a singer.[72]

The first reference to Morton in the *Eagle* appears on the second page of the
April 5, 1919, issue. Here, the first of a series of daily ads indicates that "the Great
Jelly Roll and his Jazz Band" performed nightly at the Dixie Hotel Bar and Cafe on
Jackson Street near Kerney for at least three months (see Figure 1.3).[73] Following the
ads for the extended stay at the Dixie, Morton's name disappears from the paper,
not reappearing until May 1922. It is likely that for at least part of the intervening
three years his musical activities centered around a small dance hall he took on as a
business venture after deciding to settle in Los Angeles (at least temporarily).

Morton's life as a businessman also involved pimping, gambling, and hustling.[74]
Given his prosperity during his years in Los Angeles, which was only nominally attributable to his musical activities,[75] there was clearly a market for the "sportin'
life" on Central Avenue. This was a cause of distress for the upstanding, conservative, black Angeleno establishment, which feared the community's moral standards would decline as the migration of southern blacks increased. The conser-
vatives found support for their positions in the pages of the *Eagle*, as shown in the
following passage from a 1917 article:

Figure 1.2. Jelly Roll Morton at the Cadillac Cafe, Los Angeles, 1917 or 1918. Left to right: "Common Sense" Ross, Albertine Pickins, Jelly Roll Morton, Ada "Brick-top" Smith, Eddie Rucker, Mabel Watts. From Floyd Levin's Jazz Archives. Used by permission.

The Hotel Gordon, of 750 Pacific Street, Has Moved
TO ITS NEW AND SPACIOUS BUILDING AT
606-608 JACKSON ST.
WHERE IT WILL BE KNOWN AS THE

 DIXIE HOTEL Bar and Cafe

Entertainment Every Evening by the Great Jelly Roll and his
Jazz Band — Now Open For Business — Ladies Entrance

DON'T FORGET THE ADDRESS: 606 and 608 JACKSON STREET
Right Above Kerney Street
Will announce Grand Opening later.   ALEX COCHRANE, Prop.

Figure 1.3. Hotel Gordon/Dixie Hotel. Advertisement for Jelly Roll Morton at the Dixie Hotel Bar and Cafe, *The California Eagle* (5 April 1919): 2.

The question has been asked of us what are we going to do about conditions on Central Avenue. It is claimed that gambling is flourishing on this thoroughfare like the proverbial Green Bay tree, but we surmise that the anti dice shaking ordinance will now at least put a quietus on the crap games and reduce the pernicious practice to a minimum. At any event the *Eagle* at all times stands for law and order and we must insist that Central Avenue shall have the fullest protection from those who choose to violate the law.[76]

Further efforts to crack down on corruption and vice resulted in a city ordinance requiring that all dance halls close at midnight. As the proprietor of a dance hall, Morton was frustrated by the ordinance, and to get around the restriction he "went partners with Pops Woodward, the trombone player and we opened up the Wayside Park at Leek's Lake out in Watts County. There we could stay open all night."[77] Just what Morton's business arrangement was with Reb and John Spikes, who ran the cafe at Wayside Park and were in charge of its entertainment programs, is not entirely clear. It appears that Morton was hired by the Spikeses as a kind of musical director for the amusement park.

Exactly when Morton's group started performing at Wayside Park is also a matter for speculation, but it is certain that by May 1922 his group was playing there regularly. An announcement in the *Eagle* billed a performance by "Jelly Roll's Incomparable 10-Piece Jazz Symphony" at Wayside Park featuring "Dancing from 2:00 p.m. till 3:00 a.m."[78] Subsequent notices in the paper indicate that Morton's orchestra became Wayside Park's house band for several months, playing every Thursday and Saturday at dances that were produced "Under responsible management—Good order always assured."[79] It seems that Morton played at Wayside until sometime before the end of 1922, when he left Los Angeles for Arizona.

The Wayside Park dances became a focal point of social life in Los Angeles's African-American community during the 1920s. Apparently running all afternoon, all evening, and into the early morning hours, they drew large and diverse crowds ranging from families seeking a venue for an outing or a picnic to styling nightlife types looking for some fun and action. Visiting black celebrities also found their way to Wayside Park dances on occasion. In April 1922, for example, Morton entertained Joe "King" Oliver there.[80] Some of the faces in the band were no doubt familiar to Oliver, since Morton's groups by this time were made up almost exclusively of expatriate New Orleans jazz players: Pops Woodward, Bill Johnson, Buddy Petit, Frankie Dusen, and Wade Whaley (or Waley), to name a few.[81] According to one source, Oliver himself played a "short appearance at Leake's Lake," supported by a band that included Sonny Clay on drums.[82]

Petit, Dusen, and Whaley moved to Los Angeles at the invitation of Morton and Bill Johnson, both of whom were enjoying prosperous careers and thought it would be a good investment "to bring a real New Orleans band to the coast in order to build Leek's Lake up."[83] Dressed in their sharpest clothes, Johnson and Morton went to the train station to pick up their old cronies, riding in Johnson's very fine MacFarland automobile. As Morton reports in *Mister Jelly Roll:*

We knew they would arrive in the antiquated dress habitual to New Orleans musicians, their instruments all taped up to keep them airtight and Waley's clarinet in his back pocket. . . . We were afraid somebody would see them and think they were clowns, so we rushed them to the tailors and put them in some decent-looking clothes. . . .

But, man, those guys could really play. Petit was second only to Keppard on the cornet, had tremendous power in all registers and great ideas. He was a slow reader, but if the tune was played off first, he would pick up his part so fast no one knew he couldn't read. And, as for Dusen, he was the best there was at that time on trombone. So we had a very hot five-piece band and made plenty money—$75 a night and the tips doubled the salaries.[84]

The music and the money may have been great, but Petit, Dusen, and Whaley, by Morton's account, could not adjust to the high style of West Coast living preferred by Jelly Roll, Johnson, and other transplanted New Orleans musicians. The newly arrived jazz artists would show up for gigs at Wayside Park with "a bucket of red beans and rice and cook it on the job." Morton and drummer Dink Johnson (brother of Anita Gonzales, Jelly Roll's girlfriend)[85] began to ridicule their lowbrow bandmates mercilessly. "And Buddy and Frankie blew up," recalled Morton, "threatened to kill us. Next day, they left town, without notice, and went back to New Orleans. Which shows you never fool with a New Orleans musician, as he is noted for his hot temper."[86]

The indignant departure of Petit and Dusen took place in 1922 by Morton's reckoning. As Pops Foster remembers it, Dusen did depart Los Angeles in 1922, but for different reasons than those described by Morton. According to Foster, it was Dusen's inability to make the scene musically, rather than in terms of social etiquette or style of dress, that prompted him to leave California. Dusen, Petit, and a couple of other New Orleans musicians had a band that got a job playing at a vaudeville theater, Foster says. "The first week they played their music and the people raved over them. The next week the vaudeville acts came in and they had to play music for the acts. None of them could read and that was it." Dusen reportedly caught the train back to New Orleans that same night.[87]

If there is truth to Foster's account, Dusen was but one of many players who moved to Los Angeles from New Orleans, Chicago, Texas, and other parts of the country with hopes of improved professional prospects, only to find that whatever their merits as improvisers, "syncopators," and "fakers," the particular demands of the Los Angeles musical scene were not geared to their success. Even with the rising popularity of jazz, opportunities to play "hot" jazz remained limited in Los Angeles. For a great many musicians from the South and East, a lack of music-reading ability rendered professional survival impossible. As Jack McVea explains, they "couldn't make a living here because they didn't read well enough."[88] As jazz bands increased in size and musical aesthetics changed through the 1920s, New Orleans "hot" jazz gradually transformed into the more polished and arranged big-band styles of the "swing era" of the 1930s. "Unschooled" jazz musicians faced a steady decline in marketability nationwide, but in Los Angeles, the obstacles for non- or poor-reading musicians were severely limiting from the very beginning.

Even in the playing and appreciation of "hot" jazz, the musical priorities of Los Angeles musicians and their audiences seem to have been somewhat different from those of their counterparts in other parts of the country. Because of the European art music background of most local players and the conservative aesthetic sensibilities of Los Angeles's black establishment, well-schooled local musicians with limited skills in improvisation tended to enjoy greater professional success than hot-blowing improvisers from New Orleans, Chicago, and elsewhere. For example, Reb Spikes states: "I was never much of a jazzman. I played baritone sax and I never could play a lot of hot jazz. I played a lot of counterpoint like cello parts. That's what made our music good and different from anybody else. All them other guys was jammin' and jammin', but when we'd play, I'd be carryin' a counter-melody, and I always tried to play two melodies."[89] Jack McVea's assessment of his own abilities as a jazz saxophone player reflects a similar perspective: "I wasn't a great jazzman, not a real improviser, but I really knew how to play a melody; get that right sound and phrasing."[90] One would not expect to hear comments like these from early Chicago jazz stars. Although on the basis of available phonograph recordings it is difficult to challenge Gioia's assertion that "in the 1920s there was no 'West Coast jazz,' if by that one means a distinctive regional style,"[91] the musical skills that enabled one to make it on the Los Angeles jazz scene apparently differed from those that helped one succeed in, say, Chicago. From this one might reasonably speculate that such distinctions would have been reflected, at least to some extent, in a regional distinctiveness in musical style. Perhaps the long-standing, sometimes inappropriate perception of an essential contrast between the intense, adventurous jazz characteristic of the East Coast and the more laid-back, "refined" West Coast jazz aesthetic has an even longer history than we are currently aware of, dating back to the earliest days of California jazz. The comments by Spikes and McVea and the relatively conservative cultural inclinations of the Los Angeles African-American community of the 1920s outlined in Bunch[92] and other writings would seem to support such a notion.

In any case, the musicians from New Orleans and other parts of the country who did achieve professional success in Los Angeles tended to be "schooled" musicians. Jelly Roll Morton, Kid Ory, Ernest Coycault, and Sonny Clay, for example, were all skilled readers in addition to being great improvisers, and they called upon their formal musical training not only on society dance-band gigs but in their jazz playing activities as well. Ory, who played with Morton in Los Angeles before he was a member of Morton's famous Red Hot Peppers recording bands in Chicago, told Floyd Levin in an interview that Morton "was a very tough man to work for. . . . He knew what he wanted and would not permit any variation from the arrangements he had written. They were tough to play—the tempos were difficult—lots of key changes. But he was right. The records sound great!"[93]

Sonny Clay was another talented composer/arranger/bandleader who had impressive formal musical skills and required the same of the musicians he hired for his bands. Clay learned to read music from his first music teacher, one Professor Ariola, with whom he studied while growing up in Phoenix. As Clay told John Bentley, Ariola "made me read every fly speck on the sheet music."[94] The trombonist in Clay's band, Luther Gravens, lacked comparable training and thus struggled to keep up with the demands of Clay's musical arrangements. In the early part of his tenure with Clay, Gravens was very resourceful (but not always successful) in trying to work around his limited reading skills, as illustrated in an amusing anecdote told by Clay to John Bentley:

> Though the band was playing only blues and stomps during this period the music was still arranged, which presented a small problem to current trombonist Luther Gravens. Whenever the sheet music handed him proved difficult Luther somehow managed to lose it during the course of the evening. For the balance of the night he would lean heavily towards Coycault and follow the cornet lead. After this had taken place several times Coycault became aware of what Gravens was doing and began taking liberties with the melody that left the trombonist a little distraught at what course to follow. Gravens was, however, a fine musician and was finally made to accept the fact that he had to read to maintain his spot in the band.[95]

Individual musicians responded differently to the musical demands of 1920s Los Angeles. Faced with the reality of his inadequacies as a reader but aware of his tremendous talents as a jazz trombonist, Frankie Dusen chose to leave the city and seek out a more hospitable musical environment very shortly after his arrival out west in 1922. Luther Gravens, conversely, chose to stay in Los Angeles and through diligent effort was eventually able to bring his reading skills up to the necessary level of competence.

For Jelly Roll Morton, who, like Dusen, left Los Angeles in 1922, the decision to move on had little if anything to do with musical considerations; it was, rather, a matter of personal concern. Morton left Los Angeles to follow his "paramour and muse,"[96] Anita Gonzales, to Arizona, where she was going to open a restaurant. The restaurant did not last long, and soon the couple had moved back to the West Coast, this time to San Francisco, where Morton opened a club called the Jupiter.[97] Eventually, Morton moved on to Chicago, New York, and other places before ultimately returning to Los Angeles in 1940, dying in poverty and obscurity in 1941.

Though the Los Angeles stage of Morton's career has been treated as little more than a footnote by most historians, during the five years he resided there he produced some of his most important work. According to Martin Williams, "it was probably during the California years that Morton came to understand that music was his real calling, and his composing there seems to have been prolific."[98] Entering into a publishing venture with the Spikes brothers, Morton's earliest musical manuscript, "Froggie Moore Rag," as well as "Wolverine Blues" and "Kansas City Stomp," were first published in Los Angeles. According to one source, Morton may have even made his first recordings in Los Angeles, although if this is true they were apparently never released.[99]

Trombonist Kid Ory moved west to Los Angeles in 1919. Like Morton, Ory soon became professionally connected in Los Angeles with the ubiquitous Spikes brothers, not in the area of music publishing but rather in recording. The Spikes brothers initiated their Sunshine record label by producing two recordings of Ory's band in June 1921:[100] "Ory's Creole Trombone" and "Society Blues," (along with two other sides in which Ory's Sunshine Orchestra backs up female vocalists Roberta Dudley and Ruth Lee).[101] According to Reb Spikes, he and his brother borrowed their recording equipment from the Nordskog record company, which left the original labels on the disks (explaining why these recordings are credited to Nordskog in discographies). Actually, the involvement of Nordskog and Sunshine in producing the Ory recordings is a complex and convoluted issue, detailed in an excellent article by Levin.[102] For our purposes, what is most important is that the 1921 recordings made in Los Angeles by Ory's Sunshine Orchestra have the distinction of being the first records ever made by an African-American instrumental jazz band.[103] The band for these classic sides consisted of Ory on trombone, Mutt Carey on cornet, Dink Johnson on clarinet, pianist Fred Washington, bassist Montudie Garland, and drummer Ben Borders, all of whose musical roots (with the exception of Borders) traced back to New Orleans. According to Reb Spikes, six sides were actually recorded, but four of the masters melted in the sun while being transported through the California desert.[104]

Beyond these historic recordings, Ory's five-year sojourn to Los Angeles has received little notice from jazz scholars, who have tended to treat the period almost as a hiatus between his early career in New Orleans and his illustrious later achievements in Chicago, where, most notably, he became a member of the great Louis Armstrong recording bands of the mid-1920s. Yet Ory had a very busy career in Los Angeles, especially, it would appear, from 1922 until 1924, during which time his appearances were regularly announced in the *Eagle*.

Ory's choice to head west rather than north when he left New Orleans was actually the result of a decision made by his wife. "I asked my wife if she'd rather live in Chicago or California," he recalled years later. "She thought she'd like California. I said, 'We're going to leave Thursday.'"[105]

Upon arriving in Los Angeles, Ory's first engagement was at the Cadillac Cafe on Central Avenue. He sent word to Louis Armstrong, who was still living in New Orleans at the time, to come out and join his band. Armstrong declined the offer, so the job was offered to Mutt Carey, who had been a member of Ory's band back in New Orleans. Carey settled in Los Angeles and became an important part of the city's jazz scene through the 1920s, first as a member of Ory's band and then, after Ory left for Chicago in 1924, as the leader of his own band, Papa Mutt and His Syncopators.[106] Carey would certainly have achieved wider fame had he moved on to Chicago. "Most everybody has heard of Joe Oliver and Louis Armstrong, but few ever heard of Mutt Carey in his prime," claims Preston Jackson.

"Mutt Carey, in his day, was equal to Joe Oliver. . . . I never will forget Mutt Carey."[107]

Another musician who moved to Los Angeles to play with Ory, apparently in 1922, was bassist Pops Foster. Ory sent for Pops after having a falling out with his regular bassist, Montudie Garland. As Foster remembers it, "Montudie and Ory got in a fight like they always did. Montudie went to work for the Black and Tan Band, and Ory didn't have a bass player. He wrote to me to come out. I wanted to get away from my first wife, Berta, so I went. Back then if a bandleader wanted you to play with him, he'd write and send you money for the trip. After you started working you had to pay it back."[108]

When Foster arrived, Ory's band had a regular engagement at a place called the One-Eleven Dance Hall at 111 West Third Street, a "taxi dance hall." At this type of establishment the male customers paid ten cents for the privilege of dancing with glamorous hostesses. Each dance was only about a minute long, so the band constantly had to change tunes and tempos.[109] Lionel Hampton, who also commenced his Los Angeles career with a steady job at a taxi dance hall, fondly recalls the musical challenges of the situation: "Timing was very important in that job. When the place got crowded, the manager always wanted us to speed up so the numbers would be shorter and the guys would have to pay more nickels. Since I was the drummer, I controlled the tempo, and the owner always gave the signal to me. I liked experimenting with the tempo of songs anyway, and I like things fast, anyway."[110]

Foster was perhaps less enthusiastic about taxi dance halls than Hampton and soon moved on to a job with Mutt Carey's group at the Liberty Dance Hall on Third Street near Main. But for Foster, "Los Angeles proved to be a dull place," and in 1923 he left and headed for St. Louis. He returned to Los Angeles for a few months in 1927 at the invitation of Carey, who had taken over Ory's band when Ory left for Chicago and renamed it The Liberty Syncopators. Besides Carey and Foster, the band included drummer Minor Hall, who had first moved to California from New Orleans in 1921 with Joe Oliver, returning to settle in Los Angeles permanently in 1927;[111] trombonist Leon White, formerly the drummer for the Black and Tan band;[112] and clarinetist Joe Darsenbourg.

Both during and after Foster's tenure, the Kid Ory band appears to have been continually busy. Judging by the number of engagements advertised in the *Eagle* between 1922 and 1924, they were apparently rivaled only by the Black and Tan Orchestra in popularity. Following the group's first notice in the *Eagle* in June 1922, ads for performances by Ory's Creole Jazz Band appeared regularly in the paper through 1924. The band's first mention occurs in an announcement of a "Grand Old Fashioned Picnic and Barbecue" at Rosehill Park[113] featuring music by the Black and Tan Jazz Band, with Ory's group receiving second billing. Ory has been cited as saying that during his years in Los Angeles, his was the most talked-about jazz band in the area and that the group "cut" the Black and Tan band in front of appreciative audiences on a number of occasions.[114] The Rosehill Park picnic and barbecue was likely the scene of one of these "cutting contests" between the two bands, another of which apparently occurred at an Elks picnic at Eagle Rock Park on June 19, 1924.

Between 1922 and 1924, Ory's band played at all kinds of functions, such as a "Grand Benevolent Benefit Dance" at the Moose Hall De Luxe in December 1922 and another "Grand Dance" given by the Young Men's Afro-American Republican League five days later at Normandie Hall (at Normandie and Jefferson), where the band conducted its own dance every Tuesday night. As of February 1923, Ory's group was featured three nights a week at the Hiawatha Dancing Academy, "the largest and cleanest place of amusement for the race in Los Angeles," according to "Ragtime" Billy Tucker, a well-known local promoter who co-owned and managed the Hiawatha along with M. T. Laws. Ory was also featured every Sunday at Wayside Park ("the only park and cafe in the city owned by the Race"), apparently taking over as leader of the house band following Jelly Roll Morton's departure, and had just completed a fourteen-week engagement at the Plantation Cafe, "the largest white cafe on Coast."[115] The Plantation Cafe was one of a great many clubs in Los Angeles and throughout the country where black entertainers performed for exclusively white audiences.

Ory's band was also featured during special one-day boat and train excursions to nearby destinations such as Catalina Island, San Diego, and Tijuana, Mexico. These excursions emerged as a novel feature of early-1920s black social life in Los Angeles and furnished yet another type of venue for jazz band dances. They were sponsored by the Panama Social Club and its president, M. T. Laws. Each excursion featured entertainment by a top local jazz or dance band (sometimes two) such as the Black and Tan, Wood Wilson's "Satisfied" Orchestra, or the Angel City Brass Band. Each included a picnic and barbecue, a trip to a bullfight or a baseball game, and a big dance. A "Scenic Special Trip Deluxe" train excursion to San Diego and "Tia Juana, Old Mexico," on August 5, 1922 (round-trip $5.35, $2.75 for children), featured "Music for the Entire Trip Furnished by Ed. Ory's Sunshine Orchestra."[116] The page-four advertisement in the July 29 edition of the *Eagle* is interesting both for its inclusion of a photograph of Ory and his band and for its pronouncement of Ory's Sunshine Orchestra as "the only race jazz band that has made phonograph records on the coast,"[117] an obvious reference to the Sunshine/Nordskog recordings.

In addition to his formal musical engagements, Ory is reported to have led the house band at the Ranch Club, "a jamming, after-hours spot" where resident New Orleans jazzers, local players, and touring musicians, both white and black, would congregate and jam after their regular gigs. A young Benny Goodman is reported to have sat in with Ory at the Ranch Club.[118] Some years later, it was another Los Angeles after-hours venture by Goodman, to the Paradise Cafe, that resulted in Goodman's first meeting and musical encounter with Lionel Hampton, an occasion marking the beginning of their very important musical partnership.

In 1924 (possibly as late as early 1925), Ory moved to Chicago to join King

Oliver's Creole Syncopators. He was the trombonist for Louis Armstrong's Hot Five and Hot Seven recording bands, which featured Armstrong in his prime and produced some of the greatest and most influential recordings of all time. Ory returned to Los Angeles in 1929, but musical tastes had changed with the dawning of the swing big-band era, and his style was no longer popular. By about 1933 he had moved away from music and was making his living sorting mail and running a chicken farm with his brother. In 1942 he was "rediscovered" and became an important part of the "Dixieland Revival" of the 1940s. Between 1949 and 1954, his Los Angeles–based New Orleans revival band featured trumpeter Teddy Buckner, who fondly remembers Ory as "a great guy and a superb cook." As Buckner told me, "All those guys from New Orleans could cook!" He made sure to clarify that in this case he was using the term "cook" literally rather than as a metaphor for playing music well.[119]

The Black and Tan Jazz Orchestra

There are few early jazz enthusiasts who could not tell you something about both Jelly Roll Morton and Kid Ory; there are probably just as few who *could* tell you anything about the Black and Tan Jazz Orchestra. Yet in its day the Black and Tan was at least as popular in Los Angeles as either Jelly Roll Morton's or Kid Ory's bands and may well have been more popular on the local scene than either.

As mentioned earlier, the Black and Tan Orchestra moved to Los Angeles from Texas as a ten-piece "cake-walking, ragtime brass band" in 1916 or earlier and was refashioned into a jazz band in 1918 by local trombonist Harry Southard. Renamed the Black and Tan *Jazz* Orchestra, it was reduced to a quintet and redesigned in instrumentation, repertoire, and musical style on the model of the Creole Band and other hot New Orleans jazz units. The group featured Southard, reedman Paul Howard, tuba/bass/piano player James "Tuba Jack" Jackson, drummer Leon White, and cornetist Ernest Coycault.[120] Southard and Howard were longtime Angelenos. I have been unable to determine whether Jackson and White were local products or Texans who migrated to California with the original Black and Tan Orchestra. Coycault was the hot soloist of the group and its genuine link to the New Orleans jazz tradition. Gushee describes Coycault as "a very effective ragtime player whose rhythmic verve ought to have made a great impression on any cornetists who might have heard him between 1910 and 1930."[121] Judging by a few rare recordings featuring Coycault with bands led by Sonny Clay, he appears to have been an exceptional player who, like Mutt Carey and others who moved to California and chose not to leave, was destined to historical obscurity by his West Coast address.

In 1922, Coycault was replaced in the Black and Tan by trumpeter James Porter[122] and joined a new jazz band being formed by Sonny Clay. Leon White also left the Black and Tan group to play with Clay, for whom he worked as a trombonist rather than drummer.[123] The new trumpeter, Porter, had migrated from Chicago and ultimately came to be known as "the King of the Coast."[124] He would go on to play with most of the premiere bands in Los Angeles during the twenties and thirties, including the Sunnyland Jazz Band in the mid-twenties, Curtis Mosby's Dixieland Blue Blowers in the latter part of the decade, and Les Hite's big band in the thirties. Porter was apparently a rather abrasive individual. A teenaged Teddy Buckner once got up the courage to ask him for trumpet lessons, only to be cussed out and told to go away. Years later, Buckner became a member of the trumpet section of Les Hite's big band, in which Porter played lead trumpet. Buckner found the experience rather humbling: "Having James Porter on the stand made me feel like I was playing trombone."[125]

Whether with Coycault or Porter, the Black and Tan Jazz Orchestra enjoyed tremendous popularity in the late teens and early twenties. Jelly Roll Morton and Kid Ory each claimed to rule the roost in Los Angeles during their respective tenures there, but the evidence in 1918–1924 issues of the *Eagle* indicates that the Black and Tan Jazz Orchestra was at least as popular locally as the bands of either of these jazz legends. The Black and Tan had extended nightly engagements at major nightclubs such as the Cadillac Cafe and the Dreamland Cafe; held weekly dances at the Arion Hall on East Third Street on Thursdays and at Washington and Central Hall on Mondays; performed at Sunday baseball games at White Sox Park; played at holiday balls and dances such as the 1923 Elks Thanksgiving Ball and the 1924 Iriquois Friday Morning Club's May Fete Dance, both held at Blanchard Hall; was featured on boat excursions to Catalina Island and Tijuana; and participated in fund-raising events—e.g., Social Benefit for the Delegate to the 1921 Pan-African Congress in London, held at Caldwell's Recreation Garden in Santa Monica on July 30 (an event that also featured the Westside Jazz Band and Wood Wilson's "Satisfied" Vendome Band), a "Dance for Charity Benefit" for the Eastside Mothers' Home (May 1922), the "Pilgrims Home Grand Benefit" for the black community's senior citizens' home and hospital, on May 8, 1922, and an "Educational Fund Benefit Musical Dance" in July, the latter two both at Wayside Park. Finally, the band provided entertainment at political meetings and patriotic events, such as the Washington's Birthday Grand Patriotic Ball (February 22, 1918) at the Shrine Auditorium, the Patriotic Meeting of the Republican Protective League (April 21, 1918) at the Mason Hall on Central Avenue, and a Grand Ballot Ball held at election time in November 1923 (also featuring the Sunnyland Jazz Band). In addition to all of these advertised performances, the Black and Tan Jazz Orchestra performed regularly at the One-Eleven Dance Hall at Third and Main.[126]

The entertainment programs for these fund-raising events were especially interesting. For the 1922 Pilgrims Home benefit, the band was advertised in the *Eagle* (April 29) as "The far famed and unbeatable Black and Tan Band—Nuf Sed" on a bill with "That Famous Star—Mayme [sic] Smith—Who Sings for the Okeh Record Company. . . . Here you will see and hear her in person as she sings the Crazy Blues."[127] The recording mentioned in the notice represents a major landmark in American music history. As Martin Williams explains,

> *Crazy Blues* by Mamie Smith and Her Jazz Hounds sold three million copies. . . . The success of *Crazy Blues* is, as is often said, the success of the first Negro woman singer to record an authentic blues. Unquestionably, it paved the way for recordings by even more artistically successful singers like Bessie Smith and Ma Rainey. But it also established the regular recording of Negro music of all kinds by Negro musicians.[128]

Following the success of "Crazy Blues," many record companies began recording African-American musicians in order to capitalize on the music's perceived market potential. "Race" record catalogues aimed primarily at black audiences were soon established.[129] The race record phenomenon spawned by "Crazy Blues" helped pave the way for instrumental jazz recordings by African-American musicians as well, beginning with the aforementioned classics recorded by Ory in Los Angeles in 1921. Though Chicago- and New York–based companies dominated the recording of African-American jazz during the twenties, Los Angeles became the principal recording center on the West Coast. Beginning in 1930, when Louis Armstrong recorded a number of sides for the Okeh label with the house orchestra from Sebastian's New Cotton Club in Los Angeles,[130] the city entered the mainstream of the recording industry. Between the time of Ory's pioneering 1921 recordings and the 1930 Okeh sides featuring Armstrong, several top local Los Angeles bands made recordings.[131]

Although the Black and Tan Jazz Orchestra never recorded, it broke ground at other levels. At the "Educational Fund Benefit Musical Dance" of July 1922, for example, the Black and Tan was programmed alongside a program of "classical singing and dancing." This may have been one of the first events ever in Los Angeles to include art music and jazz performers on the same bill. The only other such combination of which I know occurred some six years later during the 1928 NAACP National Convention.

The infrequent occurrence of mixed programs of jazz and art music in Los Angeles during this period is not especially surprising, given the condescending attitude toward jazz professed by many in the black Angeleno establishment. From the viewpoint of middle-class and upper-class blacks, jazz was an unsophisticated rhythmic dance and entertainment music that had no place alongside art music in the concert hall; thus, programs including both classical and jazz music were rare. John Gray, a well-known African-American pianist[132] and music teacher in Los Angeles during this period who wrote a column for the *Eagle* called "In the Music World," had the following to say about jazz in 1919:

> The popularity of Jazz is due to its appeal to the primitive in man. Itself is primitive since it consists principally of strong rhythms, and rhythm is the foundation of

music. . . . It can be observed that in many cases melody plays a very little part, indeed there are times when there is none. . . . At least we can say that Jazz, *sans* noise and *sans* harshness, or in other words, stripped of its crudeness, will leave us that basic principal of music, RHYTHM.[133]

LOS ANGELES JAZZ BANDS OF THE MID-1920s

By 1924 the Black and Tan Jazz Orchestra had fallen out of currency in the increasingly competitive Los Angeles jazz-band scene. After August of that year, the group received no further notices in the *Eagle*, with the exception of one for an appearance at the Elks Annual Picnic in Luna Park on June 19, 1926.[134] Whether the band reunited especially for this occasion or continued performing between 1924 and 1926 is unclear. In any case, a key member, saxophonist Paul Howard, left the Black and Tan Jazz Orchestra in 1924 to form his own band. Prior to that time, he had been gigging with other groups, and in 1923 he had formed a quartet, the Quality Four, for a stint at the Quality Cafe. Under the name of the pianist, Harvey Brooks, this group recorded six sides for the Hollywood label in 1924.[135] Adding a banjoist, Thomas Valentine, the Quality Four became a quintet and changed its name to the Quality Serenaders. After backing up blues singer Hazel Myers on a disastrous 1924 tour, the Serenaders returned to Los Angeles and temporarily disbanded. Howard became a member of Sonny Clay's band for a short period, there being reunited with old Black and Tan bandmates Ernest Coycault, Leon White, and James Jackson, who had also switched over to Clay's organization.

Sonny Clay

The apparent demise of the Black and Tan ensemble around 1924 seems to have had much to do with the rise of Sonny Clay as a bandleader around that same time. Of the original five members of the Black and Tan Jazz Orchestra, as seen in a 1918 photograph,[136] Coycault and White left to join Clay in 1922 (1923 at the latest), Tuba Jack Jackson had become a regular with Clay's band by 1924,[137] and Paul Howard had made his way into the Clay organization by January 1925.

Sonny Clay is by some accounts one of the great but forgotten masters of early jazz. Teddy Buckner, who played in Clay's band in the late twenties, told me, "Sonny Clay was a genius. He could walk down the street talking to you—having a conversation—and be writing an arrangement at the same time."[138] According to John Bentley, in his time, Clay's musical abilities as a composer and arranger were "favorably compared with those of his friend and contemporary, Jelly Roll Morton."[139]

Clay was born in 1899 in Chapel Hill, Texas, and moved to Phoenix, Arizona, with his family when he was nine. He began his musical career as a drummer at age eleven. Over the years he became a multi-instrumentalist, playing xylophone, trumpet, trombone, and C-melody saxophone, among other instruments, but his principal instruments were always drums and piano. In his teens he worked as a musician in dance pioneer Arthur Murray's Phoenix studio. Early on, Clay developed a fondness for Mexican music and culture, listening to Mexican bands in Phoenix playing piano in a duo with clarinetist Charlie Green in Mexicali, Calexico, and Tijuana. Clay's experiences with Mexican music influenced his musical style; Jelly Roll Morton liked to refer to the manifestations of this influence as "the Spanish tinge" in Clay's music. On record, the best example of this "Spanish tinge" is "an unexpected rumba-like phrase"[140] heard in a 1931 recording of Clay's composition "Cho-King."

Sonny Clay first met Jelly Roll Morton in Tijuana; he was hitchhiking to San Diego, and Morton happened to pick him up in his big touring car. The two became fast friends and ended up playing together frequently, with Morton on piano and Clay alternating between drums, saxophone, and xylophone.[141]

Around 1920, Charlie Green decided to move to Los Angeles to join Wood Wilson's Original Satisfied Orchestra, and Clay based himself in Tijuana for a time, shuttling back and forth across the border to San Diego for gigs. By January 1921, Green had left Wilson's group to join Reb Spikes's Famous Syncopated Orchestra, and he convinced Spikes to summon Clay to Los Angeles to play drums with the band. Clay accepted Spikes's invitation and joined the group just in time to embark upon a tour that was supposed to cover most of California. The tour was a disaster, however, and the band went broke, its members finally earning enough money for the bus fare back to Los Angeles with three one-night stands in small California towns.[142]

Back in Los Angeles, Clay struggled, gigging around with different groups and playing solo piano jobs. In July and August 1921, he filled in with Kid Ory's Sunshine Orchestra on drums, temporarily replacing the ailing Ben Borders. Clay also claims to have played with King Oliver at the Royal Gardens in Leake's Lake, "a country club–type spot in Los Angeles," during Oliver's short appearance there, also in the summer of 1921.[143]

In 1922, Clay decided to form his own jazz band. Enticing Ernest Coycault and Leon White away from the Black and Tan Jazz Orchestra, Clay formed a topflight ensemble of locally based players. At the time of the group's first recordings in 1923, the group also included "Big Boy" Leonard Davidson on clarinet, saxophonists Bob Farrell and Johnny King, banjo player Thomas Valentine, and drummer Willis McDaniel, with Clay playing piano.[144] According to Bentley, "Tremendous drive proved the asset most responsible for this new group's ease in obtaining bookings and they immediately found steady employment. . . . The year slipped by quickly and the band was beginning to enjoy tremendous popularity."[145]

Clay also made his first recordings in 1922, accompanying a young blues vocalist named Camille Allen on two songs released by the Hollywood Record Company's Sunset label. Responding to the ever-growing popularity of Clay's jazz band on the Los Angeles scene, Sunset hired the group to record two sides in 1923.

Two original compositions by Clay, "Lou" and "What a Wonderful Time," were recorded during the session, with the band going under the name The California Poppies. These recordings are extremely rare.

Clay's star continued to rise through 1923 and 1924, as "the band added to its reputation playing in the more prominent night spots in and around Los Angeles."[146] In May 1925[147] the group, billed as The Stompin' Six, recorded four more titles for Sunset and began an association with a major record company, Vocalion, recording three sessions in 1925 and 1926. The first side recorded for Vocalion was "Chicago Breakdown," but the most popular was "Bogaloosa Blues," which sold approximately 8,000 copies in Chicago on the first day of its release in that city,[148] attesting to the widespread national reputation that Clay had established by the mid-twenties. McCarthy has located references to Clay's bands in the *Chicago Defender*, one of the nation's largest African-American newspapers of the period, and the *Pittsburgh Courier*, from 1922 and 1923, respectively. In both instances, the list of band personnel includes Clay's longtime musical partner, clarinetist Charles Green (identified as "Cash Green" in the *Defender*).

Despite Clay's high level of prominence on the Los Angeles scene and even at the national level in the first half of the 1920s, his first appearance in the pages of *The California Eagle* did not occur until February 12, 1926,[149] when a front-page notice hailed his eight-piece group (which included trombonist William B. Woodman Sr. by this time)[150] as the "one and only orchestra of our group West of New York recording for Vocalion." The article continues:

> This wonderful musical organization which has made history for our group along musical lines is well worthy of the compliment paid them as without a peer for their particular line of work. . . .
>   This aggregation of men who make real music, already have attained a national reputation. It was made by playing to millions over the radio K. F. I. [sic] and highly commended from all sections of this continent.[151]

The mention of radio performances corroborates Bentley's reference to evening radio broadcasts by Sonny Clay's Stompin' Six during the mid-twenties. However, Bentley's claim that the broadcasts were heard on radio station KNX is possibly an error, assuming that the *Eagle's* reference to KFI is accurate. In any case, by the time of the 1926 *Eagle* article, Clay had already achieved unprecedented national attention for a Los Angeles–based jazz bandleader. Clay's fame was further enhanced during this period by well-known white bandleader Herb Weidoft's band, which performed many of his compositions and arrangements.[152] Weidoft capitalized on Clay's talents in much the same way that Benny Goodman capitalized on the talents of Fletcher Henderson. Clay's popularity with white audiences was also fostered by his regular nightly engagement at the Plantation Cafe in Culver City, a premiere whites-only nightspot for the rich and famous (filmmaker D. W. Griffith was a regular customer). Thus, as jazz was appropriated on a grand scale by white mainstream society beginning around the mid-twenties, the music of Sonny Clay, through his recordings and radio broadcasts and the playing of his works by leading white bands, came to have a significant impact not only locally but nationally as well.

In addition to its other activities, Clay's band remained active in Los Angeles's African-American community. Editions of the *Eagle* from 1926 indicate appearances at Arion Hall on February 22, at the grand opening of Eagle Hall (at 822 Central Avenue) on February 24, and at the Elks Annual Picnic and Barbecue at Luna Park on June 19 (a double bill with the Black and Tan Jazz Orchestra).[153] In 1927 a February edition of the paper advertised a performance of Clay's band at the Annual Pre-Lenten Benefit Dance for the St. Philip's Building Fund.[154] The band then disappears from the pages of the *Eagle* through at least the end of 1929 (where my archival search concluded).

In January 1928, Clay recorded six more sides for Vocalion, only two of which were issued. One of the unissued tracks was "Australian Stomp," presumably in homage to Clay's upcoming tour down under, where his group became "probably the first black jazz group ever to tour that continent."[155] The last of the 1928 Vocalion sessions reportedly took place only a day or two before the band's departure for Australia.[156] The Australian venture, which featured a large band (probably a ten-piece) and vocalist Ivie Anderson (who would later achieve fame through her association with Duke Ellington), was terminated abruptly when the band was deported because of rambunctious behavior by certain of its members, who most likely were accused of consorting with white women.[157] McCarthy suggests that Clay's band "must have stayed in Australia for about three months altogether,"[158] although he does not indicate a source for this information. Another Los Angeles–based musician, Teddy Weatherford, was responsible for introducing jazz to China for the first time in the 1920s.

After returning to Los Angeles, Clay restructured his band and secured an engagement at the Vernon Country Club, again playing for all-white audiences. Through 1929 and the early 1930s, he directed a new band. This group, which became the house band at the local racetrack's cafe, included a young Teddy Buckner as well as Les Hite. This was a posh gig; Buckner recalls making a base salary of $25 a night, on top of which it was not uncommon for him to pull in $60 in tips.[159] The band also had a stint in San Diego at the Creole Palace and made some film soundtracks. For club dates during this period, Clay replaced the Stompin' Six designation he had previously used for his gigging bands with the name Rhythm Demons. One of Clay's aggregations also appeared on screen in a motion picture, with the musicians paid ten dollars each "to don grass skirts and assume the identity of a Zulu band in a cafe."[160]

Clay's final recording sessions with bands took place around August 1931[161] and featured a ten-piece band dubbed the Dixie Serenaders. Clay's arrangements of "Cho-King," "St. Louis Blues," "River Stay 'Way from My Door," "When It's Sleepy Time Down South," and "Some of These Days" demonstrate his considerable talents as an arranger.

Throughout most of his life, Clay had a serious drinking problem, and his health began to deteriorate in the 1930s. His drinking, combined with economic hardships brought on by the Depression, rendered the demands of keeping a band together insurmountable, and he turned to solo piano playing and freelance work with bands to make a living. During World War II he was appointed an army band director, returning to club work on the Los Angeles scene following his discharge and reaping the benefits of the city's booming wartime economy for a time. His alcoholism and increasingly poor health, however, interfered with his ability to get and keep jobs. Following an extended hospital stay, he found work at the post office, supplementing his income by tuning pianos.

The Sunnyland Jazz Band

Almost nothing has been written about the Sunnyland Jazz Band by jazz historians, even those who have taken an interest in less prominent 1920s Los Angeles bands and musicians.[162] Furthermore, it seems that the group made no recordings. The main sources of information on the band are Berta Wood's 1956 *Jazz Journal* article based on an interview with Charlie Lawrence, "one of the few jazz musicians born in Los Angeles";[163] an undated photograph of the group;[164] and a published interview with band member Andrew Blakeney.[165]

In the Wood article, Lawrence claims that he directed the Sunnyland Jazz Orchestra, made up of himself on alto sax, James Porter on trumpet, Ashford Hardie on trombone, Buster Wilson on piano, Howard Patrick on banjo, Clarence Williams (not the New Orleans Clarence Williams) on bass, and Ben Borders on drums. With the addition of tenor saxophonist Jesse Smith, Lawrence's roster is identical to the list of musicians identified in a photograph of the group reprinted in McCarthy.[166]

Blakeney was brought to Los Angeles from Chicago to replace Porter in 1924 after Porter announced his plans to leave the group. However, when Blakeney arrived, Porter changed his mind and decided he wanted to stay. Attempts were made to reorganize the group around a two-trumpet lineup, but Blakeney wanted nothing to do with that. "I said I didn't come out here to play second trumpet, or play with anybody," Blakeney told Floyd Levin. "I was here to take [Porter's] place."[167] After just one gig alongside Porter, Blakeney left the band but stayed in Los Angeles, picking up work where he could find it. A financial settlement between him and the Sunnyland organization was worked out with the help of mediation by Reb Spikes, a close friend of Blakeney's. A short time later, Porter left the band to join Curtis Mosby's Dixieland Blue Blowers at Solomon's Penny Dance Hall, and Blakeney finally got the job he had moved to Los Angeles for in the first place, playing with the Sunnyland every Thursday night at a large dance hall at 15th and Main and at many other engagements.

Charlie Lawrence's claim that he was the leader of the Sunnyland Jazz Band[168] is at least partially contradicted by Blakeney, who reported to Levin that pianist Buster Wilson was the group's musical director and spokesperson but that the group was essentially a cooperative organization in which all members had a say in all decisions.[169]

Though information on the Sunnyland Jazz Band is scarce and the band is little remembered today, all evidence suggests that in its day it was extremely popular in Los Angeles's African-American community. Between 1924 and 1926, the group received more notices in the *Eagle* than any other jazz band, replacing the Black and Tan Jazz Orchestra as the most frequently mentioned group in that publication. Two of its earliest *Eagle*-advertised appearances were a "Pre-Halloween Masquerade Ball" and a "Grand Thanksgiving Ball" in 1923.[170] The following month the Sunnyland was one of several musical organizations involved in the "Xmas Chimes Dance and Musical Fiesta" at Washington and Central, an M. T. Laws production that ran from December 22–26 and featured "4 Days–4 Nites–3 Matinees–4 Bands–4 Chimes! The Event Unforgettable! FIRST OF ITS KIND IN LOS ANGELES." The Sunnyland band played the Christmas Eve engagement dance and the farewell ball Boxing Day Eve; the Black and Tan played the opening Saturday night dance and the "Continuous Round of Merrymaking" from 2:30 p.m. till 1 a.m. Christmas Day. Also featured, in matinee performances, was the Ferris Family Orchestra, consisting of four sisters who played piano, clarinet, violin, and drums and their saxophonist father.[171]

In 1924, in addition to the usual dances and picnics, Sunnyland was featured at an "Emancipation Celebration" at Lincoln Park Skating Rink on June 19 (with the Ferris Family Orchestra also on the bill) and played at the "Extraordinary Opening" of the Humming Bird Cafe (formerly the Quality Cafe, where Paul Howard's Quality Four had been the house band one year earlier). Located at 1143 E. 12th Street, the Humming Bird was one of the hottest nightclubs in the area, presenting vaudeville acts and dance music (see Figure 1.4).

Two of the last notices for the Sunnyland Jazz Band in the *Eagle* appear in the April 9 and 16, 1926, editions of the paper.[172] The April 9 edition includes an ad for the "Sunnyland Orchestra with Amplifiers" at the Shrine Auditorium, with a rather expensive admission charge of $1 rather than the 50 cents charged for most advertised events of this time. Though the particular type of amplification is not specified, the presence of *any* amplification in a 1926 musical performance is noteworthy.

In March 1925 the Sunnyland band began a weekly Sunday engagement at the Pavilion in Eureka Village. Located in the Eureka Mountains, Eureka Village was a suburban, resort-like residential community for African Americans. It was promoted as the "Destined Greatest Race Community Center—Buy Your Lots Now for Choice Position; They are $100 Up."[173] The Sunnyland band attracted potential home buyers to Eureka Village and provided regular entertainment for residents.

African-American neighborhoods in Los Angeles became increasingly over-

ANNOUNCEMENT EXTRAORDINARY

OPENING

SATURDAY EVENING, JUNE 7th

---THE---

HUMMING BIRD

(Formerly The Quality Café)

UNDER NEW MANAGEMENT

Entertaining and Dancing

The Management Wishes to Announce

---That---

THE HUMMING BIRD
THE GREATER SUNNY-
LAND JAZZ ORCHESTRA

Will Be An Every Night Feature
Reservations---Call FAber 5066

1143 EAST TWELFTH

UNDER MANAGEMENT TESSIE PATTERSON

Figure 1.4. Advertisement notice of opening of the Humming Bird Cafe featuring the Sunnyland Jazz Band, *The California Eagle* (6 June 1924): 10.

crowded during the 1920s as a result of rapid population growth and tightening residential restrictions. This trend, combined with escalating racial discrimination, heightened the allure of suburban areas like Eureka Village. Increased racial discrimination within the city was another factor. By mid-decade, the Ku Klux Klan wielded strong political influence in Los Angeles. The 1925 mayoral election pitted Benjamin Bledsoe, the candidate supported by the African-American community (as represented by *The California Eagle*), against George Cryer, who was strongly supported by the Ku Klux Klan. On May 2 the *Eagle* came out with a special extra issue exhorting readers to vote for Bledsoe.[174] Among the individuals who wrote articles in support of Bledsoe in this issue was Professor William T. Wilkins.

Wilkins, as mentioned earlier, was one of the top European-trained pianists and piano teachers in the community and the director of his own music school. His comments in support of Bledsoe provide an interesting perspective on the social problems connected with jazz, particularly the condescending attitudes the white community of Los Angeles displayed toward African Americans. Many whites considered jazz a symbol of the "backwardness" of blacks, and it is therefore not surprising that many in the African-American community, especially the long-established residents representing the upper echelons of black society, refused to accept jazz as a respectable musical form. Wilkins illustrated this resistance, commending Bledsoe and a group of his colleagues for the respectful and enlightened behavior shown him during a piano recital: "Judge Bledsoe and that body of intellectuals didn't ask us to render 'Your folk's good old plantation melodies' which the white people like so well. The Judge did not ask me or my pupils to play 'rag time' or 'jazz,' as the white American generally does, but he wanted to encourage us in the performance of the classics."[175]

Despite the combined efforts of the *Eagle* publishers and concerned citizens such as Wilkins, Bledsoe was defeated in the election, and George Cryer became mayor, exacerbating an already worsening racial situation.

Reb Spikes and the Spikes Brothers

The names of the Spikes brothers, John and Reb (see Figure 1.5), have already come up many times in this chapter. It is virtually impossible to discuss any aspect of early jazz in Los Angeles without some reference to them. Though the Spikes brothers are today remembered mainly for their pioneering achievements in music recording and publishing, especially through their affiliations with Kid Ory and Jelly Roll Morton, their musical endeavors in the 1920s went far beyond these areas. McCarthy goes so far as to state that "there was no corner of jazz activity in Los Angeles in which one or other of the brothers was not deeply involved."[176]

The music store John and Reb opened at 12th Street and Central Avenue in December 1919 sold sheet music, instruments, radios, Victrolas, and recordings. It also served as the headquarters for Los Angeles's African-American music community. According to Reb, "In Los Angeles, if a musician didn't know where the Spikes Brothers Music Store was, he hadn't been to Los Angeles."[177] The store "almost imperceptibly developed into a booking agency, with as many as seven or eight bands under their control"[178] and important connections to the Hollywood movie industry. Reb Spikes's own band was featured in one short film in 1927.[179] Ultimately, the booking agency spawned a black musicians' union, as Reb describes: "I supplied Negro musicians for all the Hollywood parties and motion pictures. Anytime they wanted to make a picture, and needed Negro musicians,

Figure 1.5. Jazz clarinetist and saxophonist Reb Spikes. From Floyd Levin's Jazz Archives. Used by permission.

they'd call me because we was the headquarters. We made a little change bookin' bands for those things. With all the boys comin' in here, we got to talkin' about a Union, so some of them got together, and we started one."[180]

The store also became the major outlet in Los Angeles for race records, which were all the rage among the rich and famous in Hollywood during the twenties. Reb remembers that these celebrities "would drive up in long limousines and send their chauffeurs in to ask for 'dirty records.'"[181] The "dirty" records, wild dancing, spectacular shows, and hot jazz all added up to an irresistible package of excitement and fun for the nouveau riche mavericks (and wannabes) of the Hollywood movie industry. Through the 1920s, thrill-seeking whites (otherwise known as "slummers") flocked to Central Avenue in steadily escalating numbers for top-flight black entertainment and the titillation that only African-American artistic culture seemed capable of providing. According to Bunch, the slummers were "lured by the music, the exotic notion of associating with Blacks and the desire to flaunt accepted racial conventions. . . . This practice was not meant to encourage better communication between the races. Rarely did the two groups interact."[182] At least the last part of Bunch's statement has been refuted by Jack McVea, who spent many years playing for racially mixed audiences in the clubs of Central Avenue. McVea told me, "There was no segregation in the clubs. People found out they could have more fun being mixed."[183]

The pursuit of pleasure may have been the first order of business for slummers, but for those in the business of popular entertainment a trip to the Avenue was also a research venture. The musical sounds, dance steps, fashion trends, and show routines of Central Avenue today heralded the direction of white American popular culture tomorrow, and any savvy white entertainer or show-biz entrepreneur knew better than to fall out of step.

The stomps, blues, and rags African-American jazz bands played on the latest race records and in the integrated clubs along Central Avenue, in the chic, segregated nightspots of Hollywood, and in other parts of town represented the cutting edge of West Coast music for black and white audiences alike. The Spikes brothers enjoyed a virtual monopoly on race record distribution in Los Angeles in the early 1920s and had professional ties to most of the city's major venues for African-American music and entertainment. With their music store acting as a central base of operations for their diverse business ventures, they became quite prosperous for a time and with their profits were able to branch off into more adventurous areas of the music business. The most notable of these ventures was the establishment of the Sunshine record company, which pioneered the recording of African-American instrumental jazz with Kid Ory. The brothers also owned and ran several restaurants and nightclubs during the twenties, including Reb's Club, the Dreamland Cafe, and the Wayside Park Cafe.

At some point, the music store was moved up the street to 4011 Central. Curtis Mosby, who succeeded the Spikes brothers as the leading Los Angeles–based African-American music and entertainment entrepreneur in the late 1920s, became a partner in the store, which was renamed Mosby & Spikes. In 1929, Mosby became sole owner, expanding the establishment and renaming it Mosby's Music Store.[184]

The opening of the original Spikes Brothers Music Store in 1919 coincided with Reb's return to his "hometown" of Los Angeles on a permanent basis. Born in Dallas, Texas, in 1888, the son of a middle-class businessman of mixed descent—part African, Norwegian, Irish, and native American—Reb lived in a mainly white neighborhood of Dallas as a small child but moved with his family to Los Angeles in 1897, when he was nine years old, after the family house and all his father's businesses were set ablaze in one night, presumably in a racist-inspired campaign of arson.

Reb started his musical career playing drums in a piano-drum duo with his brother John. The duo left Los Angeles around 1907 and became, by Reb's account, "a sensation around Arizona. They'd never heard drums and piano, but that's what they used to have in dance halls in Frisco. So, all the dances, black and white, and saloons, and everything, they had around there, we played."[185] Reb soon took up wind instruments and began alternating between winds and drums on jobs. The Spikes duo toured the Southwest, playing in New Mexico, Texas, and even Nogales, Mexico. As Reb recalls, "We traveled for four or five years, doin' a musical act. . . . We had chimes, marimbas, harps, saxophones, piano, trumpets, and we'd go from one instrument to another. It was the old-fashioned musical act where we'd play about seven different instruments."[186]

Their musical act was often performed in the context of a traveling medicine show or minstrel show. The entertainment programs for the medicine shows could be quite elaborate. One such show, produced by one "Doctor Ferdon," included a "ten- or twelve-piece orchestra, six or seven entertainers, comedians, a quartet, a magician, dancers, or whatever he could pick up."[187] These early experiences provided the Spikes brothers with a solid foundation for their contributions to African-American vaudeville in the 1920s. Their music was featured in the highly successful touring vaudeville show "Steppin' High," starring Hazel Myers, which played at the Philharmonic Auditorium in Los Angeles at Fifth and Olive Streets in 1924. The show was billed in the *Eagle* as "the fastest, classiest and most brilliant and scintillating jazz and musical offering that has toured the coast."[188]

After some five years of touring, Reb spent several years residing semipermanently in San Francisco in the mid-teens, mainly playing baritone saxophone for bands that were part of the exciting jazz scene on the Barbary Coast. He became a member of Sid LeProtti's So Different Orchestra, one of the finest groups of its time on the West Coast.[189] Though based in San Francisco, the So Different Orchestra occasionally had engagements in Los Angeles, such as a 1916 stint at Byron Long's Tavern at 108th and Central Avenue in Watts (later renamed the Plantation and then Jazzland). The floor show at this whites-only club also featured exhibition dancing by Rudolf Valentino, and the clientele included celebrities Charlie Chaplin and Fatty Arbuckle.[190] Blacks were able to hear the band at the

Dreamland, where it performed several nights a week in addition to its principal gig at Byron Long's. Reb also performed occasionally with local Los Angeles bands during visits to his hometown, an example being his performance at a picnic with Wood Wilson's band in 1913, documented in a photograph.[191]

Following a six-month engagement in Honolulu in 1917, Spikes and several of his So Different bandmates were drafted into the army. The members of the band who had not been drafted enlisted, and the So Different Orchestra became the resident jazz band for the 25th Infantry Division in the Pacific Islands, being restationed to Nogales, Arizona, after about a month. According to Reb, "They'd never had a jazz band in the army before."[192] After the war, Reb returned to the San Francisco area with the So Different Orchestra for an engagement at the Canary Cottage, then worked in Oakland for four or five months, where he played with Jelly Roll Morton, whom he describes as "the greatest piano player I ever heard."[193]

Reb's career shifted direction dramatically when he decided to resettle in Los Angeles permanently in 1919 and opened the music store on Central Avenue with his brother. States Reb, "I never went back up to San Francisco to stay. After that, I got into the business end of music more."[194] And it is in terms of the business end of music that Spikes made his most lasting impact. As McCarthy has noted, "Whatever the qualities of Spikes's bands during the 'twenties—and musicians have said that some at least were excellent—his activities in other directions were probably more significant in the long term in the development of jazz on the West Coast."[195]

Nonetheless, as bandleaders and players, both Reb and John Spikes were important contributors to the Los Angeles jazz scene of the 1920s, especially Reb, who led bands under several names. Reb's Legion Club 45's and Reb Spikes's So Different Orchestra, his "gigging" bands, worked four or five nights a week on average during a six- or seven-year period culminating with the onset of the Depression, which caused a severe curtailment of the Spikes brothers' activities.[196] Another group, Reb Spikes's Majors and Minors Orchestra, had a long-standing engagement at the Follies Theater on Main Street.

The Legion Club 45's were named after their main place of employment, the local Legion Club dance hall, where Reb's group furnished music both for regularly scheduled dances and for occasional special events. For example, a full-page notice in the June 4, 1926, edition of the *Eagle* advertised an extravaganza benefit for "a most worthy cause, the N.A.A.C.P. Baby Contest" held on June 10. The floor show featured "The Only Bo Didiley [sic] Dolly featuring 'Blues'" and "Sebastian's Original Cotton Club Creole Cuties—starring Mildred Washington," along with Reb's Legion 45's and other entertainers (see Figure 1.6).[197]

In addition to performing live, the Legion Club 45's recorded two sides in late 1924 for a very small label and two sides in 1927 for Columbia. The former are virtually impossible to find but are historically significant as the first records ever

N. A. A. C. P.

FOLKS:–This and next week, Gordon Manor will donate this space to a most worthy cause–the N. A. A. C. P. Baby Contest. Tho busy night and day, yet I feel it my most sacred duty to do my bit. And I sincerely hope all who read this announcement will respond to the efforts of those young people who have undertaken to stage such a wonderful show.

On the 30th day of this month, I will tell you something further abou tGORDON MANOR.

I thank you

Willise C. Gordon md

THAT BIG NIGHT

Dining, Dancing, Entertaining At Legion Club

THURSDAY EVENING, JUNE 10TH

BENEFIT OF N. A. A. C. P. BABY CONCERT

Reb's Legion Forty-Five   The Only Bo Didiley

Leslie Walton   Dolly featuring "Blues"

SPECIAL ATTRACTIONS

Sebastian's Original Cotton Club Creole Cuties—starring Mildred Washington, with Mildred and Mona Boyd, Ernestine Porter, Edna Cunningham Renee–Ellison–Renee rendering their $500.00 prize song hit, "My California Maid".

FLYING FORD

Surprise Number–We promised on our word of honor not to advertise them, but they are always a riot ! Guess Who?

ADMISSION 50 CENTS   COVER CHARGE 25 CENTS

WAITRESSES

PAULINE LEWIS	CORONA WHITE	SETH LEE
ETHEL REEVES	ANITA GRANT	PEARL SMITH
GLADYS McCURDY	EVA COLLINS	NADINE BRATTON
ELAH LEWIS	SARAH GARROTT	GLADYS SPIKES
EUGENIA WHISENANT	CORNELIA BRADFORD	

RESERVATIONS NOW

JIMMIE SMITH .... TUcker 4432
MAMIE WHITE .... MEtropolitan 3338
PAULINE LEWIS .... EMpire 1354
DR. VADA SOMERVILLE .... EMpire 1346

Figure 1.6. NAACP benefit dance featuring Reb Spikes. Advertisement notice of NAACP Baby Contest Extravaganza, *The California Eagle* (4 June 1926): 2.

made by Lionel Hampton. Hampton remembers that the two tunes recorded were "My Mammy's Blues," featuring the full eight-piece band (Hampton on drums, Reb on bass sax, Les Hite and William Calhoun on clarinets, saxophones, and vocals, plus two trumpets, trombone, and piano), and "Sheffield Blues," which Hampton describes as having been performed by a trio including him, Hite, and reedman/vocalist William Calhoun.[198] It is likely though not certain that this recording of "Sheffield Blues" is the same one referred to by Spikes in an amusing anecdote.[199] "My Mammy's Blues" was recorded again by Reb's Legion Club 45's in 1927 for Columbia, along with "Fight That Thing." According to McCarthy, "My Mammy's Blues" is the superior of the two cuts by virtue of "the powerful playing by one of the trumpeters and the drive of the whole group."[200]

Lionel Hampton and the Jazz Scene of 1920s Los Angeles

Lionel Hampton is the most famous and influential musician, nationally and internationally, to have come out of the jazz scene of 1920s Los Angeles. Born in 1908 in Birmingham, Alabama, and raised in Chicago, he went to high school with saxophonist Les Hite, three years Hampton's senior, and played drums in Hite's all-teenage band.[201] The band broke up when Hite decided to go to Los Angeles sometime in the early 1920s. As Hampton remembers, "He promised me and the other guys that he would send for us once he got himself established out there. . . . After a while, [he] wrote back and told me, 'If you come out here I'll get you a job in a big band.'"[202]

Hampton accepted the invitation, moving to Los Angeles in 1923 or 1924, when he was in his mid-teens. When he arrived, however, he found that Hite was not doing as well he had indicated in his letter. Hite had been playing with Reb Spikes but had quit to form his own group, which was not getting much work. He thought that the addition of Hampton might provide the spark needed to put the band over, but even with the talented young drummer, the group still struggled.

Soon Hampton found himself out of money and without work. He got a job as a counterman at a Culver City drugstore but did not have to keep it very long before being hired to play drums with Reb's Legion Club 45's, a job he got through a recommendation from trumpeter George Orendorff, another Chicagoan who had come out to the coast. Hite rejoined Spikes's band shortly thereafter, much to Hampton's delight. The band had a steady gig at a taxi dance hall.

When not playing with Spikes's band, Lionel Hampton often sat in with Curtis Mosby's Dixieland Blue Blowers. Mosby himself was a drummer but, according to musicians who heard him and played with him, not a very good one. In his introduction to *West Coast Jazz*, Gioia cites reports that Mosby brought in Hampton to play drums at key gigs and on recording sessions but notes that Hampton denies ever having recorded with Mosby's band.[203]

Paul Howard's Quality Serenaders, 1926–1930

In 1926, possibly as early as 1925,[204] Paul Howard, following up on his bandleading activities with the Quality Four/Quality Serenaders of 1923–24 and a short-lived band called the California Cotton Pickers, left his job with Sonny Clay's band to reform the Quality Serenaders. The new Serenaders quickly established themselves in the top echelon of black Los Angeles dance bands, and when an opening for a new drummer came along (sometime in 1926), Lionel Hampton was offered the position. He explains, "I said good-bye to Reb Spikes and Curtis Moseby [sic]. . . . The band [i.e., the Serenaders] was the most popular band among the quality black folks. . . . [They] played every dance and ball and cotillion there was. We did a good ten gigs a week and made the huge sum of fifteen dollars a week, plus tips. The music was not too exciting. It was mostly slow, romantic tunes, and I didn't beat the drums so much as I brushed them. All this was fine and mellow. We jammed together when we were off duty."[205]

When Hampton joined the Serenaders in 1926, Howard had already expanded the five-piece 1924 unit to a seven-piece band with himself and Leon Herriford (Hereford) on saxophones and clarinets, Hampton on drums, George Orendorff on trumpet, Louis Taylor on trombone, Thomas Valentine on banjo and guitar, and Harvey Brooks on piano.[206] By 1929 the Serenaders had been expanded to an eight-piece group with the addition of James Jackson on tuba. Charlie Lawrence, who played alto sax and clarinet, became the group's principal composer and arranger after replacing Herriford, on reeds, and future Ellington band member Lawrence Brown replaced Louis Taylor on trombone. This group went into the studio, first in 1929 and again in 1930, to make records for the Victor label.[207]

Beginning in 1926, Howard and his Quality Serenaders were associated with Frank Sebastian. Through 1929 they were the house band at Sebastian's New Cotton Club in Culver City, a premiere whites-only establishment for black entertainment in Los Angeles in the latter part of the 1920s that would achieve even greater fame in the 1930s. In 1928 the Quality Serenaders' prominence among Los Angeles bands led to their being included in the official entertainment for the NAACP Convention, which consisted of a "Grand Musical Review and Reception at Shrine Auditorium" headlined by the well-known soprano Florence Cole-Talbert. This event was scheduled to coincide with the opening of the glamorous Hotel Somerville.[208] Following the main concert there was a big dance in the Shrine Pavilion featuring three bands: the Quality Serenaders, Kennedy's Syncopators, and Speed Webb and His Melody Lads. Webb, a bandleader from South Bend, Indiana, based himself in Los Angeles for a period during the late 1920s and gave Teddy Buckner his start as a professional musician. Unfortunately for Buckner, Webb skipped town and hightailed it back to South Bend one day with the band's payroll, not to be seen again by Buckner for some thirty years. It was not until after the unfortunate incident that Buckner was informed that such unscrupulous behavior was typical of Webb.

On March 14, 1929, the Serenaders moved from the Cotton Club to the new Kentucky Club Cafe (2220 Central Avenue), which opened as a premiere nightspot for the African-American community and a major drawing card for the white Hollywood party set as well. The announcement of the grand opening in the *Eagle* advertises "a Galaxy of Stars and a Jam Up Review" featuring entertainer Mildred Washington in a show with a toe dancer, a tap dancer, a "silver tone blues singer," a "song bard," a famed baritone, "and dance music by Howard's Quality Serenaders." The ad invites readers to come and "see your favorite movie stars."[209]

After a year at the Kentucky, the Serenaders moved on to a short-lived residency at the exclusive Montmartre in Hollywood, a favorite and exclusive nightspot for leading Hollywood stars. The club could not survive the economic devastation of the Depression and closed in 1930. With the close of the Montmartre, the Quality Serenaders disbanded.

The work of the later versions of the Quality Serenaders has been preserved in their recordings for Victor in 1929 and 1930, including "Moonlight Blues" (Lionel Hampton's first recorded performance as a vocalist), "Overnight Blues," "New Kinda Blues," "Gettin' Ready Blues," "California Swing," "Charlie's Idea" (an arrangement of "Tiger Rag" by Charlie Lawrence), "Harlem," "Cuttin' Up," "Quality Shout," "Stuff," and "The Ramble." In assessing some of these recordings, McCarthy asserts that the band shows itself to be "a well-disciplined unit that, on recorded evidence, was by far the most professional band then playing on the West Coast." McCarthy seems to have been particularly impressed by the "well conceived, nicely balanced, and swinging" trumpet solos of George Orendorff, whom he credits as being unquestionably "the outstanding soloist of the band."[210] McCarthy also gives positive notes to the soloing abilities of trombonist Lawrence Brown and pianist Harvey Brooks. He concludes, "Of all the Californian bands recording during the late 'twenties and early 'thirties, Paul Howard's was the one most obviously in the mainstream of contemporary big band development."[211] Jazz critic Irving L. Jacobs, in a 1949 *Playback* review, went so far as to claim that "Paul Howard's Victor recording band is one of the most thoroughly underrated in the history of jazz."[212]

According to Lionel Hampton, the 1929 Serenaders recordings were produced in Culver City, where Victor had rented some film studio space from movie producer Hal Roach. Hampton's description of the session graphically portrays the challenging conditions under which many recordings were made in these early days:

> I remember it was April 1929, and it was like a steambath in that studio—to keep out the noise, they kept out the air. Every once in a while, when the musicians were about to drop, we could have a break and go out to the street for five minutes. There was a huge microphone in the middle, and the musicians moved up close or far away from it, depending on what kind of sound they wanted. That was the 1929 version of

WAY OUT WEST ON CENTRAL

"mixing." The engineer sat over in a corner trying to get the sound on wax, and you usually didn't get a good cut the first time, so you had to do it over and over until he got it. But for me this was a little piece of heaven—recording for a label that at least somebody had heard of.[213]

By the time of the Serenaders' 1930 recording sessions, Victor had set up its own recording studio in Hollywood, and the recording process went much more smoothly and efficiently than it had the previous year, with a better final product. Through a variety of unanticipated circumstances, the sessions became a show-piece for Hampton's multiple talents as a musician, with the young virtuoso not only playing drums but also singing on certain tracks ("Overnight Blues," "California Swing," and "Cuttin' Up," featuring a vocal style described by Hampton himself as "his best Louis Armstrong imitation"). He even played piano on one se-lection, "New Kinda Blues," when regular pianist Harvey Brooks arrived late for the session. Though not a pianist by trade, Hampton had taken some piano lessons with Jelly Roll Morton and had "listened to every record Earl Hines ever made" and was thus prepared for this unexpected debut.[214]

Judging from Hampton's recollections, the Quality Serenaders were a very busy band indeed, playing an average of two gigs daily, and were an integral com-ponent of black Angeleno social life during the late 1920s. "I was working steady. . . . We played for afternoon dances for the teenagers. There was a dance hall down at Fifty-fifth and Central, and all the kids went upstairs there for afternoon dances. They didn't let kids go to parties at night in those days. In the evening we played the big parties for the grown-ups."[215]

It was at one of these "big parties for the grown-ups" that Hampton met his fu-ture wife, Gladys. The event was the 1929 annual ball of the Antique Art Club, one of the biggest African-American society clubs in Los Angeles. Many club members were maids, butlers, and chauffeurs for "the rich white Hollywood folks, or porters and attendants in the 'comfort rooms' of the big stores on Rodeo Drive, and in those days if you worked for the high and mighty, you were pretty high and mighty yourself."[216] At the time Lionel met her, Gladys herself was "a career woman—worked for the movie studios as a seamstress."[217]

Though his membership in the Quality Serenaders provided a good livelihood and recording opportunities, Hampton ultimately found the situation musically stifling and decided to leave. "I wasn't content with the kind of music I was play-ing with the Quality Serenaders," he recalls. So when Les Hite, his old crony from the early Chicago days, asked Hampton to join a new big band he was putting to-gether, "I left the Quality Serenaders without thinking twice. It didn't matter to me that the country was going into a depression and that I might be better off with an established group. . . . The Quality Serenaders weren't playing my kind of music. I wanted to swing, and with my old buddy from Chicago, Les Hite."[218]

And swing they did. Les Hite's band became the number-one African-American big band on the West Coast during the Depression years and beyond, "the best known and most successful of the Californian bands of the 'thirties."[219] As the house band for Sebastian's New Cotton Club, they backed up Louis Armstrong during his extended engagement there in 1930–1931 and recorded more than a dozen sides with Armstrong during that time.[220] One of the songs, a version of Eubie Blake's "Memories of You," featured a vibraphone introduction played by Hampton—according to him, "the first time jazz had ever been played on vibes."[221] In addition to working with Armstrong, Hite's big band also backed up many other jazz stars—Fats Waller, for example—and profited from an abundance of soundtrack work and on-screen appearances in Hollywood movies, including the Marx Brothers' *A Day at the Races*.[222] In August 1936, Hampton left the band when he was "discovered" by Benny Goodman during a gig at the Paradise Cafe with a small group that also included trumpeter Teddy Buckner. His 1936–1940 membership in Goodman's famous quartet (with Teddy Wilson and Gene Krupa) catapulted Hampton to superstardom in the jazz world as a pioneer of the vibraphone. With his new celebrity status, Hampton formed a Los Angeles–based big band in the 1940s that helped elevate the careers of many local musicians, including Jack McVea and Teddy Buckner.

Curtis Mosby and the Dixieland Blue Blowers

Curtis Mosby was a musician and entrepreneur whose prominence on the Los Angeles music and entertainment scene spanned a long period, from the 1920s through the 1940s. As a leading club owner, drummer, composer, bandleader, music store owner, "man about town," and the "honorary mayor of Central Avenue,"[223] Mosby was a dominant figure in Los Angeles who "bridged the gap between . . . two generations of black music."[224] He was also a controversial figure who has been remembered with disdain and disrespect by some of his peers. According to Floyd Levin, who has interviewed many musicians who knew and worked for Mosby, the bandleader was notorious for not paying or grossly underpaying his players and was unscrupulous in other realms of his business operations.[225] Gioia writes that although "Mosby appears at first glance to be a black Renaissance man of the day," virtually all of his talents have been challenged by musicians who worked with him, saxophonist Marshall Royal among them. The scathing criticisms from his peers include assertions that Mosby "couldn't drum to save his life, completely lacked skills as a composer, called in Lionel Hampton to play drums on key gigs and recording sessions, etc."[226] Although Gioia points out that many of the criticisms levied against Mosby seem easily refutable by information found in newspapers and other primary source documents, the abundance of "acerbic comments" directed at him, "however ungrounded in the facts, nonetheless reveal the low esteem in which Curtis Mosby was held by his fellow musicians."[227]

Whatever his merits or deficiencies as a musician, businessman, or human being, Mosby's impact on the history of Los Angeles jazz cannot be ignored. Born in 1895 in Kansas City, he moved to Chicago at some point and led a dance band around 1918 before moving west to Oakland, opening a music shop there in 1921. He toured for two years with Mamie Smith's Jazz Hounds before settling permanently in Los Angeles in 1924, perhaps earlier. In Los Angeles he formed a sextet, the Dixieland Blue Blowers, which between 1924 and 1926 had a regular engagement playing for whites-only audiences at Solomon's Dance Pavilion De Luxe.[228] McCarthy cites a 1926 reference to the Blue Blowers' job at Solomon's in *Variety*, which reports the group "playing opposite a cowboy band, that is not as good."[229] The featured trumpet player with the Blue Blowers was James Porter, who left his job with the Sunnyland Jazz Band to join Mosby at Solomon's.

Mosby's Dixieland Blue Blowers reached new heights of popularity in the late 1920s, making recordings for Columbia, (1927, 1928, and 1929) and rivaling Howard's Serenaders and Sonny Clay's groups for the title of top black Los Angeles band. Going strictly by the measure of number of notices in the *Eagle* from 1927 through 1929, Mosby's group may have been the most popular of the three. However, this measure may be deceptive, because Mosby, as the unofficial "mayor of Central Avenue" and one of the most successful black businessmen in Los Angeles, probably had easier access to the media than any of his musical competitors.

By the late 1920s, Central Avenue was thriving as never before as the center of black entertainment on the West Coast. Amid rampant overcrowding (brought on by the steady flow of new immigrants and newly imposed residential restrictions), heightened racial tensions, and an overall deterioration in the standard of living in the black community, lavish new clubs and theaters were opening on the Avenue. Jazz, now generally played by bigger bands (eight to ten pieces) whose styles were beginning to foreshadow 1930s swing, was the music of choice. The passion for jazz among African Americans had grown with the music's increased status and popularity nationwide and with the diversification of the city's black community, which barely resembled the isolated, provincial, and exclusive community of a decade before. Hollywood was booming, and Central Avenue's status as a near-mandatory late-night hangout for movie stars and others in the Hollywood crowd kept climbing. The segregated, whites-only clubs featuring black entertainment expanded the realm of opportunity for jazz musicians, providing the most lucrative financial rewards despite the fact that the musicians were miserably underpaid in comparison with their white counterparts.[230]

Black entertainment, its anchor firmly planted in the music and spirit of jazz, had become big business, and Curtis Mosby became the biggest African-American entertainment mogul in late 1920s Los Angeles. Mosby's entrepreneurial skills, combined with his bandleading activities, enabled him to monopolize the scene at many levels. Following their long engagement at Solomon's, the Blue Blowers moved on to the Bronx Palm Gardens at 423 East Seventh Street.[231] Later they became the resident band at the brand-new Lincoln Theater on Central Avenue at 23rd, accompanying elaborate musical comedies and vaudeville acts[232] and playing jazz sets between acts.

In October 1927, Mosby's Blue Blowers signed a recording contract with Columbia Records. They recorded a song called "In My Dreams," written by the René brothers, Leon and Otis, Creoles from New Orleans who had settled in Los Angeles in 1922 and whose songwriting credits also included "When the Swallows Come Back to Capistrano," "Sleepy Time Down South," and "Rockin' Robin." (Leon René was also the leader of a successful Los Angeles dance orchestra in the late 1920s.) "Tiger Stomp" (actually "Tiger Rag"), "Whoop 'em Up Blues," and the excellent "Weary Stomp" were also recorded during the 1927 Blue Blowers' sessions. The personnel of the band for these sessions is somewhat in doubt,[233] but it seems clear that the hot trumpeter was the ubiquitous James Porter. A 1928 recording session for Columbia produced "Hardee Stomp" (presumably by trombonist Ashford Hardie) and "Blue Blowers Blues." Saxophonists Les Hite and Charlie Lawrence are "almost certainly" present on these sides.[234] The Blowers' final recording session for Columbia, in January 1929, resulted in "Louisiana Bo Bo" and "Between You and Me (and the Deep Blue Sea)," assessed by McCarthy as "a dismal effort, not least the vocal by an unidentified male singer accompanied by a Hawaiian guitarist."[235]

In August 1928, Curtis Mosby opened the Apex Nite Club at 4015 Central Avenue. By November 1928 this elegant club had become *the* hot spot on Central Avenue, both for well-heeled black Angelenos and for white Hollywood celebrities.[236] As was the case in other clubs in the area, including the chic Kentucky Club Cafe, which opened in 1929, the clientele at the Apex was racially mixed, although the performers were all African American.

During the Apex Club's first year, Mosby engaged the African-American actor and composer Clarence Muse to produce floor shows. The Blue Blowers worked in support of a permanent cast of entertainers that included comedian Eddie "Rochester" Anderson, future Ellington band vocalist Ivie Anderson, and tap dancer Lee Young.[237] Other stage shows at the Apex, such as "Mosby's Chocolate Revue," were co-produced by Mosby and dancer Mildred Washington and featured beautiful dancing girls, comedy acts, vaudevilles, and jazz numbers and popular songs of the day. The house band was Mosby's Blue Blowers, featuring Mosby himself on drums along with trumpeter James Porter, saxophonist Marshall Royal, and trombonist Lawrence Brown. Two Los Angeles radio stations featured live remote broadcasts of the band's nightly performances.[238] Mosby's many duties as manager of the club and man about town often precluded him from playing, and his main sub on such occasions was Lionel Hampton. The Apex Club house band recorded the soundtrack for the 1929 film *Hallelujah*.[239]

On November 1, 1929, just four days after the stock market crash, which ushered in the Great Depression, the Apex Nite Club was raided by the police and shut down. Mosby was brought to trial. According to the *Eagle,* the charges brought against him were ill-founded and were the result of racism.

> On the very face of things the attempt to crucify the Apex looked shady. It looked like a preconcocted and well laid plan to destroy this particular club, in spite of the

fact that it was conducted on a much higher plane than four-fifths of like establishments. In other words, it was a case of Mosby being a colored man; he was in somebody's way, or somebody wanted him out of the way which ever way one would want
to put it.[240]

Mosby was ultimately found innocent of the charges, and the Los Angeles Police
Commission dismissed the action that had been filed by the police to revoke his
club operating license.

CONCLUSION

Jazz historians have characterized Los Angeles before 1930 as "a provincial out-
land, separated by several thousand miles from the music centers of the country."[241] Perhaps that is what it was. Nevertheless, jazz was very much alive in Los
Angeles in the 1920s and preceding years, and the rapid growth and development
of the African-American jazz scene on and around Central Avenue came to
reflect the radical transformation of the city's black community and that community's relationship to the city as a whole. The jazz bands and their music were at
the center of African-American social life, drawing people together and fostering
a sense of communal identity in a dazzling array of diverse contexts, from after-
hours nightclubs to baby contests, political rallies to teenage dances, and society
balls to picnics. They were also at the center of controversy, bringing a loud and
unmistakable voice of change to a community intent on conserving its insular
identity but unable to do so in the face of overwhelming social, economic, and political forces. The jazz scene in Los Angeles was more than a derivative offshoot of
a national musical phenomenon. It was also a product of the dialogue between
that phenomenon and the demands, desires, and constraints of the particular
urban and cultural community in which it evolved. From Jelly Roll Morton, Kid
Ory, and Lionel Hampton to the Black and Tan Jazz Orchestra, Reb Spikes, the
Sunnyland Jazz Band, Sonny Clay, Paul Howard's Quality Serenaders, and Curtis Mosby's Dixieland Blue Blowers, the musicians and bands that swung their way
into the cultural history of Los Angeles helped to define the ethos of a city and the
collective identity of its African-American community while making some lasting
contributions to the American jazz legacy.

DISCOGRAPHY

ORY, EDWARD "KID"

1921 (June). Santa Monica, CA: Nordskog Laboratories

"Ory's Creole Trombone" and "Society Blues"(Reissues: Paradox 3, Hip HI-290–1, Jazz
Collector L-33, Assoc. Francaise des Collectioneurs de Disques du Jazz A-032)
Sunshine 3003: *Ory's Sunshine Orchestra*

Nordskog 3009: *Spikes' Seven Pods of Pepper*

Nordskog 5001: *Kid Ory's Sunshine Orchestra* (Reissue 9/1/51)

"When You're Alone" and "Krooked Blues"

Sunshine 3001 (=Nordskog 3007): *Roberta Dudley (vocalist) and Ory's Sunshine Orchestra*

"That Sweet Something Dear" and "Maybe Some Day"

Sunshine 3002 (=Nordskog 3008): *Ruth Lee (vocalist) and Ory's Sunshine Orchestra*—Kid Ory (trombone, leader); Mutt Carey (cornet); Dink Johnson (clarinet); Fred Washington (piano); Ed Garland (string bass); Ben Borders (drums)

CLAY, WILLIAM ROGERS CAMPBELL "SONNY"

1922. Hollywood: Sunset Studios

"Mama Likes To Do It" (unnumbered test pressing): Sonny Clay (piano); Camille Allen (vocals)

"Gang O' Blues" and "Punishing the Piano" (unnumbered test pressings [208 and 210?]). Sonny Clay (solo piano)

1923. Hollywood: Sunset Studios

"What a Wonderful Time" and "Lou"

Sunset (unnumbered [506?]): *The California Poppies*—Sonny Clay (piano, leader); Ernest Coycault (cornet); Leon White (trombone); "Big Boy" Leonard Davidson (clarinet); Bob Farrell, Johnny King (saxophones); Thomas Valentine (banjo): Willis McDaniel (drums)

1926 (February 2). Los Angeles

"Plantation Blues" and "Chicago Breakdown"

Vocalion 1000, 15254, or 1000, Br A-180: *Sonny Clay's Plantation Orchestra*—Sonny Clay (piano, leader); Ernest Coycault (cornet), Andrew Blakeney (cornet/trumpet); William B. Woodman Sr. (trombone); Leonard Davidson (clarinet); James Carson (clarinet, tenor saxophone); ?—Fitzgerald (banjo); Willis McDaniel (drums); Louis Dodd (alto saxophone, banjo, guitar)

1926 (Spring). Hollywood: Sunset Studios

"Jimtown Blues" and "Roamin' Around"

Sunset 1098 (673 and 676): *The Stompin' Six*

"Down and Out Blues" and "Creole Blues"

Sunset 1099 (678 and 679): *The Stompin' Six*—Sonny Clay (piano, leader); Ernest Coycault (cornet); William B. Woodman Sr. (trombone); Leonard Davidson (clarinet); Louis Dodd (banjo); Willis McDaniel (drums)

1929. Los Angeles: Brunswick Studios

"When It's Sleepy Time Down South"

Sonny Clay label, #22: *Sonny Clay's Hartford Ballroom Orchestra*

"River Stay 'Way from My Door"

Sonny Clay Label, #23: *Sonny Clay's Hartford Ballroom Orchestra*—Sonny Clay (piano, leader); "Doc" Porter, ?—Hart (trumpets); Leon White (trombone); Leonard Davidson (clarinet); Sherman Williams, Carlton Wade (saxes); Frank Watkins (banjo, vocal); Bert Holiday (brass bass); David Lewis (drums)

HOWARD, PAUL[242]

1924. Hollywood: Hollywood Studios

"Mistreatin' Daddy" and "Frankie and Johnnie Blues"

Hollywood 1008 (41 and 43): *Brooks's Quality Four*

"Down on the Farm" and "Who Will Get It?"

Hollywood 1022 (39 and 44): *Brooks's Quality Four*—Paul Howard (clarinet, alto sax); Leon Herriford (alto sax); Harvey Brooks (piano); Henry "Tin Can" Allen (drums & horn effects); Jessie Derrick (vocals on "Mistreatin' Daddy" and "Who Will Get It?")

SPIKES, BENJAMIN M. "REB"

I have been unable to find any information about Spikes's recordings beyond what is discussed in the text of the paper.

MOSBY, CURTIS

1927 (October 14). Los Angeles

"Weary Stomp" and "In My Dreams (I'm Jealous of You)"

Columbia 1191-D, J-486: *Curtis Mosby and His Dixieland Blue Blowers*

"Whoop 'Em Up Blues" and "Tiger Stomp"

Columbia 1192-D: *Curtis Mosby and His Dixieland Blue Blowers*—Curtis Mosby (drums, leader); James Porter (trumpet); Charles Hite, Leo Davis (clarinet, alto saxophone); "Bumps" Myers (tenor saxophone); Attwell Rose (violin); Henry Starr (piano, vocals); Thomas Valentine (banjo); ?—Perkins (brass bass)[243]

NOTES

A preliminary version of this paper was presented at the Pre-Conference Symposium on African American Music in California at the annual meeting of the Society for Ethnomusicology, Oakland, California, November 1990. My special thanks to Teddy Buckner, Jack McVea, Floyd Levin, John Bentley, Jacqueline Cogdell DjeDje, and Eddie S. Meadows for major contributions that have helped bring this project to its present state of completion. I am also grateful to Tom Owens, Leonard Feather, Sue DeVale, Oscar Sims, the music librarians at UCLA, Buddy

Collette, Hadda Brooks, Lonnie Bunch, and Lawrence Gushee for their various forms of assistance.

1. Ted Gioia, *West Coast Jazz: Modern Jazz in California, 1945–1960* (New York: Oxford University Press, 1992), 8.

2. Tom Stoddard, *Jazz on the Barbary Coast* (Essex, England: Storyville Publications, 1982), 60.

3. Gioia, *West Coast Jazz;* Robert L. Gordon, *Jazz West Coast: The Los Angeles Jazz Scene of the 1950s* (London and New York: Quartet Books, 1986).

4. Red Callender and Elaine Cohen, *Unfinished Dream: The Musical World of Red Callender* (New York: Quartet Books, 1985).

5. Roy Porter with David Keller, *There and Back: The Roy Porter Story* (Baton Rouge: Louisiana State University Press, 1991). Also see Hampton Hawes and Don Asher, *Rise Up off Me: A Portrait of Hampton Hawes* (New York: Coweard, McCann, and Geohegan, 1974); reprint, with new introduction by Gary Giddins (New York: Da Capo, 1974); Art Pepper and Laurie Pepper, *Straight Life: The Story of Art Pepper* (New York: Schirmer; London: Collier MacMillan, 1979); Eddie S. Meadows, *Jazz Research and Performance Materials: A Select Annotated Bibliography,* 2nd ed. (New York: Garland Publishers, 1995); and Steven Isoardi, oral histories (forthcoming, University of California Press).

6. Gioia, *West Coast Jazz,* 7–9.

7. Tom Reed, *The Black Music History of Los Angeles: A Classical Pictorial History of Black Music in Los Angeles from the 1920s-1970* (Los Angeles: Black Accent Press, 1992).

8. Bette Yarbrough Cox, *Central Avenue—Its Rise and Fall (1890–c. 1955), Including the Musical Renaissance of Black Los Angeles* (Los Angeles: BEEM Publications, 1996), 10–14, 24, 29–36.

9. Albert McCarthy, *Big Band Jazz* (London: G.B. Putnam's Sons, 1974).

10. McCarthy's main sources of information regarding these individuals and their roles in the Los Angeles jazz scene are a few short pieces from jazz periodicals of the 1950s and early 1960s, as well as interviews with the artists themselves and musicians who played in their bands. See Floyd Levin, "The Spikes Brothers: A Los Angeles Saga," *Jazz Journal* 4, no. 12 (December 1951): 12–14; Berta Wood, "Charlie Lawrence," *Jazz Journal* 9, no. 10 (October 1956): 6–7, 12; Wood, "George Orendorf: Quality Serenader: Part I—Chicago," *Jazz Journal* 10, no. 1 (January 1957): 4–6, and "George Orendorf: Quality Serenader: Part II—Los Angeles," *Jazz Journal* 10, no. 2 (February 1957): 4–6; Wood, "Paul Leroy Howard," *Jazz Journal* 10, no. 11 (November 1957): 6–8, and "Paul Leroy Howard, Part II," *Jazz Journal* 10, no. 12 (December 1957): 13–14; and John Bentley, "Sonny Clay: A Veritable Giant (Part 1)," *Jazz Research* (November/December 1962): 7–8, and "Sonny Clay: A Veritable Giant (Part 2)," *Jazz Research* (January/February 1963): 13–14.

11. See discography at the end of this chapter. My own access to some of these recordings has been made possible by jazz historian Floyd Levin, whose generosity in providing me with relevant recordings, writings, and photographs from his extensive personal jazz archive has greatly aided this project. I also have Levin to thank for contacting John Bentley on my behalf. Materials from Bentley's archives provided most of the information for my discussion of Sonny Clay and for the included discography.

12. See Levin, "The Spikes Brothers." Also see Floyd Levin, "Mystery Shrouds Kid Ory 1920s L.A. Recordings," *West Coast Rag* 3, no. 1 (November 1990): 17–20; "Untold Story of Jelly Roll Morton's Last Years (On the 50th Anniversary of His Death in Los Angeles,

California, July 10, 1941)," *West Coast Rag* 3, no. 8 (July 1991): 37–38, 40–41; and "Andrew Blakeney: Interviewed by Floyd Levin" (1989, from the personal archives of Floyd Levin); and "Kid Ory's Legendary Nordskog/Sunshine Recordings," *Jazz Journal* 46, no. 7 (1993, reprint of Levin 1990, with minor editing): 6–10.

13. Lawrence Gushee, "New Orleans–Area Musicians on the West Coast, 1908–1925," *Black Music Research Journal* 9, no. 1 (Spring 1989): 1–18.

14. Lawrence Gushee, "How the Creole Band Came to Be," *Black Music Research Journal* 8, no. 1 (1988): 83–100.

15. Lawrence Gushee, "A Preliminary Chronology of the Early Career of Ferd 'Jelly Roll' Morton," *American Music* 3 (1985): 389–412.

16. Martin Williams, *Jazz Masters of New Orleans* (New York: The Macmillan Co., 1967).

17. Alan Lomax, *Mister Jelly Roll: The Fortunes of Jelly Roll Morton, New Orleans Creole and "Inventor of Jazz"* (Reprint, Berkeley and Los Angeles: University of California Press, 1973 [1950]), 159–178.

18. Pops Foster (as told to Tom Stoddard), *Pops Foster: The Autobiography of a New Orleans Jazzman* (Berkeley and Los Angeles: University of California Press, 1971).

19. See Bette Y. Cox, "A Selective Survey of Black Musicians in Los Angeles, 1890–ca. 1945," *Black Music Research Bulletin* 10, no. 1 (Spring 1988): 8–9, for a biographical sketch of Ed Garland's career.

20. Lionel Hampton with James Haskins, *Hamp: An Autobiography* (New York: Warner Books, 1989).

21. Ibid., 28–39.

22. Stoddard, *Jazz on the Barbary Coast.*

23. Ibid., 43.

24. Cox, "A Selective Survey"; William Claxton, *Jazz West Coast: A Portfolio of Photographs* (Hollywood: Linear Publications, 1955); Leonard Kunstadt, "Some Early West Coast Jazz History—The Black and Tan Orchestra & Kid Ory's Orch.," *Record Research: The Magazine of Record Statistics and Information* 61 (July 1964): 12; William Howland Kenney, *Chicago Jazz: A Cultural History, 1904–1930* (New York: Oxford University Press, 1993).

25. Lonnie G. Bunch III, *Black Angelenos: The Afro-American in Los Angeles, 1850–1950* (Los Angeles: California Afro-American Museum Foundation, 1988).

26. Lawrence B. DeGraaf, "Negro Migration to Los Angeles, 1930–1950" (Ph.D. diss., University of California, Los Angeles, 1962).

27. Bob Rusch, "Jack McVea: Interview," *Cadence Magazine* 12, no. 4 (1986): 11–23, was also helpful.

28. Stoddard, *Jazz on the Barbary Coast,* 31–32. Sid LeProtti, an African American, was born in Oakland, California, November 25, 1886, and died August 30, 1958 (Willie Collins, personal communication, 11 July 1996). Photographs of both Sid LeProtti and the So Different Jazz Band appear in Stoddard, *Jazz on the Barbary Coast,* 164–167, 176. The band was called "So Different" because band members could play both jazz and classical music (Stoddard, *Jazz on the Barbary Coast,* 50).

29. Ibid., 118.

30. Ibid.

31. Gioia, *West Coast Jazz,* 8.

32. Stoddard, *Jazz on the Barbary Coast,* 143.

33. Bunch, *Black Angelenos.*

34. Ibid., 33.

35. Ibid., 30.

36. Ibid., 32.

37. Ibid., 30.

38. Ibid., 29.

39. Hampton, *Hamp,* 28–29.

40. Stoddard, *Jazz on the Barbary Coast,* 56.

41. Gushee, "How the Creole," 95.

42. Ibid., 96–97. The original quote is found in George Baquet, "Address to the New Orleans Jazz Club, April 17, 1948," *The Second Line* (September/October 1965).

43. Ibid., 97.

44. Eileen Southern, *The Music of Black Americans: A History,* 2nd ed. (New York: W.W. Norton and Co., Inc., 1983), 343.

45. Stoddard, *Jazz on the Barbary Coast,* 53.

46. Jack McVea, personal interview with author, 1988.

47. Bunch, *Black Angelenos.*

48. DeGraaf, "Negro Migration," 11–12.

49. Southern, *Music of Black Americans,* 339. In some circles, European art music is referred to as "classical" music. The terms are used interchangeably here, but "art" music is preferred.

50. Wood, "Paul Leroy Howard," 6.

51. Cox, "A Selective Survey," and *Central Avenue,* 14–21.

52. Stoddard, *Jazz on the Barbary Coast,* 61.

53. Ibid.

54. Gushee, "How the Creole," 95.

55. "The Angelus Moving Picture and Vaudeville" advertisement, *The California Eagle* (10 March 1916): 3.

56. Gioia, *West Coast Jazz,* 7–8.

57. See photo in Stoddard, *Jazz on the Barbary Coast,* 160. At different points in its history, the Wood Wilson Band was known by various names: the Wood Wilson Syncopators, the Wood Wilson "Satisfied" Orchestra, the Wood Wilson Satisfied Vendome Band, and the Wood Wilson Original Satisfied Orchestra.

58. Wood, "Paul Leroy Howard," 7.

59. Ibid., 6.

60. Ibid., 7.

61. "Moving Pictures and Dance" advertisement, *The California Eagle* (8 January 1916): 8.

62. Stoddard, *Jazz on the Barbary Coast,* 160.

63. Wood, "Paul Leroy Howard," 7.

64. "Get the Habit! Habit of What? of Going to the Dreamland Cafe" advertisement, *The California Eagle* (11 October 1919): 7.

65. Foster, *Pops Foster,* 122.

66. Williams, *Jazz Masters,* 50, and Gushee, "A Preliminary Chronology."

67. Spikes cites a date of 1914, but this seems unlikely; see Stoddard, *Jazz on the Barbary Coast,* 61.

68. Reed, *The Black Music,* 48.

69. Ibid., 47–48.

70. "The Cadillac Cafe" advertisement, *The California Eagle* (3 November 1917): 6.

71. Lomax, *Mister Jelly Roll*.

72. Ibid., 162.

73. "Dixie Hotel Bar and Cafe" advertisement, *The California Eagle* (5 April 1919): 2.

74. Lomax, *Mister Jelly Roll*, 164.

75. Ibid.

76. "The Question Has Been Asked," *The California Eagle* (9 June 1917): 4.

77. Lomax, *Mister Jelly Roll*, 162–163.

78. "Decoration and Memorial Day Picnic and Ball, Wayside Park" advertisement, *The California Eagle* (27 May 1922): 5.

79. "Wayside Park. Under Responsible Management—Good Order Always Assured" advertisement, *The California Eagle* (12 August 1922): 6.

80. Williams, *Jazz Masters*, 52.

81. Reed, *The Black Music*, 48.

82. Bentley, "Sonny Clay, Part 1," 8.

83. Lomax, *Mister Jelly Roll*, 163.

84. Ibid.

85. Levin, "Untold Story," 40.

86. Lomax, *Mister Jelly Roll*, 163–164.

87. Foster, *Pops Foster*, 122.

88. McVea, personal interview.

89. Stoddard, *Jazz on the Barbary Coast*, 67.

90. McVea, personal interview.

91. Gioia, *West Coast Jazz*, 8.

92. Bunch, *Black Angelenos*.

93. Levin, "Untold Story," 41.

94. Bentley, "Sonny Clay, Part 1," 7.

95. Bentley, "Sonny Clay, Part 2," 13.

96. Gushee, "How the Creole," 94.

97. Lomax, *Mister Jelly Roll*, 167.

98. Williams, *Jazz Masters*, 54.

99. Levin, "Untold Story," 40. As Levin indicates, the 1922 date often attched to those recordings is incorrect.

100. Levin, "Mystery Shrouds," 20.

101. Ibid., 17.

102. Ibid.

103. Williams, *Jazz Masters*, 206.

104. Levin, "The Spikes Brothers."

105. Williams, *Jazz Masters*, 209.

106. This is one of five Los Angeles bands reviewed in a very interesting piece, "Musicians: How and Where They Strut Their Stuff," *The California Eagle* (28 June 1928): 10. The other bands included are the Vernon Elkins Dixieland Jazz Band, which featured Elkins on cornet and was directed by Les Hite, who was to become the top swing bandleader in Los Angeles in the 1920s; the California Cotton Pickers Orchestra, led by Harry A. Southard, the former director of the Black and Tan Jazz Band; Buster Wilson's Hot Six; and Curtis Mosby's Dixieland Blue Blowers.

107. Nat Shapiro and Nat Hentoff, eds., *Hear Me Talkin' to Ya: The Story of Jazz as Told by the Men Who Made It* (New York: Dover Publications, Inc., 1955), 40.

108. Foster, *Pops Foster,* 120.

109. Ibid., 116–117.

110. Hampton, *Hamp,* 30.

111. Gushee, "New Orleans," 12.

112. Foster, *Pops Foster,* 129–130.

113. "Grand Old Fashioned Picnic and Barbecue" advertisement, *The California Eagle* (17 June 1922): 7.

114. Williams, *Jazz Masters,* 210.

115. Ibid.

116. "Scenic Special Trip Deluxe to San Diego and Tia Juana Old Mexico" advertisement, *The California Eagle* (5 August 1922): 4.

117. "Scenic Special Trip Deluxe to San Diego and Tia Juana Old Mexico" advertisement, *The California Eagle* (29 July 1922): 4.

118. Wood, "Paul Leroy Howard," 8.

119. Teddy Buckner, personal interview with author, 1988.

120. See photo in McCarthy, *Big Band Jazz,* 170.

121. Gushee, "New Orleans," 4.

122. Bentley, "Sonny Clay, Part 1," 8; and McVea, personal interview.

123. Bentley, "Sonny Clay, Part 1," 8.

124. Levin, "Andrew Blakeney," 35, 46.

125. Buckner, personal interview.

126. Wood, "Paul Leroy Howard," 7.

127. "Grand Benefit Given at Wayside Park" advertisement, *The California Eagle* (29 April 1922): 9.

128. Williams, *Jazz Masters,* 205.

129. James Lincoln Collier, *The Making of Jazz: A Comprehensive History* (Boston: Houghton Mifflin Company, 1978), 113.

130. Hampton, *Hamp,* 180–181.

131. McCarthy, *Big Band Jazz,* 167–174, 358.

132. Born in Norfolk, Virginia, John Gray moved to Los Angeles in 1910. Not only did he obtain training in music from schools in Los Angeles (e.g., the University of Southern California and the University of California at Los Angeles), but he attended l'Ecole Normale de Musique in Paris, France. He was a higly respected teacher and performer of European art music in Los Angeles; see Cox, *Central Avenue,* 19.

133. John Gray, "In the Music World," *The California Eagle* (4 October 1919): 5.

134. "Elk's Annual Picnic and Barbecue at Luna Park—Formerly Seelig Zoo—Saturday, June 19th, 1926. Greatest Attraction of the Season; Big Animal Show at 3 p.m.; Games of all Kind and Dancing—'All for One Admission'—By Golden West Lodge, No. 86, I.B.P.O.E. of W. Two Bands: Black & Tan and Sonny Clay Orchestra" advertisement, *The California Eagle* (11 June 1926): 4.

135. Wood, "Paul Leroy Howard," 7–8; and McCarthy, *Big Band Jazz,* 170.

136. McCarthy, *Big Band Jazz.*

137. Ibid., 173.

138. Buckner, personal interview.

139. Bentley, "Sonny Clay, Part 2," 14.

140. McCarthy, *Big Band Jazz,* 173.

141. Bentley, "Sonny Clay, Part 1," 8.

142. Ibid.

143. Ibid.

144. Ibid.

145. Ibid.

146. Bentley, "Sonny Clay, Part 2," 13.

147. McCarthy, *Big Band Jazz*, 173; Bentley, "Sonny Clay, Part 2," 13–14, cites a date of 1926.

148. Bentley, "Sonny Clay, Part 2," 13.

149. "Sonny Clay's Orchestra," *The California Eagle* (12 February 1926): 1.

150. According to Steve Isoardi (telephone conversation, July 1996), a jazz historian who has interviewed numerous Los Angeles jazz musicians for the UCLA Oral History Program, William Woodman Sr. moved to Los Angeles from Mississippi in 1918. Woodman had three sons who became professional musicians—trombonist Britt, pianist Coney, and William Jr., who played both trumpet and saxophone. The three brothers were the nucleus of the Woodman Brothers Band, one of several "family bands" active in Los Angeles in the 1930s; see Reed, *The Black Music*, 23. During the 1950s, Britt Woodman achieved fame as a trombonist with the Duke Ellington Orchestra.

151. "Sonny Clay's Orchestra," 1.

152. Bentley, "Sonny Clay, Part 2," 14.

153. "Washington's Birthday Dance at Arion Hall—3rd & Main—Monday, February 22—Sonny Clay's Vocalion Recording Orchestra" advertisement, *The California Eagle* (12 February 1926): 1; "Grand Opening Eagle Hall, Wednesday Night, February 24th. Music to Be Furnished by Sonny Clay" advertisement, *The California Eagle* (5 February 1926): 5; and "Elk's Annual Picnic." Curiously, the Black and Tan Band appeared in the *Eagle* for this one engagement after a two-year absence and was never seen again.

154. "Annual Pre-Lenten Dance, Benefit St. Philip's Building Fund, Knights of Columbus" advertisement, *The California Eagle* (11 February 1927): 1.

155. McCarthy, *Big Band Jazz,* 173.

156. Ibid.

157. McVea, Personal interview.

158. McCarthy, *Big Band Jazz.*

159. Buckner, personal interview.

160. Bentley, "Sonny Clay, Part 1," 8.

161. McCarthy, *Big Band Jazz*, 173, cites the date as August 1931; Bentley, "Sonny Clay, Part 2," 14, gives a date of 1929.

162. During my initial period of research for this chapter, in 1988, my preliminary findings led convincingly to the conclusion that a band called the Sunnyland Jazz Band, a Los Angeles group whose performances during the period 1923–1926 were frequently announced in the *Eagle*, was a band directed by Sonny Clay. My source for this information was Teddy Buckner, who told me in a 1988 interview that the Sunnyland Jazz Orchestra of the mid-twenties was a Sonny Clay–led organization featuring Clay on piano, Paul Howard on saxophone, and James Porter on cornet and trumpet. I had no reason to question the accuracy of Buckner's memory relative to the Sunnyland/Sonny Clay connection, but more recent findings strongly indicate that the Sunnyland Jazz Band was a separate organization having nothing to do with Sonny Clay's band, other than that both were among the most popular Los Angeles jazz bands of the mid-1920s.

163. Wood, "Charlie Lawrence," 6.

164. McCarthy, *Big Band Jazz*, 171.

165. Levin, "Andrew Blakeney."

166. McCarthy, *Big Band Jazz*, 171. The photograph, which must have been taken before trumpeter Andrew Blakeney joined the band, provides rather compelling evidence in support of Lawrence's memory of the Sunnyland group over Buckner's recollection, with the only commonality being the presence of James Porter in both personnel lists.

167. Levin, "Andrew Blakeney," 38.

168. Wood, "Charlie Lawrence," 7.

169. Levin, "Andrew Blakeney," 36–37.

170. "Sunnyland Pre-Hallowe'en Masquerade Ball. Majestic Dancing Academy. Tuesday Evening, Oct. 30th" advertisement, *The California Eagle* (26 October 1923): 2; Sunnyland Jazz Orchestra, Majestic Dancing Academy, Grand Thanksgiving Ball, Thanksgiving Night, Thurs., Nov. 29" advertisement, *The California Eagle* (23 November 1923): 4.

171. "Xmas Chimes Dance and Musical Fiesta" advertisement, *The California Eagle* (21 December 1923): 3.

172. "Carolyn Snowden and Creole Cuties to Give 30 Minutes Revue at Rho Psi Phi Dance 10 to 10:30—Sunnyland Orchestra with Amplifiers" advertisement, *The California Eagle* (9 April 1926): 1; "Silver Fox Hair Dance—Fri. Eve., April 23—$100 Given Away in Prizes to Prettiest Head of Hair—Sunnyland Jazz Orchestra Playing" advertisement, *The California Eagle* (16 April 1926): 1.

173. "All Roads Lead to—Eureka Village" advertisement, *The California Eagle* (6 March 1925): 3.

174. "Judge Bledsoe Looms a Winner," *The California Eagle* (2 May 1925): 1.

175. William T. Wilkins, "Prof. W. T. Wilkins on Bledsoe," *The California Eagle* (2 May 1925): 4. For further information about Wilkins, see Cox, *Central Avenue*, 14–18.

176. McCarthy, *Big Band Jazz*, 168.

177. Stoddard, *Jazz on the Barbary Coast*, 54.

178. McCarthy, *Big Band Jazz*, 168.

179. Ibid.

180. Stoddard, *Jazz on the Barbary Coast*, 77.

181. McCarthy, *Big Band Jazz*, 68.

182. Bunch, *Black Angelenos*, 33–34.

183. McVea, personal interview. However, it should be noted that McVea played in Los Angeles nightclubs in the thirties and later.

184. "Mosby Opens High Class Music," *The California Eagle* (1 November 1929): 2.

185. Stoddard, *Jazz on the Barbary Coast*, 57.

186. Ibid., 58.

187. Ibid., 59.

188. "Steppin' High Promises to Break All Attendance Records at Philharmonic" advertisement, *The California Eagle* (22 August 1924): 10.

189. Levin, "The Spikes Brothers," 12.

190. Stoddard, *Jazz on the Barbary Coast*, 74.

191. Ibid., 160.

192. Ibid., 75.

193. Ibid., 60.

194. Ibid., 75.

195. McCarthy, *Big Band Jazz*, 168.

196. Ibid.

197. "N.A.A.C.P. That Big Night" advertisement, *The California Eagle* (4 June 1926): 2.

198. Hampton, *Hamp*, 29.

199. See Stoddard, *Jazz on the Barbary Coast*, 77–78.

200. McCarthy, *Big Band Jazz*, 169.

201. Hampton, *Hamp*, 26. The biographical details of Hite's early life, found in McCarthy, *Big Band Jazz*, 176, present some contradictions relative to the Hampton version of Hite's life history prior to his departure for Los Angeles in the early 1920s. My account is based on the Hampton version.

202. Hampton, *Hamp*, 26.

203. Gioia, *West Coast Jazz*, 9.

204. Wood, "Charlie Lawrence," 7, 8.

205. Hampton, *Hamp*, 30.

206. McCarthy, *Big Band Jazz*, 170.

207. See Hampton, *Hamp*, 178–180, for discography.

208. Bunch, *Black Angelenos*, 32.

209. "Grand Opening Kentucky Club Cafe" advertisement, *The California Eagle* (8 March 1929): 6.

210. McCarthy, *Big Band Jazz*, 172.

211. Ibid., 169.

212. Quoted in Wood, "Charlie Lawrence," 6.

213. Hampton, *Hamp*, 30.

214. Ibid., 30–31.

215. Ibid., 32.

216. Ibid.

217. Ibid.

218. Ibid., 32, 34.

219. McCarthy, *Big Band Jazz*, 176.

220. See discography in Hampton, *Hamp*, 180–181.

221. Ibid., 38.

222. McCarthy, *Big Band Jazz*, 176–177.

223. Gioia, *West Coast Jazz*, 8.

224. Ibid.

225. Levin, personal correspondence and interview with author, 1993.

226. Gioia, *West Coast Jazz*, 9.

227. Ibid.

228. McCarthy, *Big Band Jazz*, 174.

229. Quoted in McCarthy, *Big Band Jazz*, 174.

230. Some of the very light-skinned African-American musicians such as Charlie Lawrence and Ernest Coycault were occasionally able to pass for white and play gigs with the much higher-paying white bands; see Wood, "Charlie Lawrence," 7.

231. J. B. Bass, "The Bronx Hotel," *The California Eagle* (22 July 1927): 4; "Bronx Palm Garden a Separate Institution," *The California Eagle* (22 July 1927): 8.

232. New York's New Lafayette Players was one of the first groups to present live theater at the Lincoln, which opened in 1927.

233. McCarthy, *Big Band Jazz*, 174.

234. Ibid.

235. Ibid.

236. One of the first advertisements for the Apex Nite Club appeared in the *Eagle:* "Two Big Nights! Make Your Reservations Now for Thanksgiving Eve. [sic] and Thanksgiving Nite at the Apex Nite Club" advertisement, *The California Eagle* (23 November 1928): 1.

237. "Apex Club" advertisement, *The California Eagle* (7 December 1928): 9.

238. "An Evening at the Apex Night Club," *The California Eagle* (20 September 1929): 10.

239. McCarthy, *Big Band Jazz,* 174.

240. "Apex Wins Court Fight: Apex Night Club Wins Smashing Victory As Police Commission Dismiss Charges Filed by Police to Revoke Permit," *The California Eagle* (29 November 1929): 1, 3.

241. Levin, "Mystery Shrouds," 17.

242. For complete listings of recordings made by Paul Howard's Quality Serenaders during that group's 1929 and 1930 Victor sessions (e.g. "The Ramble," "Moonlight Blues," "Charlie's Idea," "Overnight Blues," "Quality Shout," "Stuff," "Harlem," "Cuttin' Up," "New Kinda Blues," and "California Swing"), see Hampton, *Hamp,* 178–180. Also see Hampton, *Hamp,* 180–181, for a discography of recordings by Les Hite's New Cotton Club house big band featuring Louis Armstrong (listed under "Louis Armstrong and His Sebastian New Cotton Club Orchestra").

243. The accuracy of this listing of personnel, taken from Brian A. Rust, *Jazz Records: 1897–1942,* rev. ed., 2 vols. (London: Storyville Publications and Co., 1970), has been questioned on legitimate grounds in McCarthy, *Big Band Jazz,* 174. Also see McCarthy, *Big Band Jazz,* 358, for discography of reissues of some Mosby, Clay, and Howard recordings. Unfortunately, his citation format is rather sparse in terms of providing relevant and usable information.

2

"Pitchin' up a Boogie"

African-American Musicians, Nightlife, and Music Venues in Los Angeles, 1930–1945

Ralph Eastman

Most of the nation has long considered Los Angeles to be a cultural backwater. In the sphere of jazz, blues, and popular music, eastern musicians and critics erroneously claimed that the city lacked any music or musicians of consequence. In 1941, for example, well into the period that this chapter considers, *Down Beat* editor Dave Dexter dismissed all Los Angeles musicians as less competent than their eastern and midwestern counterparts.[1] This attitude took root early, and by the 1950s Los Angeles wore the bitter sobriquet "the place musicians go to die." However, a survey of the breadth and depth of Los Angeles's ignored or forgotten African-American musical heritage corrects this entrenched critical myopia. Though it is true that the city is located far from the traditional centers of jazz and blues and that, with the exception of Charles Mingus, no one of the stature of a Duke Ellington or Count Basie emerged from it, African-American musicians in Los Angeles were creating and recording vital popular music by the 1920s.

In the preceding chapter, Michael Bakan surveyed the activities of jazz musicians attracted by Los Angeles's growing African-American community early in the century.[2] As Bakan illustrates, the real architects of the local African-American music world during the twenties and thirties were primarily transplanted rather than native-born musicians. The influence of people such as Lionel Hampton and Nat "King" Cole and less-well-remembered players such as Sonny Clay, Les Hite, Curtis Mosby, the René brothers, and the Spikes brothers continued through World War II and, in some cases, far longer.

Although African Americans may have enjoyed better wages and opportunities in Los Angeles than in the South, they nonetheless met familiar patterns of racial discrimination in the city. Several members of the Los Angeles City Council were open in their advocacy for continued racial segregation.[3] Though small African-American enclaves grew in Pasadena, Long Beach, and Santa Monica, restrictive covenants confined 70 percent of Los Angeles's black population to the narrow

South Central corridor, an area that constituted only about 5 percent of the city's residential space.[4] Amazingly, the city did not receive its widespread reputation for severe housing discrimination policies until after World War II.[5]

Besides housing discrimination, blacks suffered other Jim Crow indignities within the city. Most nightclubs, restaurants, hotels, and theaters outside the city's South Central section were closed to African-American audiences, both by tradition and by the prohibitive costs of admission.[6] Clubs did, however, make strange exceptions to their racial policies. Some had separate sections from which guests of band members could watch the show.[7] They routinely admitted African-American newspaper columnists (presumably to the same segregated sections) striving to keep their community abreast of the fortunes of the featured performers, whom blacks could only see in Central Avenue appearances.[8] Community feelings about the racially based exclusionary policies of Los Angeles's clubs ran so high that when the Palomar Ballroom burned to the ground on the eve of a Count Basie appearance in September 1939, a *Los Angeles Sentinel* columnist wondered "if the rumors that Negroes were to be admitted to the affair had anything to do with the accident?"[9] Although African Americans could only attend clubs in their own districts, their clubs admitted whites. Whites tended to patronize Central Avenue on weeknights; blacks came out on weekends.[10] Hollywood stars and celebrities often frequented the most well-appointed of the South Central clubs.

Other examples of intimidation and harassment from the period under discussion include a 1940 march by twenty Ku Klux Klansmen through downtown streets to Los Angeles City Hall that went uninterrupted by police[11] and unreported in the white press. Later in the year, the same police department refused to issue the La Fiesta Club a permit to hold a dance featuring the Benny Goodman Orchestra at the Shrine Auditorium because of fears that whites, Filipinos, Mexicans, and blacks might be permitted to dance together.[12]

Los Angeles also had unwritten discriminatory practices, many subject to "arrangements" between club owners and police. In 1935 even Central Avenue's famed Club Alabam had to follow the precedent set by other area clubs in refusing to allow mixed dancing lest they face police trouble and eventual closing.[13] Other cities drafted laws to enforce racial segregation. Suburban Southgate, home of the Trianon Ballroom, had local ordinances prohibiting the "mixing of races in nightclubs, ballrooms, and restaurants."[14] In Glendale black musicians had to apply for police permits to remain within the city limits after 6 p.m. or be subject to arrest. At the 2 a.m. closing time of clubs, squad cars escorted artists with permits to the Los Angeles city line.[15] Later, as blacks moved westward, the Los Angeles police adopted a similar practice, accompanying African-American performers south to Pico Boulevard, the presumed northern boundary of their community.

Segregation within the Los Angeles locals of the American Federation of Musicians (AFM) provided another serious impediment to full employment for African-American musicians. By 1943 only two AFM union locals—New York's

Local 802 and Detroit's Local 5—admitted African Americans to full membership. There were only thirty-two black locals among the 673 AFM locals in the United States. Six hundred thirty-one limited their membership only to white musicians; eight others had "subsidiary" groupings for musicians of color.[16] This meant that virtually all of the country's largest cities—Chicago, Philadelphia, Los Angeles, and San Francisco—had segregated musicians' unions.[17] In Los Angeles, Local 47 was the union chapter for white musicians; Local 767, chartered in 1920, was for blacks. The two Los Angeles locals did not amalgamate until 1953.

With this kind of treatment routinely facing them outside of their home districts, it is no wonder that African Americans quickly created their own separate but vital community within the boundaries of the South Central area. Beginning with the repeal of Prohibition in 1933, the flurry of "beer garden" and club openings in the African-American community provided so much work that the musicians of Local 767 could even buy a new clubhouse on Central Avenue (1710 Central).[18] During the late twenties and the thirties, local audiences referred to the stretch of Central Avenue between 19th and 41st Streets as "Brown Broadway." In addition to clubs and cafes, there were several motion pictures theaters lining the twenty blocks: the Rosebud (1940 Central), Gaiety (2407 Central), A-Mus-U (35th and Central), and Tivoli (later the Bill Robinson, 4219 Central). Even after sound came to film, these movie houses employed musicians for both live stage shows between films and regularly scheduled "midnight frolics," late-night jazz and dance concerts on weekends.

The Lincoln and the Florence Mills both began as legitimate theaters. The Lincoln (2300 Central) opened in October 1927 as the largest theater on Central Avenue, seating more than 2,000 people.[19] In a prestigious start, the Lincoln engaged New York's New Lafayette Players to present live theater during its first two seasons. The Lafayette Players produced a new musical show or review every week until the hot summer months caused the un-air-conditioned theater to close. However, the ambitious live theater policy was short-lived. In 1930, to survive the worsening Depression, its owners converted the Lincoln for the presentation of talking films.[20] Although it seldom presented stage plays again, the Lincoln Theater continued as a major venue for live music on the Avenue. The smaller, more intimate Florence Mills Theater (3511 Central) celebrated the memory of the popular African-American stage star. It stood twelve blocks south of the Lincoln and was only one-third its size.[21] At its opening in December 1930, it presented black vaudeville. However, it, too, soon succumbed to the Depression and changing audience tastes and became a motion picture house. The Elks Hall, at the corner of Washington Boulevard and Central Avenue, contained a large auditorium that routinely featured dance bands and special events on weekends. Later the organization moved southward to a new facility at 3616 Central Avenue and continued staging dances and concerts throughout the war years.

Until 1928, when Dr. John Somerville built the Hotel Somerville (4225 Central) to provide first-class accommodations for African Americans, black visitors to the city had to choose between the shabby Bronx Hotel on East Seventh Street or lodging in private homes. At the time Somerville began construction, the hotel's location was twenty blocks south of the community's business center. After Somerville lost the building in the stock market crash, the new owners renamed it in honor of the poet Paul Lawrence Dunbar. The Dunbar Hotel quickly became such a glamorous landmark that it drew the community's center southward to it. "The Stem," as the strip around the Dunbar became known, was home to a thriving new business district that included the bulk of the area's prewar nightclubs.

The Dunbar itself housed a succession of nightclubs in the early thirties. The room first opened as Jack Johnson's Show Boat Cafe in October 1931 under the titular management of the former heavyweight champion. "Papa" Mutt Carey and His Syncopators served as the house band.[22] Johnson's tenure did not last out the year, and the club reopened as the Harlem Show Boat in January. This time it featured Sonny Clay's orchestra.[23] Within a year, it was the Club Ebony, and Patsy Hunter, a rising young local choreographer and producer of Avenue floor shows, led its chorus line.[24] In its final incarnation, it became the Black Derby Rathskellar and featured pianists such as Sylvester Scott and Memphis's Jesse Crump.[25] The management finally closed the club in 1935. After that, although the biggest stars in African-American entertainment were often either in residence at the hotel or holding court at its bar, audiences had to go elsewhere on the Avenue to see them perform. Guitarist Gene Phillips lived at the Dunbar in the early forties and described the exhilaration of the experience: "All the cats hung out at the bar there because that's where all the chorus girls hung out. Any night you could find Nat Cole, Duke, Cab, Basie . . . everyone who was anybody ended up at the Dunbar Bar."[26]

Drummer and bandleader Curtis Mosby settled in Los Angeles during the early twenties and was a major force in the city's black music circles for the next thirty years.[27] Mosby opened his first Apex Nite Club in Los Angeles in 1928 and a second in San Francisco in late 1930, with floor shows alternating every two weeks between the two cities.[28] He created Mosby's Blue Syncopators to play in Los Angeles under the leadership of pianist Walter Johnson while the Blue Blowers were on the road in San Francisco.[29] The move apparently caused Mosby to overreach himself, and he filed for bankruptcy within the year. After that, Mosby concentrated his activities in San Francisco, and the Blue Blowers had a successful run on the Fairbanks vaudeville circuit in Northern California.[30]

When Mosby returned to Los Angeles, in 1935, the original Apex Club was under new management and doing business as the Club Alabam. Mosby opened the New Apex Club (1063 E. 55th) fifteen blocks to the south. By this time he had long since disbanded the Blues Blowers, and he hired Buck Clayton to lead the house orchestra.[31] When the club failed, Mosby tried again with a series of smaller venues, including the Classic Bar and Grill (4253 Central) and the Cafe Beautiful (4120 Central), both of which presented music, though on a smaller scale.[32] In 1940, when Mosby took over the Club Alabam (by now Central Avenue's most celebrated nightspot), he was back in the same building that had housed his original Apex Club ten years earlier.[33]

As segregated Los Angeles clubs, restaurants, and cafes gradually relaxed their restrictions on employment, if not on admission, many—for instance, Frank Sebastian's New Cotton Club—employed African-American musicians and dancers to perform in exotically produced "black and tan" shows that came into vogue during the last years of Prohibition. When he opened his New Cotton Club in Culver City (8781 Washington) in 1926, Sebastian established his own version of the "peculiar institution" by signing personal contracts with many young musicians, both locals and transplanted midwesterners, who played the new "swing" style. These contracts bound the musicians exclusively to Sebastian and his club. Though the Cotton Club presented black orchestras with national reputations (Armstrong, Calloway, Ellington), Sebastian created the appearance of having several house bands by featuring his Los Angeles–based musicians in various configurations. He began by contracting with the members of Vernon Elkins's Dixieland Jazz Band, an established local orchestra that featured Elkins on cornet and Les Hite on reeds.[34] He also hired Paul Howard's Quality Serenaders, a nine-piece band that included Lawrence Brown, Lionel Hampton, Charlie Lawrence, George Orendorff, and Marshall Royal.[35] Sebastian simultaneously engaged Leon Herriford to lead the Whispering Serenaders, yet another band composed of this same nucleus of musicians.

By 1930 blacks could listen nightly to live half-hour radio remote broadcasts from clubs that refused their patronage. Broadcasts originating from the Cotton Club included such highlights as Lionel Hampton's first engagement at the club as a bandleader[36] and the first West Coast appearance of the Earl Hines's band;[37] they also served to build Les Hite's popularity throughout the West.[38] Hite was now the sole leader of the club's house band, and his orchestra was a successful touring attraction between San Diego and Seattle. In April 1932 a *California Eagle* columnist remarked that Hite was the most popular bandleader in the West.[39] When Les Hite made his first tour to the East in 1937, he failed to inspire similar enthusiasm, and the band remained a regional attraction. Hite continued to lead bands in Los Angeles until 1945, when he quit music to start his own business.[40]

Sebastian occasionally allowed the Orchestra and Club Revue to appear in venues in which African Americans were welcome. In his first Central Avenue appearance, at the Elks Hall in 1932, Louis Armstrong brought the entire New Cotton Orchestra and Club Revue along with him for an ecstatically received show.[41] Twice in 1934 Sebastian took Leon Herriford's Whispering Serenaders, the Revue (featuring Eddie Anderson, the Three Rockets of Rhythm, the Four Covans, and the Creole Chorus) to Central Avenue venues for charity benefits.[42] Hite brought similar packages into the Paramount Theater (626 So. Grand) and the Orpheum (Broadway and Ninth) downtown for a week each during that summer.

"Black and tan" club managers perennially revised their show policies in reaction to fluctuations in audience attendance. It was common for African-American bands and floor shows to be arbitrarily dismissed and replaced by white acts, only to be reinstated if the change did not improve business. In 1937 Sebastian sought to attract broader audiences than he felt black entertainment could draw. He renamed the club Sebastian's Club Internationale and started hiring big-name white bands.[43] When the strategy failed, Hite returned yet again to the bandstand, and Sebastian quickly booked the Louis Armstrong and Jimmie Lunceford bands for engagements. Sebastian finally sold his interest in the club and moved his operations to Hollywood, where he opened the Cubanola.[44]

In 1940 the Cotton Club reopened as the Casa Manana. The new owners gradually dropped the discriminatory practices and even went so far as to permit mixed-race dancing. As the war ended, *Down Beat* noted that the Casa Manana was possibly the first major nightclub in Los Angeles regularly operating with a nondiscriminatory patronage policy.[45]

During the late twenties, Lionel Hampton, the most famous of the original Cotton Club musicians, began earning his reputation for flamboyant showmanship there as "the world's greatest eccentric drummer."[46] He first played the vibraphone, the instrument most closely associated with him, when the Hite band supported Louis Armstrong's extended 1930–31 appearance at the club.[47] In 1935 Hampton formed his own big band and toured the West Coast, including week-long stands at the downtown Paramount Theater and Central Avenue's Lincoln Theater[48] and at the Club Araby (1063 E. 55th).[49] By 1936 Hampton's band was popular enough to open for an unlimited stand at the Cotton Club.[50] Later in the year the band, which included Teddy Buckner and Wesley Prince, began its famous residency at the downtown Paradise Club (633 So. Main),[51] where Benny Goodman first met Hampton and the idea for the Goodman Quartet was born.[52] After Hampton went with Goodman, Buckner put together a band for the Paradise job,[53] and Prince joined the King Cole Swingsters, a quartet that briefly preceded Cole's trio.

During his short tenure with Goodman, Hampton kept his own recording band together and, having jammed with the new King Cole Trio at Hollywood's Swanee Inn, cut several successful small-group sides with them in 1940.[54] Shortly after he left Goodman, Hampton made his hit recording of "Flying Home" with Illinois Jacquet and hired promising young Los Angeles players Dexter Gordon and Jack McVea. For the next fifty years, Lionel Hampton continued to be an immensely popular bandleader and vibraphonist.

Nat King Cole's popularity with both races helped make him the first major star to come out of the Los Angeles in the early days of World War II. Cole, who grew up in Chicago, came to the West Coast as the leader of the Nat Cole Swing Orchestra with the 1937 edition of *Shuffle Along.* The show played at the Lincoln Theater for a week in May[55] before it ran out of money, leaving the performers stranded far from home. Cole stayed in Los Angeles and struggled as a single, playing piano in "every beer joint from San Diego to Bakersfield."[56] In so doing, he built an enthusiastic following among African-American audiences for his unique Hines-influenced piano style. Cole's first break came when Bob Lewis of Hollywood's Swanee Inn asked him to form a quartet for a limited engagement, an unusual request in a club business that was still centered around big bands. When drummer Lee Young failed to appear, Cole, Oscar Moore, and Wesley Prince went on to set the standard for all the piano trios that followed in their wake. Lewis extended their stay at the club to six months. In that time, the group grew enormously popular among white audiences, becoming the first black musicians hired to play in other exclusive Hollywood and Beverly Hills clubs.[57] Bassist Johnny Miller, formerly with the Eddie Beale Trio, replaced Prince in September 1942 when the latter was drafted, completing the lineup of the group that became famous.[58]

The King Cole Trio recorded for Decca and for several local independent record companies, including Otis René's Excelsior Records, before Johnny Mercer signed them to his fledgling Capitol Records in 1943. During the war, record sales helped to make the trio a national phenomenon, and Cole established his reputation as a matchless ballad singer. When they were in the city, the trio played at downtown's 331 Club (which was not always hospitable to black patrons) and did occasional one-nighters on Central Avenue. In 1944 Curtis Mosby opened a breakfast club, the Last Word Cafe (4206 Central), across the street from the Club Alabam, and the King Cole Trio doubled there after hours.[59] The trio's symbolic acceptance into the American mainstream occurred when the Sunset Strip's exclusive El Trocadero named its cocktail lounge the King Cole Room and booked the group for regular appearances.[60]

The Cole Swingsters' sometime drummer, Lee Young, went on to play locally with the Eddie Barefield and Buck Clayton bands and first toured with Eddie Mollory's band behind Ethel Waters.[61] When radio personality and promoter Al Jarvis presented a quartet that featured Young along with Barefield, Eddie Beale, and Al Morgan at Hollywood's Famous Door in 1937, Freddy Doyle, a *California Eagle* columnist and bandleader, proudly noted that the group "cut" (i.e., outplayed) every white musician who jammed with them.[62] In 1941, Lester Young, Lee's older brother, returned home to the West Coast and joined Red Callender, Red Mack, and "Bumps" Myers in Lee's band for a stand at Billy Berg's Club Capri (Pico and La Cienega) in Hollywood.[63] It was in that year that *Down Beat* editor Dave Dexter wrote off all of the city's musicians except Stan Kenton as inferior to their eastern and midwestern counterparts.[64] Young, whose group (without Lester) Dexter had specifically dismissed, remembered the long-standing eastern prejudices against the West Coast: "[Y]ou never really heard of Los Angeles that much, then, where music was concerned. Everybody [jazz writers] thought all the jazz and all the better jazz musicians came from the East. The writers from *Metronome* and *Down Beat* used to segregate it. They had what they called 'West Coast Jazz'; they thought it would be different."[65] It should be noted, however, that Dexter soon moved to the city and was instrumental in the creation of Capitol Records.

The Young brothers took their band into New York's Cafe Society, but after their father died Lee returned to the West Coast.[66] He went back to the Capri and the Club Alabam, in the latter case with a band that featured Irving Ashby, Jack McVea, Charles Mingus, and Snookie Young.[67] During the war, Young worked as a staff musician at Columbia Studios and at MGM.[68] He also worked at RKO with Ashby, Barney Bigard, Benny Carter, Phil Moore, and Snookie Young on early integrated soundtrack recording sessions.[69]

Leon and Otis René, Creoles originally from New Orleans, were two other important figures in the Los Angeles music business. Leon René began his career as a bandleader, and by 1926 his Creole/Southern Syncopators were a popular local dance band. Otis earned his living as a Central Avenue pharmacist and formed a successful songwriting team with his brother.

In 1931 the René brothers participated in the creation of *Lucky Day*, an ambitious Sissle-and-Blake-style musical. The brothers composed the music and their frequent collaborator, Ben Ellison, wrote the lyrics for the show's twenty-one songs. The songs varied in style from "patter" songs to semiclassics and spirituals. Leon led the show's twenty-piece pit orchestra.[70] When it opened at the downtown Mayan Theater on December 29, 1931, *Lucky Day* co-starred Eddie Anderson and Alex Lovejoy as two simpletons who invest in a dud racehorse. The story begins in a Kentucky stable yard, then moves swiftly through several exotic locales, concluding in Hollywood. In the fashion of musicals of the period, the plot functioned simply as a device upon which to hang song, dance, and comedy routines.

The musical ran for nine weeks at a succession of major theaters—the Mayan and Orpheum downtown, the Pantages in Hollywood—for up to four performances a day before leaving for San Diego.[71] Although its advertising said that the show was going to New York after a West Coast run, there is no mention of it in standard references of New York theatrical activity, and René and other cast members were back at work in Los Angeles within weeks of the move to San Diego. René capitalized on the show's huge local success by advertising his subsequent dance band appearances as his Lucky Day Orchestra.[72]

Later in the decade, the brothers wrote songs and arranged music for Hollywood films. In 1937 the team was at Twentieth Century Fox working on Eddie Cantor's *Ali Baba Goes to Town*[73] and Bing Crosby's *Double or Nothing*.[74] Shortly thereafter, RKO won a studio bidding war for their hit popular song "Sleepy Time in Hawaii" and featured it in an Ann Sothern vehicle, *She's Got That Swing*. The studio gave the Renés full screen credit for the song, a rare occurrence for black composers.[75] When the Nelson Eddy film *Let Freedom Ring* featured Leon's song "Dusty Road," the local press heralded it as a breakthrough for African-American songwriters.[76]

The brothers continued to write popular song material. In 1939 South Central's Flash Records recorded sides by Otis René and the Four Tones.[77] Leon's Ammor Recording Corporation released performances of the brothers' material by Ceele Burke's band.[78] During World War II they capitalized on Los Angeles's wartime concentration of popular, jazz, and rhythm and blues talent by founding the city's first black-owned and operated independent record companies, Exclusive and Excelsior.[79] In 1945 Exclusive released Joe Liggins and His Honey Drippers' *The Honeydripper* (Exclusive 207), the first successful postwar recording to move away from the big-band tradition in the direction of what was to become rhythm and blues. Exclusive thus became the first important record company in the development of the city's urban blues.[80] Leon's career spanned five decades in Los Angeles's music business and concluded with his running a succession of small record companies through the early 1960s.

Drummer Alton Redd, "the brown Paul Whiteman," and his six-piece band, the Pods of Pepper, were another popular attraction, playing as the regular house band at the Tivoli Theater in the late twenties and early thirties. Redd was another African-American musician who was able to secure work in the Hollywood studios. In 1933 he worked as the drummer for Max Steiner's *King Kong* soundtrack sessions,[81] and a few years later he appeared on screen in RKO's *Alice Adams*.[82] Redd and his band played a long stand at Club Venice in 1935[83] and took up residence at Hollywood's Onyx Club (732 N. Highland) in the late thirties, broadcasting live nightly. By then his band included such future Central Avenue stars as Cee Pee Johnson, Red Mack, Jack McVea, Johnny Miller, and Marshall Royal.[84] Redd led orchestras in Los Angeles through the early forties. He was the father of Vi Redd, the saxophonist and educator.

Cee Pee Johnson, a transplanted Texan, was another popular Los Angeles bandleader during the late thirties. Because he could sing, dance, and play drums and banjo,[85] Johnson had served as the frontman with his brother Bert's Sharps and Flats band when they barnstormed through the Southwest during the early thirties. On his arrival in Los Angeles, Johnson began by playing guitar in Alton Redd's band,[86] but the charismatic performer quickly took over leadership of the group. He brought it into downtown's Del Mar Club (936 Wall) during 1940 and then back into another long residence at the Onyx, which was then doing business as the Rhumboogie Club. The band now included Dudley Brooks and Buddy Collette along with Redd.[87] Johnson's ability to persuade club owners to put in radio hookups to broadcast his performances proved so good for business that owners tended to overlook his flamboyant personal behavior.[88] By 1942 he had moved on to the Sugar Hill Club on Vine Street.[89] His career foundered after the war.

Walter "Dootsie" Williams was an important bandleader, promoter, and record company owner whose career spanned several decades. In late 1932 the nineteen-year-old trumpet player led his Harlem Dukes as the Club Alabam's house band.[90] That band was also regularly featured at Elks dances and at the Appomattox (2330 Santa Ana) and Manhattan nightclubs (11739 Parmalee) in Watts.[91] During the late thirties, Williams was one of the first African-American musicians to break the Hollywood color barrier and got bookings in clubs such as the 52nd Street Cafe[92] and North Hollywood's exclusive Grace Hayes Lodge.[93] In the early forties he led a quartet that featured pianist and vocalist Nellie Lutcher[94] into the Chez Boheme and the El Trocadero, two of Hollywood's most exclusive nightclubs.[95] Williams also ran the Savoy Ballroom (55th and Central) from 1943 until he entered the armed services. Upon his discharge, he quickly formed a small group and returned to playing South Central clubs. Once the rigid wartime hiring policies that Hollywood clubs had imposed against black musicians began to disappear, Williams's band was among the first to return. In 1949, having served as recording supervisor and staff arranger at MGM Records and several local independent companies, he started his own record label, Blue Records, which soon became Dootone, an important Los Angeles rhythm and blues label.

Pianist and vocalist Nellie Lutcher began performing on Central Avenue during the mid-thirties. She was the first African-American woman bandleader on the SS *Texas* and SS *Rex*, gambling ships anchored three miles off the coast before reformers shut them down in 1939.[96] Lutcher was one of Dootsie Williams's Four Chocolate Drops until the group disbanded when Williams entered the service. By 1945 she was again leading her own group, Nellie Lutcher and Her Swingsters.[97] Shortly after the war she signed with Capitol Records and scored a series of hit records, beginning with "He's a Real Gone Guy."

Lorenzo Flennoy, who began as pianist with Charles Echols's Ebony Serenaders,[98] had formed his own ten-piece big band by 1934.[99] He brought the band to the Elks Hall for regular Saturday afternoon dances[100] and a long series of Sunday afternoon engagements at the Lincoln Theater.[101] Flennoy worked exclusively at the Club Alabam between 1936 and 1941.[102] Ceele Burke, Red Mack, Baron Morehead, and Eddie Williams all came through Flennoy's band during that time.[103] During the war, with the demise of big bands and the popularity of the Cole trio, Flennoy cut his group down to a trio comprising himself, Eddie Williams, and Gene Phillips. They joined Meade Lux Lewis and Joe Turner at the Swanee Inn[104] and then settled in at the Casablanca Breakfast Club for a prolonged stay.[105] Eddie Williams moved on to join Johnny Moore (Oscar's older brother) and Charles Brown in the Three Blazers, and Phillips formed his own trio, the Rhythm Aces.

Through the late thirties, the South Central press enthusiastically reported each new white venue that "opened" to African-American musicians, if not audiences. By 1940 the Bal-Tabarin in Gardena, the Paradise Club and the 331 Club downtown, the Swanee Inn and the Rhumboogie Club in Hollywood, and Ciro's and the El Trocadero on the Sunset Strip had all hired black bands and entertainers to serve exclusively white audiences. Still, these "advances" were not secure; club managers continued arbitrarily to drop successful African-American bands in favor of white orchestras.

On the eve of the Second World War, Los Angeles underwent several profound social changes. In the 1938 elections, tired of corruption in city government, citizens voted a reform slate headed by mayoral candidate Fletcher Bowron into office. Central Avenue felt the chill when the reformers either shut down or sharply curtailed the city's "wide-open" nightlife and the activities of clubs and gambling dens. In May 1940 a columnist for the *California Eagle* lamented the impact of the reforms on the Stem's nightlife: "[L]ast Saturday night where all was once laughter, lights, gayety [sic] and color, with swarms of white visitors making the rounds, the old Avenue was the personification [sic] of a country graveyard."[106]

Nevertheless, several nightclubs along the Stem remained open nightly, including Mosby's Classic Bar and Grill, the Club Memo (4264 Central), the Swing-Hi Club (4259 Central), and the Elite Cafe (4520 Central). Nightclubs (and, later, after-hours "breakfast" clubs) tended to come and go quickly, either changing names and management or closing entirely. However, the Elks Hall and the Lincoln Theater featured both local and national acts throughout the war years.

As the nation edged closer to war, activists for the National Association for the Advancement of Colored People (NAACP) and other African-American leaders agitated for President Roosevelt to end discrimination against blacks in both the workplace and the military. In late June 1941, in response to A. Phillip Randolph's threatened march on the Capitol, Roosevelt finally issued an executive order to end workplace discrimination. Spurred by both the order and union support, two Los Angeles–based aircraft firms, Lockheed and Vega, opened their doors to skilled black workers for the first time in September 1941. New opportunities notwithstanding, African Americans composed an insignificant portion of the tremendous migration of workers to Los Angeles until mid-1942. By then, increased production needs and the large number of men entering the armed services had created a severe shortage of skilled workers in Los Angeles. This forced the gradual relaxation of employment barriers and made an unprecedented number of well-paying skilled and semiskilled jobs in the defense industry available to African-American workers.[107] By September 1942 most Southland defense industries were training and employing African-American men and women,[108] with Lockheed, Douglas, Kaiser, and the Long Beach shipyards becoming the largest employers of minorities during World War II.[109]

Wartime production caused the state to experience an economic boom. Per capita income in the California defense industries was 141.2 percent of the national average in 1942 ($1,214), and by 1944 it had risen to a monetary peak of $1,570 (137.4 percent of the national average). Many African Americans found the difference between their earnings in Los Angeles and what they could have earned had they remained in the South to be far greater than what these averages show.[110] Even reasonably well-established local musicians such as Lee Young and Dootsie Williams supplemented their incomes by working shifts in the war plants and shipyards.[111]

Military service and the lure of good salaries in defense work also drew young southwestern musicians to the West Coast. Pee Wee Crayton came to Los Angeles in 1937 from Austin, Texas, and moved to Oakland for defense work at the beginning of the war.[112] Lowell Fulson, of Tulsa, Oklahoma, served on a ship based in Oakland after being drafted in 1943.[113] Lloyd Glenn came to California from San Antonio, Texas, to join his family and to work for Douglas Aircraft.[114]

In 1940 the South Central corridor was bounded to the north by Little Tokyo and the city center and to the south by the Compton city line. It consisted of 130 adjoining census tracts grouped by the Los Angeles Regional Planning Commission into the Central, Avalon, Exposition, Green Meadows, Watts, Florence, University, Santa Barbara, and South Vermont tracts.[115] In the six years between 1940 and 1946, the total African-American population in Los Angeles more than doubled, yet it remained confined in an area that was already severely overcrowded. The community did not grow so much by expansion as by further consolidation within existing black areas. Of the new residents (by birth and by migration), 78 percent lived in the Central, Avalon, or Watts areas,[116] and most were crushed into a single state assembly district in the Central Avenue area.[117] The sole relief to the chronic housing shortage problem came in February 1942, when Executive Order 9066 mandated the internment of West Coast Japanese Americans. Black wartime immigrants surged northward after the forced evacuation of Little Tokyo.[118] This new demography caused the area to be referred to as "Bronzeville" during the war.

A survey of the entertainment pages of the *California Eagle* and the *Los Angeles Tribune* reveals a burst of club advertisements and openings beginning in July 1943, the peak of African-American in-migration. It was a natural response to the needs of a growing and increasingly affluent population that was excluded from venues in most of the rest of the city. Many were late-night "members-only" clubs designed to avoid laws regulating the hours of nightclub operations. These breakfast clubs sprang up in storefronts, back rooms, and second floors and opened after the regular clubs closed. Customers could buy an inexpensive membership, carry in liquor, and hear musicians jam until seven or eight in the morning. After-hours clubs became both late-night homes for touring musicians, who jammed there with locals after their regular gigs, and training grounds for the many young musicians who emerged from Los Angeles after the war.

In January 1943 Jimmy Marshall, formerly the manager of New York's Apollo Theater, took over at the Lincoln with the clear expectation of exploiting all the newly arriving talent. "I'd like to make an Apollo of the West Coast out of the Lincoln. With so many big-name bands and artists moving westward, that should not be too difficult."[119] Marshall's plans succumbed to management claims of poor box office, and he returned to the East, but the band policy remained. Besides films and stage shows, the Lincoln also held weekly jitterbug contests that featured Oliver Reeves's Big 6 Band and soon sponsored weekly amateur contests that were broadcast locally. Like those shows that the Apollo began in 1935, the Lincoln's amateur contests provided a showcase for young or newly arrived Los Angeles performers and served as an important conduit into professional jobs. A review of the Lincoln Theater's advertising reveals that the amateur contests remained in place until late in the decade. When they finally ended, Watts's Largo Theater and Johnny Otis and Bardu Ali's Barrel House continued the tradition into the fifties.

Between July and December 1943, the South Central club strip expanded well beyond the cluster around the Dunbar Hotel. For the first time, several clubs opened two miles to the north, in Bronzeville. There was the Central Annex Blue Room (1106 E. First Street) and the Indigo Breakfast Club (228 E. First) where Jack McVea's Kings of Rhythm played nightly.[120] The Creole Palace Breakfast Club (105 No. San Pedro Street) featured Roy Milton's Solid Senders and the Four Tones.[121] The Palms Breakfast Club (131 No. San Pedro) and the Cherryland Cafe (725 E. Fifth) also provided after-hours entertainment.[122]

Elihu "Black Dot" McGee, a popular Central Avenue "sportsman," opened the Casablanca Breakfast Club (2801 So. San Pedro) at the community's former northern boundary. The Casablanca was the late-night home of bandleader Lorenzo Flennoy's new trio, which included guitarist Gene Phillips.[123] In 1945, Phillips's own group, the Rhythm Aces, played a regular engagement there.[124] At the height of "The Honeydripper" craze during the summer of 1945, the club featured both Joe Liggins[125] and the Slim Gaillard Trio.[126] In the same neighborhood, at San Pedro and Jefferson Boulevard, the Rhythm Club (3403 So. San Pedro) presented Poison Gardner and Fred Harris.[127] More clubs sprang up around the Dunbar Hotel. Curtis Mosby's place, The Last Word, was across the street from the Alabam. The club featured Jack McVea in a long booking through the spring and summer of 1945.[128] There were also smaller clubs, such as the Annex Breakfast Club at 41st and Central and Kay's at 43rd and Central. The Apex Breakfast Club (4210½ Central) briefly featured Art Tatum in late 1943.[129] Black Dot McGee also held an interest in the Down Beat Room at 42nd Street and Central,[130] and the Swing Shift Breakfast Club operated a block west of Central on Vernon Avenue.

Two former Ellington vocalists, Ivie Anderson and Herb Jeffries, were popular entertainers and nightclub hosts during the war years. In failing health, Ivie Anderson left the Ellington band and returned to the city where she had been a favorite since her days at Mosby's original Apex Club. She opened Ivie's Chicken Shack (1105½ E. Vernon) just off Central Avenue. It was open from 5 p.m. until 4 a.m. and featured "chicken, steaks, wine and music."[131] Ivie's provided musicians with an alternative to Borden's Victory Pharmacy (the 54th Street drugstore) as an after-hours hangout. In 1943, before joining the Three Blazers, Charles Brown regularly played piano there. Brown recalled that Cecil Gant, stationed in Los Angeles but not yet famous for his successful wartime recording of "I Wonder," would come into Ivie's nightly to hear him play.[132]

Prior to his time with Ellington, actor/singer Jeffries, star of the "Bronze Buckaroo" series of African-American musical Westerns, worked as master of ceremonies at the Club Alabam[133] and, later, at Curtis Mosby's Classic Bar and Grill.[134] Jeffries toured the country with the Four Tones, his vocal backing group in the films,[135] and then joined Anderson in the Ellington band during 1940–41. By the fall of 1942 he was back in Los Angeles, signed to Otis René's new Excelsior Records and cutting sides with the Eddie Beale Trio.[136] He briefly ran the Black Flamingo (a name chosen, no doubt, to evoke "Flamingo," his biggest hit with Ellington) at 4505 Avalon Boulevard, a block west of Central. Although the club underwent several management and name changes (the New York Cafe and the Shadowland Breakfast Club) during the war years, it remained a consistently popular after-hours spot. During Jeffries's tenure as host in 1943, the club featured Eddie Beale.[137] Later, Jeffries was on the staff of Bronzeville's exclusive Shepp's Playhouse. As of this writing, Herb Jeffries still continues to be a musical elder statesman in the city and has recently recorded and released new material.

Blues singer Jimmy Witherspoon had fond memories of former stage and film star Alex Lovejoy's Breakfast Club (4416 3/4 Central). Before his success, Witherspoon spent his nights there where, for a thirty-five-cent admission, he heard the likes of Art Tatum, Joe Turner, and Slam Stewart.[138] Charles Brown also recalled the excitement of hearing Tatum there after hours.[139] Ten blocks further south, the Furnace Club (5432 Central) was another fixture; Jay McShann briefly served as its titular manager in 1944.[140] In the same neighborhood, the short-lived Shangri La Breakfast Club (1010 E. Slauson Avenue) presented early appearances by Johnny Moore's Blazers.[141]

At the perennial Club Alabam, Mosby hired Wynonie Harris as the permanent master of ceremonies in early 1941.[142] He brought back Lorenzo Flennoy's band, which had, under prior management, been the club's house band for four years during the thirties.[143] Pianist Flennoy's group, which included Forrest "Chico" Hamilton, Red Mack, and Eddie Williams,[144] remained in residence until April 1943, when Lee Young—who began his career as a tap dancer in an early Alabam revue—brought an eight-piece combo featuring Dexter Gordon, Eddie Hutchinson, Art Pepper, and Gerald Wiggins into the club for a short stay.[145]

In mid-1943, Mosby employed choreographer Patsy Hunter to produce Club Alabam's increasingly elaborate floor shows.[146] Lee Young evoked the club's glamour at the time:

> How can I describe it? You had to buy your ticket at a ticket window, and then you'd go in, and they had tables all around the dance floor, maybe three deep, and they had a balcony, and right on the railing they had tables all way around. I think you could get nine hundred people in there. And there was a long bar, maybe eighty, ninety feet. . . . The dance floor was about fifty feet; you could get a lot of couples on the floor. And the show—they had eight or ten chorus girls. We always had a shake dancer, chorus, comics, and a headliner, and you couldn't get near the place on Saturdays and Sundays especially.[147]

The autobiographies of Johnny Otis and Art Pepper contain equally exotic memories of the club and Avenue nightlife.[148]

Kansas City's Harlan Leonard and His Rockets, featuring Otis on drums, took over as house band in July.[149] In September 1943 Wynonie Harris left the club for the Midwest and a stint with Lucky Millinder's band.[150] When Leonard left after a year-long engagement, Mosby installed two small combos: Roy Milton's Solid Senders, the group that was to record "R. M. Blues" in 1946, and Oliver Reeves's "Big 6" Band.[151] Apparently these bookings did not work, and Ernie Fields's band quickly took over.[152] Finally, as the war was ending, Mosby contracted with Johnny Otis to form a house band.[153] Otis recruited Curtis Counce, Leonard "Lucky" Enois, Paul Quinichette, and James Von Streeter along with local players Teddy Buckner, Art Farmer, and John Pettigrew for the first of his many bands playing in the Basie style.[154] By May 1945 the quixotic Wynonie Harris, now a star because of his vocal on Millinder's hit "Who Threw the Whiskey in the Well?" was back at Club Alabam with the Johnny Otis Orchestra.[155]

Although clubs continued to open throughout the entire district, by 1945 Central Avenue's Stem was in open competition with Bronzeville for supremacy in the city's African-American nightlife.[156] In September 1944, Gordon H. "Shepp" Shepard, an African-American former Hollywood camera operator, opened Shepp's Playhouse at 204½ E. First Street, a plush two-story showplace.[157] The club debuted with Bardu Ali's Orchestra, late of the Lincoln Theater, as the house band.[158] It was home to both Eddie Heywood and an early version of Gerald Wilson's celebrated orchestra for several weeks in 1945.[159] Shepp's soon moved to a policy of staging full entertainment reviews nightly. Sammy Davis Jr. emerged from the Will Mastin Trio to become a star of these floor shows. Showman Billy Berg took over ownership of the club in late 1946.[160]

Late in the war, Foster Johnson, a "bop"-inspired tap dancer, opened the Finale Club (115 So. San Pedro), a Bronzeville after-hours spot that featured Charlie Parker after he decided to remain in Los Angeles. When that club failed, trumpeter Howard McGhee and his wife reopened it as a "bottle club" to feature the band McGhee had formed around Parker. After Parker's institutionalization, the club folded. Ross Russell claimed that the jam sessions centered around Parker made the Finale Club the West Coast equivalent of Harlem's Minton's Playhouse.[161] Sessions there were interracial and included Johnny Bothwell, Ralph Burns, Serge Chaloff, Sonny Criss, Miles Davis, Stan Getz, Hampton Hawes, Gerry Mulligan, Red Rodney, Shorty Rogers, Zoot Sims, Charlie Ventura, and Gerald Wilson. However, to McGhee's disbelief, Russell refused or neglected to record the bands, and these remarkable collaborations went undocumented.[162] A club on the Stem that featured "bop" music was Jack's Basket Room (3219 Central), which opened late in the war. It presented its "Bird in the Basket" floor shows as well as all-night jam sessions.[163] The latter showcased many of the area's younger jazz musicians.[164]

During the war, Watts was still an ethnically diverse area experiencing an influx of black residents moving southward from the city. The Brown sisters had long presented local talent there at the Little/Southeast Harlem Club (11812 Parmelee

Avenue). Marili Morden, "T-Bone" Walker's agent, remembered the Little Harlem as little more than a roadhouse, "tumble-down and tilted, and very dark out there at 114th Street and Central Avenue—quite as far out as you'd want to go in those days. Naturally the clientele was primarily black."[165] Saxophonist Big Jim Wynn, who first worked in the city in the early thirties with the Charles Echols Ebony Serenaders,[166] first brought a house band into the Little Harlem in 1936. He began a long association with T-Bone Walker, who became first the club's reigning star attraction, then a national celebrity.[167]

Joe Morris opened the Plantation Club at 108th Street and Central Avenue in April 1942.[168] The building was already a well-established Watts landmark; Reb Spikes played there in the twenties, when it was still known as Baron Long's Tavern. Later, it operated as Jazzland. The Plantation quickly had the distinction of being the only nightclub in the South Central area that presented nationally known musicians, including Erskine Hawkins, Fletcher Henderson, Andy Kirk, Jay McShann, and Joe Turner. Needless to say, Watts was a considerable distance south of the Stem in pre-freeway Los Angeles, and Morris tried to coax audiences into making the long trip by providing regular bus service along Central Avenue.[169] Toward the end of the war, however, he chose a more convenient location along the Stem for his new club, Little Joe's.[170] Apparently nothing came of this move, and within a year the Plantation began a period of sporadic closings and reopenings, eventually expiring in 1947.[171]

In 1944 Dan Grissom, a former vocalist with Jimmie Lunceford, opened The Outskirts of Town, another after-hours club, at 9624 Central Avenue in Watts.[172] In the next year Joe Turner opened his Blue Room (9900 Central) in the same neighborhood.[173]

In the city at large, racial discrimination and exclusion continued apace during the war. A 1943 *Down Beat* report noted that the management of most Hollywood-area clubs that still employed African-American bands now denied entrance even to the musicians' guests. A club representative disingenuously defended the action: "What made him [the columnist] think that Negroes are admitted, or ever have been admitted, as guests at the Palladium, the Trianon, or any of the so-called white niteries in Los Angeles? When the time comes that the American public is willing to accept Negroes as fellow-men with equal rights, the nitery men will be the first to throw open their door to Negro guests."[174]

The problem was exacerbated by friction between the large numbers of transplanted southern defense workers and servicemen of both races suddenly mingling in the city. Whites from southern states resisted the hiring and promotion of blacks in many industries, and Ku Klux Klan activity underwent a considerable revival in Los Angeles during the 1940s.[175] In the wake of the June 1943 Zoot Suit

Riots and similar violence in other cities, many Los Angeles clubs switched to a white-bands-only policy, claiming fear of continued racial strife if they employed black musicians.[176] Several did not rehire black bands until the end of the war. Only established headliners such as Louis Armstrong, Duke Ellington, or the locally popular King Cole Trio managed to break the color line during this period.[177]

In fact, it was the King Cole Trio's successful June 1944 appearance at the cocktail room of the Sunset Strip's Trocadero that signaled a gradual reopening of the city's clubs to black performers. Cole's popularity was such that when, during the summer of 1945, the neighboring Ciro's featured the Ellington band, the first African-American band to play the main room of a Sunset Strip club, the Trocadero wanted to rehire Cole to counter the appearance.[178] The success of the King Cole Trio's earlier appearance allowed Cole's management to insist that the club hire his entire touring package. The package, which consisted of Benny Carter's Orchestra, Savannah Churchill, and comic Timmie Rogers, thus became "the first all-colored show" in the club's history.[179] However, not all African-American bands were successful on the Sunset Strip. The Trocadero fired the Carter band after its first week because it allegedly played too loud on the "boogie-beat side"[180] and "didn't play enough L.A. music" to please the customers, who (the club management claimed) were used to Latin music.[181] After having his band report for work nightly without playing for the duration of his two-week contract, Carter took them into the Casa Manana. Apparently not all Angelenos wanted Latin music, because the entire Cole package reunited at the Orpheum Theater in downtown Los Angeles for a successful week-long run beginning June 21.[182] By the end of 1945, *Down Beat* observed that Roy Milton's booking at Susy-Q on Hollywood Boulevard finally signaled the end of attempts to keep African-American musicians out of jobs in Hollywood.[183] With the color barrier once again breached, the Flennoy Trio opened at the Trocadero without undue comment in January 1946.[184]

Hollywood's sole haven for African-American audiences and musicians during the war was Billy Berg's Swing Club on Vine Street. In 1942, Norman Granz, who later produced the "Jazz at the Philharmonic" concert series, determined to feature the best jazz musicians in town, without regard to color, at organized jam sessions at the club.[185] Berg admitted black patrons to these Sunday-afternoon sessions, and, though musicians may have complained about their salaries, they did not gripe about Berg's treatment of them as racial minorities.[186] By November 1942 the club was entirely nonsegregated and even allowed interracial dancing.[187] By contrast, elsewhere in the city the Casa Manana waited until August 1945 before dropping its policy of racial exclusion and permitting interracial dancing.

However, with the end of the war, production needs dropped, and male African-American workers were the first employees laid off or fired in the defense industries. Plants in Portland, Oregon, released 50 percent of their black workers, and those in San Francisco let go 25 percent.[188] Lee Young remembered the effects of the cutbacks on the Avenue: "During the war, Central was really jumping then. It was almost like Broadway. After the war, the clubs started closing. I don't know if it was hard times or what it was."[189]

It was hard times. For the balance of the decade California had an overall unemployment rate considerably higher than the rest of the country, and those blacks who could find jobs had a median income considerably lower than that of whites. In addition, their incomes were less in comparison to those of blacks in other cities than they had been during World War II.[190]

Nightlife in the African-American districts of Los Angeles continued, but not on the scale of the flush war years. For example, after repeated troubles with the Internal Revenue Service, Curtis Mosby lost control of the Club Alabam in early 1947. Mosby was then convicted of concealing assets of $17,000 while pleading bankruptcy and sentenced to three years in federal prison.[191] A series of new owners ran the spot with varying success, ultimately changing its name to the Club Congo in December 1947.[192] Mosby briefly reopened it as the Alabam in 1949, but its final failure caused him to leave the city altogether for San Francisco.[193]

The community changed in other ways as well. By January 1945 the NAACP was involved in a lawsuit against the Compton Chamber of Commerce as a result of the latter's racist campaign to "keep the colored population north of One Hundred Twenty Fifth Street."[194] African Americans won court challenges to the restrictive covenants that had contained them for so long, and the center of the community began to move south and west, away from Central Avenue. Clubs along the Stem continued to close, and with the return of interred Japanese Americans, Bronzeville again became Little Tokyo. The economic boom engendered by World War II was over, and African-American clubs and club owners were failing. However, the influence of the music and the musicians that the Avenue nurtured was just beginning to be felt.

Audiences and young musicians alike were open to the hybridization of styles that allowed for the unselfconscious experimentation that typified the period. The strict compartmentalization of musical styles (bop, rhythm and blues, swing) that became common among critics, musicians, and fans during the postwar period was not yet ingrained.[195] For instance, Gillespie and Parker shared the bill with Slim Gaillard and Harry "The Hipster" Gibson for their first West Coast club appearance. The two legends even went on to cut some record sides with Gaillard during their stay. Though the results are now mainly interesting as curiosities, this odd pairing supports the notion that there weren't arbitrary obstacles to making music at the time, certainly not within the spontaneity of jam sessions. Sadly, little of this experimentation found its way onto records, although recordings of the Jazz at the Philharmonic concerts and others from a few years later do survive.

This openness to new forms also gave rise to the beginnings of rhythm and blues. Though it is difficult to determine exactly where this synthesis first occurred, the distinctive sound of musicians working on the West Coast, specifically in Los Angeles, was the first to have a major national impact.[196] As late as 1946, when a writer pressed Joe Liggins (whose "The Honeydripper" has a strong claim for being the first rhythm and blues recording) for the name of his new style, he gamely suggested "breakdown," an older, generic term.[197] The new music did not need a name; it was an extension of older African-American traditions. The categories came later.

In this chapter I have demonstrated the wide extent of African-American musical activity in Los Angeles during the thirties and forties. As noted, the city's African-American community supported a vital and varied range of popular, Dixieland, and swing music well before the huge infusion of population and defense industry salaries that World War II occasioned. The potential for well-paying work drew African-American workers and musicians to Los Angeles during the war years, spawning what was perhaps the richest period of musical experimentation in the city's history. The fact that, after their late-1945 arrival in the city, Dizzy Gillespie and Charlie Parker jammed with Sonny Criss, Teddy Edwards, Art and Addison Farmer, Wardell Gray, Hampton Hawes, Al Killian, Dodo Marmarosa, Howard McGhee, Bobby and Jay McNeely, Charles Mingus, Roy Porter, and Chuck Thompson in South Central and Bronzeville clubs only serves to indicate the extent of the talent available in wartime Los Angeles.[198] Criss remembered: "Los Angeles was kind of wide open during the war; a lot of people coming in from the South, going into defense plants. There was new money. People hadn't had that kind of money before. They were spending it. And they just kinda found the music. Found out where the musicians were. There was never a lack of an audience, if you were in the right place."[199] Clearly, those dismissive eastern critics weren't in the right place to hear this music!

NOTES

1. Dave Dexter Jr., "Big Band Boom Has California on the Jump," *Down Beat* (15 August 1941): 3.

2. See Michael Bakan, "Way Out West on Central: Jazz in the African-American Community of Los Angeles Before 1930," chapter 1 in this volume.

3. Keith E. Collins, *Black Los Angeles: The Maturing of the Ghetto 1940–50* (Saratoga, CA: Los Angeles Century 21 Publishing, 1980), 28.

4. Ibid., 10.

5. Lawrence B. DeGraff, "Negro Migration to Los Angeles, 1930 to 1950" (Ph.D. diss., University of California, Los Angeles, 1962), 281.

6. Buddy Collette, personal interview with author, 21 December 1992.

7. Ibid.

8. "Ubangi Club Opens Here," *The California Eagle* (14 May 1937): 5A.

9. Paul McGee, "Along the Stem," *Los Angeles Sentinel* (5 October 1939): 9.

10. Art Pepper and Laurie Pepper, *Straight Life: The Story of Art Pepper* (New York: Schirmer Books, 1979), 48.

11. "Night Shirted Klansmen Stage Anti-ism Parade," *Los Angeles Sentinel* (4 April 1940): 1.

12. "Leaders Protest Dance Hall Ban," *The California Eagle* (30 May 1940): 1.

13. Harry Levette, "Behind the Scenes with Harry," *The California Eagle* (10 May 1935): 8.

14. "Trianon Bar Two Basie Men, Jimmie Sore," *Down Beat* (15 July 1943): 6.

15. Patricia Willard, liner notes, *Black California* (Savoy Records, SJL 2215, 1976).

16. " 'Not a Negro' Says Bigard," *Down Beat* (15 December 1943): 3.

17. Marl Young, "The Amalgamation of Locals 47 and 767," *Overture*, (December 1988): 8.

18. Harry Levette, "Behind the Scenes with Harry," *The California Eagle* (8 February 1935): 6; Freddy Doyle, "With Orchestras and Musicians," *The California Eagle* (13 March 1936): 11, and "With Orchestras and Musicians," *The California Eagle* (3 April 1936): 10.

19. Henry T. Sampson, *Blacks in Blackface: A Sourcebook on Early Black Musical Shows* (Metuchen, NJ: Scarecrow Press, Inc., 1980), 128.

20. "Lincoln Theatre" advertisement, *The California Eagle* (21 February 1930): 12.

21. Sampson, *Blacks in Blackface*, 21.

22. Harry Levette, "Behind the Scenes with Harry," *The California Eagle* (23 October 1931): 10.

23. Harry Levette, " 'Lucky Day' Received with Open Arms at Mayan Theatre," *The California Eagle* (1 January 1932): 10.

24. "Club Ebony Opens in Big Premiere Tonight," *The California Eagle* (9 June 1933): 9.

25. Louis V. Cole, "Chatter," *Los Angeles Sentinel* (1 November 1934): 8; "Black Derby Rathskellar" advertisement, *Los Angeles Sentinel* (16 August 1934): 6.

26. Jim Dawson, liner notes, *Gene Phillips and His Rhythm Aces* (Ace Records, CHD 169, 1986).

27. See Bakan, "Way Out West," for a discussion of Curtis Mosby's career in Los Angeles during the 1920s.

28. "Curtis Mosby's Entry in San Francisco's Amusement Circles Gets Mighty Reception," *The California Eagle* (21 November 1930): 9.

29. "At the Clubs," *The California Eagle* (8 May 1931): 10.

30. Harry Levette, "Behind the Scenes with Harry," *The California Eagle* (5 May 1933): 9.

31. "Buck Clayton Goes into Apex," *The California Eagle* (18 October 1935): 4B.

32. Freddy Doyle, "With Orchestras and Musicians," *The California Eagle* (29 January 1937): 10.

33. "Mosby to Reopen Club Alabam," *The California Eagle* (24 October 1940): 3B.

34. "Musicians," *The California Eagle* (8 June 1928): 10.

35. Gunther Schuller, *The Swing Era: The Development of Jazz 1930–1945* (New York: Oxford University Press, 1989), 393.

36. Freddy Doyle, "With Orchestras and Musicians," (3 April 1936): 10.

37. Freddy Doyle, "With Orchestras and Musicians," (30 April 1937): 5A.

38. "Les Hite Back at Cotton Club," *The California Eagle* (8 February 1935): 6.

39. "News & Views of Stage and Screen," *The California Eagle* (1 April 1932): 9.

40. John Chilton, *Who's Who of Jazz: Storyville to Swing Street*, rev. ed. (Philadelphia: The Chilton Book Co., 1979), 147.

41. Gene Woolway, "He'll Play," *The California Eagle* (20 May 1932): 1.

42. "Big Juneteenth Benefit at Alabam," *The California Eagle* (8 June 1934): 9; "Cotton Club to Aid in Legion Benefit," *The California Eagle* (7 July 1934): 7.

43. "Sebastian's Cotton Club Changes Name; Drops Colored Band, Chorus," *The California Eagle* (2 July 1937): 4B.

44. Jim Heimann, *Out with the Stars: Hollywood Nightlife in the Golden Era* (New York: Abbeville Press, 1985), 171.

45. "L. A. Nitery Drops Color Line Ban," *Down Beat* (1 August 1945): 1.

46. "Cotton Club to Aid," *Eagle*.

47. Leonard Feather, *The New Edition of the Encyclopedia of Jazz* (New York: Bonanza Books, 1962), 242.

48. "Paramount Theatre" advertisement, *The California Eagle* (3 May 1935): 6; "Lincoln Theatre" advertisement, *The California Eagle* (29 November 1935): 7.

49. "Club Araby" advertisement, *Los Angeles Sentinel* (6 June 1935): 4.

50. Freddy Doyle, "With Orchestras and Musicians," *The California Eagle* (3 April 1936): 10.

51. Freddy Doyle, "With Orchestras and Musicians," *The California Eagle* (18 September 1936): 10.

52. James Lincoln Collier, *Benny Goodman and the Swing Era* (New York: Oxford University Press, 1989), 183.

53. Freddy Doyle, "With Orchestras and Musicians," *The California Eagle* (5 March 1937): 13.

54. Dave Hyltone, "Jack Tenney Asks for New L.A. Bylaws, Expects Fight," *Down Beat* (September 1939): 32; Brian Rust, *Jazz Records, 1897–1942, 2 vols.* 5th rev. ed. (Essex: Storyville Publications and Co., 1982), 663.

55. "Lincoln Theatre" advertisement, *Los Angeles Sentinel* (6 May 1937): 4.

56. James Haskins with Kathleen Benson, *Nat King Cole* (New York: Stein and Day, 1984), 24.

57. Ibid., 22–30.

58. "King Cole Trio Loses Bassist," *Down Beat* (15 September 1942): 14.

59. Hal Holly, "Los Angeles Band Briefs," *Down Beat* (15 January 1944): 6.

60. "Notes for Show Folks," *Los Angeles Tribune* (30 April 1945): 20.

61. Freddy Doyle, "With Orchestras and Musicians," *The California Eagle* (19 February 1937): 10.

62. Freddy Doyle, "With Orchestras and Musicians," *The California Eagle* (4 November 1937): 9A.

63. "Les Young Joins Brother's Band on West Coast," *Down Beat* (1 June 1941): 13.

64. Dexter, "Big Band Boom," 3.

65. Pepper and Pepper, *Straight Life*, 46.

66. Ibid., 45.

67. "Lee Young Has New Combo Set for Swing Club," *Down Beat* (15 March 1943): 6.

68. Pepper and Pepper, *Straight Life*, 48.

69. "Studios Using Colored Musicians with Whites," *The California Eagle* (1 April 1943): 2B.

70. "Bandleader Leon René Heads 20 Piece Band of 'Lucky Day' Now Playing at the Orpheum," *The California Eagle* (26 February 1932): 10.

71. Levette, "Lucky Day."

72. "Morey's Dancing Academy" advertisement, *The California Eagle* (19 August 1932): 9.

73. "Legon Dances a Sensation in New Cantor Film," *The California Eagle* (22 August 1937): 6.

74. "René & Jones Boys Sing Band Give Effect to Movies," *The California Eagle* (5 September 1937): 8.

75. "Four Studios Bid for Renés' Song, RKO Gets Their 'Sleepy Time in Hawaii' Hit," *The California Eagle* (7 October 1937): 4B.

76. "Writes Song Sung by Eddy in New Film," *The California Eagle* (4 May 1939): 2B.

77. "Flash Records Releases Discs by Otis René and Four Tones," *The California Eagle* (30 November 1939): 4B.

78. "Ceele Burke Band on Records," *Los Angeles Sentinel* (21 December 1939): 1.

79. Ralph Eastman, "Central Avenue Blues: The Making of Los Angeles Rhythm and Blues, 1942–1947," *Black Music Research Journal* 9, no. 1 (Spring 1989): 25.

80. It should be noted that the first recording by an African-American jazz artist, Kid Ory, was released by the Spikes Brothers' Sunshine label in Los Angeles in 1921. However, the company was short-lived; see discussion in Bakan, "Way Out West."

81. David Meeker, *Jazz in the Movies*, new enlarged ed. (New York: Da Capo Press, 1981).

82. Harry Levette, "Behind the Scenes with Harry," *The California Eagle* (5 July 1935): 9.

83. Harry Levette, "Behind the Scenes with Harry," *The California Eagle* (26 April 1935): 6.

84. "Alton Redd Band on Air," *Los Angeles Sentinel* (3 August 1939): 9.

85. Collette, personal interview.

86. "Alton Redd," *Los Angeles Sentinel*.

87. "Cee Pee Johnson" advertisement, *The California Eagle* (18 December 1941): 10B.

88. Collette, personal interview.

89. Hal Holly, "Los Angeles Band Briefs," *Down Beat* (15 January 1942): 11.

90. Harry Levette, "Behind the Scenes with Harry," *The California Eagle* (2 December 1932): 9.

91. "Appomattox Club" advertisement, *The California Eagle* (31 March 1933): 9; Freddy Doyle, "With Orchestras and Musicians," *The California Eagle* (21 October 1937): 8A.

92. Freddy Doyle, "With Orchestras and Musicians," *The California Eagle* (23 July 1937): 4B.

93. "On the Beam," *The California Eagle* (5 December 1940): 3B.

94. Wilma Cockrell, "Jam Session," *The California Eagle* (31 July 1941): 2B.

95. Freddy Doyle, "Swingtime in H'wood," *The California Eagle* (4 May 1942): 2B; Hal Holly, "Los Angeles Band Briefs," *Down Beat* (15 July 1942): 12.

96. Harry Levette, "Behind the Scenes with Harry," *The California Eagle* (3 August 1939): 6, and "Behind the Scenes with Harry," *The California Eagle* (19 September 1940): 2B.

97. "Elite Cafe" advertisement, *Los Angeles Tribune* (4 July 1945): 21.

98. "Eckle's [sic] Ebony Serenaders at Tivoli Sunday," *The California Eagle* (14 November 1930): 10.

99. "Sunset Garden" advertisement, *Los Angeles Sentinel* (23 August 1934): 8.

100. "Elks Hall" advertisement, *Los Angeles Sentinel* (13 December 1934): 4.

101. "Lincoln Theatre" advertisement, *Los Angeles Sentinel* (13 December 1934): 4.

102. Freddy Doyle, "With Orchestras and Musicians," (13 March 1936): 11.

103. Freddy Doyle, "With Orchestras and Musicians," *The California Eagle* (20 November 1936): 10; Freddy Doyle, "With Orchestras and Musicians," (21 October 1937): 8A; and Cockrell, "Jam Session," (5 June 1941): 2B.

104. Hal Holly, "Los Angeles Band Briefs," (1 July 1943): 6.

105. "Casablanca Breakfast Club" advertisement, *Los Angeles Tribune* (15 November 1943): 18.

106. Harry Levette, "Behind the Scenes with Harry," *The California Eagle* (16 May 1940): 2B.

107. DeGraff, "Negro Migration," 146.

108. Ibid., 174.

109. Collins, *Black Los Angeles*, 52.

110. DeGraff, "Negro Migration," 274.

111. Hal Holly, "Los Angeles Band Briefs," (15 January 1944): 6; "Dootsie Williams" photo caption, *The California Eagle* (10 February 1943): 3B.

112. Ellen Blau, "Living Blues Interview: Pee Wee Crayton," *Living Blues* 56 (1983): 7.

113. Per Notini, liner notes, *Lowell Fulson, 1946–57* (Blues Boy Records, BB-302, 1981).

114. Attila Oess, liner notes, *Lloyd Glenn/Texas Man* (Jukebox Lil Records, JB-608, 1985).

115. Arthur Dakan, "Electoral and Population Geography of South Central Los Angeles 1932–1966" (M.A. thesis, University of California, Los Angeles, 1970), 4.

116. Ibid, 43.

117. Collins, *Black Los Angeles*, 10.

118. Ibid., 43.

119. "Ex-Apollo Manager on Lincoln Staff," *The California Eagle* (8 January 1943): 2B

120. "Indigo Breakfast Club" advertisement, *Los Angeles Tribune* (11 October 1943): 17.

121. "Creole Palace Breakfast Club" advertisement, *Los Angeles Tribune* (6 September 1943): 19.

122. "Palms Breakfast Club" advertisement, *The California Eagle* (9 December 1943):10; "Cherryland Cafe" advertisement, *The California Eagle* (10 February 1944): 13.

123. "Casablanca, Breakfast Club" announcement, *Los Angeles Tribune* (15 November 1943): 18.

124. "Casablanca Breakfast Club" advertisement, *Los Angeles Tribune* (4 May 1945): 21.

125. Eddie Burbridge, "No Fooling," *The California Eagle* (21 June 1945): 12.

126. "Casablanca Breakfast Club" advertisement, *The California Eagle* (7 September 1945): 12.

127. "Rhythm Club" advertisement, *Los Angeles Tribune* (5 February 1945): 21.

128. "Double Feather at Last Word," *The California Eagle* (16 August 1945): 14.

129. "Apex Breakfast Club Mecca for Pleasure Seekers," *The California Eagle* (9 December 1943): 10.

130. "Down Beat Room" advertisement, *The California Eagle* (1 June 1944): 12.

131. "Ivie's Chicken Shack" advertisement, *The California Eagle* (6 April 1944): 13.

132. Tom Mazzolini, "Living Blues Interview: Charles Brown," *Living Blues* 27 (1976): 23.

133. Freddy Doyle, "With Orchestras and Musicians," *The California Eagle* (27 November 1936): 10.

134. "The Classic Bar and Grill" advertisement, *The California Eagle* (23 December 1937): 6B.

135. "Jeffrey (sic) to Return for Recording Date," *The California Eagle* (18 May 1939): 2B.

136. "Herbie Jeffries Has New Record Concern," *Down Beat* (15 October 1942): 9.

137. "Black Flamingo" advertisement, *The California Eagle* (8 July 1943): 2B.

138. Arnold Shaw, *Honkers and Shouters: The Golden Years of Rhythm & Blues* (New York: Macmillan Publishing Co., 1978), 212.

139. Mazzolini, "Charles Brown," 23.

140. "Furnace Club" advertisement, *Los Angeles Tribune* (17 April 1944): 17.

141. "The Shangri La Breakfast Club" advertisement, *The California Eagle* (1 July 1943): 2B.

142. "Club Alabam" advertisement, *The California Eagle* (16 January 1941): 2B.

143. Harry Levette, "Behind the Scenes with Harry," *The California Eagle* (23 July 1937): 4B.

144. Wilma Cockrell, "Jam Session," *The California Eagle* (5 June 1941): 2B.

145. Hal Holly, "Los Angeles Band Briefs," *Down Beat* (15 June 1943): 6.

146. "Club Alabam" advertisement, *Los Angeles Tribune* (27 December 1943): 21.

147. Pepper and Pepper, *Straight Life*, 47.

148. Johnny Otis, *Listen to the Lambs* (New York: W. W. Norton, 1968), 87; Pepper and Pepper, *Straight Life*, 41.

149. Hal Holly, "Los Angeles Band Briefs," *Down Beat* (1 July 1943): 6.

150. Alyce Key, "Key Notes," *Los Angeles Tribune* (27 September 1943): 15.

151. "Club Alabam" advertisement, *The California Eagle* (2 September 1944): 2B.

152. "Club Alabam" advertisement, *The California Eagle* (14 December 1944): 21.

153. Hal Holly, "Los Angeles Band Briefs," *Down Beat* (1 March 1945): 6.

154. Otis, *Listen*, 86–87.

155. "Club Alabam" advertisement, *The California Eagle* (24 May 1945): 13.

156. Eddie Burbridge, "No Fooling," *The California Eagle* (22 March 1945): 12.

157. "Top Entertainment Is Scheduled for Shepp's Playhouse," *The California Eagle* (17 August 1944): 12.

158. "Shepp's Playhouse" advertisement, *Los Angeles Tribune* (11 September 1944): 16.

159. "Shepp's Playhouse" advertisement, *The California Eagle* (18 January 1945): 15.

160. Herman Spurlock, "Digging the Musicians," *Los Angeles Sentinel* (5 September 1946): 20.

161. Ross Russell, *Bird Lives: The High Life and Hard Times of Charlie (Yardbird) Parker* (New York: Charterhouse, 1973), 206.

162. Ira Gitler, *Swing to Bop: An Oral History of the Transition in Jazz in the 1940s* (New York: Oxford University Press, 1985), 173.

163. "Jack's Basket Room" advertisement, *Los Angeles Sentinel* (21 March 1946): 11.

164. Russell, *Bird Lives*, 201.

165. Helen Oakley Dance, *Stormy Monday: The T-Bone Walker Story* (Baton Rouge: Louisiana State University Press, 1987), 50.

166. "Eckle's [sic]," *California Eagle*, 10.

167. Per Notini, liner notes, *T-Bone Walker: The Inventor of the Electric Guitar Blues* (Blues Boy Records, BB 304, 1983).

168. Doyle, "Swingtime."

169. "Plantation Club" advertisement, *The California Eagle* (11 November 1943): 10.

170. "Jay McShann Will Open Joe Morris' New Midtown Negro Nitery, Little Joe's," *Billboard* (18 August 1945): 14.

171. Hal Holly, "Los Angeles Band Briefs," *Down Beat* (29 January 1947): 6.

172. "The Outskirts of Town" advertisement, *The California Eagle* (20 April 1944): 13.

173. "Joe Turner's Blue Room" advertisement, *Los Angeles Tribune* (31 December 1945): 19.

174. "Niteries Facing Race Problem," *Down Beat*, (3 March 1943): 6.

175. Collins, *Black Los Angeles*, 29.

176. Morroe Berger, Edward Berger, and James Patrick, *Benny Carter: A Life in American Music, Vol. 1* (Metuchen, NJ: Scarecrow Press, 1982), 229.

177. Hal Holly, "Los Angeles Band Briefs," *Down Beat* (1 May 1944): 6.

178. "Cole Trio, Carter Ork, All-Negro Unit Bought by Trocadero," *Billboard* (7 April 1945): 31.

179. "All-Colored Show Due March 22nd at the Trocadero," *Los Angeles Tribune* (12 March 1945): 18.

180. "Notes for Showfolks," *Los Angeles Tribune* (30 April 1945): 20.

181. "Troc Fired Carter, But It's Tough to Make Heave Stick," *Billboard* (14 April 1945): 11.

182. "Orpheum Theatre" advertisement, *The California Eagle* (21 June 1945): 13.

183. Hal Holly, "Los Angeles Band Briefs," *Down Beat* (15 July 1945): 6.

184. Mrs. J. T. Gipson, "Dawn 'Til Dusk," *The California Eagle* (3 January 1946): 14.

185. Haskins, *Nat King Cole*, 34.

186. Gitler, *Swing to Bop*, 162.

187. Berger, *Benny Carter*, 229.

188. Collins, *Black Los Angeles*, 24.

189. Pepper and Pepper, *Straight Life*, 48.

190. Collins, *Black Los Angeles*, 24.

191. "Curtis Mosby Convicted of Concealing Assets," *Down Beat* (7 May 1947): 11.

192. "Club Congo" advertisement, *Los Angeles Sentinel* (18 December 1947): 20.

193. "Club Alabam" advertisement, *The California Eagle* (17 February 1949): 17.

194. "NAACP Asks FBI Probe in Compton," *Los Angeles Tribune* (29 January 1945): 1.

195. Collette, personal interview.

196. Eastman, "Central Avenue."

197. "Honeydrippers Score Heavily With Swing Crowd at Shepp's," *The California Eagle* (17 January 1946): 17.

198. Robert Gordon, *Jazz West Coast: The Los Angeles Jazz Scene of the 1950s* (London: Quartet Books, 1986), 24.

199. Gitler, *Swing to Bop*, 168.

3

Oakland Blues

PART 1: ESSAY

Lee Hildebrand

Whereas southern blues traditions have been well documented,[1] West Coast blues has not received comparable scholarly attention. Blues, like other African-American musical genres, arrived in California concurrently with the new southern immigrants. By the end of World War II, Oakland had become a center of West Coast blues activity. Initially, both the music and its practitioners reflected cultural phenomena from Texas, Louisiana, Arkansas, and the Mississippi Delta.[2] However, a confluence of transformed and reinterpreted traditions from both inside and outside of California led to the development of Oakland blues. In this chapter, the history, function, and contributions of several significant artists are presented. The material is supplemented with the insider perspective of Bob Geddins, a composer, practitioner, and producer of Oakland blues, who explains the process of creating a blues recording.

Oakland has been an important blues center since World War II, having served as a launching pad for the careers of such important artists as Ivory Joe Hunter, Pee Wee Crayton, Lowell Fulson, and Jimmy McCracklin. There is little documented evidence of Oakland blues music, aside from its jazz context, before that period.

The earliest known blues band in the area was the West Oakland Houserockers, a sextet led by pianist Count Otis Matthews that also included trumpet, clarinet, guitar, bass, and drums. Matthews's style showed little of the refinement associated with his namesake, William "Count" Basie. "His people were from the Mississippi Delta; he was really from that environment," recalled Vallejo-born drummer Johnny Otis, who made his debut as a professional musician with Matthews's group in 1939. "He was steeped in boogie and blues. It was just a hard, boogie woogie blues style—very rough, very unsophisticated."[3]

Johnny Otis settled in Los Angeles in 1943, and by the late forties he was instrumental in popularizing the new rhythm and blues style with his California Rhythm and Blues Caravan, featuring vocalists Little Esther Phillips, Mel Walker, and the Robins. But he never forgot his early experience with Matthews, particularly a risque tune titled "The Signifying Monkey." In 1958, Otis adapted the number's African-derived "shave and a haircut, six bits" beat for his biggest hit, "Willie and the Hand Jive."[4]

The West Oakland Houserockers performed primarily at house rent parties; the members were too young and their music too raw for the group to secure employment at nightclubs along Seventh Street, then the hub of the East Bay's

Figure 3.1. Slim Jenkins Club, Oakland, California, 1960. Courtesy of Chris Strachwitz.

African-American community.[5] The foremost of these was the Slim Jenkins Club (see Figure 3.1), which had been opened by Louisiana-born Harold "Slim" Jenkins on the day Prohibition ended in 1933. The first-class supper club attracted a racially mixed clientele to see some of the biggest names in black popular music, including Earl Hines, the Ink Spots, and Louis Jordan.[6]

Among the local blues-oriented artists who appeared at Jenkins's club during the World War II period were Louisiana-born singer-guitarist Saunders King and Texas-born singer-pianist Ivory Joe Hunter.[7] In 1942, King, a former gospel quartet singer whose band was among the first on the West Coast to employ elements of modern jazz,[8] scored the Bay Area's first blues hit, "S.K. Blues" on Dave Rosenbaum's San Francisco–based Rhythm label. Although the company had difficulty meeting demand for the record because of the wartime shellac shortage, it sold in the tens of thousands,[9] prompting nationally established blues singer Joe Turner to record a cover version for the New York–based National label three years later. King went on to record for the Decca, Modern, Aladdin, and Galaxy labels, but his career was seriously damaged by a series of scandals involving white women and drugs.[10]

Along with Cecil Gant and Charles Brown, two fellow singer-pianists who began recording in Los Angeles during World War II, Ivory Joe Hunter helped to fashion a relaxed, jazz-informed style that has been dubbed "cocktail blues," although his repertoire also included boogie woogie. After recording for the Library of Congress in Weirgate, Texas, in 1934 and with guitarist Johnny Moore's Three Blazers (with Brown playing the piano instead of Hunter) for the Ivory label in Los Angeles in 1945, Hunter relocated to Oakland. Beginning in 1946, he made a series of 78s for Pacific Records, a label operated by disc jockey Don Hambly of Berkeley radio station KRE.[11] Hunter's 1947 Pacific recording of "Pretty Mama Blues" reached No. 1 on *Billboard*'s "Most-Played Juke Box Race Records" and "Best Selling Retail Race Records" charts.[12] The guitarist in Hunter's Oakland band was Texas-born Connie "Pee Wee" Crayton, an Aaron "T-Bone" Walker–influenced stylist. Crayton became an important blues star in his own right following the 1948 success of his instrumental "Blues After Hours," moving to Los Angeles the next year to be closer to Modern Records, for which he had recorded the tune.[13] Hunter, left Oakland in 1947 and went on to score such major rhythm and blues hits of the fifties as "I Almost Lost My Mind" on the MGM label and "Since I Met You Baby" on Atlantic.

Whereas the blues of Saunders King and Ivory Joe Hunter was jazz-imbued and basically urbane, a different variety of blues showed up in Oakland during the war years. Coming to work in the shipyards and other wartime industries, the new residents brought with them a musical style rooted in the rural South. New clubs began to emerge along Seventh Street and throughout West Oakland, as well as in North Richmond, Vallejo, and the Russell City district of Hayward.[14]

"People who could afford to spend money wouldn't go into those clubs," recalled Oakland blues tenor saxophonist "Dr. Wild" Willie Moore. "They'd go to Slim Jenkins'."[15] In these clubs, the price of entertainment, as well as life, was cheap. When Moore first began playing as a teenager in the late forties, his mother would check his shirt for bloodstains when he'd come home from engagements.[16]

"On the corner of Market and Sixteenth, there was a club called the Green Spot, and then there was the Manhattan Club," stated West Oakland resident John Noble. "They were both blood dens. On Friday nights, the ambulance and the police would sit down the street for the people to start fights. They would start bringing bodies out at 10 p.m. and wouldn't stop till 2 a.m. People were shooting, stabbing, and killing."[17]

"They tell me Tin Pan Alley's the roughest place in town./They start cuttin' and shootin' soon as the sun goes down," Texas-born vocalist Jimmy Wilson sang in 1953, vividly capturing the violent atmosphere at the period's West Oakland juke joints. Adapted by producer Bob Geddins from an earlier composition by Curtis Jones, "Tin Pan Alley" is perhaps the quintessential Oakland blues song. Although Wilson's original version is no longer available on a 45, Chicago-based bluesman Little Milton Campbell's 1973 rendition on Stax Records can be found on many jukeboxes in the area, and Oakland blues bands still get requests for the tune.[18]

Out of the turbulence of the late forties and early fifties came a distinct sound that has come to be known as "Oakland blues." Unlike the better-known Chicago variety, which came north from Mississippi, Oakland blues was rooted in the African-American musical traditions of Texas, Louisiana, and Arkansas and, ac-

Figure 3.2. Blues composer, producer, and pianist Bob Geddins. Taken in 1960, Oakland, California. Courtesy of Chris Strachwitz.

cording to Bob Geddins (see Figure 3.2), has "a slow, draggier beat and a kinda mournful sound."[19]

One week in February 1991, much ado was made about all the Grammy Award nominees from Oakland and the two who won—M. C. Hammer and En Vogue. Yet the Bay Area media gave scant attention to the death that same week of Geddins, the record producer and songwriter who had been so instrumental in putting the city's black music on the national map over forty years earlier. KGO-TV devoted just thirty seconds to his passing. The only newspaper to mention it that week was the *Oakland Tribune*—not in an obituary but in a paid funeral notice that stated simply, "He originated the Oakland blues."[20]

Although he was neither a musician nor an accomplished singer (he once recorded a novelty tune, titled "Maria's Blues," sung in a mock Italian accent, crediting himself on the label as "The Mystery Man"), Geddins played the central role in defining the Oakland blues sound. In rehearsals before recording sessions, he was able to get singers to phrase songs the way he wanted, usually by having them stretch key words through slurring. It was, in a way, an extension of his own slow, Texas-tinged speaking manner.[21]

Many of the records Geddins produced had an extremely sad, almost doomed quality. This was a conscious effect. As he explained in 1980:

I try to make everything I record sound as sad as possible. I could even take some blues records that I heard other people sing and I could probably put a different arrangement or tune to them and make them sound sadder. When black folks go to buyin' blues, they want to buy something that gives them the feeling of the old things that they went through when they were having troubles and difficulties, not when they were having good times. That's what the blues is all about.

They be thinkin' about something that happened to 'em, or the hard times they were havin', or some woman that mistreated 'em. In trying to get that over to the people so they can hear what you're talkin' about, you got to make the story sound as if the singer was really in this mood of distress or went through these problems. All the people that have had similar problems are the ones that like that stuff and are gonna buy those records.

Some people make like they don't like the blues, but if you slip around their house sometimes, you'll hear them playin' 'em. Most of your black people know something about the blues.[22]

From 1944 until the mid-1960s, Geddins recorded hundreds of singles, some gospel but mostly blues, on about a dozen of his own labels. His first company was called Big Town, and its red-and-black label design featured a silhouette of the downtown Oakland skyline. Later labels included Down Town, Irma (named for his wife), Gedison's, Veltone, and Art-Tone, most run in partnership with other local businessmen. As a small, independent producer lacking a national distribution network, Geddins often leased his productions to larger companies in Los Angeles and Chicago, including Swingtime, Modern/RPM, Aladdin, Chess/Checker, and Imperial. But he was a lamb in a den of wolves. Trusting to a fault, he was often beaten out of his masters, copyrights, and artists.[23]

Besides Jimmy Wilson's "Tin Pan Alley," Geddins's other hits included Lowell Fulson's "Three O'Clock Blues" (later covered by B. B. King), K. C. Douglas's "Mercury Boogie" (under the new title "Mercury Blues," it later became a rock hit for the Steve Miller Band and a country hit for Alan Jackson), Roy Hawkins's "Why Do Everything Happen to Me" (covered by both B. B. King and James Brown), Johnny Fuller's "Fool's Paradise" (covered by Charles Brown, Mose Allison, and Sam Cooke) and "Haunted House" (later a rock hit for "Jumpin'" Gene Simmons and a country hit for the Compton Brothers), Sugar Pie DeSanto's "I Want to Know," Jimmy McCracklin's "Just Got to Know," and Tiny Powell's "My Time after While" (covered by Buddy Guy and John Mayall). All, except the Fulson and the McCracklin songs, were either written or co-written by Geddins.[24]

Born on February 6, 1913, on a large plantation between Marlin and Waco, Texas, Geddins moved to California in 1933. During World War II, while working for the Los Angeles street maintenance department, he began hanging out at local black record shops. Impressed with the demand for blues records by the city's rapidly growing African-American population, he eventually opened his own store, which his wife managed while he was at his day job.[25]

Sometime, probably in 1943, Geddins took a month's vacation to visit his mother, who'd moved to West Oakland. A visit to Seventh Street changed his life. He recalled:

> I never seen so many people in all my life. The streets was so crowded you couldn't hardly walk down the street unless you bumped into somebody. There were people from everywhere—Louisiana, Alabama, Georgia, Mississippi, Texas, Oklahoma, Tennessee!
>
> I said to myself, "This could be a record heaven," because there was no blues records to be heard here in the Bay Area. You could hear some blues in Los Angeles, but here there was nothing. There were thousands and thousands of people working in the shipyards, and they were still calling for more. So I decided I would go and get me a job and work that month.[26]

Geddins was hired on as a burner and welder at Kaiser Shipyard in Richmond. Building an apartment downstairs at his mother's house, he moved his family to Oakland. While working as a buyer for Wolf's Record Shop on Seventh Street, he started scouting the area for artists to record. He explained: "I began going to churches and nightclubs. I went to most all the blues clubs around—Richmond, Oakland, Vallejo, San Francisco. There were pretty good bands at each place. There was a good demand for church music at the time. Finally I figured out that church music cost less money to record."[27]

Geddins's first production, recorded in the studios of San Francisco radio station KSJO (probably in 1944), was "If Jesus Had to Pray, What About Me?" by the Rising Stars quartet. He had masters and stampers made locally, then went to Los Angeles to have the records pressed by Globe Records. To save the cost of having new labels printed, he decided to use the Globe label. He ordered 7,500 records, but upon discovering that Globe was selling additional copies without his knowledge, he started his own label and pressing plant. The plant opened on April 12, 1944, at the corner of Eighth and Center in West Oakland.[28]

After losing the Rising Stars to the rival Pacific label, Geddins recorded other gospel quartets, including the Pilgrim Travelers from Los Angeles and the local Paramount Singers, but increasingly he found his attention returning to his first love—the blues—after meeting Oklahoma-born singer-guitarist Lowell Fulson in 1946.[29]

Fulson, who had ended up at Alameda Naval Air Station at the end of World War II, was walking by Geddins's pressing plant one afternoon when he heard some music and walked in. Spotting an old acoustic guitar hanging on the wall, he asked if he might play it. Within minutes, Geddins offered him his first recording contract, as well as some singing lessons. The blues singer recalled:

> Bob really taught me how to phrase the blues and not cut 'em too short. He'd say, "You're young. You got plenty wind. Hold that wind in there, boy, before you change that note." You'd be surprised by [what] a man that don't sing can tell you [about] how to sing a song. He knew what he wanted to hear, and that's what the public wanted to hear. All those voice-control things like you see me doin', I got that from him.[30]

In 1948, Fulson gave Geddins his first national hit with "Three O'Clock Blues" on the Down Town label. It went to No. 6 on *Billboard*'s "Most-Played Juke Box

Race Records" chart.[31] Fulson, however, was not satisfied with Geddins's limited distribution network. "Bob would press up a hundred and go out and sell 'em out of the trunk of his car," he explained. "He'd play 'em over the speakers in his car." Signing with Swingtime Records in Los Angeles in 1949, Fulson moved there the following year after the huge national success of "Every Day I Have the Blues." He formed a band with Ray Charles as his pianist and arranger and continued having hits into the late sixties. These included "Lonesome Christmas," "Reconsider Baby," and "Tramp." Still a popular attraction on the blues circuit, he performs in Oakland an average of once a year.[32]

During the 1950s, Geddins produced such blues artists as Jimmy McCracklin, Roy Hawkins, Jimmy Wilson, L. C. Robinson, Mercy Dee Walton, Johnny Fuller, James Reed, Willie B. Huff, and Weldon "Juke Boy" Bonner. Hawkins's recording of the Geddins tune "Why Do Everything Happen to Me?" was issued by the Modern label in Los Angeles and gave Geddins his second national hit; it went to No. 2 in 1950 on *Billboard*'s "Most-Played Juke Box Rhythm and Blues Records" and "Best Selling Retail Rhythm and Blues Records" charts.[33] Wilson's "Tin Pan Alley" was issued on Geddins's own Big Town label and went to No. 10 on the magazine's "Most Played in Juke Boxes" chart in 1953.[34] "Tin Pan Alley" featured the guitar of Geddins session regular Lafayette "Thing" Thomas, whose unique style had nearly as much to do with establishing the Oakland blues sound as did Geddins's own contributions.[35]

The Louisiana-born guitarist worked off and on with Jimmy McCracklin's band from around 1950 until his death in 1977 and played on countless Geddins recording sessions—gospel, soul, rock 'n' roll, as well as blues. Partially inspired by the playing of T-Bone Walker, Thomas made use of the low as well as the high strings during solos, employing high, ringing treble trills and volume-knob warps, and was highly propulsive when providing rhythmic accompaniment. George Hurst and particularly Johnny Heartsman elaborated on this style during the mid-1950s, and during the 1960s such Oakland rhythm and blues bandleaders as Eddie Foster, Johnny Tolbert, Eugene Blacknell, and Marvin Holmes applied it.[36]

Geddins's last national hits were San Francisco–born singer-songwriter Sugar Pie DeSanto's "I Want to Know," which placed at No. 4 on *Billboard*'s "Hot Rhythm and Blues Sides" chart in 1960,[37] and Arkansas-born singer-pianist-songwriter Jimmy McCracklin's "Just Got to Know," a No. 2 rhythm and blues hit the following year.[38] The DeSanto record was leased to Checker Records in Chicago, the McCracklin to Imperial in Los Angeles. "Everything I would get," Geddins stated, "I got took away from me somehow by another record company."[39]

Geddins had his last local hit in 1963 with former gospel singer Tiny Powell's "My Time after While," which featured the guitar and horn arrangements of Johnny Heartsman. But when Geddins refused to lease it to Chess/Checker, the Chicago company simply had one of its own artists—Buddy Guy—copy it nearly note for note. After that, Geddins produced occasional 45s into the mid-1980s, but most were vanity affairs for friends and family members, including a roller-disco novelty number.[40]

Though Geddins had bad luck, no other Oakland record producer has such a long and consistent track record. Others, however, had momentary successes. Ray Dobard's Music City label, though primarily known for its doo-wop vocal group recordings, scored in 1957 with the Johnny Heartsman instrumental "Johnny's House Party," which got to No. 13 on the rhythm and blues chart,[41] and the Heartsman-produced "Think Twice Before You Speak," recorded by singer-songwriter Al King on the Sahara label, hit No. 36 on the rhythm and blues chart in 1966.[42] Producer-arranger Ray Shanklin recorded several newer Oakland blues singers, including Sonny Rhodes and J. J. Malone, during the late sixties and early seventies for Galaxy, a division of Fantasy Records, but these were only regional hits.

Blues music enjoyed a brief spell of popularity among young whites during the sixties, especially in the Bay Area. Numerous Chicago bluesmen were imported to play at the Fillmore Auditorium and the Avalon Ballroom, both in San Francisco, yet none of the many Oakland blues players were given a piece of the action, perhaps because their styles were too far removed from the Chicago guitar and harmonica sounds that rock audiences found so appealing.[43]

The Oakland blues style, as fashioned by Bob Geddins and Lafayette Thomas, is less prominent today than it was in the fifties and sixties. As live bands were replaced by disco deejays in many black clubs during the seventies, Oakland blues moved underground and languished in the tiny beer-and-wine juke joints on the west side where it had begun. Many of the old-timers had moved away (Pee Wee Crayton and Lowell Fulson to Southern California, Johnny Heartsman to Sacramento) or had given up the music business entirely; those who remained were performing for from $12 to $15 a night. They were joined by musicians from other regions, especially Chicago and Fresno, and blues in Oakland began to take on new influences, including the use of the harmonica, an instrument previously almost foreign to Oakland blues (notable early exceptions were Sidney Maiden's harmonica work with K. C. Douglas and A. C. Robinson's with his brother L. C.). Many of the new participants were nonblack musicians.[44]

Oakland, which is said to be the most integrated city in United States, today boasts a racially mixed blues scene in terms of both band membership and audience makeup. The violence that once made blues clubs so dangerous has subsided, and since the early eighties young blacks and whites, in addition to older working-class blacks, have packed such Oakland blues bars as Eli's Mile High Club, the Deluxe Inn Cafe, and Your Place.[45]

In 1980, Troyce Key, a white Louisiana-born blues singer, leased (and later purchased) Eli's following the murder the previous year of former owner Eli Thornton. Key had recorded as a solo artist for Warner Bros. Records in the late fifties before joining a black Fresno-based blues band known as the Rhythm Rockers. Until his death in 1992, Key ran Eli's with his African-American wife, Margaret, and strived to maintain a racial balance at the club. Yet when whites began venturing there to hear the blues, some of Eli's black customers stopped coming. Margaret, who still operates the club, explains: "It's like going to a barbecue joint. Some black people think if you get a lot of white people there, it may not be too good. Most of the blacks that are regulars tend to be the kind that associate with nonblacks in their everyday lives."[46]

The banding together of black and white musicians and audiences greatly improved working conditions. When Troyce Key began to perform at Eli's under its original ownership during the mid-1970s, the whole band was paid $60 a night. "Wasn't making much of nothin,'" said Key, who cut lawns to get by. By 1992, however, he was able to boast that he paid more than that to each of the musicians in his house band.[47]

Prior to his death in 1984, pioneering Oakland blues guitarist Pee Wee Crayton frequently traveled from Los Angeles to perform at Eli's and other Oakland blues clubs (Figure 3.3). He complained at the time that, in Southern California, only white clubs would hire him. "The white kids really dig the blues," he said. "The black kids don't dig the blues too much. . . . I don't like to play in an all-black club because somebody got something bad to say if you ain't playing the Top 40." He added: "When I go to Oakland, I play the black clubs and I play the white clubs, but up there everybody goes to the same clubs, so you don't know what's a black club and what ain't."[48]

The following conversation between Bob Geddins and James C. Moore Sr. affords fascinating insight into the way Geddins once worked in the recording studio, how he coaxed vocalists into singing blues tunes *his* way—how, in essence, he created the Oakland blues.

Geddins was an inspiration to several other record producers, particularly Chris Strachwitz and James C. Moore Sr. Strachwitz picked up pointers from Geddins by observing him at work in the studio during the late fifties and went on to found Arhoolie Records, the highly successful blues and international roots music label, in 1960. Moore launched his own record company, Jasman Records, in the mid-1960s. One of his most successful Jasman releases was Sugar Pie DeSanto's early-seventies recording of the Geddins blues "Hello, San Francisco." Besides vocalist DeSanto, who had been one of Geddins's best-selling artists, the record featured the guitar of Thing Thomas. "Hello, San Francisco" was perhaps the last recording of "pure" Oakland blues of the type Geddins originated.

PART 2: A CONVERSATION WITH BOB GEDDINS

James C. Moore Sr.

This conversation with Bob Geddins, who was seventy-seven years old at the time, took place at the Society for Ethnomusicology Pre-Conference Symposium, held

Figure 3.3. Blues guitarist and singer Pee Wee Crayton. Taken at the 1980 San Francisco Blues Festival. Courtesy of Mark Sarfati.

at the Hyatt Regency Hotel in downtown Oakland on 7 November 1990. This session of the symposium, attended by approximately fifty people (scholars and local blues enthusiasts), was entitled "The Evolution of Oakland Blues" and included discussion and performance by Bob Geddins and members of the Bay Area Blues Society Band. James C. Moore Sr., a confidant and colleague of Geddins, served as chair and moderator of the session. After the introduction by Moore, Geddins gave a lecture-demonstration on the method that he used in the studio to create and record a blues song. Band member Willie Gee assisted by singing the song that Geddins composed. The presentation ended with questions from the audience.

James Moore: Good afternoon, everyone. My name is Jim Moore and I've been involved in the music scene around the Bay Area since the mid-fifties. I began as an agent, booking talent, and then I later managed talent. Later I formed a record and publishing company. I learned a lot about producing music from the gentleman who's going to be following me. I've had the pleasure of working with some very talented people in this business.[49] Black music, our blues—our American classic, I like to call it—is really the father of all popular music. Many times we've been in the studio supposedly recording a blues, without lyric, and many times the soloist has laid down his solo and somebody says, "Man, that could be a jazz tune." So it's all about music, not necessarily categories. Usually the people who put it in categories don't play anything.

But black music is an art form that's not appreciated in America quite as much as it is in Europe. We paint pictures the same as other artists who paint on canvas; we paint audio pictures. We have with us one of the greatest picture-painters on the West Coast, if not in the country, Mr. Bob Geddins—who started out, incidentally, as a radio repairman, and it was during the war that he came up with a way of fusing the filament in radio tubes. Tubes were hard to come by during the war, and he came up with a way of welding the filaments inside the tubes. Therefore, he got all of the business because he could create his own tubes. And this is how Bob met the great Lowell Fulson, and Bob recorded Lowell's first tune. I have compiled a list of 42 of the 200 tunes that Mr. Geddins has had recorded by people like Lowell Fulson, B. B. King, Roy Hawkins, Willie Huff, K. C. Douglas, Steve Miller, and Stevie Ray Vaughan; and these are actually 42 of his biggest sellers. He had about ten record labels, and what we're going to do is try and give you an idea just how creative we are. As a matter of fact, the blues gods are testing our abilities, because the original bass player wasn't able to stay. So we had to pull Mr. Domingo Balinton out of a hat; he knows nothing at all about the tune. So Mr. Geddins will come up, and this is a new tune that he has composed. He will walk you through the process of recording a song as it would happen in a recording studio. After the main track was laid down, we would usually go back, think about it—sleep on it, as we say—and the next day we might decide to add a trumpet or whatever. But anyway, here's Mr. Geddins.

Bob Geddins: Well, I will show you what happens when we get ready to record a record. First we go to the studio. Then we call a bass player. Usually they have not seen this song before. They don't know what it's all about; all they see is the words. So the first thing we do is we try to show them how the song goes [should be performed]. I can't always get it together going over it one, two, or three times. Sometimes we have to go over it for a couple of weeks before you can get the voice down. So don't look for our singing to be right up-to-date on this thing. Now, this is the blues, [so we] don't play melody—this kind of blues here is way down in the sticks, low-down blues. So they may not come out to be four bars, twelve bars, or sixteen bars. But in order for anybody to sing a blues like this, the band has to follow the singer, because this is not regular singing. This might be fourteen, thirteen, and sixteen bars. But you gotta sing it to give the song a feel.

JM: This is Mr. Willie Gee, another blues singer from Texas, just like Mr. Geddins.

BG: Now, there are two ways I can start this song. We begin with

I'm bad. I'm bad as I'm wanna be. I'm bad.

We repeat,

> *Bad as I'm wanna be.*
> *If you want to keep on living,*
> *Don't you ever mess around with me.*

Now the next lyric we do the same.

> *Bad, I'm bad as I'm going to be.*

See the "be."

> *Bad, I'm bad as I'm going to be.*
> *If you want to keep on a-livin',*
> *Don't you ever mess around with me.*

You can go down here or you can go down there. Your music come there.

> *I want everybody, to take a look at me.*
> *I don't look dangerous, but I'm tough as I can be.*
> *I got a switchblade in my pocket, I've got one hand on a gun.*
> *Cut you up if you stand, and I'll shoot you if you run.*
> *'Cause I'm bad as I'm wanna be.*
> *If you want to keep on living, don't you ever mess around with me.*

Now, when you come back to this verse, we only got two, "be" and "me."

> *Bad as I'm going to be,*

You hold that "be" up.

> *If you want to keep on a-living,*
> *Don't you ever mess around with me.*

See that? If that works, you're ready to go.

> *I smoke dynamite. I drink TNT.*
> *You know it ain't safe, messin' around with me.*
> *I may explode, I'm just like a bomb.*
> *I may blow your body into kingdom come.*
> *'Cause I'm bad. 'Cause I'm as bad as I'm gonna be.*
> *If you want to keep on living, don't you ever mess around with me.*

That's the way you get your voice down deeper. You can phrase it a little bit deeper on that drop.

> *I once knew a man, he weighed 300 pounds.*
> *He made a pass at my lady, I knocked him down to the ground.*

I tore him apart, with these bare hands.
They had to make him a coffin from a sardine can.
'Cause I'm bad.

That's the way the blues go. Now what's happening to the blues, you gotta try to write a pretty good story, it's gotta be short, and then you gotta tell folks the beginning to the ending to make it a complete story. It's all yours now. Now Jim, Willie may not be able to sing it up good like I do, but remember, if we're in the recording studio, we might have to do this twenty times.

JM: Yeah.

BG: Getting the feel of it. After twenty times, if you begin to get it, then you can sing it just like me.

Willie Gee: Like he said, this is the first time we've seen this thing. We've had a few minutes here to take a look at it, and it's going to be a little tight, but I'm going to do the best I can do with it, and we're going to work with this. We're going to work this thing in G. I think he was in C. Let's try it. I'm trying to put some highlights here so I don't get lost in the script. Let's get busy. Give me a lead.

Bad, I'm bad as I wanna be.
Well Lord I'm bad, just as bad as I wanna be.
You want to keep on living, don't ever mess around with me.

I want everybody here
To take a good look at me.
I don't look dangerous.
But I'm tough as I can be.
I have a switchblade in my pocket.
Got my hands on my gun.
I cut you if you stand.
And I'll shoot you if you run.

'Cause I'm bad, Lord I'm bad as I wanna be.
If you want to keep on living, don't ever mess around with me.

Now I smoke TNT.
And I drink dynamite.
Don't mess around with me.
I may explode, just like a bomb.
And blow your poor body, kingdom come.

Because I'm bad, I'm bad as I wanna be.
If you really wanna go on living,
You better not ever mess around with me.

Once saw me a man.
He weighed over 300 pounds.
Made a pass at my woman
And I knocked him down to the ground.

I tore him apart
With these bare hands.
I made him a coffin
Out of a sardine can.

Because I'm bad,
Bad as I wanna be,
If you want to keep on living, don't mess around with me.

Once I knew a man.
He weighed 300 pounds.
Made a pass at my lady
I knocked him down to the ground.
I tore him apart
With these bare hands.
They had to make him a coffin
Out of a sardine can

Because I'm bad.

BG: Ladies and gentlemen, that's the first time. The next time, it'll be better; the next time it'll get by; the twentieth time we'll get it right.

Bad, I'm bad as I wanna be.
Bad, I'm bad as I wanna be.
If you want to keep on living, don't you ever mess around with me.

I want everybody
To take a look at me.
I ain't a dangerous looking guy.
But I'm tough as I can be.
Switchblade's in my pocket.
Got my hand on my gun.
Cut you if you stand, and I'll shoot you if you run.

Bad, oh Lord I'm bad as I wanna be.
If you want to keep on living, don't you ever mess around with me.

I smoke dynamite.
I drink TNT.
You know it ain't safe
To mess around with me.
I may explode
Just like a bomb.
And I'll blow your body
Into kingdom come.

Because I'm bad, oh Lord I'm bad as I wanna be.
If you want to keep on living, don't you ever mess around with me.

I once knew a man.
He weighed 300 pounds.

He made a pass at me, my woman.
And I knocked him down to the ground.
Tore him apart
With these bare hands.
They had to make him a coffin
From a sardine can.

Bad, oh Lord I'm bad as I want to be.
If you want to keep living, don't you ever mess around with me.

JM: We'll use the rest of the time for questions and answers.

Q: I'm curious to know, back in the forties just after the war, how many other recording studios were there up here [Bay Area] in terms of fighting the exodus from L.A.?

BG: I was about the only real studio here at that time when we first began. Afterward there were no studios, but a few guys like R. Lee Hunt, a few folks, if they had a machine, they'd just go around and cut guys. But I actually had the first studio, first pressing plant. I'm the only black man that ever had a pressing plant. I know it all, I know pressing, I know making the ads and things, the whole works.

JM: As a matter of fact, the first recording studio was on the next corner from here on 11th Street. That was the first recording studio in Oakland.

BG: The first pressing plant was on Eighth, right off the side of the street in West Oakland. That's where I had my first label, called Big Town. The next was called Down Town, the next was called Flat—I had a bunch of them. I had about fifteen labels. The reason why I had so many labels is because they would cheat me out of my stuff, and I would put it on another label so they wouldn't take that one. They'd take that one, I would put it on another label so they wouldn't take it. They couldn't keep me down, because I would just go ahead and make me a single. When I first met Lowell Fulson, he couldn't really do the blues, but I taught him. Jimmy Wilson, and all of those guys. The only guys that could kind of sing the blues who lived here was Jimmy McCracklin. He kind of knew it from the start; the other guys I had to teach.

JM: Bob was the first man to do "The Thrill Is Gone"; that tune's been recorded many times.

BG: And B. B., they stole it, and they made millions, I made nothing.

JM: M. C. Hammer did a version of "The Thrill Is Gone."

BG: We recorded the first song, it was called "Rock Me." Do you remember? I made "Three O'Clock This Morning," that also was my record, they took that. They took everything I made.

JM: What was the problem that you had?

BG: Well, my problem was no money, you understand? I never could get ahold of enough money to pay. It costs a lot of money to press a hundred thousand records.

JM: Did you ever approach anyone to help you in financing your recordings?

BG: Well, yeah. What's the difference? You approach, you still don't make a profit after you make a little money. I went to Specialty Records, I went to Imperial, I went to Aladdin, I went to Checker Records in Chicago. I went to everybody. I had a record here, a record over there, a record here, and a record over there. Wasn't getting a handful of money, I didn't know how else I was going to get it. They just let you make a little, and if they give you too much, you might owe it on your kids.

JM: How much difference do you think there is between the blues and spiritual or gospel music?

BG: It's no difference between the two. The way blues got started, it was from spirituals. The old-time people was in slavery, and they didn't know nobody to go to, they went to the Lord. And they made it moanful and groanful, like they was begging for something, you understand? That's how spirituals started. But blues people come right along. They're going to beg about this woman. Now blues ain't nothing but a feeling. If you sing the blues, you might sing it in one feeling, and I sing it, I'll sing it with another feeling. Some can make it blue, some can make it bluer, some can make it joyful, you know what I mean? It's just a feeling, how you feel about things.

JM: Do you feel that the blues people have been stereotyped—in other words, put in a certain category?

BG: Well, you hardly ever hear about my type of blues, because my blues is a bit slower than the other people's blues. I try to give it to you so you can understand every word, and to do that, you're going to have to slow down. You know, like an old-time gospel. "Ever mess around with me." You can understand every word because I held that "ever" and I put "mess around with me."

JM: How much money do you think has been generated from your efforts, not that you got it all?

BG: Millions. Oh, I had about four—I had two that sell three million, and another one that sell a million, so I did make a little money, when everything was all over with.

JM: Well, you know Bobby, since I've known you, you've had some hard luck collecting money and people throwing you curves. But I can't ever say that I've ever seen you mad at anyone.

BG: It ain't no use. What's the use of getting mad? It ain't going to do you no good. You're just having a rough life, but I wasn't mad at nobody. I could always make some more blues.

JM: Do you think the blues is being accepted better now than it was twenty or thirty years ago?

BG: Well, about thirty years ago it was still doing pretty good. I think the blues just dropped down around '63 or '64 like that. And the bottom just dropped out. Blues, it never dropped down, it's just that people quit playing it.

JM: Have you ever noticed any difference in the acceptance of the blues among black people in any period of time as opposed to other people?

BG: Well, in the later years I think white people are catering to the blues more than black people. Most black people look like they ashamed of the blues, like it's going to show 'em up where they come from. But the white people don't care. They want to hear it because of the sound.

JM: Why?

BG: Well, white people never did understand the blues too much. They could hear black people out there hollerin' and moanin' and all that. They didn't understand it. But now they done got down to the bottom of it, and they see why we doing it. They see what kind of feelings it create.

JM: Do you think, regardless of what color you are, it might be a state of mind?

BG: What, the blues?

JM: Yeah, I mean the acceptance of the blues. Do you think it has anything to do with the way that a person feels about himself or other people? I remember Johnny Talbot, when I was recording him, when he wrote a new tune, we'd have to test it on someone. He and I thought it was a great song, so we'd test it. We'd go to a club and I'd sit in a corner, and he'd play a few standards. Then he'd play this new tune without announcing what it was, and I'd watch the people and watch their reaction. And generally speaking, the little lady that was sitting with her hair all done up in spit curls and so forth, she'd just sit there looking pretty. But the lady who was kind of heavy, who didn't particularly think she was going to dance or anything, we'd call those the real people. All of a sudden she would hit the floor. Then we knew the song had the feeling.

BG: You know, some of these people that I be talking about, I think I can teach anybody how to sing some type of a blues. It doesn't matter if I had me an Italian band right here. If you had an accordion, I'd teach you how to play the blues on the accordion. I did this song a long time ago,

> *Hello, hello Maria. Longa time you no speaka to me.*
> *Hello, hello Maria. Longa time you no speak to me.*
> *Why don't you come on home Maria,*
> *And be happy as you could be?*
>
> *Tony, he's a bigga bigga boy now.*
> *He almost done taller than your dad.*
> *Tony, Tony he's a bigga bigga boy now.*
> *He almost now taller than your dad.*
> *Every time I hear him calling you,*
> *My poor heart breaks down with [. . .].*

Q: How many women have you worked with? Or have you worked basically with men?

BG: Not too many [women]. I worked with Sugar Pie DeSanto, that's about all.

JM: About four or five. Was there any special reason you wanted to know?

Q: No, I was just interested. And another question: Was it different working with people who came from different parts of the South and different parts of the country? Say, was there any difference working with a person from Alabama as opposed to Texas?

BG: No, people from down there just got a little more of a different type of feeling, like a Delta feeling. Down in Louisiana and Texas, I'm on the Texas style, only I slowed it down. The Texas style was all pretty slow in the first place. Guys like Leroy Carr, Peetie Wheatstraw, and all those guys out, I was coming up with them all that time. Now I've been studying the blues ever since I was four years old, when you couldn't get no blues records hardly. And that's the start of getting my powerful feeling.

JM: What about the time you wanted to play guitar, and your grandmother said—

BG: —oh yeah, my grandmama [said], "That's devil music." I would have been able to play guitar, but man, every time they'd hear the guitar around the house, they busted it.

JM: Do you think perhaps that might be one reason that there's a certain stigma as far as black people are concerned, attached to the blues, because throughout the years they have been taught that it's devil's music? I had similar circumstances.

BG: [Geddins nods in agreement.]

Q: When you write your stories, and talk about blues as having a story, I wonder about your idea of the characters you have, how many different kinds of people you personify— could you talk a little bit about that? I mean, when you say that your blues are all to tell a story, you must have different characters that you think about in your stories. How many different kinds are there, and what are some of them?

BG: A story like this, this is not too deep a blues. If I was writing about a woman when she did something to you, then I would make that blues deep, deep. Low-down. I can make it, if somebody's mistreating you. I'm just writing about something happening. I'm just trying to tell the people.

JM: Can you think of a tune where you have a character, a lady, in it?

BG: Yeah, I have this blues, she says,

> *I don't want no man, if his money ain't no longer than mine.*
> *I don't want no man, if his money ain't no longer than mine.*
> *You know he ain't good for nothing but trouble,*
> *Just keep begging you all the time.*

That was one I wrote for the ladies.

> *My man have to have Cadillacs and twenty-dollar bills,*
> *He has to have all of these things so I can give my friend a thrill. Gonna give my friend a thrill.*
> *I don't want no man, if his money ain't no longer than mine.*

Q: Your style reminds me so much of Lightnin' Hopkins, and I was wondering whether you listen to him.

BG: Well yeah, I go from Lightnin' Hopkins, Muddy Waters. But I can imitate any of them. But I just don't sing good. The "Devil's Son-in-Law," I know that.

Q: Why, in your opinion, Mr. Geddins, did the independent record labels in Los Angeles have a stranglehold on the market?

BG: I'll tell you why. The first one that did it, saw it made him a heap of money, and the other ones just called it off. And every time they'd get somebody down there to do a record and it made a hit, they said, "Let's get him, because he may not make many of 'em." So they take all that money, and they just keep taking them as they come, they strip 'em. Then that's where all of those guys sold their companies for millions of dollars and got out of it when things started looking kind of dim. When they knowed they had to rob everything they could get, they're ready to get out of there.

JM: And most of those guys could not write, could not play.

BG: Every company you see in Los Angeles had a black guy in there listening to the new stuff when they'd bring it in. And he'd say, "That's good, that's it," they'd put it out. But if one come in there, he'd go, "Oh, that ain't no good," they'd send him out right away. Now they don't really need the black guy.

JM: This will conclude our session.

NOTES

1. For a discussion of southern blues, see Perry Bradford, *Born with the Blues: Perry Bradford's Own Story. The True Story of the Pioneering Blues Singers and Musicians in the Early Days of Jazz* (New York: Oak Publications, 1965); David Evans, *Big Road Blues: Tradition and Creativity in the Folk Blues* (Berkeley: University of California Press, 1982); John Fahey, *Charley Patton* (London: Studio Vista, 1970); William Ferris Jr., *Blues from the Delta* (London: Studio Vista, 1971); Charles Keil, *Urban Blues* (Chicago: University of Chicago Press, 1966); Paul Oliver, *The Story of the Blues* (New York: Chilton Blues, 1974 [1969]); and Jeff Todd Titon, *Early Downhome Blues: A Musical and Cultural Analysis* (Urbana: University of Illinois Press, 1977).

2. Lee Hildebrand, "The Thrill Goes On," *The Museum of California (Oakland)* (September/October 1982): 5, and "The Johnny Otis Story," *Express: The East Bay's Free Weekly* (12 December 1986): 18.

3. Hildebrand, "Johnny Otis," 18.

4. Ibid.

5. Ibid.

6. Hildebrand, "The Thrill," 5.

7. Ibid.

8. Ralph Gleason, "A Jazz Man and Colonna Come to Town This Week," *San Francisco Chronicle* (n.d.).

9. Ibid.

10. "Jazz Leader King's Wife Found Dead," *San Francisco Chronicle* (31 October 1942): 11; "Saunders King Shot in Fight over Girl," *San Francisco Chronicle* (25 September 1946): 11; "Witnesses Tell of Shooting of Saunders King," *San Francisco Chronicle* (1 October 1946): 9; "Saunders King Goes to Quentin for Using Dope," *San Francisco Chronicle* (4 December 1951): 17.

11. Bill Millar, liner notes, *Ivory Joe Hunter: 7th Street Boogie* (Vingaker, Sweden, Route 66 Records, 1977).

12. Joel Whitburn, *Top R&B Singles, 1942–1988* (Menomonee Falls, WI: Record Research, Inc., 1988), 200.

13. Lee Hildebrand, "Pee Wee Is a Big Man on the Blues Circuit," *San Francisco Chronicle Datebook* (27 March 1983): 40–41.

14. Hildebrand, "The Thrill," 5.

15. Ibid.

16. Lee Hildebrand, "At the Art Form's Funky West Coast Home," *San Francisco Chronicle Datebook* (15 July 1984): 70–71.

17. Lee Hildebrand, "West Side Story," *Express: The East Bay's Free Weekly* (28 September 1979): 3.

18. Hildebrand, "The Thrill," 5.

19. Ibid.

20. Lee Hildebrand, "A Life in the Blues," *Express: The East Bay's Free Weekly* (15 March 1991): 1.

21. Ibid., 1, 17.

22. Lee Hildebrand, "Been Down So Long," *The Monthly (Berkeley)* (February 1980): 2.

23. During the late 1970s, Geddins finally hired a copyright attorney, who was able to get him some of his back royalties. These included a reported $23,000 settlement from

Capitol Records for "Mercury Blues," which Steve Miller lifted from a 1948 Geddins production for blues singer K C. Douglas (originally titled "Mercury Boogie") and remade on his best-selling 1976 album, *Fly Like an Eagle;* see Hildebrand, "A Life," 17.

24. Hildebrand, "A Life," 17–18.

25. Ibid., 19.

26. Ibid., 19, 21.

27. Ibid., 23.

28. Ibid., 23–24.

29. Ibid., 24.

30. Hildebrand, "The Thrill," 5–6.

31. Whitburn, *Top R&B*, 161.

32. Hildebrand, "The Thrill," 6.

33. Whitburn, "The Thrill," 184.

34. Ibid., 450.

35. Hildebrand, "A Life," 25–26.

36. Lee Hildebrand, liner notes. *Oakland Blues* (El Cerrito: Arhoolie LP 2008, 1970).

37. Whitburn, *Top R&B*, 116.

38. Ibid., 282.

39. Hildebrand, "A Life," 26.

40. Ibid., 27.

41. Whitburn, *Top R&B*, 187.

42. Ibid., 238.

43. Hildebrand, "The Thrill," 6.

44. Ibid., 6–7.

45. Ibid., 7.

46. Lee Hildebrand, "The Audience for Blues Is a Rainbow Coalition," *San Francisco Focus* 39 (July 1992): 52.

47. Ibid., 53.

48. Hildebrand, "Pee Wee," 41.

49. In Moore's introduction to the program, he stated the following: "I've worked with King Pleasure and Jon Hendricks. Also, I've had the opportunity to contribute to the *Evolution of the Blues* [show] at Monterey. I managed Big Mama Thornton for about four years, managed and produced Sugar Pie DeSanto; this is her brother on bass, Domingo [Balinton]. In Carnegie Hall, I had the pleasure of working with Basie, Duke, Earl "Fatha" Hines, and of course Mr. Geddins. I'm very pleased to have worked with such a distinguished group of people."

4

The California Black Gospel Music Tradition

A Confluence of Musical Styles and Cultures

Jacqueline Cogdell DjeDje

In 1960, George Robinson Ricks, one of the pioneer scholars of African-American gospel music, wrote: "Chicago is the focus of activity in gospel music among Negroes. The style started here, and it is the publishing center of Negro gospel songs as well as the headquarters of the national organization and school of music. In addition, the constant influx of immigrants from many states and the regular visits of professional groups from major cities provide representative examples of style."[1]

Today, it is doubtful if gospel performers or scholars would credit Chicago as the primary center of activity for gospel music. Since its beginnings in the early twentieth century, gospel has become widespread in many cities and towns. Although the tradition is now regarded as a major art form, scholarly research on the regional development of gospel music is scant. Blues and jazz scholars commonly discuss the social and musical features of a specific region or city (for example, Mississippi Delta blues or New Orleans jazz), but this is not the case with gospel music investigators. The latter have devoted attention to individuals and the development of the genre without much reference to context, except to acknowledge Chicago as the birthplace of gospel music.[2] As a result, little is known about the history of gospel music in different urban areas or about the intercultural dynamics within regions. Also, except for musicians who have become nationally known "stars," many gospel artists have been overlooked.[3] As Joyce Beasley, a noted gospel singer who moved to the San Francisco Bay Area in 1947, says of well-known gospel musicians, "You're no greater than your foundation."[4] In her opinion, more credit needs to be given to musicians who laid the groundwork, those who nurtured the so-called stars and helped them become famous. Betty Gadling, minister of music of Allen Temple Baptist Church in Oakland, sums up the opinions of most local musicians: "Little people do a lot towards history making. It's only the big ones who get the credit. The little people lay the groundwork and the big guys walk away, all shining. They could have never developed without the support of the little people."[5]

The few investigators who have studied a specific region have concentrated primarily on the South, Northeast, and Midwest.[6] Although some in-depth works have examined Californians' contributions to the growth of gospel,[7] few scholars have explored how California as a setting or context may have affected the creativity of gospel artists.[8] Yet James Cleveland (1931–91), known as the "king" or "crown prince" of gospel, has stated that Los Angeles is the "western mecca for gospel music" and calls California "one of the states that has been able to bridge contemporary and traditional [gospel] music together."[9]

Using oral interviews, newspaper accounts, recordings, and other sources (photographs, concert programs, sheet music), in this chapter I will examine the development of gospel music in three urban areas of California: Los Angeles, the San Francisco Bay Area, and San Diego.[10] My primary focus is on activity that occurred between 1900 and 1969. I will not only pay attention to the social factors that contributed to the development of the genre in each city but also present information about noted musicians and religious institutions that supported the growth of the gospel tradition. I offer no musical analysis and little discussion of musical style. Rather, I address several questions: When and how was gospel music introduced? To what extent did Chicago musicians influence developments? What type of interchange occurred between Northern and Southern Californians? What is distinctive about gospel music in California? How did the different urban areas under investigation contribute to the uniqueness of the California gospel sound? And how can the study of gospel music in California contribute to our knowledge of the tradition in other parts of the United States?

I will also examine how African Americans with different cultural backgrounds and aesthetic values interact and create various expressive forms. The diversity and richness of the California gospel tradition becomes apparent from this confluence of ideas. For the purposes of this chapter, the development of gospel music in California is divided into four periods: 1) pre-gospel, 1900–1930; 2) beginnings of gospel, 1930–1943; 3) expansion of gospel, 1943–1955; and 4) prominence of gospel, 1955–1969. This historical outline is used only as a guide for relating social history to developments in gospel music; the activity in some of the areas in California did not fall exactly within these dates or time periods.

EARLY HISTORY OF SACRED MUSIC IN CALIFORNIA: THE PRE-GOSPEL ERA

The emergence of a large black population in California coincided with the beginning of black religious institutions in the state. In each area under study, the African Methodist Episcopal (AME) Church was the first denomination to be organized: in San Francisco during the 1850s; in Los Angeles in 1872; and in San

Diego in 1887. The establishment of Baptist, AME Zion, and Methodist Episcopal churches followed in the late 1800s. As the population increased, other
churches were founded. Noteworthy was the Azusa Street Mission, the prolonged
Los Angeles revival (1906–1909) at 312 Azusa Street, which historians and theolo-
gians mark as the genesis of Pentecostalism. Because the Pentecostal movement is
considered a wellspring in the development of gospel music,[11] its growth is
significant.

Bette Yarbrough Cox states that the first African-American musicians to perform on stage in Los Angeles were members of the Beck family (Colonel James
Alec; his wife, Loo; and their daughter, Pearl), a group of singing evangelists who
traveled throughout the United States during the 1890s. Their first performances
took place in an old hall on Fifth Street near Hill (later named the Philharmonic
Auditorium), but blacks were not allowed to attend.[12] Although a few newspaper
articles from the late twenties indicate that evangelists from Chicago visited Pentecostal churches in the San Francisco Bay Area,[13] there is no evidence to suggest
what influence these visits may have had on other church groups in the area. Thus,
it is doubtful that worship practices used in Pentecostal churches in the early 1900s
had any major impact on the performance of music in Baptist and Methodist
churches in California. Rather, those individuals who visited California to participate in the Azusa Revival but returned to the South (e.g., Charles H. Mason,
founder of the Church of God in Christ [COGIC]) probably had a more direct
influence on the later development of gospel music.

One reason for the lack of direct influence from Californians is that Pentecostals and non-Pentecostals rarely interacted in religious settings. Another reason
is that the two groups looked down on each other. A 1921 editorial in the *Western
Appeal* reflects the attitudes many blacks had toward those who attended Pentecostal churches (referred to in the article as "two-by-four churches"). Although
Harlem is the focus of the discussion, it is clear that this way of thinking applied
to most Pentecostal churches regardless of their location. Toward the end of the
article, a reference is made to churches in the San Francisco Bay Area:

> Harlem is becoming infested with a species of two-by-four churches, which meet in
> some private houses and hold some sort of hugger-mugger proceedings intended to
> launch a new sect of worshippers upon a world already too full of a confusion of
> tongues and creeds. . . .
>
> The leader of a two-by-four church is a man with the gift of gab and some de-
> gree or personal magnetism, too lazy to work at an honest trade, but loth to starve.
> He gathers around him a number of followers, mostly women, who hang upon his
> words as a divine inspiration, and deem it a privilege to support him in idleness.
>
> The moral is, of course, to stick to the established churches that are founded
> upon the doctrines of Christianity. The two-by-four church, with its lazy leader,
> should be shunned by all decent people.
>
> New York is not the only city that has an overstock of "isms," new and old. The
> bay cities have more than their share. Some of these fellows who are living off of the

earnings of the poor washwoman, and who are able to go on a thousand or more miles pleasure trip annually, should be splitting rails or clearing away the sage brush in the Imperial Valley.[14]

Ken Anderson, a member of Mount Olive Church of God in Christ in San Diego, states that Pentecostals traditionally have resisted interaction with individuals of other denominations but says changes have begun to take place in recent years:

> Our church (the COGIC), I think, has been plagued by the same traditional limitations. . . . Recently we've begun to move away from traditional things. [We had] traditional attitudes about people who perhaps weren't dressed like we think they should be dressed. [These were] the barriers we put up to keep certain people out. In the church we want to reach people, but sometimes we are so holy, until just by that, we keep others out. Some people . . . feel that they couldn't live up. Most of them just stay out simply because it just doesn't feel right to them. They say it's kind of snobbish or holier-than-thou.[15]

Betty Gadling, who has been affiliated with Baptist churches all of her life, states,

> There used to be a thing where you weren't supposed to go to Pentecostal churches. At that time, churches were much more separate than what they are now. They [Baptists] weren't supposed to go to a Pentecostal church because it wasn't the right church. They weren't Baptists, and the Baptists were biblically based because John the Baptist baptized Jesus Christ.
>
> We weren't supposed to go to them either because they did not get immersed [into the water for baptism]. That was quite a division thing with the churches. Everybody claimed to be THE CHURCH. And they just got away from that.[16]

The date that Pentecostals established churches in other California cities is not known, but by 1916 the Church of God in Christ in San Diego had a thriving religious community,[17] and by the 1920s there were at least two Pentecostal churches in the San Francisco Bay Area.[18] In addition, many blacks attended white churches, where they were accepted as members but were not given the opportunity to take on leadership roles.[19]

Newspaper articles from the first few decades of the twentieth century indicate that the religious music of urban blacks in California differed little from that performed by African Americans in other cities in the United States. Hymns, spirituals, jubilees, anthems, and European art music constituted the repertoire of most established, or so-called middle-class, black churches.[20] Accolades were given to musicians who had studied at institutions such as Fisk University or had obtained a certificate from a European organization.[21] Radio programs of sacred music featured spirituals, anthems, and folk songs by local soloists and choirs.[22] Singing groups affiliated with schools from the South—e.g., the Tuskegee Institute Singers (Alabama), Fisk Jubilee Singers (Tennessee), Camps Normal and Industrial

School Singers (Texas), the Samuel Houston College Singers (Texas), or the Prairie View Singers (Texas)—as well as professional quartets and choruses often traveled to California and gave performances throughout the state.[23] One San Francisco newspaper account about a visitor from Los Angeles who sang spirituals noted: "The down-home atmosphere is produced when the spirituals of our race are played and sung during the communion service. Mrs. Helena Smith of Los Angeles sang 'O, mourner, don't you weep when you see that ship come sailing over.'"[24]

Large-scale community events took place at prominent churches or in city auditoriums. People's Independent Church of Christ in Los Angeles (formed in 1915 by N. P. Greggs) was noted for its musical extravaganzas.[25] In the San Francisco Bay Area, several church choirs from the community competed at the Municipal Auditorium in Oakland.[26]

A significant amount of interchange occurred between black Californians and African Americans who lived in different parts of the country. It was not uncommon for ministers and evangelists from other cities to preach in California or for blacks in California to travel to conventions and events in the East and Midwest.[27] The interaction with groups from various parts of the country not only helped Californians to maintain contact with past traditions but also allowed individuals to exchange ideas and be introduced to new modes of cultural expression. For example, Californians who attended a special music concert featured at the National Baptist Convention in Denver, Colorado, on September 14, 1927, had an opportunity to experience and take pride in a part of their heritage that was probably foreign to them. An article in the Bay Area newspaper *Western American* sums up the significance of the event:

> Strident melodies and insistent rhythms of the Congo, softened through a long evolution wrought by years of chanting in the back woods of the Southern United States will be heard in Denver September 14. . . .
>
> Songs hitherto unknown outside the isolated groups worshipping in little pine churches on the edges of Alabama's swamps, in the depths of Arkansas' forests and in the midst of Georgia's cotton fields, will be sung for the first time before a representative audience.
>
> From the throats of 500 negro choristers the plaintive spirituals will throb with religious fervor through Denver's largest auditorium to make a definite contribution to America's musical history.
>
> Skilled musicians will be present to set down upon paper the melodies as they issue forth from the choir. Lyricists, too, will attend, to interpret the almost spontaneous words into verses suitable for publication.[28]

GOSPEL MUSIC HISTORY

African-American gospel music evolved as a musical form during the early twentieth century, when southerners began migrating to urban areas in search of greater economic opportunities and freedom. Once in the city, many found the rural-born spiritual to be unsatisfactory and unresponsive to their needs. Thus, a more expressive, urban form of black music came into being. The term "gospel" was applied to this genre, but it had only slight resemblance to gospel hymns of whites. Sung in an improvisational style with instrumental accompaniment, gospel gave solace and uplifted people in difficult times. It was a sacred counterpart to city blues.[29]

Although Philadelphia minister Charles A. Tindley (1851–1933) was an important figure in the early development of African-American gospel, the form crystallized during the thirties with the music of Thomas A. Dorsey (1899–1993), who is called the "father" of gospel music. Dorsey was born in northern Georgia and raised in the Baptist Church but decided to become a blues musician in his youth. During the twenties, he led his own jazz band and was a successful blues composer; he worked extensively with blues artists Gertrude "Ma" Rainey and Tampa Red (born Hudson Whitaker). When Dorsey returned to the church after surviving several life crises,[30] his experience with blues and jazz influenced his gospel compositions, which caused his religious music to be unacceptable to churchgoers, particularly those who attended established black churches. However, Dorsey's songs, like those by Tindley, were popular among black Pentecostals, who used them as models for their freely improvised congregational songs. In spite of gospel's nonacceptance by some, Dorsey became one of the leading promoters of gospel music and established several gospel organizations in Chicago, where he was based.

In California, the term "gospel" was used very loosely by the public before and during the thirties. Generally, it was applied only to "gospel preaching" or to hymns such as "Pass It On" or "Rock of Ages." The spirited jubilees and congregational songs in the character of early slave music were rarely heard in established churches, but this type of music continued to be used in Pentecostal and storefront Baptist churches. However, the performance style of "gospel" songs in the thirties was different from the music that later came to be known as gospel music. Don Lee White, a native of Los Angeles who is a church choir director, organist, and former professor of music at California State University, Los Angeles, explains:

> Back then, most gospel you heard were gospel hymns. There were the hymns like "Power and the Blood," "Brighten the Corner," "Dwelling in Beulah Land," or something that had a little rhythm to go with it—a rhythm that was changed from the printed score.
>
> Most of the time, it [the music] was accompanied with just piano. There was a little improvisation. They had the rhythm, maybe a few arpeggios or so. But most of it was basically chordal structures with a few octave runs. The accompaniment was really subservient to the singing; it didn't overshadow the singing as we hear it now.
>
> The gospel singers during that period would sing a few traditional religious songs on their program, like "The Lord's Prayer," the "Beatitudes," or "The Twenty-third Psalm." I presume that most of them had heard this music, and they were fairly well-trained vocally. So it wasn't just all gospel.[31]

During the thirties and early forties, a differentiation could be seen in the development and performance of black sacred music in various areas in California, attributable mainly to varying migration trends. Some support for gospel music had been garnered during the thirties and forties, but this did not happen in all areas of the state. Most of the activity occurred in Los Angeles, which had the largest black population. There is no evidence to indicate that individuals in other parts of the state performed gospel to any large extent in the 1930s.

Regardless of the setting, gospel musicians who traveled West had difficulty finding audiences. Blacks in urban California, like African Americans in other cities in the United States, did not readily accept this new style of singing. Many African Americans were concerned with upward mobility and preferred the more European-sounding hymns, anthems, and concert spirituals for worship rather than the African-based gospel music, which was often performed with much emotionalism and improvisation. Those who performed the former tended to be Western-educated singers with substantial training and instruction in European art music.[32] In ensembles, they sang a cappella in four-part harmony, with a clear, operalike vocal quality. The latter was music of the folk, marked by rhythms with body motions, grace notes, sliding intonation, extensive rhythmic and melodic variations, and instrumental accompaniment (drums, tambourines, etc.). White explains that in Pentecostal churches, which more than other religious denominations embodied the musical and cultural expressions of the folk,[33] "there was a lot of congregational singing. A lot of gospel hymns were not really gospel hymns, but they were kind of like old jubilee spirituals."[34] Therefore, whereas groups that performed the established forms (e.g., the Fisk Jubilee Singers, the Samuel Houston College Singers, the Prairie View Singers, and the Hall Johnson Choir) were welcomed, the same could not be said for gospel musicians.[35]

As black migration increased, the social fabric of urban areas in California changed, and new cultural traditions were brought into communities. Because social conditions and the dynamics of change affected the development of gospel music differently in various parts of the state, each area will be examined individually.

Los Angeles

Most of the activity in the early history of gospel music in California occurred in Los Angeles, where traveling evangelists and musicians often performed. Interestingly, most came from the South and the Midwest, particularly Chicago. J. C. Austin (1887–1968), pastor of Pilgrim Baptist Church in Chicago, and gospel pioneers Sallie Martin (1896–1988; see Figure 4.1) and Thomas Dorsey frequented the Los Angeles area, performing in concerts and conducting singing revivals. Once the gospel territory had been colonized, other established artists—e.g., Robert Anderson (1919–96), R. L. Knowles (1915–71), and the Roberta Martin

Figure 4.1. Gospel singer Sallie Martin (Los Angeles). Courtesy of Albert A. Goodson.

(1907–69) Singers—appeared in Los Angeles during the late 1930s and early 1940s.[36]

The growth of gospel music during the thirties and forties can be attributed in large part to the support that it received from various churches and the radio. Not only was it performed in Pentecostal and some Baptist churches, but other Protestant denominations also organized gospel choirs and sponsored gospel artists. People's Independent Church of Christ, which established one of the first gospel choirs (the N. P. Greggs Gospel Choir), became an important institution for the performance of all types of sacred music. New Hope Baptist and Phillips Temple

Colored Methodist Episcopal (CME) often had programs, and several churches organized gospel singing groups: Phillips Temple; Zion Hill Baptist; Bethel Church of Christ, Holiness; Progressive Baptist; and Emmanuel Church of God in Christ.[37]

Another trend was the growing professionalism among local gospel musicians. Although artists and groups such as the Three Sons of Thunder (Arthur Atlas Peters, Eugene Douglass Smallwood, and Earl Amos Pleasant), the E-Flat Gospel Singers, the Radio Four Gospel Singers, the Cornerstone Quartet, and the Carter Sisters never received national acclaim, they were considered stars in their hometown. Peters, Pleasant, Smallwood, and Nathan John Kirkpatrick (a singer from Long Beach, California), who occasionally sang with them, not only performed as solo artists but also directed church choirs.[38] Many of these performers were born in the South and formally trained in European art music, and these roots were reflected in their performance of gospel.[39] Thus, their gospel singing did not include much rhythmic and melodic variation.[40] Gwendolyn Cooper Lightner, who moved to Los Angeles from Chicago during the mid-1940s, describes the music community in Los Angeles during the beginnings of gospel:

> I opened the studio [Los Angeles Gospel Music Mart] and managed it. Then I . . . started to teach in the studio. There were many young people, old people, middle-aged, choir directors. Everybody was coming, because they wanted to learn how to play this music I was playing. It wasn't any gospel singers here. Rev. Peters was a gospel singer. Rev. Pleasant, and Rev. Kirkpatrick from Long Beach, and another gentleman. . . . But they did the gospel in a different way than our gospel in Chicago.
>
>   They had the gift to sing. They weren't doing a lot of [up]tempo numbers, but they sang "Precious Lord." Rev. Peters sang "The Little Wooden Church on the Hill." Now that was a gospel number written by Professor Dorsey. They did it in their style.[41]
>
>   There's a difference in what the Holiness beat was than the true gospel. Even though the Holiness can play gospel, they had the Sanctified beat. The gospel beat that Mr. Dorsey created was a different beat, but it was in the same likeness and form. Gospel music isn't necessarily fast music.[42]

On occasion, organizers of radio broadcasts featured gospel artists, as I have noted elsewhere:

> As early as 1939 a program known as the Gold Hour was heard over radio station KGFJ nightly at 6:30 pm. Sponsored by the Gold Furniture Company . . . , the program featured Floyd G. Covington as Master of Ceremonies. Mrs. A.C.H. Bilbrew, the organizer and director of the programs, instituted a gospel song night on each Wednesday evening as part of the weekly series. Initially, Norris J. Stokes, a local performer, was the featured guest. In subsequent shows other artists and groups were presented, e.g., Arthur A. Peters and His Gospel Four, the Four Harmonizer Quartet, Phillips Temple Gospel Choir (William Smallwood, director), Earl A. Pleasant, and the Women's Chorus of the Church of Christ Holiness (Mrs. O'Connor, director).[43]

In summary, gospel music in Los Angeles during the thirties and early forties was dominated by visitors, primarily from the Chicago area and the South, who traveled to the city introducing the tradition. Although several local churches established gospel choirs and the media provided some support, gospel music still was not wholeheartedly accepted by the black populace.

Local performers who made names for themselves singing gospel music in various churches during the thirties and early forties later organized and became pastors of their own churches during the mid-forties. Men such as Peters (formed Victory Baptist in 1943), Pleasant (formed Mount Moriah Baptist in 1945), and Smallwood (formed Opportunity Baptist in 1946) felt that change in religious worship and music could be initiated more effectively if they were in positions of authority. The support their churches provided helped the gospel tradition to experience enormous growth. These institutions became important centers in the social and cultural life of black Angelenos.

Also in the forties, churches that had been founded in the early 1900s took on new leadership. These new pastors not only were more responsive to the needs and desires of the new black immigrants but also had different ideas about black music and worship. William Jack Taylor, who was installed as pastor of Grace Memorial Church of God in Christ in 1941, and John L. Branham,[44] who became pastor of St. Paul Baptist in 1946, were among the innovators who introduced and implemented traditions that altered the performance and development of black sacred music in Los Angeles.

The events that took place at St. Paul are significant because they gave impetus to the gospel music tradition in Los Angeles during the forties. Coming from Chicago, Branham knew much about the style of gospel that was unique to the Midwest and the performers who were recognized for this music. Therefore, he hired two musicians—James Earle Hines, a nationally known gospel singer and choir director (see Figure 4.2), and Gwendolyn Cooper Lightner, a young gospel pianist who had also lived in Chicago and performed with established gospel musicians in that city—to develop his gospel music program.[45] What resulted was the Echoes of Eden Choir, a group organized in 1946 by Hines and Lightner that grew to more than one hundred voices. The choir made its radio debut in February 1947 on KFWB, the Warner Bros. station, with Joe Adams as producer and announcer. The program, which broadcast from 10:30 to 11:30 p.m., was eventually heard in seventeen states and had a listening audience of one million people, the largest on the West Coast.[46] Lightner describes the popularity of the program: "People came from every where. We had people [celebrities] like Hattie McDaniels, Louise Beaver, Joe Louis. Nat King Cole[47] was a friend of Rev. Branham. People would crowd into that church on Sunday night. They would get there early because we started at 10:30. And they would come to early service like at eight [o'clock] to get a good seat."[48]

Albert Goodson,[49] a Los Angeles native who, as a young man, performed with

Figure 4.2. J. Earle Hines and His Goodwill Singers (Los Angeles). Top left—clockwise:
James Earle Hines, Wilbert Pritchard, Ruth Black, Gwendolyn Cooper Lightner, and
Ernie Gladney, 1950s. Courtesy of Gwendolyn Lightner.

the Echoes of Eden Choir during the forties and fifties, describes the impact St.
Paul had on the Los Angeles community. In addition, he explains that the night
service at St. Paul was similar to one that took place in Chicago:

> In Los Angeles, most of the people here were singing hymns and very little gospel
> music. Mr. Hines was one of the first here with this new sound and this new type of
> singing. And he was an excellent singer too. St. Paul had five to seven soloists who
> could sing excellently. With all of this new music and this new sound, the voices grew

to 250 voices and nobody had ever heard a sound like that in this city. It was just something new and just made people flock.

You would have to be at St. Paul at seven or eight o'clock to get in and get a seat for the broadcast. That shows you how popular it was. The church could seat about 400 to 500 in that area. It was located at 21st and Naomi. They built this new church over here at 49th and Main [St. Paul moved in 1951], which was one of the prettiest churches at that time here in the city because it had the curtains going up like show business on stage when the choir was sitting down. The pulpit went down to the floor. People had never seen that before. So they came from far and near to see that church and hear that choir. It was just outstanding in this city. It [late-night service] was copied after a church in Chicago—Rev. Clarence Cobbs' The First Church of Deliverance.[50]

The musical training of Hines and Lightner is noteworthy, for although their backgrounds differed from those of some early gospel performers, such as Sallie Martin, their profiles were typical for gospel musicians in Los Angles during the 1930s and 1940s. Both attended music schools, were professionally trained in European art music, and did not become interested in performing gospel music until later in their careers. Also, Hines's work with the National Baptist Convention had provided him with experience and visibility prior to his arrival in Los Angeles. Lightner's piano style, which was different from that used by most early performers of gospel in Los Angeles, made such an impact that Eugene Smallwood called her "the one who put the 'ump' in gospel playing. Others played it as they saw it, but she's the one whose fingers interpreted the soul of the gospel music. She's about the 'Queen of Gospel' when it comes down to playing."[51]

The performance of gospel music at St. Paul set a standard of excellence for other religious institutions in the city. Eventually, St. Paul became a center for the performance of gospel music, and the Echoes of Eden was one of the first church choirs in the United States to popularize gospel music and make commercial recordings—"I'm So Glad Jesus Lifted Me" (Capitol 40018) in April 1947, "What Could I Do if It Wasn't for the Lord?" (Capitol 40076) in June 1947.[52] In the 1950s the choir made an album, *Revival Day: The St. Paul Church Choir of Los Angeles* (Capitol T791). St. Paul's notoriety inspired churches elsewhere in the community and the state to establish choirs, radio programs, and even television broadcasts. For example, the Voices of Victory Choir, under the direction of Thurston Gilbert Frazier,[53] performed on a weekly television program (KTTV, Channel 11) during the 1950s and made various recordings in later years, giving Victory Baptist Church enormous visibility and recognition (see Figure 4.3).[54]

In addition to the increase in the number of churches promoting gospel music, other indicators demonstrated that the tradition had expanded. The number of gospel artists and groups in Los Angeles grew tremendously during the forties and fifties. Not only did visiting artists (the Original Gospel Harmonettes, the Pilgrim Travelers, and the Sallie Martin Singers)[55] find means to reside in the city over long periods of time, but groups that originated elsewhere—the Crisp Brothers

God Willed It So

Words and Music
by
Rev. Albert Goodson

DEDICATED IN MEMORY
OF A GOSPEL GIANT
THURSTON GILBERT FRAZIER

$1.00

Published by Rev. Albert Goodson
3434 West 41st Street, Los Angeles, CA 90008

Figure 4.3. Gospel director, singer, and composer Thurston Gilbert Frazier on front cover of music score, "God Willed It So," by Albert A. Goodson, 1974 (Los Angeles). Courtesy of Albert A. Goodson.

(from Arizona), the Jubilaires (from Florida), the Kansas City Soul Revivers of Los Angeles (from Missouri), the Paul Quinn Singers (from Texas), and the Stars of Harmony (from Texas)—settled in Los Angeles permanently. Some of the groups organized in Los Angeles during this period include the Caravans of Los Angeles, the Chosen Gospel Singers, the Dave Weston Singers, the Ebony Echoes, the Golden Jubilee Singers, the Gospel Pearls, J. Earle Hines and His Goodwill

Singers, the Macedonians, the Simmons-Akers Singers, the Spiritual Five, the Victory Trio, the West Coast Jubilees, and the Zion Travelers.[56]

Most of the groups were composed of males and performed in a hard, driving style with a great deal of emphasis on rhythm, a style very similar to the quartet tradition that originated in southern states. The Simmons-Akers Singers (formed in 1948 by Dorothy Simmons and Doris Akers)[57] were one of the few nationally known Los Angeles groups that included only women. Their performance style was distinct because it was lyrical, with heavy emphasis on melody. Charles Johnson, a well-known gospel choir director who migrated to Los Angeles from Texas in the 1960s, states, "Doris's style of music is a Euro-Western kind of gospel. It's a very smooth form. The [European] rules of music greatly influenced what Doris [and her group] sings. Pretty, soft soprano voice. Very smooth, not the rough gospel sound. Very refined, a white kind of sound."[58]

In addition to quartets and small groups, community choirs had become an important medium for the performance of gospel music by the early 1950s. Following in the tradition started by Smallwood and Pleasant,[59] several large community choirs were organized. The Venerable-Smallwood Gospel Singers were formed by Smallwood and E. B. Venerable during the late forties,[60] and the Hines Goodwill Choir, with Frazier serving as Hines's assistant, was started in the fifties.[61]

A number of black Angelenos were composers who established their own publishing companies.[62] Eugene D. Smallwood is the earliest known composer-publisher of gospel music in Los Angeles. Probably because of his training in European music, Smallwood, unlike his counterparts elsewhere in the United States, not only scored his own sheet music, he prepared it fully (see Figure 4.4) rather than just providing a skeleton score (see Example 4.1). As the publishing of gospel music became a profitable business, Specialty Records (a white-owned company based in Los Angeles),[63] along with other black- and white-owned record companies in the city, began to record both Los Angeles–based artists and those who traveled to the city. Specialty used its subsidiary, Venice Music, to publish songs that were recorded and produced on its label. Kenneth Morris, owner of the Chicago publishing firm Martin and Morris Music Studio, arranged and exclusively distributed virtually all the songs recorded by Venice. Specialty was also involved in the promotion of concert tours by Los Angeles musicians through Herald Attractions, Incorporated, with Lillian Cumber as manager.[64]

The large number of quartets and choirs, as well as the enormous amount of activity that resulted from their many performances, led to the establishment of gospel unions, such as Sallie Martin's Los Angeles Gospel Choral Union and a branch of the national Interdenominational Singers Alliance, formed in 1946.[65] Events normally held on the East Coast or in the Midwest (the National Convention of Gospel Choirs and Choruses, the National Baptist Convention)[66] took place in Los Angeles more often. Gospel music performances began to occur outside the church setting more frequently—for example, Thomas Dorsey gave a

Figure 4.4. Gospel singer and composer Eugene D. Smallwood on the front cover of the score of his music composition, "Whither Shall I Go—If I Go?" 1942 (Los Angeles). Courtesy of Eugene D. Smallwood.

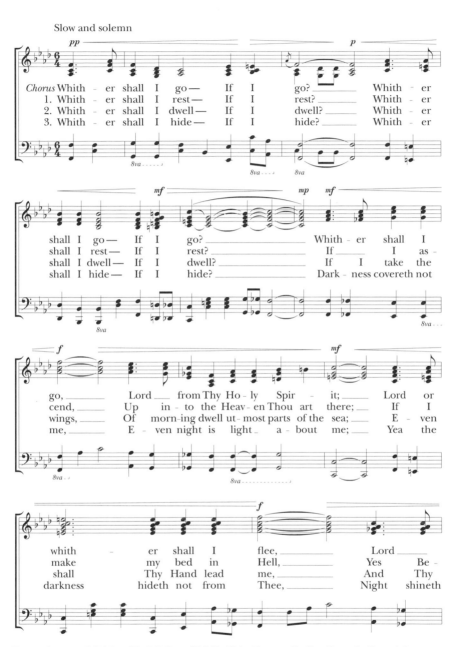

Example 4.1. "Whither Shall I Go—If I Go?" by Eugene D. Smallwood. Copyright 1942 by Eugene D. Smallwood, 10513 South Vermont Ave., Los Angeles, CA 90044.

Example 4.1.   *(continued)*

concert at Wrigley Stadium in 1946, and Herald Attractions' Gospelcade was held at the Embassy Auditorium in 1953.[67]

A distinctive performance style came to be associated with Los Angeles as black Angelenos were heard in the media, at concerts, and in conventions across the United States. Songs recorded by the Echoes of Eden Choir ("God Be with You," "Yield Not to Temptation," and "I'm So Glad Jesus Lifted Me") became signature pieces that others emulated. Though many of the songs had some melodic variation and a lively rhythm with piano and organ accompaniment, there was not a lot of emphasis on rhythm or extensive improvisation, as one would hear in the Pentecostal tradition. Lightner explains the uniqueness of the Los Angeles gospel sound:

> They say I'm a classical gospel musician. They say they can still see [hear] that touch. There's a different touch in my music. Los Angeles singers are a little bit different from Chicago. They [people in Chicago] still, in some instances, are the best, but Los Angeles [has] a little tinge or sparkle that's a little bit different than just the down-home gospel music. There've been so many people who have come in here and between the people that are still in the classical . . . when you mix it together . . . I think it has a tinge of "classical."[68]

Not only were new religious institutions established, but older ones were revitalized in response to the growth of gospel music. Weekly and monthly gospel programs were held. Service organizations were formed to meet the needs of gospel artists. Agents, promoters, disc jockeys, and others in the music business began to realize the commercial potential of black music. More important, gospel performers in Los Angeles became "stars." Foremost among these individuals was J. Earle Hines. Thus, gospel came to be regarded as an art form in its own right, a form that eventually became independent of the institution from which it evolved.

Changes in the larger black community in Los Angeles during the late 1950s and 1960s made an impact on the music world. Increased socioeconomic opportunities caused more gospel artists to migrate to Los Angeles. They came not only from the South and Midwest but also from the East (for example, Clara Ward and the Ward Singers). By the mid-1960s gospel music had become so much a part of

the city that a 1964 issue of the *Los Angeles Sentinel* included a series of articles entitled, "The New Music: Los Angeles Nears Goal of 'Gospel Capital of World.'"[69]
Thus, gospel had become a prominent part of both the sacred and secular music
communities.

The status of the gospel musician in Los Angeles was one of the major factors that affected the development of the genre during this period. Although
many of the individuals who migrated during the fifties and sixties had already
attained some renown before their move, the Los Angeles environment allowed
them the opportunity to achieve even greater recognition. After moving to the
city, some became nationally or internationally known. Among these were Bessie
Griffin, James Cleveland, Margaret Aikens-Jenkins, Clara Ward and the Ward
Singers, Isaiah Jones, Cassietta George, and Raymond Rasberry.[70] More important, Los Angeles natives achieved notoriety for their contributions. Artists
such as Albert A. Goodson (Figure 4.5), Margaret Pleasant Douroux, and Andraé Crouch are just a few who rose to fame because of their compositions and
recordings.[71]

Community choirs, quartets, and small groups continued to be popular during
the late fifties and sixties. As in earlier periods, a number of groups were formed.
In 1956 Harrison A. Johnson, a student at Los Angeles City College, formed the
Los Angeles Community Choir at the request of Joseph Matthews, a local disc
jockey who wanted a dependable group to show up for programs. More than 200
voices performed in the choir's first appearance. This success led to several recordings and television appearances. In later years, Johnson worked closely with
James Cleveland and the Southern California Community Choir, which was organized in the late sixties.[72]

Originally formed by Thurston Frazier and Gwendolyn Cooper Lightner in
1957 to raise funds for the March of Dimes, the Voices of Hope became nationally
known. In addition to releasing two recordings with Capitol Records (*We've Come
This Far by Faith*[73] and *Walk on by Faith*), the group made appearances in churches
and auditoriums throughout the country, on television, and at amusement parks
(e.g., Disneyland) in the area.[74] Because of Lightner's and Frazier's influence in
various religious and music conventions around the country, the performance style
of the Voices of Hope became prominent. Songs such as "We've Come This Far
by Faith," "The Beautiful Garden of Prayer," and "Jesus" were commonly used by
church choirs in places as far away as Georgia. Like the Echoes of Eden Choir
and the Simmons-Akers Singers, the Voices of Hope placed heavy emphasis on
melody without extensive variation or intense rhythms.[75]

Los Angeles was a haven for gospel singing groups in the fifties and sixties. The
COGICS, the Golden Jubilee Singers, the Gospel Consolaters, the Ladies of
Song, the Los Angeles Gospel Chimes, the Melody Kings, the Mighty Clouds of
Joy, and the Sweet Singing Cavaliers are just some of the small groups associated
with Los Angeles during this period. The Mighty Clouds of Joy, formed in 1960,[76]
became one of the few Los Angeles quartets to attain international fame. The

Figure 4.5. Gospel composer, director, and organist Albert A. Goodson, 1970 (Los Angeles). Courtesy of Albert A. Goodson.

group has released more than twenty-five albums and makes at least 200 appearances worldwide in a typical year. Though the Clouds' music appeals to pop, jazz, and rhythm and blues audiences, their press releases indicate that "they still maintain their message."[77] Like other performers from this period, the Clouds have received numerous awards, made many television appearances, and performed regularly at sacred and secular festivals.[78] Funk states, "In 1963, they were proclaimed the number one gospel group in America."[79]

By the late sixties, gospel music and musicians had become so much a part of the city that Los Angeles emerged as a national center.[80] The meaning of gospel music also broadened. Though many regarded it as a vehicle for worship, others, particularly nonchurchgoers and individuals who were not part of the black folk community, appreciated it as an art form. For some, the sound itself was at least as important as the message.

As the gospel music industry grew, artists no longer depended solely on religious institutions for support. Other, more lucrative sources of income became available. These opportunities included recording contracts, record sales, television, Broadway and nightclub appearances, films, national and international tours, festivals, cavalcades, extravaganzas, and other events outside the normal realm of the church. One of the reasons Bessie Griffin moved to Los Angeles in 1959 was to perform in the gospel musical *Portraits in Bronze* by Robert "Bumps" Blackwell (her agent); the production combined jazz, blues, and gospel. Later, with a group called the Gospel Pearls, Griffin became both a nightclub and television performer, appearing on *Shindig* and as a guest on shows hosted by Dinah Shore, Danny Kaye, Steve Allen, and Ed Sullivan. Although her performances in nightclubs were criticized by churchgoers, she continued to perform in secular venues because she wanted "to provide a niche for herself. After living in the shadow of Mahalia Jackson for so long, she wanted to make Bessie Griffin unique."[81]

By now, Los Angeles gospel musicians were celebrities. Anything that affected their personal lives—illness, death in the family, marriage—became front-page news, which was a departure from newspaper accounts during the thirties and forties. Also, many more tributes in honor of gospel musicians were presented during the sixties than in any other period. No longer were church officials and gospel musicians the primary organizers of events. Music industry figures entered the field, for they saw gospel as a viable business venture. True, such individuals had existed from the earliest days of gospel music, but during this period there were more of them, and they were involved on a number of different levels—from the creation to the production and distribution of the product.

Los Angeles has a rich history of gospel music, rivaling other locales in terms of its impact on the genre as a whole. Some gospel musicians in Los Angeles were regarded as innovators. The factors that most affected the development of gospel in Los Angeles were churches, individuals, and the media. Without the support of churches and various organizations, individuals such as J. Earle Hines, Gwendolyn Cooper Lightner, and Thurston Frazier would not have had the opportunity to develop their talents. Once their talents were recognized and gospel music had been accepted, artists such as Doris Akers, Bessie Griffin, James Cleveland, and others used the media to the extent that they became national stars. During the 1960s they traveled across the United States and the world, introducing innovative styles and setting new trends.

San Francisco Bay Area

It is difficult to tell when gospel music became a dominant force in the San Francisco Bay Area. Not only is documented evidence from the early years lacking,[82] but few people can recall the performance of the music prior to the 1940s, indicating that the genre probably did not make much of an impact during the early 1900s. In the thirties and early forties, traveling musicians and evangelists visited the area for performances; a few even settled.[83] Little change occurred in the type of music that was used in churches. Those in Pentecostal churches continued to perform jubilees and congregational songs, and Baptists, Methodists, and other religious groups maintained repertoires of hymns, anthems, and spirituals. The music performed by community groups provides insight about the type of music that may have been heard in churches. The Oakland Colored Chorus, formed in 1935 by William Elmer Keeton (a music teacher, conductor, and composer who arrived in Oakland in 1921),[84] featured concert spirituals, European art music, and selections from Broadway musicals. With funds from the Works Progress Administration, Keeton transformed a core group of five singers, whom he recruited from black church choirs in the East Bay, into a sixty-voice chorus that performed throughout California.[85]

Although gospel may not have been widely accepted or prominently used in most church services, some Bay Area worshipers took great pride in their congregation's musical assets, as seen in a 1938 newspaper report about Mount Pleasant Baptist Church in Berkeley: "The choir under the direction of Mrs. Bessie Mack has made great success. Peace and harmony seems [sic] to be the order of the day in this splendid choir and much improvement can be seen in these Gospel singers. Miss Willie Mae Johnson has just returned from Chicago visiting relatives and friends."[86] The inference is that since Ms. Johnson's return from her visit to Chicago,[87] there had been a significant improvement in the choir's ability to sing gospel music. Otherwise, why would the writer even mention that the choir member had been to Chicago? The statement also demonstrates the type of musical communication that took place among gospel performers at that time.

The relative dearth of gospel music in the Bay Area can be attributed to several factors. As noted, the black population in Northern California did not increase as dramatically as that of Los Angeles during the same period. Whereas Los Angeles had a large influx of immigrants who brought in new cultural traditions, Bay Area residents maintained the same type of lifestyle that had existed in previous years. Historian Lawrence Crouchett, who moved with his family into the Bay Area from Texas in 1939, states: "People lived everywhere. There was no so-called black community. It was a black community on the psychological level, but geographically there was not. The only so-called black institutions were the black nightclubs and churches. And there weren't that many people."[88]

Even more important was the mentality and attitude of blacks who lived in the Bay Area. In the thirties and early forties, Crouchett states, "the difference between San Francisco and Oakland was just like the difference between here [Bay Area] and Los Angeles. There was very little communication between the two groups. People in San Francisco stayed over there, and people over here [East Bay] stayed here. San Francisco was the monied class in the old times, and so just being there made you in a different class. Oakland was the so-called blue-collar community."[89] Yet it should be noted that many who lived in Oakland had migrated from San Francisco during the early 1900s. Betty Reid Soskin,[90] a Berkeley record-store owner who moved to the Bay Area from Louisiana in 1925, explains:

> It was an interesting childhood, because this area of California had so few blacks in it that it was pre-segregation. All of the blacks in the Bay Area could be gotten into the Oakland Auditorium. And we were spread all over. We were not living in particular districts so that our lives were somewhat unreal in a lot of ways. We came together from all parts of the area socially by choice. We saw our connectedness as blacks. But there were no areas where we had to be in, there were no schools we had to attend. There wasn't a consciousness around church for black folks. It was something you did, but I don't remember it as being that profound.[91]

Whether Bay Area residents had significant, long-term contact with gospel musicians from the Chicago area is not known, but it seems doubtful considering that there was little support for the tradition among individuals living in the Bay Area. When asked about the beginnings of gospel music in the Bay Area, Soskin states:

> During the middle and late forties, because the whole gospel movement was imported along with the black population as people came in to deal with the war. Those people who came from fundamentalist black churches in the South began to establish fundamentalist black churches on the West Coast. And during that period, the music that we began to hear publicly was a music we didn't hear as kids, because there were so few black churches.
> But that happened very fast. I mean it was just explosive, absolutely explosive. And these were largely people without a lot of status. . . . For the most part, these were people who came from farms and were people who had nothing to lose. But they did have a strong need for one another, a strong need to establish roots. And so storefront churches began to crop up all over the place. And gospel music came with that.[92]

Newspaper accounts include mention of Lillian Glenn Smith, who moved to the San Francisco Bay Area in the 1940s. Born in a small town (Kaufman) near Dallas, Texas, Smith became a celebrity in the Bay Area for her gospel singing in the late forties and early fifties. She generally sang on occasions when her husband (the Rev. H. R. Smith, pastor of New Hope Baptist Church) preached, but she also was affiliated with Temple of Truth Baptist Church.[93] According to Joyce Beasley, "Lillian Glenn Smith used to sing 'Drop Your Net and Follow Me.' The woman could roll her tongue better than anybody. We used to walk around and try to mimic her, but we couldn't do it. She was one of the noted gospel solo singers that we, as youngsters, could attribute [relate] to. She was like our mentor."[94] Like many performers, Smith took a circuitous route to the world of gospel. After studying voice for two years at Paul Quinn College in Waco, Texas, Smith was invited to perform blues. Eventually she was headlining shows at theaters in the South and had a contract with Columbia Records. By the late 1920s, Smith was a popular vaudeville singer who had composed and recorded several blues hits.[95]

The San Francisco Bay Area did not attract nationally known gospel stars as permanent residents. Rather, it was a setting in which local talent was nurtured through support from community institutions and visiting artists, who served as role models. In addition to Lillian Holmes, who was a well-known local solo artist, a few Bay Area residents performed with established gospel musicians; Charlie Mae Haynes was a member of the Sallie Martin Singers, and Odessa Perkins became one of the Ward Singers during the 1960s.[96] Small groups and quartets dominated the gospel music community from the 1940s through the 1960s. Betty Gadling states that some quartets "were allowed to sing at the churches. They had late night programs. Groups, trios, women quartets and things like that drew large crowds."[97]

Groups could be categorized into three types: 1) traveling musicians or visiting artists, 2) local independent groups, and 3) local groups that were affiliated with a church or another organization. Though many of the visiting groups and artists came from Los Angeles (e.g., J. Earle Hines and His Goodwill Singers, the Simmons-Akers Singers, the Sallie Martin Singers, and Cora Martin), performers from the Midwest and East also frequented the area, including C. L. Franklin and daughter Aretha, the Clara Ward Singers, the Davis Singers, Joe May, Mahalia Jackson, the O'Neal Twins, the Pilgrim Travelers, the Raymond Rasberry Singers, the Soul Stirrers, and the Staple Singers.

Many of the independent local groups traveled from church to church within the San Francisco Bay Area, but a few made efforts to reach larger audiences. The Paramount Singers, a men's quartet, originally formed in 1936 in Austin, Texas, and reorganized in 1944 when the members moved to San Francisco. After the move to the West Coast, the Paramount Singers performed in the Bay Area and Southern California, recorded in Hollywood in 1948, and, during the late forties and early fifties, had a regular radio broadcast on KWBR in Oakland and Berkeley.

Another local independent group, the Original Joy Spreaders of Oakland, was organized during the mid-1950s. Although the personnel changed from time to time, the core members included Estelle Vasser, Dorothy Cotton, Jimmie Bowie, Joyce Beasley, Joyce Copeland, and Doris A. Barber.[98] As a teenager, Edwin Hawkins, now regarded as the "father of contemporary gospel music," served as their piano accompanist. Beasley states, "When Ed was playing, it was a very unique situation because he could only play in one key and that was F-sharp. So we all sang in F-sharp. When you begin to see a man become famous and he's playing in all keys now, I have to tease him from time to time. Later we changed from him to Roger Payne. But Ed had that sound that was much different."[99]

Other independent groups from the Bay Area included Brother Green's Southern Sons, the California Wonders, the Choraleers, the Choralites, the Golden Keyes, the Golden Stars, the Golden West Gospel Singers, the Gospel Clouds, the Gospel Tonics, the Mighty Serenaders, the Nightingale Jubilaires, the Nunley Singers, the Oakland All Stars, the Oakland Silvertones, the Omega Aires, the Rising Stars,[100] Sons of the Soul Revivors, the Southern Travelers, the Sunlight Jubilee Singers, the Spartonaires, the Swanee River Singers, the True Light Singers, and the West Coast Corinthians.[101]

In addition to local independent groups, a number of small groups were affiliated with churches. Church pastors initiated this trend during the early 1950s. One of the first to do so was James Lee Richards, originally from Texas, who organized Evergreen Baptist Church in 1947. In 1950 he established a women's trio called the Golden Echoes to do a fifteen-minute morning radio broadcast with him on the Warner Bros. station.[102] He increased the size of the ensemble to six and in 1953 renamed it the J. L. Richards Specials. Another church group, the Andrews Sisters (formed in 1950), included director and arranger Ola Jean Andrews (the eldest), Myrta, Paula, and Sylvia. Ola Andrews, a native of Arkansas who moved to the San Francisco Bay Area in 1939, explains how the group began:

> We were in the Sunshine Band [a children's group] at Emmanuel Church of God in Christ under the leadership of Sister Bertha Robinson, who asked us to sing a song. That was our beginning. As we began to sing more and more in our local church, we were asked to sing in other churches. We entered many contests, winning first place each time. One such contest was given by KDIA. As winners of that contest we became the official KDIA SINGERS and were awarded a 15-minute broadcast every Sunday afternoon (live) for three years.
>
> Whenever the Andrews Sisters sang, there was no such thing as casual singing. It was all or nothing at all. Flora and Donna Daggao, and Beulah Mabry (cousins) joined the Sisters, and when Sylvia was living in Arizona, Jeanne King joined the Sisters. I always tried to be different. Consequently our music was ahead of the times.[103]

Ola Andrews's training and early influences had a significant impact on her career; she was one of the few musicians in the Bay Area during the fifties and sixties who were performing what was called "progressive" gospel music, which included elements from blues and jazz. Andrews states that as a child she not only listened to her uncle play jazz and "honky-tonk" music on the piano but also regularly heard popular music on recordings and the radio. In addition to taking private instruction from local teachers in the Bay Area, she attended San Francisco City College as a music major. She greatly admired Clara Ward and Marion Williams of the Clara Ward Singers, as well as the Original Gospel Harmonettes.[104] She recalls: "The person who inspired me was Clara Ward. By observation and listening to her, when she rehearsed the Ward Singers in our home, I learned how to teach harmony. As a budding musician, Clara introduced me to many of the great artists, many of whom I became friends with. I learned much about gospel music and keyboard mastery from Herbert Pickard, pianist for the Original Gospel Harmonettes."[105]

Before long the Andrews Sisters had become stars in the Bay Area. Often they were the featured singers in the Bay Area Youth Fellowship under the direction of Herman Harper (see Figure 4.6; also see discussion of Harper in note 127). They also sang at the International Youth Congress of the Churches of God in Christ in Ohio in 1959; appeared on television in Hollywood with the Original Gospel Harmonettes; made a successful tour of the eastern and southern United States; and won trophies (on several occasions) in competitions sponsored by Reid's Records. The group's notoriety led to an invitation to perform in a show (*Evolution of the Blues* with Jon Hendricks) at the Monterey Jazz Festival in the early sixties.[106] In 1962 they released an album on Capitol Records—*The Andrews Gospel Singers: Open Your Heart* (Capitol T1959).[107]

In later years, other church groups came into existence: the Dew's Specials of San Francisco, the G. L. Bedford Specials, the Lathanettes, the Macedonia Harmonettes, the Poole Sisters, the St. John Specials, and the St. Paul Specials.[108] Church groups served several functions. Mary Bolden, who migrated to Oakland in 1942 and was an early member of the Golden Echoes at Evergreen, explains:

> During the forties and I guess earlier, there wasn't a lot of choirs in the Bay Area. A lot of churches just had groups. The preacher could travel better with the group than he could a choir. And we didn't have a large choir in the first place. Then through people hearing us sing on the broadcast, we would travel from one church to another. We would do our services and then we would go to Stockton or we would go to Vallejo.
>
> There was a lot of good times in it. It was a lot of fun and it was a lot of benefit because that's what made our church grow. People were hearing us sing and hearing him preach.[109]

Because of the significant role that quartets and small groups played in the development of gospel music in the Bay Area, support for these organizations was strong. According to Odessa Perkins, a branch of the national Interdenominational Singers Alliance was established in Oakland during the late 1940s. However, when the regional meeting took place in the Bay Area in 1958, members of the organization "voted unanimously to constitute itself the new America's Singers Association. The purpose of the changed organization set up, according to President Battles, is to facilitate better, more aggressive promotion, training and organization of Spiritual and Gospel Singers in the Far West."[110]

The structure of the association is noteworthy. The entire San Francisco Bay Area was divided into several geographical units, called locals. Each local was given a number and included its own solo artists, quartets, and choirs. As in Los Angeles, the groups met monthly at different churches in the city for performances. For example, Local 3 included all groups based in Oakland, whereas Local 4 encompassed those in San Francisco.[111] "They would pay dues and have rules and regulations. They would travel from church to church and would get

Figure 4.6. Andrews Sisters gospel singers, 1960s (San Francisco). Left to right—back row: Jeanne King, Donna Daggao; middle row: Paula Andrews, Sylvia Andrews, and Flora Daggao; front: Ola Jean Andrews. Courtesy of Ola Jean Andrews.

their members from various church choirs."[112] In the early years of their existence, ministers apparently supported locals because, as Gadling reports,

> that was the way of getting a lot of people to come to the church . . . to have quartet singings. . . . Every Sunday night they had these late musicals. . . . The crowd came after church [service]. There was always a lead group, of course, that was going to be there. Most of them [music groups in the city] felt that they could come and be apart of it. . . . People would be milling around, walking and singing with the beat going, just like a regular camp meeting.[113]

Although the locals were very popular at one time, William Allums, a Louisiana native who migrated to the Bay Area in 1939, states that locals received little support from ministers in later years:

> There was a disagreement between the locals and the ministers because the locals were pulling members from the churches. Whenever the local had an engagement, members would not be at their own local church to fulfill that function. So the locals were like a traveling choir. They would give concerts and you would pay at the door.
>
> The ministers didn't like it. Locals died out several years ago because ministers wouldn't let them play in the churches anymore. What was left was for them to come to venues like the convention center. And it was hard for them to gain the muscle to get crowds to pay the bills. [Locals] died because they couldn't go into the churches.[114]

Although most churches had gospel choirs during the fifties and sixties, they did not attain fame comparable to that of the Echoes of Eden Choir in Los Angeles. As in the case of the quartets and small groups, a support organization for choirs (the Federation of Choirs) was organized in the Bay Area in 1953. However, whereas the quartets were sometimes in conflict with churches, church choirs were incorporated into the federation.[115]

Temple of Truth Baptist Church was an important place for gospel music during the 1950s. Groups from Los Angeles often performed at the church, as did local artists.[116] Beasley states that Temple of Truth "had an open season on quartet and gospel singers. They used to come and when I was a little girl, I used to go to those. They had broadcasts."[117] Mount Zion Spiritual Temple, founded in 1943 by Louisiana native Louis H. Narcisse,[118] was another major force in the community in the fifties and sixties, not only because of its charismatic leader, who was influential in social and political affairs, but also because of the church's music program.[119] Gadling states:

> He [Narcisse] was a piano player at Second Baptist in Vallejo. Then he felt the call to do something greater, and he did. He had late-night services and we would go to his church late. He had quite a large following. . . . You couldn't hardly get in there some Sunday nights, because there were visitors too. He had a very good voice, and he had one of the best gospel choirs. They were singing strong gospel music.[120]

Helen Stephens, a New Orleans native who moved to the Bay Area in the mid-fifties and at one time played piano for the 10:30 p.m. radio broadcast (station KLX) at Mount Zion, states, "[Narcisse] would have his choir and church service at night. He would have a message, and the choir would sing. And the service would last until two in the morning."[121] Other East Bay churches known for their gospel music and heard regularly on radio programs during the 1950s include St. John Baptist, Evergreen Baptist, Antioch Baptist, and McGee Avenue Baptist.[122] In the San Francisco area, choirs from Third Baptist and Macedonia were featured in newspaper reports.

During the early 1950s, music extravaganzas, festivals, and anniversaries were common; thus, gospel music could be heard both in church and nonreligious venues. For example, the Songspirational Festival sponsored by Kyles Temple AME Zion Church in Vallejo became an annual event for choirs and small groups from the Bay Area.[123] During the summer of 1954, Herald Attractions sponsored a gospel festival at the Oakland Baseball Park. As in a similar event in Los Angeles in 1953, artists from around the nation participated.[124]

Because of all the activity, it was not surprising that a choir competition became a regular event in the gospel community. This tradition began in the 1920s,[125] although the focus at that time was on all types of sacred music. The new competition began in 1954 and became an annual affair through the 1960s. Held at the Oakland Auditorium, the event was elaborately produced and sponsored by Reid's Records, an important East Bay institution. Mel and Paul Reid not only sold records and other church materials but also sponsored a radio program called *Reid's Records Religious Gems*, heard each Sunday over KRE in Berkeley.

The choirs chosen to perform in the competition were selected by votes from listeners of the radio program. Therefore, all denominations were represented. Originally, groups competed within three divisions: senior choir, gospel song, and young adult. In later years other divisions—best youth choir, best radio performance by a choir, best organ presentation, best pianist, best soloist—were added to the competition, each with its own sponsor (e.g., Hudson Funeral Home, Reid's Records, Rumford's Pharmacy).[126] Some of the Oakland churches known for having excellent choirs included St. John Baptist, Evergreen Baptist, Mount Zion Spiritual Temple, Inc., Star Bethel Baptist,[127] Greater New Hope Baptist, Bebee Memorial CME, McGee Avenue Baptist, and Temple of Truth Baptist. San Francisco choirs from El Bethel Baptist, Emmanuel Church of God in Christ, Macedonia Baptist, New St. John Missionary Baptist, and Third Baptist won awards through the years. The event was important not only because it allowed choirs from the entire community to celebrate collectively but also because it caused groups to strive for high performance levels. Trophies were "awarded on the abilities of the choirs to sing anthems, spirituals and gospel songs, with points being scored on an applause meter."[128] Also, the competition gave Reid's Records an opportunity to promote publishers of religious music; "certificates for proficiency in the interpretation of gospel music from Kenneth Morris of the Martin and Morris Music [Studio] of Chicago and Clara Ward's House of Music in Philadelphia were presented to top choir directors."[129]

During the 1950s, well-known gospel artists began to visit and perform in the Bay Area more frequently, a trend that continued into the 1960s. Also, as Bay Area performers began receiving media coverage, they visited the Los Angeles area more often, and some Southern California gospel performers came north. Though most singers from Los Angeles (e.g., James Cleveland, the Voices of Hope with Thurston Frazier and Gwendolyn Cooper Lightner) made short-term visits, some came and directed choirs over longer periods of time. The Simmons-Akers Singers directed the Upper Room Choir in Richmond during the mid-fifties.[130] Justin S. Cummins, former director of Greater Olivet Baptist Church in Los Angeles, permanently moved to the Bay Area in the early 1960s, becoming minister of music at Macedonia Baptist Church.[131] In 1955 two artists—Dorothy Love of the Original Gospel Harmonettes of Birmingham, Alabama, and Professor Alex Bradford of the Bradford Specials of Chicago—received trophies at the Spiritual Festival in the Oakland Auditorium before a crowd of some 6,000 people. The trophies were awards for outstanding educational and religious music composed and recorded during the past year.[132]

Though the city of San Francisco produced some gospel musicians (G. L. Bedford Specials, Justin Cummins), the center for gospel music in the Bay Area during the fifties and sixties was Oakland. Ola Jean Andrews states, "If you wanted a large concert turnout, you would always have to go to Oakland."[133] Stephens adds, "San Francisco is a slow place. Gospel musicians live in San Francisco, but they have everything in Oakland because people in San Francisco don't frequently go to the musicals in San Francisco. They would rather come over here [East Bay]."[134]

By the 1960s gospel was prominently heard throughout Bay Area communities and in most churches. Ephesians Church of God in Christ in Berkeley had become a major center for gospel music. Andrews, choir director at Ephesians from 1958 to 1965, was instrumental in developing the music program at the church. Her unique style of arranging and performing provided the foundation upon which other gospel musicians developed their talents. Members of Edwin Hawkins's family regularly worshiped at Ephesians, and Hawkins served as the organist for Andrews's inspirational choir. She recalls:

> We all grew up together. Edwin Hawkins was also one of my students. He would sit on the piano stool with me when he was a little boy. I didn't realize how much I'd impacted his life until he grew up and began to say what an influence I had on him. . . . I used to feature him in many of my concerts when he was a little boy. He was always in the audience wherever the Andrews Sisters were singing.
>
> I think Edwin is a very good songwriter, musician, and arranger, although he seems to favor arranging older songs. In much of his music, particularly in his earlier recorded years, I can hear much of my sound. But, of course, he has expanded and gone much further. The student always goes farther than the teacher.[135]

When Andrews left Ephesians, Hawkins took over the choir and became minister of music. In 1967 he formed a forty-member group from members of Pentecostal churches in Berkeley, San Francisco, Oakland, San Jose, and Richmond for the Annual Youth Congress of Church of God in Christ. In 1968 the group, then known as the Northern California State Youth Choir, recorded the legendary LP *Let Us Go into the House of the Lord,* which included the song, "Oh Happy Day," with Dorothy Morrison as lead vocalist.[136] Most gospel performers regard the recording of "Oh Happy Day" as the springboard for the development of contemporary gospel music.

Whereas Los Angeles had gospel community choirs as early as the 1940s, the Voices of Christ, founded by Helen Stephens in 1969, was one of the first large community choirs in the San Francisco Bay Area. It was founded in large part because of the influence of James Cleveland's Gospel Music Workshop of America.[137] Although gospel music developed slowly in the Bay Area, the foundation laid in the forties and fifties provided the necessary basis for expansion of the music in later years. As the sociocultural environment changed, there were institutions and individuals to support the growth of the tradition. Starting in the 1970s, the Bay Area came to be regarded as one of the most important areas in the United States for gospel music, and its local stars achieved world renown.

San Diego

Like the San Francisco Bay Area, San Diego was slow to develop a gospel tradition. San Diegans preferred music in the style of Oakland's Keeton Chorus over down-home gospel. In 1935, George Garner organized a San Diego Chorus to participate in Negro Achievement Day at the California Pacific International Exposition.[138] Though there is no mention of the group's repertoire, the music performed probably did not differ from that used by the Keeton Chorus. In other words, the music was probably performed in the tradition of the Fisk Jubilee Singers, with emphasis on elements associated with European art music. Garner, an internationally known tenor, was the only black member of the exposition music committee.

During the thirties, most churchgoers in San Diego did not care for gospel music. Songs by Thomas Dorsey (called "ten-cents music" because the sheet music was reasonably priced) received little respect from blacks who considered themselves to belong to the middle or upper class. De Vonne C. Morris, a native of San Diego and musician at Calvary Baptist (formed 1889), explains:

> Members preferred a more staid, a more aristocratic type of worship. And I don't mean to be negative, but that's simply the way they were. That "10-cents music," that jazzy, country music, seemed to be, for a while at least, beneath them. There were blacks who had studied music and were well able to handle anthems. . . . They just did not appreciate the simplicity, certainly not the beat of some of the gospel. Yet there wasn't that much of a beat back in the thirties. However it was different.[139]

In spite of this attitude, a few people performed songs by Thomas Dorsey during religious worship (e.g., "Precious Lord, Take My Hand").[140]

It was not until the migration of southerners into the area during the forties that interest in gospel music began to take place. As in Los Angeles, the promotion of gospel in San Diego came from church leaders. Without the support of pastors, the acceptance of any music is slow, especially when there are church members who have strong opinions about the appropriateness of certain types of music in religious worship.[141] Therefore, the fact that several San Diego churches installed pastors who were knowledgeable and strong advocates of the tradition helped the growth of gospel music in the city.

It was not until Noah E. Taylor (originally from Texas) became pastor in 1942 that the expansion of gospel music began to occur at Calvary Baptist.[142] During his tenure, a gospel chorus was formed under the direction of E. W. Brooks (Juanita Pryor and Jean Wesson were piano and organ accompanists, respectively), a Hammond organ was purchased, and a radio broadcast featuring gospel music was established; the church became San Diego's primary venue for gospel concerts by local and visiting artists. Morris states, "We had lots of quartets visiting. We also had the famous names in gospel music—Sallie Martin, Roberta Martin, Robert Anderson, J. Earle Hines, they all appeared at Calvary. Used to be quite a thing. You would see people literally walking toward Calvary on all of the side streets when there was going to be a performance by any of those named gospel singers."[143]

When S. M. Lockridge[144] (also from Texas) became pastor in 1952, Calvary's prominence as a center for the performance of gospel field was maintained. In 1959 the three existing church choirs—Vesper (young adult) Choir, Gospel Chorus, and Senior Choir—were combined into a Sanctuary Choir under the leadership of De Vonne C. Morris. The repertoire of the new choir expanded to include hymns, spirituals, and anthems, but the church continued to be a strong supporter of gospel. In addition, two small groups were formed: the Cavaleers and the Cavalettes.

It was also during the forties (under the pastorate of Caney Johnson, who moved to San Diego from Arkansas in the late thirties) that Mount Zion Baptist (formed 1900) became known as a gospel-singing church. Marvin C. Hines and Birdie Ola Braxton were instrumental in developing the gospel program; both were Texas natives who joined the church in 1943. Like Calvary, Mount Zion was one of the few places in the city where traveling gospel musicians were able to give concerts. Verneater Robinson, the daughter of Caney Johnson and a gospel musician who began to work at Mount Zion in the late forties, states, "We've had a lot of musicians come through there. Gwen Gordon, Dorothy Hines Chestang [Marvin Hines's former wife], Norma Galloway, and me. These were the most prominent ones."[145]

Quartet singing began in San Diego during the mid-forties.[146] When Exton Hullaby Sr., a native of Louisiana, and several other men formed a men's singing group (the Spiritual Kings)[147] in 1947, the music was not called gospel. C. W. Dean, a native of Texas who later joined the group, states:

> When we started, they didn't even call it gospel singing. It was called spiritual singing. The title gospel singing more or less started in the fifties, and we were the first quartet in San Diego to amount to anything. And that was back in the forties. As time passed, we did recordings [on Score Records] and things like that but nothing major, mostly local. But we did a lot of promoting gospel singing. [We promoted] artists like James Cleveland, the Soul Stirrers, Dixie Hummingbirds, Pilgrim Travelers and Swan Silvertones, Brother Joe May, the Consolers, the [Original Gospel] Harmonettes, the Blind Boys, both groups, Mississippi and Alabama. Those are all of the old timers.[148]

Several other San Diego groups came into existence around the same time and in later years: the Matthew Singers, the Friendly Five, the Silver Lights, and the

Gospel Revelators.[149] By the early fifties, not only were different service organizations established (e.g., a chapter of the Singers Alliance) to promote quartet singing in the city, but one of the quartet conventions was held in San Diego.[150]

By the 1950s gospel music had become accepted in most churches in San Diego. Gwendolyn Gordon (1919–96), a native of Florida who migrated to San Diego County in 1952, states, "When I got here, I heard churches doing it. . . . It was just about all of them."[151] Morris explains, "by the fifties and sixties when youth choirs were performing, we were able to listen to records and get different ideas about gospel music that even had a stronger beat. But by that time the congregation was kind of accepting the music. The problems that my mother had back in the thirties had very much disappeared."[152]

One of the most significant developments in San Diego gospel occurred in 1960, when Marvin C. Hines (1925–83) founded and became pastor of Pilgrim Progressive Baptist Church (Figure 4.7). Hines had already established a reputation as a gospel musician at Mount Zion and was a solo recording artist [on the Duplex and Pilgrim labels] and member of the Spiritual Kings. But his fame grew when the church started a fifteen-minute gospel and religious music radio program on XEXX, allowing him to reach thousands at one time. He was also president of the Gospel City Enterprises and Radio Network, which served more than seven states. By the mid-1960s, Hines's radio choir had become well known. Under the direction of Leroy Geter and accompanied by Charlie Mae Ralph (on piano) and Darlene Caldwell (on organ), "the choir performed in many concerts and programs in the city and throughout Los Angeles."[153] Prominent Pentecostal (Church of God in Christ) churches in San Diego that were noted for gospel singing during the sixties included St. Stephens, Jackson Memorial, and Israelite.

Although there was greater demand for gospel in churches, quartets and small groups declined in popularity in the 1960s. "The national groups became much too expensive to bring in for a church-hall concert to headline over the talent, and besides, by 1969 the church choirs were all singing gospel in the style, that twenty years before, would have been considered too avant-garde for proper church singing. Why hear a local, independent quartet sing gospel when you had it every Sunday from the youth choir in your own church?"[154]

Los Angeles had a significant impact on the development of gospel music in San Diego, much as it influenced the Bay Area gospel community. Besides the St. Paul radio broadcast, musicians and groups who traveled to Los Angeles often visited San Diego.

> Of course, we've always caught the dregs of Los Angeles. I don't think too many people booked themselves directly into San Diego. If they came from another state, they booked into Los Angeles, but while they were in California, they could give a night to San Diego. So we caught them that way. But by hearing all those groups and watching them sing would heighten your own appreciation of gospel music. And you could introduce that, or those songs that you've heard, to your choir. That would have been in the forties.[155]

Figure 4.7. Gospel singer Marvin C. Hines (San Diego). Courtesy of Berdena Mae Hines and Verneata Robinson (owner of photograph).

Los Angeles artists that frequented San Diego included J. Earle Hines, the Sallie Martin Singers, the Simmons-Akers Singers, the West Coast Jubilees, the Stars of Harmony, the Spiritual Five of Los Angeles, the Canaan Singers, and the Zion Travelers.

San Diegans also visited Los Angeles, not only to attend and perform in concerts and conventions but also to work in the media.[156] Ministers and members of churches visited each other for anniversary programs and other events. When pastors convened in Los Angeles, Oakland, San Francisco, or other cities, their church musicians accompanied them and performed at the worship services. Carl J. Anderson of Oakland preached in San Diego at Calvary Baptist for Lockridge's twenty-fifth anniversary in July 1977.[157]

Gospel musicians from San Diego were not involved in gospel music on the national level between 1930 and 1969.[158] Those who had an opportunity to become nationally known preferred to stay close to home. For example, after having some success locally and regionally,[159] the Spiritual Kings decided to disband:

> We had gone as far as we could go locally. And so nobody wanted to go on the road. We all had families and some of them [Hines and Graves] went to preaching. Some of them left the group. We just disband[ed]. . . . We sang all over California, Nevada, Arizona, New Mexico, and wasn't nothing left but go on the road nationally. But we weren't ready to make that sacrifice . . . , but we still stayed active[160] in the business by promoting and stuff like that.[161]

Like the San Francisco Bay Area, San Diego did not attract recognized gospel musicians who permanently settled in the area because it was not able to compete with the opportunities available in Los Angeles. Therefore, the city's close proximity to Los Angeles hindered as well as helped the development of gospel music in San Diego.

CONCLUSION

Gospel evolved differently in various areas of California partly because of contrasting migration trends. As blacks moved West, primarily from the South and Midwest, they took their cultural traditions with them. California gospel music developed from a combination of sources, as westerners with established traditions came into contact with southerners and midwesterners with slightly different cultural practices. Thus, the so-called European-influenced elitism of the West Coast fused with the down-home folk traditions of the South and the brassy, urbanism of the Midwest. Because Los Angeles had the largest black population, it became the standard-bearer for California gospel. Los Angeles provided a nurturing environment, and the energy that resulted from the interaction of various groups helped gospel music to develop on a large and grand scale.[162]

Chicago played a significant role in the history of the California gospel tradition. Not only were traveling musicians and evangelists from the Midwest responsible for introducing gospel in California, but a number of midwesterners eventually settled in the state, helping Los Angeles, in particular, to become a major center for gospel music. The mentorship and new ideas that Chicago musicians provided black Angelenos made gospel in Los Angeles distinct from that in other areas of the state. A permanently settled musician is in a better position to nurture or mold a young person's talent than a visitor is. The encouragement and training that Sallie Martin provided Cora Martin, Dorothy Simmons, and Doris Akers helped them become nationally known. The opportunities that Hines and Lightner gave to Frazier and Goodson enabled them to become innovators, just as the support that Frazier provided Margaret Pleasant Douroux and Andraé Crouch furthered their careers as composers. What style of gospel would Ola Jean Andrews have created if she had not interacted personally with Clara Ward, Marion Williams, and Herbert Pickard? Without mentorship from Andrews, would Edwin Hawkins have acquired the expertise to create "contemporary" gospel, a dominant force in the gospel music world since the sixties?

The interchange between Southern and Northern Californians was extensive. Los Angeles served as the hub; it was the city where many musicians were based and from which they visited other areas. As seen in the case of San Diego, close proximity to the center yielded both negative and positive consequences. Los Angeles's role in the development of gospel music in California is comparable to that of Chicago in the general history of gospel music. By the 1950s and 1960s, many of the characteristics that made Chicago a gospel center (publishing houses, headquarters for national organizations, influx of immigrants, and visits of professional groups) could be found in Los Angeles. Both were settings in which artists could develop their talents in whatever manner they desired.

Several new trends in gospel music began in California—for example, the large gospel choir tradition. Though some Los Angeles community choirs were formed during the early forties, it was St. Paul's radio choir that had the greatest impact. In addition to sparking the organization of other large church and community (mass) choirs, the group's notoriety laid the foundation for what James Cleveland was able to achieve later with the Southern California Community Choir. When Cleveland settled in Los Angeles in the sixties, he found "a rich territory from which to trigger and move gospel choir performance to a higher level."[163]

In addition, the performance style of gospel choirs changed as community choir directors began to have different expectations of their singers. Though some of the changes were the result of media exposure (most groups who performed on television and radio wanted to sound as professional as possible), I believe the California aesthetic was partly responsible for the direction the music took after the 1960s. The controlled performance and complex arrangements characteristic of large community choirs and contemporary gospel may be products of the aesthetics that existed in the music of J. Earle Hines, Doris Akers, Gwendolyn Cooper Lightner, and Thurston Frazier. Gadling explains:

> It's that they [community choir directors] require more allegiance to them. You *have* to make those meetings. You *have* to be at rehearsals. You *have* to make their engagements. At church, it's more of their [the members'] will. At church, if you don't feel like going to another church, you don't go.
>
> The fact that they [community choir directors] require you to attend all of their rehearsals means that it is a more practiced group. And of course they sound better. And they have the best organist and pianist available. Of course, the church takes

whoever comes, and they work with them. The community groups are not polished toward gearing songs to worship. They're polished towards performing.

You find that in contemporary gospel, a lot of the musicians perform well and are classically trained. There's a lot of structure in the harmony . . . that an ordinary pianist at a church cannot play.

The classically trained musician loves that type of music [contemporary gospel]. They bring their expertise with them. Of course, they can modulate and make changes and bring in substitute chords and all of that kind of stuff. That's not traditional gospel music.[164]

Los Angeles's prominence as a national media capital also affected the development of gospel. The media helped to promote the gospel music business, which caused established gospel artists to migrate to Los Angeles in greater numbers. The commercialization of gospel music was not new. Thomas Dorsey, Sallie Martin, and others depended for their livelihoods on the income they received from performing, composing, and selling sheet music. In the early years the business was controlled by blacks, and much of the activity took place in religious settings. As the media became a central part of gospel music, a new audience was created, and secular influences began to be incorporated into the music to meet the demands of the audience. As Bernice Johnson Reagon explains, " 'Oh Happy Day' became a national hit, crossing over and creating a new, broad audience for the new era of contemporary gospel."[165]

Furthermore, many of the people who controlled the media and music industry were not from the black religious community and possibly not aware of or sensitive to the norms and values of black churchgoers. Thus, tensions arose between church members and gospel musicians who performed in the church but took gospel to the world (as occurred with Griffin and Andrews). There were also conflicts between musicians who sang traditional gospel and artists who performed contemporary gospel; churchgoers believed the latter were bringing the world into the church.[166] Interestingly, this complaint is not very different from the one gospel pioneer Thomas A. Dorsey heard during the early 1900s, and it probably will continue to be a factor in gospel music.[167]

The variety of gospel music styles found in California cities not only reflects the diversity of musical tastes and interests within the black community but also reveals the characteristics of most urban areas. Within a large, dense, and heterogeneous population, a wide spectrum of attitudes and values can be found.[168] As a result, one style of music is generally not satisfactory. Several gospel offerings were available in California, so people with different musical preferences could find something to suit their tastes. Therefore, it is not surprising that a number of the different strains of gospel—the lively, spirited performance style of the Echoes of Eden Choir; the down-home, hard-driving rhythmic songs of gospel quartets in Oakland and San Diego; the European-based lyrical melodies of the Simmons-Akers Singers; and the bluesy and jazzy sound of the Andrews Sisters—enjoyed equal levels of support by members of the various communities.

This study on California indicates that gospel thrives in a dense population of blacks whose aesthetics are closely aligned with characteristics associated with black folk culture. Although a European aesthetic permeated most black communities in California during the early 1900s, the attitudes of many African Americans in Los Angeles and the East Bay changed dramatically after the migrations of the 1940s, allowing gospel music to flourish. In areas (e.g., San Francisco and San Diego) where blacks were slow or reluctant to embrace folk traditions, the development of gospel stalled until later years. Yet the fusion of African and European elements in California created a unique style that some regard as more classical than the gospel traditions of Chicago, Texas, or Louisiana. In addition, the history of gospel in California helps us to understand better how one city—in this case, Los Angeles—can serve as a catalyst and model for innovation not only in a particular region but also for other parts of the country.

NOTES

1. George Robinson Ricks, "Some Aspects of the Religious Music of the United States Negro: An Ethnomusicological Study with Special Emphasis on the Gospel Tradition" (Ph.D. diss., Northwestern University, 1960).

2. See works by Horace Clarence Boyer, "The Gospel Song: A Historical and Analytical Study" (M.A. thesis, University of Rochester, Eastman School of Music, 1964); "An Analysis of Black Church Music with Examples Drawn from Services in Rochester, New York" (Ph.D. diss., University of Rochester, Eastman School of Music, 1973); and "Contemporary Gospel Music," *The Black Perspective in Music* 7, no. 1 (Spring 1979): 5–58; Viv Broughton, *Black Gospel: An Illustrated History of the Gospel Sound* (Dorset, England: Blandford Press Ltd., 1985); Anthony (Tony) Heilbut, *The Gospel Sound: Good News and Bad Times*, rev. ed. (Garden City, NY: Anchor Books, 1975); and Pearl Williams-Jones, "Afro-American Gospel Music: A Brief Historical and Analytical Survey (1930–1970)" in *Development of Materials for a One-Year Course in African Music for the General Undergraduate Student (Project in African Music)*, ed. Vada E. Butcher (Washington, DC: College of Fine Arts, Howard University, 1970), 199–209.

3. An exception to the trend of writing about gospel as a style with little regard for regional developments is the recent work by Horace Clarence Boyer, *How Sweet the Sound: The Golden Age of Gospel* (Washington, DC: Elliott & Clark Publishing, 1995), which includes a brief survey of major gospel artists in selected locales in the United States. A section of the book entitled "The California School of Gospel" (pp. 205–212) includes discussion of performers in the Los Angeles area. However, little mention is made of context except for his comments on how artists from other parts of the United States influenced gospel music in California.

4. Joyce Beasley, personal interview with author, 28 June 1990. Beasley (1938–93), born in Beaumont, Texas, was active in several quartets (e.g., the Original Joy Spreaders, the Lathanettes, and the Spiritual Corinthians) in the Bay Area from the fifties to the seventies. She was also well known locally as a solo artist.

5. Betty Gadling, personal interviews with author, 19 June 1989 and 17 June 1990. Although Betty Gadling was born in 1926 in St. Louis, she was raised and spent most of her early life in Edwardsville, Illinois. Gadling's mother moved to California in 1944. Gadling

visited her on many occasions but did not settle in California until 1951. Gadling and her sisters organized the Poole Sisters in the mid-1950s. She states that they sang in the style of the Wings Over Jordan Choir (concert spirituals). In addition to receiving formal training in Western music in music schools on the West Coast, Gadling performed with her sisters in a group (called the Lesdinns) in France, Switzerland, Spain, and Italy between 1964 and 1967. Gadling has worked at a number of churches in the Bay Area: Union Baptist and St. John Baptist in Vallejo, California; Evergreen Baptist, where she was minister of music and one of the directors of the J. L. Richards Specials (see discussion later in this chapter); and Allen Temple Baptist, where she has served as minister of music since 1976.

6. See discussion in Jacqueline Cogdell DjeDje, "Gospel Music in the Los Angeles Black Community: A Historical Analysis," *Black Music Research Journal* 9, no. 1 (Spring 1989): 35.

7. For my previous studies on gospel music in California, see "An Expression of Black Identity: The Use of Gospel Music in a Los Angeles Catholic Church," *The Western Journal of Black Studies* 7, no. 3 (Fall 1983): 148–160; "Change and Differentiation: The Adoption of Black American Gospel Music in the Catholic Church," *Ethnomusicology* 30, no. 2 (Spring/Summer 1986): 223–252; "A Historical Overview of Black Gospel Music in Los Angeles," *Black Music Research Bulletin* 10, no. 1 (Spring 1988): 1–5; "Gospel Music in the Los Angeles Black Community: A Historical Analysis," *Black Music Research Journal* 9, no. 1 (Spring 1989): 35–79; "Black Gospel Music in Los Angeles," *UCLA Center for Afro-American Studies Report* 12, nos. 1&2 (1989): 12–13, 23; "Black Gospel Music in Los Angeles," *Los Angeles Folk Arts Newsletter* 5, no. 2 (1990): 1–2, 11; "Gospel Music in Los Angeles and the Bay Area: A Sociocultural Analysis" (paper presented at the Society for Ethnomusicology Pre-Conference Symposium on African American Music, Oakland, California, 7 November 1990); "The Beginnings of Gospel Music in the Bay Area" in *African-American Traditional Arts and Folklife in Oakland and the East Bay: A Collection of Essays*, ed. Willie R. Collins (Oakland: City of Oakland Cultural Arts Division, 1992), 1–3; "Akers, Doris," "Douroux, Margaret Pleasant," "Griffin, Bessie," "Hawkins, Tramaine," "Lightner, Gwendolyn," "Martin-Moore, Cora," and "Simmons, Dorothy Vernell" in *Black Women in America: An Historical Encyclopedia, Vols. 1 and 2*, ed. Darlene Clark Hine (Brooklyn: Carlson Publishing, 1992), 16, 353–354, 503–504, 547–548, 720–721, 751–752, and 1035–1036; interview with Sonja Williams, 5 October 1992, as part of the twenty-six-part radio series, *"Wade in the Water": African American Sacred Music Traditions*, Program 24, "'We've Come This Far By Faith': The Story of the California Gospel Movement" (Washington, DC: National Public Radio, 1994); "Los Angeles Composers of African American Gospel Music: The Early Generations," *American Music: A Quarterly Journal Devoted to All Aspects of American Music and Music in America* 11, no. 4 (Winter 1993): 412–457; "A History of Gospel Music in California, 1930–1970" (paper presented at "We'll Understand It Better By and By": A National Conference on African American Gospel Music Scholarship in Tribute to Pearl Williams-Jones, Smithsonian Institution Program in African American Culture, Washington, DC., February 5, 1993); liner notes, *The Sallie Martin Singers/Cora Martin: Throw Out the Lifeline* (Specialty Records, SPCD 7043–2, 1993); and "Pioneers and Trailblazers: Composers of the Los Angeles Gospel Sound," in *Music in the Central Avenue Community 1890–c. 1955*, ed. Bette Y. Cox (Los Angeles: BEEM Foundation, 1996), 55–60.

8. In spite of the fact that some artists have lived most of their lives in a totally new environment, generally greater attention is paid to artists' birthplace and the town/city where they were raised. This is particularly evident in the case of some Los Angeles gospel musicians—for example, Bessie Griffin (1922–89; the birth date of 1927 that appears in DjeDje,

"Gospel Music in the Los Angeles Black Community," 68, is incorrect) and James Cleveland (1931–91). Griffin's upbringing in New Orleans and life in Chicago tend to be emphasized in gospel music publications. In the case of Cleveland, most studies mention his hometown of Chicago and work in Detroit. Although the accomplishments that gave him the most notoriety (recording the gospel hit "Peace Be Still" and organizing the Southern California Community Choir, Cornerstone Institutional Baptist Church, and the Gospel Music Workshop of America) were achieved after his move to Los Angeles, rarely do scholars emphasize Los Angeles or California as a factor in his development as an artist. See discussion of these artists in Heilbut, *The Gospel Sound;* Broughton, *Black Gospel;* and Boyer, *How Sweet.* For a discussion of their achievements while living in California, see DjeDje "A Historical Overview of Black Gospel," "Gospel Music in the Los Angeles Black Community," and "Los Angeles Composers."

9. James Cleveland, personal interview with author, 29 September 1987.

10. I began my research on the history of gospel music in Los Angeles during the summer of 1987, interviewing several gospel musicians and reviewing early issues of Los Angeles black newspapers. In addition, other data (sheet music, music programs, recordings, and iconographical material) were collected to substantiate findings. Not only have I continued to identify and develop biographies on gospel figures in Los Angeles, but attention has also been given to the sociocultural history of blacks in other cities in California to determine if there are correlations between the social environment and the rise and development of certain gospel trends. In summers 1989, 1990, and 1992, I conducted research in the San Francisco Bay Area and Sacramento. Fieldwork in San Diego was done in February, June, and December 1992. This research was made possible with funding from the UCLA Institute of American Cultures, Center for African-American Studies, and Academic Senate, as well as the 1993 Los Angeles Festival. I am grateful to all of the individuals who took the time to share their life experiences with me. I also want to thank all of the research assistants from UCLA who helped me to collect, transcribe, and organize the data for this project.

11. DjeDje, "Gospel Music in the Los Angeles Black Community." Also see Boyer, *How Sweet,* pp. 12–18, for further discussion of the history of the Azusa Street Mission.

12. Bette Yarbrough Cox, *Central Avenue—Its Rise and Fall (1890–c.1955: Including the Musical Renaissance of Black Los Angeles* (Los Angeles: BEEM Publications, 1996), 7. According to Cox, Mrs. Beck had a magnificent contralto voice, and her daughter, Pearl, played guitar, tambourine and violin. Colonel Beck traveled with them but did not play an instrument. Other musicians from the late nineteenth and early twentieth centuries include Gilbert Allen and Pearl Hinds Roberts, who were "highly involved in sacred music with the early churches" (Cox, p. 7).

13. "Revival Meeting at Pentecostal Church," *Western American* (7 January 1927): 6; and "Bishop Humphrey at Penecostal [sic] Church," *Western American* (24 September 1928): 8.

14. "Two-By-Four Churches," *Western Appeal* (17 August 1921).

15. Ken Anderson, personal interview with author, 16 February 1992.

16. Gadling, personal interview, 1989.

17. Robert Fikes, Gail Madyun, and Larry Malone, "Black Pioneers in San Diego, 1880–1920," *Journal of San Diego History* 27, no. 2 (Spring 1981): 107.

18. "Where to Go Sundays," *Western Outlook* (22 April 1922): 1; and "Where to Go Sundays," *Western Outlook* (11 June 1927): 6.

19. Lawrence P. Crouchett, Lonnie G. Bunch III, and Martha K. Winnacker, *Visions Toward Tomorrow: The History of the East Bay Afro-American Community 1852–1977* (Oakland: The Northern California Center for Afro-American History and Life, 1989), 15.

20. "First A.M.E. Church Notes, Oakland," *Western Appeal* (14 October 1920): 1; "Promise and Fulfillment: A Christmas Cantata," (18 December 1920): 1; "Interesting Topic Next Sunday at Market St. Church," *Western American* (22 April 1927): 6; "Activities at Cooper A.M.E. Zion Church," *The California Voice* (25 January 1929): 2; "Activities at Cooper A.M.E. Zion Church," *The California Voice* (15 February 1929): 2; "Annual Conference at 15th St. Church," *Western American* (4 January 1929): 1; and "From 'Pasadena Section,'" *The California Eagle* (29 March 1929): 6.

21. "Fifteenth Street Church Choir Out to Win," *Western American* (16 March 1928): 1.

22. "No. Oakland Baptist Sings Over KGO on Saturday at 6:30," *Western American* (9 March 1928): 1; "Parks Chapel Goes Over Big on KTAB," *Western American* (9 March 1928): 1.

23. "Tuskegee Institute Singers to Visit California," *Western Outlook* (12 December 1914): 2; "Rev. J. E. Boyd to be Heard at Beth Eden," *The California Voice* (7 January 1922): 1; "Fisk Jubilee Singers at Hollywood Bowl," *Los Angeles Times* (16 June 1929); and DjeDje, "Gospel Music in the Los Angeles Black Community," 41–42.

24. "Third Baptist Church Happening," *Western American* (9 March 1928): 3.

25. "Pacific Coast Harmony Makers in Grand Recital at Independent Church," *The California Eagle* (3 May 1929): 1.

26. "Nine Churches Lined Up Solidly Behind Great Choir Contest: Each Urging Its Choir on to Victory," *Western American* (24 February 1928): 1.

27. "Attends Convention: Dr. Coleman to Return Thursday," *Western American* (1 October 1926): 6.

28. "Negro Songs Never Heard Before Sung at Convention," *Western American* (19 August 1927): 8.

29. Jacqueline Cogdell DjeDje, *American Black Spiritual and Gospel Songs from Southeast Georgia: A Comparative Study* (Los Angeles: Center for Afro-American Studies, University of California, Los Angeles, 1978), 5–14.

30. Michael W. Harris, "Conflict and Resolution in the Life of Thomas Andrew Dorsey" in *We'll Understand It Better By and By*, ed. Bernice Johnson Reagon (Washington and London: Smithsonian Institution Press, 1992), 165–182; and *The Rise of Gospel Blues: The Music of Thomas Andrew Dorsey in the Urban Church* (New York: Oxford University Press, 1992).

31. Don Lee White, personal interview with author, 21 July 1987.

32. Even though little discussion is given to them here, solo artists and church groups that performed art music (concert spirituals, anthems, etc.) played a significant role in the development of African-American sacred music traditions in California between 1900–1969. In Los Angeles, the Albert McNeil Jubilee Singers, a group organized in the sixties and now known worldwide, is an excellent example of the endurance of spirituals. Although the prominence of concert spirituals, hymns, and anthems has waned over the years among the black populace, the coexistence of this music with gospel has created an interesting dynamic among musicians in various black communities. Also, in spite of their lack of popularity, groups that perform black sacred art music have been highly regarded and respected by African Americans. Several church musicians indicated that it is important to include a mix of anthems, hymns, spirituals, and gospel in all worship services (Ineze Caston, personal interview with author, 23 July 1987; Gadling, personal interview, 1989;

Norma Johnson, personal interview with author, 25 June 1992; Glenn L. Jones, personal interview with author, 17 February and 29 June 1992; Dave Weston, personal interview with author, 25 July 1989; and White, personal interview).

33. White, personal interview.

34. DjeDje, "Gospel Music in the Los Angeles Black Community," 44–45.

35. DjeDje, "A Historical Overview," 1.

36. See DjeDje, "A Historical Overview," and "Gospel Music in the Los Angeles Black Community," 44–45. All of these artists were based in Chicago. Sallie Martin and Thomas Dorsey were members of Pilgrim, and Dorsey is believed to have organized the first gospel choir at Pilgrim in 1931; see "Gospel Music in the Los Angeles Black Community," 39. J. C. Austin (Junius Caesar Austin Sr.) was a black orator and minister known throughout the United States during the early twentieth century. Austin became pastor of Pilgrim Baptist in 1926 and was one of the first ministers in Chicago to welcome gospel music in the church (Paulene Keller, granddaughter of Austin, telephone interview, 24 February 1997).

37. DjeDje, "A Historical Overview," 1.

38. DjeDje, "Gospel Music in the Los Angeles Black Community," 45–46.

39. Arthur A. Peters (1907/08–75) and Earl A. Pleasant (1918–74) were born and raised in Louisiana; Eugene D. Smallwood (born 1920) is from Oklahoma. Peters attended Southern University, and Smallwood attended Los Angeles City College as music majors. All three men were singers who performed all types of music (spirituals, anthems, gospel, and European art music). For more information about these artists, see DjeDje, "A Historical Overview," "Gospel Music in the Los Angeles Black Community," and "Los Angeles Composers."

40. DjeDje, "Gospel Music in the Los Angeles Black Community," 45–46.

41. The two songs that Lightner mentions—"Precious Lord, Take My Hand" and "The Little Wooden Church on the Hill"—are performed in a slow, free manner. Only piano and/or organ accompaniment are used. Emphasis is given to the clear pronunciation of the text so that the audience is able to understand the message of the song; Eugene Douglass Smallwood, personal interviews with author, 13 January and 3 February 1988.

42. Gwendolyn Cooper Lightner, personal interview with author, 25 January 1988.

43. DjeDje, "A Historical Overview," 2.

44. John L. Branham was born in Denison, Texas, but migrated to Chicago with his family as a youngster. Before settling in Los Angeles, Branham was pastor of Calvary Baptist in San Diego; see De Vonne C. Morris, personal interview with author, 15 February, 1992. Morris (1928–93), a native of San Diego and member of Calvary, states: "Branham was a minister back in Chicago, with his brother Joseph and his father. But he was not pastoring. In 1938, he was visiting in San Diego. We [members of Calvary] were without a pastor at that time, and he agreed to fill our pulpit for 60 days. At the end of those two months, he accepted his very first ministerial assignment and became pastor of Calvary. [He left Calvary because] I assume the opportunities, the field was so much greener in Los Angeles than in San Diego." Branham was invited to serve as co-pastor of St. Paul in 1943 under the leadership of Rev. S. R. Williams. When Williams died in 1946, Branham became the senior pastor. St. Paul was founded in 1907; Cora Martin-Moore, personal interviews with author, 8 and 23 July 1987; and Lightner, personal interview.

45. James Earle Hines (1916–60) was born in Atlanta. As a young man, he attended the Cosmopolitan School of Music in Cincinnati, Ohio, and Columbia University in New York City. In the 1930s, Hines worked closely with officials of the National Baptist Convention as

a member of the Goodwill Singers and national director of the Convention Choir. During the 1940s, Hines performed with the Wings Over Jordan Choir, an organization that "won wide recognition during the 1930s–40s as a broadcasting church choir"; see Eileen Southern, *The Music of Black Americans: A History*, 2nd ed. (New York: W. W. Norton and Co., 1983), 414; and DjeDje, "A Historical Overview." After he left St. Paul in 1949, Hines not only served as minister of music at Grace Memorial and Victory for short periods but also organized the Hines Goodwill Singers and the Hines Goodwill Choir and established the Hines School of Music; see DjeDje, "Gospel Music in the Los Angeles," 50; and DjeDje, "Los Angeles Composers," 435–436. Gwendolyn Cooper Lightner was born in Brookport, Illinois. After completing high school, she attended Southern Illinois University in Carbondale, Illinois, and Lyon and Healy Music School in Chicago. In Chicago she came into contact with noted gospel musicians and eventually became a member of the Emma L. Jackson Singers. From 1968 to 1972, Lightner served as piano accompanist for Chicago gospel singer Mahalia Jackson. See further discussion of Lightner in DjeDje, "Lightner, Gwendolyn," and other works by DjeDje.

46. DjeDje, "A Historical Overview," 2.

47. After Hines left St. Paul in 1949, the choir had several directors. Cora Martin-Moore (born 1927 in Chicago), a featured soloist with the Echoes of Eden Choir as well as a solo gospel artist [she also sang with the Sallie Martin Singers] and songwriter in her own right, became director in 1958. In 1959 the Echoes of Eden Choir performed at the Hollywood Bowl with Nat King Cole. Thus, Martin-Moore was responsible for the performance at the Hollywood Bowl.

48. Lightner, personal interview.

49. Albert A. Goodson (born 1933) is one of the first Los Angeles natives to become nationally known for gospel music. Although raised as a Pentecostal, he joined St. Paul at twelve years of age and came under the influence of Hines and Lightner. He served as assistant pianist for the Echoes of Eden Choir and the Hines Goodwill Singers. He also served as choir director at Grace Memorial, Opportunity, and other churches in Los Angeles. He has performed with the Sallie Martin Singers, the Simmons-Akers Singers, the Sky Pilot Choir, the Voices of Hope, and the Ward Singers. From 1955–1961, Goodson lived in Chicago, where he served as minister of music at Fellowship Baptist Church. He returned to Los Angeles in the early sixties to direct the interdenominational Wings of Healing Gospel Choir, a group that grew from 40 to over 100 voices when he took over the leadership role. Though he has composed many songs, Goodson is most famous for "We've Come This Far By Faith," which is published in many hymnbooks and translated in several languages.

50. Albert A. Goodson, personal interview with author, 2 October 1987.

51. Smallwood, personal interview.

52. DjeDje, "A Historical Overview," 2.

53. Thurston Frazier (1930–74), a Houston, Texas, native who moved to Los Angeles with his family in the thirties, was a powerful force within the Los Angeles music community. His early music training was in European art music; he attended Los Angeles City College and sang with the Wings Over Jordan Choir. He served as music director of several church choirs but probably is best known for his work at Victory Baptist (with Peters) and Mount Moriah Baptist (with Pleasant). At Mount Moriah he had a big influence on Margaret Pleasant Douroux (daughter of Earl Pleasant), who was just beginning her career as

a songwriter; see DjeDje, "Gospel Music in the Los Angeles Black Community," 71. In 1957 Frazier and Lightner established the Voices of Hope, a community choir that became nationally known for its unique performance style and made two recordings for Capitol Records. Because of his training, Frazier was often called upon to arrange songs for songwriters. In the 1960s, Frazier and James Cleveland formed the music publishing firm Frazier-Cleveland and Company and were responsible for publishing Andraé Crouch's "The Blood (It) Will Never Lose Its Power," a gospel standard found in many church hymnals (see DjeDje, "Los Angeles Composers," 427, 455).

54. See DjeDje, "Gospel Music in the Los Angeles Black Community." In the fifties and sixties, it was common for Los Angeles churches to release their own recordings. I know of at least two recordings made by Victory Baptist: *I Sing Because I Am Happy: The Singing Shepherd and His Flock* (Victorian Records 102) and *Songs of the Shepherd and the Church Choir* (Victorian Records VL 3006). Trinity Baptist Church's Gospel Choir, under the direction of Ineze Caston, and Calvary Baptist Church's (Santa Monica) Youth-Adult and Cathedral Choirs, under the direction of Dave Weston, are among the other churches in Los Angeles that made recordings during the fifties and sixties (Caston, personal interview, and Weston, personal interview).

55. Sallie Martin used Los Angeles as her home base from the late forties to the mid-fifties. Cora Martin-Moore, Sallie Martin's daughter, settled in Los Angeles in 1947; see Martin-Moore, personal interview; and Cora Martin Moore, telephone interview with author, 2 January 1991.

56. Much of the information about quartets in California comes from Ray Funk and Allen Peters, who are well-known gospel music researchers and collectors. Lee Hildebrand also assisted me with information about groups and artists in the Bay Area.

57. Dorothy Vernell Simmons (1910–96), born in Powhatan, Louisiana, moved to Chicago with her family when she was young. As a child, she wanted to become an opera singer, but her family did not have the funds to send her to a music school. In the early 1940s, Simmons worked with Sallie Martin and Kenneth Morris (1917–89), considered the "Dean of African American Gospel Composers," at the Martin and Morris Studio. She later performed with the Martin and Morris Singers and the Sallie Martin Singers before settling in Los Angeles in 1948; see Dorothy Simmons, personal interview with author, 21 June 1988.

Doris Akers (1923–95) was born in Brookfield, Missouri. The birthdate of 1922 reported in most publications is incorrect. In a personal interview (4 September 1989), Akers stated: "I didn't see my birth certificate until a couple of years ago. Then I found out I was born in 1923 and not 1922. I was a year younger than I thought." After traveling with an evangelist in the Midwest, she settled in Los Angeles in 1945 and formed her own group, the Doris Akers Singers. Like Simmons, Akers sang with the Sallie Martin Singers. Originally, the Simmons-Akers Singers comprised three females: Simmons, Akers, and Louise Byrd of Los Angeles. They performed throughout California, traveled to other parts of the country, and made a number of recordings. Many of the songs on their recordings were composed by Akers. The Simmons-Akers Singers were active as a group until 1960, when the members decided to become solo artists and choir directors. Both Akers and Simmons were affiliated with the Sky Pilot Choir, a group of white gospel singers popular in Los Angeles during the fifties and sixties (Doris Akers, telephone conversation with author, 8 February 1988). For further discussion of the Simmons-Akers Singers, see "Simmons, Dorothy Vernell," "Akers, Doris," and other works by DjeDje.

58. Charles Johnson, personal interview with author, 2 July 1987.

59. In the early forties, Smallwood and Pleasant formed the Interdenominational Chorus. See further discussion in DjeDje, "Gospel Music in the Los Angeles Black Community," 57.

60. Ibid.

61. DjeDje, "Los Angeles Composers," 434.

62. Several Los Angeles musicians have composed and/or owned music publishing companies. Some of those from the pre-1969 period include Margaret Aikens-Jenkins, Doris Akers, James Cleveland, Andraé Crouch, Margaret Pleasant Douroux, Thurston Frazier, Albert A. Goodson, Raynaud L. Hatter Sr., James Earle Hines, Isaiah Jones Jr., Walter Lewis, Henry P. Markham, Cora Martin-Moore, Arthur A. Peters, Mary G. Rubin, Dorothy Simmons (owner of a company, not a composer), Eugene D. Smallwood, and Dave Weston. See further discussion in DjeDje, "Los Angeles Composers."

63. Specialty was founded in 1946 in Los Angeles by Art Rupe, who was a pioneer in the recording of gospel, rhythm and blues, and rock and roll; see DjeDje, "Los Angeles Composers," 428–429.

64. Ibid.

65. The National Quartet Convention, the parent organization for the Interdenominational Singers Alliance, was founded by the Blue Jays and Soul Stirrers in Chicago. See Ray Funk, personal communication with author, 1995; and Mary Smith, personal interview with author, 23 June 1992. Mary Smith, a native of Mississippi who migrated to the San Francisco Bay Area in 1941, states that she has been involved with quartets and the Singers Alliance since the early 1950s.

66. The Los Angeles Gospel Choral Union, of which Sallie Martin was president, served as host for Thomas Dorsey's National Convention of Gospel Choirs and Choruses, which met at Second Baptist Church in 1949; see DjeDje, "Gospel Music in the Los Angeles Black Community," 64. John L. Branham and the musicians at St. Paul were in charge of the music for the National Baptist Convention in 1949; Lightner, personal interview.

67. DjeDje, "Gospel Music in the Los Angeles Black Community," 62–64.

68. Lightner, personal interview.

69. Betty Pleasant, "The New Music: Los Angeles Nears Goal of 'Gospel Capital of World,'" *Los Angeles Sentinel* (23 April 1964): F15.

70. Each of these individuals had established careers before settling in Los Angeles. Born in 1925 in Lexington, Mississippi, Margaret Aikens-Jenkins spent the majority of her life in Chicago before moving to Los Angeles in 1964. Prior to her move, she not only organized and sang with two gospel groups (the Meltones and the Ladies of Song) but also established several record and publishing companies. She has composed many songs, two of her most famous being "The Only Hope We Have" and "A Brighter Day Ahead" (Margaret Aikens-Jenkins, personal interview with author, 11 January 1991).

In Memphis, Tennessee, where she is originally from, Cassietta George (1928–95) performed with a female group, the Songbirds of the South, during the forties and fifties. She later sang with the Brewster Ensemble. When she moved to Chicago in the 1950s, she sang and recorded extensively with a nationally known group called the Caravans. George moved to Los Angeles in the mid-sixties and continued with a solo performing career in gospel. See Ray Funk, liner notes, *San Francisco Bay Quartets* (Gospel Heritage 314, 1987); "Singer Cassietta George Dies," *Los Angeles Sentinel* (5 January 1995): A4; and Boyer, *How Sweet the Sound*, 225.

Born 1940 in St. Louis, Missouri, Isaiah Jones Jr. was influenced by pioneering gospel singer Willie Mae Ford Smith (his mentor) as a child. When he completed high school, he lived in Chicago, where he performed with several noted gospel musicians

(Robert Anderson, Mahalia Jackson, the Caravans, etc.). After leaving the military, he was involved in the musical *Black Nativity,* touring throughout the United States and Australia. Explaining why he settled in Los Angeles in 1965, Jones states, "[S]ome of my friends up there [the Bay Area] suggested to me that I come to Los Angeles, that all the commercial agents and all the contacts I would need are in the Los Angeles area. So that's the only reason I came to L.A., because I loved the Bay Area. I was trying to be practical at that time, since I was still in show business. I was in the theatrical world. So I came here." Jones received his formal music training from Los Angeles City College and California State University, Los Angeles. He has performed in several gospel musicals, worked with a number of popular music performers, including the Fifth Dimension and Friends of Distinction, and composed several secular pop songs. In the gospel world, he is probably best known as a composer and recording artist (Isaiah Jones, personal interview with author, 26 July 1990).

Raymond Rasberry (1932–95) was born in Akron, Ohio, and moved to Los Angeles in 1969. As a young man he studied European art music and gospel music privately and attended the Cleveland Conservatory of Music. When the opportunity arose, he decided to forgo his formal studies to become a traveling musician, working with such musicians as Wynona Carr, Beatrice Ward and the Brown Inspirational Singers, Clara Ward and the Ward Singers, and Mahalia Jackson. From 1954–69, he traveled throughout the United States with his own all-male group, the Raymond Rasberry Singers. Of his several compositions, one of his most famous is "Only What You Do for Christ Will Last" (Raymond Rasberry, personal interview with author, 25 February 1989).

Clara Ward (1924–73) and the Ward Singers moved to Los Angeles from Philadelphia during the 1960s. Ward began her gospel career during the thirties, singing with her mother, Gertrude Murphy Ward (1901–83), and sister Willa (1921–) as a trio. After a successful debut at the National Baptist Convention in 1943, the Ward Singers became nationally known, with Clara as the main soloist, piano accompanist, and arranger. In 1946 the group began recruiting other members, holding auditions in cities where they performed. Their most famous was Marion Williams, who became the lead singer on the group's greatest hits. The Ward Singers had a successful recording career and made numerous tours throughout the world before moving to Los Angeles. The group was known for flamboyant wardrobes and hairstyles and a pop-gospel repertoire in addition to the gospel standards. They performed in television and movies, on Broadway, and at jazz festivals and amusement parks (e.g., Disneyland), and they became noted for their nightclub acts in Las Vegas, Hollywood, and other cities. See "Clara Ward Singers Back from Europe After Seven Months," *Los Angeles Sentinel* (17 September 1970): B2; "Clara Ward Singers to Return Home After Seven Months European Tour," *Los Angeles Sentinel* (27 August 1970): C9; Anthony (Tony) Heilbut, *The Gospel Sound: Good News and Bad Times,* rev. ed. (Garden City, NY: Anchor Books, 1975); and Heilbut, "Clara Ward (1924–1973) and the Ward Singers" in *Black Women in America: An Historical Encyclopedia,* ed. Darlene Clark Hine (Brooklyn: Carlson Publishing, 1993), 1223–1224.

See biographical data on Bessie Griffin and James Cleveland in foregoing discussion and in works by DjeDje.

71. Margaret Pleasant Douroux, born in 1941 in Los Angeles, acquired much of her religious musical training in her father's (gospel singer Earl A. Pleasant's) church, Mount Moriah Baptist. She was also greatly influenced by contacts with Frazier and Lightner, who both worked as musicians at Mount Moriah. As a music major, she attended Southern University but received her B.A. degree in music from California State University, Los Angeles.

She composed her first song, "Give Me a Clean Heart," in 1968 and since has written more than 200 sacred songs, becoming nationally known. Her songs have become standards in gospel hymnbooks and have won awards. In 1980, Douroux established the Heritage Music Foundation, an organization whose mission is to build Gospel House in Los Angeles (a monument, hall of fame, and museum complex that would be devoted to the nurturing and preservation of gospel music).

Andraé Crouch and his twin sister, Sandra, were born in 1942 in Los Angeles. Since the publication of his first gospel song by Frazier-Cleveland and Co. in 1966, he has become an internationally known composer of both traditional and contemporary gospel. Further discussion about Crouch can be found in Jean Kidula, "The Gospel of Andraé Crouch: A Black Angeleno," chapter 9 in this volume. Also see DjeDje, "Gospel Music in the Los Angeles Black Community," 7, and "Los Angeles Composers."

72. Ray Funk, "Los Angeles Recorded Gospel Who's Who" (unpublished manuscript, 1992); and Charles Johnson, personal interview.

73. The title of the first Voices of Hope album, *We've Come This Far by Faith*, is taken from a song composed by Los Angeles native Albert A. Goodson; see foregoing discussion and DjeDje, "Los Angeles Composers."

74. DjeDje, "Gospel Music in the Los Angeles Black Community," 68.

75. The clergy and members of various churches in my hometown of Jesup (a small town located in southeast Georgia) were very slow in incorporating gospel music in worship. Though it was common to have special concerts by gospel quartets on Sunday afternoons and evenings, the music most often used in worship service included jubilees, folk or old-time spirituals, lining-out hymns, and congregational hymns found in the *Gospel Pearls* or the *Baptist Standard Hymnal*. The only gospel music heard in service was performed by local musicians, who sang songs by Charles A. Tindley (ca. 1850s–1933), Lucie Campbell (1885–1963), Thomas Dorsey, or Kenneth Morris. When, during the 1960s, gospel was finally introduced in worship, the songs performed by the Echoes of Eden Choir ("God Be With You") and the Voices of Hope ("We've Come This Far by Faith" and "The Beautiful Garden of Prayer") and music written by Doris Akers ("It Means a Lot to Know Jesus for Yourself" and "Lead Me, Guide Me") were most accepted. As a young pianist at Bennett Union Baptist Church in Jesup, I worked closely with Ruth Mallard, one of the persons responsible for introducing gospel in churches in Jesup and other small towns in southeast Georgia; Mallard learned most of her songs by attending the National Baptist Convention.

76. A press release for the Mighty Clouds of Joy—"Profile (The Mighty Clouds of Joy)," *Performing Arts (Southern California Edition)* 29, no. 2 (February 1995): P6—indicates that the group was formed in 1960, but gospel researchers and collectors give 1959 as the year that the group was organized. See Ray Funk, "Let's Go Out to the Programs (The Peacock Gospel Years)" in *Duke/Peacock Records: An Illustrated History with Discography*, comps. Galen Gart and Roy C. Ames (Milford, NH: Big Nickel Publications, 1990), 37–50; and Lee Hildebrand, "Mighty Clouds Are Mighty High," *San Francisco Sunday Examiner & Chronicle Datebook* (4 May 1980): 26–27.

77. "Profile (Mighty Clouds of Joy)."

78. Funk, "Let's Go Out" and "Los Angeles Recorded"; and Hildebrand, "Mighty Clouds."

79. Funk, "Los Angeles Recorded."

80. DjeDje, "Gospel Music in the Los Angeles Black Community."

81. Bessie Griffin, personal interview with author, 1 October 1987; DjeDje, "A Historical Overview," 3–4; "Gospel Music in the Los Angeles Black Community," 68–69; and Funk, "Los Angeles Recorded."

82. Many issues of black newspapers from the pre-1930s period of the San Francisco Bay Area are missing, and no microfilm copies exist.

83. Funk, in the liner notes for *San Francisco Bay Quartets* album, states that the Spiritual Five "was the first important quartet from out-of-town that is reported to have traveled to the Bay Area. They came to the Bay Area [from Houston] in 1937 after having been formed a few years before and immediately settled there [on the West Coast]."

84. William Elmer Keeton was born in Missouri and formally studied music at Northwestern University, earning a doctorate with honors. Keeton opened several music studios in the Bay Area; he provided instruction in piano and organ and offered courses in music history, theory, harmony, counterpoint, form and analysis, composition, and instrumentation. See Michael Fried, "Sing It, When You Can't Tell It" (unpublished manuscript, 1994).

85. Crouchett, et al., *Visions Toward*, 42; and Fried, "Sing It."

86. "Mt. Pleasant Baptist Church," *The California Voice* (9 September 1938): 2.

87. By the late 1930s, Chicago had become known as a major center for gospel music. Because noted gospel musicians lived in Chicago, many blacks throughout the United States probably felt it was the city where one could learn to perform "good" gospel music.

88. Lawrence P. Crouchett, personal interview with author, 23 June 1989.

89. Ibid.

90. At present, Betty Reid Soskin and her sons are the owners of Reid's Records. She and Melvin Reid, her former husband, established the business in 1945. Melvin Reid, a native of California, died in 1988. He was the great-great-grandson of Captain William Henry Galt, the first black captain of the state militia in Sacramento, who traveled across the continent to California from Portsmouth, Virginia, in 1861 (Betty Reid Soskin, personal interview with author, 21 June 1989). During the fifties and sixties, Melvin and his uncle, Paul Reid, were successful promoters of gospel music in the Bay Area. See Lee Hildebrand, "Sell a Joyful Noise," *Express: The East Bay's Free Weekly* (1 December 1989): 27–31 for an article about Betty Soskin and the Reid family business. Also see below for further discussion of Reid's Records.

91. Soskin, personal interview.

92. Ibid.

93. "Cooper A.M.E. Zion Church," *The California Voice* (29 August 1941): 7; "Cooper A.M.E. Zion Church," *The California Voice* (5 September 1941): 7; "Progressive Baptist Church," *The California Voice* (29 August 1941): 7; "New Hope Baptist Church," *The California Voice* (29 August 1941): 7; "New Hope Baptist Church," *The California Voice* (5 September 1941): 7; "New Hope Baptist Church," *The California Voice* (7 November 1941): 7; and "New Hope Baptist Church," *The California Voice* (28 November 1941): 7; "Shiloh Baptist Church," *The California Voice* (7 November 1941): 7; "Mt. Pleasant Baptist Church," *The California Voice* (16 July 1943): 8; "First A.M.E. Church," *The California Voice* (13 July 1951): 7; "First A.M.E. Church," *The California Voice*, (27 July 1951): 7.

94. Beasley, personal interview.

95. In the article, " 'Can't Nothing Shake Me Now': When Lillian Glenn Walked Off a Vaudeville Stage Fifty Years Ago, She Gave Up a Promising Career as a Blues Singer to 'Stand Fast for the Master,' " *Express: The East Bay's Free Weekly* (31 August 1979): 4, Lee Hildebrand states: "VJM Records in England recently reissued an album titled *Lillian Glinn*

[sic]: *Recorded 1927–1929 in Atlanta, Dallas and New Orleans.* Three Lillian Glenn sides (two of them different from those on the VJM album) are included on the more readily available Blues Classics anthology, *When Women Sang the Blues.*

96. Odessa Perkins, personal interview with author, 22 June 1990. Perkins was born in 1930 in Louisiana. She moved to Oakland in 1952.

97. Gadling, personal interview, 1989.

98. Jimmie Bowie, personal interview with author, 19 June 1990.

99. Beasley, personal interview.

100. Bob Geddins, one of the first independent record producers in Oakland, recorded the Rising Stars on his Big Town label in 1944. The success from the Rising Stars provided Geddins with funds not only to start his own pressing plant but also to record the Pilgrim Travelers, the Soul Stirrers, and the Paramount Singers. The Rising Stars is believed to be the first local Bay Area quartet to come to any prominence. See Funk, *San Francisco Bay Quartets;* Lee Hildebrand, "Saving Grace: Other Musical Styles Suffer from Fickle Fans, But Gospel Is Sustained by a Truly Faithful Audience," *Berkeley Monthly* (February 1980): 39. For further discussion of Geddins, see chaptere 3 of this volume, "Oakland Blues," by Lee Hildebrand and James Moore Sr.

101. Funk, *San Francisco Bay Quartets.*

102. "Outstanding Singing Group, the J. L. Richards Specials" photo caption, *Sun Reporter* (18 February 1961): 11; and Mary Bolden, personal interview with author, 21 June 1990.

103. Ola Jean Andrews, personal interview with author, 22 June 1992.

104. Ola Jean Andrews, telephone conversation with the author, 9 January 1993; personal letters to author, April 1995 and July 1996.

105. Ola Jean Andrews, personal interview.

106. In a 1992 personal interview with the author, Andrews stated that some members of their church were not pleased when an article appeared in the local paper about their performance at the Monterey Jazz Festival. The newspaper report described the group as the "five Andrews Sisters of Ephesians Church of God in Christ, a swinging group from a swinging church." Though the pastor of their church was not critical of the performance at the festival and believed it to "be a good testimony for [the group] to go there," church members "felt that [the Andrews Sisters] shouldn't be on that territory." At the Monterey Festival in 1963, the Andrews Sisters appeared with Bessie Griffin and the Gospel Pearls, the Georgia Sea Island Singers, Peter Paul and Mary, and other artists. See "Artists Signed for Monterey Folk Fete," *The California Voice* (5 April 1963): 4.

107. Ralph J. Gleason, "Memories of Monterey—A Great Jazz Festival," *San Francisco Sunday Chronicle* (2 October 1960): 17; "Singing Team to Mark 12th Anniversary," *Oakland Tribune* (3 May 1961); Lillian Fortier, "The Big Sound," *The California Voice* (22 September 1961); "The Folk Festival Stars for Monterey," *San Francisco Chronicle* (10 April 1963); "Gospel Singers on the Way Up," *Berkeley Gazette* (11 May 1963); and Richard Hadlock, "Folk Singer's Day—to Talk," *San Francisco Examiner* (19 May 1963): 5CH.

108. Gadling, personal interview, 1989; Bolden, personal interview; and Helen Stephens, personal interview with author, 22 June 1989.

109. Bolden, personal interview.

110. "Gospel Singers to Convene in Oakland," *Sun Reporter* (5 July 1958): 10; "America's Singers Association Formed at Gospel Singers Meeting in East Bay," *Sun Reporter* (19 July 1958): 11; and Perkins, personal interview.

111. In a personal interview, 23 June 1992, Mary Smith states that Los Angeles was Local 1, San Diego Local 2, Sacramento Local 5, and Bakersfield Local 6. Helen Stephens, in a 1989 personal interview with the author, stated that Richmond was Local 10.

112. William Allums, personal interview with author, 21 June 1989.

113. Gadling, personal interview, 1989.

114. Allums, personal interview. Although their popularity has diminished, locals have not died out completely. In a 1992 personal interview with the author, Mary Smith stated that locals still have their regular monthly meetings and annual conventions, but the number of people who participate now is much smaller than the number who were active during the fifties. The decline in the prominence of locals can also be attributed to the rise in popularity of community choirs and the Gospel Music Workshop of America (see further discussion below).

115. "Federation of Choirs," *Sun Reporter* (7 February 1953): 9; "Choir Federation at Pleasant Hill," *Sun Reporter* (14 March 1953): 12; and "Choir Federation Meets July 26," *Sun Reporter* (11 July 1953): 9.

116. "The Temple of Truth Baptist Church," *The California Voice* (27 January 1950): 7; and Beasley, personal interview.

117. Beasley, personal interview.

118. Among those who lived in the San Francisco Bay Area, Narcisse was known as His Grace King Louis H. Narcisse and often compared to Daddy Grace and Father Divine (evangelists who were prominent in black communities throughout the United States during the early decades of the twentieth century) because of his flamboyance and old-time preaching style. He is believed to have established branches of his church in Sacramento, Detroit, Houston, New Orleans, and Orlando; see "In Anniversary Celebration," *The California Voice* (7 September 1956): 7; "State Meeting," *The California Voice* (10 May 1957): 3; Lee Hildebrand, "The Departure of King Narcisse: Flamboyant Last Rites for a Legendary Oakland Preacher," *Express: The East Bay's Free Weekly* (24 February 1989): 3, 27. In a 1989 personal interview with the author, Helen Stephens stated, "It [Mount Zion] was a very booming church. It was an active church. He would sell candles and have readings. He would have you stand and he could tell you what's going to be happening in your life in the coming days. But he passed in 1989." In his early life, Narcisse was also a well-known baritone singer. "He had been a prolific recording artist during the '50s, making 78s, 45s, and one album for such labels as Jaxyson, Modern, Hollywood, Music City, Veltone, and Peacock. In 1963, musicologist Chris Strachwitz [a Bay area record store owner and producer] filmed him for a folk music documentary that was shown here and in Europe"; see Hildebrand, "The Departure."

119. "From 'The Scene and the View' by Wetumka M. Moffatt, Jr.," *The California Voice*, issues of 20 July 1962: 2; (9 November 1962: 7; and 7 October 1966: 7. See also "His Grace Bishop Louis H. Narcisse of Mt. Zion Spiritual Temple, Oakland, left . . . for Washington D. C. where he will offer prayer at Pres-elect John F. Kennedy's inauguration," photo caption, *Sun Reporter* (21 January 1961): 9; "His Grace Returns," *Sun Reporter* (18 February 1961): 11; "King Louis Narcisse Pledges Backing of AWOC," *The California Voice* (14 July 1961): 4; and "Narcisse, Mayor Christopher Get Together," *The California Voice* (2 March 1962): 5.

120. Gadling, personal interview, 1989.

121. Stephens, personal interview.

122. Most of the churches in the Bay Area had radio broadcasts, but Evergreen Baptist and St. John Baptist had two of the longest-running programs. Formerly a quartet singer, Carl J. Anderson founded St. John Baptist in the late forties. He served as pastor and di-

rector of his radio choir. Anderson and his choir were often invited to churches for performances or to participate in worship services during the fifties and sixties, and their radio program, *The Gospel Call Hour,* was considered one of the best in the area. See "Reid's Records Presents Third Annual Choir Competition at Oakland Auditorium," *The California Voice* (9 November 1956): 6; "Rev. Carl Anderson to Preach Anniversary Sermon at 3rd Baptist," *Sun Reporter* (26 October 1957): 11; "Presentation—The Outstanding Radio Choir of . . . St. John's Baptist Church," *The California Voice* (20 December 1957): 2; "Rev. Richards Concludes Anniversary at Evergreen Baptist Church," *The California Voice* (9 November 1962): 7; "Rev. Richards Celebrating 16th Anniversary at Evergreen Baptist Church," *The California Voice* (25 October 1963): 6; "Rev. Carl Anderson Honors Rev. Haynes," *Sun Reporter* (15 October 1966): 36; Bolden, personal interview; and Gadling, personal interview, 1989.

123. "Vallejo Vignette," *Sun Reporter,* issues of 28 March 1953: 11; 8 August 1953: 15; 15 August 1953: 15; 20 March 1954: 16; 10 April 1954: 15; and 17 April 1954: 10.

124. "Fifteen Thousand to Attend Gospel Festival in Oakland," *Sun Reporter* (12 June 1954): 2.

125. "Nine Churches Lined Up Solidly Behind Great Choir Contest: Each Urging Its Choir on to Victory," *Western American* (24 February 1928): 1; and "Fifteenth Street Church Choir Out to Win," *Western American* (16 March 1928): 1.

126. "First Annual Choir Competition This Sunday in Oakand," *Sun Reporter* (20 November 1954): 1; "Choirs Compete in Oakland Aud.," *Sun Reporter* (19 November 1955): 13; and "Third Annual Choir Contest at Oakland Auditorium Sunday," *Sun Reporter* (17 November 1956): 9.

127. Herman Harper was well known in the Bay Area for his ability to direct choirs. He worked with youth choirs at El Bethel Baptist (San Francisco) and Star Bethel Baptist (Oakland). His choirs were often called on to perform with noted gospel musicians when they visited the Bay Area. In 1957 his group at El Bethel was one of the few choirs from the Bay Area invited to perform at the Oakland Auditorium to welcome Detroit minister the Rev. C. L. Franklin and his daughter Aretha. In 1959 his choir at Star Bethel performed at the Oakland Auditorium with Franklin in a program in connection with the National Baptist Convention. In 1960, Star Bethel's youth choir appeared in a concert, sponsored by Paul and Mel Reid, with the Raymond Rasberry Singers, James Cleveland, and Sallie Martin. See "Reid's Records Presents Third Annual Choir Competition at Oakland Auditorium," *The California Voice* (9 November 1956): 6; "Detroit Minister to Preach at Oakland Auditorium," *The California Voice* (31 May 1957): 8; "El Bethel Youth Choir Wins Competition 2nd Time," *The California Voice* (29 November 1957): 2; "Rev. Franklin in Auditorium with Singers," *The California Voice* (4 September 1959): 6; and "Rasberry Singers in Concert," *Sun Reporter* (19 November 1960): 15.

128. "Choirs Compete in Oakland Auditorium," *Sun Reporter* (19 November 1955): 13.

129. "First Annual Choir Competition This Sunday in Oakland," *Sun Reporter* (20 November 1954): 1.

130. "Vallejo Vignette, *Sun Reporter* (20 March 1954): 16.

131. "One Hundred Voice Choir of Macedonia Baptist Church" photo caption, *Sun Reporter* (19 May 1962); and "Newcomer to Direct 100-Voice Choir at Merit Awards Program," *Sun Reporter* (24 March 1962): 16.

132. "Outstanding Composers Cited by Music Company," *Sun Reporter* (26 February 1955): 2.

133. Andrews, personal interview.

134. Stephens, personal interview.

135. Andrews, personal interview.

136. Lee Hildebrand, "Gospel's First Family," *Express: The East Bay's Free Weekly* (24 November 1978): 1, 4–5; Lee Hildebrand, "Dorothy Morrison's Happy Days," *Express: The East Bay's Free Weekly* (9 January 1980): 9; and Hildebrand, "Saving Grace."

137. Stephens, personal interview.

138. "Garner to Direct S.D. Chorus for Achievement Day," *The San Diego Informer* (17 June 1935): 1.

139. De Vonne C. Morris, personal interview.

140. Morris states that her mother used to sing Dorsey's "Precious Lord" in worship services at Calvary Baptist during the 1930s.

141. DjeDje, "Change and Differentiation," 237–238.

142. From 1938–1941, John L. Branham served as pastor of Calvary Baptist. Morris, in a personal interview, did not provide any information on whether Branham attempted to introduce gospel music in the church while he was in San Diego.

143. Morris, personal interview.

144. S. M. Lockridge, whose full name is Shadrack Meshack Lockridge, was nationally known and held several important positions in religious organizations in California. A 1977 report in the *San Diego Union* states: "Dr. Lockridge is head of the Progressive Baptist District Association, president of the California Baptist Convention and statistician of the National Baptist Convention of America. Statewide, he is known for his leadership in efforts to bring all black Baptist churches under one organization and nationally, and internationally, he is well-known as an orator." See "Dr. Lockridge to Celebrate 25 Years As Pastor," *San Diego Union* (30 July 1977): A15.

145. Verneater Robinson, personal interview with author, 31 December 1992.

146. V. M. McPherson, personal interview with author, 17 February 1992.

147. Originally, the group was known as the Spiritual Four and included Willie Pitts, Edward Graves, Willie Lee Ross, and Exton Hullaby Sr. After several months, C. W. (Corn Wallis) Dean joined, and the group became the Spiritual Five. In the late forties, other members were added: Marvin C. Hines and J. T. Rattler. In the 1950s, when the group decided to make a recording, they discovered that another group in Los Angeles was using the name "Spiritual Five." It was at that time that they decided to change their name to the Spiritual Kings. They sang a cappella in most performances but used instruments when they recorded. In 1954 the Kings performed with two nationally known groups—the Spirit of Memphis and the Dixie Hummingbirds—at a San Diego high school, drawing more than 1,000 people. See Jon Applegate, "This Is Gospel: More Than Just Prayer with a Beat," *Reader: San Diego's Weekly* 12, no. 27 (14 July 1983): 14, 16.

148. C. W. Dean, personal interview with author, 31 December 1992.

149. The Gospel Revelators were formed in 1969. Members of the group included Lester Logan (founder), Sammy Graham, Clifford Robinson, and Osefine Washington. Millard Stacy, called the utilityman (because he was able to sing baritone, tenor, or a slightly higher tenor called fifth voice), replaced Sammy Graham when Graham moved to Arizona to become a pastor. The group has recorded two albums. Like the Mighty Clouds of Joy, the Revelators perform in a "modern" quartet style characterized by tight harmonies from the backup group. Also, they always sing with instruments. See Applegate, "This Is Gospel," 1,10; and Funk, personal communication.

150. "Gospel in Songs," *The San Diego Light House* (29 September 1951): 1.

151. Gwendolyn Gordon, personal interview with author, 15 February 1992.

152. Morris, personal interview.

153. "Pilgrim Progressive Baptist Church Plans 1st Reunion," *San Diego Voice & Viewpoint* (20 November 1986): A16, A18.

154. Applegate,"This Is Gospel," 16.

155. Morris, personal interview.

156. Dean, personal interview.

157. "Dr. Lockridge," *San Diego Union;* and Bolden, personal interview.

158. Marva Hines, the daughter of Marvin C. Hines and Dorothy Hines Chestang, sang with James Cleveland's Southern California Community Choir during the seventies and eighties.

159. The Spiritual Kings "took turns traveling in their own cars, usually leaving on Friday night and returning late Sunday. Working only for a percentage of the gate receipts, never for a guaranteed amount, the Spiritual Kings did not make enough money for its members to quit their regular jobs, but they had a large local following, and they took pride in their musicianship" (Applegate, "This Is Gospel," 14, 16).

160. Dean opened his record shop (Dean's Record City) in 1959 because "there was no outlet for gospel records in San Diego" (Dean, personal interview). When he discovered that gospel would not support a business, he expanded his market to all types of music. Since its founding, Dean's Record City has become an important institution in San Diego.

161. Dean, personal interview.

162. DjeDje, personal interview with Sonja Williams.

163. Bernice Johnson Reagon, Sandra Rattley-Lewis, Judi Moore Latta, and Sonja Williams, *"We've Come This Far by Faith": The Story of the California Gospel Movement,* Program 24 of the twenty-six-part radio series *"Wade in the Water": African American Sacred Music Traditions* (Washington, DC: National Public Radio, 1994).

164. Gadling, personal interview, 1989.

165. Reagon, *We've Come This Far.*

166. Smallwood, personal interview, 1988; and Karima Haynes, "The Gospel Controversy: Are the New Songs Too Jazzy and Too Worldly?" *Ebony* 47, no. 5 (1992): 76, 78, 80, 82.

167. Harris, "Conflict and Resolution," and *The Rise of Gospel Blues.*

168. DjeDje, "Change and Differentiation," 244; and Edwin Eames and Judith Granich Goode, *Anthropology of the City: An Introduction to Urban Anthropology* (Englewood Cliffs, NJ: Prentice-Hall, 1977), 36.

PART TWO

Music and the Media

5

Insider Perspectives
on the American Afrikan Popular
Music Industry and Black Radio

Kwaku Person-Lynn

PART 1: THE POPULAR MUSIC INDUSTRY:
AN INTERVIEW WITH AL BELL

African-American music in Los Angeles has been influenced and shaped by a myriad of people from the music industry: artists, composers, and record producers. Some have resided in California since the migrations in the forties; others are more recent immigrants. Al Bell moved to Los Angeles in 1988 to become (briefly) the president of Motown Records. Before this move, he was national director of promotions, national sales manager, executive vice president, and eventual owner and board chairman of Stax Records. Describing his formal entry into the record business and the impact of Stax Records (which was well established before Motown Records) on music, Bell says: "When I went in there it was a young production company, driven by rawness and honesty. I thought it was the music everyone ought to hear, which I believed when I played the songs on the radio. I believed in that then and have seen how it has affected the whole of the music industry. I watch things [now] that are subtle and see how that's the Stax influence."[1]

Because Stax, under the guidance of Al Bell, has played such a pivotal role in the development of American popular music, his inclusion in a collection of essays on California's black music is imperative, particularly because Los Angeles is one of the major centers of the popular music industry and often regarded as the mass media capital of the world.

Al Bell began his career as a teenage disc jockey in Little Rock, Arkansas, then took similar jobs in Memphis and Washington, D.C. After a short stint with Martin Luther King's Southern Christian Leadership Conference, he held various executive positions with Stax and Motown Records and established Edge Records and Bellmark (short for Al Bell Marketing) Records after leaving Motown in late 1988. Bellmark produces all categories of African-American music and has made an immediate impact in the record industry. In 1993, Bellmark produced and distributed Tag Team's hit record "Whoomp! (There It Is)" on the Life label and Duice's "Dazzey Duks," on TMR, proving that Bell's musical and marketing instincts remain as keen as they were when he guided the careers of artists such as Isaac Hayes, Sam and Dave, and Otis Redding.

Bellmark also promotes what Bell refers to as "God-inspired music." In November 1995 the company released ten albums featuring music by the Howard University Gospel Choir, Edwin Hawkins, Walter Hawkins, Rance Allen Group, Wintley Phipps, the Church of God in Christ International Mass Choir, and several other gospel artists. In addition, the company provides opportunities for individuals to learn about the record music industry. According to Bell, "We hope . . . we'll be able to grow or aid in growing the next Berry Gordy, the next Ewart Abner, the next Al Bell, or the next young person with creative ideas that can continue to perpetuate African-American music and continue to have a positive impact on this record music industry."[2]

This interview covers several topics: Bell's career as a record company executive; major Stax artists; Stax in Los Angeles; Los Angeles and the popular music industry; the Stax sound versus the Motown sound; trends in popular music from the sixties to the nineties; future directions of black music; the impact of radio on Stax and the music industry; creativity within the music industry; and black music marketing.

Al Bell's Role in the Development and History of Stax Records

Kwaku Person-Lynn: What were your duties at Stax from the beginning of your involvement with the company to the point of ownership?

Al Bell: I started out at Stax as its national director of promotions and shortly after that became national sales manager, then became executive vice president, and then acquired a 50 percent equity interest, and ultimately acquired the entire company and became its board chairman.

I never functioned as president. My former partner, or the founder of Stax, functioned as president of Stax, but I functioned as its board chairperson. As the chairman of the board, I was chief executive officer and responsible for the overall executive duties of the company. In addition to that, I operated as the chief cook, bottle washer, janitor, and everything else that was necessary to be done to make a business function properly, particularly one that we were building. So I guess it's fair to say that I performed the normal kind of executive duties as well as whatever else had to be done to develop that business. Also, I wrote a few songs and produced a few artists and continued throughout the development of the company. I was very much involved in promotion, marketing, and distribution.

KPL: Compare your involvement in the early development of Stax to your present duties at Edge Records? What role have you played in the development of Edge Records?

AB: Well, it's quite different. Stax was a company that was founded by a white gentleman, Jim Stewart, and his sister. The "ST" is from Stewart and his sister, Estelle Axton, the "AX" in Axton. *Stax.* They had founded the company, which was basically a production company, meaning that they had a small recording studio, monaural, one-track recording studio, and some in-house community musicians who came in and played in the studio there every day. They formed a label that was called initially Satellite Records, and they had to change that name to Stax, which was ultimately distributed by Atlantic Records.

They had such artists as Carla Thomas with a hit, "Gee Whiz," and Booker T and the MGs with a hit, "Green Onions," and the Mar-Keys with a hit, "Last Night." They had also signed and were recording at that time Otis Redding. By the time I joined the company as its national director of promotions, they had had several hits on the label, although it was still basically a production company. But it had developed from the community musicians, who were primarily Booker T and the MGs, and had begun to develop in-house writers to write the songs for the various artists that they would record.

By and large, the company's initial production approach had been established. They were selling records through this distribution relationship with Atlantic Records, primarily in the South. There was an A&R director, Steve Cropper, who was the guitarist with Booker T and the MGs, and Jim Stewart and his sister were the owners and employees. When I got there, I came in as an employee, one charged with the responsibility of turning a production company around because it was in a losing situation and about to go down the tube. We came in and were successful in doing that in a reasonable period of time. We took it from 90,000 in the red to 3.5 million dollars gross in about eighteen months with about a 20 percent net before-tax earning, by sheer hard work, creativity, and a lot of imagination.

I had developed my appreciation for Stax while in radio. My background prior to Stax was radio, in addition to a small company that I had on my own, which was distributed by Atlantic Records. I had a company, Safice Records, and had the artist Eddie Floyd, along with other artists on that label and was operating it out of Washington, D.C. Eddie, if you recalled, his first big hit on Stax was "Knock on Wood." He ultimately became a writer, artist, and producer for Stax. But the point I'm making is that the company basically was started and owned by someone else, and I spent my entire involvement with Stax, attempting to take what was there, build it, develop it, organize it with a view toward building a major independent record company, having to, on a step-by-step basis, integrate my philosophy toward business into the overall business philosophy there.

If you take that and compare that to this particular situation, here's a company that I'm starting with a partner here. Well my philosophy, as well as his, were discussed prior to any development in the company. That combined philosophy is being implemented here in the inception. So we are starting off with an understanding as far as business philosophy, creative philosophy, etc., is concerned, and the company is being founded based on that philosophy. And we're able to creatively begin to put it together in that fashion. I suppose that more importantly is that we've embarked upon the development of this company with the experiences of the past, which we're blessed to have. We didn't have that in Stax. But those experiences, I venture to say, put us in a novel position in the establishment of this business here. And that probably is the clearest distinction between what happened in the development of Stax and what is happening in the development of this company.

Major Stax Artists

KPL: Who were some of the major artists on Stax? And didn't you have some comedians on another label?

AB: We had, as I mentioned, Carla Thomas, Rufus Thomas, Booker T and the MGs, the Mar-Keys, Sam and Dave, Otis Redding, Johnny Taylor, William Bell, Eddie Floyd, Albert King, Little Milton, the Staple Singers, the Emotions, the Dramatics, Isaac Hayes, Billy Eckstine, Glenn Yarborough and the Limelighters, Mike Douglass (the TV host), Black Oak Arkansas (the rock/pop group), O. B. McClinton (a black country and western singer).

We had Richard Pryor, Moms Mabley, Bill Cosby. Also, we had an Irish, a very influential young Irish singer, Lena Zalarony. We had Rance Allen on the gospel side, the Howard Lemon Singers, Maceo Woods, and numerous other gospel artists.

KPL: While you were with Stax, a concept entitled the "Memphis sound" evolved. What were the creative mechanics that developed the Memphis sound?

AB: A cross-fertilization of cultures, primarily. And I suppose the influence of the cultures as they matriculated over a period of time up the Mississippi River. The Stax sound was a small part of the overall mosaic that made up the Memphis sound, which was an integration of your mid-South jazz, as it came from New Orleans up the Mississippi to St. Louis, as it came out of Mississippi, the influence of [William] Handy and what have you. That was what the whole Memphis sound was about.

With Stax, we had the four guys that made up Booker T and the MGs. Al Jackson, who was a drummer who came from the jazz background. His father was a jazz musician, and he was a very, very outstanding drummer with the jazz and blues influences and a feel for the contemporary music of that era. We had Steve Cropper, who had basic country rock and roll kind of influences. And he was a white guitar player, who was a rhythm guitar player. Then we had Doug Don, who was the bass player who had basic country influences, and he also was white. And Booker T, who played keyboard, and he had basically a general musical influence and was the one that had the formal training because he was going to school, studying music, and ultimately got his degree in music. So it was a combination of that plus the music that's really indigenous to that area of the country, which made up the Stax sound, which was part of the Memphis sound.

Stax in Los Angeles

KPL: Stax produced an event in Los Angeles that was unprecedented at the time (1972). This was the WattStax event,[3] and you brought many artists to the Los Angeles Coliseum. What was the original thought and idea for that? What was the political significance of that event?

AB: I don't know the political significance. There was no political thought given with respect to the event. Stax was a company that was very much of and responsive to its social responsibility as it related to black America. We were major contributors to the NAACP, the Urban League, the PUSHes, the United Negro College Fund, the black colleges individually as well as the College Fund. We probably had 200 to 250 lifetime memberships in the NAACP, for example. We were all over this country doing whatever, whenever it was required for black people.

Forrest Hamilton, who ran our West Coast office, wanted to put on something here in Los Angeles to support the Watts community. Watts—I think the gentleman's name was Tommy Jacquet—had the Watts Summer Festival that they were putting on here. And Forrest called me and said, "I think this is something we ought to do. It would be great."

And he went on to tell me about Jacquet and what all of the people were doing. As we talked, it started expanding from something small to us having the audacity of putting it into a stadium out there and bringing in the whole roster of artists. Because it was getting too massive . . . we took it then from support of the Watts Summer Festival group to involvement from all of the major black groups—social groups and civil rights groups. NAACP, Urban League, etc. were all participants in the revenue generated from that event.

That was the reason that it came about. And I was glad to do it. From a business and a marketing sense, I thought it was a great opportunity for the artists. I thought it was a great opportunity for it allowed us to expose all of the artists in Los Angeles and allowed us to spend an enormous amount of money on the artists, and we could see ways of recouping it through the sale of phonograph records. Whereas individually, we could not have afforded to spend that kind of money on any individual artist. And it was allowing us to make a deep, deep dent into the Los Angeles market, just being really pragmatic about it. Influencing Los Angeles radio, popularizing the artist with the Los Angeles community, thereby making it a lot easier to promote and market subsequent releases on the artist. So from a business standpoint, I viewed that part of it, which made it kind of a happy pursuit because we had an enormous financial investment in that. We invested an inordinate amount of money. We made our money back and were able to make some contributions to the community and to these various organizations. That's what it was really all about. And I'm pleased with the success of it.

KPL: One of the auxiliary effects was that a black-owned company produced an event that practically filled the Coliseum with black faces. I was there. I witnessed it and enjoyed it. Do you feel that the event may have had some kind of threatening effect on the industry as a whole, which at that time was primarily white-owned?

AB: I think it did. I think that our motives in some instances were misread. In other instances, it probably posed itself as a threat. I have been told by some people, years after its happening, that it was in fact threatening. What you had was a combination of things going on here. You had a black company—that operated out of Memphis, Tennessee, no less—that was able to come to Los Angeles, California, and go into the stadium and put 112,000 people through the turnstiles out there in that stadium. To film it with one of your major documentary producers at that time, David Wolfer. Underwrite the cost of all of that with the finest director of documentaries in the industry at that time, and underwrite the cost of all of that, and to take that film and market it along with another major company, but spending the lion's share of the money ourselves across the United States of America. If you have the money, the talent, and the audacity to do something like that, then you have the money, talent, and audacity to get into the motion picture business with your own money, no less. *WattStax* was tremendously successful. It was the very first documentary that was entertaining. It was a first for the industry. So here is something else that's new on the horizons. And you had black folks doing that.

Another perspective is that at that time, we didn't recognize it, but Jesse Jackson was a friend, and we consulted Jesse in the development and establishment and financing of Operation PUSH. He also was a recording artist for Stax. We had a label, Truth Records, where we had Jesse Jackson and John Casandra. And Jesse was one of the principle players on stage in the WattStax event and also in the film. Well, that film was shown around these United States, and we had screenings all over the place in Washington for the senators and the congressmen, and we had them in New York, and we had them in Chicago and in Detroit. We had them for *Who's Who in the World*. The subtitle of that film was *The Living Word*. It was *WattStax: The Living Word*, and it was meant to be a reflection of what was going on in black America. And it was meant to show the music of black Americans, reflecting what was going on in black lifestyle, and black culture, and black lives.

We wanted everybody to see this. In letting everybody see that, they saw some other things that we didn't see. We showed a bigger mirror than we had intended to project, when folks looked and saw 112,000 people in this Coliseum and nobody with guns to control them. Los Angeles folks said, officials said, we can't have no guns in there. If you recall, we put our own black policemen in there with no guns. We had our black security in there with no guns whatsoever. No problems. Controlled the crowds. Nothing at all. No riots, none of this kind of stuff. And Jesse was on stage and this film going around the country with Jesse standing up there with his hands up in the air and Kim Weston singing the black national anthem and all of this kind of stuff came off as a black nationalist kind of thing, when it was about none of that (laughter). But it was perceived in some quarters to be that way.

So it was then a threat, if you view it from a purely political perspective in terms of someone amassing some awesome black political power. It was a threat as far as a minority business getting involved in the motion pictures without perhaps the correct associations. They were tongue-in-cheek. And I'm sure it caused the phonograph industry to stand back on its heels, because who would have thought of and did it make sense to go and put a lot of black artists in the Los Angeles Coliseum and expect to put 50,000 people in there at that time. No less to come out with two double-pocket albums—they were gold albums in the sales at that time. That was awesome. If you consider all of those things, I suppose that was threatening and frightening.

In retrospect, the big album we had on Richard Pryor after that . . . 'cause we had Pryor in that film . . . was called *This Nigger Is Crazy*. I suppose in retrospect, looking at myself, I would have to say, "That nigger is crazy" (laughter), to have the audacity to do something like that. But we dared to be different and quite frankly had no idea, no idea, no earthly idea of the ramifications of all of that. Had no thoughts whatsoever about any kind of historical contribution or nothing. There was no more involved than what I just told you.

There was another agenda, quite frankly, and that agenda dealt with the training of black people and putting the film together. Training black people in learning how to work behind the camera with a view toward creating a creative force that could deal with video. We knew . . . because of the amount of time we had spent in Europe watching Phillips and the rest of them developing video at that time. What we had been hearing in seminars and what have you . . . we had been participating in on this cable bit. We knew at that time what was going to happen as far as cable was concerned. We had a feeling or thoughts or visions about what was going to happen with respect to video. So I also took advantage of the opportunity to start training people to deal with video productions and get ready to start developing and creating the software for cable television. The outgrowth of that was Stax Films. We actually went into the film business. Prior to that, we had been dealing with Melvin van Peebles. Melvin had out *Sweet Sweetback's Baadasssss Song*. We were involved in parts of the financing and purchasing of that. We had gone across the country with that film without any of the film distribution outlets across the United States of America. We had several other projects that we were involved in with Melvin at that time. So I guess when you sit back and look back on it, someone not really knowing what was in our minds and what we were all about, they probably would have really been concerned about that now. I'm really thinking about that as we are talking. I guess it would be frightening.

Los Angeles and the Popular Music Industry

KPL: What inspired you to move to Los Angeles after Stax went out of business?

AB: After the close of Stax and what I recognized as a change in the influences in African-American music in 1975, which was the advent of the disco era, I moved into— went back to Arkansas. I just decided to leave the business alone. Disco was putting an emphasis on so many beats per minute, a good hook line, and deemphasizing the development of unique artists and the development of unique songs, which is what our business is all about. I thought it was a detriment to the industry and to us but couldn't do anything about it. So I went back to Arkansas, set me up a little label, and sort of kept my finger on the pulse of the industry.

Then I saw something start developing out of New York called rap music. I heard the stories being told once again and recognized that if that music became popular with today's young people, then once again we've become oriented to hearing stories in our songs. And maybe the melody would come back in. I saw that they were looking and feeling for the drum beats, the authenticity and the passion associated with the music of my era as they sampled to make their rap music. In my mind, I saw a change coming. This industry, this business is cyclical in nature. So I assumed we were back to square one and time for a fellow like me to get back into midstream. I recognized the change in the industry and realized that I would have to come out of the South this time. Stax was in Memphis, I'm there in Arkansas. This time around, there were only two places for me to go. And that was either to New York or Los Angeles.

KPL: Why did you pick Los Angeles over New York?

AB: I opted for Los Angeles because to me Los Angeles is the entertainment capital and the creative center of entertainment, period, and especially recorded music. As far as the recording music industry is concerned, all the power is in New York because it is the financial center. But I just feel more inclined to deal in Los Angeles because it's more creative here in Los Angeles, and I think more conducive for creativity. So I headed here to Southern California, pitched my tent, and went to work in 1986.

KPL: Is there anything that you can say that reflects a Los Angeles sound or California sound that is affecting black popular music?

AB: The California sound that came out of here most recently was the sound actually that was born by SOLAR Records and Dick Griffey. The contribution that SOLAR, which is [short for] the "Sound of Los Angeles," made to this industry during its development is still being felt. When you listen to "L.A." [Antonio Reid] and "Babyface" [Kenneth Edmonds] and many of these other guys out here today that are very successful, they came out of the SOLAR scene. Right now, these are the dominant African Americans in the recorded music business. So recently, the greatest impact has come from the influence of all of the creative people that were there at SOLAR Records with Dick Griffey.

KPL: Would you say that what is coming out of California is affecting black popular music as a whole nationally or globally?

AB: Well both, nationally and globally. If you just look at the impact of, even though they are not physically located here now, if you just look at L.A. and Babyface and their influences, well, you would have to say both nationally and globally. California has had that kind of impact on music for some time, Southern California in particular.

If you go back, which is what I always relate to, at least in my mind is the genesis— and I'm sure there was something before then—was back to the days of Modern Records. I think there was another label but I've forgotten the name of it. Back during those days, they recorded and perpetuated the likes of B. B. King, Lowell Fulson, and that kind of blues music. That music was coming out of Southern California. It had an impact and influence on blues music nationally and globally and many of the musicians that came after that. Those that came out of Chicago, the Muddy Waters and Howlin' Wolf and all of that, I venture to say, were influenced to a certain degree by what was coming from the likes of Lowell Fulson and B. B. King out of Southern California. You had back during that era, the Johnny Taylors—a little later on, both Johnny Taylors: the Johnny Taylor of the Sam Cooke Soul Stirrers fame and the Johnny Taylor that was the "Part-Time Love" Johnny Taylor.

Subsequent to that, or during that same period of time, you had Specialty Records, which was the label that Sam Cooke gave birth to, and you had Sam and the Valentino Brothers, and the Womack Brothers. Out of that came Bobby Womack, and Specialty gave birth to the likes of Little Richard, who was from Georgia. But you had Southern California looking around for those kind of artists and everything. Then you had Johnny Otis and all of that.

So if you just look at what has come out of California over a period of years, it's safe to say that California has had a tremendous impact on global music going back for some time. If you just look at California picking up Little Richard, then doing what it did with Richard, and Richard's influence on the Beatles and the rest of popular music, you have to contribute that in part to California or the California way of thinking.

KPL: In California, you know a lot of key players in terms of African-American executives. Do you feel that there is a large enough pool here in Southern California of African-American executives to have the business savvy and the creative intuition to help foster a new music, a new black music?

AB: No. I think that the generation of African-American executives that we've had were executives who were developed inside of these major corporations. Inside the corporations you are trained and taught that marvelous bureaucratic process. You understand how to preserve and protect your job without making waves and stepping on other people's feet or getting outside the boundaries of your job and impacting somebody else's job. So you become a specialist in that limited area of whatever it is you're doing as an executive. In order to be richly successful in developing as you and I are discussing it now, you have to really have had an opportunity to experience the lumps and bruises of understanding it from A to Z, and not specializing in one particular area. You have to understand the manufacturing, the marketing, the distribution, the production, and how all of these things have to relate.

That person generally is born from the streets. Generally speaking, this is basically a street business. The next executive, or the next big successful one, will not have been heralded by you, me, or others as a learned executive, but [it will be] some daring, persevering young person out there with the desire to make something happen in this music business and willing to work at it and take the risks and the knocks and bruises in order to cause it to happen. There are enough of those around to start another industry out here overnight.

KPL: When we talk about the area of rap, it started on the East Coast and Bronx and New York. But Los Angeles, particularly South Central and Compton, is known for starting a genre called "gangsta rap." How influential has that been in the rap industry?

AB: Well, it's been the most dominant music in the industry from a musical standpoint and from a sales standpoint. It is naturally and authentically inner-city African-American music. And it projects the rhythms or rhythm of today's young people, whether they are African American or European American or Spanish-speaking Americans, or whatever the case might be. Its message is the message of today's youth, and specifically inner-city youth. And it has really permeated the music of young people. It has impacted young people that are doing gospel music, gospel-rap music. The interesting thing about it is the rhythm that you find is not unlike the rhythm of the African-American youth of the sixties and seventies. It's the same type of feel. But it's the feel and rhythm of today's young people.

Stax Sound versus Motown Sound

KPL: How would you describe the difference between the Stax sound and the Motown sound?[4]

AB: Well, Motown was more urban. Motown was a reflection of the kind of music that you experience in the big cities, the metropolitan lifestyles. I like to always identify or define music really as a reflection of what goes on in the lives and lifestyles of a people. Motown grew out of the urbanness of Detroit, a major metropolitan industrial kind of city. And its music was a reflection of that kind of lifestyle. The Stax music was more rural America, certainly America and that lifestyle that you feel in the mid-South of this country. And that was the distinction between what was happening in Motown and what was happening at Stax.

Additionally, Motown took more of a formula kind of approach to creative production, in that they had established a very clearly defined musical approach with respect to arrangements, etc. Stax was basically free-form. Very few arrangements were [used] in Stax in the early days and even in the latter days. We did what you called "head sessions." Everybody would go in and you'd play and play until you get a groove. When you got a groove, then you had it. The [Stax] guys were allowed a little bit more than Motown to just freely express themselves, whether it was musically or otherwise. We did that until we came up with the right kind of chemistry and what we all discerned to be a hit record or a hit production. And then that was our final product. It was not in one specific category.

Motown tended to stay into the urban, general-market kind of appeal music . . . what they are calling today "crossover." We dealt with another kind of art form, which was dealing with it more in a purer sense, not looking per se for any kind of general-market commercial appreciation but just dealing with the art form, whether it was gospel, whether it was jazz, whether it was R&B. Whatever it was, we dealt with it in its purest sense as the culture of that area dictated. That's what you had.

KPL: Would you say the difference between the Stax and Motown sound could be similar to the rural and urban blues, although there was growth and evolution from those foundations? Would you juxtapose those together, or would you use another analogy?

AB: No, no, no, I think that's excellent. Rural and urban blues, rural and urban young American music. Motown at that time was dealing with young American music. We chose to believe that we were dealing with young American music at that time, even though in terms of demographic appeal we did not confine it to young America. And Motown's music was appreciated by more than just young America. But it was, as opposed to blues, rural and urban, young American music of that era. There is no question about it.

KPL: In the 1990s there's one major shift that's occurring out of California: Motown Records has a new CEO/president. He wants to shift the headquarters to New York rather than stay in Los Angeles or Hollywood. Do you think that's going to have a major effect on what Motown produces?

AB: Yes. Motown, as you and I and the rest of the world affectionately know and understand it to be, ceased to exist when Berry Gordy stepped down from the helm of creativity inside that company. That change started taking place after he relocated from Detroit to Los Angeles and expanded his horizons and started moving further into motion pictures and leaving that creative direction to others in his company. That's not a criticism, that's an observation. From that point forward, Motown, which was the essence of Berry Gordy and those that he inspired directly, didn't continue to exist. If you listen to the music, it changed. I'm not criticizing, again, [but] it changed when it was moved to Southern California. When Berry sold it, that certainly was the end of that. What you had left from that point forward, as far as I am concerned, was the asset value associated with the goodwill in that label, Motown itself—its rich, rich musical history, and the fact that it's an institution in American and global music with respect to its name.

We had Jheryl Busby to come in and do a wonderful job as he dealt with the beginning of the next era of Motown or the new chapter of Motown, and now Andre Harrell and what he's doing. We cannot associate what Busby achieved under his leadership or what Andre will achieve under his leadership with what was done in Motown when Motown was Motown/Berry Gordy. It will have to become whatever it is Motown became under Busby and whatever it will become under Andre Harrell. The problem is, they're having to live in that awesome shadow of the Berry Gordy Motown. In order to get the recognition that they should have, they're going to have do something that is uniquely outstanding from a creative standpoint. They're going to have to write their own book. It will have to be called Motown, with no real association with Motown of the past. A new mold has to be created. What is it the philosopher says? "The moving finger writes, and having writ moves on." Berry's gone.

KPL: Maybe moving to New York is part of writing that new book.

AB: Maybe. I think only time will tell.

Trends in the Popular Music Industry: 1960s–1990s

KPL: How do you compare black music of the Stax era with what you hear now in late 1980s?

AB: Night and day. During the Stax era we fortunately had an opportunity as a people and as record consumers generally to hear and purchase and sing and play all kinds of music. In the 1980s, it was limited to a few categories. And the record companies placed their marketing strategy on appealing to a narrow demographic, teenagers, which is fine. But to assume that the only people that appreciate recorded music in America were teenagers bordered on insanity. If I were to make a comparison, I would have to say what happened was insane. What was generally available, merchandised, and promoted was teen-oriented music. During the Stax era, the teen music—bubblegum, as it was called during that era—represented somewhere between 10 and 20 percent of the business. In the eighties, it was 80 percent, only because the companies focused it in that fashion. The focus during the seventies and early eighties was on a disco-oriented kind of music, strictly dance-oriented music, with little emphasis placed on listening, albeit teen music. So we were getting a narrow piece of the musical creativity that was available in the market-place.

KPL: Why do you think the record industry marketed music in that way?

AB: Honest to God, I don't know. I suppose the only thing I can attribute it to is lack of knowledge. That's the only thing I can attribute it to, because veteran record people know that the demographic that you focus on is the twenty-five to forty-nine. Teenagers rapidly become twenty-five. Teenagers rapidly grow up. You're talking about from thirteen to nineteen. You're talking about six years. They move out of that group fast. As soon as one group gets into the group, they grow and become young adults, and along comes another group. There is no stability there. And once they become adults, they put aside childish things. And they become young adults and they have a different kind of music appreciation. So there's a twenty-five-to-forty-nine grouping that you are constantly catching. When they leave the forty-nine, they always relate, too, because we appreciated it when we were young adults. Not necessarily that we appreciate it when we were teenagers.

If I understand that myself, I cannot understand why others don't understand that and that our industry focused on totally a teenage demographic during the eighties. I can only say, lack of knowledge. Not to negate the teen music. But to focus an entire industry on teen music was a travesty.

Future Directions of Black Music

KPL: Why do you think crossover was so important during the eighties?

AB: I don't know. I don't know. I really don't know. That troubled me. That really troubled me. That is one of the reasons that I went back in this business. We needed some people that appreciated the diverse art form as I do. And there are others like me, but I'm talking about myself now. I don't believe we will have anything that can be recognized in any respect as black music with some influences of the past. They say, "A tree separated from its roots will soon die." And black music has been separated from its roots, and its roots were being destroyed. Our music with its African influence that became slave music, that became spiritual, that became jubilee, that became gospel, that became blues, that became jazz, that became R&B, has been separated from its roots. If you don't know where you came from, it's impossible for you to know where you are going or how to get there as it relates to the subject.

During the late eighties, that was being destroyed, that root, the basis for our music. We have several, maybe two generations of young black Americans that have been integrated into society to a certain extent. In that integration process, they were removed from the roots of their music. So they were unable to identify with it. It was foreign to them; it was an alien. And as we moved forth, I feared it was going to become a vanishing art form, an obsolete part of our culture as a people. Perhaps with some European histor-ical appreciation only as a thing left to keep it slightly visible in our books. Dead, unless someone got out there and tried to do something about it. And in the process of that, a lot of good human beings that were endowed with the talents that God had given them to perform the gospel music, the blues music, and the jazz music were denied the right to ex-press that in America. That's what I foresaw.

One day in 1980s I saw Rod Stewart on MTV. Rod Stewart was saying that in the past white artists were primarily copying black artists and black artists were beginning to copy white artists. In other words, black artists were so interested in copying what the white artists were doing, it was not leaving anything for the white artists to borrow from the black artists. So ultimately, down the road, I didn't think there would be anything upon which to grow and build on because the black artists who were the originators and inven-tors of black music were crossing over into, I guess, pop music or whatever it was called, imitating white styles [that] were imitating black styles. But the roots and foundations were being lost, which ultimately left the music foundationless.

KLP: In the nineties, crossover doesn't seem to be as large an element now. What would you say now, in this new day and age—and you've gotten back into the business—would you say is the future of black music?

AB: In a discussion with some decision makers in this industry about a month or so ago, I heard the statement that black music is in a state of hopelessness. That is the think-ing of some of those behind the scenes as it relates to our music. I don't think so. Our music has already or always reflected what was going on in our lives and in our lifestyle. Rap music certainly indicated what was going in the lives and lifestyles of inner-city young people and our young in general. I believe out of that a new music will be born.

I see and hear discussions among musicians and hear what they're doing as it relates to what they're calling now "acid jazz." As I listen to the acid jazz, I see young people with all sorts of musical influences looking for a new way for African-American music to ex-press itself. So it is looking for a new way to express itself. That new way will be found. The young creators were confused by that whole crossover notion, because new ideas were not being born. New creativity was not allowed to be born that came from African-American youth, that came from them purely. The crossover kind of thing has played out in terms of the demands of the industry. So what has to happen is, it has to start all over again.

The challenging question is whether or not we will have independent, free-thinking entrepreneurs that can get into a position, given the control on radio and the control on distribution, to take this new music, whatever it may be, that will emerge from the young people and promote and market it successfully so as to have it impact and influence music overall. That's the big question.

KLP: It seems like a lot of the young artists today, particularly in the rap field, are rely-ing on what they call the "old school" for inspiration. Do you see that as one of the foun-dations for developing a new music?

AB: No question about it. Not only do I see it as being the foundation, but I think it has given rise to some of the finest creative minds that will have come from us. If you go back and look at what has happened to us musically, we as African Americans would cre-ate a music concept idea, only to have the European Americans adopt, adapt, or take that concept and popularize it and cause the masses to appreciate it. Which meant that as fast as we would create, it would be taken away, and we'd have to go and create something else. We haven't had an opportunity until just recently to go back and look at from whence we came. Where we came from, to understand our musical roots from a historical standpoint.

Today's young people, because of the new technology and the ability to sample, have had an opportunity to go back and examine carefully and thoroughly our music. The creators of today know where this music came from. All of the generations that preceded them had no earthly idea.

Today's young people know. I listened to acid jazz the other night that had some John Coltrane influence in it, some Thelonius Monk influence in it, and in the middle of that I heard Rufus Thomas sampled, and then I heard some B. B. King. To be able to do that successfully and creatively means that you have to have a pretty good feel for all of that. So I think out of this generation of young people probably will come our finest contribution to music or popular music.

Impact of Radio on Stax and the Music Industry

KPL: What role did black radio play in the growth and development of Stax?

AB: Obviously, as it does with all companies, absent black radio, you don't really feel that kind of popular total acceptance for black music. But more specifically, black radio, after we were able to cause the majority of black radio stations in America to appreciate our music, black radio was almost like an extension of Stax. We provided the diversification in black product that allowed them to play all kinds of music on the radio stations. Unlike Motown—Motown had basically one kind of music. We had a bit of it all. So when they wanted to play jazz, we had the product, a high-quality product, a unique product. When they wanted blues, we had the product. When they wanted rhythm and blues, we had it. And we had the stars in each one of the categories. So it played a very, very significant role.

Also, once we had the exposure, there was a great appreciation by the jocks in radio at that time for the kind of creativity that was coming out of Stax. It was basically black folk's music. And the black jocks appreciated it, because you had black jocks in control of their own destiny, so to speak, as far as music was concerned. They had a great opportunity to exploit the product.

KPL: Did pop or so-called white radio have any role at all in terms of the growth and development of Stax?

AB: I suppose somewhat. After it was popularized, our philosophy never was necessarily to place that much emphasis on pop radio except when we were dealing with pop artists. Certainly we wanted our records played on every kind of radio imaginable. That's just business. But we didn't think in terms of crossover. The approach was to go and produce a record that would be accepted and appreciated by the masses of black America, which was our base market, believing that once a significant number of black Americans purchased the music, that in fact would popularize the music and subsequently [it would] become pop. Well, it took a while. And in some instances, we never overcame it. It took a while to overcome the discrimination that goes along with black music and pop acceptance.

Otis Redding never received any significant pop air play in America till he died. When he was killed and we released "The Dock of the Bay," it became the number-one record in America and was played on pop stations all over the country. But prior to that, maybe 5 percent of the pop stations in America played Otis Redding. Isaac Hayes, for example, we had sold several million albums on several album releases prior to getting any significant pop air play. And we really didn't get any on him until "Shaft," which was the hit motion-picture soundtrack—*after* then, after we had won the Academy Award. So pop radio had some influence, but very little influence. When pop radio played our music, it was popular music at that time.

KPL: My understanding, through the interviews that I've done in Los Angeles, is that black radio in the eighties became more and more like pop radio and became more for-mulaic and more formatted. Do you think this had a harmful effect on black music as a whole?

AB: I think it was harmful, if we define harmful in the sense of restrictive. These radio stations programmed music that appealed to the demographics that we just finished talking about. That has not always been the case. Our business is generally influenced by the dictates of your major companies. Your major companies were moving in that direc-tion. So as a result, that influenced black radio. It was no longer black radio; it became "urban contemporary."

KPL: A term started by Frankie Crocker.

AB: Frankie is one of the veterans. Frankie Crocker played a significant role in the de-velopment of Stax Records, in exposing Stax Records and breaking its products in New York City, and introducing Stax Records to New York City. So Frankie Crocker has a broad-based music appreciation.

But we have a controlled industry. If there was an unwritten part of the Harvard report [on the marketing of black music], it was the part that would have emphasized the last stage of development that said, "You can control the sound of the music and control the music once it becomes yours. You then change it from what it is to what you want it to be-come and you then control it by relationships with radio stations, etc." That has happened.

Let me tell you something. The control is there now, the change in radio is there now. But I think that an in-depth examination of [the] economics [of] broadcasting in today's world and the sales and the lack of sales as well as the lack of stability in the area of sales of strictly teen-oriented music has become problematic. It may be awhile before it sur-faces to the extent that folk will admit it. And perhaps, hopefully, during this era we will begin to see some more independent companies emerge who will then begin to influence radio. And because of the economics of the situation, we will find some radio stations or a radio station and a market that will begin to play a more diverse kind of music format, popularizing that music in that particular market, thereby influencing the other radio sta-tions in that market to begin to play a broader kind of music format.

But it has changed. Black music is now pop radio, practically speaking.

Creativity Within the Music Industry

KPL: Concerning creative freedom, top executives in the A&R [Artists and Repertoire] departments at both Columbia and Warner Bros. maintain that their depart-ments select the producers, the songs and other material, the engineer, and make most of the creative decisions. They estimate that 90 to 95 percent of their artists are under this kind of A&R control. How would you compare the control that is used today with the creative control of artists at Stax during your tenure?

AB: Night and day. You're talking about two different worlds. We have an industry that's divided into segments. One segment is made up of your major conglomerate-controlled record companies. In today's world, there are basically only six of them. That's one segment of our business. And the other segment is the independent segment of the business, which is where you have the small independent companies that are owned by music buffs, entrepreneurs, and what have you that form independent companies out here and distribute their product through independent wholesalers across the country. To distinguish the difference in size in today's market, we have an industry, according to 1984 figures, that grossed $4.2 billion. The independent segment of it accounted for 15 percent, which is about $650 million. So you're talking about a $650 million side, which is where you have the free-form, creativity. On the major company side is where you have the kind of structure that you're talking about.

Appreciate the difference, though. The major companies are set up, and they have been since inception, to be manufacturers, meaning those that manufacture albums and duplicate tapes, etc., and mass-merchandising, distribution machines. They are designed to manufacture and mass-merchandise that product that has already received general market acceptance. Prior to that, they aren't necessarily obliged to waste too much energy exploiting that kind of product, which is why you see or hear them always acquiring some major act or some act that has a style that is like unto a style or an idiom that is happening in the marketplace. Rarely or ever do you see or hear of these companies creating or developing a new kind of music, a new idiom, or whatever. They are set up to acquire, to copy the "happening" producer in the marketplace, the accepted artist in the marketplace, and obliged to mass-merchandise the kinds of products that would be generally accepted by the masses of the people. That's a difference.

So as a result of that, you find A&R departments or A&R department heads with a job description and responsibility that causes them to pair an artist with a "happening," [an artist] who has had access to or has himself the kind of songs that are songs that currently happening on the national charts and currently have mass-merchandising appeal. So in order for them to be successful, operating as they are designed to operate, they almost have to function that way, unless there is a philosophy that's changed someplace else in those companies.

KPL: This eliminates the chance or opportunity for a new style, idiom, or development within music. If they are staying within the mainstream, then someone who is innovative like Sly Stone, Jimi Hendrix, Charlie Parker, or Dizzy Gillespie has less of a chance of breaking into the major companies.

AB: There is no question about it. But there are exceptions to the rule where you do have some of those artists developed in those companies . . . not as often today as it has been in the past. The independent side of the business has been—and, I suppose always will be as long as it exists—the training ground or farm club for the major companies. It is on the independent side of the industry where the new talent is created, where the new concepts are developed. Once they are developed on that side, your majors are there, and they then acquire it. We are talking about a business today that's 650 million dollars. Well, your major companies got into rap music. Well, rap was started on the independent side.

They got into disco music. Disco started on the independent side. And other kinds of music, I'm hoping, will start on the independent side.

The problem, of course, today—and appreciate that our business is cyclical in nature, if you appreciate my description and accept that of the major companies—every ten to fifteen years, we go through a cycle where we have independent companies that have grown up. The past era, it was the Staxes, the Motowns, the Atlantics, etc. Once these companies become successful and you have a group of successful producers out there, they are then acquired by the major companies because it then becomes general market. You have a new kind of music or a new sound, and it's acquired by the major companies. Well, we've just gone through that cycle, where the major companies acquired everything that was available in the marketplace.

So we are now back to square one. Square one says you have to have new entrepreneurs that need to get into the business on the independent side, creative minds to start these new independent companies, to start that new cycle all over again. And once again, hopefully, you'll have an opportunity for a new kind of talent to get back into the business. If it goes as it has been in the past and should go, we'll have a more diversified kind of music available in the marketplace. As we go forth, we'll hear a more diversified music on our radio stations, because as these companies acquire—once they finish acquiring so much, the fat gets in the middle. So they have to start trimming the fat, which means cutting off the artist roster. So those artists that are not producing and carrying their weight get trimmed, employees get trimmed, and where do they go? They go back to the independent side of the business, and the ballgame starts all over again. You once again begin to hear the broad-based diversification of American music, as opposed to what we've heard in recent years, which has been something less than that. So just appreciate that it's cyclical, and then you can understand what I'm saying and that's why you have the two segments of the industry. I hasten to say that this last time around, this last cycle, the acquisition process became so competitive that discretion went down the tubes. The independent side of the business was almost destroyed, and a void was created out there in the marketplace that is almost unbelievable.

At the same time, it is a great opportunity, especially for people like myself that understand what it is really all about and what that segment of the business is all about and thankful that, in my particular case, where I have the expertise and experience to know how to take advantage of it. The opportunities are enormous now. It costs a lot more than it did years ago, obviously, so the economics of it will make it a bit more difficult than it has been in the past. But creative people are creative people, and record people are record people, and artistic people are artistic people, and they are going to find some way, no matter what the situation is, to get their products recorded and somebody gets out here and starts the ball to rolling. And that snowball is going to accelerate as time goes along. Hopefully, we'll become a catalyst toward that end.

Black Music Marketing

KPL: In terms of black music marketing, CBS commissioned the business school at Harvard to do a study [in 1971]. I just want to ask you how influential was this study in terms of developing music marketing within the industry.

AB: I think that—and this is just my opinion—I think that the Harvard report in fact was the blueprint for the establishment of the black division in CBS and ultimately the black divisions in the phonograph business, period, particularly with regard to the major record companies. As a matter of fact, I all but know that. How did you find out about the Harvard report?

KPL: I interviewed Logan Westbrook. But originally I interviewed Verdine White of Earth, Wind and Fire, and he told me about it. Then I went to Logan Westbrook, who oversaw that whole study for CBS.

AB: The Harvard report, which Logan was involved in with another young lady out here, in my opinion was a excellent study on our approach at Stax to operating a black phonograph record company, in total. When I saw it, I thought that I was looking at Stax (laughter). Its policy, its assumption of corporate responsibility as it relates to the community—socially, politically, educationally, culturally, and otherwise. Its being responsive to the religious community and what have you. When I saw all of that in the Harvard report, I thought it very interesting. Now the approach to integrating the black music division into the corporate structure was the traditional, as far as I'm concerned. That's the way you do it.

But the study, I must say . . . while frowning in one sense, I had to applaud it in another sense, because it was very accurate—very, very accurate. And they have done a skillful job of integrating the various phases into the corporate structure of the major companies on a step-by-step basis, which included the bringing in raw—at its most basic level—as it relates to black America, in its inception. And the steps that led to the ultimate refining of it until it became no more than a part of CBS or a part of other companies. It no longer appeared to be what black America is all about but really what corporate America is all about, if you follow the drift of that. And I think they've done a very skillful job in pursuit of that goal.

KPL: My gut reaction tells me that the study may have been part of the inspiration for the ending of Stax. Is my gut reaction true? Yes or no.

AB: Do you want the truth, the whole truth and nothing but the truth, so help you God, and then ask me for a half-truth? (laughter) Yes or no. I must say that I cannot give you an absolute answer to that. However, prior to that study, our business methodology was unknown. So as a result, we had very little competition. No one knew what we were doing. So we were able to build a business at our own pace. Subsequent to the revelations in that study, the competition became much more intense. The appreciation for the potential volume that black music could generate became a threat. And in the big business world, you go for market share. And if someone has a nice-sized piece of the pie with respect to market share and you don't have that share of the pie, then your business dictates say, "take it" or "remove the threat," which leaves that share up for grabs. I'm sure that, by deducing, normal intelligence could give an accurate conclusion with respect to the matter.

KPL: You said a lot there without saying it. Since we are into it, what really put Stax out of business? I know, getting into some particulars, when Clive Davis was at CBS, in the early 1970s, it seemed to be a positive relationship developing. When he left, there was a change. I guess the whole attitude and character of CBS—I guess the study may have played a small role. The fact that the potential of black music in the general market was—the awareness of that was growing. Combined with the things I just mentioned, what really were the things that ended Stax Records?

AB: You've asked me now a very simple question, but one of the most complicated questions that you could ask me. To really give you an appreciation for the answer would require another two or three hours to establish background. But let me try to give you a feel for it.

I choose to believe that Stax was the first pure distribution deal through one of these major companies. We have now what we call P&D deals, pressing and distribution deals of companies in the industry. And Stax's involvement with CBS began as a discussion between Clive Davis and myself. The bottom line of the discussion was, we were going to distribute our product through CBS's branch distribution in the same manner and business procedure as we were distributing our product through independent wholesalers. They would only sell and distribute our product, and for that we would pay them a normal kind of fee. We were responsible for everything else with our product. That of course enhances CBS's image, getting them into the black market, because they were not into the black market at that time. And it was envisioned that the reciprocity that would come would be a further expansion of Stax's LP sales, because of CBS's ability to sell LPs at that time. With that premise, it would be logical to assume that would have been a good business deal. I choose to believe that it would have been, could have been, and should have been.

Clive Davis's untimely departure perhaps contributed to Stax's problem with CBS. We had only been in the deal about four or five months, and Clive was no longer with CBS. I choose to believe that could have been a catalyst that created the problems, because the oral agreement between Clive Davis and myself . . . had not permeated the CBS organization.

Perhaps that led to some of the problems. When I say some of the problems, I mean problems that led to the separation of Stax and CBS, that ended up embroiled in litigation. We filed an antitrust suit against CBS for 67 million dollars in 1974, alleging violation of the Sherman Patman Antitrust Act.

KPL: Why did you file that?

AB: It was our belief, based on evidence that we had available to us, that there was a concerted effort on the part of the individuals that controlled and operated CBS to practice restraintive trade and in fact put us out of business.

KPL: Are there any theories as to why?

AB: I would assume that either they concluded it was a bad business deal and/or it was a share of the market that they wanted. It was a share of the market that we had. I venture to say, if that deal had not been terminated, regardless of how it could have been done or was done, that would have been a situation where the tail would have been literally wagging the dog. CBS had the massive mass-merchandising machine, and we had the most diverse black product that was ever assembled in the history of recorded music. We had the blues, we had the gospel, we had the jazz, from the Chico Hamiltons to the Maynard Fergusons, you name it. We had it all. With their distribution machinery and with the consumer appeal of black music and the kind of music that we had, we would have continued to outbuild CBS. I do remember at one time during the relationship, when Stax distributed through CBS's branches, Stax was outbilling CBS in terms of gross volume on a monthly basis. I would assume that was probably problematic.

KPL: For them?

AB: Certainly. And it was not a deal that was enormously profitable for them because of the structure of the deal. It was not your normal label deal. This was a strict business deal. We would just use their branches for distribution. So it was not that profitable for them. They made pennies out of the deal. And we were making dollars in the deal. So I'm sure that was not too palatable from a corporate standpoint. I can imagine that led to all kinds of thoughts, and we alleged clandestine activities on their part to try to stop it. That's a part of the court records. I suppose it would be fair to say—and I really want to be clear on this—I suppose it would be fair to say that some of the people, executives in CBS, who were employed by CBS at that time, played a significant role in the demise of Stax. Very significant role.

PART 2: BLACK RADIO IN LOS ANGELES, 1980–1987:
AN INTERVIEW WITH PAM ROBINSON

Radio has been an integral part of the Los Angeles black community since the early 1900s. Special programs targeted to the black community were common-place on white-owned stations. As early as 1939 a program known as the "Gold Hour" was heard over radio station KGFJ.[5] These programs not only allowed blacks to showcase outstanding artists but also helped to unify the burgeoning black community in Los Angeles. During the 1940s and 1950s, several church ser-vices were broadcast on the air.[6]

In 1959, KGFJ became one of the first radio stations in Los Angeles and the United States as a whole to target the black community as its primary audience. Although white-owned, the station used a black music format. This approach made KGFJ an immediate success because "the black community was, at the time, fairly well condensed in Central Los Angeles. And black people listened."[7] It did not matter that KGFJ's signal strength and position on the AM dial were weak, causing its signals to bleed over onto adjacent frequencies. KGFJ always ranked among the top five in the market. It was one of the few stations in the Los Ange-les market "programming rhythm and blues. If . . . [someone] wanted to listen to R&B, KGFJ was the only game in town."[8]

With the success of KGFJ, it was not long before other stations began to target the black community, for those in the media realized that KGFJ's appeal tran-scended racial lines. More important, KGFJ's success contributed to the crossover phenomena; Top 40 and general-market stations saw that black music attracted a large audience.

During the 1970s two black-owned stations came into existence. Also, several white-owned stations (e.g., KUTE[9] and KDAY) changed formats to challenge the success of KGFJ. When KJLH-FM (the first black-owned Los Angeles radio sta-tion) started, it did not seek to compete directly against KGFJ. Rather, KJLH opted to compete head-to-head with other stations, such as Los Angeles's jazz sta-tion, KBCA. KAGB, the other black-owned station established during the 1970s, never became a factor in Los Angeles radio. Notes media observer Ron Dungee, "Either KAGB could not commit the resources required to unseat KGFJ from its position as top dog, its signal was not strong enough to be competitive, or FM radio was not yet enough of a force for KAGB to be competitive."[10]

During the mid-1970s, former Hall of Fame football player Willie D. Davis purchased KAGB and rechristened it KACE.[11] However, KACE never became a blockbuster. By the seventies, those in black radio struggled to stay afloat as more stations played black music to capitalize on the marketplace. One of the biggest factors that caused the decline in black radio's importance was the transformation of the Los Angeles black community.[12] Dungee states:

> Gone were the days when L.A.'s black community was concentrated in the inner-city area. The migration to the suburbs was underway and the core of listenership that once was the strength of KGFJ and KDAY had disbursed to the San Fernando Valley and the Inland Empire. Also gone were the days when there were only one or two sources for black music. The crossover of black music to Top 40 stations was such that it was almost impossible to determine that they were, in fact Top 40 stations.[13]

In 1994, Davis sold KACE[14] to Cox Broadcasting, the parent company of KFI-AM talk radio and KOST-FM (a white-owned station), leaving the number of African-American-owned radio stations at two—KGFJ and KJLH.

Although KACE's call letters are the same and the personnel has not been drastically altered by the sale, the station's music format has changed from adult contemporary to soul oldies. Some circles of the Los Angeles black community like the change, some do not. It seems to be evenly divided. There does seem to be a listenership among Latinos. For some reason or other, many of them [Latinas/Latinos] like oldies.

Since the beginning of the 1990s, KJLH has been KACE's direct competitor in the African-American community. At present, the music format of KJLH differs from that of KACE in that the former mixes contemporary music and oldies, providing a better balance for the breadth of African-American music. However, KKBT (The Beat) is a bigger and more successful competitor because of its larger wattage (50,000, compared to 3,000 for KJLH). Most young African Americans in Los Angeles listen to this station because it goes after that demographic and has much more money to spend.

This interview with Pam Robinson took place in Inglewood, California, on July 29, 1986. Robinson, program director of KACE during much of the 1980s, provides an insider perspective on the complexities of running a black radio station in a changing market. She not only talks about her struggles but also explains some of the strategies she was employing at that time to make KACE successful in a very competitive market. Robinson no longer works at KACE. She occasionally fills in at local adult contemporary stations and is doing voiceovers for commercials.

Programming Responsibilities

KPL: How long have you been program director at KACE?

PR: I've been program director for ten months.

KPL: What are your duties and responsibilities?

PR: As program director, I am responsible for the entire audio sound of the station, everything from the commercials to the music, the rotation of the music, the on-air presentation put together by the jocks.

Influence of KACE

KPL: Where do you see KACE in terms of the growth, development, and influence of black music in Los Angeles?

PR: In this market, I know that we've done a lot to promote new artists and go on product a lot sooner than most radio stations and not shy away from playing new products just based on the fact that the artist is new, the product is new, and you don't want to take a chance on it. As I said before, the basic philosophy for us has been, if it fits the format and it works, play it. Sales and chart consideration come into play only when I may not be as sure about a record or when I don't test records at the station. I don't hear a record and say, "Well I like this, but I'm not really sure. So let me put it in test rotation." If I go on a record, I'm on it. But I want to make sure that I'm going to go on it and give it its full support in terms of airplay and time spent before I start judging a record based on its sales.

So, in effect, if a record sounds good and I want to take a chance with it, I'm going to play it, whether that's starting out in light rotation or medium rotation. But I'll give it enough time to warrant either higher rotation or less rotation or totally off the playlist. I based that strictly on a gut feeling. So I'm not as concerned with who the artist is, if it is a new artist, if it's an artist that's not established, or if it's an artist that's had five or six bad records in a row. You have to go with what you feel. Because we don't test records, I will look at chart action and local sales before I make a decision on it.

KPL: How important is visibility in the community to the station?

PR: I think it's becoming more and more important. When you look at the fact that POWER [a Los Angeles radio station] has come into the market and they are identified as another urban station, it's important that the black stations maintain that visibility and connection with the community, because a station such as POWER is not going to do it. So we are licensed to the city of Inglewood; it is important that we are as visible as can be, given the limited budget that we have compared to what they have. But it is important.

Playlist/Format

KPL: What criteria are used to place music on your playlist?

PR: Several things go into consideration when we are looking at a record. A lot of times, immediately, it is based on feel, whether or not it fits our format, if it can slide right into the format without causing too much disruption, in terms of how things are set up. Other times it is based on chart action and local sales. The bottom line is always whether or not it fits the format.

KPL: How would you describe the format of KACE?

PR: Progressive Adult Contemporary, which is something new for us. We've been into this about six months and recently showed a three-tenths-of-a point increase in Arbitron [the primary radio ratings system]. Based on the fact that we are concentrating on more of an adult-based audience, twenty-five to thirty-four, also eighteen to twenty-four, we aren't alienating that group but concentrating less on the twelve-plus-to-seventeen audience. Basically, going more toward the adult demographics.

KPL: What was the basis for making the decision to go from urban contemporary to adult progressive?

PR: Basically, because of the overflow of Urban Contemporary music in this market, with POWER going to a more homogeneous form of Urban Contemporary with such high wattage (72,000 watts). Based on the fact that we have a limited signal, we started to realize that in order to maintain or gain a consistent qualitative audience, we had to narrow our base. We wanted to gear programming toward a specific group of people, a specific demographic, so that the POWER handicap that we had wouldn't affect us as much as if we were attempting to mass appeal such as a POWER, or KISS, or KJLH at the time.

KPL: Do you think the American market has an ethnocentric, paternalistic attitude in terms of black music? For instance, American black music has not had problems in getting airplay. But black music from Jamaica or Africa, such as Fela or Sunny Adé, or Brazil, with Gilberto Gil or Djavan—they make really good music, but they don't get airplay here. Why do you think they don't get airplay with the good music that they play?

PR: I think with each artist, the case is different. You're talking about Djavan, the music is great, but there is no English, and people have difficulty, for the most part, identifying with something they can't understand. And music is supposedly universal. But I think we've been locked into the English language so much and brainwashed into thinking that if it isn't English, it's Greek to me, no matter what it is. If you look at an artist like Djavan who has great music, his music has a great feel to it, but people have a difficulty getting into that. It's the same thing with Julio Iglesias. For all the years that he sang music and sang in his own native language, when he started singing English lyrics he was the biggest recording artist in the world. So I think that probably has something to do with it. But once again, the outlets for that kind of music in the States are so few and far between. So many people just don't hear it.

Rotation / Sales / Ratings

KPL: When you say light rotation, heavy or moderate rotation, can you define what that means?

PR: Light rotation is generally two plays a day. Medium rotation is anywhere from four to five plays a day. Heavy rotation is six or more plays a day.

KPL: It seems like artists might be restricted in length of time. What is the average length of a record you like to play?

PR: Four and a half to five minutes. Some records are as short as 3:20, 3:50. And others are as long as 6:50 or six and a half. I think the average has got to be five. To me, that's fine, because we're not a hot hit format. We aren't necessarily as concerned with how many we get into an hour's block of time so much as we're concerned that what we are playing within that hour is quality music. We're giving the listeners what they want.

KPL: What if a barrage of records came out—for instance, maybe three or four albums came out with some eight-, nine-, or ten-minute tracks? But they were really good. When Isaac Hayes came out with that album *Hot Buttered Soul,* which had "By the Time I Get to Phoenix" (I've forgotten the title), it was quite long. Would you fit them in your format?

PR: I have done that before, usually with LP cuts. It's very difficult because of the time allotted within an hour's time because of the spot [i.e., advertising] load. Sometimes our commercial load is lighter at the beginning of the week than it is at the end. So records would have a better chance at the beginning of the week. Certain records have come in and I have had to edit them, which makes you feel like a butcher because it's not [right]. You have very little right to go into someone's creative force of music and decide, "I can take this out. This is really insignificant." But if you are talking about airplay as opposed to no airplay at all, I think sometimes it's necessary, depending on the music.

KPL: How do you do sales research?

PR: We have a callout listing of about thirty stores. And each week we rotate. We call ten stores in the market, get a rating from them as to how records are selling. Also, I look at charts from *Billboard, Cash Box, R&R (Radio and Records), BRE (Black Radio Exclusive),* any impact, any trade [publication] I can get to get a balance as to what it's doing across the country. Of course, I have to tailor that to this market and look at local sales. L.A. has always been different from most other markets, depending on how fast the record is moving or how slow it is in establishing itself. There are records that are slow in establishing themselves that we will leave in and stick with because we honestly believe there's an audience out there that wants to hear it.

KPL: The ten stores that you check, are those primarily in the black community?

PR: Primarily, yes. Every now and then, we will go a little further out and deal with Northridge or some parts of North Hollywood, Orange County areas. Every now and then, depending on the record.

KPL: How important is the Arbitron rating to you as a program director?

PR: It's important in that I am always looking for a specific audience base, and it gives me a barometer from which to work. I don't live and die by Arbitron. Our sales department here doesn't live and die by that in terms of their approach to sales. They won't depend totally on Arbitron for data or information. It's always helpful.

But the main consideration when you are a station is primarily retail-based. It's how well are your retailers doing? How well do the retail clients do if they have a sale or if they run a schedule and you want to find out what the response was? Basically, it's up to the sales department to make sure the retail clients are well taken care of. They have an understanding about what to expect the first time, the second time, the third time, whenever they advertise, and look at that as a report or gauge for what we're doing in the community. Of course, Arbitron is great, but it doesn't give you a base in terms of retail from which to work.

Black Radio's Influence on Black Artists and the Music Industry

KPL: What influence do you think black radio has had on the creativity of artists— black artists?

PR: It's got to mean something, because I've talked to several artists in casual conversation. They've said, "I listen to KKGO[15] when I just want to mellow out. I listen to you guys when I want to get some ideas for songs. I listen to KJLH when I want to get my street fix." So they have different radio stations that they listen to for different reasons. I think they get ideas from the current product because they want to be at least close to what's happening, musically.

So often, as a creative artist, you may feel, "I like this and this is good to me. But is it really what people are buying now?" You can get so lost in your own creative juices that you're not really in touch with what is happening in the street or with people who are buying music, which is unfortunate, because it shouldn't be like that. Creativity should come from the soul. And you should feel, when you are writing a song, that [it] will sell based on the fact that it is good music. Unfortunately, a lot of artists use radio. I say unfortunately only because it seems unfortunate to have to depend on that to ensure record sales or ensure a place in this industry.

KPL: In terms of black radio and record companies, are there any struggles between the two in terms of the things that you want to do?

PR: Between record companies and radio stations? Oh yeah, definitely. There's always a battle here or there. Working relationships are difficult to keep on an even keel regardless of what business you're in. I think that as soon as the record company understands what it is you're trying to do—the kinds of things that they can approach you on with promotions, for example—then they will be a lot easier to work with. If someone comes to me wanting to do a promotion with Adidas tennis shoes and Run DMC, they don't know what my station is about. They don't know who my audience is. And that offends me. How can you serve me as a record company with products if you don't really know what I'm doing? You don't really know who it is I am trying to reach and what my goal is. So once the understanding is there, as far as what your role is, what my role is, yes, we can work together. For the most part we do. Ten percent of the time, sure, there are problems, as with any business.

KPL: I remember there was a problem developing during the Prince tour. I remember you (KACE) did a three-hour concert with [percussionist/singer] Sheila E and Prince. But there was a rebellion, so to speak, by black stations because they felt that they were not getting equal billing in terms of promotional items as the pop stations, or so-called white stations. Can you elaborate on that?

PR: Yes. It's really about crossover product, music, and artists. And Prince had crossed over. So, quite naturally, promotional items were scarce, far and few between. We were promised several things that never came through and learned of certain purple umbrellas that were given to the pop stations and "Purple Rain" jackets and tour jackets. All things that could be used as promotional items, I think, basically ended up staying with the staff because they didn't want the public, or they didn't want the black radio stations, to know what it was they had gotten from the record company.

So when it comes to ticket giveaways, that is just one aspect of it. The audience that you have wants to be able to depend on you for that chance to win tickets. You don't get tickets to give away, and another artist or another radio station is doing it, and it's a pop station, then there is a problem. They say, "You have only been playing Prince for three months. Whereas these radio stations were playing Prince when he was doing 'Soft and Wet,'" which was very suggestive in terms of lyrics. But we weren't ignoring Prince as an artist back then. Those are the kinds of things that upset black radio, because we have been supporting Prince all of this time. Now that he has crossed over, we get nothing. We can't give our audience something for listening, or thank them for sticking with us all of this time.

KPL: So what was the supposed action, and what do you think the result would have been if that action had been followed through?

PR: The proposed action was that, at that point, until we could sit down and talk about the inherent problem that we have with crossover artists and acts, we weren't going to play their product. As one station, that may not have mattered. If other stations were feeling that same neglect coming from the record companies and all threatened to do the same thing, then that would have made a difference. Most of them did [stop playing certain records] across the country. Black radio stations just started dropping Warner Bros. products. And it is unfortunate that it had to happen with Prince. But it happens at all record companies with all artists. It was just a way of making a statement.

There were talks after that, and there was an agreement that in the future this supposedly was not going to happen. If you got tickets for your radio station, you would be getting the same amount that a [pop station such as] KISS or a KOST or KKHR, at the time, would get. I think that for the most part, if it hasn't been followed through like that, it's been hidden quite well, because usually I'm brought two or three pairs of tickets, [and] the first thing the record company representative says [is], "Pop stations got the same amount. So this is all we got. Unfortunately, this time we did not make a big buy." There are several excuses as to why you may not get what they say they're going to try to get.

So I believe that it's been rectified in a sense. It still must go on, I'm sure. That one action shook everyone up for quite some time. But things always have a way of slipping back into old habits. Or people have a way of slipping back into old habits. So I think that at some point something like that will probably happen again, because someone will get frustrated and fed up and say, "I'm not going to deal with this anymore."

Unfortunately, the meetings and talks did not continue. There were a couple of them, two or three. But I think it's something that really needs to be dealt with quarterly. I think that radio stations and record companies really need to sit down and find out what each other's needs are. That's the best way to serve each entity.

KPL: Do you think black radio is like a second-class citizen in the industry?

PR: I think it has been viewed as that by a lot of record companies or pop departments in record companies. But I also think that black radio has had to gain respect in that people have had to stop and take notice. Had it not been for black radio, the Janet Jacksons, the Whitney Houstons, the Patti LaBelles would have never gotten any exposure. Even Teena Marie, being a white artist, she would have never gotten exposure on pop radio. She just had her first crossover record a year and a half ago. But before that, she'd never been played on white radio because she is a black artist in terms of her sound. So when you look at how long black radio stuck with Patti LaBelle, and how long black radio has stuck by Frankie Beverly and Maze, certain artists that have that mass appeal would never have gotten it without black radio. I think certain artists will never forget that. Patti LaBelle is one of them. I think she will probably always realize which side her bread is buttered. Audiences are very fickle.

But most black radio audiences like Patti for Patti, regardless of what she does. I think she has never lost really her identity in terms of her music. So I think black radio has been looked upon as a stepchild, but I also think that black radio has gained a lot of respect, because you look at the Top 10 records on the pop charts, and consistently six out of ten records are black records.

Black Radio and Formatting

KPL: One of the things I hear mumblings about in the industry is that black radio is becoming more and more like pop radio. It's becoming more formatted, more formulaic, and less experimental as it used to be. How would you comment on this?

PR: I think that's true. For the most part, black radio has adapted certain techniques used by pop radio, such as computer research, laying out a format based on computer. I think there is nothing wrong with that within black radio's scope of things. As long as black radio is not losing its originality, as long as it's not losing its desire to break new music or to break new artists. I think it depends on the station.

With us, if I can use us as an example, we are more of a Progressive Adult Contemporary, or Black Adult Contemporary, which is sometimes how we are referred to. It's time for black radio to grow up, if you look at radio generally in the market. White audiences have country, which is not to say that all audiences that are listening to country are white. But for the most part, white audiences have country, pop radio, contemporary urban music, Top 40, and adult contemporary.

Black radio has black radio. There is no sectioning off of different black audiences. All black people do not like to listen to the same radio stations. So it is time for us to start qualifying who we are, what audience we want to reach, and go for that base. For us, it is the adult audience, and we can't afford to become as formatted or as strict and restricting as contemporary urban music or Top 40 because black adult audiences are a lot more experimental. They want to hear newer music. They want to hear album cuts. Single sales are not important to them.

So I think for black radio to realize, yes, KDAY,[16] has a specific responsibility to its audience, KJLH to its audience, KACE to its audience, KUTE[17] to its audience (and it's questionable whether it's black or not anymore), KGFJ[18] to its audience. And you look at the trade layouts, there's one black chart. A black chart, period. There is no adult [black] chart. There is no contemporary urban music black chart. There is no Top 40 black chart. And that's where we are doing ourselves a disservice. I think there is too much music out there to be lumped into one category. Too much good black music.

KPL: So what do you see is the future of black radio, five, ten years down the line? Do you think it will become so formulated and scientific that it will automatically eliminate a lot of experimental black music?

PR: Not if the radio stations that are experimenting are supported by the record companies and the audiences. I think the audience is the bottom line. If the audiences are there, and the numbers are showing on Arbitron and your station is successful retailwise, then there is no way that that can dissipate. No one is going to deny success. It really depends on the success of the format.

Black Women in the Record Industry

KPL: From all the interviews I've been doing in the record and radio industry, there appear to be few black women involved. Why do you think, in terms of the oppression and everything that we've gone through, why do you think there are so few black women in top positions?

PR: I wish I knew, 'cause I sure would publish the answer. It is true that there are very few women in top positions within this industry. But I think it's getting better. I remember doing an interview about four years ago and saying the same thing. I remember right after doing the interview and talking to some people and realizing that it really wasn't getting any better. Sure, there were women that were being hired and put in positions. But for every woman hired, a woman was fired.

In this industry, it's not unusual because everyone is fired at some point. It's an industry where you can't take it personally. I've known people throughout the years that have lost jobs, male and female, because it's such a changing industry. And it's always new players and new chiefs and new everything because you're trying to stay new. It's an industry where the main focus is to stay fresh and new and up on what's happening. So a lot of people have lost their jobs, and I think with women, they have been given the opportunity. Someone within their spectrum, work spectrum, has had to have been able to say, "I believe in you. I know you know what you are doing. I have a slot for you. Let's see how it goes." Whether or not black or white men are threatened, I wouldn't even want to get into that because I think each case is individual.

But I think being a woman and knowing how difficult it is, the obstacles are not always men. Sometimes there are other women. Some women are insecure with hiring women to work for them because, basically, it was so difficult for them to get to the point where they are. It's almost like, I don't really want to give up too much information because I've worked hard to get to this point. And it's very understandable once you break it down like that. But it's unfortunate, because where does it stop? If you say [that], then the next person that comes along will feel the same way.

What I've tried to do in the short time that I've been in this position is—and even before that—is help other women gain some sort of acceptance into whatever it is they want to do. With voiceovers, a lot of times, I'm called about a particular voiceover situation. Either I can't make it for the audition or I'm not right for it, and they think that I am. And I'm saying, "I'm really not what you're looking for, but I do know someone who is." When you talk about networking, that's what it really means. There's so many network groups now where women and men get together. They talk about what they're doing, what's happening in their end of the business. But in terms of really helping each other and saying, "So and so over here has got a job. Why don't you call and see what the possibilities are? And by the way, tell them I asked you to call."

Those kind of things always help. But people have to really lighten up and let go and realize that you can't get everything. You can't get every job. You can't work in every aspect of the business. Everything is not made right, but when it is, it will come back around and you're be able to benefit from it.

KPL: This is a station that has a black woman general manager, and you are the program director. In fact, I see more women than I see anything else running around. Has that presented any obstacles at all in terms of the progress of the station?

PR: Oh no. I don't think so. I think it has helped. I know that the sales manager has a team of, I believe, four men and five women. I know that he's said, "I'd much rather have women working for me basically because women have a stamina, [an attitude] of, 'I'm not going to give up.'" When it comes to sales, I'm sure that's very important. Maybe it's been the women that he's come into contact with. Maybe that's the reason he feels that way. But I don't think it has hindered the success of the station. If anything, people have probably stopped and waited to see what the station is going to do and watched with great interest as to what we were going to do and how we were going to do it. In the recent months, it has paid off. I don't know if that's because there are more women or not. We are fortunately right now doing very well.

Trends in Black Music

KPL: In black music, every now and then, there are trends established. What are the elements that make a trend in black music which radio might promote?

PR: Give me an example.

KPL: I guess the latest trend is Prince. He's on top; he's very creative. Now there's a whole lot of other artists who are trying to sound like a Prince. What is it that radio does to help promote these kinds of trends?

PR: I don't know. It's difficult to say whether radio is following or whether the radio is leading at this point. Prince was played on black radio for years without any mass appeal or acceptance. I remember when he opened for the Rolling Stones a few years ago and was booed off the stage. He had tomatoes thrown at him. People were just adamant that he was not a rock and roll star. And now, he's one of the biggest. So I think a lot of it has to do with timing. I think a lot of it has to do with generation. I think a lot of it has to do with what particular format is popular at that time. And at that time, AOR [Adult Oriented Rock] was doing very well in this city, and Prince was black and was considered a black artist, period. That same group of people now may be into Prince. Obviously, somebody is. I don't know if it's always radio that's leading or following. But I know that media as a whole definitely has to affect the trends. That's from television to print and whatever seems to be hot at the time, everybody jumps on the bandwagon. Whether that's Patti LaBelle or Janet Jackson or Whitney Houston, who are three black women recording artists that have hit the top of the charts in the last few months consistently and have stayed there. There are trends in music. Whether or not radio leads or follows, I don't know.

I know that there are a lot of people making decisions for radio that you really wonder sometimes if they should be or not. Trends in New York go so far as to dominate the airwaves with rap music. It's a very street-oriented sound. It is a street experience, rap music. But the street experience is a lot stronger in New York than it is in L.A. So consequently, the trend of rap music. Sure it's big out here, but it's nowhere near what it is in New York. It always depends geographically where you are.

KPL: What about rap? When you drive around the black community, you hear music coming from the youth. Eighty to ninety percent of what I hear is rap. But, I understand that there are some stations, black station, who are resisting playing rap. Do you have any explanation for that?

PR: I know that we don't [play rap]. Even before we changed formats to an adult format, we didn't play rap. And that was basically a belief that the station owner had, Willie Davis. He just didn't feel that it was for this radio station, for whatever reason.[19] I think generally it depends on the format. I know that in recent months KISS has played certain rap records, but they were always rap records that have gone Top 10. In other words, they would never touch it before then. They are not in the business of building rap hits. KDAY is. They spend most of their time appealing to that listener, that audience, and rap music is very important. Because of that, they will probably continue to do well with younger audiences, because younger audiences are into that.

Even though I think it's an expressive form of music and very poetic, I think it's something that you have to be into. It's like reggae. It's specialized, and I think it's something that you personally have to want to hear all day long. Most surveys have shown that most adults don't really care about it. So if you are appealing to an adult base, you don't want to inundate yourself with rap music.

KPL: There's a lot of synthesized and computerized sounds in the sounds that we hear today. Do you feel as some people say, there's a homogeneous quality happening, there's a sameness. Do you think that's going to be harmful? How do you see that?

PR: I think that it's a lot like the disco era in that right now, it's very hot. Music is progressing to the point that a lot of it can be done on computers. And a lot of it will be. But it takes people to program computers. Just as with any synthesizer or with anything you may do in the studio, you still need to have that creative know-how in how to put it together. I think it has a lot to do with trends in music, as we were saying before. I think that it will probably have the same effect that disco did. I think it will be very popular. I think that people will sell a lot of records with it. I think it is here to stay. Computers are the wave of the future.

But I still think that music can always go back to the creative bottom line and be successful. You look at a George Benson or a Phyllis Hyman. Both of them have new releases that are ballads and very unsynthesized and will probably be major records. But there's always the listener, more than I think people want to give credit for, that is really unconcerned with a synthesized sound. Ballads are very, very hot right now. And for the summertime, that's unusual. Most radio stations don't want to play ballads in the summertime because [they think their listeners are saying,] "I've got to be moving, I've got to be popping, I want that active feel in the streets." But right now, ballad after ballad seems to be able to make it to the top of the charts. So that's an indication that synthesizers aren't always the quickest way to a hit record.

Crossover

KPL: I was at the Black Radio Exclusive conference and I've heard some discussions that are potentially harmful to some artists or black music in general. Stations are complaining about how many artists start out on black radio stations and then cross over into the pop market. Because they cross over to the so-called pop stations, some black stations feel like somebody has stabbed them in the back and will take them off the playlist. Do you think that this is a potential problem for black music and/or black artists?

PR: I think crossover has been an issue for quite some time. I think what is key is how the record company and how the artists respond after this crossover phenomenon has happened. In other words, if you are a Madonna or a Whitney Houston, both of which were played exclusively on black radio in the very beginning—Madonna much longer than Whitney. Whitney hit it big within two songs in terms of crossover. Madonna got through a whole album before anybody white realized who she was and that she was white, maybe they should check her out.

It depends on the record company. If the record company then decides to take a stand—"Now this artist is crossover, now I'm going to totally ignore black radio. Now I'm not going to give black radio any promotions when this artist comes in town. I'm not going to bring this radio station for an interview"—that, I think, is when it becomes a problem. And, yes, I do think potentially it can be a great problem. When that same record company wants you to start building another act for them, they're not going to be interested in bargaining. "We'll help you with this artist. But the next time a Whitney Houston or"—and I'm using her as an example, not to say that that's what has happened with Arista. But because she's had such phenomenal crossover success, she's a good example to use. But when that artist comes to town, you say "Hey, I'll love to do this for you. But I don't want to be stepped on when Whitney comes back. If you take her to KISS, you're going to have to bring her over here, too."

So potentially, yes, it can be a great problem. But it depends on how the company deals with it and even the artist. The artist has to make a stand and has to say this is what I want. Artists with that much to say about their career, and that much clout, can make a difference. A Lionel Richie, the same thing. It's up to him at this point to let his management know what he will and will not do. If the artists don't wake up and the record companies don't wake up and say, "Well, we can't ignore black radio," then they will have problems.

KPL: It seems today that more and more white artists are copying black music, particularly from Britain. It seems that some of the black stations are playing the white artists who are playing black music. It seems like the reverse of crossover in a way. Do you feel that incorporating white artists on a black station format gives less exposure to black artists?

PR: I can't speak for all stations. But I know here, specifically, if I go on a white artist such as a Phil Collins or Hall and Oates, basically because of its R&B feel, I'm going on it because it's a good record. If I have five spaces for good records that week and four of those five are black, and there are no other qualifying records that week coming from black artists, then he's not taking up a slot for black artists. If I had five spaces open, and I have six black records and one white record, and I put four black records on and one white record, then you could say yes. That space is taken up for what could have been a black artist's slot.

But very seldom does that happen. Not that much music comes out where you can't program it and make it more of a flavor record than part of your overall major format. Those records are used for flavor and flavor only. In this market, you have to do that because blacks don't just listen to black radio.

Reggae and Jazz on Black Radio

KPL: Why do you think such a great black musical form as reggae could not establish itself in the American market?

PR: That's difficult. I don't know. I remember at one point, reggae was getting a lot of attention because of [Bob] Marley, and a lot of attention basically because white audiences had accepted it a lot quicker than black audiences. Really, reggae artists would have preferred to have been playing to their own people, black people. I think reggae probably needs as much of an outlet as mainstream music. It's not as commercial. It's good music.

But I think it has to be programmed in such a way that people don't look at it as a different form of music. If audiences can look at it as a basic form of music, as they do with anything else, I think it would be easier to accept. When reggae is programmed, it is programmed in blocks of time—three, four, five hours at a time. That automatically makes it eclectic and different to the ear. If it were interspersed and programmed throughout the day with other forms of music, maybe it would have been identified as a recognizable form of popular music.

KPL: Where do you feel jazz is? Some people say jazz has seen its day and its appeal is limited to senior citizens. But some say just the opposite. I know at Warner Bros., they say that jazz is very healthy and is making a slight comeback. Where do you feel the jazz scene is headed?

PR: I definitely think it's making a comeback. Basically because the jazz that we do play as LP cuts, and sometimes in major rotation, medium and heavy rotations, sell quite well and are very competitive with the Top 10 or Top 20 on the charts. The Top 10 or 20 pop records or black pop records are urban records on the charts. They are very competitive. So definitely, I think more stations are opening up to certain types of jazz. Straight-ahead jazz is always a little more difficult. But when you talk about the David Sanborns and Billy Mitchells and Bob Jameses and Roy Ayerses, these are artists who are really considered mainstream jazz and are getting quite a bit of play.

KPL: I notice that the jazz artists that you mentioned, at least half of them are white artists. Do you hear, or do you see the airplay, of some of the greats, such as Miles Davis, John Coltrane, and Cannonball Adderley? These were, in terms of modern jazz, the foundation. Do black stations play them, or have they pretty much forgotten them?

PR: Well, Miles Davis is still making contemporary records. And a lot of jazz artists have said that Miles has "sold out." He's not what he used to be. It would be very difficult for me to program Miles in my regular weekly format, what he was doing ten years ago. What he's doing now, it's very easy because he's more mainstream.

But we also have a show on Sunday called *LA Sunday* where we program a lot of progressive straight-ahead jazz. And those artists do have an outlet, maybe not as much as they should. I don't think that you ever forget about the John Coltranes and the Cannonball Adderleys. But in terms of being able to program them throughout your week, it's very difficult unless you come up with a Cannonball Adderley record that he came out with a few years ago with Phyllis Hyman singing lead vocal. Then it's a lot easier to program. I think the issue comes in how easily I can fit it into the scheme of things here as opposed to whether or not it's good music. That's never the case. Jazz is an excellent form of music. But it just doesn't have a lot of outlets when you talk about progressive or straight-ahead jazz.

New Artists and African Influences

KPL: I've talked to several promotion men in the record industry, and they say in terms of new artists (a new artist's first record), maybe nine out of ten don't have a chance. They may get like a spark or glimmer of exposure and that's basically it. How would you respond to that?

PR: Nine out of ten seems relatively high. I guess they would know better than I would because I am not dealing with them on a day-to-day basis. I think that for the most part, that's probably very close to the truth in terms of radio because radio will not always take a chance on an artist. A lot of times, an artist has to depend on exposure through video first or gigging around the country as much as possible to get recognition. Then again, there's always that one record, that one hit that everybody looks for. So, in fact, an artist has been out there ten years and they get a hit record, they're considered a new artist when in all actuality they've been out there and working at it and working toward this goal.

KPL: You hear an enormous amount of music, a lot that never makes the airwaves. Knowing historically that black people came from Africa, under forced conditions, do you feel or do you hear any African influences or musical elements in the music that you hear?

PR: Definitely, some more than others. Black music has been so assimilated into the pop music culture so easily that an artist such as . . . I don't even want to name names because there are so many of them. But there are a lot of artists that are just concentrating on getting a hit, making a hit record and getting the recognition that they feel they so deserved, whereas years ago, they [may] have been a lot closer to the African culture in terms of how their music was portrayed or the kind of writing they did at the time. You look at someone like Teena Marie who is a white artist but very influenced by black music and the black music culture. She's got a song now on her album called *Bata Kata Suite.* Nothing but African and Spanish rhythms in that particular song. And she feels and seems so connected to it. But black artists for the most part, I think, have escaped that or not made a strong attempt to stick to it. Billy Ocean is an exception. He is from Trinidad and has somehow been able to keep that. And, as slight as that may be, when you listen to his music, you can still hear the Caribbean influence. So I think it is a matter of how well you can assimilate it into what you are doing, to gain that pop acceptance or black mass appeal acceptance. Those who can do it are very good at it, very successful with it.

NOTES

Two interviews were conducted with Al Bell. The first, on 19 August 1986, was used as part of my doctoral research on popular music in the United States; see Kwaku Lynn, "American Afrikan Music: Study of Musical Change" (Ph.D. dissertation, University of California, Los Angeles, 1987). The second interview was conducted on 24 February 1996.

1. Quoted in Bruce Haring, "A Soul Man from the '60s Is Back in the Groove Again," *Los Angeles Times* (21 September 1993): F1, F5.
2. Al Bell, telephone interview with author, 24 February 1996.
3. Michael Haralambos, *Right On: From Blues to Soul in Black America* (New York: Da Capo Press, 1985), 146, provides detailed information about WattStax: "The 1972 Watts Summer Festival closed with 'Wattstax,' a seven-hour show sponsored by Stax Records and Schlitz Beer, with the proceeds going to black charities. Over 100,000 people watched a parade of soul singers, including the Staple Singers, the Soul Children, Rufus and Carla Thomas and Isaac Hayes. Kim Weston sings the 'Black National Anthem' *Lift Every Voice and Sing,* and the

audience jumps to its feet and responds with the black power salute." The event was filmed and released in movie form as *WattStax*.

4. The company, Motown Records, moved to Los Angeles in the early seventies. See further discussion in Kimasi Browne, "Brenda Holloway: Los Angeles's Contribution to Motown" in this volume.

5. Jacqueline Cogdell DjeDje, "A Historical Overview of Black Gospel Music in Los Angeles," *Black Music Research Bulletin* 10, no. 1 (Spring 1988): 2.

6. Ibid., and Jacqueline Cogdell DjeDje, "Gospel Music in the Los Angeles Black Community: A Historical Overview," *Black Music Research Journal* 9, no. 1 (Spring 1989).

7. Ron Dungee, "Radio Business in the Black. KGFJ: 'The Sound of Success,'" *Los Angeles Sentinel* (27 January 1994): B9.

8. Ibid.

9. KUTE was owned by Tracy Broadcasting, the same company that owned KGFJ. In 1979, Percy Sutton's New York–based Inner City Broadcasting purchased KUTE and its sister station, KGFJ. With this change in ownership, KGFJ became a black-owned station; see Ron Dungee, "Radio Business in the Black. KGFJ—The Fall of an Empire," *Los Angeles Sentinel* (3 February 1994): B7. For further discussion of black radio in Los Angeles, see "KGFJ Celebrates 65 Years of Service in the Community," *Los Angeles Sentinel* (18 June 1992): A16, and James Bolden, "KACE Set for Move; KGFJ Goes Gospel," *Los Angeles Sentinel* (29 September 1994): A1, A17.

10. Dungee, "Radio Business: The Sound."

11. Dungee, "Radio Business: The Fall."

12. Changes in the black community greatly affected the context for music making in Los Angeles; see discussion in Ralph Eastman, "'Pitchin' Up A Boogie': African-American Musicians, Night Life and Music Venues in Los Angeles 1930–1945," chapter 1 in this volume.

13. Dungee, "Radio Business: The Fall."

14. Along with partners Quincy Jones (entertainment executive), Don Cornelius (producer of television show *Soul Train*), and Geraldo Rivera (talk-show host), Davis entered into a joint venture with Tribune Broadcasting to form what could become the largest minority-controlled broadcasting company in the United States. For details about this business venture, see discussion in Jane Hall, "Qwest to Reflect Diversity of Its TV Viewers, Partners Say," *Los Angeles Times* (17 November 1994): D2, and John Lippman and Jane Hall, "Quincy Jones–Led Group Forming TV Joint Venture," *Los Angeles Times* (16 November 1994): D1, D3.

15. During the time of this interview and earlier, KKGO was a radio station that programmed primarily jazz. In the late 1980s, KKGO changed its format and began to play only European art music (Western classical music).

16. With the rise in the popularity of rap, KDAY began specializing in rap music.

17. In 1986, Inner City decided to sell KUTE; the station no longer exists.

18. In 1986, KGFJ started its "oldies but goodies" format. As other stations embraced the oldies format, KGFJ had to reevaluate its programming. In 1994, KGFJ became a 24-hour gospel music station with its "Sweet Inspirations" programming; see James Bolden, "KACE Set for Move; KGFJ Goes Gospel," *Los Angeles Sentinel* (29 September 1994): A1, A17. However, in 1996 KGFJ was sold and became a station that programmed motivational speakers.

19. KACE was not alone in denying airplay to rap music during the 1980s. Comments by several rap artists who visited Los Angeles for a concert in the 1990s indicate that they received little support from the music industry when rap was in its formative stage. Rap

artist Def Jef states: "When I got into it [performing rap music], there was no records. There was no radio exposure or anything. There was just cassette tapes that was passed around. It was a cult thing. And then it just got broader. Now you have a rap record and you can listen to the radio and hear rap" (personal interview with author, 15 September 1990).

Concerning the issue of violence and rap, which is the reason some industry executives have given for not supporting or promoting this genre, rap artist Laquan states: "You go anywhere in the world, there's violence. You go to Saudi Arabia right now, there's violence. Violence takes place all over the world. They don't say anything about these rock concerts and all the violence that happens there. Anytime blacks get together and try to do something to better themselves or do something together, it's considered violent or negative" (personal interview with author, 15 September 1990).

On the topic of censorship, Mr. Mix of 2 Live Crew states: "I feel personally it's because I'm a black-owned company. A lot of money is being made and other people's hands ain't in the pot. So that causes a problem, especially where we're from. We live in the South. So it's a lot different than it is here [in Los Angeles]" (personal interview with author, 15 September 1990).

6

California Rhythm and Blues Recordings, 1942-1972
A Diversity of Styles

Willie R. Collins

Urban cities were the incubators for urban blues. There was Los Angeles, but every city in America that had a black population had a gospel singer or blues singer that made contributions to the style. But everybody wanted to move to Los Angeles; it was the promised land—a chance for a black person to get a job and a less virulent form of racism.

JOHNNY OTIS

Some of the most significant recordings in the history of rhythm and blues[1] were made in California between 1942 and 1972. Although many of the musicians[2] who were involved in these recordings moved West during the early twentieth century, California rhythm and blues, popularly known as "West Coast blues,"[3] evolved as a regional style in the decades of the forties and fifties. In that period a number of independent record companies (e.g., Exclusive, Specialty, Aladdin, Modern, Black & White, and Big Town)[4] produced hits that made it into the top ten (including many at number one) on the commercial charts.[5] Although these hits put Los Angeles, Oakland, and San Francisco on the map among popular music performers and promoters, few scholars include California in their discussion of the history of blues or rhythm and blues. For example, in the introduction to *The Blues: A Bibliographical Guide,* William Ferris does not list any California cities: "Each of the northern urban areas that attracted a black population has similarly produced an important blues tradition. While Chicago has the best known urban tradition, cities like St. Louis, Detroit, New York, Philadelphia, and the District of Columbia are also important blues capitals."[6] However, Mike Rowe acknowledges the significance of California: "At a time when blacks were leaving the South in their thousands to swell the urban populations of the North and West it's interesting that only two of the host areas, Chicago and California, should develop a discrete regional postwar style. Los Angeles was an exception; there a new 'race' record industry, built up from scratch, could grow and prosper in happy isolation, not hampered as other cities were by their close proximity to Chicago or New York."[7] Similarly, Lee Hildebrand contends that there is a style of blues unique to Oakland: The slow mournful ambience that Bob Geddins gave to many of his productions is one characteristic of the Oakland sound, and the other is the guitar style developed by Lafayette "Thing" Thomas.[8]

Of the major studies that have been done on urban blues and/or rhythm and blues, only Arnold Shaw's *Honkers and Shouters*[9] makes significant mention of California.[10] Much of the literature on West Coast blues focuses on individuals: interviews and articles on artists, as well as autobiographies.[11] Hildebrand has written extensively on artists in Oakland,[12] whereas Ralph Eastman has discussed musicians and music venues in Los Angeles.[13] Researchers that include mention of California in surveys of rhythm and blues are Eddie Meadows,[14] Portia Maultsby,[15] and Milton Lee Stewart.[16] Maultsby gives a stylistic description of what constitutes California rhythm and blues, whereas Meadows writes about California independent record labels and groups, 1943–1955. Stewart's "Development of Rhythm & Blues and Its Styles" includes an analysis of selected rhythm and blues songs and a general discussion of popular music.[17] Tom Reed's pictorial history of black music in Los Angeles includes mention of rhythm and blues.[18]

A number of factors account for the scarcity of studies on California rhythm and blues. Some writers and audiences deny the authenticity of West Coast blues, alleging that the modernizations in the music left it without folk roots. In discussing the transformation of California blues and several of its pioneer artists, Paul Oliver states:

> Lloyd Glenn's contemporaries, Charles Brown, the pianist, and the brothers Oscar and Johnny Moore, had popularised a bland, fluent technique. Though lacking in strength or conviction, they were capable of adapting themselves to popular ballads or boogie-blues with equal confidence. Similar in character and also coming from Texas, Floyd Dixon played a delicately melodic blues piano and sang in a plumy, sophisticated voice. They had all followed Ivory Joe Hunter out to the West Coast and together formed a style of blues which was peculiar to the region. . . .
>
> For many tastes the work of this group was too effete, but for others it was agreeably sophisticated in sound.[19]

Hildebrand argues that "much attention has been paid to modern Chicago and Memphis blues and little to Oakland maybe because it [Oakland's music] contain[s] little of that crying Mississippi guitar sound that so attracts new, white listeners to the blues."[20] Joe Williams, longtime vocalist with Count Basie, states: "The blues boom of the fifties was largely supported by young whites. They did not, of course, approve of the conditions and hardships that lent authenticity to the accents and delivery of singers from the South, but the grim and often sordid background to the music that they enjoyed undoubtedly gave it savor. In effect, the North preferred the blues of the South and measured authenticity by its Southern and rural characteristics."[21] Shaw succinctly addresses the issue: "As for scholars of the blues such as Paul Oliver and Sam Charters, R & B is suspect because of its market orientation and basically because it is not a folk art. R & B research has suffered not only from negative aesthetic and social attitudes but also from a confusion about its identity."[22] The rhythm and blues ballad style, or "cocktail" rhythm and blues, pioneered by Charles Brown falls victim to this naiveté. Johnny Otis noted his irritation with stereotypes when Brown's name came up in a discussion with a white guy who called Brown's music "Muzak blues": "Your problem is you don't know what the fuck you're talking about. You don't belong to the community and because he [Charles Brown] ain't screaming and hollering and ain't got some overalls on, you think he's not doing the blues, see?"[23]

Whenever a discussion of rhythm and blues ensues, it is important to acknowledge that some of its early practitioners were initially blues musicians who changed their performance style as African Americans migrated from the South to points in the Midwest, Northeast, and West. The transformation[24] enabled musicians to meet the demands of new audiences whose musical tastes were shaped by urban phenomena. The changes that took place in California cities are particularly noteworthy because, as Johnny Otis notes, "Los Angeles was different."[25] Not only was Los Angeles the land of opportunity, but the diverse mix of people and cultures dramatically affected the music. As the big-band era waned, West Coast musicians fused the sounds of bebop, southwestern jazz, and Louis Jordan's jump combo with those of newly transplanted Oklahoma and Texas boogie woogie and blues singer-pianists into a hybrid. Two distinct styles of rhythm and blues music emerged: "club" blues and "jump blues." The former was based on the cool, detached, piano-guitar pairing of the King Cole Trio, whereas the latter was patterned on the hot, aggressive horn sound of the Tympany Five. All the essential ingredients (shout-styled vocal blues, boogie woogie and shuffle rhythms, and tenor sax–led jump combos) were in place by the end of World War II for the conversion of blues to rhythm and blues.[26] Ralph Bass, who is known for his work with King and Chess Records, states: "The big, first surge of R&B was on the West Coast in LA, not in New York."[27]

Musicians perceive California rhythm and blues as unique for various reasons. Floyd Dixon states: "I think that 'West Coast blues' is a different flavor because [on the] West Coast—you can always tell from the drummer and the bass beat."[28] A number of musicians believe there is a causal relationship between the California climate and the style of music found in the state. Hugh Merrill states: "The agreeable, sunny life on the West Coast imparted to the music a more mellow, sophisticated flavor."[29] Gaylord Birch, an accomplished drummer, provides a fuller explanation:

> Because of different climates, you tend to react differently to nature. So that makes you play differently. On the East Coast and in the Midwest, music seems to be more energetic than the West Coast. The West Coast is more classy and laid-back. The East Coast and the Midwest are more energetic and that's attributed a lot to the cold season. You know when it gets cold, you want to do something to get warm. So consequently the cats back there could play faster and play harder and more aggressive than the cats out here in this moderate climate—the ocean and the sunshine—and

what have you. We tended to be more laid-back and the music tended to be more citified than the music from the Midwest or the East.[30]

Although it is convenient to place blues and rhythm and blues in self-contained categories based on geographical regions, the fact remains that California rhythm and blues is composed of a diversity of styles. Johnny Otis comments on the uniqueness of West Coast blues and California's contribution to the development of rhythm and blues:

> "T-Bone" Walker, Charles Brown, Lowell Fulson, Ray Charles was on West Coast—all these things together became a California influence. There's no one defined answer to some of that; it's too much input from a thousand different directions. You can't say this idiom started here in California because California was made up of black people from many places, the church was part of our heritage, gospel music and even some Caribbean input—West Indian sisters and brothers—and New York.[31]

Maultsby's description of the characteristics of California rhythm and blues provides further insight about the music's uniqueness and distinct qualities:

> The West Coast up-tempo rhythm and blues style is largely a three-component hybrid form. It combines the boogie-woogie with the driving eight-to-the bar top-hat cymbal pattern, a heavy back two and four back beat on the snare drum, a driving solo tenor saxophone, a three- and four-note rhythmic horn riff pattern, and group singing—all characteristic of the Southwest Black swing-band style of performance. The Texas blues piano stylings (triplet figures and the rolling octaves) complete the musical tripod that made up the West Coast up-tempo combo style.
>
> Most rhythm and blues combos featured a shouting-and-preaching-type blues singer. These singers drew vocal stylings from both rural blues and gospel traditions. Among the first and most popular blues vocalists of the rhythm and blues combo ensembles were Wynonie Harris, Jimmie Witherspoon, Sister Rosetta Tharpe, "Bull Moose" Jackson, and Ivory Joe Hunter.[32] All of these artists at one time or another had performed with Black swing bands.
>
> Another rhythm and blues style first popularized and recorded in Los Angeles was the solo ballad. This ballad style is unique because the stylings of both the vocalists and the piano accompaniment are derived from the blues, gospel, and jazz traditions. It initially was designed as listening or conversational music for performance in small intimate clubs and lounges. This ballad style, therefore, was sung in more of a subdued and pleading manner than the shouting and preaching style associated with vocalists of the rhythm and blues combo tradition. Cecil Gant ("I Wonder"—1945) and Charles Brown ("Drifting Blues"—1946) were the primary forces in the development of this rhythm and blues ballad. Gant performed as a single artist accompanying himself on piano. Brown also accompanied himself on piano but was influenced by the trio concept of the Nat King Cole Trio. His performances, therefore, were supported by a string bass and guitar.
>
> Although individual performers personalized their interpretation of the rhythm and blues ballad form, the vocal delivery style usually had these common features: the lyrics were delivered in a pleading, soft, and subtle conversational manner; and

vocal phrasings and melodic lines were guided by the natural rhythms (triplet and sixteenth-note patterns) of Black speech. Although the term "blues" appears in the title of many these romantic-styled ballads and the flavor often is "bluesy," the label "rhythm and blues ballad" best describes the musical quality and hybrid nature of this song form.[33]

MUSICAL STYLES

In this chapter I examine the musical styles and song texts of fifty-one commercial sound recordings made in California between 1942 and 1972. The recordings, many of which sold enough copies to be charted by *Billboard*,[34] were made primarily in three cities: Los Angeles, Oakland, and Berkeley (see Chart 6.1, Appendix B). Though the fifty-one recordings represent a selection of national and regional hits from a three-decade period, they do not include every style or artist. For example, neither Mercy Dee nor Floyd Dixon is represented. The sample includes several styles of rhythm and blues: Kansas City jazz-based; boogie woogie–based; gospel-based; and two California-based styles (a ballad style and an Oakland-based style).

The styles proposed from the selected sample are not to be considered definitive. Though some recordings defy categorization, others exhibit an overlapping of two styles. Three of the recordings are clearly country blues.[35] In addition, eight songs do not fit into any of the categories proposed. Three selections have California artists covering or imitating commercially successful styles and songs of artists outside of California. These are Little Joe Blue's "Dirty Work Going On," an imitation of B. B. King's style; Johnny "Guitar" Watson's "Those Lonely, Lonely Nights," a cover of a New Orleans song by Earl King; and Johnny Heartsman's "Johnny's House Party," inspired by Bill Doggett's "Honky Tonk." Sugar Pie DeSanto's "I Want to Know" (written by Bob Geddins), employing double-tracked voice, was inspired by Patti Page hits and designed as a crossover song aimed at the popular market. Two selections were created to generate teen dances: Jimmy McCracklin's "The Walk" and Johnny Otis's "Willie and the Hand Jive." Little Willie Littlefield's "It's Midnight" was the first hit record to use steady triplet chords, a device that was borrowed by Fats Domino and became a staple of early rock and roll. Lowell Fulson's "Tramp" (composed by Jimmy McCracklin) illustrates the soul style's influence on California rhythm and blues. Thus, the styles from this sample are not unique to California. Many of the characteristics associated with each style appear in other regions of the United States. In addition, this sample is not representative of the total output of rhythm and blues recordings made in California between 1942 and 1972.

The musicians did not exist in isolation; the audience influenced the style and direction of the music. Therefore, the recordings provide us with insight about some aspects of African American culture. Not only do they tell us something about African-American life in California during the three decades under discussion, but they demonstrate some of the adaptation strategies that blacks employed to deal with racism and living in America. However, it should be noted that the rhythm and blues recordings included here do not reflect the attitudes, values, and behavior of *all* African Americans in California. Although the market initially was limited to African Americans, California rhythm and blues could be heard throughout the United States and abroad as the distribution of the recordings widened. Whether West Coast blues interrupted the continuation of folk traditions is speculative. However, it is abundantly clear that when African Americans settled in cities, they wanted change, and that change was reflected in their behavior (dress, talk, etc.) and their music.

Kansas City Jazz-Based Rhythm and Blues

Kansas City jazz had an immense influence on California rhythm and blues. The two prominent elements in Kansas City jazz were the riff and the blues.[36] The repertoires of Count Basie and Jay McShann primarily consisted of "head" arrangements (i.e., memorized or improvised parts), with a large number of blues arrangements.[37] According to Stanley Dance, "Soloists, backed by ensemble or section riffs, were extensively featured, and particular attention was paid to the role of the rhythm section."[38] Features from Kansas City jazz can be heard in eight recordings: Saunders King's "S. K. Blues" Parts 1 and 2 (1942); Joe Liggins and His Honey Drippers' "The Honeydripper" (1945); Roy Milton's "R. M. Blues" (1946); Jimmy Liggins's "Tear Drop Blues" (1948); Jimmy Witherspoon's "Ain't Nobody's Business" (1949); Joe Liggins and His Honey Drippers' "Pink Champagne" (1950); and Jimmy Nelson's "'T' 99 Blues" (1951).

Otis, who played with the George Morrison Orchestra as well as the Harlan Leonard Orchestra (the former a southwestern band, the latter a Kansas City band), recalls the Kansas City influence and the type of music he performed in Los Angeles in 1945, when he became leader of the house band and drummer at the Club Alabam: "Big-band blues was played at the Club Alabam—strictly Kansas City, Wynonie Harris, Jimmy Witherspoon. It was Kansas City swing which is what I preferred and loved and still do. When we played and somebody was singing, instead of just guitar, you heard the horns setting a little riff or something; and the solos were very jazz oriented—they were blues soloists but they had those good flavorings of Lester Young."[39]

In June 1942, Saunders King, a vocalist and guitarist who was influenced by Charlie Christian, had a hit on the Rhythm label called "S. K. Blues," Parts 1 and 2. King's band was described as "among the most polished on the coast and they were regulars at plush clubs in Hollywood and Frisco, and also touring the 'southern chittlin' circuit."[40] "S. K. Blues" is a moderate tempo twelve-bar blues. The opening is harmonized in the horns and could be associated with the sound of a freight train (see Example 6.1). It also employs two-note riffs in the second chorus (see Example 6.2), with muted horns, jazz-influenced solos, group singing (part

Example 6.1. Excerpt from "S. K. Blues, Part 1," by Saunders King (melody for horns).

Riff (second chorus)

Example 6.2. Excerpt from "S. K. Blues, Part 1," by Saunders King (two-note riff for horns).

two), and tenor sax solos. Two musicians who identified with Kansas City, Pete Johnson and Joe Turner, covered this recording in 1945.

In 1945, Joe Liggins recorded "The Honeydripper,"[41] a smashing success that is unquestionably one of the finest examples of Kansas City–inspired rhythm and blues. "The Honeydripper" departs from the twelve-bar blues form but has all the elements of Kansas City jazz, including riffs and a vocal chorus. It has touches of Ellington, stride piano in a certain section, and a wonderful interplay of voices, producing a polyphonic texture and a lilting swing over a one-chord vamp. This piece epitomizes fun and the element of play.

The number-two song for most of 1946 was "R. M. Blues" by Roy Milton. Born in Oklahoma, Milton was influenced by the Kansas City swing bands of Count Basie and Jay McShann. Roy Milton and His Solid Senders was one of the preferred bands in Los Angeles and in other cities in the United States. "R. M. Blues" features riffs in the horn section, with the blues frills in a high tessitura; the shuffle of Camille Howard's piano; a muted trumpet solo; and an interspersion of vocal choruses with solo improvisations. Jimmy Liggins's "Tear Drop Blues" features jazz phrasing and riffs with a subdued vocal line and a bluesy piano. Jimmy Witherspoon, who sang with Jay McShann's orchestra in Los Angeles, is a versatile singer equally at home in a shouting style or in the more subdued, mellow vocal delivery used in "Ain't Nobody's Business." This selection departs from the twelve-bar-blues sentence and uses a thirty-two-bar popular-song form; nevertheless, the piano responds with blues runs, backed by the guitar and jazz phrasings from the horn section. In "Pink Champagne," Joe Liggins cleverly employs a men's vocal chorus to sing the riff in evenly accented quarter notes (see Example 6.3). The horns respond to the lead vocal chorus. Jimmy Nelson's "'T' 99" begins with a raucous yell in a four-bar introduction but quickly settles into a steady, smooth, 4/4 rhythm, with the Peter Rabbit Trio singing a riff response to the lead vocal, which combines a quasi-shouting style with a mellow approach.

In sum, Kansas City jazz was strongly apparent in California rhythm and blues. Not only was this style a favorite in a number of the upscale clubs, but many

Vocal line riff

Pink cham-pagne that   stole   my   love   from   me

Example 6.3. Excerpt from "Pink Champagne," by Joe Liggins and the Honey Drippers (vocal group singing riff).

of the musicians who helped create California rhythm and blues performed with Kansas City bands. The riffs (whether performed by instruments or by a men's vocal chorus), the blues form (with blues piano and jazz stylings), and the four-to-the-bar rhythm were present in all eight of the recordings noted here.

Boogie Woogie–Based Rhythm and Blues

Although popular in California, the boogie-based rhythm and blues (boogie-ostinato—i.e., the continuous accented figure played by the bass) is linked to the boogie woogie piano style that originated in Texas and the Southwest:

> The state of Texas, the largest and most populous in the Kansas City–Southwest area, predictably yielded the greatest number of musicians and bands. . . . Texas pianists were apt to be blues-inspired players, or boogie-woogie players. Boogie-woogie was called "Texas piano" or "fast Texas piano," and its place of origin was most likely in the honky-tonks of the pinewood and turpentine country of east Texas and southern Arkansas.[42]

Boogie woogie pianists had a repertoire of established bass figures that were played with the left hand. The figure changed in accordance with the root note of the basic tonic, subdominant, and dominant chords used in the blues. Only the recordings that include these established figures are considered here as boogie-based. For example, there are numerous recordings of West Coast blues as well as rhythm and blues that feature bass ostinatos but that do not feature the established repertoire used by boogie pianists in the twenties, thirties, and forties.

Most California boogie bands were based in large cities with significant black populations. Otis recalls: "I played in a boogie woogie band in the thirties in Oakland and Berkeley, so that was part of my molding."[43] The eight-to-the-bar and modifications of boogie woogie piano patterns were to become firmly rooted not only in California rhythm and blues bands but also in other rhythm and blues and in commercial music in general.[44]

Just as the audience played an important role in the development of the rhythm and blues ballad style, African-American listeners helped to shape modern rhythm and blues music in Los Angeles in the 1940s. Otis remembers how he used the audience's taste for boogie-based rhythm and blues and jump blues as a basis for establishing his own group:

[W]hen I saw the audience, [I said], "Oh yeah, I need to put together Count Otis Matthews's West Oakland House Rockers again; that's what these folks want." You couldn't get it; nobody was really doing that, you see, because a pure country blues thing—lot of us enjoyed it, but they [the audience] wanted other elements there. Almost all of us [Roy Milton, Jimmy Liggins, etc.] did the same thing. Pretty soon, we're playing a very bluesy style because the people asserted themselves. That's what they liked. We played "After Hours," and they would all holler and get up and say, "Yeah!" When we played boogie woogie, something set in my mind, and I said: "That's what the people want. They want this jump music, blues, these boogie woogies, that's what they love." So I cut mine's [my band] down from eight brass to two brass, from five reeds to two reeds, my piano player would have to be a boogie woogie piano player—most jazz pianists could play anything—and the guitar player was not a rhythm guitar like Freddie Green anymore. Here was a twangy T-Bone Walker–type guitar, and the afterbeat with the drums constantly. And what we were doing, we were inventing a new art form through hybridization—but we didn't know that. We thought what we were doing was to stay in the business—cutting down because we couldn't afford to have a bigger band, and maintaining certain elements of the big band.[45]

The recordings in the sample that represent boogie-based California rhythm and blues include: Louis Jordan's[46] "Caldonia" (1945); Amos Milburn's "Chicken Shack Boogie" (1948); Lowell Fulson's "Everyday I Have the Blues" (1950); Lloyd Glenn's "Old Time Shuffle Blues" (1950); Lowell Fulson's "Guitar Shuffle" (1950); Jimmy McCracklin's "Looking for a Woman" (1951); and Lowell Fulson's "Reconsider Baby" (1954).

Jordan, alto saxophonist and leader of the Tympany Five, was not only the composer of "Caldonia" (as well as many other hits) but also the biggest recording artist of the 1940s.[47] Popular among African Americans and white audiences, his recordings (e.g., "G.I. Jive") often crossed over to the pop and rhythm and blues charts. Jordan's recordings, influenced by a diversity of musical styles, run the gamut—novelty, humorous, ballads, jump blues, and boogie shuffles. In "Beans and Cornbread," with its leader/chorus form, Jordan employs a preaching style; he serves as lead vocalist, and the band becomes the congregation. The African-American spiritual "Nobody Knows the Trouble I've Seen" is used for the introduction and ending to "Nobody Knows You When You Are Down and Out," and Latin rhythms over twelve-bar blues and calypso appear in "Early in the Morning" and "Run Joe," respectively. Jordan uses both the twelve-bar blues form and the thirty-two-bar song form. But the ostinato boogie, with a smaller combo playing riffs, characterizes the majority of his hits. Approximately 35 percent of the recordings on *The Best of Louis Jordan* and more than 60 percent of his top songs from 1944–1947 are based on the ostinato boogie.

Jordan's "Caldonia" begins with the pianist playing in a boogie style using a quarter-note ostinato pattern (see Example 6.4), with a shuffle rhythm in the right hand. The rhythm is an example of a typical "stomp down" shuffle on the snare

Example 6.4. Excerpt from "Caldonia," by Louis Jordan (ostinato boogie).

snare drum

Example 6.5. Excerpt from "Caldonia," by Louis Jordan (shuffle with no backbeat).

(see Example 6.5). Also, extensive interplay takes place between the horns and the soloists in the instrumental choruses.

In Amos Milburn's "Chicken Shack Boogie," the pianist performs the boogie ostinato on an open fifth and sixth in the bass. Also, riffs are heard in the horn section, and the drummer plays a straight rhythm with heavy accents on two and four. Milburn was a visionary, influencing the nascent rock and roll of Bill Haley and others. In Fulson's rendition of "Everyday I Have the Blues," the bass line starts with a boogie ostinato; brushes join the bass for a straight four beats to the bar while Lloyd Glenn's piano makes the case for the blues. Earl Brown's alto sax responds with Glenn to Fulson's vocal line. Glenn's "Old Time Shuffle Blues" resembles Fulson's "Guitar Shuffle," a solo piece with shuffle rhythms (see Example 6.6). McCracklin's "Looking for a Woman" employs the boogie ostinato in the bass with the piano and guitar responding with a shuffle rhythm (see Example 6.7 and Figure 6.1). Boogie woogie is an important element of rhythm and blues. All of the examples of the boogie-based California rhythm and blues employ the twelve-bar blues form.

Gospel Based Rhythm and Blues

In African-American culture, the distinctions between sacred and secular music grew out of a myopic view of Christianity rather than out of the characteristics and forms of the music itself. It is not surprising that gospel music has had a significant impact on California rhythm and blues, given that so many musicians grew up singing or playing in the African-American church. It was not uncommon in the thirties and forties for a blues musician to play for a secular function on Saturday night and for church on Sunday morning. "Blues-gospel,"[48] a term not in currency by the practitioners of the music but used here for the purposes of analysis and categorization, consists of a sacred song text that employs the twelve-bar blues form.[49] The vocal style and use of the vamp for extended vocal improvisation are features from gospel music that have most influenced California rhythm and blues.

The recordings that draw on performance practices from the gospel tradition include Etta James's "The Wallflower" (1955); Jimmy McCracklin's "Just Got to Know" (1961); Little Johnny Taylor's "Part Time Love" (1963); Tiny Powell's "My Time after While" (1964); McCracklin's "Think" (1965); Al King's "Think Twice

piano

Example 6.6. Excerpt from "Old Time Shuffle Blues," by Lloyd Glenn (ostinato bass figure, left hand).

guitar

bass

Example 6.7. Excerpt from "Looking for a Woman," by Jimmy McCracklin (guitar shuffle and bass ostinato).

Figure 6.1. Blues singer Jimmy McCracklin. Courtesy of Jonathan Eubanks, photographer.

Before You Speak" (1966); Z. Z. Hill's "Don't Make Me Pay for His Mistakes"; and J. J. Malone's "It's a Shame" (1971).

In Etta James's "The Wallflower (Roll with Me Henry)," we hear a closely integrated interrelationship between the leader/chorus and harmonized vocals in intervals of thirds and sixths. Also, 12/8 meters and vocal interjections as used in the church are heard more often in this genre than in other rhythm and blues forms. For example, Little Johnny Taylor's "Part Time Love" includes the sentence, "There is one more thing I want to tell you right here." The vamp—continued vacillation on two chords (I to VI or I to V)—serves as the basis for an extended improvisation in "Part Time Love," "My Time after While," and "It's a Shame." Shouting and vocal interjections also appear in many of gospel-based rhythm and blues recordings.

California Rhythm and Blues Styles

In general, the California rhythm and blues sample comprises records that were made by California blues artists and (based on *Billboard's* charts) had national impact. Not every record fitting these characteristics could be included in the sample. For instance, only a few recordings from Lowell Fulson and Aaron "T-Bone" Walker were analyzed. In a few cases, I selected records that were not national hits because they were either regional hits or good examples of a particular style (e.g., McCracklin's "Too Late to Change," which exhibits Lafayette "Thing" Thomas's guitar style). Even though I call the sample "California Rhythm and Blues," it excludes some types of rhythm and blues. Some songs are not necessarily considered blues but are performed by artists associated with the blues. Excluded are "doo wops," honking and screaming jump blues, soul, and funk—styles that some writers might classify as rhythm and blues. Each selection was analyzed structurally (music and song text) to determine the overriding musical characteristics and influences from boogie woogie, gospel, Kansas City jazz, and other genres.

Rhythm and Blues Ballad Style   Though the Kansas City jazz–based rhythm and blues style was always associated with the Midwest, the rhythm and blues ballad style[50] (which refers not so much to form as to the manner of singing and the articulation of words) is believed to have developed in California. Admittedly, in form and style the blues ballad predates the beginnings of West Coast blues. Leroy Carr and Scrapper Blackwell's performances were a poised egress from what generally was blues with a raucous quality. Commenting on Carr's "How Long, How Long Blues," Rowe states: "The new departure was not only the piano-guitar instrumentation, which added a more sophisticated dimension to the style, but also a change of mood."[51] Charles Brown contends that the audiences that listened to the Nat King Cole Trio were influential in the development of a ballad style:

> Nat was singing the blues before, songs such as "That Ain't Right," and "Straighten Up and Fly Right." He wasn't doing the pop numbers that he did later. So in the

clubs where the white folks came, they only knew "St. Louis Blues," so the artists created songs around that with more sophistication. That was a different type of music
that they [white people] listened to, and that was acceptable to them, and you
couldn't play the real blues unless it was "St. Louis Blues." It wasn't that old Mississippi "boomty, boomty, boomty" blues. It had to have a little jazz orientation in it.
Nat's audiences were a combination of black and white. He played for the whites in
the first part of the night, and then there were after-hour clubs such as the Last Word
on Central Avenue where he would play for the blacks.[52]

Fulson gives some interesting insights on the trio format associated with the ballad
style: "Nat Cole, he was what you would call a classic white. In San Francisco,
[the] Nat Cole and Charles Brown trio style was popular. They could not hold a
house by themselves; they were playing listening music and blues, a soft modern
type of blues."[53] Otis states that the audience at the Club Alabam in Los Angeles
"was all black. We had some whites who would come, say, to the Barrel House on
Friday night for some reason, but basically it was a black audience at the Club Alabam. On Monday nights, the Hollywood crowd would come."[54] The regular audience at Ivie Anderson's Chicken Shack on Vernon and Central Avenue, where
Charles Brown first played, included African-American movie stars[55]—e.g., Hattie
McDaniel, Louise Beavers, Ethel Waters, and Bobby Short.

The context in which the music was performed also had an impact on the ballad style. In an interview with Sidran, Charles Brown states:

> Well, you know at the time they used to call this the "club blues," West Coast. Be-
> cause at the time we were playing in nightclubs, and we had to set an *atmosphere* for
> those guys who brought their girlfriends or wives in. We set the atmosphere, and you
> couldn't be too loud. You had to be mellow and play songs that set the mood for the
> drinking. Sweet numbers and the little ditties and whatnot.[56]

Gillett contends that black migration outpaced the creation of clubs available to
African Americans and that the commingling of blacks and whites within nightclubs may have led musicians to "minimiz[e] the blues content of their repertoire."[57]

The recordings representative of the rhythm and blues ballad style include
Ivory Joe Hunter's "Blues at Sunrise" (1945); Charles Brown's "Drifting Blues"
(1946); T-Bone Walker's "Call It Stormy Monday" (1948); Brown's "Trouble
Blues" (1949); Little Esther[58] with the Johnny Otis Orchestra's "Double Crossing
Blues" (1950); Percy Mayfield's "Please Send Me Someone to Love" (1950);
Charles Brown's "Black Night" (1951); T-Bone Walker's "Evening" (1957); and
Percy Mayfield's "The River's Invitation" (1952).

Although Charles Brown is considered the pioneer of the rhythm and blues
ballad style, he acknowledges Ivory Joe Hunter as a forerunner (Figure 6.2).

> Ivory Joe Hunter was older than I. I must have been 12 years old in Texas City,
> Texas, [when] Ivory Joe Hunter was living in Houston. My aunt had a little place
> called Hollywood, and on the weekend they had a "rent party." They would send for

Figure 6.2. Ivory Joe Hunter and His Band at Tappers Inn, North Richmond, c. 1944. Left to right: John Patterson, tenor saxophone; "Chuck" Walker, drums; Freddie McWilliams, emcee; Mitchell, bass; Ivory Joe Hunter, piano/vocals. Courtesy of Homer "Chuck" Walker.

> piano players to come down and play; so Ivory Joe Hunter was one of them. He was a young, nice-looking, tall man, a guy that played the piano and sang beautifully for $20 each night. He was a person that could turn around backward and play the piano with his hands on the keys.[59]

Like Brown, Hunter was exposed to classical piano and could play boogie woogie, blues, and ballads. On "Blues at Sunrise," his first commercial recording, Hunter is accompanied by Johnny Moore's Three Blazers (Charles Brown on piano, Johnny Moore on guitar, and Eddie Williams on bass). "Blues at Sunrise" is a twelve-bar blues with a soft, mellow vocal delivery, excellent blues piano accompaniment by Brown, and a jazz-inspired guitar solo that moves Hunter to remark: "Ain't the gravy good?"[60]

Charles Brown's "Drifting Blues," recorded when he was a member of the Three Blazers, defines a new direction in the rhythm and blues ballad style. According to Brown, there is a big difference between a blues singer and a blues *ballad* singer: "Well, I was more of a blues ballad singer, not a blues singer, because my numbers are more of story-ballad numbers. 'Drifting Blues' is blues, but it was kind of a ballad blues, it was a little different from these hard blues like they really sing."[61] "Drifting Blues" is what Gillett defines as "cocktail" piano playing: "[C]ocktail piano playing was common—pretty right-hand tinkling with a light rhythm from bass and brushed drums."[62] Otis, who played drums on "Drifting Blues," explains that the style of music dictated a certain type of drumming (a four on the snare drum, with brushes and interspersed accents) because the audience was listening to Brown: "When Charles Brown was singing, the audience was listening and enjoying it. That song does not lend itself to a bunch of banging—one automatically picks up the brushes and plays along. The style of drumming can be traced to Jo Jones and James Crawford."[63]

"Trouble Blues," by Charles Brown with a trio (no drummer), is a minor blues based on a modified popular song format. Says Gaylord Birch: "He [Brown] has a very deep, melodic, and hypnotic voice. He has a different way of singing—he almost sing-talks. He's very dramatic, he's an actor-vocalist as opposed to a vocal-actor. He's very much a dramatist; he's very emotional—he brings all of his essence out in his voice."[64] While performing, Brown often acted out, with hand and facial gestures, the words and meanings of songs. Brown's "Black Night," set in a minor blues-spiritual mode, begins with a gospel-tinged introduction,[65] with the blues flavor coming through as the song progresses. The accompaniment is minimal (again, no drummer), although a saxophone is added and plays in responsive fashion off the vocal line. The guitar chords chime as a church bell would for a funeral, setting the mood for the blackest night of all. Brown's existential voice articulates with pathos his plight of being alone.

Singing so that every syllable is articulated is a characteristic feature of the California blues ballad style. When asked why he emphasized diction, Brown comments:

> I had listened to Pha Terrell; see, he was a romantic balladeer. In college, the type of music we listened to was a little more high-class—from big bands like Jimmie Lunceford and Duke Ellington. I listened to him as well as Helen O'Connell, with Jimmy Dorsey. What really inspired me about her was her diction, that she said her words in such manner that they were understandable. I knew that it was important to say the words; so Nat and all of us had that way of saying the words where they would dominate and out there and front and dramatize.[66]

Floyd Dixon also believes the perfect diction of the ballad singer is a characteristic of the California rhythm and blues ballad style. "It was a cleaner blues coming out of the West Coast—accented. Articulation, and the diction was different. Take Charles Brown, for instance. When he sang, 'You taught me to love and not to forget; there is no greater love in all this world so true,' that diction and articulation and pronunciation is so good."[67]

The Johnny Otis Orchestra's "Double Crossing Blues," featuring Little Esther, established Otis as a top rhythm and blues artist in 1950, and the popularity of the recording enabled him to travel with the California Rhythm and Blues Caravan. This traveling show did much to create a consciousness of rhythm and blues in California. Otis calls "Double Crossing Blues" a happy accident; it grew out of

Jessie Mae Robinson's song, "What's the Matter Baby," and a line that was used in a song-and-dance comedy act called "Amos and Estrelita in Vaudeville," wherein Estrelita would say to Amos: "You should be in the forest fighting grizzly bears." Otis combined the two and came up with "Double Crossing Blues."[68]

Percy Mayfield's "Please Send Me Someone to Love" and "The River's Invitation" are also examples of the rhythm and blues ballad style.[69] His strength as a composer and a performer cannot be stressed enough. His voice was subtle and of medium-to-light texture, and most of his songs are confined within an octave or less. "Please Send Me Someone to Love" is based on a thirty-two-bar song form, and "The River's Invitation" is based on the twelve-bar blues form. T-Bone Walker's "Evening" bass line is a ground ostinato that continues with the A section of the thirty-two-bar chorus (AABA) format.

The so-called "cocktail" blues and the rhythm and blues ballad style should be considered identical because the music is usually accompanied by a "two-beat" rhythm. The vocal style is mellow and smooth, with the lyrics sung in an imploring manner. Both the twelve-bar blues and thirty-two-bar popular song forms are employed. Hildebrand states: "The style that is most unique to California is the so-called cocktail blues, primarily in the Los Angeles area. Piano players from Texas who came to the Los Angeles area associated with Charles Brown and Ivory Joe Hunter, who was in Oakland and Los Angeles, Floyd Dixon and Cecil Gant, who is not from Texas—that sort of soft, small-group, no-horn type of blues that I think is influenced by the King Cole Trio. Charles Brown is the most important figure in the so-called cocktail-blues genre."[70]

Oakland-Based Rhythm and Blues   As Hildebrand observes in his discussion of Oakland blues, "a different variety of blues showed up in Oakland during the war years."[71] Five selections from the sample represent Oakland-based rhythm and blues: Roy Hawkins's "Why Do Everything Happen to Me?" (1950); Jimmy Wilson's "Tin Pan Alley" (1953); Jimmy McCracklin's "Too Late to Change" (1957); Al King's recording of Fulson's "Reconsider Baby" (1964); and Sugar Pie De-Santo's "Hello, San Francisco, Part 1" (c. 1972). The selections by Hawkins, Wilson, and McCracklin are slow twelve-bar blues, with horns harmonizing the vocal line with sustained chords. Simple harmonies and arrangements, with the unique biting and wailing responsive countermelodies of Thing Thomas's guitar, are trademarks of these Bob Geddins productions. Many notes are sustained in a legato fashion. The ensemble sound of rough-hewn chords is sometimes out of sync with the standard twelve-bar blues musical sentence. In addition, there is a loose adherence to the beat. King's "Reconsider Baby" features Johnny Heartsman's guitar style, and DeSanto's "Hello San Francisco" features Thomas's guitar style. These selections are decidedly medium- to up-tempo, but the use of the sustained chords by the horn section and the guitar playing of Heartsman and Thomas contribute to the Oakland-based rhythm and blues sound. In these recordings, Thomas's debt to T-Bone Walker and his influence on Heartsman are clear.

Like Charles Brown, T-Bone Walker and Lowell Fulson are performers who represent or reflect California rhythm and blues. Walker is identified with California because his background is diverse; elements from country blues and Kansas City jazz can be heard in his music. Influenced by Lonnie Johnson, Walker led Blind Lemon Jefferson around, worked in a medicine show playing the banjo, and played with Charlie Christian. His tour with Les Hite in 1939 enabled him to move easily from blues to jazz. In early 1940 the American Record Company recorded "T-Bone Blues," featuring Walker on vocal with the Les Hite Band.[72] When asked if he was a blues or a jazz guitarist, Walker responded: "It's because I love the blues and I don't think I can play anything in the jazz world but the blues. And your blues is the foundation of your jazz. I think if it wasn't for the blues there wouldn't be no jazz."[73] Walker was able to retain features from his Texas background yet modernize the sound and use of the guitar. In fact, he was the first to popularize the electric guitar in blues. Walker's singing and guitar playing on "Mean Old World" stand alone in setting the direction for the use of the electric guitar and small combo in California rhythm and blues. "Mean Old World," recorded in July 1942, a month after Saunders King released "S. K. Blues," became a regional hit that defined the modern California rhythm and blues style.

Walker's debts to swing music and Charlie Christian are evident. His unique technique of bending the string to produce a note and holding the note over the bar (see Example 6.8) imbues the "blue notes" (flatted third, fifth, and seventh) with a human quality, so that they "talk" to the listener. Walker's sense of swing— i.e., his rhythm against the 4/4 beat (see Example 6.9)—and his phrasing give him a distinctive, easily identifiable style. Pee Wee Crayton's "Blues after Hours" owes much to Walker's guitar sound; with the pianist playing chords in a triplet rhythm, the melodies from the guitar are reminiscent of Walker's style.

Lowell Fulson, another artist whose music exemplifies California rhythm and blues, moved to Oakland in December 1943 and worked in the naval shipyard, as did many other African Americans from the South. Soon after he arrived, he picked up a guitar from a pawn shop and played for house parties. His repertoire consisted of country blues tunes—e.g., "Ain't No More Sweet Potatoes, Frost Done Killed the Vine" and "Brazo Bottom Blues"—that he had learned in Texas and Oklahoma. However, Fulson saw where the music was heading and began practicing selections such as "Caldonia." Later, Fulson met Bob Geddins and in June 1946 made his first record, "Black Widow Spider Blues." Fulson and his band played at various clubs in the Bay Area, including Aster House in Vallejo and Granny's in Richmond. The music of Saunders King and blues in the style of T-Bone Walker were popular at the mainstream establishments in Oakland. Fulson states that when he walked on the bandstand in Oak-

Example 6.8. Excerpt from "Mean Old World," by Aaron "T-Bone" Walker (holding over a flatted fifth).

Riff

Example 6.9. Excerpt from "Mean Old World," by Aaron "T-Bone" Walker (Walker's use of riff figure).

land, the musicians would all walk off because they did not perform country blues and looked down on Fulson's playing (Figure 6.3).[74]

Audiences influenced him to change his performance style: "Well, I couldn't get no gigs playing that other [country] stuff. They [audience] wanted to hear me sing the blues; but at the same time, they wanted a kind of a band sound with it. They didn't want me sitting there 'dry playing,' they wanted to be able to dance off of the blues after sitting and listening to them [the band]."[75]

Although Fulson and Walker both helped to shape the California rhythm and blues sound, Fulson retained more of the southwest country rural flavor than Walker did. Still, Fulson's "Blue Shadows" differs markedly from "Three O'Clock Blues," which was recorded just two years earlier and features his early, country style of playing. Not only was the timbre of Fulson's guitar more cutting on the later record, but he was fond of using short statements. Also, Fulson chose not to break up the beat as much as Walker did. Although Fulson's style of playing is simpler than Walker's, his melodies are more fluid, and he uses a lot of technique. Sometimes he performs short motifs with the end note accented, as in "Reconsider Baby" (Example 6.10), or he may play a motif and then respond to it at a different range. His vocals still draw on Texas influences; one can hear a little of Blind Lemon Jefferson in them. In "Blue Shadows" and "Reconsider Baby," songs that reflect Fulson's middle period, melodies are voiced in a quasi-speaking manner.

The "two-beat style" of drumming and bass playing are strong components of both forms of California rhythm and blues. Floyd Dixon states, "I think that 'West Coast blues' *is a different flavor* because of the drummer and the bass beat. It's something about a 2/4 beat."[76] The two-beat style appears in the rhythm and blues ballad "Call It Stormy Monday" by Walker and in Pee Wee Crayton's "Blues After Hours," and a variation of it is heard in Lowell Fulson's "Blue Shadows." The two-beat style is derived from jazz drumming and bass playing. Gaylord Birch, drummer with Charles Brown, explains:

> In the forties-style two-beat, wire brushes play two-beat music and put a slight back-beat with it with the hi-hat. This is a traditional style that was prominent in the forties and fifties style of drumming. The drummer sweeps across the drum with the

Figure 6.3. Blues singer Lowell Fulson. Publicity photo issued by Bullseye Blues/Rounder Records. Photograph by E. K. Waller. Courtesy of Lowell Fulson. Used by permission.

Example 6.10. Excerpt from "Reconsider Baby," by Lowell Fulson (Fulson's motif, guitar shuffle).

brushes that make a kind of a "ssss" kind of sound at the same time he makes a backbeat on two and four to emphasize those beats. Drums are not only used as timekeeper but mainly as a supportive instrument that brings different colors and intensities to the music. [In the two-beat style, drums represent the] art of being heard without being heard. It's like being felt and not being heard. So the bass is playing predominantly half notes on one and three. So every two beats; if the bass player is playing a certain way, that determines how you [the drummer] will play.[77]

The urbanization of African-American culture appeared to be more dramatic in Los Angeles than in Northern Californian cities. In Los Angeles, many African Americans not only changed the style of clothes they wore but began to walk and talk differently. Fulson explains: "You dressed with your big apple hat and your long jive chain that's hanging down from your pocket. Cats would put any kind of weight they could find, not necessarily a watch, at the end of the chain; suits, tie and shirt. Some guys would wear sports shirts with the big collar on the outside; Mr. B. (Billy Eckstine) brought out the big collar (shirt style)—they got out of those one-room country shacks and got to the city and played the part."[78] Regarding the music scene in Los Angeles in 1949, Fulson states:

> When they packaged me in L.A., there was T-Bone, "Bull Moose" Jackson, Wynonie Harris, "Big" Joe Turner, and Jay McShann with "Hot Biscuits." On the east side of Los Angeles you had clubs such as the Club Alabam, the Last Word, and the Plantation. There were blues ballads and up-tempo house-rocking stuff, Louis Jordan, and Big Joe Turner's kick-type; Wynonie Harris with the screaming and shouting–type. When my "Everyday I Have the Blues" come along, they called that mellow-type blues. I would sing "Caldonia" and "Everyday I Have the Blues" and "Blue Shadows." I made me up an instrumental in the studio called "Guitar Shuffle." I began to build up my book because of touring. I made my first tour in 1950. I left with five pieces, and when I returned I had about ten pieces; that's when I got Ray Charles. My basics was piano, alto sax (he played all of Louis Jordan and could warm up the stage). The band was paired with rhythm and blues singing groups such as the Dominoes, Orioles, Clovers, and the Moonglows.[79]

In the sixties, recordings that fit the California rhythm and blues model moved toward a 12/8 meter similar to much of gospel music. See Johnny Heartsman's "Johnny's House Party" and DeSanto's "Hello, San Francisco" for examples.

SONG TEXTS

An analysis of forty-eight song texts reveals that California rhythm and blues artists dealt with a variety of themes and subjects. Some texts reflect the realities of the African-American experience in California, but many draw from folk blues and treat themes and attitudes that date back to the slave era. Several songs are concerned with issues that relate to physical attributes.

Because many African Americans believed that the features of a white person were the ideal, it was common for blacks to invest in beauty products to change their appearance. Saunders King's last chorus of "S. K. Blues," Part 1 (1942), makes reference to a scorned lover who wants his partner to return the wig that he had purchased for her. Similarly, someone with a brown or white complexion was considered to be more beautiful than someone who was black. Walker's famous line from "T-Bone Blues"[80]—"Brown-skinned woman, who may your good man be?"—is but one example of the concern about skin color. In the last chorus of "Blues at Sunrise" (1945), Ivory Joe Hunter describes the physical attributes of a brown-skinned woman with a risqué element so common to the blues. The woman not only has brown skin and bowed legs but also "sticks way out behind."

The elements of play and laughter and the ambience of a children's song are evoked in J. J. Malone's "It's a Shame" (1971). The phrase, "It a shame, she don't love you friend," addresses the brother/friend's former lover, chastising him about his loss and the bluesman's gain.

Sexual imagery and explicit references to the sexual act, subjects common in the blues, are also found in California rhythm and blues. Liggins's "The Honey-dripper" (1945) refers to the blues singer's "main squeeze," or preferred lover. The numbers six, nine, and sixty-nine appear in Jimmy Nelson's "'T' 99 Blues" (1951) and Saunders King's "S. K. Blues," Part 2 (1942). In the final chorus of "'T' 99 Blues"—when Miss Viola Lee is remembered for her "good stuff" (sex)—the vocal chorus is changed from "T 999" to "T 969." In Saunders King's "S. K. Blues," Part 2 (1942), which is mostly instrumental, the vocalist sings the numbers three, six, and nine and states that if the woman consents to sex, he will sell her the same. The notion of the man's being a "sweet daddy" and a natural lover is seen in Lowell Fulson's "Tramp" (1967), where the singer indicates that although he does not wear continental clothes or Stetson hats, he is a lover.

References to the South or a country lifestyle are rare, and those that do appear are pejorative. For example, in Jimmy McCracklin's "Looking for a Woman" (1951) the singer meets a woman and tells her what he likes, and she responds by telling him to go back to his cotton sack. Rhythm and blues songs that refer to cities, places, and venues are also rare. Sugar Pie DeSanto's "Hello, San Francisco" (1972) and Amos Milburn's "Chicken Shack Boogie" (1948) are among the few songs that mention places. The female singer in "Hello, San Francisco" specifically talks about San Francisco's Fillmore district and "booking activities" in which her estranged boyfriend and his new girlfriend are involved. However, it is not likely that Milburn's "Chicken Shack" refers to the Los Angeles club/restaurant of that name located on Vernon and Central and owned by Ivie Anderson and her husband. The Chicken Shack, the club where Charles Brown first played professionally, was not a "hole in the wall," as the lyrics state in the first chorus of Milburn's song.

The majority of the songs deal directly or in part with infidelity in relationships. Because a large number of the blues singers are men, the "no-good woman" appears perennially. The few women (for example, Little Esther and Sugar Pie DeSanto) who have recorded blues songs sing about the infidelity of men: "Double Crossing Blues" (1950), "Hello, San Francisco" (1972), and "I Want to Know" (1960). Z. Z. Hills's "Don't Make Me Pay for His Mistakes" (1971) is concerned with a contemporary theme: a woman who mistreats her present lover, even though he is generous and supportive, because she was abused by an ex-partner. To prove his worthiness, he reminds her that he is working and providng a home for the six kids that she conceived by her former lover.

Recordings in the California rhythm and blues ballad style are noteworthy for their profundity and treatment of themes usually not associated with the blues. Percy Mayfield is the most creative poet in this style. "Please Send Me Someone to Love" (1950) is a prayerful request not only for a partner but also for peace between men and women of all races. In "The River's Invitation" (1952), Mayfield enters a dialogue with a river that personifies a peaceful home and death. The river invites him to give up his search for his lost love and join the waters. Mayfield believes he will find his lost love and vows to take her for a ride.

Bad luck and trouble, sometimes unexplainable, are the subjects of Lowell Fulson's "Everyday I Have the Blues" (1950). In it, Fulson laments that nobody loves him or cares that he has had his share of bad luck. He discusses escaping his plight by moving to another location. In "Why Do Everything Happen to Me?" (1950), a song composed by Bob Geddins and recorded by Roy Hawkins, the singer feels as if he is jinxed. Unable to do anything right, he is blue, lonesome, full of misery, and at a loss to explain why strange things continue to happen to him.

The world of the blues singer, like the world of African Americans, was not easy. The dream that California might be the land of golden opportunity, the place where African Americans would be able to achieve equal rights as musicians and citizens, was soon shattered by the harsh realities of racism. Sure, Nat King Cole's successes paved the way for black entertainers, particularly in providing opportunities to perform for white audiences. But Cole was appreciated and liked because he fulfilled a perceived stereotype of a gentlemanly black man. How much of his soul did he have sell for his popularity; how many masks did he have to wear? Was playing pop numbers to a white audience before 2:00 a.m. and the blues after hours to blacks really a good compromise?

When African-American musicians moved to California, they soon learned that all was not well. It was commonplace for artists to receive no royalties or only royalties up front for the recordings they made.[81] Not only were people who supported the musicians harassed when they patronized clubs, but law enforcement officials, in an effort to "clean up" city life, had begun by 1945 to close venues that promoted black secular music.[82] In the Los Angeles area, nightclubs and dance halls that permitted interracial fraternizing were closed.[83] The Jade Room, Florentine Gardens, and Susy-Q were among those that were shut down for fear of interracial mixing.[84] At Billy Berg's club in Hollywood, African Americans were granted permission but were not allowed to dance with whites.

Discrimination in housing and in public facilities also hampered African Americans in California cities. Because of restrictive covenant housing laws, blacks could rent or buy houses only in certain areas. California was, in the name of one of T-Bone Walker's quintessential compositions, a "Mean Old World" (1956). In addition to hiding his worries by drinking, T-Bone asserts that once he is dead he will no longer be treated "like a low-down dirty slave." Choosing death over bondage was a theme often expressed in African-American culture during the slave era. For example, the chorus to the spiritual "Oh Freedom" says: "And before I'd be a slave, I'll be buried in my grave, And go home to my Lord and be free."[85]

The songs were personal statements on conditions and attitudes that affected blacks. Thus, California rhythm and blues became and represented somebody: somebody called segregation, somebody called discrimination, somebody called a slave in the nineteenth century, somebody called trouble, and somebody that wouldn't go away in the land of golden opportunity. Fulson personalized the blues when he sang "Blue Shadows" (1950), a composition in which the blues symbolizes the singer's having lost his woman. African Americans could also find consolation in listening to California rhythm and blues. In addition to serving recreational purposes, the music offered a spiritual tonic to survival. Anyone who ever felt lonely could empathize and identify with Charles Brown when he sang "Black Night" (1951). Here, Brown bemoans not only the loss of his woman but also his lack of good friends and the apparent endlessness of his problems. The blues were bad for T-Bone Walker every day. "Call It Stormy Monday" (1948) takes us through the week—to payday on Friday, partying on Saturday, and to Sunday, when the blues and the spirituals converged, as they do in African-American culture. Walker's use of a sacred metaphor is a continuation of a trend used by earlier Mississippi Delta blues singers.

The song texts of California rhythm and blues both created new subjects and rearticulated some that had appeared earlier in folk and country blues. What seems to set West Coast blues texts apart from other blues song texts is their concern for humanity.

CONCLUSION

The fifty-one recordings examined for this study reflect the realities of the African-American experience in California. The largely black audience consisted primarily of African-American women, who supported the blues by going to clubs and purchasing recordings. Musicians listened to their audiences' likes and dislikes, which, in turn, influenced what was recorded. Although the rhythm and blues ballad style may have originated as a result of performances in clubs attended by whites, the recordings were bought overwhelmingly by African Americans.

California rhythm and blues reflects a diversity of styles, including Kansas City jazz, boogie woogie, gospel, the blues ballad, and Oakland-based rhythm and blues. Whereas performers who played Chicago and Mississippi Delta blues drew heavily from the folk traditions, musicians who played California rhythm and blues were open to other influences. Musicians in Oakland (with the exception of those who played the upscale clubs, such as Slim Jenkins), Richmond, Vallejo, the Central Valley, and San Diego performed in a style that was similar to country blues, whereas those in larger cities (Los Angeles and San Francisco) used a smoother, more urbane performance style. Although California did not prove to be the land of golden opportunity for African Americans, numerous small record labels and clubs boomed between 1942 and 1953, churning out hit after hit and gaining national distribution. More important, the three decades of California rhythm and blues, 1942–1972, spawned a diversity of musical styles that greatly influenced the history of American music.

APPENDIX A

Selected California Rhythm and Blues Recordings, 1942–1972

1942
SAUNDERS KING,   *S. K. Blues, Parts 1 and 2* (Rhythm).

1945
IVORY JOE HUNTER,   *Blues at Sunrise* (Exclusive), no. 3.[86]
LOUIS JORDAN AND HIS TYMPANY FIVE,   *Caldonia* (Decca), no. 1.
JOE LIGGINS,   *The Honeydripper* (Exclusive, Specialty), no. 1.

1946
CHARLES BROWN,   *Drifting Blues* (Philo, Aladdin), no. 2.
ROY MILTON & HIS SOLID SENDERS,   *R. M. Blues* (Juke Box), no. 2.

1948
PEE WEE CRAYTON,   *Blues After Hours* (Modern), no. 1.
K. C. DOUGLAS,   *Mercury Blues* (original label not available; Down Town, Gilt Edge).
LOWELL FULSON,   *Three O'Clock Blues* (Down Town), no. 6.
JIMMY LIGGINS,   *Tear Drop Blues* (Specialty), no. 7.
AMOS MILBURN,   *Chicken Shack Boogie* (Imperial, Aladdin), no. 7.
AARON "T-BONE" THIBEAUX WALKER,   *Call It Stormy Monday (But Tuesday Is Just as Bad)*, (Black & White), no. 5.

1949
CHARLES BROWN,   *Trouble Blues* (Aladdin), no. 1.
LITTLE WILLIE LITTLEFIELD,   *It's Midnight* (Modern), no. 3.
JIMMY WITHERSPOON,   *Ain't Nobody's Business* (Supreme), no. 1.

1950
LITTLE ESTHER & THE ROBBINS, WITH THE JOHNNY OTIS ORCHESTRA,   *Double Crossing Blues* (Savoy), no. 1.
LOWELL FULSON,   *Blue Shadows* (Swingtime), no. 1.
LOWELL FULSON,   *Every Day I Have the Blues* (Swingtime), no. 3.
LOWELL FULSON,   *Guitar Shuffle* (Swingtime).
LLOYD GLENN,   *Old Time Shuffle Blues* (Swingtime), no. 3.
ROY HAWKINS,   *Why Do Everything Happen to Me* (Modern), no. 2.
JOE LIGGINS AND HIS HONEY DRIPPERS,   *Pink Champagne* (Specialty), no. 1.
PERCY MAYFIELD,   *Please Send Me Someone to Love* (Specialty), no. 1.

1951
CHARLES BROWN,   *Black Night* (Aladdin), no. 1.

JIMMY MCCRACKLIN,   *Looking for a Woman* (Swingtime).

JIMMY NELSON,   *"T" 99 Blues* (RPM), no. 1.

1952

PERCY MAYFIELD,   *The River's Invitation* (Specialty).

1953

WILLIE MAE THORNTON,   *Hound Dog* (Peacock), no. 1.

JIMMY WILSON,   *Tin Pan Alley* (Big Town), no. 10.

1954

LOWELL FULSON,   *Reconsider Baby* (Checker), no. 3.

1955

JOHNNY FULLER,   *Fool's Paradise* (Aladdin).

ETTA JAMES,   *The Wallflower* (Modern), no. 1.

JOHNNY "GUITAR" WATSON,   *Those Lonely, Lonely Nights* (RPM), no. 10.

1956

T-BONE WALKER,   *Mean Old World* (Atlantic).

1957

JOHNNY HEARTSMAN,   *Johnny's House Party, Parts 1 & 2* (Music City), no. 13.

JIMMY MCCRACKLIN,   *Too Late to Change* (Checker).

T-BONE WALKER,   *Evening* (Atlantic).

1958

JIMMY MCCRACKLIN,   *The Walk* (Checker), no. 5.

JOHNNY OTIS,   *Willie and the Hand Jive* (Capitol), no. 3.

1960

SUGAR PIE DESANTO,   *I Want to Know* (Checker), no. 4.

1961

JIMMY MCCRACKLIN,   *Just Got to Know* (Art-Tone), no. 2.

1963

LITTLE JOHNNY TAYLOR,   *Part Time Love* (Galaxy, Ace-Chase), no. 1.

1964

AL KING,   *Reconsider Baby* (Shirley).

TINY POWELL,   *My Time After While* (Wax).

1965

JIMMY MCCRACKLIN,   *Think* (Imperial), no. 7.

1966

LITTLE JOE BLUE,   *Dirty Work Going On* (Checker), no. 40.

AL KING,   *Think Twice Before You Speak* (Sahara), no. 36.

1967

LOWELL FULSON,   *Tramp* (Kent, Modern), no. 5.

1971

Z. Z. HILL,   *Don't Make Me Pay for His Mistakes* (Hill), no. 17.

J. J. MALONE,   *It's a Shame* (Galaxy).

1972

SUGAR PIE DESANTO,   *Hello, San Francisco, Part 1* (Jasman).

Statistical Data on California Rhythm and Blues

Northern California   30.0%

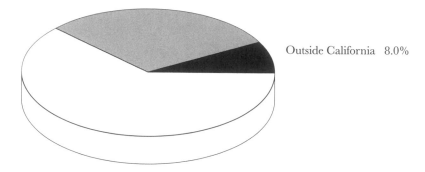

Outside California   8.0%

Southern California   62.0%

Chart 6.1. California rhythm and blues recording locales

Not Charted   28.0%

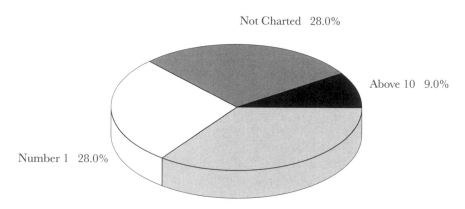

Above 10   9.0%

Number 1   28.0%

Top 10   35.0%

Chart 6.2. Performance of California rhythm and blues recordings

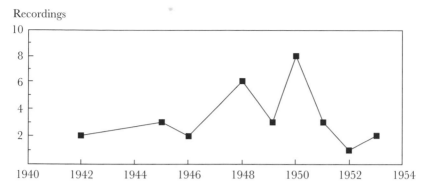

Chart 6.3. Rhythm and blues recordings by year, 1942–1953

NOTES

I could not have completed this article without the assistance of the following in-dividuals: Charles Brown, Danny Caron, Floyd Dixon, Lowell Fulson, Lee Hilde-brand, Tina Mayfield, Johnny Otis, and the late Gaylord Birch. Special thanks to Lee Hildebrand, author and critic whose knowledge, dialogue and encourage-ment were invaluable and to Jacqueline Cogdell DjeDje and Eddie S. Meadows for their advice.

1. The trade magazine *Billboard* introduced the term "rhythm and blues" (a term al-ready in use in the independent recording industry) on 25 June 1949 to refer to records in-tended for distribution in black communities; see Eileen Southern, *The Music of Black Amer-icans: A History*, 2nd. ed. (New York: W. W. Norton and Co., Inc., 1983), and Nelson George, *The Death of Rhythm & Blues* (New York: Pantheon Books, 1988). Also see Ralph Eastman, "Central Avenue Blues: The Making of Los Angeles Rhythm and Blues, 1942–1947," *Black Music Research Journal* 9, no. 1 (Spring 1989): 19–35: "While *Billboard* used the term 'in a non specific fashion to refer to the entire range of black vernacular and popular musics, the phrase was originally coined to describe a post-war urban, black ghetto style of rhythmic dance music played by small bands, frequently featuring electrified instruments and/or 'honking' tenor saxophones.'"
2. Some of these musicians include Joe Liggins (who migrated in the early thirties), Aaron "T-Bone" Walker (who moved in 1934), Roy Milton (1935), and Jimmy Witherspoon (1935).
3. Though scholars make a clear distinction between "blues" and "rhythm and blues" (particularly when sociocultural and musical differences are taken into account), many artists and others in the tradition use the terms interchangeably. However, it is not my pur-pose to investigate the transformation, conceptualization, or realization of blues to rhythm and blues.
4. For further discussion of the record companies in California that produced rhythm and blues recordings, see Portia K. Maultsby, *Rhythm and Blues (1945–1955): A Survey of Styles* (Washington, DC: The Museum of American History, Program in Black American Cul-

ture, 1986). For publications on California artists and/or recordings, see Art Rupe, "The Specialist: Specialty Records," *Blues Unlimited* 104 (October/November 1973): 6–8, and Dave Penny, "Johnny Otis Discography: 1945–1952, Part One," *Blues and Rhythm: The Gospel Truth* 21 (July 1986): 22–23.

5. Seventy-two percent of the California rhythm and blues recordings included in this analysis made the charts (see Charts 6.1, 6.2, and 6.3 in Appendix B, pp. 238–239).

6. William Ferris, "Introduction" in *The Blues: A Bibliographical Guide,* eds. Mary L. Hart, Brenda M. Eagles, and Lisa N. Howorth (New York: Garland Publishing, 1989), x.

7. Mike Rowe, *Chicago Breakdown* (London: Eddison Press, 1973), 11, 211.

8. See "Oakland Blues," by Lee Hildebrand, chapter 3 in this volume.

9. Arnold Shaw, *Honkers and Shouters: The Golden Years of Rhythm and Blues* (New York: Collier Books, 1978).

10. Some of the major works include Charles Keil, *Urban Blues* (Chicago: University of Chicago Press, 1966); Charlie Gillett, *The Sound of the City: The Rise of Rock and Roll* (New York: Outerbridge and Dienstfrey, 1970 [1983]); and Rowe, *Chicago Breakdown.*

11. *Living Blues: A Journal of the Black American Blues Tradition* and *Blues Unlimited* are two journals that have published interviews and articles on California artists. Also see Ellen Blau, "Living Blues Interview: Pee Wee Crayton," *Living Blues* 56 (Spring 1983): 5–12, 14–16; and 57 (Autumn 1983): 6–9, 36–39, 41, 43, 45, 47; Ulf Carlsson, "Trekvarts Sekel Med Musiken—Lloyd Glenn," *Jefferson* (Sweden) 67 (Winter 1984): 26–34; and "Trekvarts Sekel Med Musiken—Lloyd Glenn," *Jefferson* (Sweden) 69 (Summer 1985): 10–17; Lee Hildebrand, liner notes, *Oakland Blues* (Arhoolie LP 2008, 1970); "Pee Wee Is a Big Man on the Blues Circuit," *San Francisco Chronicle Datebook* (27 March 1983): 40–41; "The Honeydrippers Still Sound Sweet," *San Francisco Chronicle Datebook* (27 January 1985): 36–37; "The Johnny Otis Story," *Express: The East Bay's Free Weekly* (12 December 1986): 17–20; "A Life in the Blues," *Express: The East Bay's Free Weekly* (15 March 1991): 1, 17–19, 23–27, "Oakland Blues," chapter 3 in this volume; and personal interview with author, 22 July 1993. Also see Bruce Iglauer, Jim O'Neal, and Bea Van Geffen, "Living Blues Interview: Lowell Fulson," *Living Blues* 5 (Summer 1971): 19–25; and 6 (Autumn 1971): 10–20; "Ivory Joe Hunter," *Living Blues* 19 (January/February 1975): 3; Mike Leadbitter, "Roy Milton: His Life and Times," *Blues Unlimited* 108 (June/July 1974): 6; and "More Milton Facts," *Blues Unlimited* 123 (January/February 1977): 14–22; Tom Mazzolini, "Living Blues Interview: Charles Brown," *Living Blues* 27 (May/June 1976): 19–27; and "Chicago Blues in Oakland," *Living Blues* 45/46 (Spring 1980): 21–23; David Nelson, "Bob Geddins," *Living Blues* 97 (May/June 1991): 43–44; Jim O'Neal and Amy O'Neal, "Living Blues Interview: T-Bone Walker," *Living Blues* 11 (Winter 1972–73): 20–26 and 12 (Spring 1973) 24–27; Johnny Otis, *Listen to the Lambs* (New York: W. W. Norton Co., and Inc., 1968); "The Otis Tapes: 2. Pee Wee Crayton," *Blues Unlimited* 107 (April/May 1974): 8–9; "The Otis Tapes: 3. Roy Milton," *Blues Unlimited* 108 (June/July 1974): 5; *Upside Your Head! Rhythm and Blues on Central Avenue* (London: Wesleyan University Press, 1993); and personal interiew with author, 20 August 1993; Steve Rosen, "Lowell Fulson: Forty Years of Playing the Blues," *Guitar Player* 10 (November 1976): 22, 70, 74; Doug Seroff, "Roy Milton: Miltone Records," *Blues Unlimited* 115 (September/October 1975): 10–17; and Kevin Sheridan and Peter Sheridan "T-Bone Walker: Father of the Electric Blues," *Guitar Player* 11 (March 1977): 22, 48, 50, 52, 54, 56.

12. See Hildebrand, *Oakland Blues,* "Pee Wee," "Johnny Otis," "A Life," and "Oakland Blues."

13. See Eastman, "Central Avenue," and " 'Pitchin' Up a Boogie': African American Musicians, Night Life and Music Venues in Los Angeles 1930–1945," chapter 2 in this volume.

14. Eddie Meadows, "A Preliminary Analysis of Early Rhythm and Blues Musical Practices," *The Western Journal of Black Studies* 7, no. 3 (1983): 172–182.

15. Maulstby, "Rhythm and Blues."

16. Milton Lee Stewart, "Development of Rhythm & Blues and Its Styles," *Jazzforschung* 20 (1988): 89–116.

17. Ibid.

18. Tom Reed, *The Black Music History of Los Angeles—Its Roots: A Classical Pictorial History of Black Music in Los Angeles from the 1920s–1970* (Los Angeles: Black Accent Press, 1992).

19. Paul Oliver, *The Story of the Blues* (London: Chilton Book Company, 1969), 143.

20. Hildebrand, *Oakland Blues*.

21. Quoted in Stanley Dance, *The World of Count Basie* (New York: Charles Scribner's Sons, 1980), 199.

22. Arnold Shaw, "Researching Rhythm and Blues," *Black Music Research Journal* (1980): 71–73.

23. Otis, personal interview.

24. This process of transformation from blues to urban blues and/or rhythm and blues has been discussed by a number of scholars, including Keil, *Urban Blues;* Lynn Ellis McCutcheon, *Rhythm and Blues: An Experience and Adventure in Its Origin and Development* (Arlington, VA: R. W. Beatty, 1971), 73; Shaw, *Honkers,* 65, 245; Maultsby, *Rhythm,* 8; George, *The Death of,* 26; and Eastman, "Central Avenue," 19–21.

25. Otis, personal interview.

26. Eastman, "Central Avenue," 19; and Shaw *Honkers,* 245.

27. Quoted in Shaw, *Honkers,* 245.

28. Floyd Dixon, personal interview with author, 8 February 1992.

29. Hugh Merrill, *The Blues Route* (New York: William Morrow & Co., Inc., 1990), 183.

30. Gaylord Birch, personal interview with author, 21 September 1993.

31. Otis, personal interview.

32. I would argue with the inclusion of Ivory Joe Hunter and Sister Rosetta Tharpe here. "Jimmy" is the correct spelling of Witherspoon's first name.

33. Maultsby, *Rhythm,* 8.

34. See Joel Whitburn, *Top R&B Singles, 1942–1988* (Menomonee Falls, WI: Record Research, Inc., 1988). In addition to providing information obtained from artists and individuals through interviews, Whitburn was a helpful source in developing the sample and determining the year and highest number a particular recording reached on the charts. Many researchers have made ingenious uses of commercial recordings for scholarly research; see discussion in Cathleen C. Flanagan, "The Use of Commercial Sound Recordings in Scholarly Research," *Association for Recorded Sound Collections* 11, no. 1 (1979): 3–17; and Jeff Todd Titon, "Thematic Pattern in Blues Lyrics: The Evidence on Commercial Phonograph Records Since World War II," *Journal of American Folklore* 90, no. 357 (1977): 316–330. In "Researching Rhythm and Blues," p. 76, Shaw states: "Trade paper charts can be of value in a number of respects. They are obviously a better index of a record's success than either an artist's or a record producer's memory. Most researchers, including the present writer, have relied on records in studying R&B because they are more readily available."

35. Only three recordings are in the country blues style: K. C. Douglas's "Mercury Blues," Lowell Fulson's "Three O'Clock Blues," and Willie Mae Thornton's "Hound Dog."

36. Ross Russell, *Jazz Style in Kansas City and the Southwest* (Berkeley: University of California Press, 1971), 137.

37. Dance, *The World*, xvi.

38. Ibid.

39. Otis, personal interview.

40. Ray Toping, liner notes. *The First King of the Blues* (Ace Records, CHD 248, 1988).

41. In Hildebrand, "The Honeydrippers," p. 35, Joe Liggins explains: "The term 'honeydripper' refers to a man who's popular with women." The term also refers to a man's woman, as in Jimmy Nelson's " 'T' 99 Blues." See further discussion below.

42. Russell, *Jazz Style*, 74.

43. Otis, personal interview.

44. Meadows, "A Preliminary Analysis," 173.

45. Otis, personal interview.

46. Louis Jordan was not from California, but he was a major influence on the development of rhythm and blues in California and elsewhere. For a discography, see David Colebeck, "Louis Jordan Discography," *Blues Unlimited* 143 (Autumn/Winter 1982): 14–18.

47. Robert Palmer, "A Guy Named Louis," *Los Angeles Times/Calendar* (11 July 1993): 45.

48. See Michael W. Harris, "Conflict and Resolution in the Life of Thomas Andrew Dorsey," in *We'll Understand It Better By and By*, ed. Bernice Johnson Reagon (Washington and London: Smithsonian Institution Press, 1992), 165–182; and *The Rise of Gospel Blues: The Music of Thomas Andrew Dorsey in the Urban Church* (New York: Oxford University Press, 1992). Harris uses the term "gospel blues" to describe the music and performance style of Thomas Dorsey, the father of gospel music. Dorsey was also a well-known blues performer.

49. This song form is often used by gospel performers; see Rev. Oris Mays's "I Learned How to Lean on Jesus" and "Don't Let the Devil Ride," Song Bird Record 45–1126, Lion Publishing (1968); James W. Alexander and Jesse Whitaker's "Straight Street," Venice Music (1955); and Charlie Barnwell's "Holy Ghost Got Me," Excelloree Music (1961). All are examples of blues gospels. It should also be noted that some blues gospels do not use the twelve-bar blues form.

50. The recordings that I categorize as rhythm and blues ballad style employ both the twelve-bar blues form and the thirty-two-bar popular song form.

51. Rowe, *Chicago*, 13.

52. Charles Brown, personal interview with author, 14 September 1993.

53. Lowell Fulson, personal interview with author, 20 August 1993.

54. Otis, personal interview.

55. With the exception of Louis Jordan, the film industry did not employ rhythm and blues artists in great numbers. Yet most musicians were extremely proficient in a variety of musical styles. Nat King Cole appeared in interludes and in nightclub scenes in feature-length movies. Charles Brown, with the Three Blazers, appeared in a movie entitled *Along the Navajo Trail* with Johnny Shadrack (1944).

56. Ben Sidran, *Talking Jazz: An Illustrated Oral History* (Hong Kong: Pomegranate Artbooks, 1992), 149.

57. Gillett, *The Sound*, 162.

58. In 1950 she was known as "Little Esther." However in 1954, she began to use the name Little Esther Phillips.

59. Brown, personal interview.

60. Ivory Joe Hunter's statement "Ain't the gravy good" appears on the recording, "Blues at Sunrise" (1945).

61. Mazzolini, "Living Blues," 19.

62. Gillett, *The Sound,* 162.

63. Otis, personal interview.

64. Birch, personal interview.

65. Like many California rhythm and blues performers, Brown grew up in the church, playing piano at the age of eleven.

66. Brown, personal interview.

67. Dixon, personal interview.

68. Norbert Hess, "What a Diff'rence a Day Makes," *Black Music* (May 1976): 6–7.

69. Mayfield's contribution as the ordained poet of the blues will be treated later.

70. Hildebrand, personal interview.

71. Hildebrand, "Oakland Blues."

72. Albert J. McCarthy, *Big Band Jazz* (London: G. P. Putnam's Sons, 1974), 179.

73. O'Neal and O'Neal, "T-Bone Walker interview."

74. Fulson, personal interview, 19 July 1993.

75. Ibid.

76. Dixon, personal interview.

77. Birch, personal interview.

78. Fulson, personal interview, 19 July 1993.

79. Ibid.

80. See discussion of Les Hite in Michael Bakan, "Way Out West on Central: Jazz in the African American Community of Los Angeles Before 1930," chapter 1 in this volume. "T-Bone Blues," composed by Hite, was recorded in 1940 in New York and released on Varsity label #8391; it was subsequently recorded in 1956 (Los Angeles) on Atlantic compact disc #CD8020–2. "T-Bone Blues" is not included in the samples under consideration for this study.

81. Fulson, personal interview, 19 July 1993.

82. See further discussion of this issue in Eastman, "Pitchin' up a Boogie."

83. Otis, *Upside Your Head,* xxvi.

84. Brown, personal interview.

85. This spiritual probably dates back to the nineteenth century. For the complete text to "Oh Freedom," see *The New National Baptist Hymnal* (Nashville: National Baptist Board, 1977), 504.

86. The list of songs included in this discography is based on information obtained from Whitburn, *Top R&B.* The numbers listed after the name of the label (e.g., [Exclusive] no. 3) refer to the song's position on *Billboard's* R&B chart.

7

African Americans and "Lites Out Jazz" in San Diego

Marketing, Impact, and Criticism

Eddie S. Meadows

Few jazz scholars would disagree that a complete, definitive history of jazz has yet to appear, primarily because jazz historians have failed to articulate the contributions of most local and regional styles and practitioners outside of Chicago, Kansas City, New Orleans, and New York. Jazz histories continue to focus on these cities, to the exclusion of other important areas. Works on Louis Armstrong,[1] John Coltrane,[2] Duke Ellington,[3] and Charles Parker[4] permeate the literature, as do sources on Chicago,[5] Kansas City,[6] New Orleans,[7] and New York.[8] With the exception of Buddy Collette,[9] Eric Dolphy,[10] Hampton Hawes,[11] Earl Hines,[12] and Charles Mingus,[13] Californian African-American jazz musicians have received little scholarly attention, and to date no in-depth works have been published on San Diego's jazz or jazz musicians.

Like other urban areas in the United States, San Diego has an eclectic jazz community. Although bebop, big bands, and the fusion of world musics (particularly African and Brazilian) have survived, these forms do not receive overwhelming support from blacks and others in the San Diego community. Instead, "lites out jazz," a format adopted by **KIFM** radio in 1982, not only has become more popular than traditional forms but has flourished and been exported throughout the United States. In this chapter I will explore the impact of lites out jazz on San Diego African-American jazz preferences. Although the research covers the 1986–1990 period, the primary emphasis is 1986. I will assess African-Americans and "lites out jazz" in San Diego by examining the evolution of the African-American middle and upper class; presenting an historical overview of African-American jazz in San Diego; addressing marketing, impact, and criticism of the music; and interviewing radio personalities and musicians.

The popularity of "lites out jazz" in San Diego's African-American community is closely related to the socioeconomic position of blacks in the city. As blacks have become more affluent, particularly those between the ages of 25 and 34, they have become better able to participate in and support activities associated with "lites out jazz." There is a direct connection between education, income level, and the ability of black listeners to afford certain types of leisure-time activities. To illustrate how the change in socioeconomic status affected the musical tastes of African Americans in San Diego, I present background information on education and income.

EVOLUTION OF THE AFRICAN-AMERICAN MIDDLE AND UPPER CLASSES

The African-American middle and upper classes' beginnings in San Diego date to the late nineteenth century. Prior to the population increase of the 1880s,[14] "most of the new arrivals were slaves, ex-slaves, or employees of whites whom they had accompanied."[15] After the 1880s, African-American job descriptions and land ownership began to change:

> In 1880 in Georgia and Mississippi, fewer than one black farmer in one hundred owned land. As many as one in ten San Diego County blacks did. According to Robert L. Carlton, by 1860 one black farmer owned land in Temecula, while several others worked as laborers at San Luis Rey. In 1869 Fred Coleman, a black, discovered gold at Julian, initiating a gold rush. By 1880, when the county's black population numbered fifty-five, thirty-one blacks lived in Julian. In 1887 Albert Robinson built the Hotel Robinson, now the Julian Hotel, and his family operated it until 1915.[16]

By the late nineteenth and early twentieth centuries, African Americans had abandoned Julian and other rural areas of San Diego County. Most moved to the city of San Diego to escape racism and to seek better jobs and education. In 1890 the city's black population numbered 289. African Americans operated blacksmith shops, at least one saloon, a laundry, a mortuary, several restaurants, and a bakery. They published their own newspaper, and black political organizations, social clubs, and churches flourished. A few blacks were practicing physicians and attorneys, though the majority worked at menial jobs as cooks, laborers, maids, and shoeshine operators.[17]

The early twentieth century witnessed a continued increase in African-American business activity. Walter Meadows, a master jeweler from Chattanooga, Tennessee, opened a shop in 1903. The Douglas Hotel, located at 206 Market Street, was built in 1924 by African-American businessmen George Ramsey and Bob Rowe, and the Simmons Hotel, owned by Lucille House Simmons, opened in 1938. It is estimated that between 1880 and 1930 African Americans owned more than twenty businesses in downtown San Diego (an area bounded by Third and Fourth Avenues and Market and J Streets), with hotels and restaurants dominating.[18]

In spite of the successes and the continued growth of the middle and upper classes, patterns of discrimination and violence that African Americans had experienced in Julian began to recur in the city of San Diego. After 1900 the jobs available to blacks were increasingly limited to menial labor; thus, the black community grew more disadvantaged. By 1920 restrictive housing covenants had caused most African Americans to be concentrated in southeast San Diego.[19]

Between 1920 and World War II, African Americans constituted only 2 percent of San Diego's population. Most worked in mail rooms or were employed as domestics and janitors. This pattern changed with the beginning of the war. Employment opportunities expanded for both skilled and unskilled workers. Beginning in 1940, Dennis V. Allen, president of the San Diego Race Relations Society, was instrumental in securing assembly line jobs for African Americans at aircraft plants, especially at Convair and Ryan. However, even though the number of African Americans who were employed increased, their job classification did not improve significantly: "Figures for 1944 show that 3,200 black men were working for the federal government (1,500, mostly at Convair) and [in] construction (500). Another 2,000 worked in trades and services. Yet a 1946 report, 'Intergroup Relations San Diego,' noted that most positions in large firms were custodial. . . . When the war ended, 1940 employment patterns returned."[20]

After World War II, there was a substantial increase in the city's population. By 1950, San Diego's population was 334,387, with the African-American community numbering 14,904 (approximately 4.5 percent). In 1960, the black population increased to 38,980, or 6.8 percent of the total population of 573,244.[21] During the fifties and sixties, the majority of the African-American population lived in Southeast San Diego, "probably the most economically deprived areas within the city."[22] Of the ten tracts that made up the southeast section of the city, six were identified as belonging to Logan Heights, the site of the Logan Heights Rebellion in 1965.[23] During the 1960s about 80 percent of the people living in Logan Heights were members of minority groups. African Americans constituted 62.7 percent of the minorities, 49.6 of the total population.[24] Logan Heights was characterized by low incomes, large families, inadequate educational opportunities, substandard housing, and high unemployment.[25] The average family size was 3.9 persons, and more than a quarter of all families had less than $3,000 in annual income. Among persons twenty-five years and older, one-third had fewer than eight years of formal education, and 3.8 percent had none.

After the 1965 rebellion, there were dramatic improvements in the socioeconomic conditions of many blacks in San Diego. Not only did longtime residents benefit from social programs and opportunities that were made available after the rebellion, but San Diego began to attract more outsiders during the 1970s. Improved education and newly instituted social programs gave blacks access to new and better-paying jobs, which, in turn, formed the basis for the development of a more vigorous African-American middle class.[26] Concurrently, the African-American population began to scatter throughout San Diego County. The diffusion was aided by both an increase in economic wealth and the advent of fair housing laws. Instead of remaining in Logan Heights and Southeast San Diego, better-educated and economically secure African Americans began to move to areas such as Bonita, La Jolla, Rancho Bernado, and the more affluent suburbs of La Mesa, as well as to North County areas such as Poway. In order to provide a more accurate and comprehensive picture of African-American economic and educational gains in San Diego, I will present an overview of these accomplishments on a county basis rather than limiting my discussion to Logan Heights and Southeast San Diego.

San Diego witnessed gains in both population and economic activity during the 1970s. At the same time, the city's blacks enjoyed a qualitative and quantitative increase in socioeconomic status. In 1970, 62,028 African Americans lived in San Diego County; by 1980 the black population had increased to 104,452.[27] There were 56,967 males and 47,485 females in 1980. Of the total, 1,479 were in nursery school, 16,277 in kindergarten/elementary school, 7,901 in high school, and 9,602 in college. The level of education of adult African Americans during this period breaks down as follows: 5,397 elementary, 6,347 high school (1–3 years), 16,089 high school (4 years), 12,674 with 1–3 years of college, and 5,066 with a college or graduate/professional degree. See Tables 7.1 and 7.2 for the family income and mortgage payments of African Americans in San Diego in 1979.

By the late 1980s, San Diego had become known as a vacation/convention city with large populations of retirees and past and present Navy personnel. Like other urban areas in California, the city continued to have a racially diverse population.[28] The 1990 census lists 157,495 African Americans as residing in San Diego County.[29] Of that number, 85,334 were male, and 72,161 were female; 3,243 were in pre-primary education, 29,991 in elementary or high school, and 14,877 in college. The educational level breaks down as follows: 3,797 with elementary only, 10,527 with grades 9–12 but no diploma, 25,530 with some college but no degree, 7,507 with an associate degree, 7,535 with a bachelor degree, and 3,671 with a graduate or professional degree. In addition, 18,751 were in the armed forces. There were 44,119 homeowners, 95,667 renters. Table 7.3 lists household income by age for African Americans in 1989, and Table 7.4 gives mortgage payments for the same year.

The 1979–89 data indicate that both education and income improved significantly for African Americans during the decade. Whereas 5,066 possessed a college or graduate/professional education in 1979, the number grew to 11,206 by 1989. Income distribution by age was not available in the 1979 census but in the 1989 census the greatest number of income earners fell in the 25–34 age category. It is also noteworthy that whereas only 506 African Americans earned $50,000 or more in 1979, this number had increased to 8,081 by the 1989 census. The mortgage data indicate a significant change in the economic status of African Americans. In 1979 only 2,936 paid mortgages of $500 or more per month; however, by 1989 the number had grown to 9,066, including 3,778 whose mortgages ranged from $1,000 to $1,499/month and 1,595 with mortgages of $1,500/month or

TABLE 7.1   Family Income of African Americans,
San Diego County, 1979

Income ($)	Number of Families
0– 4,999	3,189
5,000– 7,499	2,497
7,500– 9,999	2,554
10,000–14,999	4,249
15,000–19,999	3,141
20,000–24,999	2,605
25,000–34,999	3,299
35,000–49,999	1,466
50,000 or more	506

California State Census Data Center 1980 Census, Summary Tape File One
(San Diego: Sandag/Sourcepoint, 1980), 1–9. Age-distribution data not
available.

TABLE 7.2   Mortgage Payments of African Americans,
San Diego County, 1979

Monthly Mortgage Payment ($)	Number of Households
0–199	1,012
200–299	1,810
300–399	1,652
400–499	1,456
500 or more	2,936

California State Data Center 1980 Census, Summary Tape File One (San
Diego: Sandag/Sourcepoint, 1980), 1–9.

more. In addition to having the greatest number of income earners, the 25–34 age
group included 4,919 people earning $35,000 or more and 1,781 earning $50,000
or more in 1989. This new wealth made it possible for African Americans in the
25–34 age group to engage in leisure activities such as "lites out jazz" concerts,
happy hours, and cruises.

JAZZ IN THE SAN DIEGO AFRICAN-AMERICAN COMMUNITY: A HISTORICAL OVERVIEW

Unlike New Orleans, Chicago, and New York, San Diego has not produced an indigenous jazz style. Instead, jazz artists who migrated to the city brought their
styles with them, and native artists assimilated these styles. The first known jazz-

TABLE 7.3   Household Income by Age, African Americans,
San Diego County, 1989

Income ($)	15–24	25–34	35–44	45–54	55–64	65–74	75+	Total
0– 4,999	452	1,078	500	413	248	204	241	3,136
5,000– 9,999	949	1,660	1,066	422	670	766	513	6,046
10,000–14,999	1,041	1,927	887	388	303	398	276	5,220
15,000–24,999	1,603	4,148	1,978	960	804	534	277	10,304
25,000–34,999	969	3,391	2,166	1,002	591	290	101	8,510
35,000–49,999	566	3,138	2,142	1,378	769	286	91	8,370
50,000–74,999	106	1,481	1,759	1,548	654	199	21	5,768
75,000–99,999	32	218	392	586	267	67	9	1,571
100,000 or more	13	82	190	307	136	6	8	742
Total	5,731	17,123	11,080	7,004	4,442	2,750	1,537	49,667
Mean	—	—	—	—	—	—	—	30,339

1990 Census of Population. Social and Economic Characteristics. California (Washington, DC: United States Department of Commerce, 1993).

TABLE 7.4   Mortgage Payments of African Americans,
San Diego County, 1989

Monthly Mortgage Payment ($)	Number of Households
0– 299	595
300– 499	1,382
500– 699	1,286
700– 999	2,407
1,000–1,499	3,778
1,500 or more	1,595

1990 Census of Population. Social and Economic Characteristics. California (Washington, DC: United States Department of Commerce, 1993).

related band in San Diego was formed in the 1890s: "A brass band organized by blacks in 1893 with thirteen musicians first performed with shiny new instruments at the corner of Seventh and H [Streets]. A desire for social recognition brought together members of the Hotel Florence Social Club. One evening in 1891 they waltzed in elegant attire into the wee hours of the morning to the music of Professor Forbes and his five piece orchestra."[30]

Most jazz groups performed and received much of their support from social organizations such as the Violet Club, a women's group founded in 1899 that admitted only the black elite of San Diego. The Acme Social Club was formed after the turn of the century, as were several other social and professional organizations.

There is little information on bands, activities, and venues in San Diego prior to the 1920s. However, substantial data have been documented for the Douglas Hotel, one of the most important meccas of African-American entertainment in San Diego from the early twenties to its demise in 1984.[31] Inside the Douglas Hotel was a club called the Creole Palace, which featured jazz bands, comedians, shake dancers, and a group known as the Creole Cuties. According to Froebel "Fro" Brigham, a jazz musician who booked acts for the club in the late 1940s and 1950s, "there wasn't another place like it. People came from L.A. just to visit the Creole Palace."[32] The club had a small cover charge and a seating capacity of several hundred in the back. It also served food and would attract outside artists.[33] Billie Holiday performed at the club, and Count Basie and Duke Ellington, when they were in town to perform at venues such as the Orpheum Auditorium, would show up and joined the band. Lionel Hampton even dined at the Creole Palace.[34] More important, the Creole Palace provided employment for jazz artists who settled in San Diego. I will now take a closer look at the contributions of some of these individuals to the city's jazz history.

Troy Floyd

In the early forties, Troy Floyd was hired to run the band at the Creole Palace.[35] Before moving to San Diego in the thirties, Floyd was a highly respected musician and bandleader of the Troy Floyd Orchestra (the house band at the Shadowland Ballroom in San Antonio, Texas) in the late twenties and occasionally toured Arkansas, Oklahoma, and Texas. Floyd was known for his performance of New Orleans–type jazz, using small band interplay and polyphonic swing with big-band orchestrations. Among his side musicians were Don Albert (trumpet) and Herschel Evans and Buddy Tate (saxophones). Schuller describes Floyd's pre–San Diego style as combining the best of Don Redman's arranging style with a blues feeling:

> We must judge Floyd's band by the only evidence available today, four sides recorded on the Okeh label in 1928 and 1929. Both pieces, "Shadowland Blues" and "Dreamland Blues," were recorded in two parts, that is, on both sides of a ten inch disc. Thus they are six-minute pieces, both slow blues, a loosely constructed forerunner of an extended piece like Ellington's "Diminuendo and Crescendo in Blue." "Shadowland," recorded in 1928, is the lesser of the two performances.[36]

Whereas the 1928 sides overemphasized the trombone playing of Benny Long, "Dreamland Blues" featured a good solo by Herschel Evans and excellent collectively improvised ensemble choruses. Schuller praises Floyd's use of rhythm and the New Orleans ensemble concept as it was incorporated into the blues.[37] Although there are no known recordings from his San Diego years, there is no reason to believe that Floyd, in San Diego, did not continue to employ the musical concepts that made him one of the premier Southwest jazz bandleaders. Floyd's original group disbanded in 1932. Thereafter he moved to San

Diego, where he married the widow of New Orleans clarinetist Jimmy Noone in 1953.[38]

Froebel "Fro" Astor Brigham

When Troy Floyd served as bandleader at the Creole Palace, he employed trumpet player Fro Brigham[39] (Figure 7.1), "who had played with Papa Celestin in New Orleans until he was drafted and wound up in the Navy Band[40] in San Diego."[41] Before moving to San Diego, Brigham was working in a Civilian Conservation Corps (CCC) camp in the South. There he read an advertisement recruiting African-American musicians into the Navy. After auditioning, he was only one of twenty-two musicians to be selected. Concerning the New Orleans–San Diego connection, Brigham states:

> I volunteered for the Navy in New Orleans. My present wife sent me a cutting from the newspaper that said they were going to organize black bands for the Navy. This was under President Truman, it was 1942. I had to pass a medical and music test. They wanted to organize a twenty-six-piece black band. They made me a recruiting officer for the New Orleans–Baton Rouge areas. After the band was organized we traveled to the Chicago, Illinois, training center (Great Lakes Center).[42] We had to learn Navy ways; thereafter we returned to New Orleans.
>
> After two years in New Orleans we were sent back to Chicago, and thereafter dispersed to other points. . . . I had a choice of Boston, Norfolk, Virginia, or San Diego. Being a country boy, I didn't know too much about California; however, I chose San Diego because the weather was cold in the other cities. I came to San Diego in 1945. . . . When I arrived in San Diego, they placed me on the Frontier Base (Point Loma). There we played parades, raised the flag, and performed for dances. The band was all black. Once established in Point Loma, I began to come to town and get acquainted.[43]

Concerning his initial attempt to sit in with bands and his eventual role as bandleader at the Douglas Hotel, Brigham states:

> After having made my reputation "sitting in" down at the Douglas Hotel, there was a man named Justin Johnson running the entertainment (he was a tap dancer). When the war ended, this man approached me about organizing the band. Mabel Rowe would send me to Los Angeles to recruit show people. Some of the people I picked up was Redd Foxx, Errol Garner, Jimmy Reed, and Joe Turner. Almost all the people on the West Coast, you got them from Los Angeles.
>
> I took over the band around 1946 and stayed until integration [in the 1950s]. The integration cut into our audience because some began to go here or there, places they had not been allowed to go. People wanted to get out and see what the other side was doing. [In the fifties], the Douglas Hotel was not doing well, and finally I went to a stage called Club Romance on C Street. Almost everything was down on C Street or Fifth Avenue.[44]

After the glory days at the Creole Palace, Brigham began an active career as leader of small groups in and around the city, continuing to perform through the

Figure 7.1. Jazz trumpeter "Fro" Brigham. Taken in the 1970s. Courtesy of "Fro" Brigham and Trina Brown.

1980s.[45] Bud Conway, who earlier worked with Earl Hines and Fletcher Henderson in Chicago, usually appeared with him on tenor saxophone. Younger musicians who gained experience with Brigham include Harold Land and Victor Gaskin.

In addition to the early New Orleans–style jazz, ballads, and swinglike compositions that he had played since the 1940s, Brigham also performed other types of music to satisfy the tastes of his listeners. He indicated that not only blacks but also white students liked blues and rock. Brigham's description of his repertoire and the musical preferences of some African Americans in the forties and fifties demonstrates that a blues/rock/jazz fusion was strong before KIFM changed its format in 1982.

> We played mostly dance music. At one time I was going in for the progressive jazz (bebop), but it was a very difficult type of music to put across in San Diego. People who came in during the war years were from blues areas—Texas, Louisiana, Arkansas—they loved that rock and roll and blues. Naturally, to try to make a buck and keep my family going, I went to rhythm and blues. Then even that got skimpy. So I went to work for Sears, then the post office. The reason why I didn't stay at the post office was that they wanted you on the job at 5:00 a.m. and sometimes I

wouldn't get home from a music job until 3:30 a.m. Then [in the 1950s] I went with the city. I worked twenty-five years for the city and retired in 1979.[46]

Throughout his career, Brigham was concerned about the preservation of African-American music. He was probably one of the earliest jazz musicians to organize a band to preserve a jazz tradition. In a 1995 interview, Brigham stated: "In the [Navy] barracks some of us would sit around and talk about preserving 100 years of music—I started one [a band] in New Orleans. I named my band Preservation, attempting to preserve the good songs of yesteryear and the good ones of today."[47] His concern with preservation was also reflected in the naming of his San Diego band, Fro Brigham and the Preservation Band.

Although Brigham remained in the San Diego area, he had national influence through the help he gave other musicians. Concerning the artists that he helped to gain national prominence, Brigham stated the following:

> Major Holly [bass], you know who picked him up from me? Oscar Peterson. Then other friends of mine, Harold Land [tenor], Herman Riley [tenor], and Leon Pettis [drummer]; he was picked up by Nat King Cole and stayed with him until King Cole passed in 1965. Charles Owens [tenor] played with Duke Ellington after leaving me, and then I had Teddy Edwards [tenor]. Then I had some piano players—Eugene Watson, exceptional, he played all types of music and worked with Walter Fuller. Bud Conway [tenor], he was a master. He had played with Fletcher Henderson and Count Basie in his younger days. He was out of Philadelphia; we sent for him to come to a smaller area and relax. Jesse Wilkins has been with me for thirty years; he sings, plays harmonica and guitar. Betty Roché, a former singer with Duke Ellington, worked with me. I picked her up in Los Angeles.[48]

As an eyewitness and participant in the making of San Diego jazz history, Brigham's observations regarding contemporary jazz musicians are insightful. He believes that record companies "package" newcomers, thereby creating a process by which both to diffuse music and make it popular. It is those in the music business who affect what is heard on radio stations such as KIFM:

> We have what we call "kingmakers" in the music business. Music is a very prosperous business. There are some people here and in Los Angeles that they take into the studio and teach them five or ten numbers. They take you out and tell the club operators, "We want you to help us out by giving some experience to this person." The companies season them for the field, they put their tapes and recordings out, disc jockeys are given words to say, and after a while people believe. They say, "This guy is good, go get one of these." The guy might only know ten to twenty numbers. Some get on tapes with less experience.
>
> It's who the kingmakers decide to distribute across the country. These bands have been fortunate to have one of those kingmakers say, "We are going to record you, we are going to do this and that." So people who are asking for this type of music have been taken in. If you tell a lie long enough, people will begin to believe it. So Kenny

G has been fortunate enough to be recorded and to be heard on KIFM. People naturally go out to Humphrey's to see him, and that's the name of the game. The music
is attracting blacks, too, because they also listen to the radio.[49]

Walter Fuller

Like Fro Brigham, Walter Fuller has been an astute observer and exponent of
African-American jazz in San Diego (Figure 7.2).[50] Before his arrival in San Diego
in 1947, Fuller played jazz in Chicago, where he led the Fletcher Henderson band
after Henderson became the chief arranger for Benny Goodman. Stanley Dance
provides the following information about Fuller:

> Walter Fuller, for many years a trumpet and vocal star of Earl Hines's famous Grand
> Terrace Band, had made a name for himself with a small group by 1946, when he
> was booked into a club called Eddy's on Second Avenue and C Street in San Diego.
> As a result of appearances in many different parts of the country he had become fa-
> miliar to servicemen, and because the city was then "loaded with sailors," he was an
> instant success. For four years he played clubs in San Diego, Los Angeles, and San
> Francisco, commuting from time to time to his Chicago home until 1950, when he
> moved his wife, Ida Mae, and daughter Rosetta (named for the song he did so much
> to make popular) to San Diego. He played at the Club Royal there for twelve years,
> and then eight years more at the Moonglow, always finding good musicians with
> which to work, among them tenor saxophonist Gene Porter (formerly with such
> leaders as Papa Celestin, Don Redman, and Benny Carter) and pianist Eugene Wat-
> son. One of his big discoveries was singer Marie Louise, who later had great success
> on records after changing her name to Georgia Carr.[51]

In a 1980 interview, Fuller said his move to San Diego "was a good investment
for me. The lifestyle was different [because] in those days, clubs closed at 12:00
a.m. I was used to playing until 4:00 in the morning."[52] When he arrived in San
Diego, Fuller states, he had a quintet and vocalist (Figure 7.3). But his drummer
and pianist returned to Chicago, and it was not easy to find replacements: "I had
the most trouble finding a pianist. Eventually I hired Adam Kato (formerly of the
Four Clefs), who remained with me for the twelve years that I played at the Club
Royal at Third and C Streets."[53] In addition to his work in clubs, Fuller performed
casuals and served on the Musician's Union's board of directors.

An examination of select Fuller recordings with Earl "Fatha" Hines reveals a
trumpet player in the mold of Louis Armstrong. The Armstrong influence sur-
faces on "Take It Easy" and "Cavernism," both recorded in 1933. Another excellent solo in the Armstrong tradition can be heard on "Rosetta," an introspective
and emotional ballad composed by Hines and Henri Woode. Fuller's ability to
string together coherent ideas over a driving rhythm section can be heard on
Lawrence Dixon's "Bubbling Over" (1933).[54] Fuller's infatuation with Armstrong's
trumpet and vocal styles continued in San Diego. The respect was mutual, because Armstrong visited him once while he was in town to perform at the Club
Royal.[55]

Figure 7.2. Jazz trumpeter Walter Fuller and band. Taken in Chicago, c.1943. Left to right: Rozell Claxton, piano; Buddy Smith, drums; Quincy Wilson, bass; Elmer Ewing, guitar; Omer Simeon, clarinet/saxophone; Nelda Dupree, vocals; Fuller, trumpet. Courtesy of Walter Fuller.

Commenting on the types of jazz artists in San Diego during the forties and early fifties, Fuller explains why some musicians decided to leave: "Jazz is different from dancing. Most players would like to play their music and not worry about [playing for] dancing, like Harold Land. He moved to Los Angeles and stuck with it."[56] After leaving San Diego, Land became one of the leading bebop/hard-bop tenor saxophonists of the period and alternated with Sonny Rollins on several of the Clifford Brown–Max Roach Quintet recordings.

Jazz from the 1950s to 1970s

From the fifties through the seventies, the African-American jazz community expanded, reflecting a diversity of artists and styles. Artists such as Brigham and Fuller continued to be active, but the period also witnessed an increase in the post-bebop styles. These, combined with the older styles, helped to produce a jazz menu to accommodate the wide-ranging jazz preferences that began to emerge in the period. An overview of some of the artists and their styles, including some who migrated to San Diego before and during the period of discussion, reveals the diversity of musical tastes in the city.

Figure 7.3. Jazz trumpeter Walter Fuller and band. Taken 1954 at the Club Royal in San Diego. Left to right: Eugene Porter, baritone saxophone; Marie Louise, vocals; Preston Coleman, bass; Fuller, trumpet; and Charlie Blackwell, drums. Courtesy of Walter Fuller.

Ray Crawford, a guitarist who was steeped in swing, bebop, and post-bebop styles, was active in San Diego during the fifties. Before moving to San Diego, he performed with Fletcher Henderson and Ahmad Jamal and recorded with Gil Evans in 1959. Walter Williams, a trumpeter who was as adept in rhythm and blues as he was in swing, moved to San Diego in the mid-fifties. Before his arrival he had performed with Les Hite, Benny Carter, Johnny Otis, and Roy Milton and from 1949–1954 led Lionel Hampton's trumpet section. The period also witnessed the arrival of Teddy Picou, grandson of Alphonse Picou (a premier New Orleans musician) and a tenor saxophonist in the Sonny Rollins mold. Calvin Jackson, a pianist, arranger-composer of film scores and jazz works, and proponent of the Teddy Wilson and Earl Hines school of piano, spent his retirement years in San Diego.[57] Jimmy and Jeannie Cheatham, exponents of blues, and Charles McPherson, an alto saxophonist and exponent of Charles Parker (and former side musician with Charles Mingus), moved to San Diego in the seventies.

Although the period witnessed an increase in the number of artists migrating to San Diego, several native and world-class artists left to seek fame and fortune elsewhere. Among these were bop saxophonist Arthur Blythe; bassist Nathan East, a blues-rock and jazz artist and member of Eric Clapton's band; and James Zollar, a trumpeter in the tradition of Clifford Brown and Freddie Hubbard.

Jazz and the Media

Jazz artists, regardless of ethnicity, received minimum media coverage before 1970. Print and broadcast outlets often failed to list upcoming jazz performances or review concerts. Information about jazz performances was often circulated only via informal networking among people who frequented a specific club or among members of a social group that hired a band to perform at a specific function. However, media coverage of jazz events increased significantly in the 1980s. Both the *San Diego Union* and the San Diego edition of the *Los Angeles Times* hired jazz critics, and two San Diego radio stations, KSDS and KIFM, began to program jazz. Tables 7.5 and 7.6 list, respectively, the AM and FM stations operative in San Diego in 1990.

The increase in San Diego's population was accompanied by an expansion of entertainment outlets. In 1980 five San Diego clubs hired jazz musicians on a consistent basis (three or more days a week), including Chuck's Steak House, which promoted fusion, and Elario's, which emphasized bebop. By 1990 more than fifteen clubs hired jazz musicians on a regular basis. Because of increased media exposure, local musicians who once might have moved to Los Angeles, New York, or Europe discovered more work opportunities in San Diego, particularly in performing "lites out jazz."

"LITES OUT JAZZ"

Insider Perspectives: Musical Structure

Conversations with jazz critics, radio personalities, and jazz musicians[58] have produced an interesting musical profile of "lites out jazz" as played by KIFM. The music often features progressions using extended harmonies (e.g., flat ninths, elevenths) and a funk, samba, or shuffle beat. Swing feel on percussion and walking bass lines are rarely heard. Both instrumental and vocal music is featured, with saxophone being the dominant lead instrument. Electronic or synthesized instruments are common. Melodies, which are primarily diatonic, tend to be emphasized over rhythm, and arrangements replace improvisation on recordings, though improvisation plays a greater role in concerts. Solos often occur over vamp sections rather than entire forms.

The music has its roots in the late-sixties style of Miles Davis and the spinoff groups that emanated from his band, including Chick Corea's Return to Forever, John McGlaughlin's Mahavishnu Orchestra, Josef Zawinul/Wayne Shorter's Weather Report, Herbie Hancock's Head Hunters, and Tony Williams's Lifetime. Individual performers such as George Benson, Bob James, Grover Washington, and Horace Silver not only contributed to this style but also inspired several San

TABLE 7.5   AM Radio Stations, San Diego County, 1990

Frequency	Call Letters	Formats	Power (watts)
550	KCR	Alternative radio	0.25
600	KKLQ	Top 40	5,000
690	XTRA(ABC)	News, sports	50,000
760	FFMB(CBS)	News, music, sports	5,000
860	XEMO	Spanish music	5,000
1000	KCEO(ABC)	News, talk	2,500
1130	KSDO(ABC)	News, sports, talk	10,000
1170	KCBQ	50s rock	50,000
1210	KPRZ	Religious	10,000
1240	KSON	Classic country	1,000 day, 500 night
1320	KGMG	Contemporary hits	500
1360	KPOP(NBC)	Hits of 40s–70s	5,000
1420	XEXX	Mexican music	5,000
1450	KOW(ABC)	Classic country	15,000

San Diego Union, "TV Weekly" (2–8 September 1990): 7.

Diego African-American jazz musicians, including Ella Ruth Piggee (vocalist),[59] Eddie Davis (vocalist), Hollis Gentry (leader of Neon and, in the late 1980s, tenor saxophonist with Larry Carlton), and the group Fattburger.

Carl Evans, an African American born February 19, 1955, in San Diego, is the co-leader,[60] keyboardist, arranger, and composer for Fattburger. He began his career as a bebop pianist. In a 1990 interview, he indicated that as a professional musician his first objective was merely to survive. Therefore, he was pleased that Fattburger was doing very well. Acknowledging the increased airplay and popularity of the "lites out jazz" format, Evans comments on the stylistic features of Fattburger's music:

> It is more palatable than melodic, it's easier to deal with, easier to hear, pleasing, not offensive to the ear at all. Some people criticize it because they say it is bland, it's unadventuresome, and all those sorts of things. They have a point there, too, but it's like any other style of music. It's individual songs and individual musicians who have a range of abilities and expertise. Some are better than others, but the style itself is basically instrumental pop music.
>
> I think the reason why it ["lites out jazz"] is popular is because there are certain people who would be considered jazz connoisseurs that realize that the type of music Miles Davis plays—or the type of music he is known for—or the type of music Coltrane plays, and Charlie Parker and these guys [play], is a lot more advanced and takes a lot more expertise than the type of music Fattburger, Spyro Gyra, or Grover Washington play. But that type of music is not for everybody, that type of music is not designed for everyone to enjoy—in that respect, it is somewhat more exclusive. The music that we, along with Spyro Gyra or Earl Klugh, play is designed for more

TABLE 7.6   FM Radio Stations, San Diego County, 1990

Frequency	Call Letters	Formats	Power (watts)
88.3	KSDS	Jazz	831
89.5	KPBS (NPR)	News, classical	2,000
90.3	XHTZ	Rock music	100,000
91.1	XTRA	Cutting-edge rock	100,000
92.1	KOWF	Modern country	3,000
92.5	XHRM	Urban/contemporary	100,000
93.3	KECR	Religious	2,000
94.1	KFSD	Classical	100,000
94.9	KKYY	Adult contemporary	22,000
95.7	XHKY	Fiesta Mexicana	18,000
95.9	KKOS	Contemporary	3,000
96.5	XYXY	Best of today/yesterday	41,000
97.3	KSON	Country	50,000
98.1	KIFM	Contemporary jazz	28,000
98.9	KSM (AFM)	UB dance	unknown
99	KCR (AFM)	Alternative	25
100.7	B-100	Contemporary	30,000
101.5	KGB	Album rock	5,000
102.1	KGMG	Classic rock	50,000
102.9	KSDO	Classic rock	32,000
103.7	KJQY	Adult contemporary	36,000
104.5	XLTN	Radio Latina	120,000
105.3	KCBQ	Oldies	29,000
106.5	KKLQ	Top 40	5,000
107.1	KMLO	Adult contemporary	3,000
107.3	XHFG	Romantic Spanish	5,000
107.9	KWVE	Religious	5,000

San Diego Union, "TV Weekly" (2–8 September 1990): 7.

people to enjoy. It's simpler, it's a little more pleasant, and it's more inclusive by design.[61]

According to Evans, Fattburger is acutely aware of the jazz structure and type of music a "lites out jazz" audience might be attracted to:

> It's simpler as far as the chord progressions, the overall movement, the imagery it is trying to project—it's simpler in every way possible. The only thing that is not simpler is the production—the recording process—due to the fact that stuff recorded in 1989 was different from something recorded in 1956. But other than that, it is mellower. Vanilla ice cream is the most popular flavor there is.[62]

An excellent example of "lites out jazz" is the Fattburger song "Good News." Composed in C minor, "Good News" has a funky, blues feel, with harmonies that fluctuate between major and minor voicings, especially thirds and sevenths (see Example 7.1, measures 10 and 11), conjunct and disjunct melodic intervals (measures 9 and 10), and repetition of form, featuring an eight-bar repeated A section, a fourteen-bar B section, and a sixteen-bar C section. Repetition of harmonies and melodic motifs permeate all sections of the composition.[63] The analysis suggests that "Good News" was composed to accentuate sameness, using repetition as a generic structural device. Because the composition was created to appeal to a mostly nonliterate (musically) population that enjoys music primarily as a complement to social activities, repetition is used both to achieve a point of reference and to ensure that the audience is not overwhelmed by the complexity of the composition.[64]

A more detailed stylistic analysis by Evans, an insider, provides greater insight about both the structure and performance of "Good News":

> This song is the title cut from our second album, entitled "Good News." It is the essence of what Fattburger is doing. First of all, it is a funky tune. You hear a Stevie Wonder–type clavinet rhythm bass for it. Then there is a flute synthesized-sound melody played on a DX7, and all the percussion mixed in the background. It has an interesting chord progression—it's a minor mode, like the stuff that Horace Silver and McCoy Tyner do, and it is also a vamp. But the movement in it, I don't know, it's kind of cyclical, so that makes it easy to move around in and to solo. There's no solo, basically, until the end of the song, because the melody and bridge are played first, and after restating the melody you get into the solo part.
>
> It's a contagious sort of funky tune, and that's one of the reasons it has remained one of our most popular songs, even to today. There's some pretty good playing on it, too. Steve Laury is playing rhythm guitar, nice, and real tasty. The drummer is not our regular drummer. The tune was co-written with Ricky Lawson, who is a drummer for Michael Jackson, who used to play with the Yellow Jackets and is one of the top studio drummers around. We have a publishing partnership, so he is the guest on the particular song. He uses the backbeat concept on this song, like he plays with Michael Jackson.
>
> It's a contagious little funky tune with a pleasant melody, with a solo by myself which has a Bach fuguelike approach. You have a contrapuntal-like solo on top of a funky feel. What I am trying to do is not play the instrument so much as to play the song. I hear people playing with phenomenal chops over a song, but it has nothing to do with the essence of the song, so I would rather play the song well, so each composition pretty much dictates to me how I'm going to take the solo.[65]

Describing the audience that is attracted to Fattburger's music, Evans states:

> A large number of people that come to hear us are, agewise, in their late twenties to early fifties, the yuppies, BMW-driving set, and Perrier-water drinking set. We have a certain amount of blues, and some Latin percussion involved with our music. So we draw a whole lot of different kinds of people together, not the audience that B. B. King would draw, but it's approaching that. I see people in their early twenties come to hear us and their parents like us too, so that' s really nice to see. [66]

Example 7.1. Excerpt from "Good News," by Carl Evans and Ricky Lawson of Fattburger (keyboard melody). Transcribed by Eddie S. Meadows.

By "approaching that," Evans means that significant numbers of African Americans have begun to attend their concerts and purchase their recordings. Fattburger's use of blues and Latin percussion effects have been designed to attract a crossover audience, because crossover artists sell more records and draw larger audiences than nonfusion, blues, or jazz groups. Evans explains that radio has played a significant role in helping to expose Fattburger's music to the larger public: "That's [radio is] where we get most of our exposure, other than live performances. . . . They [KIFM] actually put us on the map to a large degree. KSDS has helped, but mainly when we first started. Actually, the first time I heard myself on the radio was on KSDS. I am still very appreciative of that, but we get more play on KIFM due to the type of music we play."[67]

Marketing and Format

"Lites out jazz" was the brainchild of Bruce Walton, general manager of KIFM. In 1982 he initiated the format "to boost the then-struggling soft rock's station's ratings. Walton called on Art Good, then KIFM's program director, to put together a late-night radio show that would appeal to KIFM's daytime listeners."[68] The "lites out" format became an instant success with both African Americans and white listeners, leading Scotty Morache, sales manager of KIFM, to remark: "We had no idea 'lites out' would become so popular. We often laugh about it, and wish that we could have been brilliant enough to have sat down and planned all this out."[69]

In addition to using Good's talents as a disc jockey, KIFM unleashed a shrewd marketing program, including sponsorship of "lites out jazz" concerts, happy hour jazz parties at various clubs throughout a week-long period, and jazz cruises. In order to attract these listeners, many San Diego nightclubs shied away from hiring local bands not favored by KIFM.

According to Art Good, the "lites out jazz" audience includes African Americans, whites, and listeners of other ethnicities.[70] Varga describes the music as a smooth, homogenized blend of soft rock, pop, jazz, funk, and blues. In addition, Varga believes the pleasant, unobtrusive, and sweet pop jazz played by KIFM provides a perfect musical alternative for yuppies seeking something to replace the rock and roll of their youth.[71] In an interview with George Varga, Art Good explains the purpose and concept of the "lites out jazz" format:

The reason "lites out" was able to be successful is that I had many years background in soft rock programming. So rather than be a jazz person who could sit down and create an esoteric jazz show, I was steeped in soft rock and could create a jazz show for people who love soft rock. Right from the beginning I had a concept that was very consistent . . . the songs, the productions . . . my purpose is to entertain, not to educate. I'm not going to tell you every performer on a record. I still want the audience to feel like they're listening to San Diego, and not to a radio station. Can you imagine someone not into jazz hearing me say that was Bill Frisell playing guitar on the new album by Lyle Mays?

I don't care about an artist's name; it's the song. David Sanborn has a distinctive sax flavor and Earl Klugh has an interesting guitar style, but it's still the song and my talent is finding songs. Rhythm and melody are the key words, and fortunately, it (contemporary jazz) is not a fad; it's a tent—an additional part of adult life. And I don't mind having the distinction of having my area, which I'm a leader in, which is contemporary jazz.[72]

In another interview, Good gave his opinion about why jazz purists tend to look down upon contemporary jazz:

[T]hey are worried about their own medium of music; they're worried that contemporary jazz is going to swallow them up. To a certain extent, I suppose that is true except for the fact that most people coming into contemporary jazz, or who are in contemporary jazz, weren't into jazz at all. It's not that contemporary jazz is taking them and making them abandon the traditional jazz; it's not that contemporary jazz is taking all the other people and pulling them into contemporary jazz. People who for years were in rock, and they just got tired of the pounding of rock—they got older and they found this form of instrumental music that fit their life-style, plus the other types of music have not been good for the last ten years. I think rock of the seventies was better than rock of the eighties. I also think the traditionalists were protectionists.[73]

Impact

Apparently Good's analysis was correct. In 1986 the KIFM format had become so, popular that George Varga, jazz critic for the *San Diego Union*, reported that "lites out jazz" (which the station featured seven days a week from 7:00 p.m. to 1:00 a.m.) drew the highest ratings on evening radio in San Diego for listeners between the ages of 25 and 54. The pop-jazz format attracted national attention because it received consistently high ratings among listeners from all ethnic backgrounds, including African Americans.[74] On the subject of record sales, Varga stated: "Sales of jazz albums at Tower Records are up since the debut of 'lites out jazz.' And KIFM's audience of affluent young consumers has grown so large that both major and independent record companies are now using 'lites out jazz' to preview and test market albums."[75] Commenting on KIFM's national influence, radio and record jazz editor Barbara Barnes remarked: "KIFM is in the forefront of the country. Because of their success, other stations in the country are starting to do evening jazz shows. The word 'jazz' tends to turn people away because they don't know what it is. By maintaining two formats,[76] they've introduced more listeners to jazz."[77]

The impact of KIFM on the San Diego jazz market can be measured by reviewing the roster of artists and attendance figures of concerts from 1986 to 1990. Between June 13 and June 15, 1986, eight major artists competed for the time and money of local jazz/blues fans. The concerts featured Miles Davis, the Newport Jazz Festival All Stars, George Howard, B. B. King, and, in one concert, Chick Corea's Elektric Band, the Wayne Shorter Quartet, Al DiMeola, and Paco DeLucia. Although only the Howard and King concerts were financial successes, overall the concerts drew numerous African Americans. In 1986 the Humphrey's by the Sea jazz concert series, with KIFM as sponsor, drew 57,000 people for eighty-six open-air concerts by thirty-six artists in a space that seats around 1,100. The concerts featured artists such as the Crusaders, Larry Carlton, David Sanborn, and Fattburger. KIFM's success led Duke DuBois, director of national promotions for GRP Records (whose roster includes Dave Grusin and Lee Ritenour), to conclude that "the San Diego territory is by far our most successful in sales."[78] In 1989 jazz musicians such as Arthur Blythe, Dave Brubeck, Don Cherry, Chico Freeman, Ornette Coleman, and Prime Time performed in San Diego; however, these artists did not attract as many listeners as Earl Klugh, Spyro Gyra, or Kenny G did.

As the effort to present a variety of jazz concerts continued, the impact of KIFM on jazz preferences became more and more apparent. Rob Hagey, director of the San Diego Jazz Festival, had staged several festivals and produced more than thirty individual concerts by 1990. Although some of his events sold out, his jazz festival consistently operated with a deficit. In fact, from 1979 to 1985 Hagey did not receive a salary for his director duties. The financial strain eventually led him to abandon the San Diego Jazz Festival. Hagey was concerned that San Diegans of all ethnicities would reject the traditional and modern jazz artists he was featuring in favor of KIFM artists such as Earl Klugh, Spyro Gyra, ShadowFax, George Howard, Kenny G, and Hiroshima:

> If anything, there's too many jazz shows here of the same type, and there's only a certain amount of money people can spend. It's healthy that people have so much to choose from, but I wish that most of the shows this summer weren't by such sugar-coated artists.
>
> People in San Diego need to realize that jazz is not just what they hear at Humphrey's or on [KIFM's] "lites out" show. People don't realize the rich history of jazz or the important innovators like Chico Freeman, Anthony Davis, and Ornette Coleman who don't get heard on the radio.[79]

Some jazz artists in San Diego also believed that KIFM had a negative impact on the traditional jazz markets. Bruce Cameron, a trumpet player, gave the musician's perspective:

We recently played the Catamaran and did a lot of songs by David Sanborn, George Benson, and Michael Franks, but not the same songs that KIFM and all the other bands in town play. Afterwards, someone from KIFM came up and said, "You guys sound real good and people like it, but it's not really our thing!" They push the same three bands—Fattburger, Talk of the Town, and New Shooz—over and over. There's a lot more jazz people could be hearing. It's a vicious cycle.[80]

While many in the San Diego jazz community believed KIFM had a negative impact, Kenny Weisberg, promoter of Humphrey's concerts, and others were pleased with KIFM's role and support:

KIFM has helped tremendously. A lot of promoters in the rest of the country won't book Chuck Mangione because they say he's a stiff (poor draw), but here he sells out four shows in a row. In what other city would a radio station really get behind Sadao Watanabe or George Howard? I'm in constant communication with KIFM program director Bob O'Connor, who is always supportive of what we're doing.[81]

David Sanborn added, "Art Good has done more for jazz in San Diego than anyone else I know. He's really put jazz on the map."[82]

The impact of the "lites out jazz" format on the San Diego jazz community, then, has been mixed. Though KIFM helped the careers of some, it was detrimental to others. If an artist was not exposed on KIFM, the attendance at his or her concerts suffered. By 1986, San Diego concert promoters and nightclubs had begun to shy away from artists not favored in KIFM-sponsored events. The 1986 Ornette Coleman concert drew about 200 people to Sherwood Hall in La Jolla; the Toshiko Akiyoshi Big Band drew about 150 people to Montezuma Hall (a 1,000-seat venue at San Diego State University), and McCoy Tyner drew fewer than 500 people to two shows. None of the three received airplay on KIFM.

These lessons were not lost on African-American artists. "Lites out jazz" included numerous African-American artists from its inception, and KIFM-sponsored concerts and events drew significant numbers of African Americans. Therefore, several San Diego African-American artists began to modify their musical repertoires to fit these new realities. Artists such as Carl Evans, Eddie Davis, Hollis Gentry, Ella Ruth Piggee, and others began to feature a fusion pop-jazz repertoire. Although all, with the exception Eddie Davis, had roots in bebop and always had drawn large numbers of African Americans to their performances, their support base expanded when they became favorites at KIFM-sponsored events and introduced their new repertoires; they began to attract more whites to their performances. Hollis Gentry asserted: "There's been a dramatic increase in the popularity of jazz, especially in the last three years, and I attribute a lot of it to KIFM. They've harnessed a lot of random energy and provided consistent radio and live nightclub programming."[83] Gentry's observations were echoed by Ella Ruth Piggee: "KIFM has opened it up for everyone—consumer and musicians. They call what they play 'fusion jazz.' It's good music, and it's easier for people to understand. They can tap their feet and know where you are going."[84]

Both the "lites out jazz" radio format and KIFM-sponsored live performances, especially by black artists, drew significant numbers of African Americans. By extending their repertoire to include a homogenized blend of soft rock, soul, pop, jazz, funk and blues, both Gentry and Piggee made their music easier to follow. To many upwardly mobile African Americans, "lites out jazz" was more palatable because it was close to the music they heard on soul stations; they did not have to make the quantum leap from Stevie Wonder, Aretha Franklin, and Earth, Wind, and Fire to Thelonious Monk, John Coltrane, and Ornette Coleman. In addition, by attending KIFM-sponsored events, African Americans were able to mesh with mostly young, hip, white listeners who were more open and generally less inhibited than members of their parents' generation. In this context, "lites out jazz" became a catalyst not only for musical change but also, to a limited degree, for social change. By providing venues in which young African Americans and whites could meet, it helped create greater understanding and cooperation between the races.

Though many of these intangibles had a positive influence on African-American jazz preferences in San Diego, there was at least one negative impact to "lites out jazz." Because concerts by Earl Klugh, Hubert Laws, George Howard, Grover Washington, and Kenny G drew more African Americans than did concerts by Ornette Coleman, Charles McPherson, and Carmen McRae in 1986, some African Americans apparently were not connected with or had begun to reject traditional jazz artists. By giving scant support to traditional artists, San Diego African Americans limited the jazz market in San Diego and endangered traditional jazz. The result was that KIFM's definition and use of the word "jazz" became the operative concept among members of an uninformed community that had been conditioned and educated by the media.

When KIFM announced in 1991 that it was adopting the slogan "Jazz San Diego Style"[85] to describe its programming, there was an outcry from the jazz community. Although traditional jazz artists and critics had opposed the station's use of the word "jazz," KIFM decided to continue to use the term after a perceptual study of 800 listeners was conducted by the Strategic Research Company in Chicago, Illinois. The results "indicated a majority of KIFM listeners and non-listeners alike consider the music heard on the station to be jazz even though KIFM and many of the artists it features admit such a description is incorrect."[86]

Criticism

Criticism of KIFM and its effect on the preservation of traditional jazz has been leveled by a program director, musicians, and other jazz personalities. As of 1990, KIFM's only competition in San Diego was KSDS, a small, 831-watt station owned by the San Diego Community College District. Whereas KIFM had twenty-four paid employees, including radio personalities, and a $1 million annual

budget, KSDS was a training facility for San Diego City College students major-
ing in radio. Its disc jockeys were not paid, although some remained with the station for five or more years.

There were several differences between the formats of the two stations. KSDS
featured fifty minutes of mainstream, traditional jazz and ten minutes of contemporary jazz per hour. The station featured twenty-minute music segments, after
which pertinent information concerning the music, instrumentation, and personnel was provided because emphasis was placed on educating listeners. Commercials were never heard on KSDS. By contrast, KIFM provided little information
about the music that was played; only the artist's name was mentioned. After each
recording, three to five commercials would be aired. The primary concern of
KIFM was to cultivate listeners and make money, not educate. Tony Sisti, a program manager at KSDS since 1984, commented on the differences between the
two stations:

> KIFM is not a jazz station; they are an NAC (New Adult Contemporary) station.
> What they do is blend "smooth jazz" with smooth adult contemporary vocals. It's a
> very successful format, excellent format. There are good numbers, good money in
> that format all across the country. What we do and what they do are two different
> formats. We're doing the true, mainstream jazz. We are playing the masters. You
> would be hard-pressed to hear what we do on their station. They're locked into num-
> bers, they're locked into making money; they have to because they're a commercial
> entity. They are not our competition.[87]

The analysis of Dirk Sutro, jazz critic of the San Diego edition of the *Los Angeles Times*, provides further insight about the respective roles of the two stations in
the community:

> KSDS has always had an important role, but is limited by its weak signal. Even with-
> out a new transmitter, the station could vastly increase its audience by promoting
> cable FM hookups but doesn't seem able to tap this market. Most local cable systems
> carry KSDS. The station's "Jazz Live" concerts downtown, with a live radio simul-
> cast, provide a valuable outlet for top new and established local talent. Shows like
> "Percussive Profiles" and "Instrumental Women" serve to educate San Diegans
> about the history of jazz in a thorough, methodical fashion. Given KSDS's [limited]
> reach, it would be hard to imagine that they have much impact on record sales. I
> have heard that there are times when they give away free albums or tickets on the air,
> and no one calls for several minutes. In terms of defining jazz, KSDS is a shining ex-
> ample of what the city needs—a strong and steady dose of real jazz, from ragtime
> and New Orleans jazz right up through the avant garde loft players and such youth
> purists as Wynton Marsalis. The station also deserves credit for recognizing the close
> relationship between blues and jazz. Much jazz is built around blues, and the station
> plays a lot of blues, including a weekly blues show.
>
> Sheer numbers push one to the conclusion that KIFM has more impact than
> KSDS on the local scene. They have several thousand watts of power versus KSDS's
> 831, or something like that. In a sense, this means that "traditional," "mainstream,"

"straight-ahead," "acoustic" jazz, or whatever you want to call the pure jazz art, is losing ground, or at least not gaining. Meanwhile it seems as if hordes of yuppies—say 30- to 45-year-olds of all races—are searching for something more than rock and soul and turning to KIFM instead of true jazz as an alternative. This isn't bad in and of itself, but it is disappointing that real jazz, which has so much more to offer in terms of spontaneity, soul and musical profundity, doesn't get a broader hearing. [88]

Both Tony Sisti and Sutro recognized the importance of KSDS as a purveyor of "pure" jazz and as an alternative to KIFM. However, both acknowledged that KIFM had more impact in the community than KSDS.

By programming and promoting pop jazz to the exclusion of traditional jazz, KIFM created a schism that led traditional jazz artists and KSDS to criticize KIFM's use of the word "jazz" in its format. Bob O'Connor, program director of KIFM, admitted: "We're not really a jazz station. We play pop instrumental music with a jazz flavor. It's for people who don't know about jazz. Our listeners don't have the background to know who John Coltrane or Thelonious Monk are."[89]

Although O'Connor's statement helped to clarify KIFM's position, it did not lessen the impact of KIFM nor the criticism from traditional jazz artists. Anthony Ortega, a jazz musician who moved to San Diego in 1975, commented on the changes that have taken place since his arrival: "There's much more jazz activity in San Diego now than in Los Angeles. Because this is a newer city, people are more open to jazz, and it's growing by leaps and bounds. When I moved to San Diego eleven years ago, there wasn't much going on here. The only thing that bugs me is the confusion with fusion. People think they like jazz, but it's not jazz. It's fusion, which is OK, but it's not my cup of tea."[90]

Charles McPherson (former alto saxophonist with Charles Mingus), an African American who has been a resident of La Jolla, California, since 1978, did not feel that the situation in San Diego helped him: "Most of my work is on the road; I don't really make it in this town. I don't think the scene here is that healthy. It's a good place to get your thing together and leave."[91]

Joe Marillo, a tenor saxophonist in the bebop tradition, agreed that the climate was not the best for traditional jazz musicians, but he saw some positive developments: "Overall, the jazz scene is much healthier, but I'm definitely working less now than before. The reason is that when club owners ask me what type of music I play, I say 'bebop,' and they're not interested. But I have more students than I've ever had before who want to learn to play the saxophone like David Sanborn who they've heard on KIFM. So it balances out."[92]

Ron Galon, an African-American jazz radio personality for KPBS-FM at San Diego State University (SDSU) from 1973 to 1983 and host of a three-hour Saturday afternoon show on KSDS, stated:

Popularity votes aren't necessarily knowledgeable votes. What KIFM plays is contemporary shopping mall music. It's better than nothing, but—to me—it's still nothing. I always try to give recording dates so that many people can have a reference point of time on what they're hearing. And I tell them who all the sidemen on each record are, because every sideman contributed—unlike many of today's (pop jazz) records, where the sidemen only play the notes in front of them. That's why Miles got Red Garland and John Coltrane on his albums, because of what they contributed. I like to let people know that Chick Corea has a history and that he didn't just appear 10 years ago in an all-electric band.[93]

Galon was in an interesting position. KIFM's success had not negatively affected him; because he did not have to depend on his jazz show for his livelihood nor please sponsors or station managers, he was able pursue his own interests and enjoyed the fact that musicians appreciated his show. Sutro's comments summarize the criticism voiced against KIFM:

KIFM has a tremendous impact, not always positive for jazz overall. It amazes me how many people who don't know much about music think that "jazz" is what they hear on KIFM, when even the people who run the station don't claim their music is jazz. People say they like jazz, then name musicians like Kenny G, Keiko Matsui, Fattburger and the Rippingtons, whose music, regardless of what you think of it, is really electric pop or something else—it has little of the complex harmonies and melodies associated with jazz, and none of the improvisation.

On the plus side, KIFM added a regular Sunday night mainstream show two years ago after getting heat from local media and musicians. The show gives KIFM listeners a chance to hear authentic jazz. The continuing popularity of "lites out" club jazz and its many emulators must be reducing opportunities for mainstream players. For example, Chuck's Steak House in La Jolla, formerly a serious jazz room, now books light jazz. Several of the "lites out" venues, such as Humphrey's, the Embassy Suites Hotel downtown, the Catamaran, the B Street Cafe and the Hilton on Mission Bay, weren't necessarily ever known as a mainstream room; but then again, if they weren't booking light jazz, maybe they would replace it with mainstream.

KIFM could probably sprinkle a few mainstream cuts by established pop/jazz crossovers like Lee Ritenour and David Benoit into its repertoire without losing listeners. This would be a real service to jazz and jazz fans. But I think it would be wrong to blame KIFM for any lack of live mainstream jazz or opportunities in San Diego. They are a business, and without ad revenues, they would not exist and supply jobs for several San Diegans. Also, although their music is not jazz, some of it is good, and it brings enjoyment to many San Diegans. That is the true goal of music—spiritual and emotional impact. If people get interested in their brand of "jazz," chances improve that they will check out other varieties of jazz, including the real stuff. Perhaps there is some truth to this, although I suspect fans of traditional and "lites out jazz" are fairly distinct, separate groups.

A better place to lay blame is in our schools, which don't place enough emphasis on American's cultural history, including jazz. If young people are exposed to jazz more often, they will be more likely to seek it out as adults. At the college level there is hope because of a strong jazz program at SDSU.

It's hard to say what impact KIFM has on record sales, but companies like GRP, one of the largest light jazz labels, seem to regard KIFM and the San Diego market as among their major outlets. Certainly, KIFM's promotion and play of local artists like Checkfield, Mark Lessman, Hank Easton, and Spencer Nielsen has helped these artists sell more albums and stand a better chance of landing recording contracts. When cuts from their CDs are included in KIFM's playlist, there is a much greater chance that listeners will notice the music and purchase the albums.[94]

Sutro's assessment mirrors the views of Varga, Sisti, and Galon, who emphasize that the lack of support and preservation of jazz are endemic. This writer believes that the meager support for traditional jazz offered by the public in general, and by African Americans in particular, is alarming because jazz is rooted in African-American culture. This lack of support has repercussions for the preservation of an art form. Unfortunately, the criticism suggests that all segments of the population have embraced change without retaining history, thereby ensuring that marketing, packaging, and instant musical gratification will continue to push aside a significant contribution to world culture.

CONCLUSION

Although San Diego since the 1940s has had groups with styles ranging from bebop to swing, "lites out jazz," the format espoused by KIFM, dominated the 1986–1990 jazz scene. In spite of criticisms from all segments of the jazz community and an attempt to counterbalance its influence by KSDS, as of 1990 the station continued to enjoy expanding popularity in San Diego. Blessed with foresight and marketing expertise, the station wielded an influence that extended far beyond the airwaves, affecting both clubs and musicians. Clubs often refused to bring local or national bands not featured on KIFM programs. In turn, many local bands adapted their styles to fit the "lites out" format, hoping to secure club dates, play for the myriad activities sponsored by KIFM, and receive national exposure.

"Lites out jazz" also had an impact on the jazz preferences of African Americans. In the 1979–89 period, African-American incomes, education, and home-ownership increased significantly. A large number of the newly affluent were centered in the 25–34 age range and thus inclined to attend "lites out" concerts and other activities. Because "lites out jazz" appealed to what Art Good termed the "yuppie" crowd, to those Carl Evans described as "in their late twenties to the early fifties, the yuppies, BMW and Perrier-water drinking set," affordability and musical preferences were two of the most significant factors in defining the "lites out" audience.

The preference of African Americans in San Diego for "lites out jazz" might be directly related to the number and quality of African-American artists in this genre. It might also reflect an attempt by blacks to become members of the culturally homogenized society targeted by San Diego "lites out jazz." Although traditional jazz was alive in San Diego during the 1986–90 period, it was a distant second in terms of popularity to "lites out jazz."

NOTES

1. Among others, Louis Armstrong, *Satchmo: My Life in New Orleans* (New York: Da Capo Press, 1952); Robert Goffin, *Horn of Plenty: The Story of Louis Armstrong,* reprint (Westport, CT: Greenwood Press, 1978); and Albert J. McCarthy, *Louis Armstrong* (London: Cassell, 1960).

2. Among others, Bill Cole, *John Coltrane: A Musical Biography* (New York: Schirmer, 1976); Cuthbert Ormond Simpkins, *Coltrane: A Biography* (Perth Amboy, NJ: Herndon House, 1975); and Eric Nisenson, *Ascension: John Coltrane and His Quest* (New York: St. Martin's Press, 1993).

3. Among others, Stanley Dance, *The World of Duke Ellington* (New York: C. Scribner's Sons, 1970); Edward Kennedy Ellington, *Music Is My Mistress* (Garden City, NY: Doubleday, 1973); John Edward Hasse, *Beyond Category: The Life and Genius of Duke Ellington* (New York: Simon and Schuster, 1993); and Mark Tucker, *Ellington: The Early Years* (Urbana and Chicago: University of Illinois Press, 1991).

4. Among others, Lawrence O. Koch, *Yardbird Suite: A Compendium of the Music and Life of Charlie Parker* (Bowling Green, OH: Bowling Green State University Popular Press, 1988); Robert George Reisner, *Bird: The Legend of Charlie Parker* (New York: Bonanza Books, 1962); and Ross Russell, *Bird Lives: The High Life and Hard Times of Charlie (Yardbird) Parker* (New York: Charterhouse, 1973).

5. Among others, William Howland Kenney, *Chicago Jazz: A Cultural History, 1904–1930* (New York: Oxford University Press, 1993); Frederic Ramsey, *Chicago Documentary: Portrait of a Jazz Era* (London: Jazz Music Books, 1944); and Dempsey J. Travis, *An Autobiography of Black Jazz* (Chicago: Urban Research Institute, 1983).

6. Among others, Mary Lee Hester, *Going to Kansas City* (Sherman, TX: Early Bird Press, 1980); and Ross Russell, *Jazz Style in Kansas City and the Southwest* (Berkeley and Los Angeles: University of California Press, 1971).

7. Among others, Jason Berry, *Up From the Cradle of Jazz: New Orleans Music Since World War II* (Athens, GA: University of Georgia Press, 1986); Jack V. Buerkle and Danny Barker, *Bourbon Street Black: The New Orleans Black Jazzman* (New York: Oxford University Press, 1973); William Carter, *Preservation Hall: Music from the Heart* (New York: W. W. Norton and Company, 1991); and Stephen Longstreet, *Sportin' House: A History of the New Orleans Sinners and the Birth of Jazz* (Los Angeles: Sherbourne Press, 1965).

8. Samuel B. Charters and Leonard Kunstadt, *Jazz: A History of the New York Scene* (New York: Doubleday, 1962).

9. Buddy Collette, *Central Avenue Sounds Oral History Transcript, 1989–1990: Buddy Collete* (Los Angeles: Oral History Program, University of California, Los Angeles, 1993).

10. Raymond Horricks, *The Importance of Being Eric Dolphy* (Turnbridge, England: Spellmount, 1988); and Vladimir Simasko and Barry Tepperman, *Eric Dolphy: A Musical Biography and Discography* (Washington, DC: Smithsonian Institution Press, 1974; New York: Da Capo Press, 1979 [1986]).

11. Hampton Hawes and Don Asher, *Raise Up Off Me: A Portrait of Hampton Hawes* (New York: Coward, McCann, and Geohegan, 1974; reprint with new introduction by Garry Giddins, New York: Da Capo, 1979).

12. Stanley Dance, *The World of Earl Hines* (New York: Scribner, 1977; New York: Da Capo Press, 1985).

13. Charles Mingus, *Beneath the Underdog: His World as Composed by Mingus* (New York: Alfred A. Knopf, 1971); and Brian Priestly, *Mingus: A Critical Biography* (London: Quartet Books, 1971; New York: Alfred A. Knopf, 1982).

14. A comprehensive discussion of African Americans in San Diego from 1850 to 1900 can be found in Robert L. Carlton, "Blacks in San Diego County, 1850–1900" (M.A. thesis, San Diego State University, 1977).

15. Robert Fikes Jr., Gail Madyun, and Larry Malone, "Black Pioneers in San Diego: 1880–1920," *Journal of San Diego History* 27 (Spring 1981): 92.

16. Michael Andrew Lewis, "Ethnic and Racial Violence in San Diego, 1880–1920" (M.A. thesis, San Diego State University, 1991), 46.

17. Fikes, et. al., "Black Pioneers," 110.

18. Paula Parker, "Gaslamp Lore: Research Traces Role of Black Business Downtown," *Los Angeles Times* (San Diego County edition) (11 September 1979): B1–B2, and San Diego Historical Society, "Picture Story: Hotel Douglas," *San Diego Reader* (1 April 1984): J1, J9. Black businesses such as the Simmons Hotel, which was owned by Lucille Simmons from 1938–1960, flourished in San Diego until integration in the fifties and sixties, at which time businesses owned by African Americans began to be adversely affected by competition from white-owned businesses. Starting in the mid-1980s, downtown San Diego, where black businesses were once located, became part of an urban renewal program and underwent extensive redevelopment. Currently known as the Gaslamp District, the area has become a popular tourist attraction.

19. Fikes et. al., "Black Pioneers," 92–102.

20. Maurice Albert Tompkins, "Military and Civilian Aspects of San Diego During the Second World War" (M.A. thesis, San Diego State University, 1982), 92–93.

21. These statistics are based on data from the League of Women Voters of San Diego, *Dimensions in Discrimination* (San Diego: League of Women Voters of San Diego, 1965), 6.

22. Rosemary J. Erickson and Marge Austin, *Pockets of Poverty: A Study of Areas of Poverty in San Diego County, Vol. 11* (San Diego: Community Welfare Council of San Diego, 1966), 25.

23. Around the early 1900s, Logan Heights consisted of a small triangle approximately half a mile square. In the mid-1960s, the area was considered to be part of Southeast San Diego. For more details on the civil rights rebellion of 1965, see Jean E. Hoffman and Sydney D. Hammond, "A Documentary Study of the 'Logan Heights Riots' of August 1965" (A Research Project Report, San Diego State College, 1966).

24. Ibid., 60.

25. The rate of unemployment, probably the greatest single cause of poverty, was 14 percent in 1960, compared to 6.2 percent for the county as a whole, and it is believed that this had increased by 1965, "because the unskilled labor force, unlike better trained workers, tends to remain in the community even when jobs are not available"; see Erickson and Austin, *Pockets of Poverty*, 49.

26. My experience at San Diego State University (SDSU) demonstrates some of the changes that took place during the 1970s. Upon my arrival to San Diego in 1972, there were only 200–300 black students out of a total student population of 23,000. African American student activism during the mid-1970s led to the development of an educational opportunity program and a Department of African American Studies at San Diego State University. These events not only helped to increase black enrollment at SDSU (1,500–2,000 students out of 25,000) but created a more conducive environment for African-American

students. Better education led to jobs at San Diego Gas and Electric Company, in the public school system, at local colleges and universities, and in city government.

27. *California State Census Data Center 1980 Census,* Summary Tape File One (San Diego: Sandag/Sourcepoint, 1980), 1–9.

28. In 1970 there were 59,916 African Americans in the city of San Diego. Of the 876,000 persons living in the city of San Diego in 1980, there were approximately 77,700 African Americans. Thus, African Americans in 1980 constituted 9.4 percent of the total population, following the 20.7 percent of Hispanics and 11.8 percent of Asian Pacific Islanders. These data can be found in *California State Census,* 25; *Statistical Abstract of the United States* (Washington, DC: United States Department of Commerce 1980 [1994]), 46; *1970 United States Census of the Population Characteristictics of the Population California,* (Washington, DC: United States Department of Commerce, 1973), 6–103; and *General Characteristics of the Population. 1980 Census of Population Bureau of Statistics* (Washington, DC: United States Department of Commerce, 1982), 6–26.

29. The number of African Americans living in San Diego in 1990 was 104,261; see *1990 Census of Population. Social and Economic Characteristics. California* (Washington, DC: United States Department of Commerce, 1993), p. 247. A detailed breakdown of socioeconomic variables can be found in *1990 Census of Population and Housing,* Summary Tape File 3 (corrected) (San Diego: Sandag/Sourcepoint, 1990), 1–29.

30. Fikes, et. al., "Black Pioneers," 99.

31. Michael Lebarron Austin, "Harlem of the West: The Douglas Hotel and Creole Palace Nite Club" (M.A. thesis, University of San Diego, 1994), 3–7.

32. Sarah Pattee, "Creole Palace: Memories of 30s Hot Spot for San Diego Blacks Still Warm," *San Diego Tribune* (15 January 1988): D4.

33. Froebel "Fro" Astor Brigham, personal interview with author, 28 April 1995.

34. Pattee, "Creole Palace," D4; and Brigham, personal interview.

35. Russell, *Jazz Style,* 57, indicates that Troy Floyd was born in 1898 in Texas (city not known) and died in 1951 in San Diego. However, Gunther Schuller, in *The Swing Era: The Development of Jazz, 1930–1945* (New York: Oxford University Press, 1989), 883, asserts that Floyd died in the 1960s.

36. Gunther Schuller, *Early Jazz, Its Roots and Musical Development* (New York: Oxford University Press, 1968), 291–292.

37. Ibid., 292–293.

38. Nathan Pearson Jr., *Goin' to Kansas City* (Urbana and Chicago: University of Illinois Press, 1987), 45–46.

39. Brigham was the youngest of six children born to Fannie and William James Brigham in Taylor, Arkansas, October 29, 1916; he died in San Diego May 31, 1996. To my knowledge, Brigham's role in jazz history has not been chronicled.

40. Although the focus of my research is San Diego, Brigham's work in his New Orleans Navy Band and his contributions to preserving New Orleans jazz should also be noted. When I asked Brigham about famous New Orleans musicians who were members of his Navy Band, he stated: "Well, I wouldn't know them as national top men, but there were some very well thought of musicans out of New Orleans. There was a group man known as Willie Humphrey (clarinet), and he became the mainstay of the Preservation Band in New Orleans. Clyde Kerr was an excellent arranger/composer; he would have been another Duke Ellington if I could have gotten him out of New Orleans."

41. Stanley Dance, "Jazz Musicians in San Diego," *Black Music Research Bulletin* 10 (Spring 1988): 10.

42. In a personal interview, Brigham indicated that musicians from the bands of Duke Ellington, Lucky Millender, Lionel Hampton, and others mingled at the training center.

43. Brigham, personal interview.

44. Ibid.

45. Dance, "Jazz Musicians," 10.

46. Brigham, personal interview.

47. Ibid.

48. Ibid.

49. Ibid.

50. Fuller was born February 15, 1910, in Dyersburg, Tennessee.

51. Dance, "Jazz Musicians," 10.

52. Walter Fuller, personal interview with author, 30 October 1980.

53. Ibid.

54. Gunther Schuller, *The Swing Era*, 275–277.

55. Fuller, personal interview.

56. Ibid.

57. Dance, "Jazz Musicians," 10.

58. This profile is based on the music of Earl Klugh, the Crusaders, Kenny G, David Sanborn, and local groups such as Fattburger.

59. Ella Ruth Piggee died in 1990.

60. Carl Evans and Mark Hunter are the co-leaders of the quintet. Evans is the only African American in the group. It should also be noted that Evans and Gentry received their undergraduate degrees in music from the University of California, San Diego (UCSD); Gentry went on to obtain a master's degree in music from UCSD.

61. Carl Evans, personal interview with author, 6 August 1990.

62. Ibid.

63. To understand better the overall structure of "Good News," I transcribed the composition. I was unable to secure permission to use the entire score in this chapter; however, I am including my analysis of the form. My analysis is limited to the following conclusions and may not correspond to other transcriptions of the same composition. The overall form is as follows: eight-bar introduction repeats; measure 49 returns to the sign at measure 16; measure 40 then jumps to measure 50 (after the repeat sign). At measure 56, there is a four-bar repeat. In the keyboard solo, the first and second set of four-bar changes are played four times each. The last repeat is the "coda" section at measure 111; it is repeated three times.

64. This music varies stylistically from that of artists such as Charles Parker, pre-1967 Miles Davis, and John Coltrane, whose primary musical aesthetic was based on individual identity as realized throughout both composition and improvisation.

65. Evans, personal interview.

66. Ibid.

67. Ibid.

68. George Varga, "'Lites Out' Success Has Station Beaming," *San Diego Union Lifestyle Section* (20 May 1986): 18. From KIFM's inception in 1982 through 1996, the "lites out" format expanded to seventy stations throughout the United States; see Judith Michaelson, "The Wave's on Crest of Popularity," *Los Angeles Times* (6 August 1996), F1, F6.

69. Varga, "'Lites Out,'" 18.

70. Art Good, personal interview with author, 27 July 1990.

71. George Varga, "San Diego Jazz/City Becoming Rhythmic Center for a Resurgent Beat," *San Diego Union Lifestyle Section* (19 May 1986): 23.

72. George Varga, "KIFM Has a Good Feel for Pop-Jazz Format," *San Diego Union Lifestyle Section* (20 May 1986): 15–16.

73. Good, personal interview. In Los Angeles, station KTWV, which started its smooth jazz format in 1987, "grew out of the old KMET-FM, a youth-oriented rock station"; see Michaelson, "The Wave's," F6. Thus, smooth jazz stations in both San Diego and Los Angeles were originally rock stations.

74. Varga, "'Lites Out,'" 17.

75. Ibid.

76. By "two formats," Barnes means the soft rock that was performed during the day and the "lites out" that was scheduled at night.

77. Varga, "'Lites Out,'" 17.

78. George Varga, "All That Jazz," *San Diego Union* (19 May 1986): 22.

79. George Varga, "S.D. Jazz Runneth Over?" *San Diego Union Entertainment Section* (22 May 1986): 5.

80. Geogre Varga, "Musicians Jazz Up City's Scene," *San Diego Union Lifestyle Section* (21 May 1986): 12.

81. Varga, "S.D. Jazz," 6.

82. Varga, "KIFM," 16.

83. Varga, "San Diego Jazz," 23.

84. Ibid.

85. By "Jazz San Diego Style," KIFM means Fattburger, Hollis Gentry's Neon, Reel to Real, Steve Laury, Anita Baker, Luther Vandross, and Kenny G. See George Varga, "Jazz Should Be More Than a Four-Letter Word to KIFM and Listeners," *San Diego Union Entertainment Section* (30 June 1991): 2–3.

86. Varga, "Jazz Should Be," 2.

87. Tony Sisti, personal interview with author, 1 August 1990.

88. Dirk Sutro, personal letter to author, 30 October 1990.

89. Varga, "San Diego Jazz," 23.

90. Ibid., 24.

91. Ibid., 25.

92. Ibid., 24.

93. George Varga, "On KSDS, Ron Galon Plows a Timeless Path," *San Diego Union Lifestyle Section* (20 May 1986): 14.

94. Sutro, personal letter.

PART THREE

The Musician as Innovator

8

Clora Bryant

Gender Issues in the Career of a West Coast Jazz Musician

Danica L. Stein

California has always been viewed as a land of opportunity and plenty. Musicians move to the Golden State from around the United States and the world seeking jobs, new experiences and opportunities, and pleasant weather. California has a reputation for being progressive in its attitudes toward "minority" issues—including women's issues—thus attracting people from more conservative areas of the country. There is a high tolerance for and acceptance of change, of new ideas and activities. Throughout California's history, those who arrived looking for something new adapted to the diversity of the state and its urban centers. These ever-expanding urban areas (for example, Los Angeles) promised musicians many opportunities to practice their art, possibly with financial rewards unavailable elsewhere.[1]

In the 1940s, the large migration of southern blacks stimulated a preference for certain musical genres, including gospel music and rhythm and blues, and expanded the pool of jobs open to professional musicians.[2] "Popular" genres, including jazz, flourished in Southern California. Dizzy Gillespie, Charlie Parker, and other noted jazz musicians regularly performed in Los Angeles.[3] Thus, the city's African-American entertainment scene was lively, especially in the busy clubs and nightspots on Central Avenue.[4] The motion picture industry also did its part to attract professional musicians, and the advent of television brought even more opportunities.[5]

The rich African-American entertainment scene in Los Angeles in the 1940s, with its atmosphere of experimentation, tolerance, and acceptance, should have been a welcoming one for women who sought work as professional jazz musicians. But to discuss women musicians in the context of the Los Angeles jazz scene is to expose a double-edged sword: the acceptance of change and of new things meant that recognition was often fleeting, especially for women artists. There were plenty of jam sessions in the clubs, but very few women played in them. More performance options resulted in even more competition for jobs, with women musicians often being overlooked. The war years brought more performance opportunities for women when men went into the armed services, but these opportunities often caused women players to be marginalized in some way. They were looked down upon, regarded as "novelties" instead of serious jazz musicians. Female singers and pianists were accepted, but female horn players were subject to less tolerant attitudes. How did these pros and cons affect the careers of women striving to make it as professional jazz musicians in Los Angeles?

One of the talented women who performed in Los Angeles during this period was trumpet player Clora Bryant. She and her father moved to California from a small Texas town in January 1945, when she was still a teenager. Thus began her long and fascinating career as a "West Coast" artist. Fifty-plus years after her father brought her west on the train, Bryant still makes Southern California her home. She has played all over the United States and the world with an impressive array of jazz luminaries. In addition to performing, she has taught, composed, and studied music.

I was fortunate to be able to speak with Clora Bryant at length to get her story firsthand.[6] In this chapter I will discuss her life, her career, and the issues involved in being a female jazz trumpet player trying to make a living in Los Angeles. The stories of women jazz musicians are rarely told in any detail; the existing literature gives the impression that women exist in jazz only on the periphery.[7] That may have been true, to some extent, in the past. But today, more women work as professional musicians than ever before. Many of them settle in large cities such as Los Angeles to find opportunities to make a living playing music.

This chapter comprises two sections. The first, "Clora Bryant," is subdivided into three parts: her life story, including specific musical experiences ("Biography"), an overview of the people who influenced her musical development ("Her Life in Music"), and a discussion of the issues Bryant faces as a woman jazz musician ("Issues"). The second section, "Analysis," is also subdivided. In the first part, "Marginalization of Female Jazz Musicians," Bryant's experiences are used to illustrate how women jazz musicians in general are treated. In the second part, "Perceptions of Female Jazz Musicians," her experiences are used to help show how jazzwomen are viewed by others and how jazzwomen view themselves. In the third part, "Bryant's Career in Los Angeles," some of the concepts of the previous discussion are applied more directly to Bryant's experiences in Southern California.

The questions I address in the course of this chapter are: What is it like for a woman instrumentalist—who has spent most of her life in California—to pursue a career playing jazz? What issues and/or problems are important in her career, and how does she handle them? How has living in an atmosphere of tolerance and change affected her career? How is she able to take advantage of the unique opportunities offered in California while minimizing the effect of negative perceptions of female jazz artists? Can the issues discussed here be considered typical for most female jazz musicians pursuing a career in Los Angeles? These questions cannot be answered definitively here, but one story—the story of Clora Bryant—can provide some insights.

CLORA BRYANT

Biography

Bryant was born in the small, segregated town of Denison, Texas, in 1927. Her mother died when Bryant was three years old; she and her two older brothers were raised by their father. Music was a large part of her life from an early age. Her father loved music; the family owned a Victrola and records by many jazz greats, including Harry James, Louis Armstrong, Count Basie, and Duke Ellington, and young Clora was able to pick out some of the tunes on the piano. Her brother Fred, the oldest sibling, played the trumpet, although Bryant does not recall ever having heard him play. There were many opportunities in the neighborhood to listen to and participate in music making. At hometown picnics and barbecues, neighbors played guitars, sang, and danced. At the local black theaters, stage shows called "Midnight Rambles" were presented on Saturday nights after the movies. These shows, featuring local talent, included comedians, singers, small bands, and/or chorus lines. Often, performers such as T-Bone Walker were brought in from out of town to perform at the dance halls. Traveling carnivals, circuses, and minstrel shows provided yet more opportunities to hear music. In the black Baptist church, Bryant learned to sing and took part in the holiday shows and pageants. Shows, plays, and other productions were regular occurrences in her elementary school as well.

When Bryant reached high school, a new principal introduced some extracurricular activities, including band and choir. Bryant was thrilled and, in her junior year, decided to join the band. She took up the trumpet because her brother Fred had been drafted and left the instrument behind. Bryant's uncle, a saxophonist, gave her a lesson book that taught trumpet fingerings, scales, and beginning songs. She took lessons from her high school band director, working various odd jobs to pay for them, and began playing in the marching band and the swing band. During her junior year, the swing band played at proms in small towns in the area and in white clubs on the outskirts of town. By the time she graduated from high school, she was proficient enough to have won music scholarships both to Bennett College in South Carolina and to Oberlin. However, Bryant chose to attend Prairie View College outside of Houston after her high school band director recommended Bryant to his friend, the band director at Prairie View. For Bryant, the main attraction of this school was its all-female swing band, the Prairie View Coeds. The other schools did not have any kind of jazz program.

At Prairie View, Bryant majored in music and toured with the Coeds. The group played in big cities in Texas, including Austin, Dallas, Fort Worth, and Corpus Christi. In the summer of 1944 the band went on tour, starting in Florida and

Figure 8.1. Jazz trumpeter Clora Bryant, 1964. Courtesy of Clora Bryant.

ending in New York City at the Apollo Theater. In this group, Bryant had the opportunity not only to play music but also to listen to other artists, including the original Ink Spots, singer Marla Louis, and various big bands. Then, in 1945, Bryant's father got a job with a shipyard near Long Beach, and he brought her to Los Angeles.

Bryant transferred from Prairie View to the University of California, Los Angeles (UCLA), but when she arrived, in January, classes were filled; she had to wait until the spring of 1946 to begin her studies. In the meantime, Bryant satisfied her hunger for music by taking advantage of the many opportunities Los Angeles offered. She went to the movies, listened to the radio, and stood outside some of the jazz clubs along Central Avenue, as she was not yet old enough to go inside. She began playing with various small groups. Bebop was just getting its start, and Bryant was greatly affected by the new sounds she heard. She used the money earned at her gigs to buy bebop records, and she tried to emulate the trumpet players. In early summer 1946, Bryant took a job as a maid, but she quit after being invited to play with the all-female band Sweethearts of Rhythm, which had a week-long engagement at the Million Dollar Theater in downtown Los Angeles. When she got her union card, Bryant began playing at jam sessions in the clubs. After a year at UCLA, Bryant left school (she returned to UCLA when she was in her fifties and completed a bachelor's degree in music); she was back to full-time playing.

In her long and varied career, Bryant has performed in several countries and with musicians of all statures. She has received constant guidance and encouragement from her friend Dizzy Gillespie, with whom she has performed several times. Her arrival in California marked the beginning of her exposure to such artists and opportunities. In the 1940s, when Bryant first arrived in California, a small traveling band called the Queens of Swing needed a drummer; she rented a drum set, quickly learned how to play, and joined the band. By 1951 she was back to trumpet, playing behind Billie Holiday and Josephine Baker at the Club Alabam on Central Avenue. That year she also played with the first all-female band ever to appear on a musical variety television show, on which other prominent musicians appeared as guests. The show went off the air after six weeks because it lacked a sponsor. Bryant continued to perform at clubs, matinees, and jam sessions in Los Angeles and Hermosa Beach, playing with male as well as female bands. In 1953 she decided to move to New York City. There she played at the Metropole and wherever else she could sit in, making friends and contacts. She got other jobs in the area, including a stint on a television variety show that aired from Hackensack, New Jersey. During an engagement at a club called Leon's in Hackensack, Bryant met an agent, who got her work in Canada. She headed north at the end of 1953, returning to Los Angeles in 1955.

In 1957 her only recording, *Gal with a Horn*, was released on the now-defunct Mode label.[8] Around this time Bryant made another trip to Canada, where she played club dates for about a year before returning to the United States. She went to Chicago in 1958 and played in a club for one year, returned to Los Angeles in 1959 and played clubs, then went back to Canada until 1960. Upon her return to the United States, Bryant played in clubs in Denver and Sacramento. At about this time Bryant began engagements in Las Vegas, where she played at the Flamingo opposite Harry James and at the Riviera with Louis Armstrong. While playing at the Flamingo, Bryant was noticed by singer Billy Williams and invited to join his revue. This group made an appearance on *The Ed Sullivan Show* and toured the eastern seaboard from Florida to New York, performing in clubs and resorts. In 1960 she appeared in the movie *Pepe*, playing in a big band behind star Sammy Davis Jr.

In 1962 Bryant left Billy Williams's group and returned to Los Angeles. She and her brother Mel put together an act in which both sang and Bryant played the trumpet. They took the act on the road, performing with a variety of artists (including the Lennon Sisters, Phyllis Diller, Anita Bryant, and Jackie Mason) at clubs, fairs, and shows in several cities, including Phoenix and San Diego. The duo then signed a contract to perform in Australia for six weeks, playing in clubs in Melbourne and doing a television show from their hotel twice a week.

In the late 1970s, Bryant joined Bill Berry's big band, replacing the late trumpet player Blue Mitchell. Work was becoming harder to find for Bryant. In 1983 she played on the television show *Fantasy*. After leaving Berry's group, Bryant wrote a letter to Soviet leader Mikhail Gorbachev, which resulted in an invitation to perform. She played five concerts in Russia in 1989, then returned to Los Angeles. Work was still scarce. The 1992 rebellion in response to the Rodney King verdicts added another hardship to Bryant's life; she lost many of her possessions, including a baby grand piano and priceless photographs and music, when an arsonist set fire to a storage structure Bryant had been using. In March 1993, Bryant went to New York for the memorial service of her dear friend and mentor, Dizzy Gillespie. While on the East Coast she gave an interview for the swing-era archives of the Smithsonian Institution. As of this writing, Bryant is living in Long Beach, California, and working on her autobiography.

Her Life in Music

Bryant describes her years growing up as "very sheltered." Her father worked in a hardware store in Texas during her childhood and insisted that Bryant be chaperoned wherever she went. Her brother Mel usually accompanied her when she went out of the house. This was one reason Bryant decided to join the band in high school—to get out of the house and away from her brother's watchful eye. Bryant earned money to pay for trumpet lessons by babysitting and doing other small jobs. She learned to cook, clean, and take care of the house at a young age, as her older brothers and her father were away all day working. Bryant and her father moved to the Los Angeles area in the 1940s because Bryant's father had always dreamed of taking her to "Hollywood." Her brother Mel was already living in Southern California. When they arrived in Los Angeles, Mel still looked after his sister. It was he who exposed her to the exciting musical scene on Central Avenue even though she could not go into the clubs. Even when Bryant was in college, her father was protective of her. When Bryant played with the Sweethearts of Rhythm, she was invited to travel with them, but her father thought it best for her to stay home. Bryant has a great deal of respect for her father's manner of raising his children and is grateful that he taught them discipline.

Bryant says the people in her life have always been supportive of her career in music. Bryant's father encouraged her interest, and her uncle helped her by giving her the trumpet lesson book. Her husband of ten years (1949–1959), bass player

Joe Stone, always encouraged Bryant in her work. Most of Bryant's friends are musicians, but her nonmusician friends have also been supportive.

Bryant feels that in the highly male-controlled environment of jazz, men "smother" women musicians when it comes to the competitive area of performance. She observes that women have come a long way in jazz but that the situation is not really changing and that women will only progress as far as men will allow them. Though she always has a sense of having to prove herself, Bryant believes this feeling is probably common to all musicians of all levels and backgrounds, whether male or female.

Issues

Bryant feels the music world is inherently male-dominated; men are always going to try to shut women out. Being a female professional trumpet player is extremely challenging, she says, "because that is the one instrument that men feel like women are not supposed to play."[9] She reports that in her experience, female singers, pianists, and violinists seem to be more readily accepted than female horn players and that it has often been "a fight" to get jobs. As Dizzy Gillespie once told her, the trumpet is "a man's instrument, and a young man's at that."[10]

When she first started to perform in Los Angeles professionally around the time of World War II, all-female bands were popular because so many men were serving in the military. As Bryant recounts, "You didn't run into that many problems because girl bands were 'in.' The guys were in the service, so you didn't butt heads with them for gigs."[11] But female bands were treated as a novelty: "[W]e were still male-dominated, and they kept us in our little space, all-girl bands." During the time she played in female groups, Bryant concentrated on honing her skills so she could branch out from the realm of novelty into the "real" jazz world.

Bryant mentions also that she had problems getting jobs in the 1970s: "It began to get harder, not only for the girls—black girls or black female trumpet players or horn players to get work . . . but also for the black male." In Bryant's observation, "[Whites] began to try to say that jazz wasn't started by the blacks."[12] Consequently many of the available jobs were given to white male musicians. The predominance of West Coast jazz, with its smoother, less rhythmic style, was another factor in the growing scarcity of jobs for bebop players such as Bryant.

There are more subtle ways in which Bryant feels she has been overlooked or ignored. When she returned to the United States from her successful tour of Russia, she expected to be offered all kinds of opportunities to play. Instead, she received very few calls. Bryant feels she has not landed as many gigs in the Los Angeles area as she should, partly because of race and partly because "a lot of guys I know that are out there don't really relish . . . me being who I am, but they would never say it."[13] She mentions that she has been overlooked in many books about jazz in general and about women in jazz in particular and that she has been left out of jazz encyclopedias.

Even when there is no overt discrimination, gender is still an important issue. Comments are made that, though not necessarily offensive, draw attention to the fact that a musician is a woman. For example, when Bryant participated with seven male trumpeters in an April 1993 concert tribute to Dizzy Gillespie,[14] reviewer Tony Gleske wrote in the April 29, 1993, issue of the *Hollywood Reporter:* "Now it was Clora's turn. Of course, the men had showed her no quarter, they left very little for her to do. But she fooled 'em."[15] The writer meant to compliment her work, but his choice of the phrase "the men" instead of a more neutral phrase, such as "the other players" or "the other musicians," highlighted the sex of the players. Bryant's unique contribution to the concert—she was the only performer to play an original composition—drew no comment. The ballad she played was part of a suite she wrote in tribute to Gillespie. Instead of giving relevant information such as this in the review, Gleske chose to focus on the competition between Bryant and "the men."

Bryant reports that she has had "no problems" during her actual performances and that many people have been very supportive of her career. Among those who have helped her are her father, her high school principal (Mr. Frazier), her high school music teacher (Mr. Johnson), trumpet players Louis Armstrong, Harry James and Dizzy Gillespie, and many other musicians. At the Central Avenue jam sessions she was, by her own report, "the only female that would get up [and play]" and received good responses from the audiences in the clubs. When speaking about her life and career, Bryant focuses mainly on the musicians she has played with and personal anecdotes about her relationships with her musician peers.[16] It is clear that she sets high musical standards for herself.

ANALYSIS

My discussions with Bryant revealed several important issues. I have identified two main areas for discussion. These subjects are by no means unrelated but can be identified separately for convenience.[17]

The first area concerns the marginalization of women musicians, the ways they are made to feel that they are treading on exclusively male territory. Women musicians are often challenged to prove themselves in ways that male musicians are not. The second and perhaps more important area is the perception of female jazz musicians, the views that others hold of them and that they have of themselves.[18] There are many conflicting facets to this issue. For example, whereas Bryant views herself as a musician above all else, others tend to view her as a *female* jazz player. Also, people generally measure women musicians against the traditional yardstick, male musicians, even when there is no basis for a direct comparison.[19] However, Bryant stresses that this view does not bother her; she is proud to be called a "female jazz musician."

From the earliest days of jazz, women have been discouraged, at times even forbidden, from taking part in the creation of music. Women of the early twentieth century who were concerned about their reputations would not consider entering any establishment that featured jazz, much less playing the music themselves. Even in the heyday of Central Avenue, a woman would rarely venture into a club unaccompanied, and according to Bryant women instrumentalists, no matter how well known, steered clear of the jam sessions. Women who did venture into the performing arena found the range of opportunities limited. Singing and playing the piano seemed to be appropriately "feminine" pursuits, resulting in the rise of the big bands' "girl singers" and the gradual acceptance of women as jazz pianists.[20]

Jazz has always been considered the realm of men. Some male jazz musicians have even expressed the belief that women are simply incapable of speaking the "male" language of jazz, that they lack the necessary experience to create the sounds. Others have contended that women lack the physical strength and stamina needed to play certain instruments for hours at a time. Still others have equated women with jazz music; trumpet player Cootie Williams once said, "All great jazz musicians, every one of them, have had many loves and girls in their lives . . . a girl *is* jazz music. They throw something into the mind to make you produce jazz."[21] This comment clearly devalues women who play jazz.

As women began to break down traditional barriers in music and in other aspects of life, these ideas persisted. Even after the women's movement and the campaign for the Equal Rights Amendment (ERA) gained momentum,[22] attitudes of the past remained entrenched. Things have changed somewhat over the years, and today more women play jazz professionally than ever before, but the traditional views still hold.

Marginalization of Female Jazz Musicians

Before we can discuss how female musicians are made to feel as though they do not belong in the jazz world, we must look at the ways in which women are marginalized in general.[23] Women in jazz have long been contending with the use of such terms as "sideman" and "jazzman." These terms are understood to include women. This dichotomy between what is said and what is supposed to be understood is well documented in linguistics, psychology, and sociology. Susan A. Basow claims that "language plays a major role in defining and maintaining male power over women."[24] She adds that by using the masculine gender to refer to human beings in general, females are effectively ignored.[25] Although people may claim to know, for example, that "mankind" includes women, many researchers have shown that, in fact, people (especially children) perceive the use of the masculine form to refer predominantly to males.[26] In discussing the male bias in anthropology, Sally Slocum found that when the word "man" is used, "supposedly meaning human species, it is actually exactly synonymous with 'males.'"[27]

This aspect of language sets up the expectation that maleness is the rule and femaleness the exception. The message seems to be that the typical person is male and that being female is atypical.[28] In the realm of music, we hear this message expressed in such labels as "girl singer," "lady trumpet player," "female saxophonist," or "drummer gal" (phrases I have seen in reviews and articles). Such labels set the stage for the nonacceptance of women from the outset.

In jazz, nonacceptance results in the marginalization of women who attempt to become a part of the scene. There are many ways in which jazzwomen are made to feel as if they do not belong. For example, Bryant reports being fired from a big band because of the jealousy of a male trumpet player.[29] The literature is rife with stories about female instrumentalists who have been subjected to unnecessarily rigorous "auditions," which are often designed not to assess the musician's ability but to trip her up. Historically, a woman musician has had to resist being intimidated by these pressure tactics, which, according to Linda Dahl, are designed to "put her in her place," to take away her respectability and subject her to disapproval, ridicule, and sometimes ostracism.[30]

Another manifestation of marginalization is that women are simply not taken seriously as jazz musicians. Their talent or ambition may be belittled. Ellen Koskoff notes that "in many societies, including those in the West, women's musical activities, genres, instruments, and performance efforts are frequently considered by both men and women to be amateurish, unimportant, or they are simply dismissed as not music."[31] A female musician's reason for playing professionally may come into question, and assumptions may be made about her personal life. Trumpet player Jean Davis once described the attitude she encountered from bandleaders this way: "Oh, wow, here comes another girl, she's gonna get pregnant, she's gonna stop, why am I gonna waste my time."[32] Bandleaders and club owners may undermine the professionalism of a female musician by expecting her to accept substandard wages or even to work for free. Occasionally, a playing gig might include other duties as well; Bryant mentions that during a gig with the Queens of Swing at a gangster-owned club in Chicago, the musicians were expected to act as "B-girls" during breaks, to sit at the bar and encourage male patrons to buy drinks.[33]

Ignoring female musicians is another way of marginalizing them. Bryant feels she has been ignored in the literature, which may be one of the reasons she is writing her autobiography. She has mentioned the problem of not being called for jobs, especially when she has been recommended or knows she is more than qualified. This is probably the most insidious form of marginalization, because it is often very difficult to measure and evaluate.

Perceptions of Female Jazz Musicians

According to my interviews and to the literature, people appear to hold a certain view of female jazz musicians. Their gender seems to figure significantly into how they are evaluated as musicians. Their musical performance is filtered through a set of expectations and biases. Thus, they are often perceived first as women, then as musicians.[34] The question at hand is what specific elements seem to figure into the evaluation of female musicians and whether these elements have any basis in musical fact.

One criterion for evaluation is whether or not a woman player "sounds like a man." The literature is rife with reports from female musicians who mention having received the compliment, "You play like a man." In my study, Bryant spoke about Dizzy Gillespie's comparing her playing style to that of a man. The ever-present yardstick is the male musician, although it is never specified that the male musician is a *good* one. The assumption seems to be that *all* male musicians are good (confirming expectations of competence for men in general). The acid test would appear to be whether the gender of the player can be determined through listening alone; if a woman's playing cannot be distinguished from that of the standard male, then she is deemed competent, and her music is evaluated positively.

Another criterion for evaluation is the physical appearance of the female musician. Descriptions of appearance are given repeatedly in the literature. In scholarly writings about well-known artists of the past, such as Billie Holiday, male and female authors often give more space to discussions of the performer's taste in gowns and jewelry than to elements of musical style.[35] A reviewer may devote the first paragraph of an article to a thorough description of the performer's outfit, using a phrase such as "she looked stunning as she took the stage." Sheila Jordan, a singer whose career spanned several decades, gave the following account of two reviews of the same performance: "One [reviewer] said I looked great but I didn't fulfill my capacity; in other words, I didn't sing that good, but I sure looked good. The other one said I didn't look too hot but boy, could I sing."[36] Jordan also mentioned nightclub owners who "don't know anything about music—they want to know what you look like."[37] A professional harpist once told researcher Cynthia Tse Kimberlin that prospective clients often ask questions such as "Do you have blond hair?" and "Are you pretty?"[38] Bryant mentions that she has seen women musicians wearing elaborate gowns or ostentatious outfits.[39] She reports that she herself has dressed the part and thoroughly enjoyed it, wearing fancy gowns, showy jewelry, and rhinestone-studded shoes.

Assessments of physical appearance can influence the evaluation of musical competence. As illustrated by Sheila Jordan's account of the two reviews about her, it seems as though a woman who is considered attractive may not be deemed competent, but it is acceptable to deem competent a woman who is not considered attractive. This hypothesis is supported by Basow, who states that "whereas competence is a quality seen as more appropriate for males than females, physical attractiveness is a quality that is seen as more appropriate for females than males."[40] Studies have shown that women who work in male-dominated fields and are considered attractive are often regarded negatively in terms of their job performance.

In the jazz literature, this phenomenon is fairly well documented in the stories of women artists who were "attractive" but not taken seriously and therefore evaluated negatively.[41]

Another criterion for evaluation is the artist's commitment to the music. This is certainly a valid criterion in assessing any professional musician, but in the traditionally male-dominated arena of jazz certain assumptions have been made about women musicians. Historically, the assumption has been that female jazz musicians are not very committed because there are more important duties in their lives, such as taking care of their families. This assumption contributes to the perception of the female musician as a novelty, someone who cannot be taken seriously. The corollary idea is that the woman musician needs to have some kind of "act," or gimmick, as though some other form of entertainment is needed because the playing is probably not good enough. Or perhaps the feeling is that the paying customers might not take seriously a woman with a saxophone (or trumpet or other instrument), so there must be something else to hold their attention. The requirement to "have an act" forces a female artist back into the role of a novelty rather than a serious artist. Saxophonist Willene Barton expressed it this way:

> Another thing—I always thought this never happened to men—they'd say, "You've got to have an act." The fact that I'm standing on the stage playing saxophone as well as I do is enough, as far as I can see. . . . People tell me, "I can give your band a job, but you gotta have an act." What kind of act? Tell stories? Comedy? I don't dance. I certainly can't tell jokes. I sing very little. So what do they mean? The fact that I'm standing up there is an act. And you get the same thing from club owners.[42]

Bryant had an act with her brother for a six-week stint on Australian television; the duo would sing, and then she would play trumpet. She also reported that in order to get her album *Gal with a Horn* recorded, she had to sing on some tunes as well as play trumpet.[43] Although having some unique feature or gimmick can help any musician distinguish herself or himself from the others, women musicians have historically been expected to offer attractions other than their playing in order to be hired, to "really earn their money."

Judgments as to the degree of seriousness can affect the assessment of competence. If a female musician can be relegated to the position of "novelty," then she does not have to be viewed as a serious musician. Jazz critic Leonard Feather has said saxophonist Vi Redd is too often viewed not as "an available saxophonist who plays and reads well and can hold down a chair in any man's reed section, but rather as a novelty who can't really be that good."[44] The music itself becomes unimportant and may be discussed negatively, if at all. Moreover, a woman does not have to be evaluated as a serious musician if some excuse can be found as to why she plays jazz—to make extra money or to "blow off steam," for example. In this case her commitment is perceived to be low, and therefore her music must not be good. Of course, many reviewers and writers do not confess to having this bias,

so it is difficult to discern whether a negative assessment results from truly inadequate playing or from prejudices on the part of the writer.

However, these biases can sometimes lead to positive assessments, regardless of
whether they are warranted. A woman is not expected to be a good jazz player, so
when she performs well the achievement can become magnified. If she does not
perform well, she may be evaluated positively anyway for "trying hard"—i.e., trying to play like a serious jazz musician despite having the "handicap" of being a
woman. Some scholars have termed this pattern of results the "talking platypus
phenomenon." As they explain the concept, "It matters little what the platypus
says; the wonder is that it can say anything at all."[45] In any case, the musical aspects of a woman's performance often become secondary, and the assessment is
based primarily on nonmusical elements.

Bryant regards herself as a musician, not as a female musician. Unless asked
directly, she rarely mentions gender issues, preferring to discuss the music.
Other women in jazz also seem concerned primarily with the quality of the
music. Saxophonist Fostina Dixon has stated that "the women's thing is cool, but
on record the quality has to come through."[46] Trombonist Janice Robinson remarks, "I personally think that the music is the most important thing."[47] And
drummer Dottie Dodgion describes the need to concentrate on the music, not
on what others may be thinking or assuming about her: "You're a musician
first—you're going there to set up your drums because you're a drummer. And
you're going to play because you're a musician."[48] The priority, clearly, is playing good jazz.

Bryant's Career in Los Angeles

Good jazz is what draws Los Angeles–area audiences to clubs and concert halls. In
this atmosphere of tolerance, where change is welcomed and new experiences embraced, Clora Bryant has made a career of playing in clubs, in movies, and on
television. With all of these opportunities to play, what does Bryant say about her
experiences in Los Angeles?

In my interviews with her,[49] Bryant has mentioned the negative as well as the
positive aspects of pursuing her career in Los Angeles. She draws comparisons between the West Coast and the East Coast. When she arrived in California in 1945,
she was determined to make it as a professional musician. She enjoyed the Central
Avenue music scene and the pleasant weather. Bryant was not concerned with
gender issues and did not expect to encounter problems related to gender. By her
own account, she pursued her career aggressively and commanded respect, qualities she feels were necessary to accomplish her goals but that the majority of female jazz players did not have in the forties and fifties.[50] Had she stayed in New
York, she thinks, she may have received more performing opportunities and recognition.

Throughout her career, Bryant has been able to minimize the effect of negative perceptions of female jazz artists and take advantage of suitable performing opportunities, going elsewhere when jobs were not offered in Southern California. According to Gourse, extensive touring is something of an anomaly for West Coast artists: "The West Coast's paucity of major metropolitan-like cities limits such touring. . . . All West Coast musicians generally travel far less than easterners."[51] Thus, Bryant's dedication to her career was not limited by the availability (or nonavailability) of jobs in the Los Angeles area.

Were Bryant's experiences in California similar to those of other female jazz musicians, her contemporaries? Bryant feels they were not. Trombonist Melba Liston was writing music and performing with a big band in the forties and fifties, and saxophonist Vi Redd fronted her own band, but according to Bryant neither played the Central Avenue jam sessions. Many female artists were not able or willing to go on the road for extended periods. And commanding respect—an undertaking that was often impossible—was as much a part of the job for jazzwomen as playing well. As open and accepting as the attitude was and is in California, there remain limitations for female jazz performers. Bryant's career is proof that a rewarding experience is possible, but there is still a long way to go toward the complete acceptance of women who play jazz.

CONCLUSION

The experiences of one Los Angeles–area female jazz musician help us to identify some of the prominent issues facing women in jazz. By locating recurrent themes in my discussions with Clora Bryant and by consulting the literature, I isolated two areas for analysis: the marginalization of female jazz musicians and the perceptions of female jazz musicians. Within these areas, the material has shown that jazzwomen are often subjected to unfair standards of performance, to attitudes that belittle or minimalize their ability, and to views that often have nothing to do with the actual performance. The women's views of themselves and their ability are at odds with these ideas; as musicians, they simply focus on the music itself.

Attitudes toward women jazz musicians stem from the historical expectations of women in general, which mandate that women confine themselves to domestic pursuits and avoid any arena traditionally dominated by men. Men and women are expected to conform to certain stereotypical gender roles and behaviors, and when they cross the line of acceptability they leave themselves open to negative evaluation. When a woman crosses that line by pursuing a career as a jazz musician, she is not usually expected to succeed. Thus, assessments of her ability are often based less on her actual ability and more on nonmusical factors.

Clora Bryant has transcended many of these difficulties in her career in California and elsewhere. She has been able to take advantage of the unique opportunities presented in California while effectively handling issues of marginalization and negative perceptions. But effective handling of these problems does not imply that they have been resolved. For women to gain greater respect as jazz musicians, it appears, people must change their traditional beliefs about women's roles in society. Bryant is pessimistic about the rate of change in the jazz world; though jazzwomen have definitely progressed, "we're only going to get as far as [men are going to let us]."[52] In these times when diversity is celebrated and people are more aware of sexual discrimination, it is unfortunate that beliefs are not changing as quickly as words. But in California, the atmosphere of acceptance and openness continues to evolve.

In Los Angeles, it is no longer rare to hear women playing jazz. One has only to consult a jazz guide or newspaper to see that jazz is performed by many women, whether they live in town or are visiting from other parts of the country or the world. It is difficult to determine whether the number of female musicians in jazz is increasing or whether more opportunities exist for women in jazz; perhaps both of these factors are at work. Urban areas such as Los Angeles have been and continue to be vital centers for jazz. Los Angeles attracts musicians in large numbers from all over the world and provides important opportunities for women who play jazz. In the future, perhaps the growing number of female jazz musicians will help change the historical views of women's roles, and more people will be able to enjoy the most important thing—the music.

NOTES

1. Lonnie Bunch, in *Black Angelenos: The Afro-American in Los Angeles, 1850–1950* (Los Angeles: California Afro-American Museum, 1989), 9–11, discusses the lure of Los Angeles to African Americans during the late nineteenth and early twentieth centuries.

2. Eddie Meadows, personal communication to author, 9 January 1996.

3. For more information on the West Coast jazz style and artists, see Ted Gioia, *West Coast Jazz: Modern Jazz in California, 1945–1960* (New York: Oxford University Press, 1992); and Robert Gordon, *Jazz West Coast: The Los Angeles Jazz Scene of the 1950s* (London: Quartet Books, 1986).

4. For discussion of venues in Los Angeles for the performance of jazz, see Ralph Eastman, "'Pitchin' up a Boogie': African-American Musicians, Nightlife, and Music Venues in Los Angeles 1930–1945," chapter 2 in this volume.

5. For the impact of television in the life of musicians in Los Angeles, see works on the life of Nat King Cole, including Maria Cole with Louise Robinson, *Nat King Cole: An Intimate Biography* (New York: William Morrow, 1971); and Leslie Gourse, *Unforgettable: The Life and Mystique of Nat King Cole* (New York: St. Martin's Press, 1991).

6. Clora Bryant, interviews with author, 15 July 1993 and 28 December 1995. For another source of information about Bryant and her career, see Steven L. Isoardi, *Central Avenue Sounds: Clora Bryant* (Los Angeles: Oral History Program, University of California, Los Angeles, 1994).

7. In recent years, interest in the subject of women in jazz has grown. For more information, consult Leslie Gourse, *Madame Jazz: Contemporary Women Instrumentalists* (New York: Oxford University Press, 1995). Also see Danica L. Stein Hunt, "Women Who Play Jazz: A

Study of the Experiences of Three Los Angeles Musicians" (M.A. thesis, University of California, Los Angeles, 1994), which examines the careers of Clora Bryant, saxophonist Ann Patterson, and bassist Nedra Wheeler. For a guide to sound recordings made by women who were a part of jazz history, see Jan Leder, *Women in Jazz: A Discography of Instrumentalists, 1913–1968* (Westport: Greenwood Press, 1985).

8. Clora Bryant, *Gal with a Horn* (Mode Records, LP-106, 1957).

9. Bryant, personal interview, 1993.

10. Ibid.

11. Ibid.

12. Bryant, personal interview, 1995.

13. Bryant, personal interview, 1993.

14. Bryant served as musical director for the event, which took place at the Southland Cultural Center in Inglewood, California.

15. Tony Gleske, concert review, *Hollywood Reporter* (29 April 1993).

16. Bryant, personal interview, 1993.

17. I have determined these areas by culling out recurrent themes, the problems or issues that were mentioned by Bryant in my 1993 interview with her.

18. See P. A. Goldberg, "Are Women Prejudiced Against Women?" *Transaction* 5 (1968): 28–30.

19. See K. Deaux, "Sex: A Perspective on the Attribution Process" in *New Directions in Attribution Research, Vol. 1.*, eds. John H. Harvey, William John Ickes, and Robert F. Kidd (Hillsdale, NJ: L. Erlbaum Associates, 1976).

20. Bryant, personal interview, 1993.

21. Valerie Wilmer, *As Serious As Your Life: The Story of the New Jazz* (Westport, CT: Lawrence Hill and Company, 1980), 199.

22. The Equal Rights Amendment was defeated in 1982.

23. Although it could be argued that the issue at hand is how men wield power over women, I find it more useful here to discuss how the status quo affects women.

24. Susan A. Basow, *Gender Stereotypes: Traditions and Alternatives* (Pacific Grove, CA: Brooks/Cole Publishing Company, 1986), 129.

25. Ibid., 129–130.

26. Ibid., 130.

27. Sally Slocum, "Woman the Gatherer: Male Bias in Anthropology," in *Toward an Anthropology of Women*, ed. Rayna Reiter (New York: Monthly Review Press, 1975). Slocum is cited in Ellen Koskoff, *Women and Music in Cross-Cultural Perspective* (New York: Greenwood Press, 1987), 2.

28. Basow, *Gender Stereotypes*, 130.

29. Bryant, personal interview, 1993.

30. Linda Dahl, *Stormy Weather: The Music and Lives of a Century of Jazzwomen* (New York: Pantheon Books, 1984), x.

31. Koskoff, *Women and Music*, 15.

32. Quoted in Sally Placksin, *American Women in Jazz: 1900 to the Present: Their Words, Lives, and Music* (New York: Seaview Books, 1982), 232–233.

33. Sherrie Tucker, "Clora Bryant," *California Jazz Now* 3, no. 7 (1993): 5, 14, 22.

34. I do not feel that this per se is negative; it is perfectly natural, for example, to notice whether a performer is male or female. It is when one allows preconceptions to override the event—the music itself—that inaccurate observations are made.

35. See, for example, the following caption to a photograph of Billie Holiday in James Lincoln Collier, *The Making of Jazz: A Comprehensive History* (New York: Dell Publishing Co., Inc., 1978), 309: "Billie Holiday at times allowed herself to get fat. . . . But in her prime she was a true beauty, and when this stunning woman sang 'My man don't love/Treats me awful mean,' she could freeze audiences in their seats." Although Collier comments on elements of Holiday's musical style, most of the discussion is devoted to the lurid details of her personal life. In contrast, Collier's biographical treatment of Louis Armstrong (pp. 141–160) remains focused on music.

36. Quoted in Dahl, *Stormy Weather*, 242.

37. Ibid.

38. Marcia Herndon and Susanne Ziegler, eds. *Music, Gender and Culture* (New York: C. F. Peters Corporation, 1990), 224.

39. Bryant, personal interview, 1993.

40. Basow, *Gender Stereotypes*, 238. Basow cites studies showing that women who do not conform to a certain level of attractiveness frequently may be described more negatively than similarly unattractive males. See D. Bar-Tal and P. H. O'Brien, "Physical Attractiveness and Its Relationship to Sex-Role Stereotyping," *Sex Roles* 2 (1976): 123–133; T. F. Cash, B. Gillen, and D. S. Burns, "Sexism and 'Beautyism' in Personnel Consultant Decision Making," *Journal of Applied Psychology* 62 (1977): 301–310; and B. S. Wallston and V. O'Leary, "Sex Makes a Difference: Differential Perceptions of Women and Men," in *Review of Personality and Social Psychology, Vol. 2*, ed. L. Wheeler (Beverly Hills, CA: Sage, 1981), 9–41.

41. It would be misleading to say that this is always the case. It is more accurate to say that this has been a pattern and a recurrent theme throughout the history of jazz.

42. Quoted in Placksin, *American Women in Jazz*, 230.

43. Bryant, *Gal with the Horn*. As noted earlier, Bryant began singing at an early age and enjoys it. She did not start singing just because it would get her more jobs; however, singing on the album was a concession Bryant made at the time.

44. Quoted in Placksin, *American Women in Jazz*, 259. Note that again the ever-present yardstick is a man—"any" man, not explicitly a talented one.

45. Quoted in Basow, *Gender Stereotypes*, 236–237. Also see P. P. Abramson, P. A. Goldberg, J. H. Greenberg, and L. M. Abramson, "The Talking Platypus Phenomenon: Competency Ratings as a Function of Sex and Professional Status," *Psychology of Women Quarterly* 2 (1977): 123.

46. Quoted in Placksin, *American Women in Jazz*, 278.

47. Ibid., 290.

48. Quoted in Dahl, *Stormy Weather*, 224.

49. The following discussion is based on information obtained during my December 1995 interview with Bryant.

50. As mentioned earlier, Bryant was one of the very few women who performed at the jam sessions in Los Angeles.

51. Gourse, *Madame Jazz*, 210.

52. Bryant, personal interview, 1993.

9

The Gospel of Andraé Crouch

A Black Angeleno

Jean Kidula

Since its founding, Los Angeles has been considered a city of expectation and opportunity. Lonnie Bunch discusses the lure and the ideology that prompted most
people to migrate to the state: "California has always been seen 'literally and symbolically as America's golden shore, its fabled region of hope and promise.' Generations of Americans have . . . answered California's clarion call of hope and
opportunity. . . . Blacks were drawn to Los Angeles by many of the same promises
and hopes offered to their White counterparts."[1]

Los Angeles's colonists were of mixed ancestry. The city, therefore, was
founded on multiracial and multicultural understandings. It began without the
baggage of slavery as it was known in the East and without colonial masters.
Blacks used whatever opportunities were available to create a new life and environment for themselves and for the city. Sometimes blacks were invited to take jobs
originally held by members of other races.[2] As such, black immigrants to Los Angeles found a different reality from what they had known in the East and South.[3]

In this chapter I will analyze Andraé Crouch and his music against the background of his African heritage and situation in Los Angeles.[4] Crouch, a black man
in a multiracial city that traditionally has had an ambivalent relationship with its
black citizens, qualifies as a symbol of Los Angeles's character, which encompasses
integration and synthesis as well as collaboration and compromise. Crouch's
music will be presented as a synthesis of black and white, sacred and secular, tradition and innovation, reality and expectation, image and person—the same influences I see represented in Los Angeles as a city and in African Americans as a people. The representation will be analyzed in view of Crouch's background (born
1942 in Los Angeles of parents who migrated to the city); his religious affiliation
with a Pentecostal church, which represents for the African American a synthesis
and integration of African and European religious beliefs and practices; his role as
a performer of gospel music, a genre integrating sacred and secular ideas; and his
interactions with the popular music world and the expectations that were pack-

aged in the deal. As a musician and composer, Crouch had to innovate to stay in the market and stimulate the kinds of debates and writings that have been done about him.

Andraé Crouch is described as a gospel innovator primarily because he moved the genre into an urban environment intellectually.[5] The first native Angeleno to make an impact in sacred and secular music circles with black and white audiences at home and abroad, he is a singer, keyboardist, arranger, and producer who has composed more than 300 songs. Although he is credited with including secular elements in his gospel music, he did not overtly "cross over." Yet he is among the first gospel performers whose music was labeled "contemporary gospel."

Crouch's most influential period as a performer and composer lasted from the late sixties until 1984.[6] This chapter examines Crouch and his music during the peak of his popularity, which lasted from the mid-1970s to 1981, when his group disbanded. To establish the basis of the symbolism, I will include a discussion of the most pertinent components of gospel music evinced in his music, focusing on how they were perceived and interpreted by Crouch as an evolving artist.

CROUCH AND THE CHURCH

The primary institution for the black community through the 1950s was the black church.[7] C. Eric Lincoln describes black religion as "a conscious effort on the part of the black people to find spiritual and ethical value in their understanding of their history. . . . Out of his understanding of God, in the context of his own experience, man gropes for meaning and relevance. . . . When the context of that groping is conditioned by the peculiar, anomalous context of the black experience in America, that is black religion."[8]

The church was the center of black communal life. It was not only a place for worship but also provided opportunities for education. It was one of the earliest places where blacks were able to express and govern themselves freely. It is therefore not surprising that the church represented a sense of community. "Freedom" in the church, especially in those churches founded by blacks, meant that those things considered "African-derived" could be expressed.

Crouch's religious heritage is rich in characteristics regarded as African American. Crouch grew up in the Church of God in Christ (COGIC), of which he is now a pastor, and his father became pastor of a COGIC church in the Los Angeles area.[9] Chartered in 1897, COGIC drew its earliest support from individuals who were thrown out of either Baptist or Holiness churches because they ascribed to the Pentecostal doctrines advocated by William Seymour in the Los Angeles Azusa Street revivals of 1906–1909.[10] In his discussion of the beginnings of COGIC, Vinson Synan explains that the church's founders, Charles H. Mason and C. P. Jones, were Baptists who embraced Holiness doctrines and were forced to leave their original denominations to form their own church. Mason's subscription to Seymour's teachings created a rift between him and Jones, and each formed his own denomination. Mason became the leader of the COGIC and eventually retained the name. As African Americans migrated to various areas of the United States and abroad, they set up new churches; some of the founding ministers became icons in their assemblies and pastors for life. COGIC witnessed a phenomenal increase in the number of its converts, especially among the urban poor, marking the denomination as the fastest-growing Pentecostal group of the twentieth century.[11]

Horace Clarence Boyer classifies COGIC as a fundamentalist denomination because of its puritanical expectations, the congregants' belief in the fundamental inspiration of the whole Bible by God, and the form of religious worship, which includes many elements that are similar to African practices.[12] Two of these elements are dancing and possession. The highest state of worship is attained when one becomes possessed by the Holy Spirit, a trancelike state evinced by jerky body movements and involuntary cries. Repetitive singing is often used as an aid to achieve this state of trance. As such, the religious expressions of COGIC and other Holiness and Baptist denominations represent the essence of "blackness" in worship. It is from such a background that Crouch came. Thus, his exposure to Africanisms occurred in an urban setting rather than in a southern rural environment, where these practices are prominent.[13]

Music and music making in the religious context reflect the cohesive and integrative character of the black musical experience.[14] Music is related not just to religion but to the collective experiences and social situations of blacks. In emerging as the contemporary religious black genre, gospel music superseded the spiritual (a genre that evolved during slavery), but it did not displace that tradition. In fact, gospel can be seen as a continuation of the spiritual's message of hope and deliverance.

Religion has historically been the keeper of a people's tradition and the last cultural element to succumb to change. Thomas Dorsey's theory that music and religion are inseparable implies that when a people's belief system is altered, drastic changes can occur in that group's music.[15] However, change can also occur in music as a reflection of reformation or revival within a belief system. This type of activity has been the most common source of change in the music of the church. When such a movement takes place, usually the traditionalists reject the new forms as being too worldly.[16]

Karima Haynes's article "The Gospel Controversy: Are the New Songs Too Jazzy and Too Worldly?" proposes a different side of the problem: musicians may create changes in the music in hopes of reaching a wider audience and thereby bringing about revival.[17] Tradition keepers in the gospel genre are not in favor of such innovations. Religious music in general tends to emphasize tradition rather than innovation, assimilating change cautiously. Thus, the gospel controversy is not a new phenomenon.

Gospel was introduced to Los Angeles chiefly by visiting musicians and settlers from the South and Midwest. This musical form crystallized in the Chicago area and became popular through the performances and publications of Thomas

Figure 9.1. Gospel composer and singer Andraé Crouch. Courtesy of Andraé Crouch/Ramon Hervey (Hervey and Company).

Dorsey and his disciples. Dorsey is therefore referred to as the "father" of black gospel, but he was not without opposition when he introduced his innovations into the church. Only through invitations by preachers associated primarily with the National Baptist Convention was Dorsey able to share his songs. Sallie Martin is credited with introducing Los Angeles to gospel music. Jacqueline Cogdell DjeDje states that although there was initial resistance, Los Angeles gradually embraced gospel songs primarily because of performances by well-known groups and singers from the Midwest, as well as church-sponsored choirs and radio broadcasts. Some performers of this genre also founded churches, thereby establishing an outlet for their creative and performance abilities. Leading gospel practitioners and composers held music positions in various churches, teaching their music and spreading their talent.[18]

Grace Memorial Church of God in Christ, in which Crouch was raised by his pastor father, is believed to have been one of the first black churches in Los Angeles to air services on the radio.[19] As a Pentecostal church, it was well known for extensive use of music in its service. Many of the established gospel artists in Los Angeles (e.g., J. Earle Hines, Albert Goodson, Arthur Peters, Earl Pleasant, Thurston Frazier, and James Cleveland) periodically directed the choir[20] and were involved in the church during Crouch's formative years. Though Crouch acknowledges that there were many good singers at Grace Memorial who influenced him, he also listened to classical, jazz, country, rock and roll, and rhythm and blues, all of which became part of the fusion that he later was to create.[21] Aside from these musical influences, Crouch's religious heritage has propelled his compositions. Most of the singing in these churches was accompanied by a rhythm instrument, usually a tambourine. Also, some singers would performer European-style hymns during worship. Crouch recalls: "During church, I remember sitting there enthralled when sister Garnett would sing. She had a deep anointed soprano voice. She'd sing, '[E]ven me, let some drops now fall on me,' or a song like, 'I'd rather have Jesus.'"[22]

Crouch has stated that he composes and performs music from the heart, an impulse born of his religious experience; he set his "inner feelings . . . to music."[23] Because of his contacts with nonblacks in his parents' home in Pacoima,[24] he cultivated an interest in and learned to be sensitive to people from other cultures and is able to respond to their needs in performance.

Crouch attributes his own musical abilities to his religious heritage. He stated that his father vowed to God that he would take the pastorate on a full-time basis if God gave Andraé the gift of music.[25] Two weeks later, Andraé began to play. After that, he only took lessons for six months. Thus, he developed the basic skills for playing the piano on his own. Because the way he acquired his gift is in keeping with his church doctrine,[26] it is no wonder that he refuses to be referred to as an entertainer, preferring instead to identify himself as the bearer of a message.

Although Crouch's music and artistry are based in the church, it is evident that his exposure to secular genres and music from other cultures helped to shape his style. As an Angeleno, he was influenced by black musicians who came from other areas of the United States. Members of various ethnic groups, all in search of better opportunities, lived in Crouch's neighborhood. Crouch was born during a period of great migration into a city that was establishing new industries. Yet at the same time, some blacks in Los Angeles were affected by deprivations during and after World War II. It was a period of assimilation and transition.

CROUCH AND GOSPEL MUSIC

Black gospel has been described as a "tradition bearer" in that it embodies Afro-American ideology, aesthetic, and behavior.[27] Afro-American assimilation and appropriation of Christianity resulted in the creation of a new musical expression, a new personhood. Pearl Williams-Jones defines gospel as "the sum total of . . . past and present socio-economic and cultural traditions."[28] It has always been a people's music because it is performed at least once a week in church. Therefore, it serves as a symbol of black heritage, "a crystallization of the black aesthetic."[29]

Most writers agree that gospel music is the United States's contribution to hymnody and that there is a distinct difference between black and white gospel.[30] Some investigators consider gospel to be "an evolving art form"[31] shaped primarily by performers.[32] The gospel message is one of good news, hope, inspiration, and stability. Although the black and white subsets are both rooted in the revival movements of the eighteenth and nineteenth centuries, segregation laws, different cultural backgrounds, and religious affiliations created two distinct paths of development. Over time, the genres were further separated by marketing techniques that identified potential groups and artists and steered each genre in its own direction.

Black gospel is distinguished from other styles of sacred music by its performance delivery, intimate lyrics, instrumentation, and role of composer-performer. But it is linked to other black popular genres, such as blues or soul, in its personalization of each performance, which gives rise to individualized interpretations. As a result, varied renditions of the same song are given by different people; each performer reinterprets each song with every performance. The genre is therefore constantly recreating and being recreated. Both repetition and improvisation are emphasized in gospel music. Because this genre is built on performance, whether in church or in a concert hall, repetition is the framework on which improvisation builds and on which the message of the piece is reinforced and emphasized.

Crouch's performance career was launched at a time of great national unrest, during the race riots, Vietnam sit-ins, hippie subcultures, and other disturbances of the 1960s. The message needed was one of hope. Crouch worked with a drug rehabilitation center, Teen Challenge, that provided him with even more exposure to Latinos and whites. He became active in the Jesus Movement (1968–72), which led to his first performances with white gospel musicians.[33] Through these he became popular with white audiences, performing in a style later known as contemporary gospel because of its fusion of traditional gospel with secular and modern popular elements. In this section I will discuss the synthesis of elements and races in Crouch's music.

Crouch introduced gospel music to white audiences during his appearances at concerts associated with the Jesus Movement. For most of the 1960s, he was the only black performer in this movement. As Crouch continued to play for white audiences, he eventually had to give up some of the hard-edged improvisations in his performances, so much so that James Cleveland, another gospel performer, said "Andraé has bridged the gap between black and white audiences. . . . The white artists are very interested in the more soulful type of gospel music."[34] However, this performance style proved to be his downfall. Commenting on Crouch's style, Viv Broughton says: "Andraé occupies that middle ground like nobody else, with the result that a lot of his music recordings sound like a test-card sound track, but his roots go much deeper. . . . There began to be little to differentiate Andraé's style of gospel from the predominantly bland sound of the West Coast pop."[35]

In gospel there is a dialogic relationship between performer and audience that traditionally allows the audience to participate in the creative process, resulting in a merging of the two. This has always been part of the black performance aesthetic.[36] Thomas Dorsey argues that this behavior is similar to what he encountered as a blues performer, before blues was declared "secular."[37] But Dorsey acknowledges that the essence of both blues and gospel is the "revelation of personal experience" that allows the performer to "relive" and "relieve" the audience, which then shares in the spirit, feelings, and demands of the singer. This type of performance delivery allows the singer to interpret the song to fit the mood of the occasion. In this case the form, rhythm, and tempo of a piece can be altered with every performance.[38]

Gospel singing has been defined by its unique vocal style, which favors a "strained and full-throated" sound. Some of the genre's best singers possess a wide vocal range, which they often use as their distinguishing trait. Elaborate vocal improvisation works especially well in churches or venues without amplification, but a smoother tone is better suited to larger auditoriums, where amplified and electronic instruments usually accompany the singer.[39] In addition to displaying a distinct vocal quality, a gospel singer is expected to interpret the song through creative improvisation and text interpolation.[40] The dialectic relationship between the audience and the performer either dictates or is dictated by call and response, an African stylistic performance practice. The responses are usually repetitive, eliciting audience participation. This practice not only leads to new verse forms but also is thought to facilitate spirit possession.[41]

Crouch's performance style reflects his African and gospel heritage. John D. Booth comments on how performances of the same song would vary not just in concert but also in recording sessions. On stage Crouch was able to treat the same song in different ways to reach a broader audience; his band was always prepared to perform at least three versions of the same song, to be used as the occasion and mood dictated.[42] Similarly, it was not uncommon for the same song to appear on two albums with different orchestrations or different sets of vamps. His objective was to get the message to the people in the most effective performance mode and style possible. Crouch exhibited the performance practice of a black man in a black genre, giving himself the freedom to be innovative as a musician and interpret the piece in whatever manner he would like. He also invoked his religious heritage, which allowed him to create a "new" song out of an old one as the spirit led him. Like other gospel singers, he brought "church" into his performance, and this proved very effective in concert situations, even though the audience to which he marketed this music was primarily white.

According to Boyer, Crouch was the crystallizer of "contemporary gospel."[43] When he borrowed sounds from secular genres such as rhythm and blues, jazz, and soul and incorporated them into his compositions, the results were accepted by the populace. Crouch accommodated the musical mainstream by incorporating contemporary styles. In the 1970s, when disco, with its pulsating rhythm and danceable sound, was prevalent, he created a disco arrangement of "I've Got the Best" (see *The Contemporary Man* on Light Records 7115730636:6, listed in the Appendix). At the same time, he kept gospel purists at peace with ballads and traditional compositions such as "Through It All" (see *Andraé Crouch Songbook* on Virgin R 1722:11). When black gospel was identified as a separate category by *Billboard*[44] and was marketed by traditionally white labels, Crouch and Edwin Hawkins were advised to incorporate more popular music elements into their songs so the music could cross over into the secular market. When Crouch marketed his product to the black community, he tried to be more secular by including harder, more aggressive beats. For example, the song "Let's Worship Him" (see *Finally* on Light LC 5784:5) features Afro-Cuban elements and instruments. When a performer's discs were found in both the rhythm and blues and gospel sections of a record store, "the black Disc Jockey was less apt to be startled by a spiritual message than his white counterpart."[45] However, such musicians lost credibility with fundamentalist Christians,[46] who believed the inclusion of secular elements tended to "water down the natural appeal of gospel in its purest form . . . and can leave an artist without a voice and frequently misinterpreted."[47]

The lyrics of traditional gospel songs are usually based on direct quotes or paraphrases from scripture, testimonies about a personal relationship with Christ, or adoration of and supplication to God. Ideas for gospel songs may come from sermons, personal reflection, or spiritual inspiration. The need to have a new composition for church services may also be a catalyst.[48] Most of the early performers composed their own songs or Afro-Americanized existing songs. Ministers formed some of their songs at the pulpit as they emphasized a point.[49] Eileen Southern states that many gospel classics were created spontaneously and continuously as the need arose. Formal structure and content were flexible and often sacrificed for creative expression.[50] Recently, this trend has changed. Because traditionalists have an expectation about how gospel should sound, artists such as The Winans complain that the form has become standardized to such an extent that they are "hesitant to explore new directions."[51] Still, the texts are usually personalized so that they assume special meaning for both creator and reactor. In this way, the individual is able to assert himself or herself as a performer or react individually as a member of the audience yet stay within the bonds of the collective.

Keith Bernard Jenkins states that Crouch's lyrics can be divided into three periods. In the first period, which includes music from the first six albums, Crouch makes direct and explicit references to the words "Jesus," "Christ," "Lord," "God," and "Savior." In the next five albums, his lyrics become more secular. On the 1984 album, which constitutes the third period, Crouch's lyrics revert to the first style.[52]

The first albums were made when Crouch was very active in the Jesus Movement. Although he was a black musician, no one attempted to separate him from gospel singers of other races. It is only when his music was labeled as "black" by virtue of his racial heritage that his song texts were secularized.[53] Interestingly, the texts also became somewhat ambiguous because Crouch wrote gospel lyrics for tunes that were indistinguishable from the "sweet soul music" of the 1970s.[54] For example, in his song, "Bringin' Back the Sunshine," one of the verses has the following words:

Don't you worry about tomorrow
If it will ever come
For no matter where you are my love
You'll be safe in my arms.
I'll be your bridge over troubled waters.
I'll protect you from the cold.
And I want you to know that our love won't grow old.
Watch me I'll be bringing back
The beauty of my love, bringing back.

(Text used by permission.
EMI Christian Music Group.)

One has to examine closely the rest of the lyrics to discover that the song is about a relationship with God and not a secular love song. This reticulation from sacred to secular was similar to the approach taken by secular artists who had grown up in the church. To sell their music in the secular world, church musicians sometimes "secularized" texts that were originally based on sacred beliefs. Unfortunately for Crouch, his crossover lyrics did not sell well in the secular world. He was already established as a sacred musician. In fact, his greatest sales were made on the albums recorded "live," where he could be "black" without being so labeled.

Contemporary gospel songwriters began to expand on traditional gospel lyrics. No longer did they concentrate solely on scripture, adoration, supplication, and testimony. Some lyrics contained social commentaries and admonitions; in fact, many gospel innovators and singers claimed this was the heart of their message. Though Crouch was not the only performer to make these innovations during the 1970s, he was particularly noticed because of his diverse audience. It may have been Crouch's success that caused writers such as the Winans at times to avoid putting God's name in the lyrics.

It is probably Crouch's song texts that have earned him a special place in hymnals throughout the world. His songs not only follow a familiar structure (e.g., call-response and story forms) but also reflect traditional church doctrine. His most famous song among Pentecostal and Baptist groups is probably "The Blood Will Never Lose Its Power" (Example 9.1), which is based on a stanza-refrain hymn form. The lyrics are especially appropriate to Pentecostal doctrine, which places great emphasis on the power of the blood. Here, Crouch is reinforcing his church doctrine. "Through It All" (Example 9.2), which is included in many hymnals, is a slow "soul" tune whose lyrics, like a blues text, depict a hopeless situation. But this song emphasizes a message of hope, which is the basis of most gospel songs. "Through It All" is composed in a stanza-refrain form. "Soon and Very Soon," another well-known text, promises freedom. It is characteristic of Pentecostal choruses in its call-and-response textual and musical form. The constantly reiterated words "we are going to see the king," always sung in the same melody, have an almost hypnotic effect that is intended to focus the singer on the theme. One of Crouch's most famous songs, "Bless His Holy Name" belongs to a category that Wyatt Tee Walker refers to as "prayer and praise hymns of the black religious experiences."[55] Created during the hymnbook era (1885–1925), these songs have a restricted literary form with a small melodic range and are characterized by repetition as a memory device. They are sometimes just referred to as choruses.

Donna M. Cox sees Crouch's lyrics and style as part of a contemporary trend that reflects changes in the church's doctrinal emphasis on God, rather than man's problems, as a starting point.[56] Such was the case with the testimony songs used in COGIC churches earlier in the century. It is also evident that many groups in both black and white churches more recently have focused on the praise of God as a pivotal point,[57] leading to the formation of such groups as Maranatha![58]

Although gospel music is distinguished from other black religious genres by its instrumentation, it conforms to practices used in other styles of black music. For example, assigning vocal qualities to the instruments is a common practice in African and African-American cultures. The instrumentation used in the performance of gospel resembles that found in Holiness and COGIC denominations; members of these churches decided that God was to be praised with many instruments. In addition to the tambourine and drum, a variety of other instruments have been incorporated into services.

The piano came into use quite early as an accompanying instrument in gospel. From a technical standpoint, the piano has been treated as a percussion instrument, providing a rhythmic, pulsating drive in the left hand while the right hand improvises. The instrument thus has a dual responsibility. The piano also supplies chordal accompaniment that structures the harmonic overlay of the piece. In fact, some of the early composers only scored the melody with the underlying chords so the keyboardist would have an idea of the basic harmony of the piece, over which creative and spontaneous improvisation could be performed.[59] When the organ was added, it, too, took on a improvisational role. Later, other percussive instruments were added to reinforce the rhythmic elements, and the bass guitar was included to outline the harmony. As contemporary gospel developed, other instruments were added, including strings, brass, and synthesizers.

Instrumentation provides a backdrop for improvisation. In fact, a modern gospel group can be compared, especially in the vamp section, to a West African drum ensemble, with the singer as the master drummer, improvising against the background of accompanying singers and instrumentalists. The singer gives cues for movement into the next section while assessing the mood of the audience,

Example 9.1. "The Blood Will Never Lose Its Power," by Andraé Crouch. Copyright 1966, renewed 1994, by Manna Music, Inc., 35255 Brooten Road, Pacific City, OR 97135. All rights reserved. Used by permission.

Example 9.1. *(continued)*

Example 9.2. "Through It All," by Andraé Crouch. Copyright 1971 by Manna Music, Inc., 35255 Brooten Road, Pacific City, OR 97135. All rights reserved. Used by permission.

tri - als come to on - ly make me strong.
let me know that I _____ was His own.
nev - er know what faith in God could do.

Through it all, _____ Through it all, _____ I've

learned to trust in Je - sus, I've learned to trust in God;

Through it all, _____ Through it all, _____ I've

learned to de - pend up - on His Word. _____

Example 9.2. *(continued)*

which reinforces or withdraws support by the level of its participation. According to Crouch, instruments have traditionally facilitated "dancing in the spirit" and, in a way, dictate the effect of possession on worshippers. Crouch and his sister Sandra have been in a perfect position to enhance the worship experience in their church; Crouch plays keyboard while his sister performs percussion.[60] Some innovations in Crouch's productions may have been derived from his sister, who has worked for Motown Records.[61] In addition, Crouch has included many nonblacks in his groups. Since the beginning of his recording career, Latinos, white Americans, Europeans (particularly Scandinavians), and blacks with secular music backgrounds have helped to shape his middle-of-the-ground sound.[62]

The media, and more specifically the recording industry, have had a significant impact on the development of gospel music in Los Angeles. By the late 1940s, the West Coast had already become known as a recording center, with many studio musicians based there. It was not uncommon in Los Angeles for visiting artists to perform on television or cut records for one of the many record companies in the city.[63] Thus, the media not only have given gospel on the West Coast a distinctive ambience but also are partly responsible for the secularization of the genre. For Crouch, the media certainly helped him to become a world phenomenon and the prime exponent of a new musical form.[64] The media helped create new images of gospel and its performers, yet they also became the downfall of the artists who either did not conform to their requirements or were not astute or powerful enough to conquer them. Crouch took advantage of the media opportunities, which were responsible not only for creating his image but also for breaking it.

In the late 1970s, the Contemporary Christian Artist Association made a conscious effort to produce "excellent" record products.[65] The association, formed in 1978, set out to make an impression on secular popular culture. In order to be competitive, the musical product had to be of a high quality and attractive to the general public. Gospel artists would have to employ increasingly sophisticated production techniques and top-notch musicians.[66] Crouch who by now was a leading musician, signed with Light Records (a division of Word Incorporated, a leading Christian company) under producer Ralph Carmichael, who had earlier worked with Nat King Cole.[67] Carmichael helped to make Crouch's music sound more mainstream. Moreover, working with such artists as Larry Carlton, Joe Sample, and Ernie Watts allowed Crouch to become more involved with the secular and sacred music studio circuit.[68] He began to record with black secular popular stars like Stevie Wonder. Though we do not know the degree to which the musicianship of these professional studio artists helped to shape Crouch's sound, it is safe to say that his work with these individuals probably contributed to the change in his sound.

Crouch signed with Warner Brothers so he would be able to address social issues. Although of very good quality musically and lyrically, the resulting album, *Don't Give Up* (1981), did not sell as anticipated. The albums that had the largest sales were recorded live. The studio sound, which was apparent in *Don't Give Up*, removed the improvisational character to such an extent that the creative aspects of the music were lost. Thus, as Crouch sought a sound that would sell, his sales began to decline.

Though ten years lapsed between his 1984 and 1994 albums, Crouch has been active in the music industry and continues his association with secular musicians and producers such as Quincy Jones, Michael Jackson, and Ray Charles.[69] Crouch was the vocal arranger for such popular hits as Jackson's "Man in the Mirror," and his choir was featured in Madonna's "Like a Prayer." He served as a gospel consultant and even co-wrote (with Quincy Jones) some of the songs for the film *The Color Purple,* and in 1996 he and his choir were featured in the movie *A Time to Kill,* performing his arrangement of "Precious Lord Take My Hand." Crouch states that he uses secular styles in his music because he believes the church should "realize the cries of the world and begin to try and relate to them in a way that the world can understand."[70]

Boyer commends Crouch and other contemporary performers for introducing new ideas into gospel music. Prior to the contemporary era, most gospel music was based on primary chords and verse-refrain forms.[71] For example, the five-part song form used in Crouch's "Take Me Back" stretches the verse-refrain format by varying the two verses melodically and harmonically. Crouch and others also expanded traditional harmonies by introducing chord extensions and mixtures as well as faster rhythms than had been used in traditional gospel. Vamps were extended and used more frequently, and chain vamps were introduced, as in the song "Power in the Blood."[72]

Vamp I	Lord, Send Your Power (*Several times*)
Vamp II	Power (*as one syllable*) (*Several times*)
Vamp III	Pow-uh (*Several times*)

Each successive vamp was extracted from the first one. In addition to harmonic extensions and instrumental improvisations with each successive vamp, sometimes the volume of the instrumental accompaniment would be increased to dramatize the expressive emotional response. Crouch has been credited with leading the way in instrumentation. He not only added more melodic instruments (e.g., the trumpet, saxophone, harmonica, harp, and even full orchestra) but also used them to create melodic and rhythmic sound layerings, as in jazz. It is from this perspective that the creative genius of Crouch is seen; he has integrated various elements from his background and environment to produce a new form of gospel.

CROUCH SYMBOLIZED

In any culture, power is symbolized by the ability to maintain tradition. Tradition, however, is sedimented, revitalized, and recreated through innovation and the selective assimilation of new ideas and concepts, which come either from within or through contact with other people. Even with migration, meaning is preserved through the tenacity of tradition, the ability to regulate change and prevent it from becoming overpowering.

Crouch is a symbol of power because he works within the bastion of Afro-America's primary institution. In spite of the movements within the black community that opposed the dominating force of religion, the church remains the foundation on which the black image is built. However, Crouch, though he stays within the confines of the church to create his music and performance style, does not remain passive. Rather, he revitalizes the tradition and helps others to build on it literally and symbolically. His inclusion of other ethnic groups allows him to assimilate their ideas, and, where there are differences, he realizes his own blackness.

As an African American working from within the church, Crouch spreads a message of hope. This is expressed in the content of his lyrics and also in the basic form of gospel music. The church gave Crouch a platform from which to address social issues, an interest stimulated by his work in a drug rehabilitation center and his association with the Jesus Movement. His use of popular elements in white gospel forever changed the character of contemporary Christian music. Yet for Crouch and the black church, this integration of sacred and secular was not new.[73] He admits that he listened to many secular hits as he was growing up and used these ideas in his accompaniments during church services.[74] He also acknowledges the borrowings and interrelationships between sacred and secular forms of music: "Of course there is a lot of rock and roll that has been borrowed directly from gospel songs. I don't mind rock, especially if the music is done by black artists. Black musicians have soul, many of them from gospel music to begin with."[75]

The audience that first accepted him may not have been aware of the internal borrowings, but these elements have traditionally been a part of the black sacred tradition. Therefore, Crouch was not merely a tradition bearer; he expanded his horizons by adapting his traditional roots to modern situations, using contemporary elements, whether borne from secular or sacred associations, to shape his music. After he had assimilated mainstream culture, he returned to his roots for inspiration to create a new sound. Because most successful black genres evolve out of life contexts rather than the media, it is not surprising that he had to get back in touch with black people to discover the issues that needed to be addressed. Perhaps this conscious cultivation of a new sound targeted at a black audience is what caused him to stop recording for ten years.[76]

Crouch can also be compared to traditional black performers and innovators in the field. Like gospel performer Mahalia Jackson, Crouch found a following outside the black community among whites and the world in general. Just as Mahalia Jackson gained international recognition when she sang at one of John F. Kennedy's inaugural balls,[77] Crouch's career flourished because of his association with President Jimmy Carter, who regarded Crouch as a fellow "born-again" Christian. The attention from Carter helped to increase Crouch's renown. Rising popularity enabled Crouch to travel abroad spreading the gospel, exposing him to yet more influences. Crouch informed me that his first encounter with the Norwegian group Tvers was via a live radio broadcast in Los Angeles from The Church on the Way. Tvers was singing one of his compositions—and, he says, singing it better than he did. Consequently, Tvers performed at his father's church.[78] Unlike Mahalia Jackson, Crouch was late in relating to his own people. But he has a much larger repertoire of gospel genres than Jackson with which to enrich his experience and reinforce the tradition.

Like Thomas Dorsey, Crouch achieved fame by blending sacred and secular musical elements. Also, he created lyrics that spoke to people of their plight but gave them hope for a better tomorrow. He was accused of being too worldly and bringing the devil into the church. But this did not stop him, just as it did not stop Dorsey, from aggressively marketing his product. Both artists wanted the world to know about their music. But unlike Dorsey, Crouch's success came primarily among whites, which made it difficult for him to reaffirm his musical roots when he was forced to do so. The media characterized his music as "having a 'white' sound," and Crouch understands the assertion. "It was not white, but on record it came off white because I wasn't screaming and it was recorded well. Gospel music when I started out was not recorded well. My father use to tell me always put you voice in front of the mike—be clear. Many of the choirs and records back then had a sound that was not really pleasing to the ear."[79]

Like Dorsey, Crouch is a pianist. However, he acknowledges the importance of having a backup group. Because of his dependence on all types of instruments, he has moved away from Dorsey and traditional gospel music. Few of Crouch's recordings are done with just piano and organ, which is probably a reflection of his COGIC upbringing.

Crouch's music has been recorded by some of the most popular names in gospel, including James Cleveland, the first to publish Crouch's "The Blood Will Never Lose its Power," and Evie Tornquist, a widely respected contemporary white singer who more than anybody popularized "My Tribute." Crouch's songs are carefully scored to allow singers from outside the gospel tradition to capture and reproduce the nuances associated with the black aesthetic—syncopations, glides, and calls that anticipate the response.[80] For example, in measure 52 of the song, "All the Way" the score is labeled "soloist-ad lib" to help musicians who want to improvise.[81]

Yet in another, less positive sense, Crouch's work in the recording industry typifies what happens to black artists. After black performers are identified by producers, a "classic" version of a black product is produced. The black performer is then used as an indicator of the market potential of a particular genre. I believe Crouch, consciously or unconsciously, was used to commodify contemporary gospel music. His early recordings indicate that he may not have been conscious of the move. When black gospel was separated from mainstream white gospel, Crouch was consciously marketed as a black person and used as a model for new artists. Crouch's individuality nevertheless is evinced in his analysis of himself. He acknowledges his integration of sacred and secular elements (a feature that made him appealing to whites) as a means to create his own identity. But he also portrays himself as black, much as secular black musicians did in the 1960s and early 1970s.[82]

Crouch therefore is a conformist from two angles. He not only has assimilated and commodified himself to a largely white audience but also has commodified himself as a black musician. He associated with respected black musicians by signing with a secular label, Warner Brothers, which provided a platform from which to address social issues. Then, in true traditional form, he became a producer and a model for younger black performers, whom he introduced to the market either by singing with them on his tours or by promoting them.

Crouch associated himself with black culture in 1984 by making a network television appearance with then–presidential candidate Jesse Jackson. The appearance in a way symbolized the African-American identity of the genre.[83] He also has identified with his roots and his place in the workings of the black community by performing with blues musician B. B. King. His performances in secular venues with well-known singers such as Rosetta Tharpe and the Clara Ward Singers further affirm his black heritage. These performances also attest to the symbolic power of gospel as a black genre; it is embraced by black people irrespective of their religiosity, thus allowing for the integration of all aspects of black life.

Crouch is celebrated in black theology through the inclusion of his compositions in black hymnals. His songs are also included in white hymnals, so his music is sung by gospel artists in both traditions. By including hymns by black composers, white hymnists not only consciously recognize black interpretation and understanding of theology[84] but also acknowledge the contribution of blacks to Christian song.[85] Crouch thus becomes a symbol of theological assertion and confirmation, both from a black perspective and in the wider Christian world.

Crouch's music is also a symbol for Los Angeles. He was raised in Pacoima, a multiethnic, multiracial area of the city. It is therefore not surprising that he freely borrows musical ideas from so many cultures, including Latino, Polynesian, mainstream American, and African. It may be that Crouch appropriates music so that he can appeal to the diverse groups that form a part of his heritage. This may also explain why so many writers state that his music has a West Coast ambience. For example, Broughton places Crouch against the backdrop of the West Coast: "There is a complacency in his music that is more a reflection of casual California values. . . . He himself describes his studio base as the 'laid-back laboratory of the Lord'."[86]

Those who perform with him blend both sacred and secular elements, rural and urban characteristics, sophistication with simplicity, stardom with conformity. He uses his Los Angeles studio contacts to the fullest by inviting some of the best artists, sacred or secular, to record with him. Displaying the traditionalist leanings of early black Angelenos, he presents detailed written music scores instead of the sketches[87] favored by early composers of gospel music (e.g., Thomas Dorsey and Kenneth Morris). But his conscious desire to innovate demonstrates both his creative musical ability and his awareness of his black religious heritage. His Angeleno background may also be the reason for his continued attempts to record again, his belief that there is always an opportunity ahead. In the process of becoming a successful performer, he has affirmed tradition while celebrating innovation.

APPENDIX

Selected Hymnals and Songbooks Containing Songs by Andraé Crouch

Andraé Crouch & the Disciples: Keep on Singin' (Newbury Park, CA: Lexicon Music, Inc., 1971).
Songs of Andraé Crouch and the Disciples. (Newbury Park, CA: Lexicon Music, 1979).
Songs of Zion (Nashville, TN: Abingdon Press, 1981).
Finally: Songs of Andraé Crouch (Newbury Park, CA: Lexicon Music, Inc., 1982).
Lead Me, Guide Me: The African American Catholic Hymnal. (Chicago: G.I.A. Publications, Inc., 1987).
Worship the Lord: Hymnal of the Church of God (Anderson, IN: Warner Press, 1989).

Recordings by Andraé Crouch
(listed alphabetically)

Andraé Crouch Songbook, VIRGIN R 1722 (no date)
Blood Will Never Lose Its Power. Broken Vessel. I Don't Know Why. I Find No Fault in Him. I'm Gonna Keep on Singing. It Won't Be Long. I've Got Confidence. My Tribute. Oh I Need Him. Say a Little Prayer for Me. Through It All. What Makes a Man Turn His Back on God.

Autograph, LIGHT 7115710740 (1986)
All the Way. Can't Nobody Do Me Like Jesus. I Don't Know Why. I Surrender All. It's Not Just a Story. My Tribute. No Pews. Power in the Blood. You Can Depend on Me. You Don't Have to Jump. You Gave to Me. Why.

The Best of Andraé, LIGHT LS 5678 (1975)
Bless His Holy Name. Everything Changed. He Proved His Love. I Came That You Might Have Life. I Didn't Think It Should Be. I Don't Know Why. If Heaven Never Was Promised Me. I'm Coming Home. I'm Gonna Keep on Singing. It Won't Be Long. It's Not Just a Story. Jesus. Jesus Is the Answer. My Tribute. Oh I Need Him. Satisfied. Take a Little Time. That's What It's All About. You Ain't Living.

Classics Vol. 1, LIGHT 7115730601 (reissued 1991)
I Don't Know Why. I'll Be Thinking of You. I'm Gonna Keep on Singing. It Won't Be Long. I've Got Confidence. Jesus Is the Answer. Just Like He Said He Would. My Tribute. Soon and Very Soon. The Sweet Love of Jesus. Take Me Back. Tell Them. They Shall Be Mine. Through It All.

The Contemporary Man, LIGHT 7115730636 (reissued 1993)
All the Way. The Choice. Finally. It Ain't No New Thing. It's Gonna Rain. I've Got the Best. Jesus Is Lord. Let's Worship Him. Lookin' for You. O Saviour. Perfect Peace. Please Come Back. This Is Another Day. You Can Depend on Me.

Finally, LIGHT LC 5784 (1982)
All the Way. Everybody's Got to Know. Finally. He's Waiting. Let's Worship Him. My Tribute. Sweet Communion. That's Why I Need You. We Are Not Ashamed. We Need to Hear from You.

His Best, AVL 620 LoooC (reissued 1991)
Bless His Holy Name. I Surrender All. I'm Gonna Keep on Singing. It Won't Be Long. I've Got Confidence. Jesus Is the Answer. My Tribute. Satisfied. Soon and Very Soon. Take Me Back. This is Another Day. Through It All. I'll Be Thinking of You.

I'll Be Thinking of You, LIGHT 5763 0000C (1979)
Bringin' Back the Sunshine. Dreamin'. I've Got the Best. Jesus Is Love Medley. Lookin' for You. Thinking of You. Touch Me.

Just Andraé, LIGHT LS 5598 o/p (1973)
Bless His Holy Name. Come on Back My Child. God Loves the Country People. If Heaven Never Was Promised Me. In Remembrance. It's Not Just a Story. Lord You've Been Good to Me. Lullaby of the Deceived. That's What It's All About. What Does Jesus Mean to You. You Ain't Living.

Keep on Singing, LIGHT LS 5546 o/p (1971)
Along Came Jesus. I Don't Know Why Jesus Loved Me. I Must Go Away. I'm Coming Home Dear Lord. I'm Gonna Keep on Singing. I've Got Confidence. Jesus. My Tribute. Take a Little Time. What Ya Gonna Do.

Live at Carnegie Hall, LIGHT LC 5602 (1973)
Can't Nobody Do Me Like Jesus. Halleluya. He Looked Beyond My Faults. I Didn't Think It Could Be. I Don't Know Why. It Won't Be Long. Jesus Is the Answer. You Don't Know What You Are Missing.

Live in London, LIGHT LS 5717 0000C (1978)
Bless the Lord. I Just Want to Know You. I Surrender All. If I Was a Tree. I'll Keep Loving You. Just Like He Said He Would. Power in the Blood. Praise God, Praise God. Revive Us Again. Soon and Very Soon. Tell Them. This Is Another Day. Well Done. You Don't Have to Jump. No Pews. You Gave to Me.

Mercy, QWEST 9–45432–4 (1994)
Give It All Back to Me. God Still Loves Me. He's the Light (of the World). The Lord Is My Light. Love Somebody Like Me. Mercy. Nobody Else Like You. Say So. This Is the Lord's Doing (Marvelous). We Love It Here.

More of the Best, LIGHT LC 5795 0000C (1982)
I Just Wanna Know You. I'll Be Thinking of You. It's Gonna Rain. Jesus Is Lord. Please Come Back. Praises. Quiet Times. Soon and Very Soon. The Sweet Love of Jesus. You Shall Be Mine.

No Time to Lose, LIGHT LC 5863 0000 (1984)
Always Remember. Got Me Some Angels. His Truth Still Marches On. Jesus Come Lay
Your Head on Me. Livin' This Kind of Life. No Time to Lose. Oh It Is Jesus. Right Now.
Somebody Somewhere Is Praying.

Soulfully, LIGHT LS 5581 o/p (1972)
Everything Changed. He Proved His Love for Me. I Came That You Might Have Life. It
Won't Be Long. Leave the Devil Alone. Oh I Need Him. Satisfied. Through It All. Try One
More Time. You Don't Know What You Are Missing.

Take Me Back, LIGHT LS 5637 (1974)
I'll Still Love You. It Ain't No New Thing. Just Like He Said He Would. Saviour. Stop and
Give the Saviour a Call. Take Me Back. Tell Them. You Can Depend on Me.

Take the Message Everywhere, LIGHT LS 5504 (1971)
The Blood Will Never Lose Its Power. Broken Vessel. Everywhere. He Never Sleeps. I'll
Never Forget. I've Got It. No Not One. Precious Lord Take My Hand. Wade in the Water.
What Makes a Man Turn His Back on God.

This is Another Day, LIGHT LC 5683 (1976)
All That I Have. The Choice. My Peace I Leave with You. Perfect Peace. Polynesian Praise
Song. Quiet Times. Soon and Very Soon. This Is Another Day. We Expect You. You Gave
to Me.

We Sing Praises, LIGHT 7115730628 (no date)
All That I Have. Bless His Holy Name. Bringin' Back the Sunshine. Dreamin'. I'll Still Love
You. Polynesian Praise Song. Praises. Quiet Times. Sweet Communion. That's Why I
Needed You. Touch Me. We Are Not Ashamed. We Need to Hear from You.

NOTES

1. Lonnie Bunch, *Black Angelenos: The Afro-American in Los Angeles, 1850–1950* (Los Angeles: California Afro-American Museum Foundation, 1988), 10.

2. Ibid., 20–21.

3. See John Caughey and Laura Caughey, *Los Angeles: Biography of a City* (Los Angeles:
University of California Press, 1977) for further discussion on the unique characteristics of
the city of Los Angeles.

4. Though a number of studies have been published on Andraé Crouch and his contributions to gospel music, to my knowledge no one has examined how his career is sym-
bolic or is a reflection of the city of Los Angeles. For studies that include information on
Crouch, see the following: John D. Booth, "The Music of Andraé Crouch and the Disci-
ples" (Master's thesis, The New Orleans Baptist Theological Seminary, 1974); Horace
Clarence Boyer, "Contemporary Gospel Music," *The Black Perspective in Music* 7, no. 1
(Spring 1979): 5–58, and "Crouch, Andraé," in *The New Grove Dictionary of American Music*,
Vol. 1, eds. H. Wiley Hitchcock and Stanley Sadie (London: Macmillan Press, 1986), 549;
Walter Burrell, "The Gospel According to Andraé Crouch," *Ebony* 37, no. 11 (September
1982): 57, 59–60; Andraé Crouch, *Through It All* (Waco: Word, 1974); Sherry Sherrod

DuPree, "Andraé Crouch," in *Biographical Dictionary of African-American, Holiness-Pentecostals, 1880–1990* (Washington, DC: Middle Atlantic Regional Press, 1989), 65; Tony Heilbut, *The Gospel Sound: Good News and Bad Times* (New York: Simon and Schuster, 1971); Hervey and Company, *Andraé Crouch: Biography* (Los Angeles: Hervey and Co., 1992); Lee Hildebrand, "Progressive Gospel Music in California: A Tale of Two Families" (unpublished manuscript, 1993); Keith Bernard Jenkins, "The Rhetoric of Gospel Song: A Content Analysis of the Lyrics of Andraé Crouch" (Ph.D. dissertation, Florida State University, 1990); Ed Ochs, "Andraé Crouch: '. . . they are afraid to make a change,'" *Billboard* 92, no. 39 (27 September 1980): G6, G22; Robert Palmer, "B. B. King/Andraé Crouch Double Bill," *New York Times* (29 June 1986): 63; and Patrick Salvo, "New King of 'Pop Gospel'," *Sepia* 25, no. 12 (December 1976): 50–54.

5. See Boyer, "Crouch, Andraé." Boyer discusses Crouch but also alludes to other gospel singers who have undergone criticism when they incorporated secular elements in their compositions and performances. See Karima Haynes, "The Gospel Controversy: Are the New Songs Too Jazzy and Too Worldly?" *Ebony* 47, no. 5 (March 1992): 76, 78, 80, 82. Haynes and Boyer have gotten similar explanations from other musicians, who express a desire to convey their message to people who would otherwise not listen to religious music. Rejection comes primarily from mainstream black churches. For further discussion on contemporary trends and the secularization of gospel music, see Paul Baker, "The Secularization Dilemma," *Billboard* 92, no. 39 (September 1980): G5, G26; Roxanne Brown, "The Glory of Gospel: Will the Message Be Lost in the Contemporary Sound?" *Ebony* 43, no. 7 (May 1988): 60, 62, 64, 66; Lisa Collins, "Gospel Turns Inward: Finding Success in Secular Markets," *Billboard* 104, no. 15 (1992): 28; Don Light, "Gospel Enters the Mainstream—1967," *Billboard: The World of Gospel Music*, Section 2 (14 October 1967): 8, 45; Edward Morris, "Gospel Meeting Spotlight Need for Secular Strategy," *Billboard* 94, no. 10 (1982): 3, 53; and Jerry Wood, "A Joyful Noise Rises to New Heights," *Billboard* 91, no. 30 (1979): R3, R16.

6. Crouch released an album entitled *Mercy* in 1994. Thus, there was a ten-year span of nonproductivity. See "Mercy . . . Mercy . . . Mercy: It's Andraé Crouch in Full Effect," *L.A. Focus* (5 March 1995): 19, 23. In 1996 Warner Alliance released *Tribute: The Songs of Andrae Crouch*, featuring performances by leading gospel artists (Crouch himself also appears on the album).

7. See Milton C. Sernett, ed., *Afro-American Religious History: A Documentary Witness* (Durham, NC: Duke University Press, 1985), for further discussion on the history of black religion.

8. C. Eric Lincoln, ed., *The Black Experience in Religion*, (Garden City, NY: Anchor Press, 1974), 2.

9. See Booth, "The Music of Andraé Crouch" and Crouch, *Through It All*, for more details; David Urbanski, "The Preacher's Life," *Contemporary Christian Music* 19, no. 8 (February 1997): 24–29.

10. For further discussion of the Azusa Street Revival movement, see Jon Michael Spencer, "The Heavenly Anthem: Holy Ghost Singing in the Primal Pentecostal Revival (1906–1909)," *The Journal of Black Sacred Music* 1, no. 1 (Spring 1987): 1–33; and Horace Clarence Boyer, *How Sweet the Sound: The Golden Age of Gospel.* (Washington, DC: Elliott and Clark Publishing, 1995).

11. Vinson Synan, *The Twentieth Century Pentecostal Explosion: The Exciting Growth of Pentecostal Churches and Charismatic Renewal Movements* (Altamonte, FL: Creation House, 1987), 75–86.

12. Horace Clarence Boyer, "An Analysis of Black Church Music with Examples Drawn from Services in Rochester, New York" (Ph.D. dissertation, The Eastman School of Music, 1973), 3, 155–177.

13. See Eileen Southern, *The Music of Black Americans: A History,* 2nd ed. (New York: W. W. Norton & Co., 1983); and Harry Eskew and Paul Oliver, "Gospel Music" in *The New Grove Dictionary of Music and Musicians,* Vol. 7, ed. Stanley Sadie (London: Macmillan, 1980), 549–559. Southern, Eskew, and Oliver trace some of the practices in the Church of God in Christ (COGIC) and other Pentecostal churches to "shouts" in the "invisible institution."

14. Wyatt Tee Walker, *"Somebody's Calling My Name": Black Sacred Music and Social Change* (Valley Forge, PA: Judson Press, 1979), 17.

15. Michael W. Harris, *The Rise of Gospel Blues: The Music of Thomas Andrew Dorsey in the Urban Church* (New York: Oxford University Press, 1992), 97.

16. Revival movements where such phenomena probably took place include the Great Awakenings of the eighteenth and nineteenth centuries as well as the Los Angeles Azusa Street Revival of 1906–1909.

17. Haynes, "The Gospel Controversy," 76.

18. Jacqueline Cogdell DjeDje, "Gospel Music in the Los Angeles Black Community: A Historical Overview," *Black Music Research Journal* 9, no. 1 (Spring 1989): 35–79.

19. It should be noted that the radio broadcast sponsored by St. Paul Baptist Church and the Echoes of Eden Choir in 1947 preceded that produced by Grace Memorial. See DjeDje, "Gospel Music," and "A Historical Overview of Black Gospel Music in Los Angeles," *Black Music Research Bulletin* 10, no. 1 (Spring 1988): 1–5.

20. Much of this information comes from DjeDje, "Gospel Music," "A Historical Overview," and "Los Angeles Composers of African American Gospel Music: The First Generations," *American Music: A Quarterly Journal Devoted to All Aspects of American Music and Music in America* 11, no. 4 (Winter 1993): 412–457.

21. Bob Doerschuch, "Backstage with Andraé Crouch," *Contemporary Keyboard* (1979): 6–14.

22. Booth, "The Music of Andraé Crouch," 20.

23. Salvo, "New King."

24. Pacoima, a suburb of Los Angeles, is located in the San Fernando Valley.

25. Booth, "The Music of Andraé Crouch," 39.

26. Within the black church, it is not uncommon for people to state that they received gifts (i.e., talents or abilities) or songs during prayer or by the moving of the spirit.

27. Mellonee V. Burnim, "The Black Gospel Tradition: A Complex of Ideology, Aesthetic, and Behavior" in *More Than Dancing: Essays on Afro-American Music and Musicians,* ed. Irene V. Jackson (Westport, CT: Greenwood Press, 1985), 147–167. Burnim describes ideology as the definition of blackness; aesthetics as the affirmation of blackness; and behavior as the demonstration of blackness. She discusses how these three concepts shape and regulate gospel music and move it away from mere music to something deeper. Also see discussion in Pearl Williams-Jones, "Afro-American Gospel Music: A Brief Historical and Analytical Survey (1930–1970)" in *Development of Materials for a One Year Course in African Music for the General Undergraduate Student (Project in African Music),* ed. Vada E. Butcher (Washington: U.S. Department of Health, Education, and Welfare, 1970), 201–219.

28. Williams-Jones, "Afro-American Gospel Music: A Brief," 202. For more details and musical examples on gospel, see Boyer, "Contemporary Gospel" and "A Comparative Analysis of Traditional and Contemporary Gospel Music" in *More Than Dancing: Essays on*

Afro-American Music and Musicians, ed. Irene V. Jackson (Westport, CT: Greenwood Press, 1985), 127–146.

29. Pearl Williams-Jones, "Afro-American Gospel Music: A Crystallization of the Black Aesthetic," *Ethnomusicology* 19, no. 3 (September 1975): 373–386.

30. Jon Michael Spencer, *Black Hymnody: A Hymnological History of the African American Church* (Knoxville: University of Tennessee Press, 1992).

31. Haynes, "The Gospel Controversy," 82.

32. Williams-Jones, "Afro-American Gospel Music: A Brief," 210.

33. See Janice D. Terrell, "The Growth of Contemporary Christian Music in the Last Ten Years (1973–1983)" (M.A. thesis, American University, 1984); and Paul Baker, "Jesus Music: A New Dimension in Pop and Gospel," *Record World* 2 (1 October 1977): 12, 88, 98.

34. Viv Broughton, *Black Gospel: An Illustrated History of the Gospel Sound* (New York: Sterling Publishing Co., 1985), 117.

35. Ibid., 117–118.

36. See Jacqueline Cogdell DjeDje, "Change and Differentiation: The Adoption of Black American Gospel Music in the Catholic Church," *Ethnomusicology* 30, no. 2 (Spring/Summer, 1986): 231–232.

37. Harris, "The Rise of Gospel Blues," 100.

38. Boyer, "Contemporary Gospel Music."

39. Ibid., 23.

40. Further discussion of gospel music characteristics can be found in Boyer, "A Contemporary Gospel Music," and Williams-Jones, "Afro-American Gospel Music: A Brief."

41. Paul Oliver, Max Harrison, and William Bolcom, *The New Grove. Gospel, Blues and Jazz with Spirituals and Ragtime* (New York: W. W. Norton and Co., 1980 [1986]), 195–199.

42. Booth, "The Music of Andraé Crouch."

43. Boyer, "A Comparative Analysis."

44. Light, "Gospel Enters Mainstream."

45. Terrell, "The Growth of Gospel," 121.

46. See Boyer, "An Analysis of Black Church Music," for a discussion on the belief system of fundamentalists.

47. Collins, "Gospel Turns Inward," 28.

48. DjeDje, "Los Angeles Composers," 420–421.

49. Horace Clarence Boyer, "II. Black Gospel Music" in *The New Grove Dictionary of American Music*, Vol. 2, eds. H. Wiley Hitchcock and Stanley Sadie (London: Macmillan Press, 1986), 254–261.

50. Southern, *The Music of Black Americans*, 217.

51. Haynes, "The Gospel Controversy," 80.

52. Jenkins, "The Rhetoric of Gospel Song."

53. See Terrell, "The Growth of Gospel," 11–140. Terrell reports that in 1981, record labels such as Word made a deliberate effort to reach a secular market. One of the ways companies targeted the black community was to put famous black musicians on a "black gospel" label. Crouch was one of the leading candidates at the time.

54. Palmer, "B. B. King/Andraé Crouch."

55. Wyatt Tee Walker, *Spirit that Dwells in the Deep Woods: The Prayer and Praise Hymns of the Black Religious Experience* (New York: Martin Luther King Fellows Press, 1987). See the Appendix at the end of this chapter for a list of the hymnals, songbooks, and recordings where Crouch's songs can be found.

56. Donna McNeil Cox, "Contemporary Trends in the Music Ministry of the Church of God in Christ," *The Journal of Black Sacred Music* 2, no. 2 (Fall 1988): 23–28.

57. Terrell, "The Growth of Gospel," 90.

58. Former musicians in Crouch's band are members of Pentecostal congregations— e.g., Church on the Way in Van Nuys, California, and Calvary Chapel in Costa Mesa, California—that encouraged this approach to worship. Maranatha! began in Calvary Chapel.

59. DjeDje, "Los Angeles Composers," 422.

60. Andraé Crouch, personal communication with author, 30 May 1993, and 2 June 1993. The discussion here is also based on my personal observation of worship services at Christ Memorial COGIC in 1993. It should be noted that Crouch was installed as senior minister of Christ Memorial in September 1995, after the deaths of his father, Benjamin Crouch, and older brother, Benjamin Crouch Jr., in 1994 and early 1995, respectively. In spite of the demands on his time, Crouch indicates that he "does not plan to curtail his music career"; see Jerry Crowe, "Meet *Pastor* Andraé Crouch," *Los Angeles Times* (21 September 1995): F1, F4; and Aldore Collier, "Gospel Star Andraé Crouch Takes Pulpit of Late Father's Church," *Jet* 88, no. 23 (16 October 1995): 32–33, 36–38.

61. Sandra Crouch, personal communication with author, 18 May 1993.

62. The all-white group Sonlight accompanied Crouch during the 1970s. Bill Maxwell of this group has been Crouch's longtime co-producer.

63. See DjeDje, "Los Angeles Composers," 428–429, for a discussion of the role of Specialty Records in the development of gospel in Los Angeles.

64. Hildebrand, "Progressive Gospel." Other writers see Crouch and Hawkins as the leaders of this movement.

65. "Mercy . . . Mercy," 19.

66. Terrell, "The Growth of Gospel".

67. Nat King Cole (1917–1965) was perhaps the first black male singer since Louis Armstrong to attract worldwide recognition. Cole, a popular singer and jazz pianist, was successful in crossing over to white audiences because of his vocal style; see discussion of Cole in Willie R. Collins, "California Rhythm and Blues Recordings, 1942–1972: A Diversity of Styles,"chapter 6 in this volume. Cole's voice is sometimes described as smooth or "liquid" and more accessible to white audiences than the down-home, "earthy" tones associated with most black singers of the period. Cole began to gain popularity in the 1940s and has continued to draw acclaim posthumously. For more information, see Bill and Richard Dobbins, "Cole, Nat 'King'" in *The New Grove Dictionary of American Music and Musicians*, Vol. 1, eds. H. Wiley Hitchcock and Stanley Sadie (London: Macmillan Press, 1986), 466; and Leslie Gourse, *Unforgettable: The Life and Mystique of Nat King Cole* (New York: St. Martin's Press, 1991).

68. Hildebrand, "Progressive Gospel," 17.

69. "Mercy . . . Mercy."

70. Andraé Crouch, personal communication.

71. Boyer, "A Comparative Analysis."

72. This analysis of "Power in the Blood" is based on a discussion in Boyer, "A Comparative Analysis," 137.

73. Dorsey had a very successful career in the secular world before he decided to devote his life entirely to the promotion of gospel music. See Michael W. Harris, "Conflict and Resolution in the Life of Thomas Andrew Dorsey" in *We'll Understand It Better By and By*, ed. Bernice Johnson Reagon (Washington and London: Smithsonian Instituition Press, 1992), 165–182, and "The Rise of Gospel Blues."

74. Crouch, *Through It All*, 25.

75. Salvo, "New King," 51.

76. "Mercy . . . Mercy."

77. Willie J. Jennings, "When Mahalia Sings: The Black Singer of Sacred Song as Icon," *The Journal of Black Sacred Music* 3, no. 1 (Spring 1989): 6–13.

78. Because Crouch's name is known worldwide, many international groups have performed at his father's church.

79. "Mercy . . . Mercy," 19.

80. The sheet music by early gospel composers included only a brief sketch or outline of the melody and chords; see more discussion in DjeDje, "Los Angeles Composers," 422.

81. See music score for "All the Way" in the songbook *Finally: Songs of Andraé Crouch* (Newbury Park, CA: Lexicon Music, Inc., 1982), 53.

82. Motown Records, a black record company formed in 1959 by Berry Gordy, was successful because Gordy made a conscious effort to market black artists and their music to the general white public. Some of Motown's most successful singers gained international acclaim, and black music became entrenched in the popular mainstream. For more information, see Marian Smith Holmes, "Berry Gordy and the Magic That Was Motown," *Smithsonian* 25, no. 7 (1994): 82–96. Also see Kimasi Browne, "Brenda Holloway: Los Angeles's Contribution to Motown," chapter 10 in this volume.

83. For a discussion of the relationship of identity to gospel music, see Jacqueline Cogdell DjeDje, "An Expression of Black Identity: The Use of Gospel Music in a Los Angeles Catholic Church," *The Western Journal of Black Studies* 7, no. 3 (1983): 148–160.

84. Jeremiah A. Wright Jr., "Music as Cultural Expression in Black Church Theology and Worship," *The Journal of Black Sacred Music* 3, no. 1 (Spring 1989): 1–5.

85. Spencer, "Black Hymnody."

86. Broughton, "Black Gospel," 119.

87. See DjeDje, "Los Angeles Composers," 422.

10

Brenda Holloway

Los Angeles's Contribution to Motown

Kimasi L. Browne

A featured solo vocalist during Motown's formative years (c.1964–1968), Brenda Holloway was an anomaly in every realm of her life. A singer, songwriter and instrumentalist, Holloway was viewed as beautiful, outspoken, and a fashion innovator. She was the only female artist among the opening acts on the Beatles' 1965 North American tour. With her producers, Hal Davis and Marc Gordon, she created a new sound, and she was the first West Coast artist to sign with Motown. This signing proved very significant, because in 1972, four years after Holloway quit the music business, Motown moved its entire operation, including many of its major stars, to Southern California.

Holloway's experiences and her contribution to the Motown cultural epic are singular. An irrepressible individual not to be molded, she took a unique approach to her singing, performances, and career. Female singers at Motown were often acquiescent and conformed to the mold fashioned by Berry Gordy Jr., and the star makers at Motown. They were not allowed to compose songs, produce records, or participate in any creative endeavors except singing—and then, only their assigned parts. Ironically, several other Motown singers (for example, Diana Ross, Martha Reeves, Tammi Terrell, and Gladys Knight) went on to become international recording stars and celebrities. Holloway did not reach this plateau. She ended her career after only four years.

The aim of this chapter is to identify the circumstances and issues that caused Holloway to be regarded as special and different, to examine how she achieved this status, and to elaborate on her career as one of the featured artists at Motown. It is not intended to be a biography or comprehensive study of her music. It does not include musical analyses nor a discussion of performance practice. In order to contextualize Holloway's distinctiveness, the chapter will include brief comparison with some of her Motown contemporaries. The primary concerns will be to identify her accomplishments, the factors associated with her ascendance to stardom, and her professional decline and return to private life.[1]

REVIEW OF THE LITERATURE

Although numerous sources on Motown exist,[2] the amount of material on Holloway is minuscule, partly because Holloway has been out of the music industry for more than twenty-five years and partly because she has been overshadowed by other Motown singers. Far less has been written about her than about Diana Ross, Martha Reeves, Tammi Terrell, or Gladys Knight. During the 1960s and 1970s, articles about her appeared in black music publications such as *Soul*.[3] Also, Holloway was frequently seen on television, and her records were regularly played on radio.

Literature about the life and work of Brenda Holloway has appeared primarily in the popular press. No known academic works have discussed her contributions. The available literature is limited but helpful. Writers have examined her from several perspectives, all of them casting her as an anomaly to some extent. Unfortunately, some of these works are speculative and unreliable.

Peter Benjaminson's *The Story of Motown*, the first corporate history of Motown, focuses on Holloway's California origins and her signing with Motown, which differed from all other signings (as I shall describe). He writes that she was an important contributor to the early Motown sound. However, his discussion is only one page long.[4]

Gerri Hirshey's book *Nowhere to Run* mentions Holloway only in passing, usually pairing her with Kim Weston, another Motown singer who was important but didn't have enough hit records to merit extensive national press coverage. Hirshey gives a very thorough overview of soul music and Motown in particular.[5] She provides significant data (five pages' worth) on Mary Wells, who like Holloway was a production prodigy of Smokey Robinson and Gordy. Wells's and Robinson's success helped motivate Holloway to record for Motown.

Where Did Our Love Go: The Rise and Fall of the Motown Sound, by Nelson George, characterizes Holloway as an independent, determined, rebellious, and exotic beauty who pushed her way into Motown and stormed out when things did not go her way. George's discourse, approximately three pages in length, includes a letter Holloway wrote to Gordy articulating the issues surrounding her departure from Motown.[6]

Don Waller's analysis of Holloway is consistent with the popular view of her career. Like George, he is overwhelmed by Holloway's physical features. In *The Motown Story*, which includes five short paragraphs on Holloway, Waller writes, "If good looks could kill, Brenda Holloway would've put half the male population of her native Los Angeles on the critical list. Voluptuous, and with a voice to match, it's not hard to see why she's what you might call a cult figure."[7]

One of the few works to give an insider's perspective on Holloway is Mary Wilson's biography, *Dreamgirl: My Life as a Supreme*. Wilson recounts a near-brawl between Holloway and Diana Ross and confirms that Holloway was a sought-after act when the Supremes were still "wannabes," prior to the group's record-breaking string of five consecutive number-one recordings between 1964 and

1966. Because of Holloway's popularity in early 1964, the Supremes were allowed to accompany Holloway on what would be their first of many national tours.[8]

Sharon Davis's *Motown: The History*, a British historical account of Motown, is quite comprehensive, though not a scholarly work. She includes many facts, details, and photographs on all of the Motown artists; however, her section on Holloway contains inaccuracies. Davis writes, "When Brenda took a day trip to Detroit to audition for Berry Gordy, who was looking for another Mary Wells, he personally signed her to his company."[9] All of the extant literature, including Holloway's personal account, depict a different scenario.[10] In spite of these problems, Davis's coverage (about two pages in length) gives interesting biographical and contextual information on Holloway.

David Bianco's *Heat Wave: The Motown Fact Book* discusses the details of the Motown phenomenon, including salient material on Holloway. This information, quoted in articles about her, amounts to only half of a column; however, his discography provides a useful foundation, even though it is incomplete.[11] Spider Harrison's one-page article "Brenda Holloway: The 'Every Little Bit Hurts' Lady Is Back" includes contextual data about Holloway's Los Angeles life and an account of her "discovery" by Gordy.[12]

The *Penguin Encyclopedia of Popular Music's* entry on Holloway is brief but accurate.[13] In *Soul Music: Who's Who*, Ralph Tee says Holloway's recording "Just Look What You've Done" (1967) is one of the first of a handful of records to shape the face of disco music of the early 1970s.[14] A brief entry on Holloway also appears in the *Guinness Encyclopedia of Popular Music*.[15]

Recent publications also shed light on Holloway's significance. Dennis Hunt's 1994 *Los Angeles Times* article "R&B's Brenda Holloway Still Has a Song to Sing" reintroduces Holloway to Los Angeles readers as a former Motown diva.[16] Berry Gordy's *To Be Loved: The Music, the Magic, the Memories of Motown, An Autobiography* verifies Holloway's importance to Motown's efforts to enter the white record-buying market. Gordy's discussion corroborates her pivotal role in the initial success of the Supremes.[17] His work also serves as a reliable source for contextual material on the evolution of Motown. A special record-industry salute to Gordy[18] includes the article "Gordy Speaks: The Billboard Interview" by Adam White.[19] The other articles in *Billboard*[20] address specific issues regarding Motown's development and Gordy's innovations and contributions. Holloway is mentioned as co-writer (with Gordy) of the song "You've Made Me So Very Happy."[21]

However, there remain few comprehensive sources on Brenda Holloway. To fill this gap, I conducted a series of personal and telephone interviews with Holloway, two in July 1993 and one each in November 1993 and January and March 1994. The preponderance of information herein is taken from these interviews.[22]

Works that discuss the musical aspects of soul music are also few in number. In his article, "Soul: A Historical Reconstruction of Continuity and Change in Black Popular Music," Robert Stephens not only examines Motown as a dominant force in the panorama of African-American popular music but also discusses how the music is eclectic and defiant, resisting standardization.[23] The genre of soul music is defined by Portia Maultsby in her articles "A Healthy Diversity Evolves from Creative Freedom" and "Soul Music: Its Sociological and Political Significance in American Popular Culture."[24] Her works have been used to establish an understanding of the relationship between the historical development of soul music and the larger social, political, and cultural themes embedded within it.[25]

MOTOWN

The term "Motown" refers to two phenomena. One is the Motown Record Corporation, started in Detroit, Michigan, in 1959 by Berry Gordy Jr., an African-American man born in Detroit in 1929. An $800 loan allowed him to build one of the most successful independent, black-owned record companies in history. Before he started Motown, Gordy worked as a jazz record-store owner, door-to-door cookware salesman, prizefighter, and Lincoln-Mercury assembly plant worker. Also, he co-wrote and produced hit records for rhythm and blues singers Jackie Wilson ("Reet Petite" 1957, "To Be Loved" 1957, and "Lonely Teardrops," 1958) and Marv Johnson ("You've Got What It Takes" 1959). "Reet Petite," Gordy's first song to be recorded and released, was a pop hit. Wilson states, " 'Reet Petite' was my first record. It never even charted on the R&B charts. It went pop and sold a quarter of a million. 'To Be Loved' was my first R&B chart-song."[26] Gordy was also responsible for Wilson's first national number-one pop hit recording, "Lonely Teardrops."

Gordy's greatest success came when he signed teenagers from the inner city of Detroit, first to the Tamla record label and later to the Motown, Gordy, V.I.P. and Soul labels. After a four-year period, these teens began to have consistent hits on the national record charts: Barrett Strong ("Money" 1959), the Miracles, featuring Smokey Robinson ("Shop Around" 1960, "You've Really Got a Hold on Me" 1963), the Marvelettes ("Please Mr. Postman" 1961, "Playboy" 1962), Mary Wells ("Two Lovers" 1962, "You Beat Me to the Punch" 1962), the Contours ("Do You Love Me" 1962), Little Stevie Wonder ("Fingertips, Part. 2" 1963), Marvin Gaye ("Stubborn Kind of Fellow" 1962, "Pride and Joy" 1963), and Martha and the Vandellas ("Heat Wave" 1963, "Quicksand" 1963).[27]

The term "Motown" also refers to the sound or musical characteristics associated with Gordy's company in the early 1960s. The Motown sound was a composite of 1950s rhythm and blues, soul, gospel, and Euro-American popular music. Detroit musicians, writers, producers, arrangers, and singers developed the sound in a small group of brick two-story bungalows[28] where Woodrow Wilson Avenue meets West Grand Boulevard. One of the buildings that housed the recording studios was open and operated twenty-four hours a day, seven days a week. A sign that still hangs outside on the converted house reads: "Hitsville, U.S.A."

Mikal Gilmore and Robert Witmer state that the Motown sound differed from the music of other regional centers of black popular music, such as Chicago, Memphis, and New York, in its greater reliance on conventions of mainstream Anglo-American urban popular music (such as sophisticated arrangements with large studio orchestras, usually including strings) and a muting of the more vigorous characteristics of African-American music and performance. The lyrics were of broader appeal and couched in less esoteric imagery than those of other black styles.[29] As a black genre, Motown has been singled out because of its widespread acceptance among whites.[30]

However, the characteristics that distinguish black music are also present in the Motown sound. Features such as call-and-response, offbeat rhythmic patterns, constant metronomic pulse, relaxed vocal styles, diatonic scales with lowered third, fifth, and seventh tones (blue notes), and melodic elements derived from spirituals, blues, jazz, and gospel can be heard on most Motown recordings. Even when non-Motown artists perform Motown songs with completely new arrangements and productions, these elements are still present in the music.[31]

Motown established a regional genre that Gordy labeled "The Detroit Sound" and "The Sound of Young America" (he registered these slogans as trademarks of the Motown Record Corporation). The Detroit sound differed from black popular music produced in other regions of the country during the 1960s. Stax Records produced a "Memphis" sound that was more closely associated with black folk culture.[32] This music typically featured a basic rhythm section with a sparse sound built around the Hammond B-3 electric organ used in black gospel music, as well as horn arrangements built on harmonies resembling those used by gospel choirs and lead vocalists, who sang in a raspy, preaching style. Singers often fused the mournful, wailing qualities of the blues (slides, hollers, whoops, and screams). The Memphis sound was considered to be "dry" because a minimum of echo was placed on the lead vocal, whereas the Motown sound was a "wet" sound—sophisticated, elegant, and more closely aligned with the mainstream sounds such as those produced in New York's Brill Building.[33]

Stax's roster included producers Isaac Hayes and David Porter and artists Rufus Thomas, Johnny Taylor, Carla Thomas, Eddie Floyd, Booker T and the MGs, the Staple Singers, Otis Redding, and Sam and Dave. Ironically, Stax was owned by Jim Stewart, who was white, as were the principal guitar player, Steve Cropper, and bass player, Donald "Duck" Dunn, whose playing contributed to the distinctiveness of the Stax sound. Al Bell joined the staff and eventually became chair of the board and part-owner of the company.[34] Stax is important because it appealed to the masses of African Americans and was Motown's most competitive rival for black audiences and mainstream listeners who preferred "authentic black music." Whereas Stax's Stewart sought an exclusively black audience, Motown's Berry Gordy had a vision of breaking down stereotypical barriers, especially on national television.

In the 1960s there were several regional strains of soul music and other labels that competed with Motown for the ears and dollars of black America. These included but were not limited to New York's Atlantic Records (Aretha Franklin and Wilson Pickett), Chicago's Chess Records (Billy Stewart, Jackie Ross), the Okeh label of CBS (Major Lance), Constellation Records (Gene Chandler), and Vee Jay Records (Betty Everett, Jerry Butler, and the Four Seasons).[35] James Brown, from Augusta, Georgia, was the quintessential soul artist of the era; he recorded for Cincinnati's King Records and, later, for Polydor.

Several record companies whose artists went on to have national hits were influential in the Los Angeles soul music market. Among these were Money Records (Don Julian and the Larks' "The Jerk," Bettye Swann's "Don't Wait Too Long" and "What Can It Be?" and Mary Love's "Turn My Bitter Into Sweet"). Swann later had a national number-one pop hit, "Don't Touch Me" (1969), on Capitol Records. Major mainstream labels who recorded black groups and became Hollywood institutions include Liberty Records (Ike and Tina Turner), ABC-Paramount Records (The Impressions and Ray Charles), and RCA Victor Records (Sam Cooke). Before signing with Motown, Brenda Holloway released records in Los Angeles on the Brevit, Catch, Donna/Delphi, Minasa, and Snap labels.

In spite of this competition in the music industry, Motown was unique among both black and white record companies largely because Gordy did not limit his creative vision. He wanted Motown songs and recording artists on Broadway, in movies, and in nightclubs.[36] Motown went on to crash social barriers and defy categorization. As Thomas Bowles puts it, "There are three names that are instantly recognizable the world over—Mickey Mouse, Coca-Cola and Motown."[37] Gordy sold Motown in 1988 to MCA but retained the publishing arm, Jobete Music, Inc., which controls the Motown song catalog. The record company was subsequently sold in 1993 to Polygram, the British music conglomerate. In 1995, Andre Harrell was appointed CEO. Harrell decided to move the business operations of Motown to New York City, where he is based, marking the end of more than twenty years in Los Angeles for the company.[38]

Robert Witmer and Anthony Marks summarize Motown's formula for success:

> Producers and writers such as Norman Whitfield, Smokey Robinson, and the Holland-Dozier-Holland team created a sophisticated form of "pop-soul," which blended the mannerisms and emotion of soul with the bright attractiveness of mainstream pop. Recordings by Diana Ross and the Supremes, the Jackson Five, and the Temptations were among the most successful in the 1960s. The company remains successful, although the strident arrangements and reverent offbeats that made the Motown sound distinctive are no longer company hallmarks.[39]

LOS ANGELES

Los Angeles has played a significant role not only in Brenda Holloway's career but also in the history of Motown. Although Holloway was born in Atascadero, a small town in Central California near San Luis Obispo, she was raised and educated in Los Angeles. It was here that she received her musical training, first heard the Motown sound, was discovered by Berry Gordy Jr., and signed her Motown contract. Her initial hit records, which were recorded in Los Angeles, laid the foundation for Motown's West Coast sound. Many of the hits of the seventies and eighties, including records by the Jackson Five, the Commodores, High Energy, Rick James, Teena Marie, and Diana Ross, were recorded in Motown's Hitsville studio on Poinsettia Avenue in West Hollywood. Motown's presence on the West Coast adds to the illustrious two-hundred-year history of blacks in the City of Angels. Although the first settlement of blacks in Los Angeles dates to the eighteenth century, I will focus here on developments that occurred in the Watts section of South Central Los Angeles from the 1900s to the 1960s, for it is this period that relates to the topic of discussion.

Watts was established during Los Angeles's "Golden Era." It was attractive to blacks because of its inexpensive housing, which was deemed undesirable by whites in the community. By the mid-1920s African Americans were such an important factor in Watts that many white citizens, including members of the Ku Klux Klan, feared it would become a black town; some residents of Los Angeles called the area "Nigger Heaven." To avoid the possibility of having to contend with an African-American mayor, or at least with black political influence, whites convinced the city of Los Angeles to annex Watts.[40]

This annexation was followed by waves of migration from the thirties to the sixties, which brought the black population of Los Angeles to 650,000. Racism and housing discrimination forced thousands of blacks to concentrate in small sections of Los Angeles, where there were not enough jobs and little space to live comfortably. These conditions, which resembled those facing blacks in other urban centers in the United States, led to the civil disturbance in Watts. Erupting on August 11, 1965, the unrest left 34 people dead, 1,032 wounded, and 3,952 arrested, with millions of dollars in property damage.[41]

Prior to the 1900s, much of the music performed by black Angelenos was imitative of Euro-American traditions. This changed to some extent during the Golden Era, when major jazz and blues stars visited the city to perform in the many nightclubs that lined Central Avenue, the thriving hub of black life.[42] When large numbers of African Americans migrated to Los Angeles during the 1930s and 1940s, even more changes began to take place, as migrants introduced new sacred and secular musical tastes. These audiences demanded music dominated by African features rather than by the Euro-American elements that had been prominent in local black music. Black musicians in Los Angeles thus began to produce their own music. In some instances, especially in black churches, musicians were invited to the city to meet the demand.[43]

In spite of these changes, a European aesthetic continued to permeate the music in the city; a "clean Los Angeles sound" had developed. This trait was apparent not only in West Coast jazz, which came into existence during the 1950s, but also in some black churches. For example, the worship experience of middle-class blacks who belonged to African Methodist Episcopal (AME) and Presbyterian churches did not change.[44]

The fifties were also the years in which Los Angeles emerged as the nation's primary media center. The glamour of Hollywood and the television industry lured migrants seeking fame and entertainment, establishing Los Angeles as an international city and making blacks and whites "special" just for living there. As opportunities opened for blacks to perform, those outside their community began to patronize the music, causing the audience for black music to expand into the millions. Because Los Angeles served as the center of the record industry, it became a model for outsiders. Whereas styles created during the thirties and forties were brought in by traveling musicians, by the late 1940s and early 1950s Los Angeles recording artists began to set the trends followed by the nation, and musical activity that once occurred in other regions now began to take place in Los Angeles.[45]

BRENDA HOLLOWAY

Childhood and Music Training

Brenda Holloway was born on June 26, 1946. In 1948 her parents, Wade and Johnnie Mae Holloway, moved with Brenda and her infant brother, Wade Jr., to Watts. Her sister, Patrice, was born there three years later. The Holloways lived in a modest home on Bandera Street between 92nd and 97th Streets. It was in this neighborhood that Simon Rodia built the now-world-famous Watts Towers, at 109th Street and Wilmington Avenue. Growing up, Holloway used to see Rodia at work: "As children, we used to watch this little man, Simon Rodia, while he was erecting the Watts Towers. We laughed at him and said, 'Oh God, what is this little junk man doing, collecting all that broken glass and bottles and junk?' After the towers were finished, we knew we had a genius among us."[46]

Music played a pivotal role in Holloway's childhood. She always loved music, because it had an effect on her and on other people through her. She began playing violin at seven years old and later became accomplished on viola, cello, string bass, and flute. Holloway became fluent on flute and was gifted on the piano. She was also a talented composer; she could hear a melody in her mind and sit down to the piano and create an accompaniment even though she was not trained in piano.[47]

Holloway was an anomaly in a community whose musical devotion was divided among gospel, spirituals, blues, rhythm and blues, and other styles. She was one of the few who loved classical (European art) music: "As far back as I can remember, I've always loved music. I always loved to hear Gypsy violin played. I had a sound like a Gypsy. A lot of people loved that sound. I just loved classical music, Mozart, and Beethoven."[48]

She received little support for her talents from people in her neighborhood, which comprised poor and working-class families. Unlike most of the children in

her community, who shunned homework and congregated on the streets to talk
and play with each other, Holloway played music for hours each day after school.
She was serious about her "instrument time": "I would go into the backyard and
I'd practice my violin. All the neighbors would shout, 'Oh, please make her stop!'
The dogs would be barking, because they would throw me out of the house.
They'd say, 'This black girl playing a violin in the ghetto? You're not real!' But I
just kept on, because that's what I wanted. . . . I always was a loner."[49]

During her childhood, Holloway performed several styles of music, including
jazz. She recalls, "I had a jazz group and I played the upright bass, which was very
funny and comical because I was so little. I was playing that big, big bass, and I
had to have someone carry it to the concerts for me, because it was so big."[50]

Because Holloway excelled as a musician, she was involved with several music
organizations. She performed violin in second grade in the 92nd Street Elementary School orchestra, viola in the Markham Junior High School orchestra, flute
in the Markham marching band, and cello in the Jordan High School orchestra.
When she was fifteen years old and in tenth grade, she was singled out by her orchestra conductor, Mr. Jamison, who told her she was gifted and urged her to
study violin at the University of Southern California (USC) Conservatory of
Music. He went to Watts on Saturdays and drove her to USC. This exposure
helped to mold her view of herself, and she began to understand how she fit in her
environment. After her Saturday studies at USC, she says, "I was full. I went home
and listened to Mozart and Beethoven. I was thinking, 'I can get out of the ghetto.
I don't have to stay here! If I can practice hard enough, I can get out of here.'
That was my goal, and I did."[51]

In addition to her school music ensembles, Holloway performed in the sacred
orchestra at Zion Hill Baptist Church, the Los Angeles High School orchestra,
and the Southern California Symphony. The latter meant the most to her. "When
they auditioned five hundred people for this orchestra, they had to narrow it down
to 150. Only seven out of the 150 were black. I was one of the black violinists. That
was one of the most tremendously beautifully put-together orchestras that I have
ever played in."[52]

As impressive as Holloway was as an instrumentalist, it was her singing that
made her famous. As a child, she sang to get attention. In addition to singing to
her mother, she sang to insurance salesmen and bill collectors, anyone who would
listen. As she grew older, she sang while washing dishes or mopping the kitchen
floor. Holloway's mother often compared her to her sister, Patrice, referring to
Patrice as "pretty" and Brenda as a "good singer." She made her first public performance as a singer at Bright Star Baptist Church[53] on Pace Avenue and 92nd
Street in Watts when she was twelve years old. A neighbor, Mrs. Black, was on her
way to church one day and asked Holloway if she would like to attend church with
her. Once in church and moved by the impassioned singing, Holloway asked if she
could sing a solo: "I went with Mrs. Black to church, I asked her can I sing. I was

about eleven or twelve. The people loved me. . . . I think I sang 'Precious Lord.' That was the first I ever remember singing in public."[54]

Holloway also sang in neighborhood Pentecostal and Apostolic churches[55] and in the choir at her own St. John Methodist Church, which stood on Wilmington Avenue at 97th Street, just around the corner from her home. Unlike churches in the African Methodist Episcopal and African Methodist Episcopal Zion (AME Zion) denominations, St. John had been established by whites before blacks moved into the area. When the racial makeup of the neighborhood changed, St. John's congregation became black, but its denominational affiliation and order of service were governed by the white Methodist church. Thus, the worship experience tended to be solemn, restrained, and nearly emotionless. The music was precisely arranged, with little variation; most songs were taken from the Methodist hymnal or the European art music sacred repertoire.

Although the music performed at St. John was not entirely reflective of the community that lived in Watts during the fifties and sixties, this church experience greatly influenced Holloway: this is where she began her classical voice training. She occasionally performed solos (what she calls "fill-ins") in the choir and regularly sang in the tenor and alto sections. The repertoire included performances of large classical works such as George F. Handel's oratorio *The Messiah*.

As a teenager, Holloway listened to records by the Miracles and Mary Wells and dreamed of the day when she would become a recording artist on Motown Records. Although her dream seemed far-fetched, many of the activities in which she participated seemed to prepare her for a career in popular commercial music. In addition to singing in her high school chorus, she performed with a group that included Walter and Wallace Scott, who later joined the Whispers. The students would pay to hear them sing at lunchtime.[56]

In high school she became a professional singer, forming a group called the Wattesians (for Watts).[57] The group consisted of Priscilla Kennedy, Barbara Williams, Pat Hunt, Holloway, and her sister, Patrice, who was about eleven or twelve years old. Eventually Brenda Holloway became part of a small network of singers who were regularly called to do session work in Hollywood and other Los Angeles–area recording studios. She sang background vocals for such legends as Sam Cooke, Bobby Womack, Ray Charles, Ike and Tina Turner, Barry White, Merry Clayton, Joe Cocker, Mac Davis, Johnny Rivers, Darlene Love, the Blossoms, Edna Wright, and Gloria Jones; she also sang background on Patrice's record, "The Del Viking" (recorded when Patrice was twelve). In addition, Holloway made several records (released on Minasa Records) as part of the duet Hal and Brenda.[58]

Holloway's schedule was hectic and atypical for a teenager. Most of her high school peers did not work, and those who did often worked part-time in a neighborhood store. Holloway not only worked nearly every day but also toured locally with her sister, Patrice. She would record after school until six or seven in the evening, go home, sleep, and then go to a session at midnight and record until six the next morning before she went to school.[59] Hunter Hancock, a white disc jockey on radio station KGFJ-AM (which catered to black listeners in Los Angeles), sponsored record hops and often brought artists to the black high school gymnasiums, Hancock was very influential in the careers of up-and-coming local acts. Patrice Holloway was regularly booked at these hops to promote "The Del Viking." Brenda was one of her backup singers and "go-go" dancers.

> Hunter Hancock was not a guy that was prejudiced. He played black music and he broke black songs in the L.A. area. He was an instrument that was used to promote black artists in that day. His record hops would be for black audiences. He was so popular [that] if he played your record consistently, he could make it a hit. There was a black guy by the name of Herman Griffith, also on KGFJ at night. If those two played your songs, you would have a hit.[60]

Even while gaining professional singing experience, Holloway continued her formal music education. She studied with Donna Williams, a private vocal coach, who taught her how to control pitch, sustain tone, manipulate melismas, breathe (i.e., sing from the diaphragm and control air dispersal), and care for and maintain her vocal apparatus. After graduating from Jordan High School, Holloway enrolled in the music program at Compton Community College, where she received training that reinforced what she had learned from Williams, skills that helped to prepare her for the demanding singing career that was to come.

Career

"When I was in Watts," Holloway recalls, "I said, 'Mom I'm going to be on Motown. I'm going to get on Motown Records.' She said, 'Sure you are. You're three thousand miles away, you're in Watts, and Motown is in Detroit. Think about that, Brenda.' I said, 'I am! I'm going to be on Motown.' And I was, I was their first West Coast artist.[61]

All of the events in Holloway's life—her desire to be famous, her love for classical music, her musical training, her stage work, her professional recording experience—helped to prepare her for a career as an entertainer. However, certain experiences were more prominent than others. For example, her relationship with Hal Davis,[62] her manager/producer and former recording partner, was especially important because he was responsible for her eventual meeting with Gordy. Through a business connection, Davis was able to gain admission to a disc jockey convention in the posh Coconut Grove of the Ambassador Hotel in Los Angeles's Miracle Mile district on Wilshire Boulevard. Davis took Holloway there with the express purpose of meeting Gordy, who was expected to be attending the convention:

> The convention was held in 1963 at the Coconut Grove. Hal told me I was going to go down there. He said, "It might not be possible for you to meet Berry, but what I want you to do is dress up in that sexy pants suit and look your best and sing." So I went there and sang Mary Wells's song, "My Guy."[63] Everybody said, "Listen to that

girl; she can sing!" I sang from ten in the morning until almost four. I was seventeen years old, and I didn't get tired. I kept on telling everybody, "I want to meet Berry Gordy. I don't [know] if he's here." Hal Davis got back to me and said, "Berry's here, but I don't know where, just keep singing."

Later, I was talking to this gentleman. I said, "You know, I'm getting tired, because I'm supposed to be singing for Berry Gordy. I wish he would hurry up and come." He left. After about forty minutes, he came back and said, "I like the way you sing." I said, "I'm glad that you like the way I sing, but I'm supposed to be here to sing for Berry Gordy." He said, "I am Berry Gordy." I said, "You're Berry Gordy!" I almost went through the floor.[64]

Holloway states that she waited for Gordy's response then and there, wondering if he liked her enough to sign her to Motown. She tried to be poised and not show her impatience. Then, Gordy said the words she had dreamed of hearing: "He said, 'I like you, and I want to sign you up.' I got on the phone, and I said, 'Call my mother, call my mom. Tell her to come, to put on the best clothes she has and let's sign this contract.'"[65]

Holloway was in her senior year in high school when she met Gordy and somewhat naive about the music business. "He mentioned a contract, but told me that I wouldn't be able to perform until I completed high school. When he said, 'contract,' I wasn't thinking about consulting a lawyer, a doctor, nobody! As long as it was Berry offering it, I said, 'Sign me up today,' and Berry Gordy did."[66]

In collaboration with Marc Gordon,[67] Davis produced Holloway's first Motown recording, "Every Little Bit Hurts" (1964), a song Holloway did not want to record. She cried throughout the session because she felt the final record should be released by Barbara Wilson, the singer who sang on the demonstration tape.[68] This mood and behavior became a pattern for all of Holloway's future recording sessions: "On all of my slow songs, I would think about a lot of the problems that were going on in my life. I was always sad. It was a way for me to release. I could vent my feelings on wax. I never went into the studio happy. I didn't want to cut 'Every Little Bit Hurts.' I was very, very upset."[69]

"Every Little Bit Hurts" was recorded at Armand Steiner Recording Studio on Highland Avenue between Sunset Boulevard and Melrose Avenue in Hollywood. The song's composer, Ed Cobb, was a member of the Four Preps, a pop harmony group.[70] Davis and Gordon used Four Preps pianist Lincoln Mayorga on Holloway's sessions. At the time Cobbs composed "Every Little Bit Hurts," he was developing a cross-cultural sound, which, Holloway says, distinguished Cobb from other songwriters of that time: "He came up with a totally different sound. It was more R & B than the R & B people, and black people are supposed to be the rhythm nation, right? He did not fit the regular mold of a white writer. [His lyrics were] so thoughtful."[71]

Holloway was enrolled at Compton College when "Every Little Bit Hurts" hit the charts. According to Spider Harrison, "By the time Holloway first heard the single on the radio, it was already a huge hit on the East Coast."[72] Holloway recalls, "The whole thing happened so fast and it was somewhat frightening."[73] When the record became a national hit, Dick Clark called Detroit to ask Motown if Holloway could tour with his "Caravan of Stars." Being an ingenious business-man, Gordy had his sister, Esther Edwards, convince Clark's assistant, Roz Ross, to allow the Supremes to go on the tour with Holloway.[74] "Every Little Bit Hurts" was Motown's hottest new release at the time. Barney Ales, Motown's sales execu-tive, telephoned Gordy from Chicago: "Brenda's record is out there kickin' ass. . . . Chicago came in for another five thousand on Brenda. . . . We're hot, my man."[75] Motown told Clark's office, "If you want Brenda Holloway, you're going to have to take the Supremes."[76] This was before the Supremes had any million-selling records. In her memoirs, Diana Ross writes:

> "Where Did Our Love Go" wasn't scheduled to be released until sometime in the summer. In the meantime, they had booked us on a tour called "Dick Clark's Cara-van of Stars." We were only twenty years old at the time, and we desperately wanted to be included. There were so many big names, and we wanted to be among them. Somehow, Berry Gordy succeeded in booking us on that tour, but we were not men-tioned separately in any of the press releases. The ads read, "Gene Pitney! The Shirelles! Brenda Holloway! and Others!" That was us—"Others."[77]

Mary Wilson recalls a business meeting in which Esther Edwards told her, "Motown managed to get you [the Supremes] on the Dick Clark tour only be-cause he wanted Brenda Holloway. I told him to take you too, and he agreed."[78]

On that first tour, Holloway discovered she was different from the other ladies at Motown: she was treated like a "West Coast" girl by the "East Coast" girls. They did not understand why Holloway, with only one hit and no road experience, had re-ceived top billing when they had worked so hard. Holloway's excitement about her new stardom came to a grinding halt when she nearly came to blows with Diana Ross during the "Caravan of Stars" tour over a can of hair spray. Mary Wilson writes of the episode: "Brenda Holloway and Diane were getting along fine on this trip until Diane insisted that Brenda had stolen her can of hair spray. Brenda denied the charge, but the two of them went back and forth about it until the Shirelles came to Brenda's defense, confirming that Brenda had the same can of spray since the tour started."[79] Holloway's own recollection conveys her indignation:

> I had my wig all fixed and I needed some spray. Diane had the spray and it was my spray. Just because she was Diane, or because she was older, she didn't feel like I was supposed to use it. I said, "Well, that's my spray." We really got into a big problem, and we almost got into blows about that, because that was mine. We were going to fight over a can of hair spray. Shirley of the Shirelles settled it. She said, "Well, if you bother Brenda, then I'm going to bother you. You'd better give her that spray." She did. Nothing else like that happened anymore. They were just going to take advan-tage of me because I was younger than everybody.[80]

Discord became familiar to Holloway. When she traveled to Detroit to record, she often stayed for months at a time, but she never settled there, continuing to live in Los Angeles. In Detroit she gained a reputation for being hard to get along with. "Holloway was labeled as a troublemaker because she was outspoken on occasions. This put a strain on her working relationship with writers and producers, like Holland, Dozier and Holland."[81] When she commuted to Detroit to record, there was routine dissonance. She was looking for a certain sound and did not want the Motown producers to shape her. She was perceived as temperamental, as having an attitude that boasted, "I can do my own thing." Yet she was anything but arrogant. Upon meeting other Motown performers, she was as star-struck as any fan: "When I went to Motown, it was like Disneyland to me. Even though I was an artist and a part of the family, I was saying, 'Oh wow, Mary Wells! Smokey Robinson! I was just grasping for breath. Stevie Wonder! *I* am with *this* family?' "[82]

In time, Holloway's classical training and musicianship set her apart from her Motown compatriots. She inspired jealousy because of her ability to play different instruments. Once, when Holloway was an opening act for the Temptations, she had just finished performing on her violin and was receiving a series of standing ovations when David Ruffin of the Temptations told her not to go back out on stage again. She didn't, until someone else encouraged her to go out and acknowledge her audience. Holloway feels this was typical of her experiences with some of her Motown peers. "It seemed like I was a threat to them because I was a different type of act. I was different, and I think that they saw my potential even more than I saw my potential. I was with five men, just one single woman with a violin. They probably felt that after a while I wouldn't be starting their shows; they would be starting mine."[83] Holloway told Davis, "I came from a different cultural background from the others—I liked to play the violin and cello—it made me appear strange to them."[84]

Many, but certainly not all, members of the Motown family came from impoverished backgrounds. The Supremes, the Temptations, Martha Reeves, Stevie Wonder, and others spent their earliest years in poor, crowded black ghettos. Even Berry Gordy's family was on welfare for a short time.[85] Hunger for a better life and fear of returning to poverty were two of the key motivating factors that inspired the creativity of Motown artists and drove them to succeed. Ross writes: "Rats, roaches, guts and love. That was how Berry Gordy described Motown in the early days. He was talking about the nitty-gritty of life. Creating Motown and making it a success was a massive undertaking, a bold dream, a courageous vision. And Berry Gordy had what it took to do it."[86]

According to Holloway, the people at Motown believed she was in a different class; they never regarded her as poor, even though she came from a black inner-city environment, as they had. However, Holloway saw her own family as middle class, not lower class. Prior to the Watts rebellion, poverty in California did not necessarily include rats, roaches, tenements, and squalor as it did in older, neglected areas of the rural South and urban North. Poverty in California more closely resembled middle-class life in other U.S. cities. Los Angeles's black ghetto was relatively clean. Though it had become crowded as a result of the migrations of the early 1960s, most people lived in one- or two-story dwellings, whereas in the East many of the poor lived in high rise tenements. The projects that housed many of the low-income families in Los Angeles's black community were also different from their eastern counterparts. In the early 1960s, the Los Angeles Housing Authority maintained the buildings and grounds. The units were thoughtfully designed and had ample living space, colorful shrubbery, front and back yards, centralized playgrounds, and recreation centers. The exteriors and interiors were painted at reasonable and regular intervals; the lawns were cut on a biweekly basis, and the shrubs were regularly trimmed. The dwellings were relatively safe environments for families with small children. There was very little crime in those days.[87] Holloway was poor but not lower class: "Even though I came from the ghetto, I did not have a 'poverty stricken' story. I was never really poor. I always had clothes, my mother always owned a house, we were never in the projects. We were just middle-class poor people. It was just a step above poverty. I was [from] another class, and they [other Motown artists] were not quite ready for that."[88]

Holloway's career at Motown was distinct in other ways as well. She brought her classical training with her. Although she was one of several Motown artists who had been classically trained as a vocalist,[89] Holloway was the only one who also performed as an instrumentalist. She was possibly one of the few entertainers in the United States to include classical violin in a pop music stage act. Holloway's musicianship influenced the way she approached her career. She would practice the same song for hours and hours until she felt it was correct.

> I would practice songs for over a week. I would get it perfectly. My skills for practicing and perfecting and being precise and diction from my classical background, I brought different skills. I never got tired, and I never wanted to do anything else. That's all I had done in my classical background, is practice. That's all I did in Watts. I practiced in the yard, I practiced in my bedroom, I practiced in the bathroom, I practiced at school, and on Saturday, that was my pattern.[90]

Holloway's performance style also distinguished her from other black female singers of the 1960s. She expressed and enunciated her words clearly, which was important in soul music because so much emphasis was placed on the lyrics. Although Holloway did not sing "message songs," she interpreted Smokey Robinson's[91] lyrics with remarkable precision.

After her tapes were recorded, Holloway states, Gordy would have Detroit-area Motown artists peruse them because her diction was so good. Marvin Gaye and Diana Ross were two of the singers who benefited from studying her tapes.[92] Says Holloway, "Diane was unique. She studied me. There were things I picked up from Mary Wells. I couldn't be Mary Wells, even though I gleaned a lot from her,

I still had my own sound. So, no matter how much Diana Ross studied me, she could never be me, and I could never be her. I was honored that she would even accept Berry's advice to study my tapes."[93] However, in 1988 Holloway told Sharon Davis that the imitation (or adaptation) of her sound left her feeling exploited: "They let the Supremes study my tapes and take songs from me."[94]

According to Holloway, before she signed with Motown, little attention was given to fashion or costumes for the artists.[95] In the early sixties, Motown was a small, struggling company. Money was reinvested in equipment, distribution, radio airplay, advertising, and recording. The budget for fashion was perfunctory. Holloway had no personal interest in fashion. However, her mother, Johnnie Mae Holloway, had a flair for what looked good on her daughter and zealously enjoyed shopping for her and dressing her. In 1964, Brenda Holloway was considered the most glamorous female act at Motown. "Fashion separated us. After all, I was coming from the glamour capitol. I wore more advanced stage clothes. The others copied my wardrobe. The clothes I wore were expensive, and they had no money in those days. Motown was just beginning to hit and they had not started spending money on costumes."[96]

Holloway's mother arranged for her to have access to a local dress shop, which developed into a very beneficial situation. She could go into Roxie's Unique Dress Shop on the corner of Compton Boulevard and El Segundo Boulevard in Compton and select anything off the rack. The proprietor used Holloway to advertise the establishment; in return, Holloway was given carte blanche and her own fashion designer. Anything not in stock would be special-ordered so that her apparel would be perfect from head to toe. Holloway believes she brought big-city fashion to Motown: "When I got to Motown, they were shocked because I was a star amongst stars, because I dressed as a star. They didn't have the funds to go out and purchase any and everything, as I did. California clothes hadn't even been seen in Detroit."[97]

As the most visible and, arguably, the most successful of the Motown artists, Diana Ross is the archetypal example of the pop music woman of fashion. Ross studied fashion design and costume illustration at Cass Technical High School in Detroit. She designed the costumes and styled hair for the Supremes from the beginning of their career until they became stars. However, her sense of world-class fashion seemed largely undeveloped in early Motown publicity photographs and album covers. On the Supremes' *Where Did Our Love Go* (1964) album cover, members of the group are wearing plain green sleeveless dresses. It was not until their *I Hear a Symphony* (1966) album cover that the famous glamour-girl image begins to surface. Nonetheless, when the Motown story is told, it is the Supremes, and Diana Ross in particular, who emerge as the purveyors of fashion.

Yet it was Holloway who initially acquainted Ross with California fashion. After returning from the Dick Clark 1964 tour, Holloway took Ross to the shops in Hollywood. Holloway even took Ross to her hairdresser in the Manchester district of Los Angeles.[98] It was on Holloway's *Every Little Bit Hurts* (1964) album cover that the glamorous Motown image first appeared. Wearing a floor-length pink evening gown with long white formal gloves, Holloway created the elegance that was later implemented by the other Motown singers, most successfully by Ross.

Female entertainers often use physical beauty as an asset. Brenda Holloway was thought to be so alluring on stage that she frequently found herself the object of anger from female fans whose boyfriends or husbands had become too enthusiastic toward her (see Figure 10.1). The men who have written about Holloway have emphasized her physical attributes. For example, Nelson George raves: "Holloway was the most beautiful woman ever signed to Motown. Her skin had a striking bronze hue. Her hair was bouncy and straight, with curling ends that highlighted oval, almost Oriental eyes, and full, sensual lips. In any dress, but particularly the tight gold and silver sequined outfits she often performed in, this Atascadero, California, native was a head-turner. In fact, her figure helped her get signed to Motown."[99]

When Holloway discusses her physical qualities, she is more audacious than any of her male commentators: "I was very sexy at the time. My skin couldn't breathe unless it was exposed! My costumes were made for sex appeal—and not for women. In fact, women wanted to pull me off the stage and knock my teeth out because they thought I was flirting with their men. I was influenced by Tina Turner, but when I was touring the southern states, trying to be like her, Smokey Robinson told me not to do it again. He said, 'You have a voice, you don't need to act like her.'"[100]

Had a voice, indeed. Holloway's vocal style was very relaxed, yet she was able to create tension and exercise control. She was masterful in her ability to produce warm, rich timbres. She had perfect pitch, developed from years of playing stringed instruments. With innovative articulation, a deft control of dynamics, and a flair for dramatic performances, Holloway was a singer's singer. Davis refers to her as "the deeply soulful Mistress of Emotion."[101] Highly skilled at delaying resolutions of phrases by sustaining notes, interpolating melismas, and improvising expressions, Holloway formulated her own sound and style. Although she was influenced by Mary Wells, Sarah Vaughn, Teresa Brewer, Morgana King, and Jerry Butler, Holloway forged her own style, manipulating her alto/tenor voice over an extensive range of intensity. In her characteristic declamatory delivery, it was not uncommon for her to emote both passion and pain (listen, for example, to her recording of Smokey Robinson's classic, "Who's Loving You" (1964).[102]

Holloway's vocal performance on her second Motown single, "I'll Always Love You" (1964), exemplifies her gospel inflections, impassioned phrasing, and dynamic approach to singing. This recording was important to Holloway's career, because it followed her first hit record, "Every Little Bit Hurts," and her performances on the Dick Clark Caravan of Stars tour. However, as the Supremes' record sales began to ascend, Motown recalled all competing singles. "I'll Always Love You" was one of the retracted records.

Figure 10.1. Soul singer Brenda Holloway. Photo taken in 1960s. Courtesy of The Rudy Calvo Collection.

Motown's policy was to build one act at a time. When the Supremes were taking off, the company would pull in records so that the Supremes could go for a million. When I asked why my records were being pulled, Berry Gordy just kept telling me, "Wait your time." My records would go out of stock, and stores were told to reorder. It was usually at a crucial point when the singles could not be got, so they weren't played and didn't go into the charts.[103]

"When I'm Gone" was released in 1965, as was "Operator." These tracks were written and produced by Smokey Robinson for Mary Wells, who left Motown in 1964 at twenty-one years old. As a teenager, Holloway had idolized both Wells and Robinson. Her success with these two songs fulfilled her dream to sing like Wells on Motown. She sang in Wells's soft, husky tones, not unlike Robinson's own vocal style. Holloway became very close to Robinson and was relaxed when working with him.

The year 1965 was momentous for Holloway for several other reasons. As a resident of Watts, she experienced the 1965 Watts rebellion firsthand. She also toured North America with the Beatles as the only female on the tour. She also moved out of Watts into the affluent Westside community of Los Angeles.

On August 11, 1965, when the Watts uprising erupted. Holloway was at home, locked in, afraid for her life:

> The Watts Riot seemed like the end of the world. Tanks were driving down our streets, no cars—just National Guards with guns. We were so afraid that the National Guardsmen would kill us. I didn't feel like a star. I felt like dead meat. That's why I called Berry. I said, "I'm so afraid, I can't live in Watts anymore. I feel like I might lose my life. My family might be killed." His famous words followed, "Alright, alright, whatever you need," in his soft speaking voice. He sent me the down payment for a new house so we could move. That's why I love him so much. He said, "O.K., I'll send it to you, and you guys get out of there." We moved within two weeks to South Hauser [Boulevard] in West Los Angeles near Pico [Boulevard] and Fairfax [Avenue].[104]

Still in pursuit of her childhood dreams, Holloway was a survivor; the civil disturbance did not daunt her. She moved out and up.

In several ways, Holloway was to follow in the footsteps of her Motown predecessor, Mary Wells. Both sang with Marvin Gaye (see Figure 10.2), and both opened for the Beatles—Wells on the group's 1965 British tour, Holloway on the North American tour in August 1965. It was three days after the Watts rebellion erupted that Holloway performed at the Beatles' now-famous Shea Stadium concert (August 14, 1965).[105] The tour was arranged by Jackie de Shannon, who had performed on the group's European tour. Holloway traveled on the Beatles' private jet and was treated with respect and affection. She recalls, "They liked my music, but it wasn't a Brenda Holloway tour. They showed me that they loved me and that they appreciated me and they were glad I was there. They paid me and treated me like a queen. Everyday John would ask me what I wanted to eat. We would go to a different state everyday because we were flying. We'd get bored. So Ringo would pick up a pillow and we would just throw pillows until they turned into feathers. We had so much fun. I didn't sense any type of prejudice from the Beatles."[106]

The life of a pop star is not without its ups and downs. When Holloway speaks of why she left the music industry in 1968 at twenty-two years old, she

Figure 10.2. Brenda Holloway performing with Marvin Gaye, c.1966–67. Courtesy of The Rudy Calvo Collection.

sheds light on the darker side of the glamour and fame. Several factors precipitated Holloway's demise at Motown. Living in California, she was simply too far away from Detroit. She felt her career was mishandled by the International Talent Management, Inc., Motown's artist-management subsidiary. Her loss of faith in Motown's ability to treat her fairly was brought to a head when her recording dates and material were assigned to other singers. "That was the thing that got me most angry," she says. "I would be on my way to Detroit, and if Gladys Knight got there before me, first-come, first-serve. That was the problem. At that time, Motown was totally business. Being so young, so inexperienced, and so impatient, I couldn't wait, I wanted it right then. That's why I left."[107]

Being located in Hollywood turned out to be a disadvantage to Holloway's career. In a letter to Gordy, she complained that Motown acts in Detroit were getting television and film opportunities in Hollywood; yet she, despite living there, got no Hollywood bookings.[108] She told Davis she was "treated like dirt" because Motown did not want her to be as big as the other artists, possibly because she came off as too masculine: "When they couldn't handle me they stayed away."[109] In retrospect, Holloway says, "Again, it was first-come, first-serve. The people in Detroit were the ones that got the opportunities. I was not kept abreast. I guess my talent was so big to them. I had Hal Davis and Marc Gordon out here, but we were just novices. They just left us out here on our own. We didn't even know the resources that were available to us. The business part was handled in Detroit. I was not in Detroit and I didn't get a lot of opportunities that the other artists got."[110]

Holloway states that she began to feel despondent because the Supremes, the Four Tops, and the Temptations were getting jobs and touring and she was not. She felt she was an anomaly at Motown, a situation that was exacerbated by the erratic progress she had made in her career by 1967.

> It was like I was on hold. Berry would say to me, "I'm grooming you for Vegas." I didn't want my career to start up and then fall down and then go back up. I didn't want to be like that, on a roller coaster. I was up on the charts, in the number five position on the Top Ten. It would go down to no recording dates, no engagements, nothing. I would go from a high-high to a low-low, a depressed state, even.[111]

During this period, Holloway's doctor prescribed sleeping pills to help her cope with her hectic touring schedule and the pressures of performing. However, because of her concerns over the way her career was being handled and the emotional pain that resulted, the sleeping pills became a means to escape. Fearing that she might lose her life to drug addiction, Holloway decided to leave the entertainment industry. She was unable to see who she really was or the vastness of her potential. She recalls, "I just didn't have time to wait. I was rushing, because I was young, and I didn't want to wait. I didn't fall from grace. I couldn't see the total vision. I couldn't see what Berry Gordy was trying to do with me. I had a lot of fears about Vegas, because that was an area and a territory that no one at Motown had been into.[112] I didn't know who Brenda was or the potential that I had in me. It could be because I came from Watts, and I didn't put enough value on me. When you're seventeen, you're nervous. You always feel like you're not enough."[113]

One day in 1968, Holloway's frustration came to a head. She called her mother in Los Angeles and told her of her depression and unhappiness. Her mother told her nothing was worth her unhappiness and suggested that she get her things and sneak out of Detroit on a plane. She recalls: "I just walked out. I was actually in the middle of a recording session with Smokey Robinson when I ran away to Los Angeles. He later called me there. I told him I didn't want to be with Motown anymore. There was no future for me because there was a long span when I was doing nothing. Then when Gladys Knight came in to do my songs that was the straw that broke the camel's back."[114] When her contract expired, Motown wanted to renew, but Holloway would not sign. She considered herself a true success for having gotten out of her contract alive and in one piece.[115]

Holloway instructed Motown to report that she left the company to sing gospel. It was not true, however; she became a born-again Christian after leaving Motown. A televangelist, Arthur Blessit, witnessed to her on Sunset Boulevard. In front of the Whiskey a Go Go nightclub, she prayed to receive Jesus. Holloway married a preacher, Alfred Davis, in 1969. That year she became the first artist to successfully sue Motown.[116]

Davis and Holloway lived in Los Angeles and Inglewood. Holloway became a devoted mother, forsaking her celebrity status and lifestyle. The couple had four daughters. Three—Beor, Unita, and Christy—sing in a group with their cousin called "4 You." The youngest daughter, Donna, is in high school. Her oldest daughter, Beor, says of her mother: "We haven't known anything other than just her being 'Mommy.' We haven't known the star part of her. She was there for everything. Field trips, cuts, scrapes, bruises, arguments, little fights, sleepovers, birthday parties, everything. She's never missed anything. Basketball games, softball games, singing, when my sisters sang for their school, dance competitions, she was there for everything."[117]

Since leaving Motown, Holloway has recorded for Invictus Records (1968) and Music Merchant Records (1972), companies owned by Holland, Dozier and Holland. Her recordings include a gospel album, *Brand New* (Birthright 4xt 70206, 1980); a duet with Jimmy Ruffin, "On the Rebound" (1988); the single "Give Me a Little Inspiration" (1988); and a CD album recorded in Great Britain, *All It Takes* (1988) on Motorcity Records, produced by Ian Levine.

In 1993, Holloway decided to return to public life and began speaking to youngsters, encouraging them to stay in school. She gave a concert at Crozier Junior High in Inglewood in December 1993;[118] performed with Blood, Sweat and Tears at the Normandie Casino in Gardena, California, in 1994; and was a guest lecturer at UCLA's Department of Ethnomusicology in November 1993. On that occasion she spoke about her Motown career, showed videos of her television performances, and performed some of her classic songs. She was well received, though most of those in the audience had been born after her career ended.[119] She announced at that time that she was returning to the recording studio and negotiating a recording contract.

She has gone full-circle, from a child hoping to meet Berry Gordy Jr. and sign with the company that put out records by Smokey Robinson and Mary Wells to being a Motown legend herself. Though Holloway has remained separate and unique, she, like all of her Motown contemporaries, has earned a place in history. In this respect, Holloway is not an anomaly.

RECORDINGS BY BRENDA HOLLOWAY
(LISTED CHRONOLOGICALLY BY RELEASE DATE)[120]

Singles

1962.   Echo/Hey Fool. Donna/Delphi 1358.

1962.   Echo, Echo, Echo/Game of Love. Donna/Delphi 1366.

1962.   I Told You Baby/I'm Gonna Find Myself a Guy (by the Wattesians). Donna/Delphi 1371.

1963.   You're My Pride and Joy/I Never Knew You Looked So Good Until I Quit You (by Brenda Holloway and Jess Harris). Brevit 641.

1963.   I Ain't Gonna Take You Back/You're My Only Love. Catch 109.

1963.   It's You/Unless I Have You (by Hal Davis and Brenda Holloway). Minasa 6714.

1963.   It's You/Unless I Have You (by Hal Davis and Brenda Holloway). Snap 6714.

1964.   Every Little Bit Hurts/Land of a Thousand Boys. Tamla 54094. March 26.

1964.   Every Little Bit Hurts/Land of a Thousand Boys. Stateside 307. June (released in the United Kingdom).

1964.   Sad Song/I'll Always Love You. Tamla 54099. July 3.

1965.   When I'm Gone/I've Been Good to You. Tamla 54111. February 9.

1965.   When I'm Gone/I've Been Good to You. Tamla Motown 508. April (released in the United Kingdom).

1965.   Operator/I'll Be Available. Tamla 54115. May 14.

1965.   Operator/I'll Be Available. Tamla Motown 519. June (released in the United Kingdom).

1965.   You Can Cry On My Shoulder/How Many Times Did You Mean It? Tamla 54121. August 24.

1965.   Together Till the End of Time/Sad Song. Tamla 54125. November.

1966.   Together Till the End of Time/Sad Song. Tamla Motown 556. March (released in the United Kingdom).

1966.   Stay in School Play It Cool. Tamla T-Special Project 211L-206312. August.

1966.   Hurt a Little Every Day/Where Were You? Tamla 54137. July.

1966.   Hurt a Little Every Day/Where Were You? Tamla Motown 581. November (released in the United Kingdom).

1966?   Till Johnny Comes/Where Were You? Tamla 54144. Not Released.

1967.   Just Look What You've Done/Starting the Hurt All Over Again. Tamla 54148. March 9.

1967.   Just Look What You've Done/Starting the Hurt All Over Again. Tamla Motown 608. May (released in the United Kingdom).

1967.   You've Made Me So Very Happy/I've Got To Find It. Tamla 54155. August 17.

1967.   You've Made Me So Very Happy/I've Got To Find It. Tamla Motown 622. September (released in the United Kingdom).

1969.   Just Look What You've Done/You've Made Me So Very Happy. Tamla Motown 700. June (released in the United Kingdom).

1972. Let Me Grow. Music Merchant 1001.[121]
1972. Some Quiet Place. Music Merchant 1001.[122]
1973. Every Little Bit Hurts/Just Look What You've Done. Motown Yesteryear Series 512.
1973. When I'm Gone/You've Made Me So Very Happy. Motown Yesteryear Series 515.
1980. Giving Love. Birthright 201.
1988. Give Me a Little Inspiration. ZYX (Nightmare) 5857 (released in Germany).
1988. Give Me a Little Inspiration. Nightmare 53 (United Kingdom. 12-inch single).
1989. On the Rebound. Nightmare 73 (United Kingdom. 12-inch single).
1990. Hot and Cold. Motorcity 56 (United Kingdom. 12-inch single).

Albums

1964. *Every Little Bit Hurts.* Tamla 257. July. Reissued as Motown 5242 ML
       I've Been Good To You. Sad Song. Every Little Bit Hurts. Too Proud To Cry.
       Who's Loving You? Land of a Thousand Boys. Suddenly. Embraceable You.
       Unchained Melody. A Favor for a Girl. (You Can) Depend on Me, Can I.
1968. *The Artistry of Brenda Holloway.* Tamla Motown TML 11083. November (released in
       the United Kingdom).
1978. *The Best of Tobe Milo Productions: The Beatles in Person, Sam Houston Coliseum, August 19,*
       1965. Tobe Milo VC 4795.
1980. *Brand New.* Birthright 4023. (Gospel Album).
1988. *All It Takes.* Motorcity Records 59 (released in the United Kingdom).
       All It Takes. Fighting for What's Right. You've Made Me So Very Happy. You
       Gave Me Love. Every Little Bit Hurts. Give Me a Little Inspiration. Hot and
       Cold. On the Rebound (Duet with Jimmy Ruffin).
1991. *Greatest Hits and Rare Classics.* Motown CD 3746354852.
       Every Little Bit Hurts. Who's Lovin' You. When I'm Gone. Just Look What
       You've Done. You've Made Me So Very Happy. Hurt a Little Everyday. Starting
       the Hurt All Over Again. How Many Times Did You Mean It. Operator. I'll
       Always Love You. Unchained Melody. I'll Be Available. I've Been Good to You.
       Where Were You? You Can Cry on My Shoulder. A Favor for a Girl (with a Love
       Sick Heart). Together Till the End of Time.
1992. *Motortown Uncovered, Volume 2* (Various Artists). Ville CD 102.
       Breaking My Poor Heart in Two (Reconsider). Recorded in 1968.
1993. *The Plain Beatles 2. The Houston Complete Concert: August 19, 1965.* Great Dane CD
       9304 (released in Italy).
       Shake. (I Can't Get No) Satisfaction. Put Your Head on My Shoulder (Revised
       version of "You Can Cry on My Shoulder"). I Can't Help Myself (Sugar Pie,
       Honey Bunch).

NOTES

1. This chapter could never have been realized without the guidance of Jacqueline
Cogdell DjeDje, my mentor; the assistance of Gordon Thiel and Steve Fry of the UCLA
Music Library; Victor Cordova, former director of the UCLA Archives of Popular Music;
Itibari M. Zulu of the UCLA Center for African-American Studies; Rudy Calvo; Opal
Jones; Patrice Bivens; my family; and the generosity of Brenda Holloway.

2. The following works include discussion and information about Motown: Reginald J. Bartlette, *Off the Record: Motown by Master Number, 1959–1989* (Ann Arbor, MI: Popular Culture, 1991); Ashley Brown and Michael Heatley, *The Motown Story* (London: Orbis Publishing, 1981); Kimasi L. Browne, "The Musicology of Motown: New Horizons in Popular Music Research" (Paper delivered at the Society for Ethnomusicology, Southern California Chapter, California State University, Dominguez Hills, 7 March 1992), "The Urge to Innovate: Musical Innovation in the Motown Sound" (Unpublished paper, 1994), and "Variation in the Vocal Style of Brenda Holloway: Soul Singer and 1960s Motown Recording Artist" (M.A. thesis, University of California, Los Angeles, 1995); Sharon Davis, *"I Heard It Through the Grapevine." Marvin Gaye: The History* (Edinburgh: Mainstream Press, 1991); Gerald Lyn Early, *One Nation Under a Groove: Motown and American Culture* (Hopewell, NJ: Ecco Press, 1995); Jon Fitzgerald, "Motown Crossover Hits 1963–1966 and the Creative Process," *Popular Music* 14 (1995): 1–12; Ben Fong-Torres, *The Motown Album* (New York: St. Martin's Press, 1990); Berry Gordy Jr., *To Be Loved: The Music, The Magic, The Memories of Motown, An Autobiography* (New York: Warner Books, 1994); Ian Hoare, "You Can Make It If You Try: The Motown Story," in *The Soul Book*, ed. Ian Hoare (New York: Dell, 1976); Wayne Janick, "Mary Wells: Motown's First Great Star" *Discoveries* 68 (January 1994): 27–29; Joe McEwen and Jim Miller, "Motown" in *The Rolling Stone Illustrated History of Rock and Roll*, ed. Jim Miller (New York: A Random House/Rolling Stone Press Book, 1976, 1980), 235–249; David Morse, *Motown and the Arrival of Black Music* (New York: Macmillan, 1971); "Motown" in *The Penguin Encyclopedia of Popular Music*, ed. Donald Clarke (New York: Viking Penguin, 1989), 832; Martha Reeves and Mark Bego, *Dancing in the Street: Confessions of a Motown Diva* (New York: Hyperion, 1994); Raynoma Gordy Singleton, *Berry, Me and Motown: The Untold Story* (Chicago: Contemporary Books, 1990); A. (Dr. Licks) Slutsky, *Standing in the Shadows of Motown: The Life and Music of Legendary Bassist James Jamerson* (H. Leonard, 1989); Charles E. Sykes, "A Conceptual Model for Analyzing Rhythmic Structure in African-American Popular Music (D. Mus. Ed. Dissertation, Indiana University, 1992); J. Randy Taraborelli, *Motown: Hot Wax, City Cool and Solid Gold* (Garden City: Doubleday and Co., 1986); and Tony Turner with Barbara Aria, *Deliver Us from Temptation* (New York: Thunder's Mouth Press, 1992).

3. I read articles in the *Soul* newspaper when they were first published during the 1960s. Unfortunately, this publication has been discontinued, and the original volumes are not available in any of the Los Angeles public or academic libraries. I have a few issues in my personal library. See Karen Price, "Holland & Dozier: Motown's Money," *Soul* (15 September 1966): 14, and "Showin' Soul," *Soul* (February 1968).

4. Peter Benjaminson, *The Story of Motown* (New York: Grove Press, 1979).

5. Holloway is mentioned in Gerri Hirshey, *Nowhere to Run* (New York: Times Books, 1984), 140, 180, and 198. Mary Wells is discussed on pp. 140–145. The section on Motown is contained in several chapters, pp. 117–227.

6. Nelson George, *Where Did Our Love Go? The Rise and Fall of the Motown Sound* (New York: St. Martin's Press, 1985), 155–158.

7. Don Waller, *The Motown Story* (New York: C. Scribner, 1985), 80.

8. Mary Wilson, *Dreamgirl: My Life As a Supreme* (New York: St. Martin's Press, 1986), 129, 146 and 148.

9. Sharon Davis, *Motown: The History* (London: Guinness Pub., 1988), 42.

10. See Davis, *Motown*, 41–43, for a discussion of Holloway's signing the Motown contract. The contrasting account is that Holloway was discovered by Gordy at a disc jockey convention in the Ambassador Hotel on Wilshire Boulevard in Los Angeles. There are also

inconsistencies about the date. Whereas Holloway says 1963, other printed accounts indicate 1964; see David Bianco, *Heat Wave: The Motown Fact Book* (Ann Arbor: Popular Culture, 1988), 36.

11. Bianco, *Heat Wave*, 36–37.

12. Spider Harrison, "Brenda Holloway: The 'Every Little Bit Hurts' Lady is Back," *Black Radio Exclusive* (25 November 1988): 23.

13. See "Brenda Holloway," in *The Penguin Encyclopedia of Popular Music*, ed. Donald Clarke (New York: Viking Penguin, 1989), 555.

14. Ralph Tee, *Soul Music: Who's Who* (Rocklin: Prima Publishing, 1992), 117.

15. Colin Larkin, "Brenda Holloway," in *The Guinness Encyclopedia of Popular Music*, ed. Colin Larkin (Chester: New England Publishing Associates, 1992), 1171–1172.

16. Dennis Hunt, "R&B's Brenda Holloway Still Has a Song to Sing," *Los Angeles Times* (15 July 1994): F18.

17. Gordy, *To Be Loved*, 198.

18. "Berry Gordy: The Man Who Built Motown. The Billboard Salute," *Billboard* 106, no. 45 (5 November 1994): 61–68.

19. Adam White, "Gordy Speaks: The Billboard Interview," *Billboard* 106, no. 45 (5 November 1994): 63–64, 66, 68, 72, 82, 84, 86.

20. This is a *Billboard* special issue on Berry Gordy and Motown. See Paul Sexton, "Nowhere to Run: Motown Music Casts an Intercontinental Shadow," *Billboard* 106, no. 45 (5 November 1994): 74, 80.

21. "The Top 30 Songs Written by Berry Gordy," *Billboard* 106, no. 45 (5 November 1994): 86.

22. To date, my master's thesis is the only work that examines the music and life of Holloway in a comprehensive manner. For advertisements and articles about Brenda Holloway and Motown, see "Looking Like a Million Seller . . . When I'm Gone by Brenda Holloway," advertisement, *Billboard* 77, no. 16 (17 April 1965): 31; KGFJ advertisement, *Los Angeles Sentinel* (18 March 1965): B11; KGFJ advertisement, *Los Angeles Sentinel* (1 April 1965): B5; KGFJ advertisement, *Los Angeles Sentinel* (29 April 1965): B5; "Motor Town Show on to Washington," *Los Angeles Sentinel* (3 June 1965): B9; and Dennis Hunt, "R&B's Brenda Holloway." See the discography at the end of this chapter for a list of records that Holloway has released. Rudy Calvo was an important resource for the contextual data in this project. As a professional memorabilia collector and authority on Holloway's life and career, he provided me with articles from the popular press, photographs, and recordings.

23. Robert W. Stephens, "Soul: A Historical Reconstruction of Continuity and Change in Black Popular Music," *The Black Perspective in Music* 12, no. 1 (Spring 1984): 21–43.

24. Portia K. Maultsby, "A Healthy Diversity Evolves From Creative Freedom," *Billboard* 91 (9 June 1979): BM 10, 22, and 28, and "Soul Music: Its Sociological and Political Significance in American Popular Culture," *Journal of Popular Culture* 17, no. 2 (1983): 51–60.

25. For further discussion of soul music and artists who perform soul, see "Jerry Butler: History's Hottest Iceman," *Ebony* 25, no. 2 (December 1969): 64–66, 68, 70; "Jerry Butler: Some Cool Words About the 'Iceman,'" *Sepia* 19, no. 7 (July 1970): 48–53; "Soul Music" in *The Penguin Encyclopedia of Popular Music*, ed. Donald Clarke (New York: Viking Penguin, 1989), 1097; Phyl Garland, *The Sound of Soul* (New York: Pocket Books, 1969); Michael Haralambos, *Right On: From Blues to Soul in Black America* (New York: Da Capo Press, 1979); Arnold Shaw, *The World of Soul: America's Contribution to the Pop Music Scene* (New York: Cowles

Book Co., 1970); and *Black Popular Music in America: From the Spirituals, Minstrels, and Ragtime to Soul, Disco, and Hip-Hop* (New York: Schirmer Books, 1986).

26. Arnold Shaw, *Honkers and Shouters: The Golden Age of Rhythm and Blues* (New York: Collier Books, 1978), 443.

27. Much of this information has been taken from George Albert and Frank Hoffman, *The Cash Box Black Contemporary Singles Charts, 1960–1984* (Metuchen: Scarecrow Press, 1986).

28. In the early years, Gordy lived in a converted upstairs apartment in this building, out of which lunch was served to his staff by a hired cook.

29. Mikal Gilmore and Robert Witmer, "Motown," in *The New Grove Dictionary of American Music, Vol. 3,* ed. H. Wiley Hitchcock and Stanley Sadie (New York: Grove Dictionaries of Music, 1986), 283.

30. For other works that include discussion of African-American popular music, see Donald Clarke, ed., *The Penguin Encyclopedia of Popular Music* (New York: Viking Penguin, Inc., 1989); Nelson George, *The Death of Rhythm and Blues* (New York: Pantheon, 1988); Charles Gillett, *The Sound of the City* (New York: Dell, 1972); Rochelle Larkin, "The Soul Message," in *The Sounds of Social Change,* ed. R. Serge Denisoff and Richard A. Peterson (Chicago: Rand McNally, 1972), 92–104; Portia K. Maultsby, *Rhythm and Blues (1945–1955): A Survey of Styles* (Washington: National Museum of American History, Smithsonian Institution, 1986), and "The Impact of Gospel Music on the Secular Music Industry," in *We'll Understand It Better By and By,* ed. Bernice Johnson Reagon (Washington and London: Smithsonian Institution Press, 1992), 19–33; and Arnold Shaw, *The World of Soul, Honkers and Shouters, Black Popular Music in America, Dictionary of American Pop/Rock* (New York: Schirmer Books, 1982), and "Rhythm & Blues in California," *Black Music Research Bulletin* 10, no. 1 (Spring 1988): 11–12.

31. For a more detailed discussion of the historical development and musical features associated with African-American music, see Imamu Amiri Baraka [Leroi Jones], *Blues People: Negro Music in White America* (New York: William Morrow, 1963); Eileen Southern, *The Music of Black Americans: A History,* 2nd ed. (New York: W. W. Norton and Co., Inc. 1983); and Mellonee V. Burnim and Portia K. Maultsby, "From Backwoods to City Streets: The Afro-American Musical Journey," in *Expressively Black: The Cultural Basis of Ethnic Identity,* ed. Geneva Gay and Willie L. Baber (New York: Praeger, 1987), 109–136.

32. For extended discussion of Stax Records and the "Memphis Sound," see Peter Guralnick, "Sweet Soul Music" (New York: Harper and Row, 1986), and Robert M. Bowman, "Stax Records: A Historical and Musicological Study" (Ph.D. Dissertation, Memphis State University, 1993). Also see discussion in Kwaku Person-Lynn, "Insider Perspectives on the American Afrikan Popular Music Industry and Black Radio: Interviews with Al Bell and Pam Robinson," chapter 5 in this volume.

33. The Brill Building producers included Leiber and Stoller, Bacharach and David, Goffin and King, Mann and Weil, and Phil Spector, who has been likened to Berry Gordy Jr.

34. In later years, Bell moved to California, where he served for a short time as president of Motown.

35. A black-owned company, Vee Jay Records, released the Beatles' first American album. Ewart Abner, former president of Vee Jay, eventually became president of Motown Records. Jerry Butler recorded five albums for Motown between 1976 and 1978, including a duet with Thelma Houston, "Thelma and Jerry" (Motown M-887P1, 1977); see discussion in "Jerry Butler: History's Hottest Iceman" and "Jerry Butler: Some Cool Words About the 'Iceman.'" Frankie Valli and the Four Seasons recorded one Motown record, "Chameleon" (MoWest MW 108-L, 1972).

36. Gordy, *To Be Loved,* 209.

37. Thomas Bowles made this statement to me in a personal telephone interview in January 1994 and again in person in Detroit in May 1994. Thomas "Doctor Beans" Bowles, a manager at International Talent Management, Inc. (ITMI), was also road manager for the Supremes, the Four Tops, and the Miracles, developer and road manager of the Motortown Revue, and the baritone saxophone player on most of the Motown hit records ("Baby Love" 1964, "Stop! In the Name of Love" 1965, "Dancing in the Streets" 1964, "Bernadette" 1966, and "Fingertips" 1963).

38. See James Bates, "Polygram to Buy Motown Deal Worth $325 Million," *Los Angeles Times* (4 August 1993): D1, D10; J. R. Reynolds, "Harrell Gets Nod As Motown CEO," *Billboard* 107, no. 41 (14 October 1995): 8; and Eric L. Smith, "Familar Face on Old Label: Harrell Finds It Mo' Better at Motown," *Black Enterprise* 26, no. 5 (December 1995): 20.

39. Robert Witmer and Anthony Marks, "Soul Music," in *The New Grove Dictionary of American Music Vol. 4,* ed. H. Wiley Hitchcock and Stanley Sadie (New York: Grove's Dictionaries of Music, 1986), 263–264.

40. Lonnie Bunch, III, *Black Angelenos: The Afro-American in Los Angeles, 1850–1950* (Los Angeles: California Afro-American Museum, 1988), 35. According to Bunch, Watts was annexed circa 1929.

41. Patricia Carr Bowie, "The Cultural History of Los Angeles, 1850–1967: From Rural Backwash to World Center" (Ph.D. dissertation, University of Southern California 1980), 371–372.

42. See discussion in Michael B. Bakan, "Way Out West on Central: Jazz in the African American Community of Los Angeles Before 1930," chapter 1 in this volume; Ralph Eastman, "Central Avenue Blues: The Making of Los Angeles Rhythm and Blues, 1942–1947," *Black Music Research Journal* 9, no. 1 (Spring 1989): 19–34.

43. See Jacqueline Cogdell DjeDje, "A Historical Overview of Black Gospel Music in Los Angeles," *Black Music Research Bulletin* 10, no. 1 (Spring 1988): 1–5, "Gospel Music in the Los Angeles Black Community," *Black Music Research Journal* 9, no. 1 (Spring 1989): 35–79; and Ralph Eastman, "'Pitchin' Up a Boogie'": African-American Musicians, Night Life and Music Venues in Los Angeles 1930–1945," chapter 2 in this volume.

44. I was born and raised in Los Angeles. As a native, I am personally familiar with the worship styles used in the different denominations during the fifties and sixties because I often visited these churches.

45. DjeDje, "A Historical Overview" and "Gospel Music."

46. Brenda Holloway, personal interview with author, July 1993.

47. Holloway's compositions, collaborations with her sister, Patrice, were published by Jobete Music and have been recorded by her, Diana Ross and the Supremes, and Blood, Sweat and Tears.

48. Holloway, telephone interview with author, March 1994.

49. Holloway, personal interview, July 1993.

50. Ibid.

51. Holloway, telephone interview, March 1994.

52. Ibid.

53. Most of the Baptists in Los Angeles's black community adhered to the worship traditions of the rural southern church. Worship services in the South were inspired and demonstrative but somewhat restrained.

54. Holloway, telephone interview, March 1994.

55. Holloway sang in Greater Grace Memorial Church of God in Christ (45th Street and Compton Avenue), a Pentecostal church in Los Angeles that was well known during the forties and fifties for its support and promotion of gospel music (see discussion of Grace Memorial in DjeDje, "Gospel"). Those who attended Pentecostal and Apostolic churches used an African approach to worship. Services were generally loud, with unrestrained audience participation. Congregants would stand and sing, wave their hands, sway their bodies, and shout out praises of encouragement to participants—e.g., "Sing that song, child" and "Hallelujah!" Music making would include vigorous handclapping, shouting, or "holy" dancing, with music performed on tambourines, electronic music instruments, and drums. The choir and audience would sing up-tempo "sanctified" or "holy roller" songs that included many elements associated with African performance practice: call and response, improvisation, heterophony (where several people sing the same melody with slight variations), text and melodic interpolations (adding in words such as, "oh yes"), and the "high hoo." The "high hoo," a term coined by black music historian Horace Clarence Boyer, occurs when a tonic or dominant note is sustained at a loud volume while the choir and/or congregation continues to sing the melody. I observed Boyer demonstrate the "high hoo" at a meeting of the Society for Ethnomusicology in Oxford, Mississippi, in October 1993.

56. Harrison, "Brenda Holloway," 23.

57. The Wattesians (with Holloway as a member) recorded and released "I Told You Baby/I'm Gonna Find Myself a Guy" (Donna/Delphi 1371, 1962).

58. Holloway recorded a duet single with Hal Davis as Hal and Brenda: "It's You"/"Unless I Have You" (Minasa 6714, 1963).

59. Holloway, personal interview, July 1993.

60. Holloway, telephone interview, March 1994.

61. Holloway, personal interview with author, July, 1993.

62. Hal Davis co-produced Holloway's initial hits at Motown; he eventually became an established producer and songwriter at Motown. He headed Motown's first California office and was known in Los Angeles as "Mr. Motown"; see Gordy, *To Be Loved*, 243. One of Davis's crowning achievements was co-producing and co-writing the Jackson Five's number-one hit, "I'll Be There" (1970), which has become a standard within the popular music world.

63. Although Holloway recollects this song to be "My Guy," it is chronologically impossible for this to have been the case. "My Guy" was released in March 1964, the same month that "Every Little Bit Hurts" was released. The song was possibly one of Wells's earlier releases from 1962 or 1963.

64. Holloway, personal interview, July 1993

65. Ibid.

66. Harrison, "Brenda Holloway," 23.

67. Marc Gordon produced a series of hits for the Fifth Dimension, including their *Stoned Soul Picnic* (1968) album on Soul City Records. With Hal Davis, Gordon produced most of Holloway's early recordings, laying the foundation for Motown's West Coast sound. In addition to "Every Little Bit Hurts," they produced "I'll Always Love You" (1964), Holloway's composition "Land of a Thousand Boys" (1964), "Sad Song" (1964), the standard "Unchained Melody" (1964), and her British hit "Together Till the End of Time" (1965).

68. Instead of cutting the original record herself, Holloway believed Barbara Wilson (wife of Frank Wilson, a Motown producer and co-writer of "You've Made Me So Very Happy"), whom Ed Cobb had hired to make the demonstration tape, should have been given the opportunity to release the recording; Holloway, personal interview, July 1993.

69. Holloway, telephone interview, March 1994.

70. Ed Cobb composed Holloway's second release, "I'll Always Love You" (1964), and wrote and produced "Dirty Water" (1968) by the Standells. Cobb is important because he was one of the first white songwriters at Motown. He also had hit songs by future Motown writer, producer, and singer Gloria Jones ("Heartbeat" 1965) and the British rock duo Soft Cell ("Tainted Love" 1982).

71. Holloway, telephone interview, March 1994.

72. Harrison, "Brenda Holloway," 23.

73. Holloway, personal interview, July 1993.

74. Gordy, *To Be Loved,* 198.

75. Ibid., 199–200.

76. Holloway, personal interview, July 1993.

77. Diana Ross, *Secrets of a Sparrow: Memoirs* (New York: Villard Books, 1993), 115–116.

78. Esther Edwards is quoted in Wilson's autobiography, *Dreamgirl,* 148. After the Supremes became famous, Motown used their fame to its advantage. When Dick Clark requested the Supremes, Gordy negotiated other up-and-coming acts to accompany them; see Ross, *Secrets,* 127.

79. Wilson, *Dreamgirl,* 143.

80. Holloway, personal interview, July 1993.

81. Davis, *Motown,* 42.

82. Holloway, personal interview, July 1993.

83. Ibid.

84. Davis, *Motown,* 42.

85. Berry Gordy Sr., *Movin' Up: Pop Gordy Tells His Story* (New York: Harper & Row, 1979), 128.

86. Ross, *Secrets,* 96.

87. This information is based on personal observation. I lived in the Pueblo Del Rio municipal housing projects from 1956–70.

88. Holloway lived near the Jordan Downs housing project; personal interview, July 1993.

89. Martha Reeves, personal interview with author, August 1993. Martha Reeves (lead singer of the Motown group Martha Reeves and the Vandellas) sang opera in high school. I interviewed her in Detroit in summer 1993 while directing the Motown Historical Museum Oral History Project.

90. Holloway, telephone interview, March 1994.

91. Bob Dylan has called Smokey Robinson the greatest living American poet; see Michael Lydon, *Rock Folk* (New York: Dial Press, 1972), 69–83.

92. Holloway states that Marvin Gaye later told her about the benefits he received from studying her tapes. Ross imitated Holloway's phrasing and interpretational style on the song "Bah Bah Bah," which is included on the album *Reflections* (Motown 665, 1967) by Diana Ross and the Supremes. The song was co-written by Holloway and her sister, Patrice, and was also recorded by Suzee Ikeda (MoWest MOW 5004F, 1971).

93. Holloway, personal interview, July 1993.

94. Davis, *Motown,* 42.

95. Holloway, personal interview, July 1993.

96. Ibid.

97. Ibid.

98. Ibid.

99. George, *Where Did Our Love Go,* 157.

100. Davis, *Motown,* 42.

101. Ibid., 267.

102. "Who's Loving You" is on Holloway's only Motown album released in the United States, *Every Little Bit Hurts* (Tamla 257, 1964). See discography for her other albums.

103. Davis, *Motown,* 42.

104. Holloway, personal interview, July 1993.

105. For detailed discussion of the Beatles' North American tour, see Mark Lewisohn, *The Beatles Live!* (New York: Henry Holt and Company, 1986), *The Beatles Day by Day: A Chronology 1962–1969* (New York: Harmony, 1987), and *The Complete Beatles Chronicle* (New York: Harmony Books, 1992). A live recording of Holloway performing on this tour can be heard on *The Plain Beatles 2: The Houston Complete Concert: August 19, 1965* (Great Dane CD 9304, 1993).

106. Holloway, personal interview, July 1993.

107. Holloway, telephone interview, March 1994.

108. George, *Where Did Our Love Go,* 156–157.

109. Davis, *Motown,* 42.

110. Holloway, telephone interview, March 1994.

111. Ibid.

112. Prior to signing with Motown in 1964, the Four Tops had performed in Las Vegas. However, Motown had no demonstrated experience in Las Vegas in the mid-1960s.

113. Holloway, personal interview, July 1993, and telephone interview, March 1994. Holloway was twenty-two years old when she left Motown.

114. Davis, *Motown,* 43.

115. Ibid.

116. Ibid., and Holloway, personal interview, July 1993.

117. Beor Davis, personal interview with author, July 1993.

118. Guillermina Haro, "One Time Motown Star Visits Crozier's Drama Class Students," *Topic Sun Newspaper* (15 September 1993).

119. A video of this event has been deposited in the Ethnomusicology Archive at UCLA.

120. Music archivist Rudy Calvo was the resource for much of this discography.

121. According to Rudy Calvo (personal communication, 1995), Music Merchant titles were issued with duplicate record numbers.

122. Ibid.

APPENDIX: SOURCE MATERIALS AND GUIDE TO AFRICAN-AMERICAN MUSIC, MUSICIANS, AND CULTURE IN CALIFORNIA

Compiled by David Martinelli

These source materials gather information related to African-American music, musicians and culture in California. Books and articles included here have been selected with the following criteria:

1. They relate to musicians who have made contributions to African-American musical genres and have lived in California, settled in California, were born in California, or had significant careers or personal experiences in California.
2. They relate to African-American musical genres in general and/or to musical genres in which African Americans have participated within the geographical boundaries of the State of California.
3. They provide social and historical contexts for African-American life in California. These sources are included in a separate section that is meant not to be a complete reference source in itself but rather an adjunct to the musical references.

The entries are restricted primarily to books and periodical articles. I have not included a comprehensive listing of newspaper articles and record reviews. However, some music-related articles from newspapers and other sources not necessarily associated with music are included. Entries include book-length studies, articles in academic journals, interviews with musicians, one-page profiles, blurbs, editorials, musical analysis, articles or books by musicians, biographies, autobiographies, discographies, bibliographies, etc.

Jazz articles outnumber all others, simply because it is easier to keep track of individual artists as opposed to groups (which may break up) and because of reference sources such as the *New Grove Dictionary of Jazz*. As of yet, there is no *New Grove Dictionary of Soul, Funk and Hip-Hop*.

RESEARCH METHODOLOGY

Because this topic is vast, the research methodology has been a combination of meticulous procedure and random chance. Among other sources, I have used *The Music Index, The New Grove Dictionaries of Music, American Music,* and *Jazz,* various other bibliographies and reference sources (most of these are included in the "Reference" section), bibliographies included in books and articles relating to African-American music in California, and searches through periodicals such as *The Black Perspective in Music, The Black Music Research Journal, Down Beat, Rolling Stone, Melody Maker, Spin, Guitar Player, Option, Keyboard,* and many others. Sources have also been taken from research papers, collections, and bibliographies provided by Jacqueline Cogdell DjeDje, Eddie S. Meadows, Lee Hildebrand, Steve Loza, Ralph Eastman, Michael Bakan, Willie Collins, Kimasi L. Browne, Betty Blair, Jay Keister, Andy Krikun, Javier Pacheco, Idella Watts, and the author. Other people who have provided information include Ali Jihad Racy, James Makubuya, and Kwaku Person-Lynn.

FORMAT

The source materials have been divided into three main sections. The first includes all entries relating to music and musicians. This has been further divided into three sections:

1. Reference sources (bibliographies, dictionaries, etc.)
2. Discographies
3. General (i. e., everything else)

The second section includes all the entries relating to the social and historical context of the African-American presence in California. It has been divided into two subsections: Reference and General.

The third section contains a list of newspapers and periodicals that have generally not been searched but that contain useful information for researchers.

The general bibliographical format is as follows:

Books: Author. Date. *Title.* Place of Publication: Publisher.
Book articles: Author. Date. "Article title" in *Book Title,* edited by Name of Editor. Place of Publication: Publisher, page numbers.
Periodical articles: Author. Date. "Article title," *Periodical* volume(Issue): page numbers.

At the end of each entry is bracketed information that includes:
Musical genre/type of context-Geographical location-annotation (if applicable)

KEY TO ABBREVIATIONS

CA = California
LA = Los Angeles
NGDM = *The New Grove Dictionary of Music*

NGDAM = *The New Grove Dictionary of American Music*
NGDJ = *The New Grove Dictionary of Jazz*
SD = San Diego
SF = San Francisco

CONCLUSION

It is hoped that these source materials will be useful for those researchers whose focus is California and those who are doing research on musicians associated with California. This compilation of sources is not intended to be all-inclusive, and I recognize that some of the entries are clearly of more use to the researcher than others. Finally, I would like to thank Professors Jacqueline Cogdell DjeDje and Eddie S. Meadows for coming up with the idea for such a work and for providing me with materials and guidance along the way. Though the actual work involved in compiling this may at times have been tedious, the nature of the material I was dealing with made this a compelling project.

PART 1. SOURCE MATERIALS

MUSIC

Reference

0001. Anderson, Robert, and Gail North. 1979. *Gospel Music Encyclopedia.* New York: Sterling Publishing Co., Inc. [Gospel-CA]

0002. Carner, Gary, comp. 1990. *Jazz Performers: An Annotated Bibliography of Biographical Materials.* Westport, CT: Greenwood Press. [Jazz-CA]

0003. Charters, Samuel B. 1963. *Jazz New Orleans 1885–1963.* New York: Oak Publications. [Jazz-CA-has entries for CA musicians such as Mutt Carey, Kid Ory]

0004. Chilton, John. 1979. *Who's Who of Jazz: Storyville to Swing Street,* rev ed. Philadelphia: The Chilton Book Co. [Jazz-CA]

0005. Clarke, Donald, ed. 1989. *The Penguin Encyclopedia of Popular Music.* New York: Viking Penguin. [Popular Music-CA-Includes avant-garde jazz artists and obscure British bands, dismisses rap as an unmusical fad]

0006. Clayborn, Charles Eugene. 1982. *Biographical Dictionary of Jazz.* Englewood Cliffs, NJ: Prentice-Hall, Inc. [Jazz-CA]

0007. DeLerma, Dominique-Rene. 1982. *Bibliography of Black Music, Volume 3: Geographical Studies.*Westport, CT: Greenwood Press. [General Music-CA-Has 10 entries on CA]

0008. Eckland, K. O. 1986. *Jazz West, 1945–1985: The A–Z Guide to West Coast Jazz Music.* Carmel, CA: Cypress. [Jazz-CA]

0009. Ewen, David. 1949. *American Composers Today: A Biographical and Critical Guide.* New York: H. W. Wilson. [Art Music-LA-W. G. Still]

0010. Floyd, Samuel, and Martha J. Reisser. 1983. *Black Music in the United States: An Annotated Bibliography of Selected Reference and Research Materials.* Millwood, NY: Kraus. [General Music-CA-has 5 entries on collections in CA]

0011. Fry, Stephen M., comp. and ed. 1988. *California's Musical Wealth: Sources for the Study of Music in California.* Los Angeles (?): The Southern California Chapter, Music Library Association. [General Music-CA]

0012. Fry, Stephen M., comp., with the assistance of Jeannie Pool. 1985. *The Story of the All Women's Orchestras in California, 1893–1951: Bibliography.* Northridge, CA: Department of Music, California State University, Northridge. [General Music-CA]

0013. Harris, Sheldon. 1979. *Blues Who's Who: A Biographical Dictionary of Blues Singers.* New Rochelle, NY: Arlington House Publishers. [Blues-CA-Has info on CA-based musicians]

0014. Herzhaft, Gérard. 1992. *Encyclopedia of the Blues.* Translated by Brigitte Debord. Fayetteville: University of Arkansas Press. [Blues-CA-has entry on California with list of performers' names]

0015. Hitchcock, H. Wiley, and Stanley Sadie, eds. 1986. *The New Grove Dictionary of American Music.* New York: Grove's Dictionaries of Music. [General Music-CA]

0016. Horn, David. 1977. *The Literature of American Music in Books and Folk Music Collections.* Metuchen, NJ: Scarecrow Press. [General Music-CA-Extensive discussion of black music titles in all genres]

0017.———. 1988. *The Literature of American Music in Books and Folk Music Collections, Supplement 1.* Metuchen, NJ: Scarecrow Press. [General Music-CA]

0018. Jackson, Irene V. 1979. *Afro-American Religious Music: A Bibliography and a Catalogue of Gospel Music.* Westport, CT: Greenwood Press. [Gospel-CA]

0019. Kernfeld, Barry, ed. 1988. *The New Grove Dictionary of Jazz.* New York: Grove's Dictionaries of Music. [Jazz-CA]

0020. Limbacher, James L. 1981. *Keeping Score: Film Music, 1972–1979.* Metuchen, NJ: Scarecrow Press. [Film Music-LA-Oliver Nelson, Chico Hamilton]

0021. Limbacher, James L., and H. Stephen Wright. 1991. *Keeping Score: Film and Television Music, 1980–1988.* Metuchen, NJ: Scarecrow Press. [Film Music-LA-Nelson, Hamilton, Herbie Hancock]

0021a. McCoy, Judy. 1992. *Rap Music in the 1980s: A Reference Guide.* Metuchen, NJ: Scarecrow Press. [Rap-CA]

0022. Meadows, Eddie S. 1981. *Jazz Research and Reference Materials: A Select Annotated Bibliography.* New York: Garland. [Jazz-CA-has entries for several CA-based musicians]

0023.———. 1995. *Jazz Research and Peformance Materials: A Select Annotated Bibliography.* New York: Garland. [Jazz-CA-Books only, includes section on West Coast Jazz and has entries for several CA-based musicians]

0024. Meeker, David. 1981. *Jazz in the Movies,* new enlarged edition. New York: Da Capo. [Jazz-LA-Alphabetical by film, has index of performers]

0025. Nite, Norm N. 1974. *Rock On: The Illustrated Encyclopedia of Rock 'n' Roll, The Solid Gold Years.* New York: Thomas Y. Crowell Co. [Rock-CA-Has CA people]

0026. Oliver, Paul, Max Harrison, and William Bolcom. 1986 [1980]. *The New Grove Gospel, Blues and Jazz with Spiritual and Ragtime.* New York: W. W. Norton and Company. [Gospel/Blues/Jazz-CA]

0027. Sadie, Stanley, ed. 1980. *The New Grove Dictionary of Music and Musicians.* New York: Grove's Dictionaries of Music. [General Music-CA]

0028. Southern, Eileen. 1982. *Biographical Dictionary of Afro-American and African Musicians.* Westport, CT: Greenwood Press. [General Music-CA]

0029.————. 1983. *The Music of Black Americans: A History*, 2nd ed. New York: W. W. Norton and Co. [General Music-CA]

0029a.————. 1997. *The Music of Black Americans: A History*, 3rd ed. New York: W. W. Norton and Co. [General Music-CA]

0030. Stambler, Irwin. 1989. *The Encyclopedia of Pop, Rock, and Soul*. New York: St. Martin's Press. [Popular Music/Rock/Soul-CA-Has entries for Natalie Cole, Larry Graham, Sly Stone, Pointer Sisters, War]

0031. Vann, Kimberly R. 1990. *Black Music in Ebony: An Annotated Guide to the Articles on Music in Ebony Magazine, 1945–1985*. Chicago: Center for Black Music Research, Columbia College. [General Music-CA]

Discography

0032. Boenzli, R. 1961. *Discography of Howard McGhee*. Basle, Switzerland: n.p. [Jazz-LA]

0033. Bruyninckx, Walter. n. d. *Modern Jazz Discography: Bebop/Hard Bop/West Coast*. n.p. [Jazz-CA-At least 6 volumes]

0034.————. n. d. *Progressive Jazz: Free, Third Stream, Fusion*. n.p. [Jazz-CA-At least 6 volumes]

0035.————. 1985. *Traditional Discography; Traditional Jazz 1897–1985. Origins/New Orleans/Dixieland/Chicago Styles*. Menchelen, Belgium: Copy Express. [Jazz-CA-6 volumes]

0036. Campbell, Robert L. 1994. *The Earthly Recordings of Sun Ra*. Redwood, NY: Cadence Books. [Jazz-CA-has references to Sun Ra's activities on the West Coast, including the film *Space is the Place*]

0037. Colebeck, David. 1982. "Louis Jordan Discography," *Blues Unlimited* 143: 14–18. [Blues/R & B-LA]

0038. Evensmo, Jan, Per Borthen, and Ib Skovsted Thomsen. 1982. *The Alto Saxophone, Trumpet, and Clarinet of Benny Carter, 1927–1946: With a Critical Assessment of All His Known Records and Broadcasts*. Hosle, Norway: Jan Evensmo. [Jazz-CA]

0039. Godrich, John, and Robert M.W. Dixon. 1969. *Blues and Gospel Records 1902–1942*. London: Storyville Publications. [Blues/Gospel-CA]

0040. Hayes, Cedric J. 1973. A *Discography of Gospel Records 1937–1971*. Denmark: Karl Emil Knudsen. [Gospel-CA-Mighty Clouds of Joy, many other CA artists]

0041. Hildebrand, Lee. 1995. "Johnny Otis Discography" in *Colors and Chords: The Art of Johnny Otis*. San Francisco: Pomegranate Books, pp. 121–128. [Blues/Jazz-LA]

0042. Hoffman, Coen. 1985. *Man of Many Parts: A Discography of Buddy Collette*. Amsterdam: Micography. [Jazz-LA-includes interview with Collette]

0043. Hunter, Roger, and Mike Davis. 1986. *Hampton Hawes: A Discography*. Manchester, England: Manyana Publications. [Jazz-LA]

0044. Jepsen, Jørgen Grunnet. 1957. *Kid Ory*. Copenhagen: n.p. [Jazz-LA]

0045. Laughton, Bob, and Cedric Hayes. 1983. "Mahalia Jackson: Recordings to 1959," *Blues Unlimited* 144: 40–42. [Gospel-LA-includes material recorded in LA]

0046. Leadbitter, Mike, and Neil Slaven. 1968. *Blues Records, January 1943 to December 1966*. London: Hanover Books. [Blues-CA-Has CA people]

0047. Lindenmaier, H. L., and H. J. Salewski. 1983. *The Man Who Never Sleeps: The Charles Mingus Discography, 1945–1978*. Freiburg, Germany: n.p. [Jazz-LA]

0048. Lord, Tom. 1992–. *The Jazz Discography.* West Vancouver: Lord Music Reference Inc. [Jazz-CA-Multivolume discography in process of being published]

0049. Nieus, R. 1986. *A Discography of Dexter Gordon.* Jambes, Belgium: n.p. [Jazz-LA]

0050. Penny, Dave. 1986. "Johnny Otis Discography: 1945–1952, Part One," *Blues and Rhythm: The Gospel Truth* 21 (July): 22–23. [Blues-LA]

0051. Reichardt, Uwe. 1986. *Like A Human Voice: The Eric Dolphy Discography.* Schmitten, West Germany: Norbert Ruecker. [Jazz-LA]

0052. Ruppli, Michel. 1982. *Charles Mingus Discography.* Frankfurt: Norbert Ruecker. [Jazz-LA]

0053. ———. 1986. *The Clef/Verve Labels: A Discography.* New York: Greenwood Press. [Jazz-LA-LA-based labels, 2 vols.]

0054. ———. 1991. *The Aladdin/Imperial Labels: A Discography.* New York: Greenwood Press. [R & B-LA-LA-based record labels]

0055. Rust, Brian. 1978. *The American Record Label Book.* New Rochelle, NY: Arlington House. [General Music-CA-Includes discussion of "race records" of the 1920s and 1930s]

0056. ———. 1982. *Jazz Records, 1897–1942,* 5th ed. rev., 2 vols. Essex: Storyville Publications and Co., Ltd. [Jazz-CA]

0057. Salemann, D., D. Hartmann, and M. Vogler. 1987. *Sonny Criss, 1943–1952: Solography, Discography, Band Routes, Engagements in Chronological Order.* Basle, Switzerland: n.p. [Jazz-CA]

0058. Schlouch, Claude. 1983. *In Memory of Wardell Gray: A Discography.* Marseille, France: n.p. [Jazz-LA]

0059. Sjøgren, Thorbjørn. 1986. *Long Tall Dexter: The Discography of Dexter Gordon.* Copenhagen: n.p. [Jazz-LA]

0060. Skovgaard, I., and E. Traberg. 1984. *Some Clark Bars: Sonny Clark: A Discography.* Copenhagen and Madrid: n.p. [Jazz-LA]

0061. Weber, H., and G. Filtgen. 1984. *Charles Mingus: Sein Leben, Seine Musik, Seine Schallplatten.* Gauting, Germany: n.p. [Jazz-LA]

0062. Whitburn, Joel. 1988. *Top R & B Singles, 1942–1988.* Menomonee Falls, WI: Record Research Inc. [R & B-CA]

0063. Wilbraham, Roy. 1967. *Charles Mingus: A Biography and Discography.* London: n.p. [Jazz-LA]

0064. Wild, David, and Michael Cuscuna. 1980. *Ornette Coleman 1958–1979: A Discography.* Ann Arbor, MI: Wildmusic. [Jazz-CA-includes biography]

General

0065. Aaron, Charles. 1993. "Sir Real," *Spin* 9(7) [October]: 50–56. [Rap-Long Beach-Snoop Doggy Dogg]

0066. ———. 1995. "California Dreaming," *Spin* 11 (April): 142–148, 215–216. [Rap-LA-On LA rap and rappers]

0067. Adler, Bill. 1991. *Rap: Portraits and Lyrics of a Generation of Black Rockers.* New York: St. Martin's Press. [Rap-LA-Ice-T, NWA, Ice Cube, Tone Loc, Young MC]

0068. Aldin, Mary Katherine. 1988. "It Depends on What You Call a Living: The Blues Scene in Los Angeles," *Living Blues* 80 (May/June): 24–27. [Blues-LA]

0069. ———. 1989a. "Blues News From L.A.," *Blues and Rhythm* 46 (September): 9. [Blues-LA-Part of a continuing series of articles]

0070. ———. 1989b. "Blues News from L.A.," *Blues and Rhythm* 47 (October): 15. [Blues-LA]

0071.————. 1989c. "My Whole Thing Was Playing Music: Joe Louis Walker," *Living Blues* 87 (July/August): 14–20. [Blues-SF]

0072. Allen, Harry. 1991. "Righteous Indignation," *The Source* 19 (March/April): 48–53. [Rap-Bay Area-Paris]

0073. Allen, William Duncan. 1989. "An Overview of Black Concert Music and Musicians in Northern California from the 1940s to the 1980s," *Black Music Research Journal* 9 (Spring): 81–92. [Art Music-Bay Area]

0074. Anderson, Gene. 1994. "The Genesis of King Oliver's Creole Jazz Band," *American Music* 12(3): 283–303. [Jazz-LA-has section on CA]

0075. Andrews, Ernie. 1993. *Central Avenue Sounds Oral History Transcript*. Los Angeles: Oral History Program, University of California, Los Angeles. [Jazz-LA-Interviewed by Steven L. Isoardi, 78 pp.]

0076. Anonymous. 1941. "Les Young Joins Brother's Band on West Coast," *Down Beat* 8 (June 1): 13. [Jazz-LA]

0077.————. 1942. "Herbie Jeffries Has New Record Concern," *Down Beat* 9 (October 15): 9. [Jazz-LA-Brief news item]

0078.————. 1942. "King Cole Trio Loses Bassist," *Down Beat* 9 (September 15): 14. [Jazz-LA-Brief news item]

0079.————. 1943. "Lee Young Has New Combo Set for Swing Club," *Down Beat* 10 (March 15): 6. [Jazz-LA]

0080.————. 1943. "Niteries Facing Race Problem: L.A. Columnist Takes Slam at Discrimination," *Down Beat* 10 (March 1): 6. [Jazz-LA]

0081.————. 1943. "Trianon Bars Two Basie Men, Jimmie Sore," *Down Beat* 10 (July 15): 6. [Jazz-South Gate-Snooky Young, Sweets Edison]

0082.————. 1945. "Cole Trio, Carter Ork, All-Negro Unit Bought by Trocadero." *Billboard*, p. 31, April 7. [Jazz-LA]

0083.————. 1945. "LA Nitery Drops Color Line Ban," *Down Beat* 12 (August 1): 1. [Jazz-LA-extremely brief news item]

0084.————. 1945. "Troc Fired Carter, But It's Tough to Make Heave Stick." *Billboard*, p. 11, April 14. [Jazz-LA-Benny Carter]

0085.————. 1949. "Boppers 'Rowdy', Shrine Joins Philharmonic Aud. in Banning Concerts," *Variety* 173 (February 2): 37. [Jazz-LA]

0086.————. 1949. "Empire, Berg's, Be-bop's Hollywood Homes, Close," *Down Beat* 16 (May 6): 9. [Jazz-LA]

0087.————. 1949. "King Cole Decorates His New Home," *Ebony* 4 (April): 26–29. [Popular Music-LA]

0088.————. 1950. "Ivie Anderson," *Metronome* 66 (February): 13. [Jazz-LA]

0089.————. 1952. "Frisco Bars Robeson: Follows Seattle Ban," *Variety* 186 (April 30): 58. [Art Music-SF]

0090.————. 1952. "Ivory Joe Hunter," *Ebony* 7 (July): 41–45. [Blues-Oakland]

0091.————. 1952. "Los Angeles to Have Negro Symphony Group," *Music of the West* 8 (October): 13. [Art Music-LA]

0092.————. 1952. "Nat Cole," *Metronome* 68 (October): 13. [Jazz-LA]

0093.————. 1953. "Talented T-Bone Walker," *Ebony* 8 (October): 59–64. [Blues-LA]

0094.————. 1954. "Notes on the West Coast Scene," *Record Changer* 13(Summer): 29. [Jazz-CA-Has names of people who were in CA during that era]

0095.————. 1955. "Early Coast Jazz Days Told in Files of 'Tempo,'" *Down Beat* 22 (September 21): 47. [Jazz-CA-Index of stories published in *Tempo Magazine*, West Coast jazz journal 1933–1940]

0096.————. 1955. "That Hollywood Question (Negroes Represented Seldom in Musician's Union and Never in the Critical Field)," *Metronome* 71 (November): 50. [Jazz-LA]

0097.————. 1956. "Frisco Columnist Raps White Tooters for Nixing Merger with Negro Local," *Variety* 205 (December 19): 58. [Jazz-SF]

0098.————. 1957. "Fatha Hines Settles Down," *Ebony* 12 (October): 63–68. [Jazz-Bay Area-Earl Hines's decision to stay in Bay Area]

0099.————. 1959. "The West Coast Scene," *Down Beat* 26 (November 12): 15–17. [Jazz-LA/SF]

0100.————. 1960. "The Soul of Ray Charles," *Ebony* 15 (September): 99–107. [Popular Music-LA]

0101.————. 1961. "Frisco's Masonic Temple Turns Down Miles Davis Benefit Show for NAACP," *Variety* 222 (May 3): 1. [Jazz-SF]

0102.————. 1964. "West Coaster Sees Big Shift of Jazz to L.A.," *Down Beat* 31 (June 4): 11. [Jazz-LA-West Coaster is Jack Wilson]

0103.————. 1966. "Jazz and Watts Youth," *Down Beat* 33 (April 7): 12–13. [Jazz-LA]

0104.————. 1966. "Lurning in Watts," *Down Beat* 33 (December 1): 12. [Jazz-LA]

0105.————. 1967. "West Coast Enjoys Jazzmen Explosion," *Down Beat* 34 (April 6): 13. [Jazz-CA-Elvin Jones lived in SF]

0106.————. 1968. "James Cleveland: King of Gospel," *Ebony* 24 (November): 74–82. [Gospel-LA]

0107.————. 1969. "The Chambers Brothers," *Ebony* 24 (October): 162–169. [Rock-LA]

0108.————. 1969. "The Edwin Hawkins Singers: 'Oh, Happy Day!'" *Sepia* 18 (August): 66–68. [Gospel-Bay Area]

0109.————. 1970. "Black Musicians Blast L.A. Studio Policies," *Down Beat* 37(13): 11. [Jazz-LA]

0110.————. 1970. "Black Musicians in H'wood Pitch for a 25 Percent Quota," *Variety* 258: 53. [Film Music-LA]

0111.————. 1970. "Where It Was: 1970 Edition, Los Angeles, Calif.," *Jazz Report* 7: 3–4. [Jazz-LA]

0112.————. 1973. "Andrae Crouch and Disciples Dedicated," *Lyric Magazine* 6(1): 10, 27. [Gospel-LA]

0113.————. 1973. "Jacksonmania Hits Watts," *Soul* 7 (January 29): 13. [Popular Music-LA]

0114.————. 1973. "Tower of Power Profile," *Down Beat* 40 (November 8): 34–35. [Rock/Soul-Oakland]

0115.————. 1973. "War: Seven Escapees from the Night Shift," *Rolling Stone* 137 (June 21): 16. [Rock/Soul-LA]

0116.————. 1974. "Chambers Brothers: It's Time Again So Get Ready for Good Vibes," *Soul* 9 (August 5): 11. [Rock/Soul-LA]

0117.————. 1975. "Ivory Joe Hunter," *Living Blues* 19 (January/February): 3. [Blues-CA]

0118.————. 1978. "Head and Christian Shops: Unusual Distribution for Herb Jeffries," *Billboard* 90 (December 2): 86. [Jazz-LA]

0119.————. 1982. "Edwin Hawkins," *New Christian Music Magazine* 7: 16. [Gospel-Bay Area]

0120.————. 1986. "Love Alive," *Jefferson* 73: 28–29. [Gospel-CA-Walter Hawkins]

0121.————. 1986. "Oh Happy Day," *Jefferson* 72: 32–33. [Gospel-CA-Edwin Hawkins]

0122.————. 1986. "Tramaine and the Family: Jesus Is the Way," *Jefferson* 75: 28–29. [Gospel-CA-Tramaine Hawkins]

0123.————. 1988. "Amy, Curtis (Edward)," *NGDJ* 1: 21. [Jazz-LA]

0124.————. 1988. "Dickerson, (Lowell) Dwight," *NGDJ* 1: 288. [Jazz-LA]

0125.————. 1988. "Garrett, Donald (Rafael)," *NGDJ* 1: 419–420. [Jazz-Bay Area]

0126.————. 1988. "Jeffries, Herb," *NGDJ* 1: 612. [Jazz-LA]

0127.————. 1988. "Johnson, Plas (John, Jr.)," *NGDJ* 1: 624–625. [Jazz/Studio-LA]

0128.————. 1988. "Lasha, Prince," *NGDJ* 2: 12. [Jazz-LA]

0129.————. 1988. "Lewis, Herbie," *NGDJ* 2: 26. [Jazz-LA]

0130.————. 1988. "Marable, Larry," *NGDJ* 2: 81–82. [Jazz-LA]

0131.————. 1988. "Nightclubs and Other Venues," *NGDJ* 2: 176–247. [Jazz-El Cerrito, LA, Oakland, SD, SF, Squaw Valley-lists nightclubs in these cities]

0132.————. 1988. "Perkins, Carl," *NGDJ* 2: 302–303. [Jazz-LA]

0133.————. 1988. "Porter, Roy," *NGDJ* 2: 326. [Jazz-LA]

0134.————. 1988. "Preston, Don(ald Ward)," *NGDJ* 2: 331. [Jazz-LA]

0135.————. 1988. "Reverend James Cleveland's Father's Day Tribute," *ACC Church News* 23 (June 19): 1. [Gospel-LA-A.C.C.=A Corporation for Christ]

0136.————. 1988. "Tapscott, Horace," *NGDJ* 2: 517. [Jazz-LA]

0137.————. 1988. "Thompson, Chuck," *NGDJ* 2: 534–535. [Jazz-LA]

0138.————. 1988. "Zappa, Frank," *NGDJ* 2: 653. [Jazz/Rock-LA]

0139.————. 1991. "Cop Rock," *Rock and Roll Confidential* 87 (April): 1–2. [Rap-LA-NWA]

0140.————. 1991. "Editorial: Ice Cube's Unabashed Espousal of Violence Crosses the Line," *Billboard* 103 (November 23): 8. [Rap-LA]

0141.————. 1992. "'Cop Killer' Pulled from Body Count LP," *Melody Maker* 68 (August 8): 3. [Rock-LA]

0142.————. 1992. "Cop Killer's Bullet," *Musician* 168 (October): 111. [Rock-LA-Body Count]

0143.————. 1992. "Eyewitness News (The Source's James Bernard Interviewed on Los Angeles Riots and Rap Music)," *Rock and Roll Confidential* 98 (June): 1–3. [Rap-LA-Ice Cube]

0144.————. 1992. "Ice Cube Relights LA Flames," *Melody Maker* 68 (November 14): 5. [Rap-LA-discusses *The Predator*]

0145.————. 1992. "Ice-T-'Police sent bombs during "Cop Killer" row'," *Melody Maker* 68 (August 22): 2. [Rock-LA]

0146.————. 1992. "It's Not a Black Thing (Billboard's Editorial Calling Ice Cube's *Death Certificate* Racist)," *Rock and Roll Confidential* 94 (January): 1–2. [Rap-LA]

0147.————. 1992. "News: Cop Killer Claims More Victims," *Melody Maker* 68 (September 12): 2. [Rap-LA-Boo-Yaa Tribe]

0148.————. 1992. "Police on My Back: Ice-T and Jello Biafra," *Spin* 8 (September): 72–75. [Rock/Rap-LA]

0149.————. 1993. "Gun Amok," *Melody Maker*, p. 41, December 25. [Rap-LA/Bay Area-Ice Cube, Ice-T, Paris, Compton's Most Wanted, Cypress Hill, Snoop Doggy Dogg, Tupac Shakur]

0150.————. 1993. "La diva du gospel," *Soul Bag* 132: 16. [Gospel-CA-Tramaine Hawkins]

0151. Ansell, Derek. 1994. "Charlie Haden," *Jazz Journal International* 47 (October): 10–12. [Jazz-LA]

0152. Applegate, Joe. 1983. "This is Gospel: More Than Just Prayer With a Beat," *San Diego Reader* 12(27): 1, 10, 12–14, 16–19. [Gospel-SD]

0153. Armbruster, Greg. 1984. "Joe Sample: Painter in Sound and Time," *Keyboard* 10 (April): 44–45, 48, 55–59. [Jazz-LA]

0154. Armitage, J. 1985. "Benny Carter: le roi," *Bulletin du Hot Club de France* 332: 1. [Jazz-LA]

0155. Arvey, Verna. 1984. *In One Lifetime: William Grant Still*. Fayetteville: University of Arkansas Press. [Art Music-LA]

0156. Asher, Don. 1977. "Jazz Pianist Hampton Hawes Dead at 49," *Rolling Stone* 242 (June 30): 35–36. [Jazz-LA]

0157. Atkinson, Nicole. 1993. "Henry Starr: Musical Marvel," *From the Archives* 4(3): 7. [?Oakland]

0158. Atteberry, Phil. 1994. "Conte Candoli Interview," *Cadence* 20 (November): 19–22. [Jazz-LA]

0159. Auerbach, Brian. 1986. "Profile: United Front," *Down Beat* 53 (February): 45–47. [Jazz-SF]

0160.———. 1988. "Gentle Persuasion: The Artistry of Flutist James Newton," *Option* (January/February): 44–46. [Jazz-LA]

0161. Auerbach, Susan. 1988. "From Louisiana to Los Angeles: Creole La-La Dances," *Los Angeles Folk Arts* (Winter): 1, 4. [Zydeco-LA]

0162. Baggelaar, Kristin, and Donald Milton. 1976. *Folk Music: More Than a Song*. New York: Thomas Y. Crowell Company. [Folk/Blues-CA-Odetta Gordon]

0163. Baggenaes, Roland. 1972. "Dexter Gordon: Interview," *Coda* 10(7): 2–5. [Jazz-LA]

0164. Baird, Jock. 1991. "M. C. Hammer: Rappin' With Roland," *Roland Users Group* 9(1): 30–34. [Rap-Oakland]

0165. Baker, David, Lydia Belt, and Herman Hudson. 1978. *The Black Composer Speaks*. Metuchen, NJ: Scarecrow Press. [Art Music-Berkeley/LA-Interviews with Olly Wilson, Oliver Nelson]

0166. Baker, Paul. 1979. "Setting the Good Word to Modern Music," *Billboard* 90 (July 28): R4, R12, R18. [Gospel-CA]

0167. Balliet, Whitney. 1983. *Jelly Roll, Jabbo, and Fats: Nineteen Portraits in Jazz*. New York: Oxford University Press. [Jazz-CA-Jelly Roll Morton and Ornette Coleman]

0168. Barackman, Michael. 1980. "Rick James' Funky Realism," *Rolling Stone* 309 (January 24): 20–21. [Soul-LA-He lived in LA for a while]

0169. Barnett, Anthony. 1988. "Crouch, Stanley," *NGDJ* 1: 257. [Jazz-LA]

0170. Barrell, A. 1980. "Last of the Line: An Appreciation of Barney Bigard," *Footnote* 11(6): 4. [Jazz-LA]

0171. Barros, Paul de. 1983. "Tony Williams: Two Decades of Drum Innovation," *Down Beat* 50 (November): 14–16. [Jazz-SF]

0172. Battestini, C., and J. P. Battestini. 1979. "Barney Bigard," *Bulletin du Hot Club de France* 273: 6. [Jazz-LA]

0173.———. 1980. "Benny Carter (quelques precisions)," *Bulletin du Hot Club de France* 281: 4. [Jazz-LA]

0174.———. 1980. "Marshall Royal: allons à l'essential," *Bulletin du Hot Club de France* 284: 10. [Jazz-LA]

0175.———. 1981. "Harry 'Sweets' Edison," *Bulletin du Hot Club de France* 288: 12. [Jazz-LA]

0176. Beck, Frederick A. 1988. "Wilson, Gerald (Stanley)," *NGDJ* 2: 631–632. [Jazz-LA]

0177. Benjaminson, Peter. 1979. *The Story of Motown.* New York: Grove Press. [Popular Music-LA-Brenda Holloway]

0178. Bentley, John. 1962. "Sonny Clay: A Veritable Giant (Part 1)." *Jazz Research* (November/December): 7–8. [Jazz-LA]

0179.———. 1963. "Sonny Clay: A Veritable Giant (Part 2)." *Jazz Research* (January/February): 13–14,. [Jazz-LA]

0180. Bentson, Kelli. 1985. "Sisterhood: Exene Cervenka and Wanda Coleman," *Option* (July/August): 42–43. [Rock/Poetry-LA]

0181. Berg, Chuck. 1977. "Dexter Gordon: Making His Great Leap Forward," *Down Beat* 44 (February 10): 12–13, 38, 42–43. [Jazz-LA]

0182. Berger, Edward. 1988a. "Carter, Benny," *NGDJ* 1: 189–191. [Jazz-LA]

0183.———. 1988b. "Edison, Harry ('Sweets')," *NGDJ* 1: 324–325. [Jazz-LA]

0184. Berger, Monroe, Edward Berger, and James Patrick. 1982. *Benny Carter: A Life in American Music, Vol. I & II.* Metuchen, NJ and London: The Scarecrow Press and the Institute of Jazz Studies, Rutgers University. [Jazz-LA]

0185. Berle, Arnie. 1981. "Kenny Burrell: A Pillar of Mainstream Jazz," *Guitar Player* 15 (April): 58–60, 62, 64, 66, 68, 70, 72. [Jazz-LA]

0186. Bernard, James. 1990. "NWA," *The Source* 16 (December): 34. [Rap-LA]

0187.———. 1991a. "Ice Cube: Building a Nation," *The Source* 27 (December): 32–34. [Rap-LA]

0188.———. 1991b. "West Coast Hip-Hop Round Up," *Spin* 6(10) [January]: 82. [Rap-CA]

0189. Bernstein, Charles M. 1983. "The Traditional Roots of Billy Higgins," *Modern Drummer* 7(2): 20–23, 74–75. [Jazz-LA]

0190.———. 1985. "Shelly Manne: The Last Interview," *Modern Drummer* 9(1): 14. [Jazz-LA]

0191. Bianco, David. 1988. *Heat Wave: The Motown Fact Book.* Ann Arbor: Popular Culture. [Popular Music-LA-Brenda Holloway]

0192. Bigard, Barney. 1986. *With Louis and the Duke.* New York: Oxford University Press. [Jazz-LA-Autobiography of clarinetist Barney Bigard, describes his stay in Los Angeles during the 1960s]

0193. Billingham, Alf. 1990. "M. C. Hammer: Cleaning Up Rap's Image," *Melody Maker* 66 (June 2): 16–17. [Rap-Oakland]

0194. Birnbaum, Larry. 1977. "Jimmy Smith: Sermonizing in the '70s," *Down Beat* 44 (December 15): 22–23, 57. [Jazz-LA]

0195.———. 1982. "Eddie Cleanhead Vinson," *Down Beat* 49 (October): 28–30. [Jazz-LA]

0196.———. 1991a. "Frank Morgan: Bebop Is a Lovesome Thing," *Down Beat* 58 (April): 16–18. [Jazz-LA]

0197.———. 1991b. "The Soul of the Church: David Murray and James Newton," *Down Beat* 58 (November): 24–25. [Jazz-LA]

0198.———. 1992. "Aster Aweke," *Musician* 164 (June): 25. [Ethiopian Popular Music-SF-Brief profile]

0199. The Bishop of Hip-Hop. 1991. "Yeah, That's Funkee: Del Tha Funkee Homosapien," *The Source* 27 (December): 39. [Rap-Oakland]

0200. Bishop, John. 1991. *California Artists: At the Crossroads.* Sacramento: California Arts Council. [Folk/Traditional-LA-Garifuna]

0201. Blackwell, Mark. 1991. "Niggaz4dinner," *Spin* 7 (September): 55–57, 101. [Rap-LA-NWA]

0202.————. 1994. "Artist of the Year Runners-up: Dr. Dre," *Spin* 9(10) [January]: 36. [Rap-LA]

0203. Blair, Iain. 1995. "Harvey Kubernik: Spoken-Word Pioneer," *Mix* 19 (September): 113–114, 119–122. [Jazz-LA-Buddy Collette]

0204. Blau, Ellen. 1983a. "Living Blues Interview: Pee Wee Crayton," *Living Blues* 56 (Spring): 5–12, 14–16. [Blues-CA]

0205.————. 1983b. "Living Blues Interview: Pee Wee Crayton," *Living Blues* 57 (Autumn): 6–9, 36–39, 41–47. [Blues-CA]

0206. Block, Stephen. 1990. "Pitch-class Transformation in Free Jazz," *Music Theory Spectrum* 12(2): 181–202. [Jazz-LA-analyzes Ornette Coleman's "Lonely Woman," recorded in LA]

0207. Bloom, Steve. 1981. "Facing the Facts with Earth, Wind & Fire," *Down Beat* 48 (September): 15–17, 66. [R & B-Carmel Valley]

0208.————. 1992. "Cypress Hill: as Dope as You Wanna Be," *High Times* (March): 38. [Rap-LA]

0209. Blum, Joe, and Jock Baird. 1982. "James Newton: Mystery Roots and the Solo Flute," *Musician Player and Listener* 46 (August): 65–68. [Jazz-LA]

0210. Blumenthal, Bob. 1980. "Arthur Blythe: Refreshing Traditions," *Down Beat* 47 (April): 25–26, 64. [Jazz-LA]

0211. Bogle, Donald. 1980. *Brown Sugar: Eighty Years of America's Black Female Superstars.* New York: Da Capo. [Popular Music/Jazz-CA-Ivie Anderson]

0212. Booth, John D. 1974. "The Music of Andraé Crouch and the Disciples." Master's thesis, New Orleans Baptist Theological Seminary. [Gospel-LA]

0213. Bourne, Mike. 1971. "George Duke: The Whole Gamut," *Down Beat* 38 (October 28): 14, 35. [Jazz-Bay Area/LA]

0214.————. 1977. "Benny Carter: His Royal Majesty of Reeds," *Down Beat* 44 (February 24): 20–21, 50. [Jazz-LA]

0215.————. 1985. "Bobby McFerrin: The Voice," *Down Beat* 52 (May): 20–22. [Jazz-LA/SF]

0216. Boyer, Horace Clarence. 1964. "The Gospel Song: A Historical and Analytical Study." Master's thesis, Eastman School of Music, University of Rochester. [Gospel-LA-Brief mention of the names of gospel performes who resided in LA: Cleveland, Akers, Griffin]

0217.————. 1973. "An Overview: Gospel Music Comes of Age," *Black World* 23(1): 42–48, 79–86. [Gospel-LA-Akers, Cleveland, Hawkins]

0218.————. 1979. "Contemporary Gospel Music," *The Black Perspective in Music* 7(1): 5–58. [Gospel-CA-Has information on Edwin Hawkins]

0219.————. 1985 "A Comparative Analysis of Traditional and Contemporary Gospel Music" in *More Than Dancing: Essays on Afro-American Music and Musicians*, edited by Irene V. Jackson. Westport, CT: Greenwood Press, pp. 127–146. [Gospel-LA-Andrae Crouch, Edwin and Walter Hawkins]

0220.————. 1986a. "Akers, Doris (Mae)," *NGDAM* 1: 23. [Gospel-LA]

0221.————. 1986b. "Cleveland, James L.," *NGDAM* 1: 457. [Gospel-LA]

0222.————. 1986c. "Crouch, Andrae (Edward)," *NGDAM* 1: 549. [Gospel-LA]

0223.————. 1986d. "Gospel Music II: Black Gospel Music," *NGDAM* 1: 254–261. [Gospel-CA]

0224.————. 1986e. "Hawkins, Edwin R.," *NGDAM* 2: 353. [Gospel-Bay Area-includes all the Hawkinses]

0225.————. 1986f. "Ligon, Willie Joe," *NGDAM* 3: 86. [Gospel-LA-Sang with Mighty Clouds of Joy]

0226.————. 1986g. "Martin, Sallie," *NGDAM* 3: 180. [Gospel-LA]

0227.————. 1995. *How Sweet the Sound: The Golden Age of Gospel.* Washington, D.C.: Elliot & Clark Publishing. [Gospel-CA-Has section on California School of Gospel, and other references to CA gospel artists]

0228. Bradley, Sam Y. 1979. "Profile: Ernie Watts," *Down Beat* 46 (May 3): 35–36. [Jazz/Studio-LA]

0229. Breckow, John. 1973. "Four Sheets in the Wind." *Whiskey, Women, And . . .* (February): 14–20. [Blues-CA-Pee-Wee Crayton]

0230. Briegleb, Ann M., Max Harrell, Mantle Hood, and Gertrude Robinson. 1985. *UCLA's Institute of Ethnomusicology, 1961–1974.* Los Angeles: Oral History Program, University of California, Los Angeles. [Music Education-LA]

0231. Britt, Stan. 1988. "Gaillard, Slim," *NGDJ* 1: 414. [Jazz-LA]

0232.————. 1989. *Dexter Gordon: A Musical Biography.* New York: Da Capo Press. [Jazz-LA]

0233. Broughton, Viv. 1985. *Black Gospel: An Illustrated History of the Gospel Sound.* Dorset, UK: Blandford Press, Ltd. [Gospel-LA-Includes brief references to gospel in LA—e.g., discussion about Andraé Crouch, all the Hawkins, Cleveland, Ligon]

0234. Broven, John. 1975a. "Behind the Western Sun: I. Earl Palmer," *Blues Unlimited* 115: 4–8. [Blues-LA]

0235.————. 1975b. "Louis Jordan 1908–1975," *Blues Unlimited* 113: 17. [Blues/R & B-LA-Obituary]

0236.————. 1984. "All for One: Harold Battiste," *Blues Unlimited* 146: 4–15. [Blues/Rock-LA]

0237. Brown, Clarence. 1976. "Bessie Griffin," *Lyric: A Magazine of Fine Arts* 7(3): 7–9, 17. [Gospel-LA]

0238. Brown, Geoff. 1976a. "Duke of Funk," *Melody Maker* 51 (August 14): 14. [Funk-LA-George Duke]

0239.————. 1976b. "Oh What a Lovely War," *Melody Maker* 51 (June 12): 34. [Rock/Soul-LA-War]

0240. Brown, Roxanne. 1988. "The Glory of Gospel: Will the Message Be Lost in the Contemporary Sound?" *Ebony* 43(7): 60, 62, 64, 66. [Gospel-CA-has info on Cleveland, Crouch, Hawkins, Sallie Martin]

0241. Browne, Kimasi. 1995. "Variation in the Vocal Style of Brenda Holloway: Soul Singer and 1960s Motown Recording Artist." Master's thesis, University of California, Los Angeles. [Soul-LA]

0242. Bryant, Clora. 1981a. "Trumpetistically Speaking," *Jazz Spotlite News* 2(3): 7. [Jazz-LA]

0243.————. 1981b. Trumpetistically Speaking," *Jazz Spotlite News* 2(4): 112–114. [Jazz-LA]

0244.————. 1986. "Liner Notes," *Be-Bop and Beyond* 4(3): 3. [Jazz-LA-An excerpt from "Jazz Is: Black Attitudes and Emotions"]

0245.————. 1988. "Clora Bryant's First Stroll Down Central Avenue," *IAOJA Newsletter* (February): 6. [Jazz-LA]

0246.————. 1994. *Central Avenue Sounds Oral History Transcript.* Los Angeles: Oral History Program, University of California. [Jazz-LA-Interviewed by Steven L. Isoardi]

0247. Budds, Michael J. 1986a. "Mathis, Johnny," *NGDAM* 3: 193. [Popular Music-SF]

0248.————. 1986b. "Turner, Tina," *NGDAM* 4: 427–428. [Rock-LA]

0249.————. 1986c. "Wilson, Nancy," *NGDAM* 4: 538–539. [Popular Music-LA]

0250. Bullock, Paul, and David Hoxie. 1982. "Buddy Collette Interview," *Jazz Heritage Foundation* III(1). [Jazz-LA]

0251. Burgess, A. Ace. 1976. "Can Gospel Rock? No!, James Cleveland, Yes! Mighty Clouds," *Jet Magazine* 1(6): 24–26. [Gospel-LA]

0252. Burke, Tony, and Dave Penny. 1985a. "Big Joe Turner," *Blues and Rhythm: The Gospel Truth* 11: 4. [Jazz/Blues-CA]

0253.————. 1985b. "Big Joe Turner," *Blues and Rhythm: The Gospel Truth* 12: 4. [Jazz/Blues-CA]

0254.————. 1985c. "Les Hite's Orchestra 'T-Bone Blues', 1935–42," *Blues and Rhythm: The Gospel Truth* 9: 8. [Jazz-LA]

0255. Burke, Tony, Dave Penny, and Tony Watson. 1986. "The Great Gates: 'Home Town Boy,'" *Blues and Rhythm: The Gospel Truth* 21: 14–15. [Blues-LA-Ed Gates]

0256. Burns, Jim. 1967. "West Coast Sounds," *Jazz Journal* 20 (November): 26–27. [Jazz-LA]

0257.————. 1968. "Slim and Slam," *Jazz Journal* 21 (September): 4. [Jazz-LA-Slim Gaillard]

0258.————. 1969. "Bird in California," *Jazz Journal* 22 (July): 10–12. [Jazz-LA-Charlie Parker]

0259.————. 1972. "Dexter Gordon 1942–1952," *Jazz Journal* 25 (April): 22–24, 39. [Jazz-LA]

0260.————. 1986. "Central Avenue Breakdown," *Blues and Rhythm: The Gospel Truth* 21: 4–13. [R & B-LA]

0261. Burrell, Walter Price. 1974. "Rev. James L. Cleveland: King of Gospel," *Black Stars* 3(12): 24–29. [Gospel-LA]

0262. Burrell, Walter Rico. 1982. "The Gospel According to Andrae Crouch," *Ebony* 37(11) [September]: 57–60. [Gospel-LA]

0263. Butterfield, Herbie. 1961. "Wardell Gray," *Jazz Journal* 14 (October): 1–3. [Jazz-LA]

0264. Buzelin, J. 1977. "Johnny 'Guitar' Watson," *Jazz Hot* 334 (February): 30. [Blues-LA]

0265. Caldwell, Hansonia L. 1988. "Music in the Lives of Blacks in California: The Beginnings," *Black Music Research Bulletin* 10(1): 5–7. [General Music-CA]

0266. Callender, Red, and Elaine Cohen. 1985. *Unfinished Dream: The Musical World of Red Callender.* New York: Quartet Books. [Jazz-LA]

0267. Cambell-Ingram, Sharon. 1991. "James Cleveland (1931–1991): A Tribute," *Rejoice!* 3(3): 26–27. [Gospel-LA]

0268. Campbell, Robert L. 1995. "Patty Waters Interview," *Cadence* 21 (March): 13–23, 107. [Jazz-LA/Bay Area/Santa Cruz]

0269. Carducci, Joe. 1993. *Rock and the Pop Narcotic,* rev. ed. Los Angeles: 2.13.61. [Rock-CA-Mentions several CA-based rock artists]

0270. Carles, P. 1964. "West Side Story (California)," *Jazz Magazine* 113 (December): 74–77. [Jazz-CA]

0271. Carlsson, Ulf. 1984a. "Jimmy McCracklin: Steppin' Up in Class," *Living Blues* 62: 1. [Blues-Oakland]

0272.————. 1984b. "Trekvarts sekel med musiken: Lloyd Glenn," *Jefferson* 67 (Winter): 26–34. [Blues-CA]

0273.————. 1985. "Trekvarts sekel med musiken: Lloyd Glenn," *Jefferson* 69 (Summer): 10–17. [Blues-CA]

0274. Case, B. 1982. "Most Unfortunate: Like A Fox," *The Wire* 1: 8. [Jazz-LA-Interview with Harold Land]

0275. Case, Brian. 1979. "The Funker Who Found His Right Voice," *Melody Maker* 54 (June 30): 46. [Jazz-LA-James Newton]

0276.————. 1981. "California, Here I Come," *Melody Maker* 56 (April 4): 28. [Jazz-LA-Teddy Edwards]

0277. Casey, Mary E. 1980. "The Contribution of the Rev. James Cleveland to Gospel and Music Education." Master's (?) thesis, Howard University. [Gospel-LA]

0278. Charles, Ray. 1978. *Brother Ray.* New York: Dial. [Soul/R & B/Popular Music-LA]

0279. Charles, T. 1953. "The West Coast Cats Wig and Wail," *Metronome* 69 (December): 17+. [Jazz-CA]

0280. Charone, Barbara. 1974. "War: A Street Rod on the Boulevard of Soul," *Rolling Stone* 164 (July 4): 14, 30. [Rock/Soul-LA]

0281. Charters, Ann. 1970. *Nobody: The Story of "Bert" Williams.* New York: Macmillan. [Vaudeville-SF]

0282. Chilton, John. 1988. "Clayton, Buck," *NGDJ* 1: 220–221. [Jazz-LA]

0283. Chirazi, Steffan. 1994. *Faith No More: The Real Story.* Sussex: Castle Commons. [Rock-LA]

0284. Choisnel, Emmanuel. 1972. "La scene du gospel à Oakland," *Soul Bag* 22/23: 51–52. [Gospel-Oakland]

0285. Choisnel, Emmanuel, and Lee Hildebrand. 1972a. "Johnny Heartsman," *Soul Bag* 22/23: 17–18. [Blues-Oakland]

0286.————. 1972b. "Orchestres et Musiciens de la Baie de San Francisco," *Soul Bag* 22/23: 6[Blues-Bay Area]

0287. Clark, Rick. 1994. "Ted Hawkins," *Pulse!* 129 (August): 45. [Folk-LA]

0288. Clarke, Stanley. 1992. "LA's Top Scorer," *EQ* 2(6): 50–54. [Film Music-LA]

0289. Clayton, Buck. 1987. *Buck Clayton's Jazz World.* New York: Oxford University Press. [Jazz-LA-has chapter on LA and West Coast]

0290. Claxton, William, ed. 1954. *Jazz West Coast: A Portfolio of Photographs.* Hollywood, CA: Linear Productions. [Jazz-CA]

0291. Clinco, Paul. 1972. "Living Blues Interview: Big Joe Turner," *Living Blues* 10: 20–26. [Blues-CA]

0292. Cobb, Mark. 1984. "Interview: Harold Land." *Bebop and Beyond* (November/December). [Jazz-LA]

0293. Cohen, Elaine. 1984a. "Horace Tapscott Talking: A Legacy to Pass On, Part I," *Cadence* 10 (July): 8–10, 18. [Jazz-LA]

0294.————. 1984b. "Horace Tapscott Talking: A Legacy to Pass On, Part II," *Cadence* 10 (August): 12–14. [Jazz-LA]

0295. Cole, Maria, and Louie Robinson. 1971. *Nat King Cole: An Intimate Biography.* New York: William Morrow. [Popular Music/Jazz-LA]

0296. Cole, Pat. 1994. "Hip Hop Herbie," *Down Beat* 61 (June): 16–20. [Jazz-LA-Herbie Hancock]

0297.————. 1995a. "Defending the Bottom Line: Robert Hurst & John Patitucci," *Down Beat* 62 (April): 28–31. [Jazz-LA]

0298.————. 1995b. "George Duke: Radio Formats Be Damned!" *Down Beat* 62 (May): 26–28. [R & B/Popular Music-SF]

0299. Collette, Buddy. 1993. *Central Avenue Sounds Oral History Transcript, 1989–1990: Buddy Collette.* Los Angeles: Oral History Program, University of California, Los Angeles. [Jazz-LA-Interviewed by Steven L. Isoardi, 2 vols., over 700 pages, very in-depth]

0300. Collins, D. Jean. 1983. "Interview With Adele Sebastian," *Uraeus: The Journal of Unconscious Life* 2(4): 36–43. [Jazz-LA]

0301. Collins, Lisa. 1991a. "In the Spirit: Edwin Hawkins Gives Thumbs-Up to 10th Music & Arts Seminar," *Billboard* 103 (July 13): 65. [Gospel-LA]

0302.———. 1991b. "In the Spirit: For Many, the Rev. Cleveland Personified Gospel Music," *Billboard* 103 (March 9): 66. [Gospel-LA-Obituary]

0303. Collins, Willie. 1988. "The Role of Music and Social Occasions in the Continuance of Afro-American Cultural Identity" in *Home and Yard: Black Folk Life Expressions in Los Angeles,* edited by Nancy McKinney. Los Angeles: California Afro-American Museum, pp. 28–31. [General Music-LA]

0304.———. 1990a. "The Blues: At Home and Alive in Los Angeles," *Los Angeles Folk Arts Newsletter* 5(2): 1, 3, 9. [Blues-LA]

0305.———. 1990b. "Here and Now: Willie Dixon Is the Blues," *Los Angeles Folk Arts Newsletter* 5(2): 3, 9. [Blues-LA]

0306.———, ed. 1992. *African-American Traditional Arts and Folklife in Oakland and the East Bay.* Oakland: Sagittarian Press. [Gospel/Blues/Sacred Music-Oakland]

0307. Conrad, Tom. 1994. "Meditations and Divine Offerings: Charles Lloyd," *Down Beat* 61 (April): 34–37. [Jazz-Big Sur/Santa Barbara]

0308. Considine, J. D. 1992. "Fear of a Rap Planet: The Biggest Style of the Last Decade Has a Problem with Attitude," *Musician* 160 (February): 34–43, 92. [Rap-CA-Ice Cube]

0309. Cook, David, and Keith Moerer. 1989. "N. W. A.—Art or Irresponsibility," *BAM Magazine* 15(8): 28. [Rap-LA]

0310. Cook, Eddie. 1982. "Red Holloway," *Jazz Journal International* 35 (December): 17. [Jazz-LA]

0311. Cooke, J. 1988. "Eric Dolphy," *Jazz Monthly* 11(11): 25. [Jazz-LA]

0312. Cooper, E. H. 1927. "Rag in the Barbary Coast." *Dance Magazine* (December). [Jazz-SF]

0313. Cooper, G. S. 1991. "Rev. Cleveland's GMWA Legacy Lives On," *Cash Box* 55 (August 17): 7. [Gospel-LA]

0314. Coss, Bill. 1962. "Back to Stay: Howard McGhee," *Down Beat* 29 (January 18): 20–21. [Jazz-LA]

0315. Costello, Mark, and David Foster Wallace. 1990. *Signifying Rappers: Rap and Race in the Urban Present.* New York: The Ecco Press. [Rap-LA-Includes perspectives on LA rappers; authors are obsessed with the fact that they are suburban white guys who like rap]

0316. Cox, Bette Y. 1988. "A Selective Survey of Black Musicians in Los Angeles, 1890–ca. 1945," *Black Music Research Bulletin* 10(1): 7–10. [Musicians-LA]

0317.———. 1995. *The Musical Renaissance of Black Los Angeles, 1890–1955.* Los Angeles: California Afro-American Museum. [Jazz-LA-Program notes for museum exhibition]

0318.———. 1996a. *Central Avenue—Its Rise and Fall (1890–c.1955), Including the Musical Renaissance of Black Los Angeles.* Los Angeles: BEEM Publications. [General Music-LA-Includes oral histories of Sam Browne, Jester Hairston, Marion Downs Smith, Ivan Browning, W. G. Still, Leroy Hurte, Maurice McGehee, Albert McNeil, Marshall Royal, Teddy Buckner, Eddie Beal, Buddy Collette, Marl Young, others; also has history of Central Avenue, information on musicians unions, music education]

0318a. Cox, Bette Yarbrough. 1996b. "Early Jazz in Los Angeles—(the 1920s and 1930s)," in *Music in the Central Avenue Community, 1890–c. 1955,* edited by Bette Y. Cox. Los Angeles: BEEM Foundation, pp. 34–41. [Jazz-LA]

0318b. Cox, Bette Y. 1996c. *Music in the Central Avenue Community 1890–c. 1955.* Los Angeles: BEEM Foundation. [General Music-LA]

0319. Crisafulli, Chuck. 1993. "Intro New Groove Review: Rage Against the Machine," *Guitar Player* 27 (July): 12. [Metal/Rap-LA]

0320.———. 1995. "Warren G's Home Studio," *Musician* 204: 80–82. [Rap-LA]

0321. Cronbach, Lee. n.d. "Musical Training and Compositional Motivation of Two Gospel Musicians: Interviews with Rev. James Cleveland and Charles May." Unpublished manuscript. [Gospel-LA]

0322.———. 1981/82. "Two Pieces on Tonal Stratification in Black American Music Structural Polytonality in Contemporary Afro-American Popular Music," *Black Music Research Journal:* 15–33. [Gospel-LA-Analyzes James Cleveland piece]

0323. Cross, Brian. 1993. *It's Not About a Salary: Rape, Race, and Resistance in Los Angeles.* New York: Verso. [Rap-LA]

0324. Crouch, Andraé, with Nina Bell. 1974. *Through It All.* Waco, TX: Word Books. [Gospel-LA]

0325. Crouch, Stanley. 1979. "Bringing Atlantis Up to the Top," *Village Voice* 24 (April 16): 65–67. [Rock/Jazz-SF/LA-mentions Sly Stone and Arthur Blythe very briefly]

0326. Crouchett, Lorraine J. 1987–88. "William Elmer Keeton and the Oakland Colored Chorus: Musical Pioneers of the WPA Era," *Oakland Heritage Alliance News* 7(4): 1–6. [Spirituals/Art Music-Oakland]

0327. Crowther, Bruce. 1980. "The Bill Berry Story," *Jazz Journal International* 33 (February): 12–13. [Jazz-LA]

0328.———. 1985. "Brothers in Brass," *Jazz Journal International* 38 (October): 16–17[Jazz-LA-Pete and Conte Candoli]

0329. Cuney-Hare, Maud. 1974 [1936]. *Negro Musicians and Their Music.* New York: Da Capo. [Art Music-LA-Hyers sisters]

0330. Curry, John. 1988. "Mitchell, Red," *NGDJ* 2: 114–115. [Jazz-LA]

0331. Dahl, Bill. 1989. "Video Review: Ernie Andrews: Blues for Central Avenue," *Living Blues* 20 (May/June): 49–50. [Blues-LA]

0332. Dahl, Linda. 1984. *Stormy Weather: The Music and Lives of a Century of Jazzwomen.* New York: Pantheon. [Jazz-LA-Melba Liston, Clora Bryant]

0333. Daly, Steven. 1992. "Heroes on a Roll," *Spin* 7 (March): 20. [Rap-Oakland-Short bio on Disposable Heroes of Hiphoprisy]

0334. Dance, Helen Oakley. 1987. *Stormy Monday: The T-Bone Walker Story.* Baton Rouge: Louisiana State University Press. [Blues-LA]

0335. Dance, Stanley. 1970. *The World of Duke Ellington.* New York: Da Capo. [Jazz-LA-Has interview with Lawrence Brown, LA resident]

0336.———. 1974. *The World of Swing.* New York: Scribner's. [Jazz-CA-Benny Carter]

0337.———. 1979. "Red Callender," *Coda* 167 (June 1): 9. [Jazz-LA]

0338.———. 1980. *The World of Count Basie.* New York: Scribner. [Jazz-LA-Buck Clayton, Snooky Young, Harry Edison]

0339.———. 1985. "Jimmie Noone Junior," *Jazz Journal International* 38 (July): 18–19. [Jazz-SD]

0340.———. 1988. "Jazz Musicians in San Diego," *Black Music Research Bulletin* 10(1): 10–11. [Jazz-SD]

0341. Dane, Barbara. 1965. "The Chambers Brothers Do That Real Thing," *Sing Out* 15(4): 22–24. [Rock-LA]

0342. Darden, Bob. 1990. "Laurraine Goreau and Just Mahalia, Baby," *Rejoice: The Gospel Music Magazine* 2(3): 20–23. [Gospel-LA-Talks about Goreau in CA]

0343. Darter, Tom. 1977. "George Duke: Master of Many Keyboards," *Contemporary Keyboard* 3 (July): 32–33, 36–38, 53. [Jazz/Rock/Pop-SF]

0344.———. 1979. "George Duke," *Contemporary Keyboard* 5 (October): 36–39, 46, 50–64. [Jazz/Rock/Funk-Bay Area]

0345. Darwen, N. 1986. "Slim Gaillard," *Blues and Rhythm: The Gospel Truth* 21: 15. [Jazz-LA]

0346. Daverat, X. 1989. "Billy Higgins: la Batterie c'est l'Infini," *Jazz Magazine* 383 (June): 55. [Jazz-LA]

0347. Davis, Clive. 1974. *Clive*. New York: William Morrow. [Rock-CA-Includes perspectives on Sly Stone]

0348. Davis, Francis. 1983. "David Murray: Tenor Energy," *Down Beat* 50 (June): 24–26. [Jazz-Berkeley/LA]

0349.———. 1986. *In the Moment: Jazz in the 1980s*. New York: Oxford. [Jazz-LA-Arthur Blythe, David Murray]

0350. Davis, Mark H. 1978. "The Black Sacred Song," *The Western Journal of Black Studies* 2(2): 138–141. [Gospel-LA-Includes photo of the Voices of Victory (Victory Baptist Church Choir)]

0351. Davis, Mike. 1992. *City of Quartz: Excavating the Future in Los Angeles*. New York: Verso. [History-LA-Briefly mentions John Carter and Horace Tapscott]

0352. Davis, Sharon. 1988. *Motown: The History*. London: Guinness. [Popular Music-LA-Brenda Holloway]

0353. Davis, Zeinabu Irene, with Clora Bryant. n.d. *Trumpetistically, Clora Bryant*. Manuscript. [Jazz-LA-Clora Bryant reference materials: articles, books, media]

0354. DeCurtin, Anthony, and Alan Light. 1991. "Opinion: N.W.A. has gone to a hateful extreme on *Efil4zaggin*," *Rolling Stone* 613 (September 19): 32. [Rap-LA]

0355. Deffaa, Chip. 1990. "The Blues Is Nothing but Personal: Jimmy Witherspoon," *Living Blues* 93 (September/October): 16–19. [Blues-LA]

0356. DeLapp, Jennifer. 1995. "An Index to James M. Trotter's *Music and Some Highly Musical People*," *Black Music Research Journal* 15(1): 109–136. [Art Music-Sacramento/SF-Hyers Sisters]

0357. DeLerma, Dominique. 1984. "A Concordance of Scores and Recordings of Music by Black Composers," *Black Music Research Journal*: 60–140. [Art Music-CA-Jester Hairston, Robert Owens, W. G. Still, Olly Wilson]

0358. Dery, Mark. 1988. "Notes from the Underground," *Keyboard* 14 (October): 28. [Rock/Industrial-SF-Beatnigs]

0359.———. 1992. "Fresh Licks: Guitar Finds a Funky Home in Hip-Hop," *Guitar Player* 26 (October): 96–103. [Rap-Bay Area-Disposable Heroes of Hiphoprisy]

0360. DeVaney, Byron. 1991. "Street Beat," *Cash Box* 54 (July 27): 10. [Rap-LA-DJ Quik]

0361. Deveaux, Scott. 1985. "Jazz in Transition: Coleman Hawkins and Howard McGhee, 1935–1945." Ph.D. dissertation, University of California, Berkeley. [Jazz-LA]

0362.———. 1987. "Conversation with Howard McGhee: Jazz in the Forties," *The Black Perspective in Music* 15(1): 64–78. [Jazz-LA-Talks about LA, California]

0363.———. 1988. "McGhee, Howard (B.)," *NGDJ* 2: 63. [Jazz-LA]

0364. Dexter, Dave. 1941. "Big Band Boom Has California on the Jump," *Down Beat* 8 (August 15): 3, 23. [Jazz-LA]

0365.———. 1950. "The Great Dixieland Renaissance in Hollywood," *Melody Maker* 26 (March 11): 3. [Jazz-LA]

0366.————. 1969. "Smogtown: The Los Angeles Story," *Billboard* 81 (December 27): 116–118, 120. [Jazz/Rock-LA-in 75th anniversary supplement]

0367. Di Perna, Alan. 1991. "The Bad: Fishbone Hooking into the Mainstream," *Guitar Player* 25 (August): 38–42. [Rock-LA]

0368.————. 1991. "Jazzin' the Blues With Charles Brown," *Musician* 150 (April): 80. [Blues-LA]

0369.————. 1993. "Five-String Freestyle: Fishbone's Norwood Fisher," *Musician* 179 (September): 55, 58. [Rock-LA]

0370. DJ Zen. 1993. "The Hill That's Real," *Urb* 3(30): 64–65. [Rap-LA-Cypress Hill]

0371. DjeDje, Jacqueline Cogdell. 1983. "An Expression of Black Identity, The Use of Gospel Music in a Los Angeles Catholic Church," *The Western Journal of Black Studies* 7(3): 148–160. [Gospel-LA]

0372.————. 1986. "Change and Differentiation: The Adoption of Black American Gospel Music in the Catholic Church," *Ethnomusicology* 30(2): 223–252. [Gospel-LA]

0373.————. 1988. "A Historical Overview of Black Gospel Music in Los Angeles," *Black Music Research Bulletin* 10(1): 1–5. [Gospel-LA]

0374.————. 1989a. "Black Gospel Music in L. A.," *The CAAS Report* 12(1 & 2): 12–13, 23. [Gospel-LA]

0375.————. 1989b. "Gospel Music in the Los Angeles Black Community: A Historical Overview," *Black Music Research Journal* 9 (Spring): 35–79. [Gospel-LA]

0376.————. 1990a. "Black Gospel Music in Los Angeles," *Los Angeles Folk Arts Newsletter* 5(2): 1, 2, 11. [Gospel-LA]

0377.————. 1990b. "Los Angeles: A City of Opportunity for African American Musicians" in *Who We Are: A Reader for Young People,* edited by Amy Suber. Los Angeles: UCLA World Arts and Cultures Program for the 1990 Los Angeles Festival, pp. 24–25. [General Music-LA]

0378.————. 1992. "The Beginnings of Gospel Music in the Bay Area" in *African-American Traditional Arts and Folklife in Oakland and the East Bay,* edited by Willie Collins. Oakland: Sagittarian Press, pp. 1–3. [Gospel-Oakland]

0379.————. 1993a. "Akers, Doris" in *Black Women in America: A Historical Encyclopedia,* edited by Darlene Clark Hine. Brooklyn: Carlson Publishing, p. 16. [Gospel-LA]

0380.————. 1993b. "Douroux, Margaret Pleasant" in *Black Women in America: A Historical Encyclopedia,* edited by Darlene Clark Hine. Brooklyn: Carlson Publishing, pp. 353–354. [Gospel-LA]

0381.————. 1993c. "Griffin, Bessie" in *Black Women in America: A Historical Encyclopedia,* edited by Darlene Clark Hine. Brooklyn: Carlson Publishing, pp. 503–504. [Gospel-LA]

0382.————. 1993d. "Hawkins, Tramaine" in *Black Women in America: A Historical Encyclopedia,* edited by Darlene Clark Hine. Brooklyn: Carlson Publishing, pp. 547–548. [Gospel-Bay Area]

0383.————. 1993e. "Lightner, Gwendolyn Cooper" in *Black Women in America: A Historical Encyclopedia,* edited by Darlene Clark Hine. Brooklyn: Carlson Publishing, pp. 720–721. [Gospel-LA]

0384.————. 1993f. "Los Angeles Composers of African American Gospel Music: The First Generations," *American Music* 11(4): 412–457. [Gospel-LA-Includes biographies and indexes of published works]

0385.————. 1993g. "Martin-Moore, Cora" in *Black Women in America: A Historical Encyclopedia,* edited by Darlene Clark Hine. Brooklyn: Carlson Publishing, pp. 751–752. [Gospel-LA]

0386.————. 1993h. "Simmons, Dorothy" in *Black Women in America: A Historical Encyclopedia*, edited by Darlene Clark Hine. Brooklyn: Carlson Publishing, pp. 1035–1036. [Gospel-LA]

0386a. DjeDje, Jacqueline Cogdell. 1996. "Pioneers and Trailblazers: Composers of the Los Angeles Gospel Sound," in *Music in the Central Avenue Community, 1890–c. 1955*, edited by Bette Y. Cox. Los Angeles: BEEM Foundation, pp. 55–60. [Gospel-LA]

0387. Dobbins, Bill. 1988. "Smith, Jimmy," *NGDJ* 2: 470–471. [Jazz-LA]

0388. Dobbins, Bill, and Richard Wang. 1986. "Cole, Nat 'King,'" *NGDAM* 1: 466. [Jazz/Popular Music-LA]

0389. Doerschuk, Bob. 1977a. "Billy Preston: Gospel/Rock Keyboardist," *Keyboard* 3 (February): 24–25. [Gospel/Rock-LA]

0390.————. 1977b. "Richard 'Groove' Holmes: Swinging Jazz Organist," *Contemporary Keyboard* 3 (February): 14, 15, 36. [Jazz-CA-briefly mentions California]

0391.————. 1978a. "Jimmy Smith," *Contemporary Keyboard* 4 (August): 26–28, 35–36. [Jazz-LA]

0392.————. 1978b. "Les McCann," *Contemporary Keyboard* 4 (September): 26–28, 30, 52. [Jazz-CA]

0393.————. 1978c. "Lonnie Jordan: Multi-Keyboardist with War," *Contemporary Keyboard* 4 (June): 14, 54. [Popular Music-San Pedro/Compton]

0394.————. 1979a. "Backstage with Andraé Crouch," *Contemporary Keyboard* 5 (August): 6–14. [Gospel-LA]

0395.————. 1979b. "Joe Sample: Branching Out after 25 Years with the Crusaders," *Contemporary Keyboard* 5 (August): 44–47. [R & B/Jazz-LA]

0396.————. 1982. "A Visit with Earl Hines," *Keyboard* 8 (April): 38–52. [Jazz-SF]

0397.————. 1988a. "Jazz Pianist Billy Childs: Burning up the Keys," *Keyboard* 14 (November): 90–96. [Jazz-LA]

0398.————. 1988b. "Jimmy Smith: These Hands Are Weapons," *Keyboard* 14 (April): 74–80. [Jazz-LA]

0399.————. 1991. "Hard Hits & Soft Drinks: Keyboardist Michael Buckholtz Nails M. C. Hammer's Crossover Rap," *Keyboard* 17 (October): 88–99, 111. [Rap/Popular Music-Oakland]

0400.————. 1994. "The Zappa Legacy," *Keyboard* 20 (April): 52–68. [Rock-LA-George Duke]

0401.————. 1995. "Hancock: From Miles Davis to Interactive Media (and Everything in Between)," *Keyboard* 21 (June): 48–58. [Jazz/Popular Music-LA-Herbie Hancock]

0402. Doherty, Harry. 1977. "In the Lap of the Gods?" *Melody Maker* 52 (August 6): 8–9. [Rock-LA-Little Feat]

0403. Douglass, William. 1993. *Central Avenue Sounds Oral History Transcript*. Los Angeles: Oral History Program, University of California. [Jazz-LA]

0404. Douroux, Margaret Pleasant. 1977. *About My Father's Business: The Ministry of Reverend Earl Amos Pleasant, 1918–1974*. Thousand Oaks, CA: Earl A. Publishing Co. [Gospel-LA]

0405.————. 1983. *Why I Sing*. Thousand Oaks, CA: Earl A. Pleasant Publishing Co. [Gospel-LA]

0406.————. 1987. "Benefits of Using Scripture in Song," *Message: A Christian Magazine of Contemporary Issues* 53(1): 5, 12. [Gospel-LA]

0407. Drozdowski, Ted. 1994. "Smokey Wilson," *Pulse!* 126 (May): 33. [Blues-LA]

0408. DuPree, Sherry S. 1989. "Andraé Crouch" in *Biographical Dictionary of African-American, Holiness-Pentecostals, 1880–1990*. Washington D.C.: Middle Atlantic Regional Press, p. 65. [Gospel-LA]

0409. Dyson, Michael Eric. 1991. "Performance, Protest, and Prophecy in the Culture of Hip-Hop," *Black Sacred Music* 5(1): 12–24. [Rap-LA-NWA, Ice Cube]

0410. Eastman, Ralph. 1989. "Central Avenue Blues: The Making of Los Angeles Rhythm and Blues, 1942–1947," *Black Music Research Journal* 9 (Spring): 19–33. [R & B-LA]

0411. Easton, Carol. 1973. *Straight Ahead: The Story of Stan Kenton.* New York: Morrow. [Jazz-CA]

0412. Eckstine, Roger. 1990. "Playing for the Audience: Big Jay McNeely," *Living Blues* 93: 23–28. [Blues-LA]

0413. Ehrlich, Dmitri. 1993. "Not Just Blowing Smoke: Cypress Hill light up on 'Black Sunday,'" *Rolling Stone* 662 (August 5): 16. [Rap-LA]

0414.————. 1995. "Hip-Hop Street Smart," *Pulse!* 141 (September): 93–94, 97. [Rap-LA-Priority Records]

0415. Eisner, Ken. 1980. "Unsung Heroes," *The Berkeley Monthly* 10 (February). [Jazz-Bay Area]

0416. Ellington, Duke. 1973. *Music Is My Mistress.* New York: Da Capo. [Jazz-LA-Has information on *Jump for Joy*, which premiered in LA. Includes original program]

0417. Ellis, Andy. 1995. "T-Bone Special: A Lesson in Blues," *Guitar Player* 29 (August): 79–83. [Blues-LA-T-Bone Walker]

0418. Ellis, C. 1969. "Some West Coast Bands of the 1920s," *Storyville* 21: 100–103. [Jazz-CA]

0419. Ellison, Mary. 1985. "The Honey Dripper: A True Survivor—Joe Liggins," *Juke Blues* 3: 4–5. [Blues-CA]

0420. Elwood, P. F. 1961. "The Role of San Francisco in Jazz History," *Metronome* 78 (August): 11–15. [Jazz-SF]

0421. Embree, Edwin Rogers. 1944. *13 Against the Odds.* New York: Viking. [Art Music-LA-W. G. Still]

0422. Emge, Charles. 1943. "'Not a Negro,' Says Bigard," *Down Beat* 10 (December 15): 3. [Jazz-LA-Barney Bigard]

0423.————. 1949a. "Jim Crow in L.A. Local 47 to Face Legal Showdown," *Down Beat* 16 (October 21): 1. [Jazz-LA]

0424.————. 1949b. "L.A. Council Votes Down Anti-Discrimination Law," *Down Beat* 16 (November 4): 3. [History-LA]

0425.————. 1951a. "Jazz' Most Underrated Musician? Benny Carter," *Down Beat* 18 (May 18): 2, 16. [Jazz-LA-Good article]

0426.————. 1951b. "Move Grows to Scrap L.A.'s Jim Crow Union," *Down Beat* 18 (June 15): 1, 19. [Jazz-LA]

0427.————. 1952. "Jazz Moves Underground in L.A. and is Prospering," *Down Beat* 19 (August 13): 8. [Jazz-LA]

0428. Endress, G. 1973. "Lady Trane," *Jazz Podium* 22(2): 16. [Jazz-LA-Alice Coltrane]

0429.————. 1984. "James Newton," *Jazz Podium* 33 (April): 6–9. [Jazz-LA]

0430.————. 1985. "John Carter," *Jazz Podium* 34: 4–6+. [Jazz-LA]

0431. Ephland, John. 1989. "Tony Williams: Still, the Rhythm Magician," *Down Beat* 56 (May): 20–23. [Jazz-Berkeley-Brief reference to Berkeley]

0432. Ertegun, Nesuhi. 1954a. "Jazz West Coast . . . A History and Development" in *Jazz West Coast: A Portfolio of Photographs,* edited by William Claxton. Hollywood: Linear Publications, n.p. [Jazz-LA]

0433.————. 1954b. "Modern Jazz: West Coast Brand," *Record Changer* 13 (Summer): 18–19. [Jazz-CA]

0434.————. 1954c. "The San Francisco Style Today," *Record Changer* 13 (Summer): 16–17. [Jazz-SF]

0435. Everett, Victor. 1995. "Gangsta Rap: Eve of Destruction?" *BAM Magazine* 458 (May 5): 28–30. [Rap-LA-DJ Quik]

0436. Farmer, Art. 1995. *Central Avenue Sounds Oral History Transcript.* Los Angeles: Oral History Program, Univeristy of California, Los Angeles. [Jazz-LA]

0437. Farrakhan, Louis. 1992. "Are the Police Present in the Community to Serve and Protect?" *The Final Call* 11 (August 24): 20–21, 32. [Rock-LA-Body Count, mentions "Cop Killer"]

0438. Faxio, Lorraine M. 1985. "The Music Program of the Works Progress Administration: A Documentation and Description of Its Activities with Special Reference to Afro-Americans" in *More Than Dancing: Essays on Afro-American Music and Musicians,* edited by Irene V. Jackson. Westport, CT: Greenwood Press, pp. 239–269. [Art Music-LA-Has information on WPA sponsored concerts in LA]

0439. Feather, Leonard. 1961. "The Enduring Benny Carter," *Down Beat* 28 (May 25): 15–16. [Jazz-LA]

0440.———. 1963. "Gerald Wilson," *International Musician* 62 (July): 18. [Jazz-LA]

0441.———. 1966a. "Watts: Jazz Bears Order Out of Chaos," *Melody Maker* 41 (September 3): 6. [Jazz-LA]

0442.———. 1966b. "Westward Ho! The Jazz Cry of the Sixties," *Melody Maker* 41 (March 26): 8. [Jazz-CA]

0443.———. 1967a. "Black Blues in Studios," *Down Beat* 34(3): 13. [Jazz-LA-Race and the studios]

0444.———. 1967b. "The New Life of Ray Brown," *Down Beat* 34 (March 9): 24–26. [Jazz-LA]

0445.———. 1970. "Shelly: The Whole Manne," *Down Beat* 37 (December 10): 16–17. [Jazz-LA]

0446.———. 1973. "The Pointer Sisters: A New Pointer View," *Down Beat* 40 (October 25): 16–17. [Popular Music-Oakland]

0447.———. 1978. "Piano Giants of Jazz: Nat 'King' Cole," *Contemporary Keyboard* 4 (April): 57. [Jazz-LA]

0448.———. 1979. "Piano Giants of Jazz: Hampton Hawes," *Contemporary Keyboard* 5 (July): 84. [Jazz-CA]

0449.———. 1981. "Interview: Ornette Coleman," *Down Beat* 48 (July): 16–19, 62–63. [Jazz-LA]

0450.———. 1984. "Blindfold Test: John Carter," *Down Beat* 51 (November): 47. [Jazz-LA]

0451.———. 1987. *The Jazz Years: Earwitness to an Era.* New York: Da Capo. [Jazz-LA-Clora Bryant/Melba Liston/Vi Redd; also has chapter on CA]

0452. Fein, Art. 1990. *L.A. Musical History Tour: A Guide to the Rock and Roll Landmarks of Los Angeles.* Boston: Faber and Faber. [Rock/R & B-LA-Has photos and captions of former residences, record companies, clubs, churches, death sites, and graves of many black CA artists]

0453. Ferguson, Jim. 1984a. "The Artistry and Versatility of Ron Eschete," *Guitar Player* 18 (May): 62, 64, 66, 69, 70, 144. [Jazz-LA]

0454.———. 1984b. "Eddie Duran: San Francisco's Elder Statesman of Bebop," *Guitar Player* 18 (April): 54, 56, 58, 61. [Jazz-SF]

0455. Figone, Richard John. 1988. "The Growth of the San Francisco Bay Area's Black Music Community During World War II." Master's thesis, San Francisco State University. [General Music-SF]

0456. Fish, Scott K. 1981a. "Ed Blackwell: Singin' on the Set," *Modern Drummer* 5(8): 14–17, 42–43, 56, 86, 88, 91. [Jazz-LA]

0457.———. 1981b. "James Bradley, Jr. Feels So Good," *Modern Drummer* 5(6): 14–17, 61, 82–83, 86, 92. [Jazz-LA]

0458. Fissinger, Laura. 1985. *Tina Turner.* New York: Ballantine. [Rock-LA]

0459. Flaherty, Liam. 1990. "King Arthur's Court," *Option* 31: 54–57. [Jazz-LA-Interview with Arthur Blythe]

0460. Flans, Robyn. 1981. "Harvey Mason," *Modern Drummer* 5(5): 10–13, 50, 64. [Jazz/Studio-LA]

0461.———. 1994. "Dr. Dre's Cheron Moore Up and Comer," *Modern Drummer* 18 (July): 30–33, 104, 107–110. [Rap-LA]

0462.———. 1995a. "Alvino Bennett: The Quintessential Sideman," *Modern Drummer* 19 (September): 76–85. [Studio-LA]

0463.———. 1995b. "Moyes Lucas: The Right Man for the Job," *Modern Drummer* 19 (August): 76–89. [Rock/Popular Music-LA]

0464. Flippo, Chet. 1973. "Crusaders: Contemporary . . . After 21 Years," *Rolling Stone* 138 (July 5): 18. [Jazz-LA]

0465. Floyd, Samuel A., and Marsha J. Reisser. 1989. "On Researching Black Music in California: A Preliminary Report About Sources and Resources," *Black Music Research Journal* 9 (Spring): 109–115. [General Music-CA]

0466. Fong-Torres, Ben. 1973. "The Rolling Stone Interview: Ray Charles," *Rolling Stone* 126 (January 18): 28–36. [Soul/R & B/Popular Music/Country-LA]

0467.———. 1977. "Natalie Cole," *Rolling Stone* 241 (June 16): 52–57. [Popular Music-LA]

0468.———. 1990. *The Motown Album.* New York: St. Martin's Press. [Soul-LA-Has section on Brenda Holloway]

0469. Forlenza, Jeff. 1994. "Cypress Hill's DJ Muggs," *Mix* 18 (April): 160–163. [Rap-LA]

0470. Forte, Dan. 1994. "Joe Louis Walker: Left Coast Blues Rebel," *Guitar Player* 28 (October): 31, 34. [Blues-SF]

0471. Foster, Pops. 1971. *Pops Foster: The Autobiography of a New Orleans Jazzman (as Told to Tom Stoddard).* Berkeley: University of California Press. [Jazz-LA-Did some work in LA in the late 20s]

0472. Fowler, Dr. William L. 1975. "New Hope for the Abstract Truth: Oliver Nelson," *Down Beat* 42 (April 24): 10–11, 43. [Jazz-LA]

0473. Franklin, A. David. 1986. "Los Angeles: Incubator of Jazz Talent," *Jazz Educators Journal* 18(2): 12–14. [Jazz-LA-Gordon, Mingus, Cherry, Dolphy, Zoot Sims, Art Pepper]

0474. Fredrickson, Scott. 1988. "Anderson, Ivie (Marie)," *NGDJ* 1: 23. [Jazz-LA]

0475. Fricke, David. 1991. "Black and Bruised," *Rolling Stone* 614 (October 3): 68–69. [Rock-LA-Fishbone]

0476. Fried, Michael. 1994. "Sing It, When You Can't Tell It." Unpublished manuscript. [Spirituals-CA]

0477. Frith, Simon. 1991. "Down by Law," *Village Voice* 36 (July 2): 84. [Rap-LA-NWA]

0478. Funk, Ray. 1990a. "Let's Go out to the Programs (The Peacock Gospel Years)" in *Duke/Peacock Records: An Illustrated History with Discography,* edited by Galen Gart and Roy C. Ames. Milford, NH: Big Nickel Publications, pp. 37–50. [Gospel-LA-Mighty Clouds of Joy]

0479.———. 1990b. "Let's Go out to the Programs," *Rejoice!* 2(4): 16–25. [Gospel-CA-Peacock Records, mentions several CA artists]

0480.————. 1992. "Los Angeles Recorded Gospel Who's Who." Unpublished manuscript. [Gospel-LA]

0481. Gaillard, Slim. 1968. *I Was There*. London. [Jazz-LA]

0482. Gallagher, Bill. 1976. "John Handy: Taking the Bible Out of the Brothels," *Down Beat* 43 (February): 20, 43. [Jazz-Bay Area]

0483. Garbarini, Vic. 1994. "Branford Marsalis Knows Why the Caged Bird Sings," *Musician* 189 (July): 40–50, 91, 93. [Jazz/Showbiz-LA]

0484. Gardner, Barbara. 1964. "The Baby Grows Up," *Down Beat* 31 (November 19): 18–20, 36–39. [Popular Music-LA-Nancy Wilson, barely mentions west coast]

0485. Gardner, Mark. 1967a. "Epilogue for Elmo," *Jazz Journal* 20 (July): 7. [Jazz-LA-Elmo Hope]

0486.————. 1967b. "Sonny Clark pt. 1," *Jazz Monthly* 12 (February): 21–22. [Jazz-LA]

0487.————. 1967c. "Sonny Clark pt. 2," *Jazz Monthly* 13 (March): 28–30. [Jazz-LA]

0488.————. 1988a. "Land, Harold (de Vance)," *NGDJ* 2: 7. [Jazz-LA]

0489.————. 1988b. "Richardson, Jerome (C.)," *NGDJ* 2: 376–377. [Jazz-SF]

0490. Gart, Galen. 1986. *First Pressings Vol. 1 & 2*. Milford, NH: Big Nickel Publications. [Popular Music/R & B/Rock-LA-The history of R & B as seen through Billboard Magazine]

0491. George, Lynell. 1992. *No Crystal Stair: African-Americans in the City of Angels*. New York: Verso. [History/Jazz/Gospel-LA-John Carter, James Cleveland]

0492. George, Nelson. 1985. "Inspirational Sounds Hit the Dance Floor: A & M Breaks Tramaine Hawkins, Qwest Pushes Winans," *Billboard* 97 (November 2): 57. [Gospel-Bay Area]

0493.————. 1985. *Where Did Our Love Go? The Rise and Fall of the Motown Sound*. New York: St. Martin's Press. [Popular Music-LA-Brenda Holloway/Discusses Motown in LA]

0494.————. 1988a. *The Death of Rhythm and Blues*. New York: Pantheon Books. [Popular Music-LA]

0495.————. 1988b. "Nationwide: America Raps Back," *Village Voice* 33(3) [January 19]: 32–33. [Rap-LA-Reference to LA's Rap Commission and Rap radio, Ice-T]

0496. Gerber, Alain. 1966. "Butler, à l'ouest le meilleur," *Jazz Magazine* 131 (June): 48–52. [Jazz-LA-Frank Butler]

0497. Gest, D. 1973. "A Powerful Tower of Soul," *Soul* 8 (August 6): 14. [Soul/Rock-Oakland-Interview with Tower of Power]

0498. Gibbs, V. 1974. "Success Is Diffcult but War Is Hell," *Crawdaddy* 40 (September): 66–68. [Rock/Soul-LA-War]

0499. Giddins, Gary. 1982. "Weatherbird: New Music—The L. A. Franchise," *Village Voice* 27 (December 7): 74–75, 96. [Jazz-LA-Jazz Festivals]

0500.————. 1987. *Celebrating Bird: The Triumph of Charlie Parker*. New York: Beech Tree Books. [Jazz-LA]

0501.————. 1989a. "The Tambourine Stuck on the Wall: Jazz and Poetry," *Village Voice* 34 (June 27): J1–J12, J21–J29. [Jazz-LA-Kamau Daa'ood, others]

0502.————. 1989b. "Weatherbird: Bumper Crop," *Village Voice* 34 (March 21): 86. [Jazz-LA-John Carter]

0503. Gilbert, Andrew. 1992. "Henry Franklin: Interview," *Cadence* 18 (November): 5–7. [Jazz-LA]

0504.————. 1993. "Roberto Miguel Miranda: Interview," *Cadence* 19 (April): 5–8, 109. [Jazz-LA]

0505. Gilbert, Mark. 1985. "Joe's Mode," *Jazz Journal International* 38 (August): 8–9. [Jazz-SF-Joe Henderson]

0506.———. 1994. "Joshua Redman," *Jazz Journal International* 47 (April): 6–8. [Jazz-Berkeley]

0507. Gill, Chris. 1994. "Punk Days Revisited: Slash Returns to His Roots," *Guitar Player* 28 (January): 104–107. [Rock-LA]

0508.———. 1995a. "Slash's New Band Shakes Up the Ranks," *Guitar Player* 29 (May): 65–70. [Rock-LA]

0509.———. 1995b. "T-Bone Walker: Electrifying the Blues," *Guitar Player* 29 (August): 72–78, 84, 86. [Blues-LA]

0510. Gillespie, Dizzy, and Al Fraser. 1979. *To Be or Not . . . to Bop*. New York: Da Capo. [Jazz-CA-Has reminescences of West Coast]

0511. Gillett, Charlie. 1975. *Making Tracks, Atlantic Records and the Growth of a Multi-Billion Dollar Industry*. New York: E. P. Dutton. [General Music-LA-Has section on West Coast]

0512. Ginibre, Jean Louis. 1968. "Los Angeles 68 de A a z," *Jazz Magazine* 156–157 (July/August): 18–30. [Jazz-LA]

0513. Gioia, Ted. 1992. *West Coast Jazz*. New York: Oxford University Press. [Jazz-CA-Parker, Gray, Gordon, Hawes, Criss, Edwards, Porter, Wilson, Pepper, Coleman, Dolphy, Mingus, Clifford Brown, Land, Hamilton]

0514. Gitler, Ira. 1960. "Mingus Speaks, and Bluntly," *Down Beat* 27 (July 21): 29–30, 67–68. [Jazz-LA]

0515.———. 1961. "Dexter Gordon: The Time for Recognition," *Down Beat* 28 (November 9): 16–17. [Jazz-LA]

0516.———. 1966. *Jazz Masters of the Forties*. New York: Macmillan Co., Inc. [Jazz-LA-Has sections on Dexter Gordon, Wardell Gray, Parker and Gillespie in CA, Brown/Roach, numerous other CA references]

0517.———. 1967. "Ever-ready Teddy Edwards," *Down Beat* 34 (July 27): 21–22. [Jazz-LA]

0518.———. 1985. *Swing to Bop*. New York: Oxford University Press. [Jazz-CA-Chapter 5 is entitled "California" and has reminesences from Red Callender, Zoot Sims, Benny Bailey, Howard McGhee, Sonny Criss, Joe Albany, Barney Kessel, Jimmy Rowles, Ross Russell, Earl Coleman, Dexter Gordon; other CA references throughout the book]

0519. Gittins, Ira. 1988. "Dressed to Kill," *Melody Maker* 64 (May 14): 48–49. [Rock-LA-Faith No More]

0520.———. 1993. "Griot On." *Melody Maker* (June 5): 11. [Rap-LA-Freestyle Fellowship]

0521. Glassman, Marc. 1986. "Charles Mingus' Destiny," *Coda* 206: 12–13. [Jazz-LA]

0522. Gleason, Ralph. 1949a. "Can Hampton Help Boost Sagging West Coast Biz?" *Down Beat* 16 (June 17): 18. [Jazz-SF-Lionel Hampton]

0523.———. 1949b. "Cats Should Try a Novel Approach—Please Public," *Down Beat* 16 (July 1): 12. [Jazz-CA]

0524.———. 1949c. "Quite a Few Good Things Suddenly Happen in S.F.," *Down Beat* 16 (January 28): 13. [Jazz-SF]

0525.———. 1950a. "Frisco Dancery Sets Up Two-Way Jim Crow Policy," *Down Beat* 17 (June 30): 18. [Jazz-SF]

0526.———. 1950b. "Louis, Ory Make Frisco Look Like Basin Street," *Down Beat* 17 (January 13): 18. [Jazz-SF]

0527.———. 1953. "San Francisco Officials Throw JATP Concerts Out of City Auditorium," *Down Beat* 20 (December 2): 1. [Jazz-SF]

0528.————. 1955. "Coast Counts Its Labels and Says: 'There Is, too, a San Francisco Jazz,'" *Variety* 197 (February 2): 1+. [Jazz-SF]

0529. Goddet, Laurent. 1977. "David Murray," *Jazz Hot* 343 (November): 11–15. [Jazz-Berkeley/CA]

0530. Goggin, Jim, and Peter Clute. 1994. *The Great Jazz Revival: A Pictorial Celebration of Traditional Jazz*. Sacramento: Donna Ewald Publisher. [Jazz-SF-SF Jazz Revival]

0531. Goines, Kevin. 1992. "The Phunky Feel Ones," *Nommo* 23 (February): 18, 30. [Rap-South Gate-Cypress Hill]

0532. Gold, Jonathan. 1993. "Day of the Dre," *Rolling Stone* 666 (September 30): 38–42, 109, 124. [Rap-LA-Dr. Dre/Snoop Doggy Dogg]

0533. Goldberg, Joe. 1965. *Jazz Masters of the Fifties*. New York: Macmillan. [Jazz-Mingus, Ornette Coleman, Ray Charles]

0534.————. 1992. "The Finest Pieces of Silver," *Musician* 168 (October): 34–36, 110. [Jazz-LA-Horace Silver]

0535.————. 1993. "Benny Carter's Eight Decades," *Musician* 180 (October): 22, 24. [Jazz-LA]

0536. Goldberg, Michael. 1980. "Tower of Power: Pro Blowing Section," *Down Beat* 47 (February): 22–23, 62, 64, 65. [Rock/Soul/Funk-Oakland]

0537.————. 1992. "Michael Jackson: The Making of the 'King of Pop,'" *Rolling Stone* 621 (January 9): 32–37. [Pop-Santa Ynez Valley-talks about his house which is located in CA]

0538.————. 1993. "Tony! Toni! Toné!" *Musician* 181 (November): 62, 64, 78. [R & B-CA]

0539. Goldman, Erik L. 1990. "Hamza El Din: The Hiss of the Desert," *Option* 34 (September/October): 50–53. [Folk/African-Bay Area-Originally from Sudan, lived in Bay Area, worked with the Grateful Dead]

0540. Gonzales, Michael A. 1995. "The Baby Maker," *Pulse!* 137 (May): 46–53, 109. [Soul-LA-Isaac Hayes; he moved to LA in 1977]

0541. Gordon, Robert. 1986. *Jazz West Coast*. New York: Quartet Books. [Jazz-CA-Gillespie/Parker, Brown/Roach, Hawes, Hamilton, C. Perkins, Land, Pepper, Coleman, Dolphy]

0542. Gordy, Berry Jr. 1994. *To Be Loved: The Music, The Magic, The Memories of Motown, an Autobiography*. New York: Warner Books. [Soul-LA-References to CA, Brenda Holloway]

0543. Gore, Joe. 1990. "Intro: The Rocky Road to Suicide," *Guitar Player* 24 (December): 18. [Rock-LA/Venice-Suicidal Tendencies, Rocky George]

0544. Gourse, Leslie. 1991. *Unforgettable: The Life and Mystique of Nat King Cole*. New York: St. Martin's Press. [Popular Music-LA]

0545.————. 1993. *Sassy: The Life of Sarah Vaughan*. New York: Scribner's. [Jazz-LA]

0546.————. 1995. *Madame Jazz: Contemporary Women Instrumentalists*. New York: Oxford University Press. [Jazz-CA-Has short chapter on CA]

0547. Gray, Herman. 1988. *Producing Jazz: The Experience of an Independent Record Company*. Philadelphia: Temple University Press. [Jazz-Bay Area-Discusses operations of Bay Area–based Theresa Records, an independent jazz label/Pharoah Sanders]

0548. Green, J. 1983. "The Seeds Are Set: Wind College," *Bebop and Beyond* 1(5): 8. [Jazz-LA]

0549. Green, Tony. 1995. "Ben Harper: You Can't Fool the Blues," *Guitar Player* 29 (December): 27–28. [Blues-CA]

0550. Green, William E. 1994. *Central Avenue Sounds Oral History Transcript*. Los Angeles: Oral History Program, University of California. [Jazz-LA]

0551. Greensmith, B. 1979. "Plas Johnson," *Blues Unlimited* 133: 12. [Jazz/Studio-LA]

0552. Gridley, Mark C. 1988a. "Cherry, Don(ald Eugene)," *NGDJ* 1: 204–205. [Jazz-LA]

0553.————. 1988b. "Haden, Charlie," *NGDJ* 1: 468. [Jazz-LA]

0554.————. 1988c. "Henderson, Joe," *NGDJ* 1: 516. [Jazz-SF]

0555. Griffith, Mark. 1994. "Artist on Track: Billy Higgins," *Modern Drummer* 18 (August): 84–85. [Jazz-LA]

0556. Grigson, L., and A. Morgan. 1962. "Carl Perkins," *Jazz Monthly* 8 (July): 11–15. [Jazz-LA]

0557. Gross, Terry. 1992. "Interview with Ice-T" in *Inside the L.A. Riots: What Really Happened and Why It Will Happen Again*, edited by Don Hazen. New York: Institute for Alternative Journalism, pp. 126–127. [Rap-LA]

0558. Grossman, Jay. 1975. "War: Back from the Streets with a Smile," *Rolling Stone* 193 (August 14): 18. [Rock-LA]

0559. Grove-Humphries, Stephen, and Phillip Hanson. 1982. "Teddy Edwards," *Jazz Journal* 35 (May): 12–13. [Jazz-LA]

0560. Guccione, Bob Jr. 1993. "Interview: Ice-T," *Spin* 9 (July): 70–75, 92–93. [Rap-LA]

0561. Guevara, Ruben. 1985. "The View from the Sixth Street Bridge: The History of Chicano Rock" in *The First Rock & Roll Confidential Report*, edited by Dave Marsh. New York: Pantheon, pp. 113–26. [R & B/Rock-LA-Influence of black R & B on Chicano artists]

0562. Guralnick, Peter. 1980. "Ray Charles" in *The Rolling Stone Illustrated History of Rock & Roll*, edited by Jim Miller. New York: Random House, pp. 109–112. [Soul/R & B-LA]

0563.————. 1986 [1994]. *Sweet Soul Music: Rhythm and Blues and the Southern Dream of Freedom*. New York: Harper and Row. [R & B-LA-Mostly on Stax but includes info on LA]

0564. Gushee, Lawrence. 1985. "A Preliminary Chronology of the Early Career of Ferd 'Jelly Roll' Morton," *American Music* 3(4): 389–412. [Jazz-LA]

0565.————. 1988. "How the Creole Band Came to Be," *Black Music Research Journal* 8(1): 83–100. [Jazz-LA]

0566.————. 1989. "New Orleans-Area Musicians on the West Coast, 1908–1925," *Black Music Research Journal* 9 (Spring): 1–18. [Jazz-CA]

0567. Haas, Robert, ed. 1972. *William Grant Still and the Fusion of Cultures in America*. Los Angeles: Black Sparrow Press. [Art Music-LA]

0568. Hadlock, Richard. 1965. *Jazz Masters of the Twenties*. New York: Macmillan. [Jazz-CA-some references to CA]

0569. Hague, Doug. 1962. "Los Angeles Jazz Scene," *Jazz Journal* 15 (July): 25–26. [Jazz-LA-Pops Foster]

0570.————. 1963. "Los Angeles Jazz Scene," *Jazz Journal* 16 (February): 12, 14. [Jazz-LA]

0571. Hall, Stanley. 1983. "Chester Thompson: Up for the Challenge," *Modern Drummer* 7 (January): 14–17, 64–67. [Jazz/Rock-LA]

0572. Hamilton, A. 1987. "Hampton Hawes: Letting a Beat Go By," *The Wire* 37: 26. [Jazz-LA]

0573. Hampton, Dream. 1995. "Eazy-E: 1963–1995," *Spin* 11(3) (June): 42. [Rap-LA]

0574. Hampton, Lionel, with James Haskins. 1989. *Hamp: an Autobiography*. New York: Warner Books, Inc. [Jazz-LA-Has chapter on Hollywood]

0575. Hansen, Barry. 1980a. "Doo-Wop" in *The Rolling Stone Illustrated History of Rock & Roll*, edited by Jim Miller. New York: Random House, pp. 83–91. [R & B-LA-Penguins/Platters/Coasters]

0576.————. 1980b. "Rhythm and Gospel" in *The Rolling Stone Illustrated History of Rock & Roll*, edited by Jim Miller. New York: Random House, pp. 15–18. [R & B-LA-Hank Ballard]

0577. Hansen, H. 1980. "Die Gitarre zum Sprechen gebracht: Johnny 'Guitar' Watson ein Symbol der 'Schwarzen' Rock-Musik," *Neue Musikzeitung* 4: 13. [Blues-LA]

0578. Haralambos, Michael. 1979. *Right On: From Blues to Soul in Black America.* New York: Da Capo. [Blues/Soul-CA-Mentions some artists who worked in CA]

0579. Haro, Guillermina. 1993. "One Time Motown Star Visits Crozier's Drama Class Students." *Topic Sun Newspaper* 72 (September 15). [Popular Music-LA-Brenda Holloway]

0580. Harris, Carter. 1995. "The Pharcyde," *Pulse!* 143 (November): 34. [Rap-LA]

0581. Harrison, Max. 1962. "Backlog Ten: Wardell Gray," *Jazz Monthly* 8 (May): 19. [Jazz-LA]

0582.———. 1988. "West Coast Jazz," *NGDJ* 2: 612. [Jazz-CA]

0583. Harrison, Spider. 1988. "Brenda Holloway: The 'Every Little Bit Hurts' Lady Is Back." *Black Radio Exclusive* (November 25): 23. [Popular Music-LA]

0584. Harvey, S. 1990. "Cover Story," *Cash Box* 53 (June 2): 3. [Rap-Oakland-MC Hammer]

0585. Haskins, James, with Kathleen Benson. 1984. *Nat King Cole.* New York: Stein and Day. [Popular Music/Jazz-LA]

0586. Hawes, Hampton. 1967. "In My Opinion," *Jazz Journal* 20 (November): 38, 40. [Jazz-LA]

0587. Hawes, Hampton, and Don Asher. 1972. *Raise Up Off Me: A Portrait of Hampton Hawes.* New York: Coward, McGann, and Geoghegan. [Jazz-CA]

0588. Hawthorn, Maggie. 1981. "Chet Baker," *Down Beat* 48 (October): 24–27, 63. [Jazz-LA]

0589. Hazell, Ed. 1988a. "Blythe, Arthur," *NGDJ* 1: 131. [Jazz-LA]

0590.———. 1988b. "Bradford, Bobby (Lee)," *NGDJ* 1: 142. [Jazz-LA]

0591.———. 1988c. "Carter, John (Wallace)," *NGDJ* 1: 191–192. [Jazz-LA]

0592.———. 1988d. "Coltrane, Alice," *NGDJ* 1: 235. [Jazz-LA]

0593.———. 1988e. "Hill, Andrew," *NGDJ* 1: 524. [Jazz-CA]

0594. Heilbut, Anthony. 1980. "New Signs on the Gospel Highway," *The Nation* 230(18): 565–568. [Gospel-CA]

0595.———. 1985. *The Gospel Sound: Good News and Bad Times.* New York: Limelight Editions. [Gospel-LA-James Cleveland]

0596. Heimann, Jim. 1985. *Out With the Stars: Hollywood Nightlife in the Golden Era.* New York: Abbeville Press. [General Music-LA]

0597. Helland, Dave. 1995. "Those Who Can, Teach," *Down Beat* 62 (May): 22–24. [Jazz-LA-Mentions Charlie Haden, Roscoe Mitchell (Cal Arts), Gerald Wilson (UCLA)]

0598. Henderson, A. 1990. "New Faces," *Cash Box* 54 (August 11): 54. [Rap-Compton-Compton's Most Wanted]

0599. Hennessey, Mike. 1966. "Cherry's Catholicity," *Down Beat* 33 (July 28): 14–15. [Jazz-LA-Don Cherry]

0600.———. 1982a. "First Bass pt. 1," *Jazz Journal International* 35 (July): 8–9. [Jazz-LA-Ray Brown]

0601.———. 1982b. "First Bass pt. 2," *Jazz Journal International* 35 (August): 10–11. [Jazz-LA-Ray Brown]

0602. Hennessey, Thomas Joseph. 1973. "From Jazz to Swing: Black Jazz Musicians and Their Music, 1917–1935." Ph.D. dissertation, Northwestern University. [Jazz-CA]

0603. Hentoff, Nat. 1995. "Max Roach and Clifford Brown: Dealers in Jazz," *Down Beat* 62 (June): 40. [Jazz-CA-Originally published May 4, 1955]

0604. Hershon, Robert. 1986. "James Newton: Learning From Other Cultures," *Jazz Journal International* 39 (June): 14–15. [Jazz-LA]

0605.———. 1992. "Horace Tapscott," *Jazz Journal International* 45 (July): 10–11. [Jazz-LA]

0606. Hervey and Company. 1992. *Andraé Crouch: Biography.* Los Angeles: Hervey and Company. [Gospel-LA]

0607. Hess, Norbert. 1975. "They Call Me Mr. Cleanhead: Eddie Vinson," *Blues Unlimited* 114: 4–6. [Blues-LA]

0608.———. 1976s. "I Didn't Give a Damn if Whites Bought It! The Story of Ralph Bass," *Blues Unlimited* 119: 17–24. [Blues-LA/Bay Area]

0609.———. 1976b. "Screamin' Jay Hawkins," *Blues Unlimited* 121: 4–14. [R & B-LA (?)]

0610.———. 1976c. "What a Diff'rence a Day Makes." *Black Music* (May): 6–7. [Blues-CA-Esther Phillips]

0611.———. 1977. "'I Ain't Bessie': The Story of Linda Hopkins," *Blues Unlimited* 124: 12–13. [Blues-LA/Bay Area]

0612. Hicks, Hilary Clay. 1990. "Going Through Hell for Mahalia: The Story of a Hollywood Star," *Rejoice: The Gospel Music Magazine* 2(3): 17–19. [Gospel-LA]

0613. Hildebrand, Lee. n.d. "Progressive Gospel Music in California: A Tale of Two Families." Unpublished ms. [Gospel-LA]

0614.———. 1968. "Little Johnny Taylor," *Blues Unlimited* 55 (July): 9–10. [Blues-LA/Bay Area]

0615.———. 1969a. "Little Joe Blue," *Blues Unlimited* 66 (October): 10. [Blues-Bay Area]

0616.———. 1969b. "Tiny Powell," *Blues Unlimited* 66 (October): 14. [Blues/Gospel-Oakland]

0617.———. 1971. "Jimmy McCracklin Today," *Blues Unlimited* 83 (July): 11. [Blues-Oakland]

0618.———. 1978. "Gospel's First Family," *Express: The East Bay's Free Weekly* 1 (November 24): 1, 4–5. [Gospel-Oakland-Hawkins Family]

0619.———. 1979a. "'Can't Nothing Shake Me Now'." *Express: The East Bay's Free Weekly* 1 (August 31): 4. [Gospel-Oakland-Lillian Glenn]

0620.———. 1979b. "A Dose of Mainline Soul," *Express: The East Bay's Free Weekly* 1 (August 17): 8. [Soul-Oakland-Maze, Frankie Beverly]

0621.———. 1979c. "The Elements of Style," *Express: The East Bay's Free Weekly* 2 (December 7): 10. [Soul-LA-Earth, Wind and Fire]

0622.———. 1979d. "North Richmond Blues," *Express: The East Bay's Free Weekly* 1 (February 9): 1, 4–5. [Blues-Richmond-Minnie Lou Nichols, Ollie Freeman]

0623.———. 1979e. "West Side Story," *Express: The East Bay's Free Weekly* 1 (September 28): 3. [Blues-Oakland]

0624.———. 1980a. "Been Down So Long." *The Monthly* 10 (February): 41–43. [Blues-Oakland-Bob Geddins]

0625.———. 1980b. "Dorothy Morrison's Happy Days." *Express: The East Bay's Free Weekly* 2 (January 25): 9. [Gospel-Oakland-Dorothy Morrison, Hawkins Family]

0626.———. 1980c. "The Gentlemen of Soul," *Express: The East Bay's Free Weekly* 2 (July 4): 8. [Soul-LA/Oakland-The Whispers]

0627.———. 1980d. "Saving Grace." *The Monthly* 10 (February): 39, 43. [Blues/Gospel-Oakland-Bob Geddins, Hawkins Family]

0628.———. 1981a. "Progressive Gospel at the Crossroads," *M. I.: Musician's Industry* 3 (September): 33–36. [Gospel-LA/Oakland-Andraé Crouch/Hawkins Family]

0629.———. 1981b. "Sugar Is Sweet," *Express: The East Bay's Free Weekly* 3(37) [July 10]: 8. [Blues/Soul-SF-Sugar Pie DeSanto]

0630.———. 1982a. "Bobby McFerrin Is the Jazziest Singer Around," *San Francisco Magazine* (August): 95–99. [Jazz-SF]

0631.————. 1982b. "The Thrill Goes On," *The Museum of Oakland (California)* (September–October): 5–7. [Blues-Oakland]

0632.————. 1983a. "Black and Blue," *Express: The East Bay's Free Weekly* 5 (April 29): 1, 12–14. [Jazz-Oakland-Ed Kelly]

0633.————. 1983b. "Z. Z. Hill, Blues Survivor," *Express: The East Bay's Free Weekly* 5 (July 15): 13. [Blues/Soul-LA]

0634.————. 1985. "Roots," *Express: The East Bay's Free Weekly* 7(46) [August 30]: 41–44. [Blues-Oakland/Fresno-Troyce Key, J. J. Malone]

0635.————. 1986a. "The Glamorous Life," *Express: The East Bay's Free Weekly* 8(25) [March 28]: 1, 7–11. [Soul/Jazz-Oakland-Sheila E.]

0636.————. 1986b. "Housewrecker," *Express: The East Bay's Free Weekly* 8(44) [August 8]: 16. [Soul-LA-Solomon Burke]

0637.————. 1986c. "The Johnny Otis Story," *Express: The East Bay's Free Weekly* 9 (December 12): 17–20. [Blues-LA/Oakland]

0638.————. 1986d. "The Message," *Express: The East Bay's Free Weekly* 8(50) [September 19]: 1, 12, 14–16. [Gospel-Oakland-Tramaine Hawkins]

0639.————. 1987a. "Living Blues Interview: Katie Webster pt. 1," *Living Blues* 74: 12–17. [Blues-Oakland]

0640.————. 1987b. "Living Blues Interview: Katie Webster pt. 2," *Living Blues* 75: 36–40. [Blues-Oakland]

0641.————. 1989a. "The Departure of King Narcisse: Flamboyant Last Rites for a Legendary Oakland Preacher." *Express: The East Bay's Free Weekly* 11 (February 24): 3, 27. [Gospel-Oakland]

0642.————. 1989b. "Sell a Joyful Noise." *Express: The East Bay's Free Weekly* 12 (December 21): 27–31. [Gospel-Berkeley-Betty Reid Soskin]

0643.————. 1990. "Not for Me to Say," *Express: The East Bay's Free Weekly* 12(49) [September 14]: 28–29. [Popular Music-SF-Johnny Mathis]

0644.————. 1991. "A Life in the Blues," *Express: The East Bay's Free Weekly* 13 (March 15): 1, 17–19, 23–27. [Blues-Oakland-Bob Geddins]

0645.————. 1992a. *Hammertime.* New York: Avon Books. [Rap-Oakland-Hammer]

0646.————. 1992b. "Jimmy McCracklin's Oakland Blues" in *African-American Traditional Arts and Folklife in Oakland and the East Bay,* edited by Willie Collins. Oakland: Sagittarian Press, pp. 9–11. [Blues-Oakland]

0647.————. 1993a. "Juke Joint Rambles, Midnight Crawls" in *Bay Area Blues.* San Francisco: Pomegranate Artbooks, pp. 7–11. [Blues-Bay Area]

0648.————. 1993b. "The Return of Funk," *Express: The East Bay's Free Weekly* 16(12) [December 31]: 20. [Soul-Vallejo-Con Funk Shun]

0649.————. 1994. *Stars of Soul and Rhythm & Blues.* New York: Billboard Books. [Soul/R & B-CA-Has entries for numerous CA-based Soul and R&B artists]

0650.————. 1995a. "A Unique American Life" in *Colors and Chords: The Art of Johnny Otis.* San Francisco: Pomegranate Artbooks, pp. 7–21. [Blues-LA/Oakland/Sebastopol]

0651.————. 1995b. "Legacy," *Express: The East Bay's Free Weekly* 17(48) [September 8]: 1, 10–12, 17–19. [Jazz-Berkeley-Joshua Redman]

0652. Hildebrand, Lee, with Henry Kaiser. 1984. "Jimmy Nolen: A Rare Interview with James Brown's Longtime Sideman—The Father of Funk Guitar," *Guitar Player* 18 (April): 34, 36, 38–39, 41–42, 44–45. [Blues-LA]

0653. Hildebrand, Lee, and Judith Moore. 1984. "Merry Christmas Baby," *Express: The East Bay's Free Weekly* 7(10) [December 14]: 1, 27–31. [Blues-LA/Berkeley-Charles Brown]

0654. Hill, George H. 1986. *Black Radio in Los Angeles.* Carson, CA: Daystar Publishing Co. [Radio-LA]

0655. Hochman, Steve. 1990. "Hammerin' Out the Hits," *Rolling Stone* 582/583 (July 12–26): 29. [Rap-Oakland-MC Hammer]

0656.————. 1991. "NWA: Keeping Attitude Alive," *Musician* 149 (March): 58–61. [Rap-LA]

0657. Hogan, Patricia. 1978. "Sonny Criss: 10/23/27–11/19/77," *Cadence* 3 (January): 30. [Jazz-LA-Letter to the editor]

0658. Holdship, Bill. 1991. "Reality Check," *Spin* 7(4) [July]: 51–52, 90. [Rock-LA-Fishbone]

0659. Hollis, Larry. 1988. "Bertha Hope," *Cadence* 14 (November): 18–23. [Jazz-CA-Wife of Elmo Hope, who worked in CA for a while]

0660. Hollis, Larry, and Eddie Ferguson. 1987. "Barney Kessel," *Cadence* 13 (August): 5–18, 30[Jazz-LA]

0661. Holly, Hal. ca. 1942–1947. "Los Angeles Band Briefs," *Down Beat.* [Jazz-LA-Continuing series of articles]

0662.————. 1949. "Ory, Berg Join Forces in New Vine Street Nitery," *Down Beat* 16 (November 4): 8. [Jazz-LA-Kid Ory]

0663.————. 1951. "Jazz Series Lecture Hits Ignorance of Legit Critic," *Down Beat* 18 (November 30): 8. [Jazz-LA-About UCLA Jazz course taught by N. Ertegun]

0664. hooks, bell. 1993. "Interview: Ice Cube," *Spin* 9 (April): 78–82. [Rap-LA]

0665. Horricks, Raymond. 1988. *The Importance of Being Eric Dolphy.* Turnbridge, England: Spellmount. [Jazz-LA]

0666. Hosiasson, Jose. 1988. "Ory, Kid," *NGDJ* 2: 277. [Jazz-LA]

0667. Howland, Don. 1993. "No Sell Out," *Spin* 8 (March): 40–41. [Rap-Bay Area-Paris]

0668. Hubbart, J. E. 1961. "Los Angeles Blues," *Jazz Report* 1 (February): 14. [Blues/Jazz-LA]

0669. Hubner, Alma. 1977. "Kid Ory" in *Selections from the Gutter: Jazz Portraits from the "Jazz Record,"* edited by Art Hodes and Chadwick Hansen. Berkeley: University of California Press, pp. 112–115. [Jazz-LA]

0670. Hurricane (?). 1995. "Hurricane vs. Dolomite," *Grand Royal* 2: 100–102. [Rap-LA-Rudy Ray Moore]

0671. Hutcherson, Bobby. 1971. "About the Vibes," *Crescendo International* 9(9): 24. [Jazz-CA]

0672. Hyltone, David. 1939. "Jack Tenney Asks for New L.A. Bylaws, Expects Fight," *Down Beat* 6(9): 32. [Jazz-LA]

0673. Ice-T, with Heidi Siegmund. 1994. *The Ice Opinion: Who Gives a Fuck?* New York: St. Martin's Press. [Rap-LA-Ice-T]

0674. Iglauer, Bruce, Jim O'Neal, and Bea Van Geffen. 1971a. "Living Blues Interview: Lowell Fulson," *Living Blues* 5 (Summer): 19–25. [Blues-CA]

0675.————. 1971b. "Living Blues Interview: Lowell Fulson," *Living Blues* 6 (Autumn): 10–20. [Blues-CA]

0676. "I. R." 1985. "Where Are They Now?" *Rolling Stone* 456 (September 12): 56. [Rock-LA-Chambers Brothers]

0677. Isherwood, Martin. 1993. "Harold Land," *Jazz Journal International* 46 (July): 12–13. [Jazz-LA]

0678. J-Blunt. 1991. "The Dopest Dope: The Eleven Most Important Tributes to Marijuana in Hip-Hop," *High Times* 192 (August): 45, 67. [Rap-LA-Tone Loc, Yo-Yo, Cypress Hill]

0679. Jackson, Blair. 1995a. "Broun Fellinis: Something Old, Something New," *Mix* 19 (June): 162, 165–169. [Jazz-SF]

0680.———. 1995b. "Classic Tracks: 'Birdland' by Weather Report," *Mix* 19 (June): 163, 173–175. [Jazz-LA-Recorded at Devonshire Studios in LA]

0681.———. 1995c. "Little Feat: A Whole Lotta Guank!" *Mix* 19 (June): 108, 111–117. [Rock-LA]

0682.———. 1995d. "Tuck and Patti: Small is Beautiful," *Mix* 19 (August): 181, 186–190. [New Age-Menlo Park]

0683. Jackson, Irene V., comp. and ed. 1981. *Lift Every Voice and Sing: A Collection of Afro-American Spirituals and Other Songs.* New York: The Church Hymnal Corp. [Gospel-LA-Doris Akers]

0684. Jackson-Brown, Irene. 1991. "Developments in Black Gospel Performance and Scholarship," *Black Music Research Journal* 10(1): 36–42. [Gospel-CA-Review of literature, has some info on CA people]

0685. Jackson, Robert "Scoop". 1992. "The Real Deal on 'Cop Killer,'" *The Final Call* 11 (August 24): 5. [Rock-LA-Body Count]

0686. James, Darryl. 1992. "A Day in the Hood: Rolling with Shorty the Pimp," *Rap Sheet* (August): 18–21. [Rap-Oakland-Too Short]

0687. James, Etta, and David Ritz. 1995a. "The Etta James Story: Rage to Survive," *Essence* 26(2): 61–62, 114, 116. [Blues-LA]

0688.———. 1995b. *Rage to Survive.* New York (?): Villard Books. [Blues-LA]

0689. James, M. 1960. *Ten Modern Jazzmen: An Appraisal of the Recorded Works of Ten Modern Jazzmen.* London: pub. unknown. [Jazz-LA-Includes Wardell Gray]

0690.———. 1963. "Sonny Clark," *Jazz Monthly* 9(3): 5. [Jazz-LA]

0691.———. 1973. "Order and Feeling, Discipline and Fire: An Introduction to the John Carter and Bobby Bradford Quartet," *Jazz and Blues* 3 (April): 6. [Jazz-LA]

0692. James, Michael. 1988. "McPherson, Charles," *NGDJ* 2: 71. [Jazz-SD]

0693. James, S. L. 1988. "Contributions of Four Selected Twentieth-Century Afro-American Classical Composers: William Grant Still, Howard Swanson, Ulysses Simpson Kay, and Olly Wilson." Ph.D. dissertation, Florida State Univeristy. [Art Music-CA]

0694. Jarrett, Michael. 1995. "Ornette Coleman Interview," *Cadence* 21 (October): 5–9. [Jazz-LA]

0695. Jenkins, Keith Bernard. 1990. "The Rhetoric of Gospel Song: A Content Analysis of the Lyrics of Andraé Crouch." Ph.D. dissertation, Florida State University. [Gospel-LA]

0696. Jennings, Dave. 1988. "Beat Revolution," *Melody Maker* 64 (November 26): 35. [Rock/Industrial-SF-Beatnigs]

0697. Jennings, Russ. 1987. "Composers on Campus: Mills College, Where the Avant-Garde Is Traditional," *Option* L2 (January/February): 38–39. [Art Music-Oakland-Anthony Braxton]

0698. Jeske, Lee. 1982. "John Carter," *Down Beat* 49 (November): 18–20. [Jazz-LA]

0699.———. 1983a. "Don: The Cherry Variations," *Down Beat* 50 (June): 18–20. [Jazz-LA]

0700.———. 1983b. "James Newton," *Down Beat* 50 (April): 24–26. [Jazz-LA]

0701.———. 1988a. "Farmer, Art(hur Stewart)," *NGDJ* 1: 354–355. [Jazz-LA]

0702.———. 1988b. "Hutcherson, Bobby," *NGDJ* 1: 549. [Jazz-CA]

0703. Johnson, Adrienne. 1994. "For Some in Entertainment Their Conscience Is All the Way Live." *Turning Point* (August–September–October): 30–31. [Rap-LA-On Al Bell, owner of Bellmark Records]

0704. Johnson, Hall. 1940. "Spirituals, Reels, Hoe Downs and Blues" in *Music and Dance in California*, edited by Jose Rodriguez. Hollywood: Bureau of Musical Research, pp. 170–176. [Folk/Traditional-CA]

0705. Johnson, Marilynn S. 1993. *The Second Gold Rush: Oakland and the East Bay in World War II.* Berkeley: University of California Press. [History/Blues/Zydeco-Oakland-"Discusses music in black communities of Oakland and Richmond"—Collins]

0706. Johnson, Martin. 1995. "Pharoah's Return: Pharoah Sanders," *Down Beat* 62 (April): 20–23. [Jazz-Oakland-Pharoah met Gnawa musicians in California]

0707. Jones, Andrew. 1990. "Global Villager: Don Cherry's Musical Journey," *Option* 35 (November/December): 64–67, 161. [Jazz-LA]

0708. Jones, Glenn L. 1980. "A Position Paper on Gospel Music." Unpublished manuscript. [Gospel-SD]

0709. Jones, Isaiah Jr. 1973. "Who'll Be the Next Queen of the Gospel Singers?" *Lyric: A Magazine of the Fine Arts* 6 (October): 22–23. [Gospel-LA-Bessie Griffin]

0710. Jones, LeRoi. 1967. *Black Music.* New York: Quill. [Jazz-LA-has article on Bobby Bradford]

0711. Jost, Ekkehard. 1981. *Free Jazz.* New York: Da Capo. [Jazz-LA-Ornette Coleman]

0712. Joyce, Mike. 1978. "Helen Humes: Interview," *Cadence* 3 (January): 6, 8, 17–18. [Jazz-CA]

0713. Judd, Anne. 1967. "Barney Goin' Easy," *Jazz Journal* 20 (September): 4–7. [Jazz-LA-Barney Bigard]

0714. Kalbacher, Gene. 1984. "The Return of Jon Faddis," *Down Beat* 51 (October): 18–20. [Jazz-Oakland]

0715.———. 1989. "Profile: Harry 'Sweets' Edison," *Down Beat* 56 (March): 44–46. [Jazz-LA]

0716. Karrah. 1988. "Marshall Royal," *Cadence* 14 (March): 20. [Jazz-LA]

0717. Katz, Jon. 1993. "The News: Time Warner Runs Up the White Flag," *Rolling Stone* 651 (March 4): 40–41. [Rap/Rock-LA-Ice-T]

0718. Keller, David. 1981. "Eric Dolphy: The Los Angeles Years." *Jazz Times* (November). [Jazz-LA]

0719.———.1982. "Horace Tapscott." *Jazz Times* (October): 8–9. [Jazz-LA]

0720.———. 1983. "Roy Porter Interview," *Jazz Heritage Foundation* 4(5). [Jazz-LA]

0721.———. 1984. "The Carter Years: John Carter—Jazz & America." *Jazz Times* (July): 12+. [Jazz-LA]

0722. Kelley, Robin D.G. 1994. *Race Rebels: Culture, Politics, and the Black Working Class.* New York: The Free Press. [Rap-LA-Has chapter on LA rap music]

0723. Kelso, Jackie. 1993. *Central Avenue Sounds Oral History Transcript.* Los Angeles: Oral History Program, University of California. [Jazz-LA]

0724. Kemp, Mark. 1989. "Beatnigs," *Option* 24 (January/February): 69. [Rock/Industrial-SF-later became Disposable Heroes of Hiphoprisy]

0725. Kemper, P. 1979. "Pharoah Sanders: Zwishcen Mythos und Logos," *Jazz Podium* 28 (December): 6–12. [Jazz-SF]

0726. Kernfeld, Barry. 1988a. "Braxton, Anthony," *NGDJ* 1: 147–148. [Jazz/New Music-Oakland]

0727.————. 1988b. "Dolphy, Eric (Allan)," *NGDJ* 1: 296–297. [Jazz-LA]

0728.————. 1988c. "Hamilton, Chico," *NGDJ* 1: 474. [Jazz-LA]

0729.————. 1988d. "Manne, Shelly," *NGDJ* 2: 80. [Jazz-LA]

0730.————. 1988e. "Mingus, Charles (Jr.)," *NGDJ* 2: 110–112. [Jazz-LA]

0731.————. 1988f. "Mitchell, Blue," *NGDJ* 2: 113. [Jazz-LA]

0732.————. 1988g. "Murray, David," *NGDJ* 2: 148–149. [Jazz-Berkeley/LA]

0733.————. 1988h. "Neidlinger, Buell," *NGDJ* 2: 163–164. [Jazz-LA]

0734.————. 1988.i "Nelson, Oliver (Edward)," *NGDJ* 2: 165–166. [Jazz/Film Music-LA]

0735.————. 1988j. "Newton, James," *NGDJ* 2: 172. [Jazz-LA]

0736.————. 1988k. "Pepper, Art(hur Edward, Jr.)," *NGDJ* 2: 301. [Jazz-LA]

0737.————. 1988l. "Redman, (Walter) Dewey," *NGDJ* 2: 366. [Jazz-LA/SF]

0738.————. 1988m. "Sanders, Pharoah," *NGDJ* 2: 413–414. [Jazz-Bay Area]

0739.————. 1988n. "Vinson, Eddie 'Cleanhead,'" *NGDJ* 2: 580. [Jazz-LA]

0740. Kimberley, Nick. 1985. "The Genius of Brother Ray," *The Wire* 17 (July): 26–29. [Soul/R & B-LA-Ray Charles]

0741. King, B. B. 1975. "My Ten Favorite Guitarists," *Guitar Player* 9 (March): 22–23. [Blues-LA-Talks about T-Bone Walker]

0742. Klett, Shirley. 1986a. "Roy Porter: Interview pt. 1," *Cadence* 12 (September): 5–11. [Jazz-LA]

0743.————. 1986b. "Roy Porter: Interview pt. 2," *Cadence* 12 (October): 5–11. [Jazz-LA]

0744. Koch, Lawrence. 1988a. "Gray, Wardell," *NGDJ* 1: 448. [Jazz-LA]

0745.————. 1988b. "Vinnegar, Leroy," *NGDJ* 2: 580. [Jazz-LA]

0746. Koechlin, D. 1979. *50 ans de jazz avec Barney Bigard*. Darnetal, France: n.p. [Jazz-LA]

0747. Kofsky, Frank. 1969. "Horace Tapscott," *Jazz and Pop* 8 (December): 16–18. [Jazz-LA]

0748.————. 1970. *Black Nationalism and the Revolution in Music*. New York: Pathfinder Press. [Jazz-CA-Discusses club scene in LA in the 50s and 60s, mentions Tapscott-Carter-Bradford]

0749.————. 1977. "The State of Jazz," *The Black Perspective in Music* 5(1): 44–66. [Jazz-Sacramento]

0750. Kolb, E. 1984. "John Handy Interview," *Cadence* 10 (June): 15. [Jazz-Bay Area]

0751. Korall, Burt. 1966. "The Charles Lloyd Quartet: Roots and Branches," *Down Beat* 33 (June 16): 20–21. [Jazz-SF]

0752.————. 1986. "That Old New Feeling: Bud Shank," *Down Beat* 53 (September): 23–25. [Jazz-LA]

0753. Kozak, R. 1977. "Success Comes Late to Johnny 'Guitar' Watson," *Billboard* 89 (July 16): 34. [Blues-LA]

0754. Kriss, Eric. 1976. "Backstage with Floyd Dixon," *Contemporary Keyboard* 2 (January/February): 49. [Blues-SF]

0755. Kubernik, Harvey. 1975. "Acid Queen," *Melody Maker* 50 (October 11): 26–27. [Rock/Soul-LA-Tina Turner]

0756. Kunstadt, Len. 1964. "Some Early West Coast Jazz History—The Black & Tan Orchestra and Kid Ory's Orchestra," *Record Research* 61 (July): 12. [Jazz-CA]

0757. Lake, Steve. 1974a. "Lee Way," *Melody Maker* 49 (May 18): 55. [Rock-LA-Interview with Arthur Lee]

0758.————. 1974b. "Rock Giants From A–Z; Sly Stone: Frisco's Spaced Cowboy," *Melody Maker* 49 (May 4): 31–32. [Rock-SF]

0759. Lamb, Cindy. 1985. "Hollerin' Hoodoo: Screamin' Jay Hawkins," *Option* F2 (January/February): 49. [R & B-LA]

0760. Lambert, Eddie. 1988a. "Brown, Lawrence," *NGDJ* 1: 157–158. [Jazz-LA]

0761.———. 1988b. "Woodman, Britt," *NGDJ* 2: 638. [Jazz-LA]

0762. Lambert, Stu. 1990. "Control Zone: Dr. Beat," *Melody Maker* 66 (June 16): 46. [Rap-LA-Dr. Dre]

0763. Larkin, Colin 1992. "Brenda Holloway" in *The Guinness Encyclopedia of Popular Music*, edited by Colin Larkin. Enfield: Guinness Publishing Ltd., pp. 1171–1172. [Soul-LA]

0764. Larkin, Rochelle. 1970. *Soul Music!* New York: Lancer Books. [Soul-CA-5th Dimension, Sly Stone]

0765. Larson, Steve. 1988. "Hawes, Hampton," *NGDJ* 1: 504. [Jazz-LA]

0766. Laskin, David L.L. 1989. "Anthony Braxton: Play or Die," *EAR* 14 (3) [May]: 40–46. [Jazz/New Music-Oakland-Brief reference to Mills College]

0767. Leadbitter, Mike. 1974. "Roy Milton: His Life and Times," *Blues Unlimited* 108: 6. [Blues-LA]

0768. Leadbitter, Mike, and Neil Slaven. 1977. "More Milton Facts," *Blues Unlimited* 123 (January/February): 14–22. [Blues-LA-Roy Milton]

0769. Lee, Peter, and David Nelson. 1990. "If I Miss 'Em on the Piano, I'll Catch 'Em on the Guitar: Rockin' Tabby Thomas," *Living Blues* 91 (May/June): 10–15. [Blues-LA/SF]

0770. Lee, William F. 1980. *Stan Kenton: Artistry in Rhythm*. Los Angeles: Creative Press. [Jazz-CA]

0771. Lees, Gene. 1992. *Jazz Lives: 100 Portraits in Jazz*. Buffalo, NY: Firefly Books. [Jazz-CA-Benny Carter, Harry "Sweets" Edison, Ray Brown, Ernie Andrews, Harold Land, Art Farmer, Horace Silver, Benny Golson, Cedar Walton, Billy Higgins, Charlie Haden, John Clayton, Jeff Clayton]

0772. Lerner, David. 1982. "Alice Coltrane: Jazz Pianist, Inspirational Organist," *Keyboard* 8 (November): 22–27. [Jazz/Inspirational-LA-Has address for Vedantic Center]

0773. Lesnik, Richard. 1981. "Charles McPherson," *Cadence* 7 (February): 5–8, 15, 18. [Jazz-SD]

0774. Levenson, Jeff. 1987. "Arthur Blythe's Creative Challenge," *Down Beat* 54 (October): 23–25. [Jazz-LA]

0775.———. 1988. "The Understated Elegance of Art Farmer," *Down Beat* 55 (January): 22–24. [Jazz-LA]

0776.———. 1989. "Ray Charles: What'd I Say," *Down Beat* 56 (January): 16–19. [R & B-LA-mentions Lowell Fulson, Ruth Brown]

0777. Levi, Titus. 1986a. "Billy Higgins," *Option* K2 (November/December): 47–48. [Jazz-LA]

0778.———. 1986b. "Butch Morris: Freedom of Expression," *Option* I2 (July/August): 44–47. [Jazz-LA/Oakland]

0779.———. 1986c. "Horace Tapscott: Keeping It Lit," *Option* J2 (September/October): 37–38. [Jazz-LA]

0780.———. 1986d. "John Carter's Clarinet: 'Where I Should Have Been All the Time,'" *Option* G2 (March/April): 42–43. [Jazz-LA]

0781.———. 1987. "Profile: Vinny Golia," *Down Beat* 54 (May): 45–46. [Jazz/New Music-LA]

0782.————1990. "New Music and Jazz in LA" in *Los Angeles Festival Program Book*, edited by Barbara Allen. Los Angeles: McTaggart-Wolk, pp. 38–43. [Jazz/New Music-LA-Red Callender, Buddy Collette, Ornette Coleman, Tapscott, John Carter, Bob Bradford, Vinny Golia]

0783. Levin, Floyd. 1951. "The Spikes Brothers: A Los Angeles Saga," *Jazz Journal* 4 (December): 12–14. [Jazz-LA-Reb & Johnny Spikes]

0784.————. 1979a. "Ed 'Montudie' Garland: Legend of Jazz, pt. 2," *Jazz Journal International* 32 (July): 5–6, 13. [Jazz-LA]

0785.————. 1979b. "Ed 'Montudie' Garland: Legend of Jazz, pt. 3," *Jazz Journal International* 32 (August): 15, 17, 19–20. [Jazz-LA]

0786.————. 1979c. "Ed 'Montudie' Garland: Legend of Jazz, pt. 4," *Jazz Journal International* 32 (September): 5–6. [Jazz-LA]

0787.————. 1982a. "Sweet Anita Mine: The Untold Story of Jellyroll Morton's Final Years, pt. 1," *Jazz Journal International* 35 (January): 14–15. [Jazz-LA]

0788.————. 1982b. "Sweet Anita Mine: The Untold Story of Jellyroll Morton's Final Years, pt. 2," *Jazz Journal International* 35 (February): 26–27. [Jazz-LA]

0789.————. 1985. "Festival Roundup: Sacramento," *Jazz Journal International* 38 (September): 18–19. [Dixieland-Sacramento]

0790.————. 1990. "Mystery Shrouds Kid Ory 1920s L. A. Recordings," *West Coast Rag* 3(1): 17–20. [Jazz-LA]

0791.————. 1991. "Untold Story of Jelly Roll Morton's Last Years (On the 50th Anniversary of His Death in Los Angeles, California, July 10, 1941)," *West Coast Rag* 3(8): 39–41. [Jazz-LA]

0792.————. 1993. "Kid Ory's Legendary Nordskog/Sunshine Recordings," *Jazz Journal International* 46 (July): 6–10. [Jazz-Santa Monica]

0793.————. 1995a. "The Forgotten Ones: Spud Murphy," *Jazz Journal International* 48 (February): 13. [Jazz-LA]

0794.————. 1995b. "I Wish I Could Shimmy Like My Sister Kate: The First Recorded Hit of the Jazz Age," *Jazz Journal International* 48 (January): 16–17. [Jazz-LA-Kid Ory]

0795. Levin, Michael, Nat Hentoff, and Leonard Feather. 1956. "Dissonant Thirds," *Down Beat* 23(18): 16, 50. [Jazz-CA-Hampton Hawes]

0796. Levine, Dave. 1981a. "Portraits: Reggie Smith," *Modern Drummer* 5(7): 68–70, 74. [Jazz/Baseball-LA]

0797.————. 1981b. "Shelly Manne," *Modern Drummer* 5(7): 10–13, 62–67. [Jazz-LA]

0798. Lewis, Alwyn, and Laurie Lewis. 1993a. "Jeff Hamilton: Interview," *Cadence* 19 (August): 11–17. [Jazz-LA]

0799.————. 1993b. "Ray Brown: Interview," *Cadence* 19 (September): 13–20. [Jazz-LA]

0800.————. 1994a. "Bill Berry Interview," *Cadence* 20 (February): 5–14, 21, 36. [Jazz-LA]

0801.————. 1994b. "Jeff Clayton Interview," *Cadence* 20 (May): 15–20, 26, 104. [Jazz-LA]

0802.————. 1995a. "Benny Green Interview," *Cadence* 21 (February): 5–16. [Jazz-Bay Area]

0803.————. 1995b. "Kim Richmond Interview," *Cadence* 21 (July): 17–24. [Jazz-LA]

0804. Light, Alan. 1991a. "Beating up the Charts," *Rolling Stone* 610 (August 8): 65–66. [Rap-LA-NWA]

0805.————. 1991b. "Hot Rapper: Ice-T Busts a Movie," *Rolling Stone* 604 (May 16): 83–87. [Rap/Hollywood-LA]

0806.————. 1991c. "James Cleveland: 1931–1991," *Rolling Stone* 601 (April 4): 14. [Gospel-LA]

0807.————. 1991d. "New Faces: Paris," *Rolling Stone* 597 (February 7): 22. [Rap-Bay Area-Paris]

0808.————. 1992a. "Ice-T: The Rolling Stone Interview," *Rolling Stone* 637 (August 20): 28–32, 60. [Rap/Metal-LA-discusses "Cop Killer"]

0809.————. 1992b. "L. A. Rappers Speak Out," *Rolling Stone* 633 (June 25): 15, 21. [Rap-LA-Ice-T/Janet Jackson/Kid Frost/Yo-Yo/Jody Watley/B-Real/Vanessa Williams/Tupac Shakur]

0810.————. 1992c. "Rappers Sounded Warning: The violence in Los Angeles didn't surprise those who were paying attention," *Rolling Stone* 634/635 (July 9–23): 15–18. [Rap-LA]

0811.————. 1993a. "Ice-T's Declaration of Independence," *Rolling Stone* 652 (March 18): 19, 31. [Rap/Rock-LA]

0812.————. 1993b. "Words From the 'Home' Front," *Rolling Stone* 657 (May 27): 20. [Rap-LA-Ice-T]

0813. Lind, Jack. 1966. "John Handy: Back up the Ladder," *Down Beat* 33 (May 19): 21–22. [Jazz-Bay Area]

0814. Lindenmaier, H. Lukas. 1980a. "James Newton: A Short Talk," *Cadence* 6 (February): 5–6. [Jazz-LA]

0815.————. 1980b. "John Carter: Interview," *Cadence* 6 (February): 11–12, 43. [Jazz-LA]

0816. Lipsitz, George. 1990. *Time Passages: Collective Memory and American Popular Culture.* Minneapolis: University of Minnesota Press. [R & B/Rock-LA-has chapter on East LA]

0817.————. 1992. "Against the Wind: Dialogic Aspects of Rock and Roll," *NARAS Journal* (Spring). [Blues-Oakland]

0818. Liska, A. James. 1982. "Sarah Vaughan: I'm Not a Jazz Singer," *Down Beat* 49 (May): 19–21. [Jazz-LA]

0819. Litweiler, John. 1975. "Dewey Redman: Coincidentals," *Down Beat* 42 (November 6): 14–16, 38. [Jazz-LA/SF]

0820.————. 1984. *The Freedom Principle: Jazz after 1958.* New York: Quill. [Jazz-LA-Has information on Ornette Coleman, others]

0821.————. 1992. *Ornette Coleman: A Harmolodic Life.* New York: William Morrow and Co. [Jazz-LA]

0822. Lock, Graham. 1985. "Viva la humans!" *The Wire* 19: 36. [Jazz-LA-Charlie Haden]

0823.————. 1988. *Forces in Motion. Anthony Braxton and the Meta Reality of Creative Music.* London: Quartet Books. [Jazz/New Music-Oakland-References to Mills College]

0824.————. 1990. "An Eye for Rhythm, an Ear for Colour," *The Wire* 78 (August): 16–18. [Jazz/New Music-LA-Vinny Golia]

0825.————. 1994. *Chasing the Vibration: Meetings with Creative Musicians.* Devon, UK: Stride. [Jazz-LA-Horace Tapscott]

0826.————, ed. 1995. *Mixtery: A Festschrift for Anthony Braxton.* Devon, UK: Stride. [Jazz/New Music-Oakland-Has references to Mills College]

0827. Loder, Kurt. 1990. *Bat Chain Puller.* New York: St. Martin's Press. [Blues-LA-Has chapter on Ted Hawkins]

0828. Lomax, Alan. 1973 [1950]. *Mister Jelly Roll: The Fortunes of Jelly Roll Morton, New Orleans Creole and "Inventor of Jazz."* Berkeley: University of California Press. [Jazz-SF/LA]

0829. Long, B. 1987. "Rhythm and Blues," *Cash Box* 53 (December 30): 20. [Rap-LA-Ice-T]

0830. Long, D. 1983. "Harry 'Sweets' Edison: Interview," *Cadence* 9 (March): 5. [Jazz-LA]

0831. Lott, Tommy. 1993. "Coltrane, Alice" in *Black Women in America: A Historical Encyclopedia*, edited by Darlene Clark Hine. Brooklyn: Carlson Publishing, pp. 268–269. [Jazz-LA]

0832. Lowe, Curtis. 1985. *Merger of AFM Locals 6 and 669.* Manuscript. [Unions-SF]

0833. Loza, Steven. 1993. *Barrio Rhythm: Mexican American Music in Los Angeles.* Urbana: University of Illinois Press. [R & B/Popular Music-LA]

0834.———. 1994. "Identity, Nationalism, and Aesthetics among Chicano/Mexicano Musicians in Los Angeles" in *Selected Reports in Ethnomusicology, Volume X: Musical Aesthetics and Multiculturalism in Los Angeles*, edited by Steven Loza. Los Angeles: Department of Ethnomusicology and Systematic Musicology, UCLA, pp. 51–58. [Rap/R & B-LA]

0835. Loza, Steven, Milo Alvarez, Josefina Santiago, and Charles Moore. 1994. "Los Angeles Gangsta Rap and the Aesthetics of Violence" in *Selected Reports in Ethnomusicology, Volume X: Musical Aesthetics and Multiculturalism in Los Angeles*, edited by Steven Loza. Los Angeles: Department of Ethnomusicology and Systematic Musicology, UCLA, pp. 149–161. [Rap-LA-Ice Cube/ALT]

0836. Lynn, Kwaku. 1987. "Amerikan Afrikan Music: A Study of Musical Change." Ph.D. dissertation, University of California, Los Angeles. [General Music-CA-Has discussion of black radio in LA]

0837. Lyons, Jimmy. 1978. *Dizzy, Duke, the Count, and Me: The Story of the Monterey Jazz Festival.* San Francisco: California Living Books. [Jazz-Bay Area]

0838. Lyons, Len. 1976a. "Hampton Hawes Challenging the Charts, on Wood," *Down Beat* 43 (December 16): 23, 57. [Jazz-LA]

0839.———. 1976b. "Horace Silver: Father of Funk," *Contemporary Keyboard* 2 (January/February): 18–19, 38. [Jazz-LA-briefly mentions LA]

0840.———. 1976c. "Moving Into Tomorrow: Azar Lawrence," *Down Beat* 43 (October 7): 16–17. [Jazz-LA]

0841.———. 1977. "The L.A. Four: Journeymen United," *Down Beat* 44 (September): 18–19, 57. [Jazz-LA]

0842.———. 1979. "George Cables: Rising Young Jazz Pianist," *Contemporary Keyboard* 5 (May): 14, 56. [Jazz-LA]

0843. M, Grace. 1994. "Outside-In: Lost in L. A. With Bobby Bradford" in *Selected Reports in Ethnomusicology Volume X: Musical Aesthetics and Multiculturalism in Los Angeles*, edited by Steven Loza. Los Angeles: Department of Ethnomusicology and Systematic Musicology, UCLA, pp. 223–233. [Jazz-LA]

0843a. M, Grace. 1996. "African American Musical Traditions in Los Angeles: Ethnographic Portraits of Four Musicians." M. A. Thesis: UCLA. [Jazz-LA-Bradford, Collette, Newton, Tapscott]

0844. Macnie, Jim. 1995. "Fracturing the Mainstream: Stephen Scott and Eric Reed," *Down Beat* 62 (June): 22–25. [Jazz-LA-Reed is from LA]

0845. Malone, Bönz. 1990. "Planet Janet Rock," *Spin* 6(4) [July]: 31–32. [Rap-LA-On LA rap label Delicious Vinyl]

0846.———. 1991. "Radio Graffiti: Cypress Hill," *Spin* 7 (September): 22. [Rap-LA]

0847. Mandel, Howard. 1977. "Sonny Criss: Up from the Underground," *Down Beat* 44 (March 10): 20, 40–41, 46. [Jazz-LA]

0848.———. 1983. "Dewey Redman: Nobody's Foil," *Down Beat* 50 (February): 18–20, 46. [Jazz-LA/SF]

0849.————. 1985. "David Murray: Searching for the Sound," *Down Beat* 52 (October): 26–28. [Jazz-Bay Area/LA-his mother played with Ed Hawkins]

0850.————. 1986. "Butch Morris: Conducting the New Tradition," *Down Beat* 53 (October): 26–28, 61. [Jazz-LA/SF]

0851.————. 1987. "Charlie Haden's Search for Freedom," *Down Beat* 54 (September): 20–23. [Jazz-LA]

0852.————. 1995a. "Back from Hell," *Down Beat* 62 (June): 36. [Jazz-LA-Sonny Simmons]

0853.————. 1995b. "Harmolodic Convergence," *Pulse!* 143 (November): 36–45, 120. [Jazz-LA-Ornette Coleman, briefly mentions LA]

0854. Mansfield, Horace. 1985. "Trumpetistically Speaking," *Be-Bop and Beyond* (November/December): 8–16. [Jazz-LA-Clora Bryant]

0855. Manus, Willard. 1995. "Blues for Central Avenue," *Jazz Journal International* 48 (February): 10–12. [Jazz-LA-Has reminesences by Central Avenue musicians]

0856. Marcus, Greil. *Mystery Train,* 3rd ed. 1990. New York: E. P. Dutton. [Rock-SF-Has a chapter on Sly Stone]

0857. Marlowe, D. 1989. "Hip-Hop News," *Cash Box* 52 (March 11): 26. [Rap-Oakland-On Oakland rapper Too Short]

0858. Marmorstein, Gary. 1988. "Central Avenue Jazz: Los Angeles Black Music of the Forties," *Southern California Quarterly* 70(4): 415–426. [Jazz-LA]

0859. Marra, Charles. 1973. "Art Pepper: I'm Here to Stay," *Down Beat* 40 (March 1): 16–17. [Jazz-LA]

0860. Marsh, Dave. 1980. "Sly and the Family Stone" in *The Rolling Stone Illustrated History of Rock & Roll,* edited by Jim Miller. New York: Random House, pp. 314–319. [Rock-SF]

0861.————. 1986a. "Charles, Ray," *NGDAM* 1: 405–407. [Soul/R & B/Popular Music-LA]

0862.————. 1986b. "Cooke, Sam(uel)," *NGDAM* 1: 490–491. [Soul-LA]

0863.————. 1986c. "War," *NGDAM* 4: 475. [Rock-LA/South Bay]

0863a. Marsh, Dave. 1993. *Louie Louie . . . the History and Mythology of the World's Most Famous Rock 'n' Roll Song.* New York: Hyperion. [Rock-LA-Richard Berry]

0864. Marsh, Dave, and Phyllis Pollack. 1989. "Crackdown on Culture: Wanted for Attitude," *Village Voice* 34 (October 10): 33–37. [Rap-LA-NWA vs. cops, PMRC]

0865. Marsh, Graham, and Glyn Callingham, eds. 1992. *California Cool: West Coast Jazz of the 50s and 60s, the Album Cover Art.* San Francisco: Chronicle Books. [Jazz-CA]

0866. Marshall, James. 1994. "Larry Williams: Rock 'n' Roll Pimp," *High Times* (January): 60. [R & B-Oakland/LA]

0867. Martin, D. C. 1992. "Tramaine Hawkins," *Jazz Magazine* 412 (February): 13. [Gospel-Bay Area]

0868. Mathieson, Kenny. 1990/1991. "Quincy Jones: The Dude Is Back," *The Wire* 82/83 (December/January): 50–53, 74. [Film Music/Jazz/Popular Music-LA]

0869. Mathur, Paul. 1993. "Everlast Will & Testament," *Melody Maker* (July 24): 36–37. [Rap-LA-Cypress Hill, House of Pain]

0870. Mattingly, Rick. 1988. "Moore, Eddie," *NGDJ* 2: 129. [Jazz-SF]

0871. Maultsby, Portia. 1986. *Black American Popular Music: Rhythm and Blues, 1945–1955.* Washington D.C.: Smithsonian Institution. [R & B-LA]

0872. Mazzolini, Tom. 1975. "Living Blues Interview: Floyd Dixon," *Living Blues* 23 (September/October): 14–21. [Blues-CA]

0873.————. 1976. "Living Blues Interview: Charles Brown," *Living Blues* 27 (May/June): 19–27. [Blues-CA]

0874.————. 1980. "Chicago Blues in Oakland," *Living Blues* 45/46 (Spring): 21–23. [Blues-Oakland-Profiles of Mississippi Johnny Waters and Sonny Lane]

0875.————. 1984. "Bob Kelton: Early Oakland Blues," *Living Blues* 62: 14–16. [Blues-Oakland]

0876. McAdams, Janine. 1991. "2Pac Files Claim Against Oakland," *Billboard* 103 (November 30): 20. [Rap-Oakland-Tupac Shakur]

0877. McCabe, Monica. 1992. "Commentary: The govt. did Crack Down on 'Cop Killer,'" *Billboard* 104 (October 3): 8. [Rock-LA-Body Count]

0878. McCarthy, A. J. 1970. "In Memoriam Maxwell Davis, 1916–1970," *Jazz Magazine* 190: 13. [Jazz-LA]

0879.————. 1974. *Big Band Jazz.* London: G. B. Putnam's Sons. [Jazz-CA-Has extensive section on West Coast]

0880. McCormick, Moira. 1993. "Faces: Rage Against the Machine," *Musician* 171 (January): 20. [Metal/Rap-LA]

0881. McDonnell, Evelyn. 1991. "Bum Rush the Locker Room," *Musician* 151 (May): 30–32. [Rap-LA-Yo-Yo]

0882.————. 1993. "Native Tongues: New poets with a rock & roll attitude," *Rolling Stone* 662 (August 5): 20. [Poetry-LA-Wanda Coleman]

0883. McEwen, J. 1977. *Sam Cooke: A Biography in Words and Pictures.* New York: n.p. [Soul-LA]

0884. McEwen, Joe, and Jim Miller. 1980. "Motown" in *The Rolling Stone Illustrated History of Rock & Roll,* edited by Jim Miller. New York: Random House, pp.235–248. [Soul-LA-Briefly mentions LA]

0885. McLarney, Bill. 1970. "Urge to Merge: The Harold Land–Bobby Hutcherson Quintet," *Down Beat* 37 (February 5): 14–15. [Jazz-CA]

0886. McNamara, Helen. 1964. "Travelin' Man," *Down Beat* 31 (June 4): 13–15. [Jazz-LA-Buck Clayton]

0887. McNeely, Big Jay. 1993. *Central Avenue Sounds Oral History Transcript.* Los Angeles: Oral History Program, University of California, Los Angeles. [Jazz-LA-89 pp.]

0887a. McNeil, Albert J. 1996. "The People's Independent Church of Christ: An Historical Overview of the Musical Activities, circa 1940–1960," in *Music in the Central Avenue Community, 1890–c. 1955,* edited by Bette Y. Cox. Los Angeles: BEEM Foundation, pp. 10–25. [Gospel-LA]

0888. McRae, Barry. 1965. "Barney Bigard," *Jazz Journal* 18 (April): 14–15, 39. [Jazz-LA]

0889.————. 1980. "David Murray: A Progress Report," *Jazz Journal International* 33 (September): 27–28. [Jazz-CA]

0890.————. 1988. *Ornette Coleman.* London: Apollo Press Ltd. [Jazz-LA]

0891. Meadows, Eddie. 1983. "A Preliminary Analysis of Early Rhythm and Blues Musical Practices," *The Western Journal of Black Studies* 7(3): 172–182. [R & B-LA-Has information on LA labels and groups]

0892. Mehegan, John. 1957. "Jazz Pianists, 4: Hampton Hawes: an Analysis," *Down Beat* 24 (July 25): 17. [Jazz-LA]

0893. Meltzer, Richard. 1987 [1970]. *The Aesthetics of Rock.* New York: Da Capo. [Rock-LA-has references to Arthur Lee/Love]

0894. Mendelsohn, John. 1995. "NWA Manager Jerry Heller Tells His Side," *BAM Magazine* 458 (May 5): 14, 60. [Rap-LA]

0895. Merrill, Hugh. 1990. *The Blues Route: From the Delta to California, A Writer Searches for America's Purest Music.* New York: Morrow. [Blues-CA-Has chapter on CA, incl. Johnny Otis, Cheathams, Jimmy McCracklin, Margie Evans, Cleanhead Vinson]

0896. Merrill-Mirsky, Carol. 1986. "Girls' Handclapping Games in Three Los Angeles Schools," *Yearbook for Traditional Music* 18: 47–59. [Children's Music-LA-Musical examples, biblio]

0897.———. 1988. "Notes from the Playground: Children's Singing Games," *Los Angeles Folk Arts* 3(1): 5, 4. [Children's Music-LA]

0898. Metalitz, Steve. 1974. "Spotlight on George Duke: An Underrated Mother," *Down Beat* 41 (November 7): 14, 43. [Jazz/Rock-LA/Bay Area]

0899. Mettler, Mike. 1994. "Tony Toni Toné: Small Hands, Wiggin' Grooves," *Guitar Player* 28 (June): 18. [R & B-Oakland]

0900. Mico, Ted. 1991. "Ice-T: The Original Gangster," *Melody Maker* 67 (September 28): 44–45. [Rap-LA]

0901. Milkowski, Bill. 1988. "Profile: Joe Louis Walker," *Down Beat* 55 (October): 44. [Blues-SF]

0902. Millar, Bill. 1975. *The Coasters.* London: Star Books. [R & B-CA-West coast R&B group]

0903. Miller, Doug. 1995. "The Moan Within the Tone: African Retentions in Rhythm and Blues Saxophone Style in Afro-American Popular Music," *Popular Music* 14(2): 155–174. [R & B-CA-Mentions some CA-based artists]

0904. Miller, Jim, ed. 1980. *The Rolling Stone Illustrated History of Rock and Roll.* New York: Random House. [Rock/R & B/Gospel/Soul-CA]

0905.———. 1986. "Phillips, Esther," *NGDAM* 3: 557. [Blues-LA]

0906. Miller, Paul Eduard. 1942. "Ivie joined the Duke for four weeks, stays with band for 12 years," *Down Beat* 9(14): 31. [Jazz-LA/Gilroy-Ivie Anderson]

0907. Mills, B. 1985. *Tina.* New York: n.p. [Rock-LA-Tina Turner]

0908. Mills, David. 1990. "The Gangsta Rapper: Violent Hero or Negative Role Model?" *The Source* 16 (December): 30–40. [Rap-LA-On NWA, Ice-T, and other LA rappers]

0909. Miner, Stephen Dorian. 1995. "Jambay," *Relix* 22 (August): 44. [Rock-SF]

0910. Mingus, Charles. 1971. *Beneath the Underdog.* New York: Penguin Books. [Jazz-LA]

0911. Mitchell, Elvis. 1994. "G Whiz," *Spin* 10(7) [October]: 79–80. [Rap-Long Beach-Warren G]

0912. Mitchell, Rico. 1988. "Horace Tapscott," *Down Beat* 55 (January): 13. [Jazz-LA]

0913. Moerer, Keith. 1989. "How the West Was Won," *BAM Magazine* 15(8): 20, 25. [Rap-LA]

0914. Moon, Tom. 1992a. "Front Man: Branford Marsalis," *Musician* 168 (October): 7. [Jazz-LA-talks about Tonight Show]

0915.———. 1992b. "The Joshua Reed," *Musician* 175: 21–22. [Jazz-Bay Area-Joshua Redman]

0916. Moore, Carlos. 1982. *Fela Fela: This Bitch of a Life.* London: Allison and Busby. [Afro-Beat-LA-Fela was influenced by an LA woman named Sandra]

0917. Moore, Steve. 1973. "Little Feat: Still Out There Among the Great Unknown Bands," *Rolling Stone* 140 (August 2): 22. [Rock-LA]

0918. Morgan, Alun. 1954. "Survey of West Coast Jazz," *Melody Maker* 30 (December 25): 3. [Jazz-CA]

0919.———. 1956. "Wardell Gray," *Jazz Monthly* 1(12): 7. [Jazz-LA]

0920.———. 1978. "The West Coast Discoveries," *Jazz Journal International* 31 (March): 26–27, 37. [Jazz-LA]

0921. Morgan, Joan. 1992. "Mother of Pearl," *Spin* 8 (July): 49. [Rap-LA-Yo-Yo]

0922. Morgenstern, Dan. 1967. "Flexible Chico," *Down Beat* 34 (June 15): 18–19. [Jazz-LA-Chico Hamilton; he did the score for Polanski's *Repulsion*]

0923.————. 1967. "From Hillbilly to Avant-Garde: A Rocky Road," *Down Beat* 34 (March 9): 20–21, 42. [Jazz-LA-Charlie Haden]

0924. Morris, Chris. 1991a. "The Blitz: Critical Conditions: Ice Cube's *Certificate* Spawns Mixed Reports from Music Writers," *Billboard* 103 (November 30): 73. [Rap-LA]

0925.————. 1991b. "TV Host Barnes Pumps out $23 Million Suit Against N.W.A.," *Billboard* 103 (July 13): 9, 89. [Rap-LA]

0926.————. 1992a. "The Blitz: Bill Adler Booklet Refutes *Blacks and Jews* Assertions (*Jew on the Brain* published to refute Nation of Islam Publication *The Secret Relationship Between Blacks and Jews*)," *Billboard* 104 (June 27): 35. [Rap-LA-Ice Cube]

0927.————. 1992b. "The Blitz: TV a Platform for Rapper's Reactions to Riot as Ice-T, Chuck D, MC Ren and others speak out," *Billboard* 104 (May 16): 65. [Rap-LA]

0928.————. 1992c. "'Cop' Removal Satisfies Foes, to a Point," *Billboard* 104 (August 8): 1, 83. [Rock-LA-Body Count]

0929. Morthland, John. 1975. "Little Feat: Beyond the Valley of the Punks," *Creem* 7 (September): 47–48. [Rock-LA]

0930.————. 1986. "James, Etta," *NGDAM* 2: 530. [Blues-LA]

0931. Mueller, Andrew. 1992. "Lollapalooza 2: One Nation Under a Groove," *Melody Maker* 68 (August 15): 10–13. [Rock/Rap-LA-Ice Cube]

0932. Muse, Clarence. 1940. "The Negro's Rise" in *Music and Dance in California,* edited by Jose Rodriguez. Hollywood: Bureau of Musical Research, pp. 177–182. [Folk/Traditional-CA]

0933. Nasreddin-Longo, Ethan L.J. 1995. "Selfhood, Self-Identity, Complexion, and Complication: The Contexts of a Song Cycle by Olly Wilson," *Black Music Research Journal* 15(1): 75–92. [Art Music-Berkeley]

0934. Neely, Kim. 1993. "Lollapalooza '93," *Rolling Stone* 662 (August 5): 13–14. [Rock-LA-Fishbone]

0935. Nelson, David. 1991. "Bob Geddins," *Living Blues* 97 (May/June): 43–44. [Blues-Oakland-Obituary]

0936. Nelson, Havelock. 1992a. "2Pac Takes an Activist Stance on His Solo Set (Album: 2Pacalypse Now)," *Billboard* 104 (February 29): 19, 24. [Rap-Oakland-Tupac Shakur]

0937.————. 1992b. "Artist Developments: MC Ren Rips It," *Billboard* 104 (August 8): 19. [Rap-LA]

0938. Nelson, Havelock, and Michael Gonzales. 1991. *Bring the Noise: A Guide to Rap Music and Hip-Hop Culture.* New York: Harmony Books. [Rap-CA-NWA, Ice-T, Ice Cube, Digital Underground, MC Hammer]

0939. Newman, Mike. 1977. "Monk Montgomery: The First Man to Record on Bass Guitar," *Guitar Player* 11 (September): 26–27, 56, 58, 60, 64. [Jazz-LA-Briefly mentions LA]

0940. Nicholson, J. D., and Derrick Semler. n.d. "JD Nicholson and the West Coast Blues," *Blues And Rhythm: The Gospel Truth.* 63: 4–8. [Blues-LA-Includes discography]

0941. Nilsson, Charley. 1985. "The King of Gospel," *Jefferson* 70: 10–11. [Gospel-LA-James Cleveland]

0942. Nolan, Herb. 1975. "Just Call Me Cleanhead," *Down Beat* 42 (May 8): 16, 29. [Jazz-LA-Eddie "Cleanhead" Vinson]

0943.————. 1976. "Blue Mitchell: Able to Leap All Genres With a Single Blast," *Down Beat* 43 (May 20): 19–20, 44. [Jazz-LA]

0944.————. 1978. "Chico Hamilton: Pulsation Personified," *Down Beat* 45 (April 20): 19, 40. [Jazz-LA]

0945. Norment, Lynn. 1992. "Hammer: 'Too Legit to Quit': The Fight for a New Image and a $20 Million Home," *Ebony* 47(5) [March]: 36–42. [Rap-Oakland]

0946. Notini, Per, and Ulf Carlsson. 1984. "Living Blues Interview: Jimmy McCracklin," *Living Blues* 62: 2–13. [Blues-Oakland]

0947. Nurullah, Shanta. 1978. "Vi Redd: Interview," *Cadence* 3 (January): 3, 5, 16–17. [Jazz-LA]

0948. Obrecht, Jas. 1982. "Johnny 'Guitar' Watson: 'Razor-Blade-Totin' Guitar'," *Guitar Player* 16 (February): 68–84. [Blues-LA-Definitive article on Watson]

0949. Occhiogrosso, Peter. 1975. "Emissary of the Global Muse: Don Cherry," *Down Beat* 42 (October 9): 14–15, 39. [Jazz-LA]

0950.———. 1976. "Profile: Stanley Crouch, David Murray," *Down Beat* 43 (March 25): 38–39. [Jazz-LA]

0951. Ochs, Ed. 1980. "Andrae Crouch: ' . . . they are afraid to make a change,'" *Billboard* 92(39) [September 27]: G–6, G–22. [Gospel-LA]

0952.———. 1980. "The Reverend James Cleveland: We Want to Reach a Wider Range of People," *Billboard* 92(39) [September 27]: G6, G22. [Gospel-LA]

0953. Ochs, Michael. 1984. *Rock Archives*. Garden City, NY: Doubleday/Dolphin, 1984. [Rock-CA-Nat Cole, Hank Ballard, 50s LA R & B, Ray Charles]

0954. O'Dair, Barbara. 1988. "Flash: Ice-T and No Sympathy," *Spin* 4(5) [August]: 18. [Rap-LA]

0955. Odell, Michael. 1990. "Niggers With Attitude: Shootout in the City of Angels," *Melody Maker* 66 (May 19): 28–29. [Rap-LA]

0956. Okin, E. 1984. "Benny Carter: The Cat With Nine Lives," *The Wire* 9: 16. [Jazz-LA]

0957. Oliver, Paul. 1979. *The Story of the Blues*. London: Chilton Book Company. [Blues-CA-Has chapter on West Coast]

0958.———. 1986. "Walker, T-Bone," *NGDAM* 4: 469–470. [Blues-LA]

0959. O'Neal, Jim, and Amy O'Neal. 1972. "Living Blues Interview: T-Bone Walker," *Living Blues* 11: 20–26. [Blues-CA]

0960.———. 1973. "Living Blues Interview: T-Bone Walker," *Living Blues* 12 (Spring): 24–27. [Blues-CA]

0961. Ostransky, Leroy. 1988a. "Royal, Ernie," *NGDJ* 2: 398. [Jazz-LA]

0962.———. 1988b. "Royal, Marshall (Walton)," *NGDJ* 2: 398. [Jazz-LA]

0963. Osumare, Halifu. 1992. "Sacred Dance/Drumming: African Belief Systems in Oakland" in *African-American Traditional Arts and Folklife in Oakland and the East Bay*, edited by Willie R. Collins. Oakland: Sagittarian Press, pp. 17–21. [Sacred Music-Oakland]

0964. Otis, Johnny. 1968. *Listen to the Lambs*. New York: W. W. Norton. [LA-R & B/History]

0965.———. 1974a. "The Otis Tapes: 2, Pee Wee Crayton," *Blues Unlimited* 107: 8–9. [Blues-Oakland]

0966.———. 1974b. "The Otis Tapes: 3, Roy Milton," *Blues Unlimited* 108: 5. [Blues-LA]

0967.———. 1993. *Upside Your Head! Rhythm and Blues on Central Avenue*. Hanover, NH: Wesleyan University Press. [R & B-LA]

0968. Ouellette, Dan. 1995. "Jimmy Smith: The B-3 Messiah," *Down Beat* 62 (January): 30–33. [Jazz-Sacramento]

0969. Owen, Frank. 1990a. "Bust a Groove," *Spin* 5 (January): 32–33. [Rap-LA-Young MC]

0970.———. 1990b. "Hanging Tough," *Spin* 6 (April): 32–34. [Rap-LA-Interview with Ice Cube and Eazy-E]

0971. Owens, Thomas. 1988a. "Burrell, Kenny," *NGDJ* 1: 171–172. [Jazz-LA]

0972.————. 1988b. "Criss, Sonny," *NGDJ* 1: 255. [Jazz-LA]

0973.————. 1988c. "Handy, John (Richard, III)," *NGDJ* 1: 479–480. [Jazz-Bay Area]

0974.————. 1988d. "L. A. Four," *NGDJ* 2: 4. [Jazz-LA-Bud Shank/Almeida/Ray Brown/Flores]

0975. Pagani, D. 1984. "Art Farmer: Interview," *Cadence* 10 (May): 10. [Jazz-LA]

0976.————. 1985. "Melba Liston: Interview," *Cadence* 11 (September): 5. [Jazz-LA]

0977. Palmer, Robert. 1978. "Soul Survivor Ray Charles," *Rolling Stone* 258 (February 9): 11–14. [Soul/R & B/Popular Music-LA]

0978.————. 1980. *Baby, That's Rock and Roll.* N.p.: Harvest. [Rock/R & B-LA-On songwriters Leiber & Stoller]

0979. Pareles, Jon. 1985. "Singing the Gospel." *Dial* (January): 24–27. [Gospel-CA]

0980.————. 1986. "Little Feat," *NGDAM* 3: 92. [Rock-LA]

0981. Patrick, James. 1988. "Parker, Charlie," *NGDJ* 2: 286–291. [Jazz-LA]

0982. Patterson, Willis C., comp. 1977. *Anthology of Art Songs by Black Composers.* New York: E. B. Marks. [Art Music-Berkeley-Has songs by Berkeley composers Robert Owens and Olly Wilson]

0983. Patton, Chris. 1994. "Denzil Foster and Thomas McElroy: From Oaktown to Your Town," *Mix* 18 (June): 88, 92–96. [R&B-Oakland]

0984. Pearl, Bernie. 1985. "Eaven Blues: Blues Star Willie Dixon's Got a Mission Here on Earth," *Option* D2 (September/October): 24–25. [Blues-Glendale]

0985. Pepper, Art, and Laurie Pepper. 1979. *Straight Life: The Story of Art Pepper.* New York: Schirmer Books. [Jazz-LA-Describes Central Avenue scene of 1940s, life in San Quentin, West Coast jazz of the 50s, 60s, and 70s]

0985a. Parkins, William Eric. 1996. *Droppin' Science: Critical Essays on Rap Music and Hip Hop Culture.* Philadelphia: Temple University Press. [Rap-CA]

0986. Person-Lynn, Kwaku. 1992. "Rap Music: Afrikan Music Renaissance in America" in *African Musicology: Current Trends, Volume II,* edited by Jacqueline Cogdell DjeDje. Los Angeles: African Studies Center, University of California, Los Angeles, pp. 99–113. [Rap-LA-mentions west coast rappers, NWA, Ice Cube, Ice-T, Tone Loc]

0987. Petrie, Gavin, ed. 1974. *Black Music.* London: Hamlyn. [Popular Music-CA-Ray Charles, Pointer Sisters, Billy Preston]

0988. Philips, Chuck. 1993. "2Pac's Gospel Truth," *Rolling Stone* 668 (October 28): 22. [Rap-Oakland-Tupac Shakur]

0989.————. 1994. "The Big Mack," *Spin* 10(5) [August]: 48–52, 96. [Rap-LA-Suge Knight]

0990. Piccarella, John. 1986a. "Earth, Wind and Fire," *NGDAM* 2: 6–7. [R & B-LA]

0991.————. 1986b. "Love," *NGDAM* 3: 118. [Rock-LA]

0992. Pielke, Robert G. 1986. *You Say You Want a Revolution: Rock Music in American Culture.* Chicago: Nelson-Hall. [Rock-CA-Has chapter on California. Chapter on CA doesn't relate to black music. Other parts of the book mention black CA musicians]

0993. Placksin, Sally. 1982. *American Women in Jazz, 1900 to the Present: Their Words, Lives, and Music.* New York: Seaview Books. [Jazz-LA-Has profiles of Ivie Anderson, Melba Liston, Clora Bryant, Vi Redd]

0994.————. 1993. "Liston, Melba" in *Black Women in America: A Historical Encyclopedia,* edited by Darlene Clark Hine. Brooklyn: Carlson Publishing, pp. 724–727. [Jazz-LA]

0995. Poggi, Isotta. 1993. "Turiyasangitananda, Swami" in *Encyclopedia of African American Religions,* edited by Larry J. Murphy, Gordon Melton, and Gary L. Ward. New York: Garland Publishing, p. 768. [Jazz-LA-Alice Coltrane]

0996. Pollack, Phyllis. 1992. "Body Countdown: Ice-T vs. Dan Quayle The Police The PMRC Tipper Gore City Councils The F. B. I. Congress . . . " *Rap Sheet* (August): 35. [Rock/Metal-LA]

0997. Porter, Bob, and Mark Gardner. 1968a. "The California Cats pt. 1," *Jazz Monthly* 158 (April): 7–10. [Jazz-CA-Sonny Criss]

0998.———. 1968b. "The California Cats pt. 2," *Jazz Monthly* 159 (May): 6–8. [Jazz-CA-Sonny Criss]

0999. Porter, Lewis. 1984. "Jazzwomen: 'You Can't Get Up There Timidly,'" *Music Educators Journal* 71 (October): 42–51. [Jazz-LA-On Alice Coltrane, resident of Woodland Hills]

1000.———. 1988a. "(3) Barney Bigard," *NGDJ* 1: 107–108. [Jazz-LA]

1001.———. 1988b. "Gordon, Dexter (Keith)," *NGDJ* 1: 442. [Jazz-LA]

1002. Porter, Roy, with David Keller. 1991. *There and Back: The Roy Porter Story.* Baton Rouge: Louisiana State University Press. [Jazz-LA-incl. Discography]

1003. Potter, Jeff. 1985. "Uniquely, Chico Hamilton," *Modern Drummer* 9 (April): 18–21, 68–75. [Jazz-LA]

1004.———. 1988. "Bobo, Willie," *NGDJ* 1: 131–132. [Latin Jazz-CA]

1005. Poulson-Bryant, Scott. 1992. "Soul on Ice," *Spin* 7 (March): 33–37, 82. [Rap-LA-Ice Cube]

1006. Price, Simon. 1993. "Rage Against the Machine," *Melody Maker* 69(7) [February 13]: 6–7. [Metal/Rap-LA]

1007. Priestly, Brian. 1982. *Mingus: A Critical Biography.* New York: Da Capo Press. [Jazz-LA-Includes discography]

1008.———. 1988. "Morgan, Frank," *NGDJ* 2: 133. [Jazz-LA]

1009. Primack, Bret. 1979. "Eddie Moore," *Down Beat* 46 (February 22): 37–39. [Jazz-SF]

1010. Push. 1989a. "Niggers With Attitude: Street Hassle," *Melody Maker* 65 (August 5): 42–43. [Rap-LA-Ice Cube]

1011.———. 1989b. "NWA: Shot by Both Sides," *Melody Maker* 65 (November 4): 32–34. [Rap-LA]

1012.———. 1990. "Digital Underground: S Marks the Spot," *Melody Maker* 66 (April 7): 40. [Rap-Berkeley]

1013.———. 1991. "Ice Cube: Life in the Kill Zone," *Melody Maker* 67 (April 6): 37. [Rap-LA]

1014.———. 1993. "Push Raps with the Disposable Heroes of Hiphoprisy." *Melody Maker* (July): 29. [Rap-SF]

1015. Radio Pete. 1978. "Jimmy Witherspoon: Interview," *Cadence* 3 (January): 9–10. [Blues-LA]

1016. Raether, Keith. 1977. "Ornette: Bobby Bradford's Portrait of an Emerging Giant," *Jazz Magazine* 1(3): 43–46. [Jazz-LA]

1017. Ratliff, Ben. 1991. "Taking Charge: Conductor Butch Morris' Structured Chaos," *Option* 41 (November/December): 42–46. [Jazz/New Music-LA/Oakland]

1018. Reder, Alan. 1989. "The Good Life: Charles McPherson at Home with His Horn," *Option* 28 (September/October): 54–57. [Jazz-SD]

1019. Reed, Tom. 1992. *The Black Music History of Los Angeles—Its Roots.* Los Angeles: Black Accent Press. [General Music-LA-"A classical pictorial history of Black music in Los Angeles from the 1920's-1970"]

1020. Reisner, Robert George. 1962. *Bird: The Legend of Charlie Parker.* London: Quartet Books. [Jazz-LA-Charlie Parker]

1021. Rensin, David. 1975. "Little Feat: Giant Steps Across the Sea," *Rolling Stone* 184 (April 10): 11–12. [Rock-LA]

1022. Ressner, Jeffrey. 1989. "New Faces: The D. O. C.," *Rolling Stone* 564 (November 2): 30. [Rap-LA]

1023.———. 1990. "Hammer Time," *Rolling Stone* 586 (September 6): 46–50, 96. [Rap-Oakland]

1024. Ressner, Jeffrey, and Lonn M. Friend. 1991. "The Rolling Stone Interview: Slash," *Rolling Stone* 596 (January 24): 24–30, 51–52. [Rock-LA]

1025. Reynolds, Christopher. 1988. "The Gospel Truth: Two Choir Directors Approach 'Joyful Noise' Spirit Differently," *San Diego Union*, Section D (February 7): 1, 6. [Gospel-SD]

1026. Ricard, Jean-Paul. 1991. "Retour sur le petit maître," *Revue D'Esthétique* 19: 41–44. [Jazz-LA-Hampton Hawes]

1027. Rinzler, Paul. 1988a. "Cables, George (Andrew)," *NGDJ* 1: 179. [Jazz-LA]

1028.———. 1988b. "Coker, Dolo," *NGDJ* 1: 225. [Jazz-LA]

1029. Ritz, David. 1991. *The Life of Marvin Gaye.* New York: Da Capo. [Soul-LA]

1030.———. 1993a. "Sexual Healing," *Rolling Stone* 665 (September 16): 38–43, 82. [Popular Music-LA-Janet Jackson]

1031.———. 1993b. "Viva la Divas," *Rolling Stone* 660–661 (July 8–22): 64–69, 130. [Popular Music-Oakland-En Vogue]

1032. Rivelli, Pauline, and Robert Levin. 1970. *The Black Giants.* New York: World Publishing Co. [Jazz-CA-Has articles on many jazz artists, including Bobby Bradford, John Carter, Horace Tapscott, Pharoah Sanders]

1032a. Ro, Ronin. 1996. *Merchandising the Rhymes of Violence.* New York: St. Martin's Press. [Rap-CA]

1033. Robbins, Ira. 1988. "Suicidal Tendencies: Calling the Shots," *Rolling Stone* 538 (November 3): 21. [Rock-LA/Venice]

1034. Roberts, Chris. 1992. "Guns N' Roses: Knockin' on Britain's Door," *Melody Maker* 68 (May 30): 26–27. [Rock-LA-Slash; he hates LA]

1035. Roberts, Jim. 1988. "Verdine White: Back in the Spotlight With Earth, Wind & Fire," *Guitar Player* 22 (October): 60–66. [Rock/R & B-LA]

1036. Roberts, John Storm. 1979. *The Latin Tinge: The Impact of Latin American Music on the United States.* Tivoli, NY: Original Music. [Latin Jazz-CA-Bobo, Santamaria, Tjader, Kenton, others]

1037.———. 1988. "Tjader, Cal(len Radcliffe, Jr.)," *NGDJ* 2: 539–540. [Latin Jazz-SF]

1038. Robinson, J. Bradford. 1988a. "Baker, Chet," *NGDJ* 1: 53–54. [Jazz-LA]

1039.———. 1988b. "Brown, Ray(mond Matthews)," *NGDJ* 1: 159–160. [Jazz-LA]

1040. Robinson, Leroy. 1964. "Gerald Wilson," *Jazz* 3 (September): 12–14. [Jazz-LA]

1041. Robinson, Louie. 1972. "Quincy Jones: Man Behind the Music," *Ebony* 27 (June): 92–94, 96–97, 100, 102. [Film Music/Jazz/Popular Music-LA]

1042.———. 1974. "The Enduring Genius of Ray Charles," *Ebony* 29 (October): 125–134. [Popular Music-LA]

1043.———. 1975. "The Funky Sound of War," *Ebony* 30 (March): 84–92. [Popular Music-LA]

1044. Rock, H. 1978. "Arthur Blythe: Interview," *Cadence* 3 (March): 7. [Jazz-LA]

1045. Rodriguez, Jose, ed. 1940. *Music and Dance in California.* Hollywood: Bureau of Musical Research. [General Music-CA]

1046. Rodriguez, Luis. 1980. "Eastside Sound," *Q-vo* 2(7): 27–29, 67, 76–78. [Rock/R & B-LA-African/European/Latino interaction]

1047. Romero, E. 1981. "Prince Lawsha: a Short Talk," *Cadence* 7 (June): 10. [Jazz-LA]

1048. Rona, Jeffrey. 1983. "Pro Session: James Newton's Solo on 'Feeling': A Flute Transcription," *Down Beat* 50 (April): 56–57. [Jazz-LA]

1049. Ronin Ro. 1992. "Riding Shotgun." *The Source* (September): 32–36. [Rap-LA-on Latino and Samoan rappers, Kid Frost, Boo-Yaa Tribe]

1050. Rose, Tricia. 1994. *Black Noise: Rap Music and Black Culture in Contemporary America.* Hanover, NH: Wesleyan University Press. [Rap-CA-Analyzes many CA-based rappers]

1051. Rosen, Steve. 1976. "Lowell Fulson: Forty Years of Playing the Blues," *Guitar Player* 10 (November): 22, 70, 74. [Blues-Oakland]

1052. Rosenthal, David. 1983. "Wynton Kelly, Elmo Hope, Sonny Clark: Three Neglected Jazz Piano Greats of the 1950s," *Keyboard* 9 (June): 56–61. [Jazz-CA-Hope and Clark worked in CA for a while]

1053. Rosner, Lora. 1992. "Billy Higgins: Making the Music One," *Modern Drummer* 16 (February): 26–29, 102–110. [Jazz-LA]

1054. Rowland, Mark. 1991. "Ice-T: The Code of Many Colors," *Musician* 154 (August): 66–71. [Rap-LA]

1055.———. 1993a. "Crap Killer," *Musician* 171 (January): 37–40. [Rap/Rock-LA-Ice-T]

1056.———. 1993b. "Michael Franti: Hero of Hiphoprisy," *Musician* 171 (January): 66, 68, 94. [Rap-Bay Area]

1057.———. 1995. "Twilight of the Guitar Gods? Edward Van Halen & Slash Show There's Life After the '80s," *Musician* 196 (March): 40–48. [Rock-LA]

1058. Royster, Philip M. 1991. "The Rapper as Shaman for a Band of Dancers of the Spirit: U Can't Touch This," *Black Sacred Music* 5(1): 60–67. [Rap-Oakland-Hammer]

1059. Ruffin, W. 1974. "Eleven Men Form a Pillar of Music," *Soul* 9 (September 16): 12–13. [Rock/Soul-Oakland-Tower of Power]

1060. Rule, Greg. 1993. "Tony Toni Toné: Past and Present Collide on *Sons of Soul*," *Keyboard* 19 (November): 16. [R & B-Oakland]

1061.———. 1994a. "The Good, the Bad, and the Noisy," *Keyboard* 20 (May): 30–40. [Rap-Bay Area-Del tha Funkee Homosapien]

1062.———. 1994b. "Timothy Christian Riley, Tony Toni Toné: The Sons of Soul Redefining the Funk," *Drum!* 4 (January/February): 45–49. [R & B-Oakland]

1063. Rupe, Art. 1973. "The Specialist," *Blues Unlimited* 104: 6–8. [Blues-LA-Specialty Records]

1064. Rusch, Bob. 1977. "Buck Clayton: Interview," *Cadence* 3(6): 11. [Jazz-LA]

1065.———. 1978. "Chet Baker Interview," *Cadence* 4 (August): 3. [Jazz-LA]

1066.———. 1981. "Dexter Gordon: Interview," *Cadence* 7 (November): 5. [Jazz-LA]

1067.———. 1986a. "Buell Neidlinger: Interview," *Cadence* 12 (June): 5. [Jazz-LA]

1068.———. 1986b. "Jack McVea: Interview," *Cadence* 12 (April): 11–23. [Jazz-LA]

1069.———. 1987a. "Al McKibbon," *Cadence* 13 (March): 13. [Jazz-LA]

1070.———. 1987b. "Jerome Richardson," *Cadence* 23 (December): 5–18, 24, 88. [Jazz-SF]

1071.———. 1987c. "Leroy Vinnegar: Interview," *Cadence* 13 (March): 5–16+. [Jazz-LA]

1072.———. 1989. "Eddie Gale Interview," *Cadence* 15 (October): 13–18, 92. [Jazz-San Jose]

1073.———. 1993a. "Gerry Wiggins: Interview," *Cadence* 19 (March): 9–12, 32. [Jazz-LA]

1074.———. 1993b. "Michael Vlatkovich Interview," *Cadence* 19 (November): 5–8. [Jazz/Latin-LA]

1075.———. 1994a. "Glenn Spearman Interview," *Cadence* 20 (May): 5–14. [Jazz-Bay Area]

1076.———. 1994b. "Teddy Edwards Interview," *Cadence* 20 (April): 5–18. [Jazz-LA]

1077.———. 1995a. "Bill Perkins Interview," *Cadence* 21 (November): 5–20. [Jazz-LA]

1078.————. 1995b. "Frank Strazzeri Interview," *Cadence* 21 (September): 5–18. [Jazz-LA]

1079. Russell, B. 1980. "Jelly Roll Morton: An Interview with Barney Bigard," *Footnote* 11(6): 15. [Jazz-LA]

1080. Russell, Ross. 1970. "Sonny Simmons," *Jazz Hot* 267 (December): 16–17. [Jazz-LA]

1081.————. 1972a. "Yardbird in Lotus Land pt. 1," *Jazz Hot* 280 (February): 8–9. [Jazz-CA-Charlie Parker]

1082.————. 1972b. "Yardbird in Lotus Land pt. 2," *Jazz Hot* 281 (March): 10–11. [Jazz-CA-Charlie Parker]

1083.————. 1973a. *Bird Lives!* New York: Charterhouse. [Jazz-CA-Has several chapters on California]

1084.————. 1973b. "West Coast Bop," *Jazz and Blues* 3 (May): 8–11. [Jazz-CA]

1085. Rye, Howard. 1988. "Davis, (Thomas) Maxwell," *NGDJ* 1: 271. [Jazz-LA]

1086. Sacre, Robert. 1995. "Negro Spirituals and Gospel Songs: Indexes to Selected Periodicals," *Black Music Research Journal* 15(2): 141–246. [Gospel-CA-Indexed by artists, includes articles in out of print journals]

1087. Salvo, Patrick. 1976. "Andrae Crouch: New King of 'Pop Gospel,'" *Sepia Magazine* 25(12): 50–54. [Gospel-LA]

1088. Salzman, Ed. 1958. "The Real Bay City Jazz," *Saturday Review* 41 (July 12): 39. [Jazz-SF]

1089. Sandow, Gregory. 1989. "Rock and Roll Quarterly: Gettin' Hard in Cali," *Village Voice* 34 (April 4): RR 12–13. [Rap-LA-On L. A. Rap, NWA, Ice-T, Tone Loc]

1090.————. 1995. "Dr. Dre," *Spin* 11(1) [April]: 62. [Rap-LA]

1091. Santino, Jack. 1986. "Thornton, Big Mama," *NGDAM* 4: 393. [Blues-LA]

1092. Sawyer, Eugene T. 1923. "Old-Time Minstrels of San Francisco: Recollections of a Pioneer," *Overland Monthly* 81 (October): 5–7. [Minstrelsy-SF]

1093. Scheurer, Timothy. 1991. *Born in the U. S. A.* Jackson: University Press of Mississippi. [Popular Music/Rock-CA-Mentions California artists in passing]

1094. Schneider, Wayne. 1988. "Hite, Les," *NGDJ* 1: 529. [Jazz-LA]

1095. Schrock, Marion D. 1989. "Aspects of Compositional Style in Four Works by Olly Wilson," *Black Music Research Journal* 9 (Spring): 93–108. [Art Music-Bay Area]

1096. Schuller, Gunther. 1988a. "Coleman, Ornette," *NGDJ* 1: 229–231. [Jazz-LA]

1097.————. 1988b. "Morton, Jelly Roll," *NGDJ* 2: 136–139. [Jazz-LA]

1098.————. 1989. *The Swing Era: The Development of Jazz 1930–1945.* New York: Oxford University Press. [Jazz-CA-Nat Cole, Earl Hines, Lionel Hampton, Benny Carter, Paul Howard, Sonny Clay, Curtis Mosby, other CA references]

1099. Semler, Derrick. 1984. "J. D. Nicholson," *Living Blues* 62: 3. [Blues-Oakland]

1100. Senna, Danzy. 1994. "Violence is Golden," *Spin* 10(1) [April]: 42–47. [Rap-Oakland-Tupac Shakur]

1101. Seroff, Doug. 1975. "Roy Milton and Miltone Records," *Blues Unlimited* 115: 10–17. [Blues-LA]

1102. Shapiro, Nat, and Nat Hentoff, eds. 1955. *Hear Me Talkin' to Ya: The Story of Jazz as Told by the Men Who Made It.* New York: Dover. [Jazz-CA-Brief comments on west coast]

1103. Shaw, Arnold. 1970. *The World of Soul: Black America's Contribution to the Pop Music Scene.* New York: Cowles. [Soul-CA-Has chapter on West Coast]

1104.————. 1974. *The Rockin' '50s: The Decade that Transformed the Pop Music Scene.* New York: Hawthorne Books. [Popular Music/R & B-CA]

1105.————. 1978. *Honkers and Shouters: The Golden Years of Rhythm and Blues.* New York: Collier Books. [R & B-LA-Includes a short section on the development of independent record companies in Los Angeles, and interview with Bob Geddins]

1106.————. 1980. "Researching Rhythm and Blues," *Black Music Research Journal:* 71–79. [R&B-CA-Mentions CA artists and record labels]

1107.————. 1986. *Black Popular Music in America.* New York: Schirmer Books. [Popular Music/R & B/Blues-CA]

1108.————. 1987. *The Jazz Age: Popular Music in the 1920s.* New York: Oxford University Press. [Jazz-LA-Jelly Roll Morton]

1109.————. 1988. "Rhythm & Blues in California," *Black Music Research Bulletin* 10(1): 11–12. [R & B-CA]

1110. Shaw, Russell. 1978. "Little Feat: Spectacular Sextet," *Down Beat* 45 (June 15): 20, 52, 60. [Rock-LA]

1111. Sheehan, Tom. 1993. "Mechanic Street Preachers," *Melody Maker* 69(35) [August 28]: 10–11. [Metal/Rap-LA-Rage Against the Machine]

1112. Sheridan, Chris. 1979. "The Contemporary Art of Pepper," *Jazz Journal International* 32 (September): 9. [Jazz-LA]

1113.————. 1979. "A Fresh Sea Breeze from the West," *Jazz Journal International* 32 (July): 22–23. [Jazz-CA-Interplay Records]

1114.————. 1980. "Ornette Coleman on Record Part 1," *Jazz Journal International* 33 (November): 22–23. [Jazz-LA-reviews LA-period recordings]

1115. Sheridan, Kevin J. 1977. "Pee-Wee Crayton: In the Forefront of West Coast Blues," *Guitar Player* 11 (July): 22, 74. [Blues-Oakland]

1116. Sheridan, Kevin, and Peter Sheridan. 1977. "T-Bone Walker: Father of the Electric Blues," *Guitar Player* 11 (March): 22, 48–56. [Blues-LA]

1117. Shindler, Merril. 1977. "Guitar Watson: Is this here mother for real?" *Rolling Stone* 242 (June 30): 46–48. [Blues-LA]

1118. Shoemaker, Bill. 1989. "Anthony Braxton: The Dynamics of Creativity," *Down Beat* 56 (March): 20–22. [Jazz/Art Music-Oakland-Mills College]

1119. Shurman, Dick. 1991. "Guitar Shorty: Blues on the Flip Side," *Living Blues* 95 (January/February): 23–27. [Blues-LA]

1120. Shurman, Dick, and Jim O'Neal. 1975. " 'People Like Me'—Floyd Dixon on Record," *Living Blues* 23 (September/October): 20–21. [Blues-LA]

1121. Shuster, Fred. 1991. "L.A.'s China Club," *Down Beat* 58 (February): 26–27. [Nightclubs-LA]

1122.————. 1993. "The Reluctant Power Broker," *Down Beat* 60 (July): 16–20. [Jazz-LA-Branford Marsalis]

1123.————. 1994a. "Charlie Haden: Risk Your Life for Everyone," *Down Beat* 61 (August): 16–19. [Jazz-LA]

1124.————. 1994b. "Solidarity, L. A.-Style: Black Note," *Down Beat* 61 (May): 26–29. [Jazz-LA]

1125.————. 1995. "Freddie Hubbard: When Your Chops Are Shot," *Down Beat* 62 (October): 22–25. [Jazz-LA-He lives in LA]

1126. Siders, Harvey. 1966a. "The Latinization of Cal Tjader," *Down Beat* 33 (September 8): 21–23. [Latin Jazz-SF]

1127.————. 1966b. "Sonny Criss: One-Horn Man," *Down Beat* 32 (May 19): 27–29. [Jazz-LA]

1128.————. 1968. "Hamp's New Blues," *Down Beat* 35 (October 17): 16–17, 41. [Jazz-LA-Hampton Hawes, lived at 19307 Broadacres, Compton]

1129.————. 1973a. "The Crusaders: Four of a Kind," *Down Beat* 40 (July 19): 16–17. [Jazz-LA]

1130.————. 1973b. "Drum Schticks, Pt. 1," *Down Beat* 40 (March 15): 15–17. [Jazz/Latin Jazz-CA-Willie Bobo, Shelly Manne]

1131.————. 1973c. "Drum Schticks, Pt. 2," *Down Beat* 40 (March 29): 18, 31. [Jazz/Latin Jazz-CA-Willie Bobo, Shelly Manne]

1132.————. 1973d. "Group Therapy," *Down Beat* 40 (May 10): 17–19, 45–46. [Jazz-LA-Hampton Hawes, Jimmy Smith]

1133.————. 1973e. "Splendor in the Brass: A Roundtable Discussion with Mike Barone, Red Callender, Sweets Edison, Benny Powell," *Down Beat* 40 (February 1): 13–16, 31. [Jazz-LA]

1134. Sidran, Ben. 1992. *Talking Jazz: An Illustrated Oral History.* Petaluma, CA: Pomegranate Artbooks. [Jazz-CA-Frank Morgan, Horace Silver, Charles Brown, Joe Sample, Don Cherry, Bobby McFerrin]

1135. Siegmund, Heidi. 1992. "Ernie C: Down with the Count," *Guitar Player* 26 (July): 14–15. [Rock/Metal-LA-Body Count]

1136. Sievert, Jon. 1977. "Chester Thompson: Keyboardist for Tower of Power," *Contemporary Keyboard* 3 (March): 16, 38–43. [Rock/Soul-Oakland]

1137. Sigerson, Davitt. 1986a. "Coasters," *NGDAM* 1: 460–461. [R & B/Popular Music-LA]

1138.————. 1986b. "Sly and the Family Stone," *NGDAM* 4: 242–243. [Rock-SF]

1139. Silsbee, Kirk. 1993a. "Richard Grossman Interview (Part One)," *Cadence* 19 (September): 5–12. [Jazz-LA]

1140.————. 1993b. "Richard Grossman Interview (Part Two)," *Cadence* 19 (October): 11–17. [Jazz-LA]

1141. Silvert, Conrad. 1978a. "Joe Zawinul: Wayfaring Genius, pt. 1," *Down Beat* 45 (June 1): 13–15. [Jazz-Pasadena]

1142.————. 1978b. "Joe Zawinul: Wayfaring Genius, pt. 2," *Down Beat* 45 (June 15): 52–53, 56, 58. [Jazz-Pasadena]

1143.————. 1980. "Old and New Dreams," *Down Beat* 47 (June): 16–19, 61. [Jazz-LA/SF-Blackwell, Cherry, Haden, D. Redman]

1144. Simmen, Johnny. 1975. "Crystal Clear," *Coda* 12(5): 25. [Jazz-LA-Benny Carter]

1145.————. 1978. "Sonny Clark," *Coda* 126 (August 1): 16. [Jazz-LA]

1146.————. 1985. "Maxwell Davis (14 janvier 1916–18 septembre 1970)," *Bulletin du Hot Club de France* 323: 3. [Jazz-LA]

1147. Simosko, Vladimir, and Barry Tepperman. 1971. *Eric Dolphy: A Musical Biography and Discography.* New York: Da Capo Press. [Jazz-LA-Has information on the LA jazz scene of the 1940s and 1950s. Discography includes recordings done by LA bands in the 40s and 50s]

1148. Simpson, Ralph Ricardo. 1964. "William Grant Still: The Man and His Music." Ph.D. dissertation, Michigan State University. [Art Music-LA]

1149. Sinclair, Robin. 1980. "Britt Woodman Today," *Jazz Journal International* 33 (March): 7–8. [Jazz-CA]

1150. Singleton, Raynoma Gordy. 1990. *Berry, Me, and Motown: The Untold Story.* Chicago: Contemporary Books. [Soul-LA-Has chapter on Hollywood]

1151. Skelly, Richard. 1992. "Sonny Rhodes: Disciple of the Blues," *Living Blues* 102 (March/April): 12–21. [Blues-Bay Area]

1152. Slater, Jack. 1973. "They Update the Past," *Ebony* 29 (December): 103–113. [Popular Music-Oakland-Pointer Sisters]

1153. Slattery, Paul Harold. 1969. "A Comparative Study of the First and Fourth Symphonies of William Grant Still." M.A. thesis, San Jose State University. [Art Music-LA]

1154. Slutsky, Allan. 1995. "Profile: Robert White, 1936–1994: A Motown Requiem," *Guitar Player* 29 (March): 31–34. [Soul-LA]

1155. Smith, Andrew. 1992a. "Disposable Heroes of Hiphoprisy: Fear and Loathing on the Campaign Trail," *Melody Maker* 68 (November 14): 26–28. [Rap-SF]

1156. ———. 1992b. "House of Pain: One Jump Ahead," *Melody Maker* 68 (October 10): 40–41. [Rap-LA]

1157. ———. 1993a. "'Check This Out Moms, I've Set a Time Bomb,'" *Melody Maker* (February): 6–7. [Rap-LA-Ice-T]

1158. ———. 1993b. "Genius Bordering on Insanity," *Melody Maker* (June 5): 42–43. [Rock-LA-Fishbone]

1159. ———. 1993c. "Ice Cube: The Predator's Decision Is Final," *Melody Maker* (January 16): 32–33. [Rap-LA]

1160. Smith, Arnold Jay. 1977a. "Mongo Santamaria: Cuban King of Congas," *Down Beat* 44 (April 21): 19–20, 48. [Latin Jazz-SF]

1161. ———. 1977b. "Sarah Vaughan: Never Ending Melody," *Down Beat* 44 (May 5): 16–17, 44. [Jazz-LA]

1162. Smith, B. 1976. "Art Farmer," *Coda* 144 (January/February): 2. [Jazz-LA]

1162a. Smith, Catherine Parsons. 1996. "William Grant Still: 'Dean of Afro-American Composers,'" in *Music in the Central Avenue Community, 1890–c. 1955*, edited by Bette Y. Cox. Los Angeles: BEEM Foundation, pp. 42–54. [Art Music-LA]

1163. Smith, Danyel. 1991. "Digital Underground: Just for the Funk of It." *The Source* (December): 22–27. [Rap-Bay Area]

1164. ———. 1992a. "Dreaming America," *Spin* 8 (December): 106. [Rap-Oakland]

1165. ———. 1992b. "Dreaming America," *Spin* 8 (September): 112. [Rap-LA-DJ Quik]

1166. ———. 1993a. "Dreaming America," *Spin* 8(10) [January]: 73. [Rap-Oakland-Hammer]

1167. ———. 1993b. "Dreaming America," *Spin* 9 (July): 91. [Rap-LA-Yo-Yo]

1168. ———. 1993c. "Party Out of Bounds," *Rolling Stone* 669 (November 11): 64–65. [Rap-LA-Cypress Hill, House of Pain, Funkdoobiest]

1169. ———. 1994. "Dreaming America: Hip Hop Culture," *Spin* 9 (February): 77. [Rap-Oakland-Tupac Shakur]

1170. Smith, Edwin. 1992. "Catching Up with Andrae Crouch," *Rejoice!* 4(4): 7–9. [Gospel-LA]

1171. Smith, Fletcher. 1995. *Central Avenue Sounds Oral History Transcript.* Los Angeles: Oral History Program, University of California, Los Angeles. [Jazz-LA]

1172. Smith, Gregory E. 1988a. "Clark, Sonny," *NGDJ* 1: 217–218. [Jazz-LA]

1173. ———. 1988b. "Hope, (St.) Elmo (Sylvester)," *NGDJ* 1: 537–538. [Jazz-CA]

1174. Smith, Mat. 1988. "Hell Street Blues," *Melody Maker* 64 (February 6): 24–26. [Rock-LA-Faith No More]

1175. ———. 1992. "Fishbone: Babylon's Burning," *Melody Maker* 68 (July 11): 10–11. [Rock-LA-on Riots]

1176. Smith, Miyoshi. 1989. "Lawrence 'Butch' Morris," *Cadence* 15 (July): 13–18. [Jazz-LA/SF]

1177. ———. 1992. "John Carter: Interview," *Cadence* 18 (May): 5–13, 27. [Jazz-LA]

1178.————. 1995. "Horace Tapscott Interview," *Cadence* 21 (August): 5–18. [Jazz-LA]

1179. Smith, Phylise Lorraine. 1991. "Los Angeles African-Americans: Expressions of Cultural Identity Through Participation in West African Dance." M.A. thesis, University of California, Los Angeles. [Traditional-LA]

1180. Smith, R. J. 1995. "Charles Wright Expresses Himself," *Grand Royal* 2: 94–95. [R & B-LA-Watts 103rd Street Band]

1181. Smith, Roger Len. 1995. "Little Feat: Still Runnin'," *Relix* 22 (August): 36–37. [Rock-LA]

1182. Smith, T. A. 1991. "D. O. C.: Rappin' Discord into Harmony," *Cash Box* 55 (September 7): 19. [Rap-LA]

1183. Son of Neckbone (?). 1995. "Eric Bobo! The Grand Royal Interview with Son of Neckbone," *Grand Royal* 2: 110–113. [Rap/Latin Jazz-CA-Son of Willie Bobo]

1184. Southern, Eileen. 1977. "Conversation With Olly Wilson: The Education of a Composer, Part I," *The Black Perspective in Music* 5(1): 90–103. [Art Music-Bay Area]

1185.————. 1978. "Conversation With Olly Wilson: The Education of a Composer, Part II," *The Black Perspective in Music* 6(1): 56–70. [Art Music-Bay Area]

1186.————. 1986a. "Still, William Grant," *NGDAM* 4: 311–312. [Art Music-LA]

1187.————. 1986b. "Wilson, Olly (Woodrow)," *NGDAM* 4: 539. [Art Music-Berkeley]

1188. Spellman, A. B. 1966. *Four Lives in the Bebop Business.* New York: Limelight Editions. [Jazz-LA-Has information on Ornette Coleman's early years in Los Angeles]

1189. Spencer, Jon Michael. 1990. *Protest and Praise: Sacred Music of Black Religion.* Minneapolis: Fortress Press. [Gospel-LA-Discussion of the Azusa Street Mission that was held in LA]

1190.————. 1991. "Introduction," *Black Sacred Music* 5(1): 1–11. [Rap-LA-mentions LA rappers]

1191.————. 1994. "William Grant Still: Eclectic Religionist," *Black Sacred Music* 8(1): 135–156. [Art Music-LA-Several mentions of LA]

1192. Spencer, Jon Michael, ed. 1992. *The William Grant Still Reader: Essays on American Music. A Special Issue of Black Sacred Music, Volume 6, Number 2.* Durham, NC: Duke University Press. [Art Music-LA-Includes introduction by Spencer, foreward by Olly Wilson, numerous writings by Still, bibliography]

1193a. Stanley, Lawrence A., ed. 1992. *Rap: The Lyrics.* New York: Penguin. [Rap-CA-Has lyrics to songs by Above the Law, Boo-Yaa Tribe, CPO, Cypress Hill, Digital Underground, Disposable Heroes of Hiphoprisy, DJ Quik, D. O. C., Eazy-E, Ice Cube, Ice-T, MC Hammer, Mellow Man Ace, NWA, Paris, Tone Loc, Too Short, Yo-Yo, Young MC]

1193. Stancell, Steven. 1996. *Rap Whoz Who: The World of Rap Music.* New York: Schirmer Books. [Rap-CA]

1194. Steif, B. 1959a. "Calif. Atty. General's Merger Order to White and Negro Frisco AFM Locals," *Variety* 216 (November 4): 59+. [Jazz-SF]

1195.————. 1959b. "Calif. Atty. Gen.'s 'reasonable time' Stance on White-Negro AFM Merger," *Variety* 217 (December 2): 57–58. [Jazz-CA]

1196. Stein Hunt, Danica. 1994. "Women Who Play Jazz: A Study of the Experiences of Three Los Angeles Musicians." M.A. thesis, University of California, Los Angeles. [Jazz-LA-Clora Bryant, Ann Patterson, Nedra Wheeler]

1197. Steiner, Fred. 1986. "Jones, Quincy (Delight, Jr.)," *NGDAM* 2: 594. [Film Music/Jazz/Popular Music-LA]

1198. Stephens, Robert W. 1984. "Soul: A Historical Reconstruction of Continuity and Change in Black Popular Music," *The Black Perspective in Music* 12(1): 21–43. [Soul-CA-Discussion of Motown and Jump combos of southwest]

1199. Stephenson, William. 1992. "The Many Tongues of Branford." *Jazziz* (July): 78–85. [Jazz-LA-Branford Marsalis, musical director of Jay Leno show]

1200. Stephney, Bill. 1991. "Fundamental Hip-Hop," *Rock and Roll Confidential* 85 (January/February): 1–2. [Rap-CA]

1201. Stern, Chip. 1979. "Arthur Blythe," *Musician* 19 (January/February): 44–48. [Jazz-LA]

1202.———. 1991. "Charlie Haden's Basic Values," *Musician* 154 (August): 60–65. [Jazz-LA]

1203. Stevens, Charles. 1994. "Traditions and Innovations in Jazz," *Popular Music and Society* 18 (2): 61–78. [Jazz-LA-Ornette Coleman]

1204. Stevenson, Robert. 1984. "Los Angeles," *NGDM* 11:107–115. [General Music-LA-briefly mentions some gospel people]

1205.———. 1988a. "Local Music History Research in Los Angeles Area Libraries, Part I," *Inter-American Music Review* 10(1): 19–38. [General Music-LA-Los Angeles Public Library, USC Doheny Library, reference to the Los Angeles journal *The Pacific Coast Musician*, 1911–1948]

1206.———. 1988b. "Music in Southern California: A Tale of Two Cities," *Inter-American Music Review* 10(1): 39–111. [General Music-San Diego: Cradle of California Music, Los Angeles: The First Biennium and Beyond-LA]

1207. Stewart, Milton Lee. 1988. "Development of Rhythm and Blues and Its Styles," *Jazz-forschung* 20: 89–116. [R & B-CA-Has info on CA artists and record labels]

1208. Stewart, Rex. 1972. *Jazz Masters of the Thirties.* New York: Da Capo. [Jazz-CA-Benny Carter, L. Brown]

1209. Stewart, Zan. 1979. "Horace Tapscott," *Musician Player and Listener* 21 (November): 54–57. [Jazz-LA]

1210.———. 1984. "Ernie Watts: Watts' Happening," *Down Beat* 51 (November): 26–27, 59. [Jazz-LA]

1211.———. 1985. "The Quincy Jones Interview," *Down Beat* 52 (April): 16–19, 49. [Popular Music-LA]

1212.———. 1986. "Kenny Burrell: Boppin' the Blues," *Down Beat* 53 (July): 20–22. [Jazz-LA]

1213.———. 1993. "Believe the Hype: Joshua Redman," *Down Beat* 60 (June): 26–29. [Jazz-Berkeley]

1214.———. 1995a. "Kevin Eubanks: Sorry, No Sell-Out," *Down Beat* 62 (November): 26–29. [Jazz-LA]

1215.———. 1995b. "Lost in LA: The Legends Who Stayed Behind," *Down Beat* 62 (September): 20–23. [Jazz-LA-Ernie Andrews/Bobby Bradford/Conte Candoli/Buddy Collette/Teddy Edwards/Harold Land/Horace Tapscott/Gerald Wilson]

1216.———. 1995c. "Ray Brown: King of the Road," *Down Beat* 62 (July): 22–25. [Jazz-LA]

1217.———. 1995d. "The Spirit of Collaboration: Melba Liston & Randy Weston," *Down Beat* 62 (February): 22–24. [Jazz-LA]

1218.———. 1995e. "Wayne Shorter: 'What Is It We Haven't Done Before?'" *Down Beat* 62 (October): 16–21. [Jazz-LA]

1219. Stoddard, Tom. 1970. "Black Jazz on the West Coast," *Storyville* 27 (February/March): 97–104. [Jazz-CA]

1220.———. 1982. *Jazz on the Barbary Coast.* Chigwell, Essex: Storyville Publications. [Jazz-Bay Area]

1221. Stolder, Steve. 1988. "Johnny Otis' Uptown Suite." *BAM Magazine* (February 26): 44. [R & B/Blues/Popular Music-LA]

1222. Strauss, Neil. 1992. "Ice-T: It's a Dick Thing," *Option* 43 (March/April): 74–79. [Rap/Metal-LA]

1223.————. 1993. "Phar Out," *Spin* 9 (April): 22–23. [Rap-LA-Pharcyde]

1224. The Stud Brothers. 1989. "Ice-T: Rhyme Pays," *Melody Maker* 65 (February 18): 35. [Rap-LA]

1225.————. 1990. "Ice-T: Fear and Loathing in L. A.," *Melody Maker* 66 (February 3): 46–47. [Rap-LA]

1226. Sugerman, Danny. 1991. *Appetite for Destruction*. New York: St. Martin's Press. [Rock-LA-Guns n' Roses/Slash]

1227. Summers, Russ. 1988. "Elements of Style: Composer, Musician, and Living Legend Ornette Coleman," *Option* 21 (July/August): 37–40. [Jazz-LA]

1228. Sutherland, John. 1986. "Contemporary's West Coast Revival," *Coda* 206 (February 1): 8–11. [Jazz-CA-Contemporary Records]

1229. Tabatabai, Behzad. 1992. "Trying to Fight (for) the Cause: Muslim Rappers Mix Dawah and Contemporary Music," *Al-Talib* 2 (February): 13. [Rap-LA-on Al-Jihad records]

1229a. Talalay, Kathryn. 1997. *Composition in Black and White: The Life of Philippa Schuyler*. New York: Oxford University Press. [Art-Music-LA]

1230. Tannenbaum, Rob. 1990. "Up from the Underground: Digital Underground's Rappers Hawk Their New Sex Packets," *Rolling Stone* 576 (April 19): 27. [Rap-Berkeley]

1231.————. 1992. "The Disciples of Pot: Cypress Hill says marijuana's getting a bad rap," *Rolling Stone* 631 (May 28): 18. [Rap-South Gate]

1232. Taylor, Arthur. 1993. *Notes and Tones: Musician-to-Musician Interviews*. New York: Da Capo. [Jazz-CA-Hampton Hawes, Ornette Coleman, Don Cherry]

1233. Teagarden, Norma. 1994. *Grand Lady of Piano Jazz: Norma Teagarden; with Introductions by Cyra McFadden and Marilyn Unsworth*. Berkeley: Regional Oral History Office, The Bancroft Library, University of California. [Jazz-Berkeley-Interviewed by Caroline Crawford]

1234. Tercinet, Alain. 1986. *West Coast Jazz*. Marseilles: Parentheses. [Jazz-CA]

1235. Terrell, Janice D. 1984. "The Growth of Contemporary Christian Music in the Last Ten Years (1973–1983)." Masters thesis, American University. [Gospel-LA-Andraé Crouch]

1236. Terry, Carol D. 1987. *Sequins and Shades: The Michael Jackson Reference Guide*. Ann Arbor, MI: Pierian Press. [Popular Music-LA-Includes bibliography, chronology, discography]

1237. Theroux, Gary. 1988a. "Ayers, Roy (E., Jr.)," *NGDJ* 1: 46. [Jazz-LA]

1238.————. 1988b. "Gordon, Joe," *NGDJ* 1: 442–443. [Jazz-LA]

1239. Thompson, Leon Everette. 1966. "A Historical and Stylistic Analysis of the Music of William Grant Still and a Thematic Catalog of His Works." Ph.D. dissertation, University of Southern California. [Art Music-LA]

1240. Thompson-Peters, Flossie E. 1979. *The Shepherd: A Biography of Dr. Arthur A. Peters*. Los Angeles: Atlas Press. [Gospel-LA]

1241. Tiegel, Eliot. 1969. "The State of Blues West Coast Style," *Billboard* 81(33) [August 16]: S5–S6, S28. [Blues-CA]

1242. Tobler, John. 1973. "Forever Changes," *Melody Maker* 48 (December 29): 12–13. [Rock-LA-Interview with Arthur Lee]

1243. Tolleson, Robin. 1987. "Profile: Nathan East," *Down Beat* 54 (February): 47–48. [Studio-SD/LA]

1244.————. 1988. "Bobby McFerrin: Beyond Scat, Promise Fulfilled," *Down Beat* 55 (June): 20–21. [Jazz-SF]

1245.————. 1994. "Patrice Rushen: Looking for the Magic," *Mix* 18 (June): 89, 183, 185. [Jazz/R&B-LA]

1246. Tompkins, L. 1962. "The Dexter Gordon Story," *Crescendo* 1 (4): 4. [Jazz-LA]

1247.————. 1978a. "Ernie Royal," *Crescendo International* 16 (May): 22. [Jazz-LA]

1248.————. 1978b. "Ernie Royal," *Crescendo International* 16 (July): 14. [Jazz-LA]

1249. Townley, Ray. 1973. "War," *Down Beat* 40(19): 14, 36. [Rock-LA]

1250.————. 1974. "Sugarcane's . . . got da blues," *Down Beat* 41 (November 22): 13, 39. [Blues-LA-Sugarcane Harris]

1251.————. 1975a. "Bennie Maupin: Not to be Confused with Bernie Taupin," *Down Beat* 42 (May 22): 17–18, 60. [Jazz-LA-mentions West Coast]

1252.————. 1975b. "The Herculean Tenor of Joe Henderson," *Down Beat* 42 (January 16): 18–20, 40–41. [Jazz-SF-briefly mentions CA]

1253. Townsend, L. 1982. "James Newton: Young Lion." *Jazz Times* (December): 10–11. [Jazz-LA]

1254. Tracy, Jack. 1976. "Rhythm + Rosin = Royalty: Ray Brown," *Down Beat* 43 (January 29): 12–13, 33. [Jazz-LA]

1255. Trageser, Jim. 1990. "Sweet Baby Blues: Jeannie and Jimmy Cheatham," *Living Blues* 93 (September/October): 10–14. [Blues-SD]

1256.————. 1993. "My Music Is Blues Because That's Where It Comes From: Earl Thomas," *Living Blues* 111 (September/October): 26–32. [Blues-SD]

1257. Traill, Sinclair. 1979. "The Shelly Manne Story," *Jazz Journal International* 32 (August): 21–23, 26. [Jazz-LA]

1258. Trakin, Roy. 1991a. "Fishbone Swims Upstream to Spawn Punk-Funk Hybrid," *Musician* 151 (May): 34–40. [Rock-LA]

1259.————. 1991b. "Young M. C.'s Move," *Musician* 157 (November): 26–28. [Rap-LA]

1260. Trotter, James M. 1968 [1881]. *Music and Some Highly Musical People.* New York: Johnson Reprint Corp. [Art Music-LA-Hyers sisters]

1261. True, Everett. 1992. "Axe of Faith: Disposable Heroes of Hiphoprisy," *Melody Maker* 68 (September 26): 42–43. [Rap-SF]

1262.————. 1993. "Freezer Jolly Good Fellow!" *Melody Maker* (April 3): 36–37. [Rap-LA-Ice Cube]

1263. Tucker, Sherrie. 1993. "Clora Bryant," *California Jazz Now* 3(7): 5, 14, 22. [Jazz-LA]

1264. Turman, Katherine. 1992. "Ice-T on the 3 Rs: Rap, Rock, and Racism," *Rap Sheet* (September): 1, 25. [Rap/Rock-LA]

1265.————. 1995. "Coiled and Ready," *Rolling Stone* 706 (April 20): 53–55, 96–97 [Rock-LA-Slash]

1266. Turner, Bez. 1975. "T-Bone Walker 1910–1975," *Blues Unlimited* 113: 17. [Blues-LA-Obituary]

1267. Turner, Gregg. 1984. "Time for the Chambers Brothers," *Creem* 15(9) [February]: 21–22. [Rock-LA]

1268. Turner, Tina, with Kurt Loder. 1986. *I, Tina.* New York: William Morrow. [Rock/R & B-LA]

1269. Tyler, Bruce M. 1992. *From Harlem to Hollywood: The Struggle for Social and Cultural Democracy, 1920–1943.* New York: Garland Publishing. [General Music-LA]

1270. Tynan, Jack. 1995. "The Return of Art Pepper," *Down Beat* 62 (July): 40, 42. [Jazz-LA-Originally published April 14, 1960]

1271. Tynan, John. 1956a. "Buddy Collette," *Down Beat* 23 (November 28): 18. [Jazz-LA]

1272.————. 1956b. "Chico Hamilton," *Down Beat* 23 (March 21): 12. [Jazz-LA]

1273.————. 1958. "The Red and Whitey Blues," *Down Beat* 25 (May 29): 19, 45. [Jazz-LA-Red Mitchell]

1274.————. 1960a. "Les McCann and the Truth," *Down Beat* 28 (September 15): 20–21. [Jazz-LA]

1275.————. 1960b. "Ornette: The First Beginning," *Down Beat* 27 (July 21): 32–33, 58. [Jazz-LA-Summarizes his LA days]

1276.————. 1961. "Bitter Hope," *Down Beat* 28 (January 5): 16. [Jazz-LA-Elmo Hope, he hates LA]

1277.————. 1962a. "Curtis Amy: Gettin' Into It," *Down Beat* 29 (December 6): 22–23. [Jazz-LA]

1278.————. 1962b. "Facing Challenges: Gerald Wilson," *Down Beat* 29 (January 4): 18–19. [Jazz-LA]

1279.————. 1962c. "Portrait of a Jazz Success: Shelly Manne," *Down Beat* 29 (July 5): 20–22. [Jazz-LA]

1280.————. 1962d. "Teddy Edwards: Long, Long Journey," *Down Beat* 29 (May 24): 18–19, 42. [Jazz-LA]

1281.————. 1963. "Take Five," *Down Beat* 30 (April 11): 40. [Jazz-LA-Prince Lasha, Sonny Simmons]

1282.————. 1964. "Art Pepper's Not the Same," *Down Beat* 31 (July 30): 18–19, 40. [Jazz-LA]

1283.————. 1995. "Nat Cole: Eye on Commercial Success," *Down Beat* 62 (October): 34–35. [Jazz/Popular Music-LA-Originally published May 2 and May 6, 1957]

1284. Ullman, Michael. 1982. *Jazz Lives: Portraits in Words and Pictures.* New York: Perigee Books. [Jazz-CA-Dexter Gordon, Horace Silver]

1285.————. 1988. "Higgins, Billy," *NGDJ* 1: 523. [Jazz-LA]

1286. Underwood, Lee. 1975a. "Pepper's Painful Road to Pure Art," *Down Beat* 42 (June 5): 16–17, 34. [Jazz-LA]

1287.————. 1975b. "Profile: Buell Neildlinger and Don Preston," *Down Beat* 42 (April 10): 28–29. [Jazz-LA]

1288.————. 1975c. "Profile: Harvey Mason," *Down Beat* 42 (August 14): 32. [Studio-LA]

1289.————. 1975d. "Profile: Oscar Brashear," *Down Beat* 42 (December 18): 42. [Jazz-LA]

1290.————. 1976. "The Crusaders: Knights Without Jazz," *Down Beat* 43 (June 17): 12–13, 40–41. [Jazz/Soul-LA]

1291.————. 1977. "George Duke: Plugged-in Prankster," *Down Beat* 44 (March 10): 14–15, 34, 36. [Jazz-Bay Area]

1292.————. 1979a. "Bobby Hutcherson: Cruisin' Down Highway One," *Down Beat* 46 (April 19): 14–16. [Jazz-CA]

1293.————. 1979b. "Profile: Abraham Laboriel," *Down Beat* 46 (May 3): 34–35. [Jazz-LA]

1294.————. 1979c. "Profile: Rodney Franklin," *Down Beat* 46 (May 17): 34. [Jazz-Berkeley]

1295.————. 1981. "George Cables," *Down Beat* 58 (August): 27–31, 70. [Jazz-LA]

1296. Urmann, R. 1988. "Ulrichsberger Kaleidophon," *Jazz Podium* 37 (August): 38. [Jazz-LA-Roberto Miranda]

1297. Vacher, Peter. 1986. "Teddy's Ready: Teddy Edwards," *Coda* 210 (October 1): 7. [Jazz-LA]

1298.————. 1988a. "Callender, Red," *NGDJ* 1: 181–182. [Jazz-LA]

1299.————. 1988b. "Edwards, Teddy," *NGDJ* 1: 325. [Jazz-LA]

1300. Vale, V., and Andrea Juno. 1991. "Wanda Coleman" in *Angry Women*, edited by V. Vale and Andrea Juno. San Francisco: RE/Search, pp. 118–126. [Poetry-LA]

1301. Various. 1963. "The Need for Racial Unity in Jazz: A Panel Discussion," *Down Beat* 30 (April 11): 16–21. [Jazz-LA-L. Feather, G. Shearing, G. Wilson, R. Mitchell, James Tolbert, J. Tynan]

1302. Vera, Billy. n.d. "The Aladdin Records Story," *Mosaic Records Brochure* 12: 23–26. [Blues/R & B-LA]

1303. Vercelli, Gary G. 1978. "Jack Wilson: Ivory Innovator," *Down Beat* 45 (March 9): 18, 42. [Jazz-LA]

1304. Vickers, Tom. 1975. "Johnny 'Guitar' Watson's Disco Blues," *Rolling Stone* 199 (November 6): 17. [Blues-LA]

1305. Vignes, Michelle. 1993. *Bay Area Blues/Photographs by Michelle Vignes; Text by Lee Hildebrand*. San Francisco: Pomegranate Artbooks. [Blues-Bay Area]

1306. Voce, Steve. 1982a. "Art Pepper: The Living Legend Moves On," *Jazz Journal International* 35 (August): 20–21. [Jazz-LA]

1307.———. 1982b. "Slim Gaillard," *Jazz Journal International* 35 (October): 20. [Jazz-LA]

1308.———. 1982c. "The Tenorist and Composer Benny Golson in Conversation with Steve Voce," *Jazz Journal International* 35 (December): 8–9. [Jazz-LA]

1309. Voigt, Jon. 1988. "Counce, Curtis (Lee)," *NGDJ* 1: 251. [Jazz-LA]

1310. Waller, Don. 1985. *The Motown Story.* New York: C. Scribner. [Popular Music-LA-Brenda Holloway]

1311. Warren, Bruce. 1989. "Bird Is Dead: Long Live Frank Morgan," *Option* 25 (March/April): 50–53. [Jazz-LA]

1312. Washington, E. V. 1995. "Mercy . . . Mercy . . . Mercy: It's Andrae Crouch in Full Effect," *L.A. Focus* 1 (March 5): 19, 23. [Gospel-LA]

1313. Watson, Ben. 1993. *Frank Zappa: The Negative Dialectics of Poodle Play.* New York: St. Martin's Press. [Rock/R & B-LA-Has info on Sugarcane Harris, Johnny "Guitar" Watson, George Duke]

1314. Weber, Mark. 1977a. "Bobby Bradford," *Coda* 157 (September/October): 2–5. [Jazz-LA]

1315.———. 1977b. "John Carter," *Coda* 157 (September/October): 8–10. [Jazz-LA]

1316. Weihsmann, Helmut. 1991. "Re: Jazzfilm Steve Lacy und John Carter/Bobby Bradford: Peter Bull und seine Filme ueber Jazzmusiker," *Jazz Podium* 40 (April): 8–10. [Jazz-LA]

1317. Weiss, J. 1983. "Horace Tapscott: L'autre West Coast," *Jazz Magazine* 321 (September): 28–29+. [Jazz-LA]

1318. Welding, Pete. 1979. "Art Pepper: Rewards of the Straight Life," *Down Beat* 46 (December): 16–19. [Jazz-LA]

1319. Werbin, Stuart. 1973. "The Nine Lives of Sly Stone," *Rolling Stone* 142 (August 30): 30–31. [Rock/Soul-SF]

1320. Westfield, N. Lynne, and Harold Dean Trulear. 1994. "Theomusicology and Christian Education: Spirituality and the Ethics of Control in the Rap of Hammer," *Black Sacred Music* 8(1): 218–238. [Rap-Oakland]

1321. Whitcomb, Ian. 1985. "Legends of Rhythm and Blues" in *Repercussions: A Celebration of African-American Music*, edited by Geoffrey Haydon and Dennis Marks. London: Century Publishing, pp. 54–79. [R & B-LA-Lloyd Glenn, Joe Turner, Willie Mae Thornton, Lowell Fulson, Jay McNeely, Charles Brown, Johnny Otis]

1322.————. 1986. "The Platters," *NGDAM* 3: 577–578. [R & B-LA]

1323. White, Don Lee. 1987. "A Written Report on An Oral History of Music in the Black Community of Los Angeles, 1895–1950." Unpublished manuscript. [General Music-LA-Includes good information on LA black churches and performance groups]

1324. White, William D. 1989. "David Murray Interview," *Cadence* 15 (May): 5–10. [Jazz-LA/SF]

1325. Widders-Ellis, Andy. 1991. "Slash: The Hands Behind the Hype," *Guitar Player* 25 (December): 38–54. [Rock-LA]

1326. Wiggins, Gerald. 1993. *Central Avenue Sounds Oral History Transcript.* Los Angeles: Oral History Program, University of California. [Jazz-LA-Interviewed by Steven L. Isoardi]

1327. Wild, David. 1988a. "Lawrence, Azar," *NGDJ* 2: 15. [Jazz-LA]

1328.————. 1988b. "Maupin, Bennie," *NGDJ* 2: 94. [Jazz-LA]

1329.————. 1988c. "Simmons, Sonny," *NGDJ* 2: 452. [Jazz-LA]

1330.————. 1991. "Natalie Cole's Unlikely Smash," *Rolling Stone* 613 (September 19): 19–21. [Popular Music-LA]

1331. Williams, J. Kent. 1988. "Butler, Frank," *NGDJ* 1: 174. [Jazz-LA]

1332. Williams, Jean. 1976. "Tapscott Taps Out a New System," *Billboard* 88 (April 10): 22. [Jazz-LA]

1333. Williams, Martin. 1964. "Dial Days: A Conversation with Ross Russell," *Down Beat* 31 (December 3)): 15–17. [Jazz-CA-Dial records]

1334.————. 1967. *Jazz Masters of New Orleans.* New York: The Macmillan Co. [Jazz-LA-Kid Ory, Jelly Roll Morton, Mutt Carey]

1335.————. 1992. *Jazz Changes.* New York: Oxford University Press. [Jazz-LA-has chapters on Ornette Coleman and Dial Records]

1336. Williams-Jones, Pearl. 1979. "Black Gospel Blends Social Change and Ethnic Roots," *Billboard* 91 (July 28): R12, R16, R18. [Gospel-CA-Has CA people, Cleveland etc.]

1337. Willoughby, Bob. n.d. *Jazz in L. A.* n.p.: Nieswand Verlag. [Jazz-LA-photo book]

1338. Wilmer, Valerie. 1960. "Joe Gordon," *Jazz Journal* 13 (September): 4–6. [Jazz-LA]

1339.————. 1965. "Lawrence Brown Talks to Valerie Wilmer," *Jazz Monthly* 11 (April): 18. [Jazz-LA]

1340.————. 1967a. "Harry Edison: Sweet Talking," *Jazz Monthly* 13 (November): 6–8. [Jazz-LA]

1341.————. 1967b. "There'll Always Be Blues," *Down Beat* 34 (July 13): 23–25. [Blues-CA-Jimmy Witherspoon]

1342.————. 1976a. "Plas: Rhythm of the Tenor," *Melody Maker* 51 (September 11): 42. [Jazz/Studio-LA-Plas Johnson]

1343.————. 1976b. "What the Butler Plays," *Melody Maker* 51 (September 4): 35. [Jazz-LA-Frank Butler]

1344.————. 1977. *As Serious As Your Life.* Westport, CT: Lawrence Hill & Company. [Jazz-CA-Ornette Coleman. Has numerous other references to California]

1345.————. 1991. *Jazz People.* New York: Da Capo. [Jazz-LA-Has chapters on CA musicians Buck Clayton, Howard McGhee, Billy Higgins, and Art Farmer]

1346. Wilson, Burt. 1986. *A History of Sacramento Jazz, 1948–1966: A Personal Memoir.* Canoga Park, CA: Burt Wilson. [Jazz-Sacramento]

1347. Wilson, Gerald. 1995. *Central Avenue Sounds Oral History Transcript.* Los Angeles: Oral History Program, University of California, Los Angeles. [Jazz-LA]

1348. Wilson, John S. 1966. *Jazz: The Transition Years, 1940 to 1960*. New York: Appleton, Century, Crofts. [Jazz-CA-Mentions some West Coast people]

1349. Wilson, Tony. 1968. "R & B Meets Psychedelia: That's Sly and the Family Stone," *Melody Maker* 43 (August 10): 5. [Rock/Soul-SF]

1350. Wisckol, Marty. 1981. "Profile: Charles McPherson," *Down Beat* 48 (June): 52–53. [Jazz-SD]

1350a. Wolff, Daniel. 1995. *You Send Me: The Life and Times of Sam Cooke*. New York: Morrow. [Soul-LA]

1351. Wood, Berta. 1956. "Charlie Lawrence," *Jazz Journal* 9 (October): 6–7, 12. [Jazz-LA]

1352.———. 1957a. "George Orendorf: Quality Serenader; Part I—Chicago," *Jazz Journal International* 10 (January): 4–6. [Jazz-LA-brief reference to LA at the end of article]

1353.———. 1957b. "George Orendorf: Quality Serenader; Part II—Los Angeles," *Jazz Journal* 10 (February): 4–6. [Jazz-LA]

1354.———. 1957c. "Paul Leroy Howard," *Jazz Journal* 10 (November): 6–8. [Jazz-LA]

1355.———. 1957d. "Paul Leroy Howard Part 2," *Jazz Journal* 10 (December): 13–14. [Jazz-LA]

1356. Wood, Gerry. 1979. "Joyful Noises Rises to New Heights," *Billboard* 91(July 28): R3, R18. [Gospel-LA-Makes reference to Los Angeles, Nashville, and Waco-Andrae Crouch]

1357. Woodard, Josef. 1987. "Don Preston: Synthesizer from Apocalypse Now to Zappa," *Down Beat* 54 (August): 25–27. [Jazz-LA-John Carter]

1358.———. 1988a. "The Herbie Hancock Interview," *Down Beat* 55 (June): 16–19. [Jazz-LA-He lives in LA]

1359.———. 1988b. "Present at the Creation: Bassist Charlie Haden," *Option* 21 (July/August): 41–43. [Jazz-LA]

1360.———. 1991a. "Career Swings: Stanley Clarke," *Down Beat* 58 (November): 30–31. [Jazz/Film Music-LA]

1361.———. 1991b. "John Carter's Last Frontier," *Musician* 153 (July): 24–26. [Jazz-LA]

1362.———. 1992a. "The Resurrection of Charles Lloyd," *Musician* 170 (December): 28, 30. [Jazz-LA/Montecito]

1363.———. 1992b. "The Revolution Might Be Televised: *Tonight Show* Band," *Down Beat* 59 (September): 22–26. [Jazz-LA-Branford Marsalis]

1364. Woodlief, Mark. 1990. "Def and Dangerous: N.W.A.'s Social Realism," *Option* 30 (January/February): 50–53. [Rap-LA]

1365. Woodman, William. 1993. *Central Avenue Sounds Oral History Transcript*. Los Angeles: Oral History Program, University of California. [Jazz-LA-Interviewed by Steven L. Isoardi]

1366. Woolley, Stan. 1987. "Melba Liston," *Jazz Journal International* 40(2): 20–21. [Jazz-LA]

1367.———. 1988a. "Liston, Melba (Doretta)," *NGDJ* 2: 44. [Jazz-LA]

1368.———. 1988b. "McKibbon, Al(fred Benjamin)," *NGDJ* 2: 66. [Jazz-LA]

1369.———. 1995. "Ray Brown," *Jazz Journal International* 48 (December): 6–7. [Jazz-LA]

1369a. Wynn, Ron. 1985. *Tina: The Tina Turner Story*. New York: Macmillan. [Soul/Rock-LA]

1370. Yanow, Scott. 1984. "George Duke: Dukin' Out the Hits," *Down Beat* 51 (November): 16–19, 57. [Jazz-SF]

1371.———1988a. "Duke, George," *NGDJ* 1: 316. [Jazz-Bay Area]

1372.———. 1988b. "McCann, Les(lie Coleman)," *NGDJ* 2: 58–59. [Jazz-CA]

1373. Young, Marl. 1988. "The Amalgamation of Locals 47 and 767," *Overture* (December): 8–9. [Jazz-LA]

1373a. Young, Marl. 1996. "The Amalgamation of Local 47 and Local 767: A Follow up of a January, 1989, Article in Overture," in *Music in the Central Avenue Community, 1890–c. 1955*, edited by Bette Y. Cox. Los Angeles: BEEM Foundation, pp. 26–33. [Unions-LA]

1374. Yukich, Ray. 1991. "Los Angeles Bluesman J. D. Nicholson," *Living Blues* 95 (January/February): 36–40. [Blues-LA]

1375. Zappa, Frank. 1982. "Zappa on Watson," *Guitar Player* 16 (February): 69. [Blues-LA-Johnny Guitar Watson]

1376. Zappa, Frank, with Peter Occhiogrosso. 1989. *The Real Frank Zappa Book*. New York: Poseidon Press. [Rock/R & B-LA/Antelope Valley-Zappa had an integrated R & B band in Lancaster in the late 50s]

1377. Zipkin, Michael. 1978a. "Charlie Haden: Struggling Idealist," *Down Beat* 45 (July 13): 27–28, 56–57. [Jazz-LA]

1378.———. 1978b. "Patrice Rushen: Rushen to the Top," *Down Beat* 45 (March 9): 16–17, 46. [Jazz-LA]

1379.———. 1979. "Profile: Ed Kelly," *Down Beat* 46 (January 11): 34–35. [Jazz-Oakland]

CULTURE

Reference

1380. Abajian, James. 1974. *Blacks and Their Contributions to the American West: A Bibliography and Union List of Library Holdings Through 1970*. Boston: G. K. Hall. [Bibliography-CA-has section on music and dance]

1381.———. 1977. *Blacks in Selected Newspapers, Censuses, and Other Sources: An Index to Names and Subjects*. Boston: G.K. Hall. [Directory-CA]

1382. *Bay Area Black Almanac*. 1983. Palo Alto, CA: Bay Area Almanac. [Reference-Bay Area]

1383. Bischof, Phyllis. 1984. *Afro-Americana: A Research Guide to Collections at the University of California, Berkeley*. Berkeley: The General Library and the Department of Afro-American Studies, UC Berkeley. [Collections-Berkeley]

1384. Brown, Tanya D. 1991. *San Diego State University Resource Directory of Ethnic Community Organizations in San Diego*. San Diego: San Diego State University Educational Opportunity Program. [Directory-SD]

1385. Brown, Tanya D., and Veronica N. Hargrove. 1991. *The San Diego County Ethnic Business Directory: A Comprehensive Resource Directory of Ethnic-Owned Businesses in San Diego County*. San Diego: Ethnic Resources Unlimited. [Directory-SD]

1386. California Institute of Public Affairs. 1981. *Ethnic Groups in California: A Guide to Organizations and Resources*. Claremont: California Institute of Public Affairs. [Reference-CA-Has entries for Africans, Afro-Americans, Arabs, Cape Verdeans, Copts, Cubans, Puerto Ricans]

1387. *Directory of San Diego County Churches, Synagogues and Religious Organizations*. n.d. San Diego: San Diego Ecumenical Conference. [Directory-SD]

1388. Dumaux, Sally, comp. 1978. *Ethnic and National Collections in the Los Angeles Area*. Los Angeles: Southern California Answering Network, LA Public Library. [Directory-LA]

1389. *East Bay Colored Business Directory*. 1930. n.p.: W.J.D. Thompson and Kelly Williams Publishers. [Directory-Bay Area]

1390. Hart, James. 1987. *A Companion to California*. Berkeley: University of California Press. [Reference-CA]

1391. Hewlett, Rene A., and Max J. Williams. 1948. *Negro Who's Who in California*. n.p.: "Negro Who's Who in California" Publishing Co. [Reference/Biography-CA]

1392. Hill-Scott, Karen, and Alice Walker Duff. 1990a. *Facilities: The Mapping of Cultural and Arts Facilities in the City of Los Angeles*. Los Angeles: City of Los Angeles. [Urban Planning-LA]

1393.————. 1990b. *Historic Cultural Monuments: A Review of Historical Monuments to Identify Potential Cultural Facilities*. Los Angeles: City of Los Angeles. [Urban Planning-LA]

1394.————. 1990c. *Los Angeles Cultural Masterplan*. Los Angeles: Submitted to the City of Los Angeles by Morris McNeill, Inc. [Urban Planning-LA]

1395.————. 1990d. *The People of Los Angeles: Technical Report for the City of Los Angeles Cultural Masterplan*. Los Angeles: City of Los Angeles. [Urban Planning-LA]

1396. Hyatt, Marshall, comp. and ed. 1983. *The Afro-American Cinematic Experience: An Annotated Bibliography and Filmography*. Wilmington, DE: Scholarly Resources, Inc. [Film Industry-LA]

1397. Jones, Tobbie T. Jr., and Paul H. DeVan. 1982. *Who's Who Among Black Women in California 1981–82*. Inglewood: Who's Who Among Black Women in California. [Biography/Reference-CA]

1398. La Brie, Henry G., III. 1973. *The Black Newspapers in America: A Guide*, 3rd ed. Kennebunkport, ME: Mercer House Press. [Newspapers-CA]

1399. LaFond, Deborah, and Phyllis Bischof. 1988. *Afro-Americana: A Guide to Collections at the University of California at Berkeley, Supplement to the 1984 Edition*. Berkeley: The General Library University of California at Berkeley, 1988. [Collections-Berkeley]

1400. Langley, Henry G., comp. *San Francisco Directory, 1860–1879*. San Francisco: H. G. Langley. [Directory-SF]

1401. *The Los Angeles Negro Dictionary and Who's Who (1930–1931)*. 1930. Los Angeles: The California Eagle Publishing Company. [Reference/Biography-LA]

1402. Murphy, Larry, J. Gordon Melton, and Gary L. Ward, eds. 1993. *Encyclopedia of African American Religions*. New York: Garland Publishing. [Religion-CA]

1403. Nunis, Doyce Blackman. 1973. *Los Angeles and Its Environs in the 20th Century: A Bibliography of a Metropolis*. Los Angeles: The Ward Ritchie Press, 1973. [Bibliography-LA-Compiled under the auspices of the Los Angeles Metropolitan History Project. Foreward by Mrs. Fletcher Bowron with an introduction by D. B. Nunis Jr.]

1404. *The Official California Negro Directory and Classified Buyer's Guide: A West Coast Directory (1942–1943)*. 1942/1943. Los Angeles: New Age Publishing Co. [Directory-CA]

1405. "Proceedings of the Colored Conventions in California" in *Proceedings of the Black State Conventions, 1840–1855, Volume II*, edited by Philip S. Foner and George E. Walker. 1979–1981. Philadelphia: Temple University Press, pp. 110–203. [History-CA]

1406. *Proceedings of the State Convention of Colored Citizens of the State of California, Sacramento, 1855, 1856, 1865*. 1969. San Francisco: R & E Research Associates. [History-CA/Sacramento]

1407. Sawyer, Frank B., ed. 1967. *Directory of United States Negro Newspapers, Magazines, and Periodicals in 42 States*. New York: U.S. Negro World. [Directory/Newspapers-CA]

1407a. *Resource Directory of Ethnic Community Organizations in San Diego County*, 4th ed., 1990. San Diego: Office of Educational Opportunity and Ethnic Affairs, San Diego State University. [Directory-SD]

1407b. *The San Diego Ethnic Business Directory*. 1991–1994. San Diego: Ethnic Resources Unlimited. [Directory-SD-2 vols.]

1408. "Southeast San Diego Organizations & Clergymen." N.d. Unpublished manuscript, San Diego Public Library, California Room. [Directory-SD]

1409. Szwed, John F., and Roger D. Abrahams. 1978. *Afro-American Folk Culture: An Annotated Bibliography of Materials from North, Central and South America and the West Indies.* Philadelphia: Institute for the Study of Human Issues. [Bibliography-CA-Has 12 entries on California]

1410. Tilghman, Charles F., comp. 1917. *Colored Directory of the Leading Cities of Northern California, 1916–1917.* Oakland: n.p. [Directory-CA-names, addresses, occupations of heads of households, advertisements, photos of homes, statistical information]

General

1411. Adams, Chris. 1990. "Going for the Good," *Christianity and Crisis* 50(1) [February 5]: 8–9. [Religion-SF]

1412. Adams, Dorothy. 1931. "Life in the Mining Camps of the Yuba River Valley." M.A. thesis, University of California, Berkeley. [History-CA]

1413. Adams, Russell. 1964. *Great Negroes Past and Present.* Chicago: Afro-American Press. [Biography-CA]

1414. Adler, Patricia. 1977. "Watts: From Suburb to Black Ghetto." Ph.D. dissertation, University of Southern California. [History-LA]

1415. Albert, Elena I., and Marc Primus. 1976. *How California Got Its Name.* San Francisco: n.p. [History-Oakland]

1416. Albrier, Frances. *Determined Advocate for Racial Equality.* 1977/1978. Berkeley: Regional Oral History Office, Bancroft Library. [History-Bay Area]

1417. Alexander, Charles. 1914. *The Battles and Victories of Allen Allensworth.* Los Angeles: n.p. [History-Allensworth]

1418. American Association of University Women. 1975. *Heritage Fresno—Homes and People.* Fresno: Pioneer Publishing Co. [History-Fresno]

1419. Anderson, Frederick. 1976. "The Development of Leadership and Organization Building in the Black Community of Los Angeles from 1900 through World War II." Ph.D. dissertation, University of California. [History-LA]

1420. Anderson, Garland. 1927. *From Newsboy and Bellhop to Playwright.* San Francisco: n.p. [Biography-SF]

1421. Angelou, Maya. 1970. *I Know Why the Caged Bird Sings.* New York: Random House. [Autobiography-SF]

1422. Anonymous. 1944. "Negro Wakes in Los Angeles," *California Folklore Quarterly* 3(4): 326–328. [Anthropology-LA-"description of 4 West Indian Negro wakes witnessed in 1939"]

1423.————. 1952. "The Story of 'Nigger Nate,'" *The Southern California Rancher* (May). [History-SD]

1424. Anthony, Earl. 1971. *The Time of the Furnaces: A Case Study of Black Student Revolt.* New York: Dial Press. [History-LA-San Fernando Valley College]

1425. Aptheker, Herbert. 1951. *A Documentary History of the Negro People in the United States.* New York: Citadel. [History-CA]

1426. Austin, Michael Lebarron. 1994. "Harlem of the West: The Douglas Hotel and Creole Palace Nite Club." M.A. thesis, University of San Diego. [History-SD]

1427. Bagwell, Beth. 1982. *Oakland: The Story of a City.* Novato, CA: Presidio. [History-Oakland]

1428. Bakunin, Mikhail Alexandrovich. n.d. *The Catechism of the Revolutionist by Mikhail Alexandrovich Bakunin.* Oakland: The Party. [Social Issues-Oakland-Introduction by Eldridge Cleaver, put out by Black Panthers]

1429. Bass, Charlotta A. 1960. *Forty Years: Memoirs from the Pages of a Newspaper.* Los Angeles: Charlotta A. Bass. [History-LA-Based on information from the California Eagle]

1430. Beasley, Delilah L. 1918. "Slavery in California," *Journal of Negro History* 3 (January): 33–54. [History-CA]

1431.————. 1919. *The Negro Trail Blazers of California.* Los Angeles: Times Mirror Printing and Binding House. [History-CA-Author was a journalist who wrote a weekly column on the activities of blacks in California. Photos of individuals, including some musicians (i.e. Hyers Sisters)]

1432. Bell, Howard H. 1967. "The Negro in California, 1849–1859," *Phylon* X (Summer): 151–160. [History-CA]

1433. Belous, Russell. 1969. *America's Black Heritage.* Los Angeles: Los Angeles County Museum of Natural History. [History-CA]

1434. Bennett, Lerone Jr. 1979a. "Mystery of Mary Ellen Pleasant pt. 1," *Ebony* 34(6) [April]: 90–96. [Biography-SF]

1435.————. 1979b. "Mystery of Mary Ellen Pleasant pt. 2," *Ebony* 34(7) [May]: 71–86. [Biography-SF]

1436. Benson, J. J. 1906. "San Bernardino, California," *Alexander's Magazine* 3 (December): 111–113. [History-San Bernardino]

1437. Bernard, James. 1990. "Doin' the Knowledge: My Last Dying Breath," *The Source* 16 (December): 28–29. [History-LA-Interview with Geronimo Pratt]

1438. Berwanger, Eugene H. 1967. *The Frontier Against Slavery: Western Anti-Negro Prejudice and the Slavery Extension Controversy.* Urbana: University of Illinois Press. [History-CA-Has chapter on California]

1439.————. 1981. *The West and Reconstruction.* Urbana: University of Illinois Press. [History-CA]

1440. Bing, Léon. 1991. *Do or Die.* New York: Harper Collins. [Social Issues-LA-on LA Gangs]

1441. Bond, Max J. 1972. *The Negro in Los Angeles.* San Francisco: R & E Research. [History-LA-Reprint of 1936 Ph.D. Dissertation (USC)]

1442. Bonner, Thomas D., ed. 1972. *The Life and Adventures of James P. Beckwourth.* Lincoln: University of Nebraska Press. [Biography/History-CA]

1443. Bontemps, Arna, and Jack Conroy. 1945. *They Seek a City.* Garden City: Doubleday. [History-CA]

1444.————. 1966. *Anyplace but Here.* New York: Hill and Wang. [History-CA]

1445. Bowers, George. 1930. "Will Imperial Valley Become a Land of Opportunity for Negro Citizens?" *Southern Workman* 59 (July): 305–313. [History-Imperial Valley]

1446. Bowie, Patricia Carr. 1980. "The Cultural History of Los Angeles, 1850–1967: From Rural Backwash to World Center." Ph.D. dissertation, University of Southern California. [History-LA]

1447. Branch, Edgar M. 1969 *Clemens of the Call: Mark Twain in San Francisco.* Berkeley: University of California Press. [History-SF-brief mentions of blacks in SF]

1448. Broussard, Albert S. 1981. "Organizing the Black Community in the San Francisco Bay Area, 1915–1930," *Arizona and the West* 23 (Winter): 335–354. [History-SF]

1449.————. 1984a. "Oral Recollection and the Historical Reconstruction of Black San Francisco, 1915–1940," *The Oral History Review* 12: 63–80. [History-SF]

1450.————. 1984b. "The Politics of Despair: Black San Franciscans and the Political Process, 1920–1940," *The Journal of Negro History* 69 (Winter): 26–37. [History-SF]

1451.————. 1993. *Black San Francisco: The Struggle for Racial Equality in the West, 1900–1954.* Lawrence, KS: University Press of Kansas. [History-SF]

1452. Brown, William Henry. 1970. "Class Aspects of Residential Development and Choice in the Oakland Black Community." Ph.D. dissertation: University of California, Berkeley. [History-Oakland]

1453. Bullock, Paul, ed. 1969. *Watts: The Aftermath—An Inside View of the Ghetto by the People of Watts.* New York: Grove Press. [History-LA]

1454. Bunch, Lonnie G., III. 1987. *Allensworth: An Enduring Dream.* Los Angeles: California Afro-American Museum. [History-Allensworth]

1455.————. 1988. *Black Angelenos: The Afro-American in Los Angeles, 1850–1950.* Los Angeles: California Afro-American Museum. [History-LA-Book to accompany exhibit of the same title, June 11 1988–March 6, 1989, CAAM, 600 State Drive, Exposition Park, LA]

1456. Burma, John H. 1963. "Interethnic Marriage in Los Angeles," *Social Forces* 42(2): 156–165. [Social Issues-LA]

1457. Carlton, Robert. 1974. "Blacks in San Diego County in the 1880s." Historical research paper, San Diego State University, Department of History. [History-SD]

1458.————. 1975a. "Blacks in Los Angeles County in the 1870s: A Social Profile." Historical research paper, San Diego State University, Department of History. [History-LA]

1459.————. 1975b. "Blacks in San Diego County: A Social Profile, 1850–1880," *Journal of San Diego History* 21 (Fall): 7–20. [History-SD]

1460.————. 1977. "Blacks in San Diego County, 1850–1900." M.A. thesis, San Diego State University. [History-SD]

1461. Cartland, Earl. 1948. "A Study of the Negroes Living in Pasadena." M.A. thesis, Whittier College. [History-Pasadena]

1462. Case, Frederick E. 1972. *Black Capitalism: Problems in Development, A Case Study of Los Angeles.* New York: Prager Publishers. [Social Issues-LA]

1463. Caughey, John, and La Ree Caughey. 1976. *Los Angeles: Biography of a City.* Berkeley: University of California Press. [History-LA]

1464. Chaplin, Julia. 1993. "Peace 'Trane," *Spin* 9(2): 24. [Religion-SF-Church of John Coltrane]

1465. Chapman, John L. 1967. *Incredible Los Angeles.* New York: Harper and Row. [History-LA]

1466. Clar, Mimi. 1959. "Negro Beliefs," *Western Folklore* 18(4): 332–334. [Folklore-LA]

1467. Cleaver, Eldridge. 1968. *Soul On Ice.* New York: Dell. [History-CA]

1468. Cohen, Jerry, and William S. Murphy. 1966. *Burn Baby Burn: The Los Angeles Riot: August 1965.* New York: Dutton. [History-LA]

1469. Cole, Lewis. 1994. "Hyperviolence: A Generation of Kids in Richmond, Calif., Is Growing Up in the Shadow of Guns, Drugs and Violence," *Rolling Stone* 696: 106–113, 138. [Social Issues-Richmond]

1470. Collier, Ras M., ed. 1992. *Rodney King and the L.A. Rebellion: Analysis and Commentary by 13 Independent Black Writers.* Newport News, VA: UBCS. [History-LA]

1471. Collins, Keith E. 1980. *Black Los Angeles: The Maturing of the Ghetto 1940–50.* Saratoga, CA: Los Angeles Century 21 Publishing. [History-LA]

1472. Coltrane-Turiyasangitananda, A. 1977. *Monument Eternal.* Los Angeles: Vedantic Book Press. [Inspirational/Religious-LA]

1473. Conot, Robert E. 1968. *Rivers of Blood, Years of Darkness.* New York: Morrow. [History-LA]

1474. Constantine, Alex. 1993. *Blood, Carnage, and the Agent Provocateur: The Truth About the Los Angeles Riots and the Secret War Against L.A.'s Minorities.* Los Angeles: Alex Constantine. [History-LA-Conspiratorial view of LA Riots]

1475. Crouchett, Lawrence P. 1987. "Assemblyman W. Bryon Rumford: Symbol for an Era," *California History* 66(1) [March]: 12–23, 70–71. [Biography-Bay Area]

1476.————. 1988/1989. "Black Precedents in Oakland Cultural History," *Oakland Heritage Alliance News* 8(4): 7–8. [History-Oakland]

1477. Crouchett, Lawrence P., Lonnie G. Bunch III, and Martha Kendall Winnacker. 1989. *Visions Toward Tomorrow: The History of the East Bay Afro-American Community 1852–1977.* Oakland: The Northern California Center for Afro-American History and Life. [History-Bay Area]

1478. Crouchett, Lorraine J. 1988/1989. "Delilah Beasley, Trail Blazer," *Oakland Heritage Alliance News* 8(4): 1–6. [Biography-CA]

1479. Dakan, Arthur. 1970. "Electoral and Population Geography of South-Central Los Angeles 1932–1966." M.A. thesis, University of California, Los Angeles. [Social Issues-LA]

1480. Daniels, Douglas Henry. 1980. *Pioneer Urbanites: A Social and Cultural History of Black San Francisco.* Philadelphia: Temple University Press. [History-SF]

1481. Davison, Berlinda. 1921. "Educational Status of the Negro in the San Francisco Bay Region." M.A. thesis, University of California, Berkeley. [History-SF]

1482. DeGraaf, Lawrence. 1962. "Negro Migration to Los Angeles, 1930–1950." Ph.D. dissertation, University of California, Los Angeles. [History-LA]

1483.————. 1970. "The City of Black Angels: The Emergence of the Los Angeles Ghetto, 1890–1930," *Pacific Historical Review* 39(3): 323–352. [History-LA]

1484.————. 1975. "Recognition, Racism, and Reflections on the Writing of Western Black History," *Pacific Historical Review* 42 (February): 22–51. [History-CA]

1485. Delay, Peter J. 1924. *History of Yuba and Sutter Counties, California.* Los Angeles: Historic Record Company. [History-CA-References to AME church, Yuba City (p. 183) and negro miners and suburb of Smartsville called Timbuctoo (p. 209)]

1486. Dellums, C. L. 1973. *International President of the Brotherhood of Sleeping Car Porters and Civil Rights Leader.* Berkeley: Regional Oral History Program, the Bancroft Library. [History-Oakland]

1487. Derrick, John. 1906. "Booker T. Washington Orphanage of California," *Colored American Magazine* 10 (March): 171–172. [History-CA]

1488. Douroux, Margaret Pleasant. 1979. "Christian Principles that Motivate and Enhance Academic Education Among Black Children." Ph.D. dissertation, University of Beverly Hills. [Religion-LA]

1489.————. 1985. *Find the Kingdom.* Thousand Oaks, CA: Rev. Earl A. Pleasant Publishing Co. [Religion-LA]

1490. Draper, Hal. 1946. *Jim Crow in Los Angeles.* Los Angeles: Workers Party. [History-LA]

1491. Du Bois, W.E.B. 1913. "Colored California," *Crisis* 6 (August): 182–183. [History-CA]

1492. Duberman, Martin Bauml. 1988. *Paul Robeson: A Biography.* New York: Alfred A. Knopf. [Biography-CA-Mentions his trips to CA]

1493. Duniway, Clyde. 1906. "Slavery in California After 1848," *American Historical Association Annual Reports for the Year 1905* 1: 243–248. [History-CA]

1494. Eaton, Eddie. 1990. *In Search of the California Dream: From Houston, Texas to Richmond, California, 1943.* Berkeley: Regional Oral History Office, the Bancroft Library, University of California. [History-Richmond-Interviewed by Judith K. Dunning]

1495. Eddington, Neil Arthur. 1967. "The Urban Plantation: The Ethnography of an Oral Tradition in a Negro Community." Ph.D. dissertation, University of California, Berkeley. [History-SF/Oakland]

1496. Edwards, Malcolm. 1977. "The War of Complexional Distinction: Blacks in Gold Rush California and British Columbia," *California Historical Quarterly* 56 (Spring): 34–45. [History-CA]

1497. Elman, Richard M. 1967. *Ill-at-Ease in Compton.* New York: Pantheon Books. [Social Issues-Compton]

1498. Ervin, James M. 1973. *The Participation of the Negro in the Community Life of Los Angeles.* San Francisco: R & E Research Associates. [Social Issues-LA]

1499. Evans, Veichal J. 1983. "Chester Himes on Miscegenation," *The Western Journal of Black Studies* 7(2): 74–77. [Social Issues-LA-Mentions LA]

1500. Far West Surveys. 1961. *San Francisco–Oakland Metropolitan Area Population Report of White, Negro, and Other Races.* San Francisco. [History-Bay Area]

1501. Fikes, Robert, Gail Madyun, and Larry Malone. 1981. "Black Pioneers in San Diego 1880–1920," *Journal of San Diego History* 27(2): 91–114. [History-SD]

1502. Finney, Ronald LeRoy. 1972. "The Black Press in Los Angeles." M.A. thesis, University of California, Los Angeles. [Newspapers-LA]

1503. Fisher, James A. 1966. "A Social History of the Negro in California 1860–1890." M.A. thesis, Sacramento State University. [History-CA]

1504.———. 1969. "The Struggle for Negro Testimony in California, 1851–1863," *Southern California Quarterly* 51(4) [December]: 313–324. [History-CA]

1505.———. 1971. "The History of the Political and Social Development of the Black Community in California, 1850–1950." Ph.D. dissertation, University of California, Los Angeles. [History-CA]

1506. Fogelson, Robert M. 1967. "White on Black: A Critique of the McCone Commission Report on the Los Angeles Riots," *Political Science Quarterly* 82(3): 337–367. [History-LA]

1507. Folb, Edith. 1972. "A Comparative Study of Urban Black Argot." Ph.D. dissertation, University of California, Los Angeles. [Folklore-LA-Based on research in south central LA]

1508. Foner, Philip S. 1970. *The Black Panthers Speak.* Philadelphia: Lippincott. [History-Oakland]

1509.———. 1976. "Reverend George Washington Woodbey: Early Twentieth Century Black Socialist," *Journal of Negro History* 61 (April): 136–157. [Biography-SD]

1510. Forbes, Jack. 1966. *Afro-Americans in the Far West.* Berkeley: Far West Laboratory. [History-CA]

1511. Foster, Stephen. 1903. "Los Angeles Pioneers of 1836," *Historical Society of Southern California Journal* 6: 80–81. [History-LA]

1512. France, Edward Everett. 1974. *Some Aspects of the Migration of the Negro to the San Francisco Bay Area Since 1940.* San Francisco: R & E Associates. [History-SF]

1513. Francis, Robert Coleman. 1928. "A Survey of Negro Business in the San Francisco Bay Region." M.A. thesis, University of California, Berkeley. [History-SF]

1514. Franklin, John Hope, with Alfred A. Moss Jr. 1994. *From Slavery to Freedom: A History of African-Americans* (7th ed.). New York: McGraw-Hill. [History-CA-Has references to CA]

1515. Franklin, William E. 1963. "The Archy Case: The California Supreme Court Refuses to Free a Slave," *Pacific Historical Review* 32(2) [May]: 137–154. [History-CA]

1516. Garcia, Mikel Hogan. 1985. "Adaptation Strategies of the Los Angeles Black Community, 1883–1919." Ph.D. dissertation, Univeristy of California, Irvine. [History-LA]

1517. Garcia, Mikel, and Jerry Wright. 1989. "Race Consciousness in Black Los Angeles, 1886–1915," *The CAAS Report* 12(1 & 2): 4–5, 42–43. [History-LA]

1518. Gibbs, Mifflin W. 1968 [1902]. *Shadow and Light.* New York: Arno Press. [History-CA]

1519. Goode, Kenneth G. 1974 [1973]. *California's Black Pioneers: A Brief Historical Survey.* Santa Barbara: McNally & Loftin. [History-CA]

1520. Gooding-Williams, Robert, ed. 1993. *Reading Rodney King/Reading Urban Uprising.* New York: Routledge. [History-LA]

1521. Gordon, Dan. 1990. "Los Angeles County: 10 Billion Dollars a Year in Government Spending," *The Crisis* 98(3): 17–19, 38–39. [Social Issues-LA]

1522. Grenier, Judson, ed. 1978. *A Guide to Historic Places in Los Angeles County.* Dubuque, Iowa: Kendall/Hunt. [History-LA-Prepared under the auspices of the History Team of the city of Los Angeles]

1523. Grigsby, Eugene J. 1989. "The Rise and Decline of Black Neighborhoods in Los Angeles," *The CAAS Report* 12(1 & 2): 16–17, 44. [Social Issues-LA]

1524. Harding, Frank, ed. 1965. *Anarchy Los Angeles.* Los Angeles: Kimtex Corporation. [History-LA-On Watts riot, includes photos and essays, magazine format]

1525. Harris, Le Roy E. 1974. "The Other Side of the Freeway: A Study of Settlement Patterns of Negroes and Mexican-Americans in San Diego, California." Ph.D. dissertation, Carnegie Mellon University. [History-SD]

1526. Hashe, Janis. 1990. "A Tale of Two Cities: Los Angeles 2000: Can the Dream Be Realized, Part 1 of 2," *Crisis Magazine* 98(5): 22–23, 29. [Social Issues-LA]

1527. Hausler, Donald. n.d. "Blacks in Early Oakland, 1850–1900." Unpublished manuscript, Oakland Public Library. [History-Oakland]

1528. Hazen, Don, ed. 1992. *Inside the L.A. Riots: What Really Happened and Why It Will Happen Again.* New York: Institute for Alternative Journalism. [Rap/Social Issues-LA-has interview with Ice-T]

1529. Heath, G. Louis, ed. 1976a. *The Black Panther Leaders Speak: Huey P. Newton, Bobby Seale, Eldridge Cleaver and Company Speak Out Through the Black Panther Party's Official Newspaper.* Metuchen, NJ: Scarecrow Press. [History-Oakland]

1530.————. 1976b. *Off the Pigs!: The History and Literature of the Black Panther Party.* Metuchen, NJ: Scarecrow Press. [History-Oakland-Kim Il-Sung expressed support for Panthers in 1970]

1531. Helper, Hinton Rowan. 1855. *The Land of Gold: Reality Versus Fiction.* Baltimore: n.p. [History-SF]

1532. Herbert, Solomon J. 1990. "Blacks Who Migrated West Between 1915 and 1945," *Crisis Magazine* 98(2): 24, 26–27, 45. [History-LA/CA]

1533. Hippler, Arthur E. 1974. *Hunter's Point: A Black Ghetto.* New York: Basic Books. [History-SF]

1534. Ho, Christine. 1989. "Transnational Social Systems of Afro-Trinidadians in Los Angeles," *The CAAS Report* 12(1 & 2): 10–11, 44. [Anthropology-LA]

1535. Hoffman, Jean E., and Sydney D. Hammond. 1966. "A Documentary Study of the 'Logan Heights Riots' of August 1965." Research Project Report: San Diego State College. [History-SD]

1536. Holdredge, Helen O'Donnell. 1953. *Mammy Pleasant.* New York: Putnam. [Biography-SF]

1537. Hollenweger, Walter J. 1972. *The Pentecostals.* Minneapolis: Augsburg Publishing House. [Religion-LA-Translated from German into English by R. A. Wilson. Has section on the Los Angeles Revival]

1538. Howay, F. W. 1939. "The Negro Immigration into Vancouver Island in 1858," *British Columbia Historical Quarterly* 2 (April): 101–113. [History-CA-"discusses the reasons behind the California exodus."]

1539. Hughes, Ronald Elliot. 1977. "Race and Social Class Consciousness Among Black Workers: A Study of Ideological Contradictions." Ph.D. dissertation, University of California, Los Angeles. [Social Issues-Long Beach]

1540. Imole Olumo Akinwale. 1987. *16 Beliefs of the Imole Olumo Akinwale Yoruba Temple.* Los Angeles: Imole Olumo Akinwale Yoruba Temple. [Religion-LA]

1541. Jackson, Elizabeth Kate. 1989. "Contemporary Black Film, Television, and Video Makers: A Survey Analysis of Producers." Ph.D. dissertation: Northwestern University. [Film Industry-LA-Based on research on producers in the LA area]

1542. Jackson, Inez. 1978. *History of Black Americans in San Jose.* San Jose: Garden City Women's Club. [History-San Jose]

1543. Johnson, Charles S., Grace Jones, and Herman H. Long. 1944. *The Negro War Worker in San Francisco: A Local Self-Survey.* San Francisco: n.p. [History-SF]

1544. Johnson, Margaret. 1953. "The Negroes in West Berkeley" in *Immigration and Race Problems, 1949–1953, Part II,* edited by George Hedley. Oakland: Mills College Department of Economics and Sociology, 865–899. [History-Berkeley]

1545. Jones, Woodrow Jr., and Mitchell F. Rice. 1979. "Race, Social Class, and Attitudes Toward Urban Transportation: A Comparative Study of Four Cities," *The Western Journal of Black Studies* 3(1): 39–42. [Social Issues-SD-Atlanta, Baltimore, Boston, San Diego]

1546. Jurmain, Claudia, and James Rawls, eds. 1986. *California: A Place, A People, A Dream.* San Francisco and Oakland: Chronicle Books and the Oakland Museum. [History-CA]

1547. Katz, William L. 1974. *Eyewitness: The Negro in American History.* Belmont, CA: Pitman Publishing Corp. [History-CA]

1548.———. 1986. *Black Indians: A Hidden Heritage.* New York: Atheneum. [History-CA]

1549.———. 1987. *The Black West, 3rd ed.* Seattle: Open Hand Publishing. [History-CA]

1550. King, Celes III. 1989. *Black Leadership in Los Angeles: Celes King III, Vols. I and II.* Los Angeles: University of California, Los Angeles Oral History Program and Institute of American Cultures and Center for Afro-American Studies. [History-LA]

1551. Lapp, Rudolph M. 1964. "The Negro in Gold Rush California," *The Journal of Negro History* 49 (April): 81–98. [History-CA]

1552.———. 1966. "Negro Rights Activities in Gold Rush California," *California Historical Quarterly* 45(1) [March]: 3–20. [History-CA]

1553.———. 1968. "Jeremiah B. Sanderson, Early California Negro Leader," *The Journal of Negro History* 53 (October): 321–333. [Biography-CA]

1554.———. 1977. *Blacks in Gold Rush California.* New Haven: Yale University Press. [History-CA]

1555.———. 1979. *Afro-Americans in California.* San Francisco: Boyd and Fraser Publishers. [History-CA]

1555a.———. 1987. *Afro-Americans in California,* 2nd ed. San Francisco: Boyd and Fraser Publishing Co. [History-CA]

1556. Larrie, Reginald. 1977. "William Leidesdorff: San Francisco Millionaire," *Encore* 6 (June 6): 3. [Biography-SF]

1557. LeFalle-Collins, Lizzetta. 1988. "Home and Yard: Black Folk Life Expressions in Los Angeles" in *Home and Yard: Black Folk Life Expressions in Los Angeles,* edited by Nancy Mc-Kinney. Los Angeles: California Afro-American Museum, pp. 10–17. [Arts-LA]

1558. Lewis, Earl. 1990. "Acting in Their Own Interests: African-Americans and the Great Migration," *Crisis Magazine* 98(2): 18–22, 44–45. [History-LA]

1559. Lewis, Frank. 1967. "Original Town of Weed," *The Siskiyou Pioneer and Yearbook* 3: 5–10. [History-Weed]

1560. Lewis, Michael Andrew. 1991. "Ethnic and Racial Violence in San Diego, 1880–1920." M.A. thesis, San Diego State University. [History-SD]

1561. Lifton, Sarah. 1994. "Man of Color: The Incredible Life of John Alexander Somerville," *USC Trojan Family Magazine* 26(3): 35–41. [Biography-LA]

1562. Ligon, Alfred M. 1981. "Ancient and Modern Initiation," *Uraeus: The Journal of Unconscious Life* 2(2): 4, 46–48, 51–52. [Metaphysics-LA]

1563.————. 1984. *All Lights the Light Oral History Transcript.* Los Angeles: Oral History Program, University of California, Los Angeles. [Metaphysics-LA-Interviewed by Ranford B. Hopkins]

1564. Lincoln, Charles Eric. 1973. *The Black Muslims in America.* Boston: Beacon Press. [Social Issues-LA-has section on LA, LA newspaper Herald-Dispatch]

1565. Lockwood, Charles, and Christopher B. Leinberger. 1988. "Los Angeles Comes of Age," *The Atlantic Monthly* 261(1): 31–56. [Social Issues-LA]

1566. Lortie, Francis N. Jr. 1973. *San Francisco's Black Community, 1870–1890: Dilemmas in the Struggle for Equality.* San Francisco: R & E Research Associates. [History-SF]

1567. LuValle, James E. 1987. *Founding President of UCLA's Graduate Students Association Oral History Transcript.* Los Angeles: Oral History Program, University of California, Los Angeles. [History-LA-Interviewed by Ranford B. Hopkins]

1568. Madhubuti, Haki, ed. 1992. *Why L.A. Happened: Implications of the '92 Los Angeles Rebellion.* Chicago: Third World Press. [Social Issues-LA]

1569. Marinacci, Barbara, and Rudy Marinacci. 1980. *Take Sunset Boulevard: A California Guide.* San Rafael, CA: Presidio Press. [Social Issues-LA]

1570. Marx, Wesley. 1962. "The Negro Community: A Better Chance," *Los Angeles* 3 (March): 38–41. [Social Issues-LA]

1571. Mason, William, and James Anderson. 1969a. "The Los Angeles Black Community, 1781–1940," in *America's Black Heritage,* edited by Russell E. Belous. Los Angeles: Los Angeles County Museum of Natural History, History Division, Bulletin No. 5, pp. 42–64. [History-LA]

1572.————. 1969b. "Los Angeles Black Heritage," *Museum Alliance Quarterly* 8 (Winter): 4–9. [History-LA]

1573. Mason, William, and Roberta Kirkhart Mason. 1976. "The Founding Forty-Four," *Westways* 68(7): 20–23. [History-LA]

1574. Mayer, Robert. 1978. *Los Angeles: A Chronological and Documentary History, 1542–1976.* Dobbs Ferry, NY: Oceana Publications, Inc. [History-LA-Howard B. Furer, Series Editor-American Cities Chronology Series]

1575. Mayer, Robert, comp. 1978. *San Diego: A Chronological and Documentary History, 1535–1976.* Dobbs Ferry, NY: Oceana Publications. [History-SD]

1576. McEntire, Davis, and Julia R. Tarnpol. 1950. "Postwar Status of Negro Workers in San Francisco," *Monthly Labor Review* 70 (June):. [History-SF]

1577. McGee, Henry W. Jr. 1989. "Affordable Housing vs. Racial Integration," *The CAAS Report* 12(1 & 2): 6–9, 45. [Social Issues-LA]

1578. McGroarty, John. 1921. *Los Angeles, From the Mountains to the Sea*. Chicago: American Historical Society. [History-LA]

1579. McKeever, Michael. 1985. *A Short History of San Diego*. San Francisco: Lexikos. [History-SD]

1580. McPherson, James. 1965. *The Negro's Civil War*. New York: Pantheon Books. [History-CA-Brief mention of CA]

1581. McWilliams, Carey. 1973. *Southern California: An Island on the Land*. Santa Barbara and Salt Lake City: Peregrine Smith, Inc. [History-CA]

1582. Meredith, Mamie. 1931. "Negro Patois and Its Humor," *American Speech* 6: 317–321. [Folklore-CA]

1583. Milner, Christina, and Richard Milner. 1972. *Black Players: The Secret World of Black Pimps*. Boston: Little, Brown. [Social Issues-SF]

1584. Mitchell-Kernan, Claudia. 1971. *Language Behavior in a Black Urban Community*. Berkeley: University of California Language Research Laboratory. [Linguistics-Oakland]

1585. ———. 1972. "Signifying and Marking: Two Afro-American Speech Acts" in *Directions in Sociolinguistics*, edited by John Gumperz and Dell Hymes. New York: Holt, Rinehart, and Winston, pp. 161–179. [Linguistics-Oakland]

1586. Mitchell-Kernan, Claudia, and M. Belinda Tucker. 1989. "Views on Marriage and Family Among Black Southern Californians," *The CAAS Report* 12(1 & 2): 18–22. [Social Issues-CA]

1587. Montesano, Philip M. 1967. "San Francisco in the Early 1860s: Social and Cultural Life of the Negro Community," *Urban West* 1 (November–December): 15–16. [History-SF]

1588. ———. 1968. "The Amazing Dr. Ezra Johnson," *Urban West* 1(January–February): 21–26. [Biography-SF]

1589. ———. 1973a. "San Francisco Black Churches in the 1860s: Political Pressure Group," *California Historical Society* 52(2): 145–152. [History-SF/LA/CA]

1590. ———. 1973b. *Some Aspects of the Free Negro Question in San Francisco, 1849–1870*. San Francisco: R & E Research Associates. [History-SF]

1591. Moore, Shirley. 1989. "The Black Community in Richmond, California." Ph.D. dissertation, University of California, Berkeley. [History-Richmond]

1592. Morgan, Neil Bowen (1924), and Tom Blair. 1976. *Yesterday's San Diego*. Miami: E. A. Seeman Publications. [History-SD]

1593. Morris, De Vonne. 1989. "Calvary Baptist Church." Unpublished manuscript. [History-SD-"excerpt from the centennial church history booklet"]

1594. Murphy, Larry George. 1973. "Equality Before the Law: The Struggle of Nineteenth-Century Black Californians for Social and Political Justice." Ph.D. dissertation, Graduate Theological Union. [History-CA]

1595. ———. 1979. "The Church and Black California: A Mid-Nineteenth Century Struggle for Civil Justice," *Foundations* 18: 165–183. [History-CA]

1596. Musere, Jonathan. 1991. "Southern Californians' Attitudes to Immigrants: Blacks Compared to Other Ethnic Groups." Ph.D. Dissertation, University of California, Los Angeles. [Social Issues-CA]

1597. Nash, Gerald D. 1985. *The American West Transformed: The Impact of the Second World War.* Bloomington: Indiana University Press. [History-CA-Has chapter, "Blacks in the Wartime West"]

1598. Nelson, Howard J. 1983. *The Los Angeles Metropolis.* Dubuque, IO: Kendall/Hunt Publishing Co. [Geography-LA]

1599. Newman, Lucille F. 1969. "Folklore of Pregnancy: Wives' Tales in Contra Costa County, California," *Western Folklore* 28(2): 112–135. [Folklore-Contra Costa]

1600. Newton, Huey P. 1972. *To Die for the People: The Writings of Huey P. Newton.* New York: Random House. [History-Oakland]

1601. Nicholls, William L. 1966. *The Castlemont Survey: A Summary of Results.* Oakland: Department of Human Resources. [History-Oakland]

1602. Nteziryayo, Antoine. 1982. "International Migration of Talent: Africans in Southern California." Ph.D. dissertation, University of California, Los Angeles. [Social Issues-CA]

1603. Outterbridge, John W. 1993. *African-American Artists of Los Angeles Oral History Transcript.* Los Angeles: Oral History Program, University of California, Los Angeles. [Art-LA-635 p.]

1604. Parker, Elizabeth, and James Abajian. 1974. *A Walking Tour of the Black Presence in San Francisco During the Nineteenth Century.* San Francisco: Afro-American Historical and Cultural Society. [History-SF]

1605. Patterson, Beeman Coolidge. 1967. *The Politics of Recognition: Negro Politics in Los Angeles, 1960–1963.* Ph.D. dissertation, University of California, Los Angeles. [History-LA]

1606. Paul, Jan. 1977. "Allen Allensworth: The Man and the Movement," *Encore* 6 (May 23): 3. [History-Allensworth]

1607. Pearlstone, Zena. 1990. *Ethnic L.A.* Beverly Hills, CA: Hillcrest Press. [Social Issues-LA]

1608. Peters, "Gene" Raymond. 1971. *Profiles in Black American History: A Community History Book, San Diego City and County, 1950–1971.* San Diego: "Gene" Raymond Peters. [History-SD]

1609. Peterson, Raoul C. 1973. "Garveyism in California: A Lady Remembers." *Core Magazine* (Fall/Winter): 20–22. [History-CA]

1610. Pittman, Tarea Hall. 1974. *NAACP Official and Civil Rights Worker.* Berkeley: Regional Oral History Office, Bancroft Library. [History-Oakland]

1611. Porter, Kenneth W. 1971. *The Negro on the American Frontier.* New York: Arno Press. [History-CA]

1612. Pride, Armistead Scott. 1950. "A Register and History of Negro Newspapers in the United States: 1827–1950." Ph.D. dissertation: Northwestern University. [Newspapers-CA-Has 64 entries for CA]

1613. Pulliam, Roger C. 1978. "Allan Bakke vs. Regents of the University of California: Analysis and Implications," *The Western Journal of Black Studies* 2(1): 18–23. [Social Issues-CA]

1614. Rabinovitz, Francine F. 1975. *Minorities in the Suburbs: The Los Angeles Experience.* Boston: Massachusetts Institute of Technology, Joint Center for Urban Studies. [Social Issues-LA]

1615. Ramsey, Eleanor Mason. 1977. "Allensworth: A Study in Social Change." Ph.D. dissertation, University of California, Berkeley. [History-Allensworth]

1616. Ramsey, Eleanor M., and Janice S. Lewis. 1980/1988. "A History of Black Americans in California" in *Five Views: An Ethnic Sites Survey for California.* Sacramento: The Resources Agency, Department of Parks and Recreation, pp. 57–101. [History-CA/LA-Includes Bibliography and historical sites survey]

1617. Rashidi, Runoko. 1986. "Men Out of Asia: A Review and Update of the Gladwin Thesis," *Journal of African Civilizations* 8(2): 248–263. [History-CA-Black presence in ancient California]

1618. Ray, Mary Ellen Bell. 1985. *The City of Watts, California: 1907 to 1926.* Los Angeles: Rising Publishing. [History-LA]

1619. Record, Wilson. 1963. *Minority Groups and Intergroup Relations in the San Francisco Bay Area.* Berkeley: n.p.. [Social Issues-SF]

1620. Richards, Eugene S. 1941. "The Effects of the Negro's Migration to Southern California Since 1920 Upon His Socio-cultural Patterns." Ph.D. dissertation, University of Southern California. [History-CA]

1621. Ridenour, Ron. 1965. *The Fire This Time: The W.E.B. DuBois Clubs View of the Explosion in South Los Angeles.* Los Angeles: W.E.B. DuBois Clubs. [History-LA]

1622. Rischin, Moses. 1973. "Immigration, Migration, and Minorities in California" in *Essays and Assays: California History Reappraised,* edited by George H. Knoles. San Francisco: California Historical Society, pp. 65–77. [History-CA]

1623. Robbs, Lloyd Franklin Sr. 1990. "The Aura of Equal Opportunity: A Study-Profile Concerning Affirmative Action." Ph.D. dissertation, Claremont Graduate School. [Social Issues-LA-Based in LA area]

1624. Robinson, Beverly J. 1988. "Vernacular Spaces and Folklife Studies Within Los Angeles' African American Community" in *Home and Yard: Black Folk Life in Los Angeles,* edited by Nancy McKinney. Los Angeles: California Afro-American Museum, pp. 19–27. [Arts-LA]

1625. Rodriguez, Joseph A. 1983. "From Personal Politics to Party Politics: The Development of Black Leadership in Oakland California, 1900–1950." M.A. thesis, University of California, Santa Cruz. [History-Oakland]

1626. Rossa, Della. 1969. *Why Watts Exploded: How the Ghetto Fought Back.* New York: Merit Publishers. [History-LA]

1627. Royal, Lurie A. Jenkins. 1989. "A Study of Factors Related to Black Adolescent Pregnancy in the County of Los Angeles, California." MSW dissertation, California State University, Long Beach. [Social Issues-LA]

1628. Ruff, Paradine, and Emory J. Tolbert. 1982. *From Beacon Light to Thirty-First Street: A Pictorial History of Black Seventh-Day Adventists in San Diego.* n.p. [Religion-SD]

1629. Sales, Timothy. 1989. "Blacks in Los Angeles: A Brief History of Central Avenue." *Los Angeles Conservancy* (September–October): 4–5. [History-LA]

1630. Santino, Jack. 1989. *Miles of Smiles, Years of Struggle: Stories of Black Pullman Porters.* Urbana: University of Illinois Press. [History-CA]

1631. Savage, W. Sherman. 1945. "The Negro on the Mining Frontier," *Journal of Negro History* 30 (January): 30–46. [History-CA]

1632.———. 1946. "Early Negro Education in the Pacific Coast States," *Journal of Negro Education* 15 (Winter): 134–139. [History-CA]

1633.———. 1976. *Blacks in the West.* Westport: Greenwood Press. [History-CA]

1634. Schlesinger, Marilyn Ruth. 1960. "Riddling Questions from Los Angeles High School Students," *Western Folklore* 19(3): 191–195. [Folklore-LA]

1635. Seale, Bobby. 1970. *Seize the Time: The Story of the Black Panther Party and Huey P. Newton.* New York: Random House. [History-Oakland]

1636. Sears, David O., and John B. McConshay. 1973. *The Politics of Violence: The New Urban Blacks and the Watts Riot.* Boston: Houghton Mifflin. [History-LA]

1637. Shephard, Rodney, and Yvonne Shephard. 1990. "Watts: Twenty-Five Years Later," *Not Forsaking the Assembling* (October): 16–17, 43. [History-LA-Religious publication obtained from Trinity Baptist Church]

1638. Simpson, George Eaton. 1974. "Black Pentecostalism in the United States," *Phylon* 35(2): 203–211. [Religion-LA]

1639. Singleton, Calvin. 1958. "Negro Folk Beliefs Collected in Los Angeles," *Western Folklore* 17(4): 277–279. [Folklore-LA]

1640. Siracusa, Ernest. 1964. "The Negro in Gold Rush California," *Journal of Negro History* 49 (April): 81–98. [History-CA]

1641.————. 1969. *Black 49ers: The Negro in the California Gold Rush, 1848–1861.* A typed essay on microfilm, Bancroft Library, UC Berkeley. [History-CA]

1642. Skjeie, Sheila M. 1973. "California and the Fifteenth Amendment: A Study of Racism." Ph.D. dissertation: Sacramento State University. [History-CA]

1643. Smith, J. Owens. 1978. "The Bakke Decision: A Flagrant Denial of Human Rights," *The Western Journal of Black Studies* 2(4): 244–255. [Social Issues-CA]

1644. Smythe, William E. 1907. *History of San Diego, 1542–1907.* San Diego: The History Company. [History-SD]

1645. Somerville, John Alexander. 1942. *Man of Color: An Autobiography of J. Alexander Somerville: A Factual Report of the Status of the American Negro Today.* Los Angeles: Morrison Printing and Publishing Company. [Autobiography-CA]

1646. Soulé, Frank, John H. Gihon, and James Nisbet. 1966 [1854]. *The Annals of San Francisco.* Palo Alto: Lewis Osborne. [History-SF]

1647. Spoehr, Luther W. 1973. "Sambo and the Heathen Chinese: California's Racial Stereotype in the Late 1870s," *Pacific Historical Review* 42(2) [May]: 185–204. [History-CA]

1648. Stanford, E. Percil. 1978. *The Elder Black.* San Diego: Center on Aging, San Diego State University. [Social Issues-SD]

1649. Stevenson, Alva Moore, and Dale E. Treleven. 1989. "Black Leadership in Los Angeles Oral History Project," *The CAAS Report* 12(1 & 2): 14–15. [History-LA]

1650. Strohm, Susan Mary. 1989. "Black Community Organization and the Role of the Black Press in Resource Mobilization in Los Angeles." Ph.D. dissertation, University of Minnesota. [Social Issues-LA]

1651. Struhsaker, Virginia F. 1975. "Stockton's Black Pioneers," *Pacific Historian* 19 (Winter): 347–355. [History-Stockton]

1652. Sutter, Alan. 1972. "Playing a Cold Game: Phases of a Ghetto Career," *Urban Life and Culture* 1(1): 77–91. [History-SF]

1653. Sweeting, Anthony. 1992. "The Dunbar Hotel and Central Avenue Renaissance, 1781–1950." Ph.D. dissertation, University of California, Los Angeles. [History-LA]

1654. Tackett, Marnesba. 1988. *Black Leadership in Los Angeles Oral History Transcript.* Los Angeles: Oral History Program, University of California, Los Angeles. [History-LA-Interviewed by Michael S. Balter]

1655. Tate, Will D. 1976. *The New Black Urban Elites.* San Francisco: R & E Research Associates. [Social Issues-Oakland]

1656. Taylor, Quintard. 1977. "Blacks in the American West: An Overview," *The Western Journal of Black Studies* 1(1): 4–10. [History-LA/CA]

1657. Teiser, Ruth. 1969. "Black Muslims Turn to Baking," *Bakers Weekly* 216 (January 13): 26–28. [Social Issues-Richmond]

1658. Thurman, A. Odell. 1973. *The Negro in California Before 1890*. San Francisco: R & E Research Associates. [History-CA-Reprint of M. A. Thesis, College of the Pacific, Stockton, 1945]

1659.————. 1975. "The Negro in California Before 1890," *Pacific Historian* 19: 321–345. [History-CA]

1660.————. 1976. "The Negro in California Before 1890," *Pacific Historian* 20: 52–66. [History-CA]

1661. Thurman, Sue Bailey. 1952. *Pioneers of Negro Origin in California*. San Francisco: Acme Publishing. [History/Biography-CA]

1662. Todd, Charles Frederick. 1976. *Cable Television and Minority Ownership: A Case Study of the Franchise Process*. Los Angeles: n.p. [Social Issues-LA/Compton]

1663. Tolbert, Emory. 1975. "Outpost of Garveyism and the UNIA Rank and File," *Journal of Black Studies* 5 (March): 233–253. [History-CA]

1664.————. 1980. *The UNIA and Black Los Angeles: Ideology and Community in the American Garvey Movement*. Los Angeles: Center for Afro-American Studies, University of California, Los Angeles. [History-LA]

1665. Tompkins, E. Berkeley. 1972. "Black Ahab: William T. Shorey, Whaling Master," *California Historical Quarterly* 51 (Spring): 75–84. [Biography-SF]

1666. Tompkins, Maurice Albert. 1982. "Military and Civilian Aspects of San Diego During the Second World War." M.A. thesis, San Diego State University. [History-SD]

1667. Tong, Yasmin Theresa. 1992. "In the Middle: Mediating Black-Korean Conflict in South Central Los Angeles." Ph.D. dissertation, University of California, Los Angeles. [Social Issues-LA]

1668. Tryman, Donald. L. 1977. "A Typology of Black Leadership," *The Western Journal of Black Studies* 1(1): 18–22. [Social Issues-CA-Has info on Karenga, Panthers]

1669. Turiyasangitananda, A. C. 1981. *Endless Wisdom*. Los Angeles: Avatar Book Institute. [Inspirational/Religious-LA-Alice Coltrane]

1670. Tyler, Bruce Michael. 1983. "Black Radicalism in Southern California, 1950–1982." Ph.D. dissertation, University of California, Los Angeles. [Social Issues-CA]

1671. Verge, Arthur C. 1988. "The Impact of the Second World War on Los Angeles, 1939–1945." Ph.D. dissertation, University of Southern California. [History-LA]

1672. Vivian, Octavia B. 1956. *The Story of the Negro in Los Angeles County*. Compiled by the Federal Writer's Project of the WPA. [History-LA]

1673. Walters, Bishop Alexander. 1917. *My Life and Work*. New York: n.p. [History-SF-"devotes a chapter to Walters' San Francisco residency"]

1674. Weatherwax, John M. 1976 [1954]. *The Founders of Los Angeles*. Los Angeles: Bryant Foundation. [History-LA-Printed for Aquarian Spiritual Center]

1675. Weaver, John D. 1980. *Los Angeles: The Enormous Village*. California: Capra Press. [Social Issues-LA]

1676. Weber, David J. 1974. "A Black American in Mexican San Diego," *Journal of San Diego History* 21(4): 7–209. [History-SD]

1677. Wheeler, B. Gordon. 1993. *Black California: The History of African-Americans in the Golden State*. New York: Hippocrene Books. [History-CA]

1678. Widaatalla, Ahmed Mohammed. 1970. "Effect of Racial Change on the Tax Base of the City of Compton." Ph.D. dissertation, University of California, Los Angeles. [Social Issues-Compton]

1679. Wilkerson, Margaret. 1972. "Black Theatre in the San Francisco Bay Area and in the Los Angeles Area: A Report and Analysis." Ph.D. dissertation, University of California, Berkeley. [Theater Arts-SF/LA]

1680. Wollenberg, Charles. 1970. *Ethnic Conflict in California History.* Los Angeles: n.p.. [Social Issues-CA]

1681.————. 1976. *All Deliberate Speed: Segregation and Race Exclusion in California Schools.* Berkeley: n.p. [History-CA]

1682. Wolpert, Stuart. 1989. "A Tale of Two Cities: Promise or Problems for the City of the 21st Century," *UCLA Magazine* 1(1): 60–65. [Social Issues-LA]

1683. Youngstedt, Scott Matthew. 1989. "Resisting Racism and Constructing Cultural Identity: African Americans and the Imole Olumo Akinwale Yoruba Temple in Los Angeles." M.A. thesis, University of California, Los Angeles. [Social Issues-LA]

Periodicals

The following periodicals provide further sources of information on African-American music and life in California. The citations include the name of the periodical, place of publication, dates of publication (if known), format, and remarks.

Accent L.A. Los Angeles. Los Angeles black community paper.

African Connection Newspaper. Los Angeles. Newspaper dealing with African community.

Al-Talib. Los Angeles. 1990–current. Newspaper of Muslim Student Union, UCLA.

BAM. Los Angeles. 1994 = vol. 20. Free newspaper dealing with local music events.

Bay Area Blues Letter. 1980s. Newsletter.

Bay Blues. San Francisco. 1980s. Magazine.

Bayou Talk. Moreno Valley, CA. "A Cajun Creole Community Newspaper."

Beacon. Oakland. 1945-?. Newspaper.

Berkeley Gazette. Berkeley. Newspaper.

Berkeley Monthly. Berkeley. Magazine.

Billboard. New York. 1894–current. Trade newspaper.

Black Music. England. 1970s–early 1980s. Magazine

Black Music Review. Tokyo. Magazine.

Black Panther. Oakland. 1967–1980. Newspaper of the Black Panther Party.

Black Politics. Berkeley. 1968–1969. Newspaper.

Black Radio Exclusive. 1980s–current. Trade newspaper.

Black Stars. Chicago. 1970s. Magazine.

Blues and Rhythm: The Gospel Truth. Leeds, England. 1984–current. Magazine.

Blues and Soul. England. 1970s–current. Magazine

Blues Unlimited. London. 1963–1987. Magazine. Has numerous articles on CA-based musicians.

California Eagle. Los Angeles. 1897–current. Los Angeles black community newspaper.

California History. San Francisco. 1922–current. Journal.

California Voice. Oakland. 1919–current. Newspaper.

Cash Box. Trade newspaper.

City. San Francisco. 1970s. Magazine.

City Life. Oakland. Magazine. Entertainment guide.

Comet. San Diego. Newspaper.

Drum! San Jose. ca. 1992–current.

East Bay Reporter. Oakland. Newspaper.

East Oakland Times. Oakland. Newspaper.

Ebony. Chicago. 1945–current. Magazine.

Egypt Times. Los Angeles. Newspaper.

Elevator. San Francisco. 1865–1898. Newspaper.

Ethiopian Tribune. North Hollywood. 1994–current. Newspaper for Ethiopian Americans.

Express: The East Bay's Free Weekly. Berkeley. 1991 = Vol. 13. Newspaper.

The Final Call. Chicago. 1992 = Vol. 12. Nation of Islam newspaper.

Free Lance. San Francisco. 1916. Newspaper.

From the Archives. Oakland. 1990–current. Periodical.

Goldmine. 1970s–current. Magazine.

Jazz Now. Oakland. 1980s–current. Magazine.

Jazz Times. 1970s–current. Magazine.

Jefferson. Stockholm. 1968–current. Magazine

The Knowledge Broker. Long Beach. Newsletter. "Monthly calendar of events serving the Afrikan community of Los Angeles and the surrounding areas."

L.A. Jazz Scene. North Hollywood. Free newspaper dealing with local jazz artists and events.

LA Village View. 1994 = Vol. 8. Free weekly entertainment newspaper. Changed name to *New Times* in 1996.

L.A. Watts Times. 1991 = Vol. 14. Newspaper.

LA Weekly. 1978–current. Weekly free entertainment newspaper.

Living BluesLetter. University of Mississippi. Newsletter. Has information on California events.

Los Angeles Reader. 1994 = Vol. 16–17. Newspaper. Free weekly entertainment guide. Changed to *New Times* in 1996.

Los Angeles Sentinel. 1933–current. Newspaper.

Los Angeles Times. 1881–current. Biggest newspaper in Los Angeles.

Los Angeles Tribune. 1940–1960. Newspaper.

Mirror of the Times. San Francisco. 8/22—12/12 1857. Newspaper from Pacific Slope.

Muhammad Speaks. Chicago. 1961–1975. Newspaper. Newspaper of the Nation of Islam.

New Age. Los Angeles. 1903–1926. Newspaper.

New Times. Los Angeles. 1996–current. Free weekly entertainment guide.

The Night Times. Berkeley. Early 1980s. Newspaper.

Nommo. Los Angeles. 1992 = Vol. 23. Newspaper of African Student Union at UCLA.

Oakland Daily Evening Tribune. Newspaper.

Oakland Daily Times. Newspaper.

Oakland Enquirer. Newspaper.

Oakland Herald. 1943–? Newspaper.

Oakland Heritage Alliance. Newspaper.

Oakland Independent. 1929–1931. Newspaper.

Oakland Post. 1966–1967, 1972–1986. Newspaper. Related to Berkeley tri-city port.

Oakland Sunshine. 1900–1923 or 1915–1922. Newspaper.

Oakland Times. 1923–1930. Newspaper.

Oakland Tribune. Newspaper.

The Official Central Avenue District Directory: A Business and Professional Guide. Los Angeles. 1940.

Pacific Appeal. San Francisco. 1862–1880. Newspaper.

Pacific Coast Appeal. San Francisco. 1898–1925 or 1901–1906. Newspaper.

People's News Service. Los Angeles. 1969–1970. Newspaper. Continued by *Black Panther.*

Performing Arts. San Francisco, San Diego, Orange County. "*Performing Arts* magazine is published monthly by Performing Arts Network, Inc. to serve musical and theatrical attractions in Los Angeles, Orange County, San Francisco, San Diego, and Houston."

Rap Sheet. Los Angeles. ca. 1992–current. Newspaper. Has numerous articles on CA-based musicians.

Reader: San Diego's Weekly. Free newspaper.

Record World. Trade newspaper.

Rhythm and Blues. New York. 1950s–1960s. Magazine.

Rock and Soul. New York. 1970s–1980s. Magazine.

San Diego Downtown Newsweekly. Newspaper.

San Diego Evening Tribune. Newspaper.

The San Diego Informer. Newspaper.

San Diego Lighthouse. Newspaper.

San Diego Tribune. Newspaper.

San Diego Union. 1868–current. Newspaper

San Diego Voice and Viewpoint. Newspaper.

San Francisco Bay Guardian. 1960s–current. Newspaper.

San Francisco Chronicle. 1869–current. Newspaper.

San Francisco Examiner. Newspaper.

San Francisco Vindicator. 1887–1915. Newspaper.

San Francisco Weekly. 1980s–current. Newspaper

Sentinel. San Francisco. 1890. Newspaper.

Soul. Los Angeles. 1960s–1970s. Newspaper.

Soul Bag. Paris. 1968–current. Magazine.

The Source. New York. ca. 1989–current. "The Magazine of Hip-Hop Music, Culture, and Politics"; has numerous articles on CA-based musicians.

Southland Blues. Long Beach. 1989–current. Periodical. Details blues events in southern California.

Spokesman. San Francisco. 1931–1935. Newspaper.

Stockton Press. Stockton. 1944–? Newspaper.

The Sun Reporter. San Francisco. 1944–? Newspaper.

Tri-County Bulletin. San Bernardino. 1945–? Newspaper.

Turning Point. Los Angeles. 1993–current. Free magazine. "Of, by, and for the L.A. County African American Community."

The Uganda American Focus. 1994 = Vol. 4. Newsletter. Has information on Ugandan-Americans, includes California activities.

Uraeus: The Journal of Unconscious Life. Los Angeles. ca. 1981–?. Journal. Published by Aquarian Spiritual Center.

Urb. Hollywood. 1993 = Vol. 3. Periodical. Magazine of hip-hop culture and music.

Vibe. New York. 1990s–current. Magazine.

Vindicator. San Francisco. 1884–1906. Newspaper.

Western American. Oakland. 1926–1929. Newspaper.

Western Appeal. San Francisco. 1918?–1927. Newspaper.

Western Outlook. Oakland. 1894–1924 or 1896–1928. Newspaper.

ADDENDUM

Music

1684. Barney, Deborah Smith. 1993. "Martin, Sallie," in *Black Women in America: A Historical Encyclopedia*, edited by Darlene Clark Hine. Brooklyn: Carlson Publishing, pp. 750–751. [Gospel-LA]

1685. Borgo, David. 1996/97. "Emergent Qualities of Collectively Improvised Performance," *Pacific Review of Ethnomusicology* 8 (1) (Winter): 23–40. [Jazz-LA]

1686. Caldwell, Hansonia L. 1996. *African American Music—A Chronology, 1619–1995*. Los Angeles: Ikoro Communications, Inc. [General Music-CA-LA-SF]

1687. Chamberland, Carol P. 1996 "The House That Bop Built," *California History: The Magazine of the California Historical Society* 65 (3) (Fall): 222–235. [Jazz-SF]

1688. Fried, Michael. 1996. "W. Elmer Keeton and His WPA Chorus: Oakland's Musical Civil Rights Pioneers of the New Deal Era," *California History: The Magazine of the California Historical Society* 65 (3) (Fall): 236–249. [Spirituals-Art Music-Oakland]

1689. Haralambos, Michael. 1985. *Soul Music: The Birth of a Sound in Black America*. New York: Da Capo Press (Reprint ed. Originally published as *Right On: From Blues to Soul in Black America*. London: Eddison Press, 1974). [Blues/Soul-CA]

1690. Heilbut, Anthony, 1993. "Ward, Clara, and the Ward Singers," in *Black Women in America: A Historical Encyclopedia*, edited by Darlene Clark Hine. Brooklyn: Carlson Publishing, pp. 1223–1224. [Gospel-LA]

1690a. Hildebrand, Lee. 1996. "West Oakland Nightlife Reunion," *Express: The East Bay's Free Weekly* (April 19): 6, 8. [Blues-Oakland]

1691. Jackson, Joyce Marie. 1993. "Jackson, Mahalia" in *Black Women in America: A Historical Encyclopedia*, edited by Darlene Clark Hine. Brooklyn: Carlson Publishing, pp. 620–623. [Gospel-LA]

1691a. Keyes, Cheryl L. 1996. "Rap," in *Encyclopedia of African-American Culture and History*, edited by Jack Salzman, David Lionel Smith, and Cornel West. New York: Macmillan Library Reference USA, pp. 2266–2269. [Rap-CA]

1692. Merrill-Mirsky, Carol. 1988. "Eeeny Meeny Pespsdenny: Ethnicity and Gender in Children's Musical Play." Ph.D. dissertation, University of California, Los Angeles. [Children's Music-LA]

1692a. Morgan, Pat. 1996. "Youngblood," *Express: The East Bay's Free Weekly* 18 (34) (May 31): 1, 8–10, 12–13. [Blues-Oakland—Alvin "Youngblood" Hart, Elmer Lee Thomas]

1693. Tucker, Sherrie. 1996/97. "West Coast Women: A Jazz Genealogy," *Pacific Review of Ethnomusicology* 8 (1) [Winter]: 5–22. [Jazz-CA-Brief discussion of Clora Byrant, Hadda Brooks, Dexter Gordon, Melba Liston, Ginger Smock, Violet Wilson]

Culture

1694. Bragg, Susan. 1996. "Knowledge Is Power: Sacramento Blacks and the Public Schools, 1854–1860," *California History: The Magazine of the California Historical Society* 65 (3) (Fall): 214–221. [History-Sacramento]

1695. Caesar, Clarence. 1996. "The Historical Demographics of Sacramento's Black Community, 1848–1900," *California History: The Magazine of the California Historical Society* 65 (3) (Fall): 198–213 [History-Sacramento]

1696. Chang, Edward T., and Russell Leong, eds. 1994. *Los Angeles Struggles toward Multiethnic Community: Asian American, African American and Latino Perspectives.* Seattle: University of Washington Press. [Social Issues-LA]

1697. Irvin, Dona L. 1992. *The Unsung Heart of Black America: A Middle-Class Church at Midcentury.* Columbia. University of Missouri Press. [History-Oakland]

1698. Lemke-Santangelo, Gretchen. 1996. *Abiding Courage: African American Migrant Women and the East Bay Community.* Chapel Hill: University of North Carolina Press. [History-Bay Area]

1698a. Leonard, Kevin Allen. 1996. "Los Angeles," in *Encyclopedia of African-American Culture and History*, edited by Jack Salzman, David Lionel Smith, and Cornel West. New York: Macmillan Library Reference USA, pp. 1647–1650. [History-LA]

1699. Moore, Joe Louis. 1996. "In Our Own Image: Black Artists in California, 1880–1970," *California History: The Magazine of the California Historical Society* 65 (3) (Fall): 264–271. [History-CA]

1700. Moore, Shirley Ann Wilson. 1996. "African Americans in California: A Brief Historiography," *California History: The Magazine of the California Historical Society* 65 (3) (Fall): 194–197. [History-CA]

1701. Moses, H. Vincent, and Celena Turney, eds. 1997. *Our Families/Our Stories: From the African American Community, Riverside, California.* Riverside: Riverside Museum Press [History-Riverside]

1702. Moss, Rick. 1996. "Not Quite Paradise: The Development of the African American Community in Los Angeles through 1960," *California History: The Magazine of the California Historical Society* 65 (3) (Fall): 222–235. [History-LA]

1703. Pitt, Leonard, and Dale Pitt. 1997. *Los Angeles A to Z: An Encyclopedia of the City and County.* Berkeley: University of California Press. [Reference-History-LA]

1703a. Salzman, Jack, David Lionel Smith, and Cornel West, eds. 1996. *Encyclopedia of African-American Culture and History.* New York: Macmillan Library Reference USA. [Reference-History-CA]

1704. Sides, Josh. 1996. "Battle on the Home Front: African American Shipyard Workers in World War II Los Angeles," *California History: The Magazine of the California Historical Society* 65 (3) (Fall): 250–263. [History-LA]

1704a. Tate, Gayle T. 1996. "Los Angeles Watts Riot of 1965" in *Encyclopedia of African-American Culture and History*, edited by Jack Salzman, David Lionel Smith, and Cornel West. New York: Macmillan Library Reference USA, pp. 1650–1651. [History-LA]

1705. Waldinger, Roger, and Mehdi Bozorgmehr. 1996. *Ethnic Los Angeles.* New York: Russell Sage Foundation. [Social Issues-LA]

1706. Waymon, Carrol W. 1997. *Being Black in San Diego—Anytown USA.* San Diego: W. W. Publications. [History-SD]

PART 2. GUIDE TO SOURCE MATERIALS

The guide is divided into two sections: music and culture. In the music section, one can find information on individual musicians, musical groups, record labels, genres (e.g., blues, jazz, gospel, soul, and rap), venues, and other topics related to major cities and the state of California. Sources dealing with individuals or musical groups are listed under the musician's or group's name. For example, sources on M. C. Hammer are listed under "Hammer" and not "Oakland." Sources dealing with a genre or topic in a geographical area are listed under that area's names. For example, Bette Cox's "A Selective Survey of Black Musicians In Los Angeles" is found under "Los Angeles: General Music."

In the culture section, the names of different cities and geographical areas in California are listed; the city/geographical headings are then subdivided into topics like history, biography, religion, newspapers, and social issues.

After each entry in the guide is one or more numbers; the number(s) identify a specific item in the "Source Materials." For example, the number 1431 refers to Delilah Beasley's *The Negro Trail Blazers of California* (1919).

MUSIC

Above the Law: 1193a
Aikens-Jenkins, Margaret : 0384
Akers, Doris: 0216, 0217, 0220, 0373, 0375, 0378, 0379, 0384, 0683
Albany, Joe: 0518
Alley, Vernon: 1687
ALT: 0835
Amy, Curtis: 0123, 1277
Anderson, Ivie: 0088, 0211, 0474, 0906, 0993, 1690a
Andrews, Ernie: 0075, 0331, 0771, 1215
Aweke, Aster: 0198
Ayers, Roy: 1237

B-Real (*see also* Cypress Hill): 0809
Bailey, Benny: 0518
Baker, Chet: 0588, 1038, 1065
Ballard, Hank: 0576, 0953
Bartlett, Elmer Lee: 0318
Bass, Ralph: 0608
Battiste, Harold: 0236
Bay Area (*see also* Oakland; San Francisco)
  Art Music: 0073
  Blues: 0286, 0647, 1305
  Jazz: 0415, 0837, 1220
Beal, Eddie: 0318
Beatnigs (*see also* Michael Franti): 0358, 0696, 0724
Benjamin, Fannie: 0318
Bennett, Alvino: 0462
Berry, Bill: 0327, 0800
Berry, Richard: 0863a
Beverly, Frankie: 0620
Bigard, Barney: 0170, 0172, 0192, 0422, 0713, 0746, 0888, 1000
Bilbrew, Mrs. A. C.: 0318, 0373

CULTURE

Oakland
  History: 0705, 1415, 1427, 1452, 1476, 1486, 1495, 1508, 1527, 1529, 1530, 1600, 1601, 1610,
    1625, 1635, 1697, 1698
  Linguistics: 1584, 1585
  Social Issues: 1428, 1655
Pasadena
  History: 1461
Richmond
  History: 0705, 1494, 1591, 1698
  Social Issues: 1469, 1657
Riverside
  History: 1701
Sacramento
  History: 1406, 1694, 1695
San Bernardino
  History: 1436
San Diego
  Biography: 1509
  Directory: 1384, 1385, 1387, 1407a, 1407b
  History: 1423, 1426, 1457, 1459, 1460, 1501, 1525, 1535, 1560, 1575, 1579, 1592, 1593, 1608,
    1644, 1666, 1676, 1706
  Religion: 1593, 1628
  Social Issues: 1545, 1648
San Francisco
  Arts: 1679
  Biography: 1420, 1421, 1434, 1435, 1536, 1556, 1588, 1665
  Directory: 1401
  History: 1447, 1448, 1449, 1450, 1451, 1480, 1481, 1495, 1512, 1513, 1531, 1533, 1543, 1566,
    1576, 1587, 1589, 1590, 1604, 1646, 1652, 1673
  Religion: 1411, 1464
  Social Issues: 1583, 1619
San Jose
  History: 1542
Stockton
  History: 1651
Weed
  History: 1559

CONTRIBUTORS

MICHAEL B. BAKAN is assistant professor of ethnomusicology at Florida State University and director of Sekaa Gong Hanuman Agung (FSU Balinese Gamelan). He formerly taught ethnomusicology at Bowling Green State University. Bakan received a B.Mus. in percussion performance from the University of Toronto and M.A. and Ph.D degrees in ethnomusicology from the University of California, Los Angeles (UCLA). His publications include "Demystifying and Classifying Electronic Music Instruments," *Selected Reports in Ethnomusicology* (1990); "Lessons from a World: Balinese Music Pedagogy and the Teaching of Western 'Art' Music," *College Music Symposium* (1993–1994); "Music of Southeast Asia," *Multicultural Perspectives in Music Education* (1996); "Asian Traditions: Balinese Music," *Making Connections: Multicultural Music Traditions and National Standards in Music Education* (1997); and "Polycultural Polyrhythms: World Music Percussion Compilations," *Ethnomusicology* (1997). He is writing a book on the Balinese *gamelan beleganjur.* Bakan has composed numerous *gamelan,* jazz, cross-cultural, and electronic pieces and is a professional jazz drummer.

KIMASI L. BROWNE is a Ph.D. candidate in ethnomusicology at UCLA specializing in African-American music of the 1960s. He holds an A.A. degree in Fine Arts from Citrus College, a B.A. in music composition from California State Polytechnic University, Pomona, and an M.A. in ethnomusicology from UCLA. His master's thesis is entitled "Variation in the Vocal Style of Brenda Holloway: Soul Singer and 1960s Motown Recording Artist" (1995). His research includes fieldwork in Detroit, Los Angeles, London, and Toronto. His publications include "Marvin Gaye: Culture Bearer of an African-American Musical Tradition" in *Fourth Annual Tribute to Marvin Gaye*, Detroit (1993); "The Circle of Reciprocity Between Runners and Musicians at the Halfway Point of the L.A. Marathon" in *Selected Reports in Ethnomusicology* (1994); and "The Intercultural Nexus Between the Music of Motown and the Beatles," *Intercultural Music* (1997). He teaches an

African-American music performance ensemble at UCLA and is conducting research on 1970s northern soul music in Britain.

WILLIE R. COLLINS is a cultural specialist working in public sector ethnomusicology and folklore. His activities include presenting and documenting California's folk and traditional artisans and artists. He holds a B.A. in American history from UCLA, an M.A. in music composition from the University of California, Santa Barbara (UCSB), and a Ph.D. in ethnomusicology from UCLA. His dissertation, "Moaning and Prayer: A Musical and Contextual Analysis of Chants to Accompany Prayer in Two Afro-American Baptists Churches in Southeast Alabama," was completed in 1988. He has taught at both UCSB and Tuskegee University. His publications include "An Ethnography of the Moan-and-Prayer Event in Two African-American Baptist Churches in Southeast Alabama," *African Musicology: Current Trends* (1992); "Putting on the Bit Hat: Labor and Lore among Oakland's Red Caps" and "Jazzing Up Seventh Street: Musicians, Venues and Their Social Implications in West Oakland" in *Selected Essays on West Oakland* (1997); and four edited monographs: *The Pacific Wave: A Collection of Essays on Pacific Islanders in Los Angeles* (1989); *African-American Traditional Arts and Folklife in Oakland and the East Bay: A Collection of Essays* (1992); *Chinese Traditional Arts and Folklife in Oakland* (1993); and *Chicano/Mexicano Traditional and Contemporary Arts and Folklife in Oakland* (1995.) His ongoing research interests include African-American labor lore as well as religious and secular musics.

JACQUELINE COGDELL DJEDJE (coeditor) is professor of ethnomusicology at UCLA and a scholar of African and African-American music. She received a B.A. from Fisk University and M.A. and Ph.D. degrees in ethnomusicology from UCLA. Her research includes fieldwork in Jamaica, the United States, and West Africa (Burkina Faso, Côte d'Ivoire, Ghana, Liberia, Niger, Nigeria, Senegal, The Gambia, and Togo). She has published two monographs—*American Black Spiritual and Gospel Songs from Southeast Georgia: A Comparative Study* (1978) and *Distribution of the One String Fiddle in West Africa* (1980)—and three anthologies: *African Musicology: Current Trends: A Festschrift Presented to J. H. Kwabena Nketia, Vol. 1* (1989, coedited with William G. Carter) and *Vol. 2* (1992), and *Selected Reports in Ethnomusicology, Vol. 5. Studies in African Music* (1984, coedited with J. H. Kwabena Nketia). Her published articles include "An Expression of Black Identity: The Use of Gospel Music in a Los Angeles Catholic Church," *The Western Journal of Black Studies* (1983); "Women and Music in Sudanic Africa," *More than Drumming* (1985); "Change and Differentiation: The Adoption of Black American Gospel Music in the Catholic Church," *Ethnomusicology* (1986); "Gospel Music in the Los Angeles Black Community: A Historical Overview," *Black Music Research Journal* (1989); "Los Angeles Composers of African American Gospel Music: The First Generations," *American Music* (1992); "Music and History: An Analysis of Hausa and Dagbamba Fiddle Traditions," *African Musicology: Current Trends* (1992); several entries on gospel musicians in *Black Women in America: A Historical Encyclopedia* (1993); and "The Music of West Africa,"

Garland Encyclopedia of World Music, Africa Volume (1997). She is writing a book on fiddle traditions in West Africa and blacks in the United States.

RALPH EASTMAN is professor of humanities and director of the theater program at Mt. San Antonio Community College, Walnut, California. In addition, he has taught the history of American popular music at several Southern California colleges. He was educated at Antioch College (B.A.), Trinity College (M.A.), and UCLA (M.F.A.). In the summer of 1985 he was a National Endowment for the Humanities Fellow at the Center for Black Music Research, Columbia College, Chicago. His publications include "Country Blues Performance and the Oral Tradition," *Black Music Research Journal* (1988), and "Central Avenue Blues: The Making of Los Angeles Rhythm and Blues, 1942–1947," *Black Music Research Journal* (1989).

LEE HILDEBRAND, journalist and critic, specializes in African-American music. He is the author of *Hammertime* (1992) and *Stars of Soul and Rhythm and Blues* (1994) and coauthor (with Mary Lovelace O'Neal) of *Colors and Chords: The Art of Johnny Otis* (1995). He has published widely in newspapers and magazines, including *Express: The East Bay's Free Weekly*, the *San Francisco Chronicle*, the *Oakland Tribune*, *Blues Unlimited*, and *Living Blues*. Among his numerous articles are essays on Charles Brown, Solomon Burke, Andraé Crouch, Sugar Pie DeSanto, Sheila E., Lowell Fulson, Bob Geddins, the Hawkins Family, Johnny Heartsman, Joe Henderson, John Lee Hooker, Etta James, Joe Liggins, Little Richard, Nellie Lutcher, Percy Mayfield, Jimmy McCracklin, Bobby McFerrin, David Murray, Jimmy Nolen, Johnny Otis, Joshua Redman, Jimmy Smith, Little Johnny Taylor, Timex Social Club, Willie Mae "Big Mama" Thornton, Too Short, Johnny "Guitar" Watson, Katie Webster, the Whispers, and Tony Williams.

JEAN KIDULA, a Ph.D. candidate in ethnomusicology at UCLA, is also a lecturer of music at Kenyatta University. She holds a master of music degree from East Carolina University and a bachelor of education degree from the University of Nairobi. Her master's thesis was titled, "The Effects of Syncretism and Adaptation on the Christian Musics of the Logoli." Her publications include "Unity and Diversity in Music," *Selected Reports in Ethnomusicology* (1994) and "The Appropriation of Western-derived Music Styles into Kenyan Traditions: A Case Study of Some Nairobi Christitian Musics," *Pacific Review of Ethnomusicology* (1996)

DAVID MARTINELLI holds a B.A. degree in composition and an M.A. in ethnomusicology from UCLA. He specializes in improvised music and is an active performer in several world music ensembles. His M.A. thesis, "The Cosmic-Myth Equations of Sun Ra: An Examination of the Unity of Music and Philosophy of an American Creative Improvising Musician," is one of the first scholarly works on this important musician. Martinelli is a lab technician for the UCLA Departments of Ethnomusicology and Music and an independent researcher.

EDDIE S. MEADOWS (coeditor) is professor of music at San Diego State University (SDSU) and a specialist in African-American music, especially jazz. He holds a Ph.D. in music education, with a research focus on musical preference, from Michigan State University. He has done postdoctoral work in ethnomusicology at UCLA and conducted fieldwork in Ghana. In addition to teaching at SDSU, he has held visiting professorships at Michigan State; UCLA; the University of California, Berkeley; and the University of Ghana, Legon. Among his publications are *Theses and Dissertations on Black American Music* (1980); *Jazz Reference and Research Materials* (1981); *Jazz Research and Performance Materials: A Select Annotated Bibliography*, 2nd ed. (1995); "Prolegomenon to the Music of Horace Silver," *Jazzforschung* (1986); "The Miles Davis/Wayne Shorter Connection: Continuity and Change," *Jazzforschung* (1988); and "Africa and the Blues Scale: A Selected Review of the Literature," *African Musicology: Current Trends, Vol. 2.* (1992). He has published several encyclopedia entries and numerous book and record reviews. His current research is focused on transformations in jazz.

JAMES C. MOORE SR., artist manager, songwriter, record producer, and president of Jasman Records and Eroom Music Publishing Company, has been very active in promoting the careers of San Francisco Bay Area musicians. Among the artists he has assisted are Sugar Pie DeSanto, Jayne Kennedy, and Willie Mae "Big Mama" Thornton. He "discovered" Thornton in Richmond, California, and helped promote her climb back to success by booking her for the 1964 Monterey Jazz Festival, a six-week European tour in 1966, and a Carnegie Hall performance in 1967. Moore studied acting at Contra Costa College, where he produced noon concerts for artists such as Freddie Hubbard and Sonny Rollins. He still manages and produces Sugar Pie DeSanto.

KWAKU PERSON-LYNN is a lecturer in Africana Studies at California State University, Dominguez Hills (CSUDH). He received his undergraduate degree from CSUDH and his M.A. and Ph.D. degrees from UCLA. His dissertation, "American Afrikan Music: A Study of Musical Change," was completed in 1987. Among his publications are *First Word: Black Scholars Thinkers Warriors, Vol. 1* (1996) and several articles in popular journals. A second book, entitled *On My Journey Now: The Narrative of Dr. John Henrik Clarke*, and a novel, *Stepping on the Crown*, are in progress, as is the second volume of his first book. Person-Lynn has much experience in the music industry as a record producer and owner of a production and publishing company. Also, he has hosted and produced radio program *Spirit Flight* and the thirty-hour weekend special *Afrikan Mental Liberation Weekend* for Los Angeles station KPFK. He has taught at Compton College; California State University, Los Angeles; Immaculate Heart College; and UCLA Extension.

DANICA L. STEIN holds a B.M. in music theory from the Eastman School of Music and an M.A. in ethnomusicology from UCLA. She has studied jazz history, theory, and arranging. Her research on Los Angeles–based female jazz musicians culminated in a thesis entitled, "Women Who Play Jazz: A Study of the Experiences of Three Los Angeles Musicians," in which Clora Bryant was featured. Stein's research interests include cross-cultural music styles, jazz vocal styles, East African musical genres, and native American music and dance. She is an active performer, composer, and researcher.

INDEX

Compositor:	Impressions Book and Journal Services, Inc.
Text:	10/12 Baskerville
Display:	Baskerville
Printer and binder:	Edwards Brothers, Inc.